The

JEWISH
EXPERIENCE

As old as the Bible: Jewish clay jar, wheel-turned, pulled handles, discovered by Israeli archaeologists and dated by them to the period 800–586 B.C., when much of the text of the Hebrew Bible was written.

The
JEWISH
EXPERIENCE

Edited by
Norman F. Cantor

CASTLE BOOKS

Copyright acknowledgements appear on page 483.

Published by
Castle Books,
a division of Book Sales, Inc.
114 Northfield Avenue
Edison, New Jersey 08837

Printed in the United States of America

ISBN 0-7858-1128-1

Library of Congress Cataloging-in-Publication Data

The Jewish experience / edited by Norman F. Cantor.
    p.   cm.
    Includes index.
    ISBN 0-06-270124-X
    1. Jews—Biography. 2. Jews—History—Sources. 3. Judaism—History—Sources. 4. Jews—Fiction. 5. Jews—
Civilization. I. Cantor, Norman F.
DS115.J35   1996
909'.04924—dc20   96-14552

Over 3,000 years of Jewish culture, history and thought are brought to life in Norman F. Cantor's *The Jewish Experience*. Containing selections from more than 100 written texts as well as more than 50 illustrations—this extraordinary collection includes short stories, essays, novels, biographies, memoirs and other first-person accounts. In addition, the book includes Professor Cantor's insightful commentary that puts the selections into context. As such, it assembles expressions and descriptions of Jewish feeling and reason, hope and despair, expectation and disappointment, and ambition and love throughout history and throughout the world.

Each of the book's ten parts is devoted to a specific theme in Jewish culture and experience: Living on the Edge, Growing Up, Maturing and Dying, Divine Intoxication, Victims and Martyrs, Hoping and Coping, Women, Striking Back, Icons and Alternative Intimations.

Here you will find both the familiar and the obscure—everything from Maimonides on the difference between Judaism and Christianity to Philip Roth on sex and money in Newark, from Franz Kafka on the coming of the Messiah to Letty Cotten Pogrebin on the Hollywood image of the American Jewish Woman, and from Primo Levi on Auschwitz to Irving Howe on New York's Lower East Side.

In short, *The Jewish Experience* is a unique evocation of Jewish voices expressing Jewish concerns, beliefs and ideas from the Patriarchs to today.

To the Memory of
My Father's Family in Belarus
Who Died in the Holocaust 1941–45
And Whom I Never
Had the Chance to Know
This Book Is Dedicated

A world without Jews is a world
devoid of humanity.

CONTENTS

PART FIVE: VICTIMS AND MARTYRS

PART SIX: HOPING AND COPING

PART SEVEN: WOMEN

PART EIGHT: STRIKING BACK

PART NINE: ICONS

PART TEN: ALTERNATIVE INTIMATIONS

PREFACE

I wish to express my appreciation to the Quality Paperback Book Club for adopting and recommending to its huge membership my edited *The Medieval Reader* (HarperCollins, 1994) as a main selection. This choice demonstrated that a novel, thematically organized volume of instructive texts and pictures on a serious and complex subject can find a substantial and diverse audience these days.

The generous budget for copyright permission provided by HarperCollins Reference has allowed me to roam freely and avidly through the vast textual and pictorial resources of the Jewish past and use the best material I could find during a year of research without worrying about budgetary limitations.

In the course of my research, I was delighted to find original redactions and good translations of important Jewish writings of various kinds that were published many years ago by small publishers in limited editions and are long since out-of-print and accessible only in the very best libraries. I feel privileged to have had the opportunity to rescue this writing from obscurity and make it deservedly available to a wide audience.

Especially I hope that one of the consequences of this book will be to make many thousands of readers more conscious of how wonderfully imaginative and original Jewish writing was in the period from 1880 to 1940, an age of Jewish Renaissance monstrously cut short by the Holocaust and regretfully repressed after 1945 by shifting intellectual and political trends.

I happily acknowledge the assistance and encouragement of my editor at HarperCollins Reference, Robert Kaplan, and my literary agent Alexander Hoyt.

My former secretary, Nelly Fontanez, not only assisted in finding books and assembling the bulky manuscript, but also began the tedious and troublesome task of obtaining the copyright permissions. This difficult work has been completed by my current secretary, Eloise Jacobs-Brunner.

Mindy Cantor made many valuable suggestions as to this book's contents.

Mr. James Ricco assisted in selecting the pictures; and Art Resources, the Jewish Museum of New York, and the Jewish Theological Seminary were very cooperative in providing publishable prints.

The half dozen synagogue groups in the New York, Boston, Detroit, and Cleveland areas who invited me to discuss *The Sacred Chain* (1994) gave me some new ideas as what should go into this kind of book.

New York University partly funded the secretarial and research support for this book.

Above all, I wish to thank the staffs of the Bobst Library of New York

University, the Firestone Library of Princeton University, and of the Hebrew Union College Library in New York, for their generous cooperation and admirable patience, as well as the many publishers and authors who have granted copyright permissions. "May your hands be strengthened."

Sag Harbor, New York

GENERAL INTRODUCTION

The verifiable recorded history of the Jews (Hebrews) extends from the time of King David's establishment of the capital of his kingdom in Jerusalem around 1000 B.C. to the present.

Jewish historical identity thereby spans three millennia of complex and dramatic vicissitudes. Among the other peoples of the world, only the Chinese have a comparably long, continuous, and scientifically demonstrable development. For those (I am not one of them) who believe in the historicity of the Hebrew Bible's accounts of Jewish history before King David, known Jewish history extends back to the time of Abraham and Moses (commonly estimated at somewhere between 1200 and 1500 B.C.).

Historians and archaeologists do not agree on the question of origins of the Jews. Some see the Bible's attributions of Patriarch Abraham's origins to Mesopotamia designating the Tigris-Euphrates Valley (Iraq) as the place of Jewish beginnings. Others believe that the Hebrews were desert nomads, one of a wave of such people over several millennia, who pushed their way out of Saudi Arabia into neolithic Canaan (what is today Israel) with its beckoning rich urban enclaves. Still others believe that the Jews emerged as an innovative religious sect and/or a group of social rebels from among the Canaanites themselves.

Whatever the origins and early narrative of Jewish history, its course after 800 B.C. is well established, at least in outline, by modern historical scholarship. Following the death of King Solomon (around 900 B.C.)—King David's ambitious successor and the builder of the First Temple in Jerusalem—the ancient Hebrew kingdom split into the northern kingdom of Israel and the southern monarchy of Judea, with Jerusalem as its capital.

In the eighth century, Israel was conquered by a Mesopotamian power and most of its people appear to have been deported to Mesopotamia, where they lost their identity. Following the conquest of Judea by yet another Mesopotamian empire in the sixth century B.C., the majority of Judea's population was similarly deported to the Tigris-Euphrates Valley (what is today Iraq). But there they retained their identity and developed further their monotheistic, puritanical religion in communal synagogues in absence of the Temple in Jerusalem. In Iraq, the draft of what today constitutes most of the Hebrew Bible was written, or at least compiled and edited.

Then in the fifth century B.C., Mesopotamia came under rule of Persian kings whose attitudes toward the Jews was benign. A minority of the exiled Jewish population returned to Jerusalem, and with the encouragement and support of Iranian officials, commenced building the Second Temple in Jerusalem. By this time (around 400 B.C.) the majority of Jews actually lived in the Diaspora (Galut) of the Eastern Mediterranean. Under the succeeding Hellenistic rulers of the Greek-speaking eastern Mediterranean, the Jews prospered and their number greatly increased.

In Judea itself, the final text of the Bible was edited by Ezra and his colleagues (fourth century B.C.). Splits along both religious and political lines developed within the Jewish community. The main issue was what kind of daily life the Bible legislated and whether there was an oral as well as a written law allegedly stemming from Moses. This religious, legal, and ethical dispute was complicated by a successful war of independence led by the Maccabean family against the Hellenistic Syrian empire.

By the time Judea was incorporated into the Roman Empire in 63 B.C., the most vocal and determined, if not the most numerous, Judean religious group were the Pharisees, the rabbinical founders of what is today Orthodox or Halachic ("legal") Judaism.

The Jews prospered greatly under liberal Roman rule, spreading from the Eastern Mediterranean to Rome and as far as Marseilles and experiencing a population boom to the extent that by the middle of the first century A.D., approximately 8 to 10 percent of the Roman Empire's fifty million people were Jews. In Alexandria, the largest Greek-speaking Mediterranean city, one-third of the million inhabitants were Jews, for the most part practicing a relaxed, Hellenistically acculturated, philosophically refined Judaism that anticipated today's Reform Judaism.

The favorable condition of the Jews under benign Roman rule was interrupted first by political rebellions in Judea in A.D. 66–70, which led to the destruction of the Second Temple, extensive mortality, and exile of a large part of the Jewish population from the ancestral homeland. A second desperate rebellion in A.D. 132 led to the complete expulsion of the Jews from all the southern parts the country. Twenty years earlier an internecine feud in Alexandria between Jews and pagans—which generated anti-Semitic motifs that still endure—had turned into a Jewish disruption severely repressed by the Roman authorities. Liberal Alexandrian Judaism went into steep decline along with a severe reduction in Jewish population and prosperity in the great Egyptian city.

The Pharisaic rabbis meanwhile had withdrawn to schools and synagogues in the far north of Judea and had reinvigorated the age-old Mesopotamian centers as well. By A.D. 500, in these two locations were compiled varying recessions of the Talmud, the code of Orthodox Jewish law; and it was the Babylonian Talmud that became the textual foundation of Orthodox Halachic (codified) Judaism from the Middle Ages to the present time.

The second cause of Jewish decline in late antiquity was the emergence of the Christian Church, which was originally an obscure Judean sect that was turned into a world religion open to Gentiles by a maverick Pharisaic rabbi from Asia Minor. A fierce competition between Christianity and Judaism to gain pagan converts followed in the second and third centuries, with the Christian Church prevailing. Finally after A.D. 312, with the ascension of the first Christian Roman emperor, the Christian state religion of the Mediterranean world used political and legal power to turn the Jews into a repressed, depressed, and segregated minority. By A.D. 400 there were only two million Jews in the world.

The condition of the Jews improved in most of the Germanic successor states, particularly France, that emerged after the collapse of the Roman Empire in Western Europe in the fifth century. While most Jews were small farmers and humble craftsmen, many Germanic kings found the elite group of Jewish merchants and bankers highly useful to their underdeveloped economies and protected the Jewish communities with their rabbinical-mercantile leadership from persistent attack by Christian bishops.

Around A.D. 600, at both ends of the Mediterranean in Germanic Spain and in the surviving East Roman (Byzantine) Empire, there was active state persecution of Jews fomented by Christian leaders. Therefore, in the seventh century, Jews welcomed the triumph of the invading Muslim Arabs and gave assistance to the invaders as they conquered Egypt and Mesopotamia and most of Spain.

Under Muslim rule in the Mediterranean from the eighth to twelfth centuries, Jews were officially deemed second-class citizens who had to pay a special tax. But in practice, Muslim rule was relatively benign toward Jews, and especially in Spain and Egypt, Jews prospered greatly in the management of trading companies whose activities stretched as far as India. In Muslim Spain, some Jews came to hold important political positions. Spain was also the focus of a Jewish intellectual renaissance stimulated by Greek and Arabic science, philosophy, and medicine and the imitation of Arabic poetry in Hebrew.

A reversal of Jewish fortunes occurred in Muslim Spain in the twelfth century with the rise to power of fundamentalist Muslim sects who migrated from North Africa. In most of Christian Europe, the Jewish position rapidly deteriorated in the twelfth century due to the persistent efforts of Church leaders to segregate and repress the Jews, spontaneous pogroms by Christian mobs inspired by militant devotion, and a lack of interest in protecting Jews on the part of Christian monarchs who no longer—in the developing capitalist economy of Western Europe—needed Jewish services in commerce and banking.

At the end of the thirteenth century, Jews were expelled from England and most of France and moved eastward into Germany. Here they adopted the German language, which, with the addition of some Hebrew words and written in Hebrew letters, became modern Yiddish. In the sixteenth century, adverse economic circumstances and Church-inspired pogroms drove the Jews further eastward, into Poland, where they were welcomed by the dukes and the lords not only for their customary commerce and banking, but also as estate agents and managers, to control and exploit the Polish and Ukrainian peasantry.

The adverse social and political conditions of the Jews in late medieval Europe stimulated rabbinical withdrawal from their previous immersion in Greek philosophy and rationalist culture. Along with the full-scale social triumph of Orthodox, Talmudic Judaism in the segregated communities headed by a rabbinical-mercantile elite, a mystical, astrological, demonological antirationalist pastiche, the Kabbalah, became the dominant Jewish higher culture in the late Middle Ages.

In Christian Spanish kingdoms that had emerged in the thirteenth centuries with the steady pushing back of the Muslim Arabs, Jews initially found a place as merchants, bankers, and government officials. But around 1400, as Church influence fomented a vehement and sometimes violent campaign to convert the Jews, the disappointment of some Jewish intellectuals with regnant anti-rationalistic Kabbalist culture worked together with Church pressure to bring about mass Jewish conversion to the Catholicism in the fifteenth century.

Jewish converts (Marranos) in the fifteenth and sixteenth centuries played a major role in the Spanish intellectual renaissance as well as early modern international capitalism. By 1492 out of a million or more Spanish Jews that had existed in 1400, there were less than one hundred thousand still loyal to their old faith. Church leadership, among which converted Jews were prominent, persuaded the Spanish monarchy to prohibit the practice of Judaism and to offer a choice of conversion or exile. Only forty thousand Jews chose the latter option, moving first to Portugal and then in the sixteenth century mostly to hospitable Protestant Holland (and from there back to England) and to the tolerant Muslim Turkish empire.

Although militant Spanish church leaders, through the vehicle of the court of the Inquisition between 1480 and 1530, sought to show that many Marranos were in fact crypto-Jews, in fact only about five thousand Iberian Jews ever suffered loss of life or property at the hand of the Inquisition.

The status and condition of the Jews in Slavic lands, at first so promising, rapidly declined in the later seventeenth century. The prosperity and freedom of Jews in early modern Poland and its satellite Ukrainian territory abruptly ended in 1648, with a rebellion by Ukrainian Cossack mercenary bands that led to widespread slaughter and vast destruction of Jewish property.

The Polish and Ukrainian Jewish communities in the eighteenth century went into steep decline along with the political enfeeblement of the Polish nobility whom they served. The political partitions of Poland in the later eighteenth century brought two-thirds of the Polish, Ukrainian, and Belerusan Jews under the rule of the hostile and intolerant Tsarist Russian Empire, The other Jews came under the somewhat more benign rule of the Austro-Hungarian and Prussian (German) states.

By the early nineteenth century, the condition of the Jews in the eastern Pale of Settlement of the Russian Empire, where they were mostly confined by the Tsarist government, had become desperate due to economic deterioration and massive Jewish population growth. In 1800 there were still only three million Jews in the world; by 1900 there were eleven million, with the growth mainly within the Russian and Austro-Hungarian territories.

The misery of the Jewish East European masses was somewhat alleviated by the therapeutic evangelical religious movement of Hasidism, which was at first combated by the Orthodox rabbis because it threatened their authority and then collaborated with by Halachic leadership by 1860. In the 1880s, just as the overtures of the Industrial Revolution and rapid urbanization of the Russian Empire began to alleviate the Jewish economic plight, the hostile Tsarist government, Jewish involvement in revolutionary organizations, and increasing anti-Semitism and popular pogroms once again threatened Jewish security. The response was not only a massive migration to America (1880–1917)—principally to New York City—of some three million Eastern European Jews, but also the beginning of settlement in Turkish Palestine by small groups committed to socialist agricultural settlements whose ambiance was intended to reform Jewish character away from the behavioral traits of exile and ghetto, and toward an emancipated New Jew.

In Western Europe, especially Germany, England, and France, Jews in the nineteenth century accepted the governments' enlightened offers of emancipation and full civil rights in return for Jewish participation in the general educational, business, and professional life of secular society. The majority of Jews accepted this bargain and espoused the Haskala (enlightenment, modernization) with its commitment to secular culture and the centralized state.

By 1914, in Germany and in the German-speaking parts of the Austro-Hungarian empire, Jews had come to play a prominent role in science, law, industry, and publishing as well as in banking and commerce. The emergence of Reform Judaism in Germany (and later the United States) offered a more liberal, modernized from of Judaism that made participation of Jews in secular life much easier. But this updated Judaism still did not satisfy perhaps half of German Jews and many Jews in France. Hundreds of thousands of Jews became fully assimilated into secular culture and society and ceased to practice any religion when they did not convert outright to Christianity—more often for reasons of professional or business advancement than religious persuasion.

This widespread assimilation did not arrest the resurgence of popular and political anti-Semitism in the late nineteenth century. In some respects it stimulated Judeophobia.

Jewish fate since World War I has been an extremely polarized one. Jews in the United States (and to a slightly lesser extent in Canada and Latin America) achieved freedom, prosperity, and success by 1910 similar to that of Jews in German-speaking countries. Jews in the Soviet Union, who played a very important role in the leadership of the Bolshevik Revolution, experienced the obliteration first of their community's political leadership in the Stalinist purges of the 1930s and then of their Yiddish cultural elite, while ordinary Jews did well in the professions, the military, and commerce.

An international Yiddish-based literary renaissance, concentrated especially in Odessa and New York since around 1890, had run its course by the 1930s. Jews in Poland, where three million still lived in 1939, continued in a condition of ambient political and religious hostility and general poverty that could no longer be alleviated by immigration after the United States closed its doors in 1917.

The small Jewish community in Palestine, coming under British rule in 1917, struggled in the 1930s and 1940s against both the British and the Arabs and in 1948 gained independence and security by fact of military heroism, with some political help from the U.S.A. In the next fifteen years, Israel absorbed almost a million refugees forced from Arab countries, as well as a million refugees from war-torn Europe. A military triumph over the Arabs in 1967 led to the establishment of a triumphalist Greater Israel.

The most fundamental fact of Jewish life in the twentieth century was the Hitlerian Holocaust of the early 1940s that reduced Jewish world population from seventeen to eleven million—the devastation falling mainly in Eastern and Central Europe. Demographic recovery has been slow, given a Jewish penchant to small families, except for very devout Orthodox Jews. By 1995 Jewish population was somewhere between fourteen and fifteen million. However, Jewish roles in business, learning, and the arts are immensely greater than this trivial population figure would indicate, precipitating renewed anti-Semitic jealousy.

Two recent further developments of importance were the emigration to Israel of a half-million Jews from the disintegrating Soviet Union in the late 1980s; and the rapid assimilation, extreme secularization, and loss of identity of perhaps half of American Jews as the century grows to a close, just as Jews become the wealthiest ethnic group in the country.

Scholars involved in the new Judaic Studies department of American universities, who have chosen to ally themselves with the more conservative Jewish religious and political groups in American society, may question a statement here and there in the preceding summary of Jewish history, but in general the patterns as outlined from 800 B.C. to the end of the twentieth century are universally recognized by educated people.

But this historical narrative is given only as a handy contextual summary for *The Jewish Experience*.

This book is not an attempt to offer a narrative of Jewish history. There is no need to do that. I have already done that in *The Sacred Chain* (HarperCollins, New York 1994; and in a somewhat modified text, London 1995).

While this book, like *The Sacred Chain*, aims to get at the reality of the Jewish experience through the ages, it does so by an entirely different method and from a significantly alternative perspective.

Organized topically and categorically rather than chronologically, *The Jewish Experience* offers through more than 100 selections from written texts of every conceivable genre, many at considerable length, and fifty pictures, a kaleidoscopic view of Jewish behavior and consciousness through multiple times and places.

If we deign to employ the jargon of current debates among historians and social scientists, *The Jewish Experience* takes a strong *phenomenological* (also called relativist and constructivist) rather than the *essentialist* (traditional, legitimating, establishmentarian) approach to the pursuit of understanding the construct of Jewish personality, mind, behavior, and sensibility.

This book does not presume to legislate, or at least withholds dictating explicit judgment on what is essentially Jewish, as communicated by religious, historical, ethnic, and cultural data. This book assembles expression and descriptions of Jewish feeling and reason, hope and despair, expectation and disappointment, and ambition and love over long periods of time and in a great many places. If the people called Jews did or said something, it is within the scope of this book.

Out of these vibrations, impulses, and messages, and from reception of these brilliant phenomena, the reader will construct his own composite memory of Jewish experience and his own image of a Jewish nature relative to these bits and bites of information.

I have organized the material into ten parts reflective of modes of behavior and patterns of sensibility. Each part begins with a brief thematic Introduction. I have introduced each particular selection with enough background to provide the necessary information for attentive reading. The reader who immerses herself in this book will come away with a sophisticated understanding of the Jewish experience through diverse times and places, even without reading other books.

Each part is devoted to a specific theme in Jewish culture and experience, and within each part the placement of the selections follows the unfolding of thematic script. But random access to the selections in possible from the detailed Table of Contents and the Index.

I have sought to liberate and authenticate the voice of ordinary people—they, too, are Jews—and to balance and circumscribe authority with the passions and the expectations of those existing outside the establishment.

The wisdom of rabbis and the formulations of other sages and leaders are sufficiently included. But the intimate feelings of ordinary people, the personal insight of secular writers, and the nay-sayings of rebels and nonconformists are eagerly drawn upon in this book to throw upon the screen of memory the residue of things that happened to, or were devised or perceived by, those singular, distinctive people called Jews. Turning these pages should generate for Jew and Gentile alike discovery and recognition of the surprising joys and agonizing dreads that have fallen like a nimbus and penumbra about the unique people called Jews.

Jews are what Jews do and say. That is the existential principle on which this book is based.

Jewish doings and sayings fall within ten patterns of behavior and consciousness that translate into the ten parts of this book

Part One of the book exhibits examples of the Jewish sensibility, however derived, of living on the edge, the feeling of ambiguity and ambivalence, the sense of being Other.

Part Two gives many instances of growing up among Jews, roughly covering the span of human life from ages ten to thirty as marked by optimism and discovery or at least expectation and determination.

Part Three details the sense of frustration, disappointment, and regret that comes with maturing and growing older, and culminates with the Jewish careful observance of death of an individual.

Part Four gives representative examples of Jewish intoxication with divine power and majesty over three millennia, and interpretations of divine omnipotence and providence.

Part Five exhibits the various ways that Jews have served as victims and martyrs in their history through their psychological and artistic responses to this deprivation and terror.

Part Six shows diverse ways that Jews have persisted in hoping and coping with life and society in the context of the threat of discrimination and persecution.

Part Seven illustrates the behavior, consciousness, and treatment of Jewish women over time and in various places.

Part Eight shows Jews striking back against adversity and enjoying small or great moments of revenge, victory, or epiphany.

Part Nine highlights individual Jews who have assumed iconic dimensions and whose names have assumed totemic power.

Part Ten presents intimations about many things in Jewish culture and society worthy of scrutiny and consideration that, while lying now outside the conventional mainstream, may become more central in the future.

The individual parts focus on thematic formations that are critically important and provide avenues of understanding that chronology and homiletics will not uncover. Taken together, this menu of highlights penetrates into just about every facet of Jewish thought and behavior.

Within each part, the chronological arrangement of selections is normally superseded by a thematic, topological progression, which is signaled by its Introduction, and the head notes to each of its selections, and becomes fully evident upon the reading of the selections. Thematic connections transcend the narrow bounds of chronology. What happens in the life of a people is much more solidly connected by moral, intellectual, biological, and psychological substance than the happenstance of temporal sequence. Even the category of space is relatively artificial compared to these deeper affiliations. So in this book we are concerned with the molecular dimensions of cultural energy, ethnic identity, behavioral similitude, and universality of consciousness, much more than with the superficial unities projected by time-lines and spatial gatherings.

There are two certain things to be said about the past. First, it lies malleable and subject to our perception, contemplation, and intellectual reconstruction. The past is an object of mind, and open to our imposing of structured meaning upon it. Second, the past is something in which we ourselves are immersed. Our own culture and society not only emerged out of the past, but are still actively engaged in their behavioral heritage and intellectual legacy. Past and present are thus doubly fused—by the imposition of our own meaning upon the past, and by our interactive relationship with historical derivations. The Jewish past, like the history of any other people, is characterized by these two dimensions.

Because of the long and enduring Jewish history, because of the intricate pattern of events that occurred within it, and because the Jews are now at a critical point in their history—in which the two main Jewish communities in the United States and Israel are experiencing difficult challenges about the future of each—the intellectual and moral confrontation of present-day observers with the Jewish past in an especially demanding, stimulating, and prickly one. From pulpit and lecture platform, from magazines, and from books, the inevitable resistance to recognizing the complexity of the Jewish past and the immense diversity of forms of behavior and structures of consciousness of life within it presses onward. This book offers a countervailing data base, opposing the simplification of the Jewish past with revelation of its intrinsic diversity and multifaceted unfolding.

Conventionally the history and sociology of the Jews has been presented as a series of predictable tableaus, like a many-times renewed television series, in which the musical theme played under the opening credits already signals the repeated tropes that offer no surprises and merely reinforce the familiar. This book by the breadth and variety of its selections and its thematic, rather than temporal and spatial, organization offers precognitive surprises and unconventional insights.

That is one good thing this book will provide. Another is the personal pleasure that reading widely in cultural and social material illuminating individual lives always offers. By exploiting the privilege of perceiving the hopes and passions, the triumphs and disappointments, and the loves and estrangements that shape lives, the special pleasure that comes with knowing the stories and mindsets of particular individuals is made accessible to us.

Der Jurist mit seinem bůch
Der Jud mit seinem gsůch
Vnd das vnder der frawen fürtsich
Die drew geschyr
Machen die ganntzen welt yr.

H W

Jews in European society: Woodcut from Germany, 1520. A christian jurist (*left*) with a Jewish banker (*center*) and the banker's wife (*right*).

PART ONE

LIVING ON THE EDGE

INTRODUCTION

Jews are marginal people. They live on the edge. Ambivalence, ambiguity, and contradiction are most frequently exhibited by them, among the other characteristics. If permitted, they adapt and assimilate readily. They belong intimately to the society in which they live.

They adhere to and are fastened to the prominent culture, political ideology, behavioral pattern, and normal social structure of the particular country in which they live or work. And yet not entirely—they hold something back; they keep a reserve. They live also in an internal realm, a bit out of synch, marginally at odds with the dominant ambiance and empowered structure, sometimes more blatantly than at other times.

Jews often appear the most normal and conforming of groups within a society—nowadays in summer they dress in tennis whites and in winter in ski stretchpants and expensive parkas—and yet there is an air of the Other about them. They live on the edge between normality and conformity on the one side and independence, dissent, rebellion, and deviance on the other.

French and German anti-Semitic literature and art in the early years of the twentieth century foisted up Jews the image of the common rat—scurrying around remorsefully, scavenging furtively at the table of the Western Civilization, and eating away at the sinews of Gentile Christian culture and society. Thus were stamped Jew-rats to be gotten rid of. The image of Jews as rats became a piece of Nazi iconology, preparing for and justifying the Holocaust: This ugly pest must be removed as systematically, swiftly, and fully as possible, and polite society will not question the most thorough and violent methods to effect this task. Particularly conservative Catholics in the 1930s, like the English poet and critic, T. S. Eliot, and the French novelist, Celine, agreed that Jews were rats.

But the Jew is not a rat, not a selfish dirty scavenger, not an enemy of comfortable society. Rather the Jew is like the domestic house-cat who belongs intimately to and purrs along joyfully with families and groups of the master race—so loyal, so positively concerned, so grateful, so comforting. But the cat—unlike the domesticated dog—always holds something back, always follows some interior message, some reserved commitment. The cat-like Jew intimately belongs to family and group and yet retains at least a modicum of independence, preserves some mysterious inner goal: He or she can withdraw loyalty unanticipated and may choose to move along elsewhere and give love to another.

The rabbis, the Zionists, and the Judaic Studies salons will ascribe this Jewish marginality entirely to the conditioned response by Jews to their history of victimization in the Diaspora, and to the current persistent hostility of 200 million surrounding Arabs back in their homeland. Jews have been disappointed so often, been betrayed so frequently, and experienced roller-coaster vicissitudes in so many times and places, it is said, that they learned to sustain an anticipatory emotional edge of defensive sensitivity to sudden reversal of fortune and ambivalent observation of *Goyim*. The latter are friend today and persecutor tomorrow. The Jews are not essentially cat-like holder-backs of full commitment to the society in which they live, it will be claimed by the Jewish establishment: Bitter historical experience made them that way and fortunate enduring of experience will change behavior, indeed has already changed it.

There is no more common a motif in Jewish history and literature than the Jew as the Other—marginal, on the edge.

Jewish ambivalence and ambiguity; Jewish commitment and restraint—everywhere this condition of Jewish marginality prevails. Even in the midst of peace and prosperity, Jewish sensibility is different. Angularity, irony, and ambiguity are central to it. Even when the Jew can submerge into the establishment, he keeps a bit of distance and edginess.

He plays the game, but quietly keeps score by his own criteria. The bottom line on his scorecard may be the same as anyone else's, but also may not. That special Jewish feeling is one of pursuing and often gaining success in accordance within the established parameters, but still viewing the parameters from a different perspective. The Jew hears the beat of a different drummer amidst the leitmotif of the prevailing symphony; the Jew hears a subliminal trumpeter's discordant note even while joining in the orchestrated harmony.

Jewish Business

Jerome Weidman's *I Can Get It for You Wholesale* (1937) is the finest novel ever written about the struggling small Jewish businessman who apes his successful Gentile competitor's lifestyles, doesn't quite make it, and lapses into bankruptcy. In the excerpt, the established world rejects the upstart Jewish intruder as wholly as he tries to belong to it. And as much as he identifies externally with this world, he lives intensely according to his own peculiar vision and hopes. He has his own agenda and methods.

"Hello? Hello, McKee?"

"Talking."

"This is Bogen, McKee. Bogen of Apex Modes."

"Oh, yes. How are you, Bogen?"

"Fine. Listen, McKee, what's this I hear about you not wanting to ship us? What is it, a gag?"

"No gag, Bogen. I'm sorry, but it's true."

"Why?"

"Your account has been slow for months, Bogen. And we've checked you way above your credit limit. I'm sorry, Bogen, but we can't send you another yard of goods until we get a check."

"Don't be like that, old man. We've got orders to fill. Send us the goods, and you'll get a check on the tenth. What do you say, McKee?"

"Sorry, Bogen, it's no dice."

"Look here, McKee. You can't do a thing like that to us. Why, we've done over seventy-five thousand dollars worth of business with you during the past year, haven't we? After doing business with you like that, don't tell me you're going to cut us out just because we're slow on one bill, are you, McKee?"

"It's not one bill, Bogen, and you know it.

You've been slow with us for months. We've carried you, but we can't do it any longer. Your balance is too big right now, as it is."

"Oh, come, now, McKee. Be a sport, will you?"

"Sorry, Bogen. With somebody else, maybe we would. But there's no room for fine feelings in the way *you* do business, Bogen, and you know it."

"Aah, now, McKee, listen. You—"

"No go, Bogen. The way you wrote your contract, there's no room for that. You wrote the rules, Bogen, remember that. We're just playing your way, that's all."

"Oh, come on, McKee. Don't tell me you're still holding against me those allowances we took last year. I'll tell you what. I'll send you a check on account right away. I'll put a check for five hundred in the mail right away. What do you say?"

"Sorry, Bogen. That's all you've been giving us for months, just on-account payments. We want a check in full, to clean up your balance immediately, or we don't ship."

"But McKee—!"

"Sorry, Bogen. Not an inch of goods till we get your check."

All of a sudden, while I was holding the phone in my hands, it occurred to me that here I was, begging, actually *begging,* a thick-headed Irish *putz* like that to sell me goods. The realization that I was crawling in front of anybody made me so sore, that for a few seconds I couldn't talk straight. But when I spoke, it was in a low, clear voice, so he shouldn't miss a word.

"You know what you can do, McKee?" I said.

"What?"

"You can go right straight to hell," I said. "I'll get all the goods I want from some other place."

I wanted to say a lot more, but I didn't have time. I had to beat him to the punch. I slammed the receiver down on the hook. Nobody was going to slam receivers down on *me.*

As I got into the elevator, I had to laugh a little to myself. Not that I was in what you could call a happy frame of mind. But it was a little funny, the way the whole thing was working out, just like in a movie. I'd even gotten to the stage where I was buying her a diamond bracelet!

But that's as far as the similarity went. Because while I'd been willing to let her think I was a rummy and she'd been taking me over, I had my limits, too. The bracelet was the last payment.

And as a payment it was going to be strictly C.O.D.

I knew that once I got my mind concentrated on this thing it would begin to work out. I should have done it long before, instead of wasting so much time. Now, if she wanted the bracelet, she knew what she had to do. I'd made *that* plain. No tickee, no shirtee.

I had to admit, though, that there was a little pleasure in that laugh, too. There was a certain satisfaction in knowing that you could actually afford to go out and *buy* a diamond bracelet. I liked milestones like that.

But even that little bit of pleasure was knocked out of me when I saw the elevator pass my floor.

"Twenty-nine!" I said sharply.

"Sorry, sir," the operator said, giving me a look out of the corner of his eye. "You have to call your floor, sir."

That was a nice way to start off a morning. You can always count on some eighteen-dollar-a-week punk to put you in a nice cheerful frame of mind. You pay ten thousand dollars a year for a loft, and the elevator operators don't even remember what floor you're on. But when Christmas comes around they're there with the gimme act. Well, wait till Christmas came. I'd get him a gift. A fur-lined jockstrap I'd get him. The little jerk.

"I'll stop on the way down, sir."

"Thanks," I said. "That's goddam nice of you."

I opened the door into the showroom and stopped. Half a dozen credit men were standing around Babushkin, all talking at the same time.

"Well, well, well," I said, grinning at them from the doorway. "Good morning, gentlemen. What is this, a convention?"

They turned around quickly, and looked at me. I recognized McKee of Dommelick and Hazzard of Mandel. Before I could spot the others, Babushkin let out a cry and came toward me.

"Harry!"

In all the time I'd known him, this was the first time I'd ever seen him look happy.

"What's going on here?" I said, coming into the showroom. "What's up?"

He opened his mouth to tell me, but the others beat him to it.

"Gentlemen, *please!*" I said, holding up my hand. "One at a time."

"Look here, Bogen—"

It was McKee talking.

"We-ell! Good morning, Mr. McKee," I said, bowing a little toward him and smiling. "I'm glad to see we're still on speaking terms. No hard feelings, eh?"

He clamped his teeth around his cigar so hard that his face looked like it was made out of little crossword puzzle squares.

"Cut the comedy, Bogen," he said out of the other corner of his mouth.

"Okay," I said, running my hand over my face and wiping off the smile. "Look how serious I am!"

"Harry!" Babushkin cried, "they say—"

"Listen, Bogen," McKee interrupted.

"That's my specialty," I said, turning back to him. "What do you want?"

"We want our money," one of the others said.

"Yeah, we want our dough."

"You're way past due," McKee said. "We want our bills paid."

I looked around at all of them, and then back at McKee.

"You'll get your dough," I said.

"Yeah? When?"

"The same as you always got it. In a couple of days, when my collections come in. What are you guys hollering about? You'll get your dough."

"Yeah? We been hearing that for a long time, Bogen."

"We want it now."

"We want checks, Bogen, and we want them now."

I looked at them quickly, hesitating. But in a moment I had made up my mind. This was no time to crawl. There was only one way to play this.

"That's just too bad about you guys," I said. "You'll get your dough when my collections come in, and not before. How do you like that?"

McKee took the cigar out of his mouth and took a step toward me.

"I'll tell you how we like it," he said. "We're calling a creditors' meeting this afternoon."

"Suits me," I said. "Call a meeting and I'll show you guys that this is a one hundred percent liquid business. You'll get your dough. What are you guys hollering about? What am I all of a sudden, the first dress manufacturer on Seventh Avenue that was ever slow in his payments? Go ahead, call your meeting. I'll be glad of the chance to show the whole creditor body the kind of a business we got here. Go ahead. Call your meeting for tomorrow morning first thing."

"Nothing doing," McKee said. "This afternoon."

"I can't make it today," I said. "Make it tomorrow morning."

Can you beat that? Here I am on the home stretch, I've got an appointment with Martha to go pick out the bracelet, so of all the days in the year, these bastards have to pick this day to get tough!

"No, Bogen," McKee said, "that meeting is for this afternoon."

"Sorry, gentlemen. I've got an appointment with a buyer this afternoon. Make it for tomorrow morning, and I'm with you."

Babushkin put his hand on my arm.

"Go ahead, Harry. Make it for this afternoon. Let's see what's what. Make it for this afternoon, Harry."

"Your partner's right, Bogen. You better be there this afternoon."

If those rummies thought I was going to take the chance of ruining a four months' foundation by letting them throw me off my stride *now*, they were crazy.

"Listen, you guys," I said, talking tough. "We've got thirty thousand dollars' worth of sun tan dresses on the racks. I've got an appointment this afternoon with the buyer for the biggest mail-order house in the country. Just remember that it's getting on toward the end of the summer. If we don't move those dresses off our racks now, they'll never move. And if we get stuck with all those dresses, then you guys'll be up the creek for good. You'll *never* get your dough. This buyer is interested and it looks like she'll take the whole lot. She's making a Chicago train at three o'clock this afternoon. Tomorrow is too late. Buyers don't wait, and you guys know it. That's why I can't go to that meeting this afternoon. You guys call that meeting for tomorrow morning, any time tomorrow, I don't care, and I'll be there."

"Nothing doing, Bogen. We're on to your tricks. That meeting is for this afternoon."

"Well," I said with a shrug, "that's just too bad about you guys. Because I'm not gonna be there."

"Oh, no? If you're not there, Bogen, it's going to be just too bad about *you*, not us."

"Yeah?"

"Yeah."

"Don't frighten me, gentlemen. What are you gonna do, kidnap me and carry me there?"

"We don't have to kidnap you, Bogen. If you're not at that meeting this afternoon, we'll put you into bankruptcy."

"Aah, stop the oil, will you? Who do you think you're talking to, a kid?"

"I'm warning you, Bogen. If you're not there, we're going to file a petition against you."

"Go ahead, file!" I said, tipping my hat back on my head and waving my hand at them. "You guys can't bluff me. This business is liquid and we can pay one hundred cents on the dollar. You guys aren't scaring me."

"We're warning you, Bogen."

"Stop the crap, will you?" I said. "You're losing weight."

The ringing of the telephone woke me. I looked at my watch. Twenty after seven. Who could be calling me at this hour? I took the receiver off the little table beside the bed.

"Hello?"

"Hello, Harry? Who's this, Harry? Is that you, Harry?"

It was Babushkin, his voice full of excitement.

"Yeah, Meyer, it's me. What's the matter?"

"Oh, thank God, Harry. I been trying to get you since last night. Why didn't you come back to the office? Where were you all night? I been ringing you all night till after one. I thought maybe I'd get you in if I called this morning, so I—"

"For God's sakes, Meyer," I cried. "Stop hollering like that. I'm not deaf. What happened? What are you talking about?"

"They filed a petition, Harry. They—"

"They *what?*" I yelled.

"They filed a petition like they said they'd—"

"Why, the dirty son of a bitches!"

"Harry! Harry, what—?"

"Meyer!" I said sharply. "*Meyer!*"

"Yeah, Harry, what—?"

"Shut up," I barked, "and listen, will you?"

"All right, Harry, what—?"

"Shut-*up!*" I shouted. "And *listen,* will you?"

No answer.

"Hello? Hello, Meyer?"

"Hello," he said in a lower voice.

"Where are you now?" I asked.

"Home."

"When were you in the place last?"

"Yesterday in the afternoon. Right after the meeting. I went back. I thought maybe you'd be there, Harry. I wanted to tell you—"

"What happened at the meeting? They ask you any questions?"

"Yeah, they—"

"What'd they ask? What'd they ask you?"

"All about the business. They asked about the orders, how many we had on hand, how much stock we had, how much was out at contractors, how—"

"Anything else?"

"Yeah, a few other things. Nothing special, just a few things about—"

"They ask anything about withdrawals?"

"Withdrawals?"

"Yeah, yeah, withdrawals. They ask anything about us taking out any money, or anything like that?"

"No, Harry, they didn't—"

Well, that was something.

"All right, Meyer," I said. "You can tell me the rest when I see you. Right now, just listen. You listening?"

"Yeah, Harry, I'm—"

"All right," I said. "You're home now, right?"

"That's right, Harry."

"It's now"—I looked at my watch—"half-past seven. How long does it take you to come down from the Bronx?"

"I don't know, a half hour, maybe a little longer, maybe a little less. Why?"

"Well, say a half hour," I said. "Don't you leave the house until eight or a few minutes after, understand? Then come right down to the place. That means you ought to get there about eight-thirty. Right?"

"Yeah, I suppose so."

"All right," I said. "When you get there, don't speak to anybody. Keep your mouth shut and don't say a word. Just go right into my private office. I'll be waiting there for you. Understand?"

"Yeah."

"So remember, Meyer, before I hang up. Leave your house at about eight, and when you get to the place, don't talk to anybody, *nobody,* understand? Just go right into my private office. I'll be there. Okay?"

"Okay, Harry."

"Now, remember, don't talk to anybody."

"Okay, Harry."

"Okay," I said, "I'll see you at eight-thirty."

I hung up and hopped out of bed. I picked up the house phone and spoke to the doorman. "Get me a cab. I'll be down in ten minutes. Have it waiting for me."

I dressed quickly, but carefully. I don't care what's going on, I still don't like to look like I went to sleep in my clothes.

"Fourteen Hundred Broadway," I told the driver. "Go over to Broadway, and then down. Stop at the first newsstand."

The first two didn't have it. But I knew one of them further downtown would have it.

"Got a *Daily News Record?*" I asked at the next one.

"Yes, *sir.*"

"All right," I told the driver. "Now Fourteen Hundred."

Not that I thought Babushkin was kidding or anything like that. But I just didn't think they'd really do it. I thought they were trying to bluff me. There it was, though, on page six, under Business Troubles.

APEX MODES, INC. 1400 BROADWAY. Harry Bogen, Pres. An involuntary petition in bankruptcy was filed yesterday against Apex Modes, Inc., manufacturers of women's and misses' evening wear. The petitioning creditors were D. G. Dommelick & Co., $12,039.50, Mandel Laces, Inc., $8,422.29, and Commercial Factors Corp., $5,500.00. The creditors' committee, headed by Earle J. McKee of D. G. Dommelick & Co., has retained the accounting firm of Seidman & Turletzky to make an audit of the books of the debtor concern. Liabilities are estimated at $80,000.00.

The showroom door was locked, but I had a key. As I opened it, the Holmes signal went off. A man in a derby, with a cigar in his mouth, jumped up from the couch when I came in.

"Hey, there," he called, "where do you—?"

"It's okay," I said, walking over to the Holmes box and giving the answering signal. "Keep your pants on. My name is Bogen. I'm the president of the firm. Who're you?"

"I'm the custodian. You can't—"

"It's okay," I said, "it's okay. Just don't get excited. I'm not walking out with anything. Here's my card."

While he read it, I went into the office. I sat down at the switchboard and dialed a number. There was no answer. It was still too early. I reached for the telephone book to look up his home number, when the board buzzed. I plugged in.

"Hello," I said.

"Hello? Who's this, Bogen? That you, Bogen?"

"Yeah, Golig. I just called your office. But there was no answer."

"Yeah, well, listen. I was eating breakfast just now, and I was looking through the paper, and I saw it. I called you right away."

That's the kind of a lawyer to have.

"That's fine," I said. "I'm glad you called. Can you come right down here?"

"Sure."

"How soon can you be here, Golig?"

"What time is it now, ten after eight? I'll just call one of my girls at her home and tell her where I'm going, and then I'll come right down. I'll be there about half past, maybe a few minutes later, maybe twenty to nine."

"Okay, Golig," I said. "I'll be here waiting. I'll have Babushkin here, too."

"All right. How does it look, Bogen?"

"I'll tell you when I see you," I said. "But don't worry about a fee, Golig. I've got *that* salted away."

"I wasn't worrying about it, Harry." Maybe he wasn't. "I'll be right down."

For the next call I connected an outside wire to my private phone and went in to make it. I closed the door and sat down at my desk and dialed Riverside 9–0437.

She answered the phone right away. And her voice was wide-awake, too.

"Hello, Martha?"

"Yes, Harry."

Her voice was something else besides wide-awake. It was a perfect ad for an electric refrigerator.

"I'll tell you why I called you, Martha."

"Why?"

"We'll have to postpone that shopping trip for a couple of days," I said. "In fact, I won't be seeing you for a little while."

"I thought that's why you called," she said.

Apparently she read the papers, too.

"Interesting little paper, the *News Record,* isn't it?" I said.

"It's not bad," she said. "It gives you the news. Short and sweet."

"Well, don't believe everything you read, Martha."

"No?"

"No-o-o," I said, spreading the word out. "When I see you in a few days I'll give you the real story." And something else, besides.

"I'll bet it'll be good."

"You can place that bet," I said angrily. "You won't lose any money on it."

Who the hell was she, to start kicking?

"If that's a guarantee," she said, "you'd better put it in writing. According to the *Daily News Record,* your word isn't so good today."

"It's good enough for me," I said, and slammed the receiver down.

There was a commotion out in the showroom. I opened the door to take a look. Babushkin was arguing with the custodian.

"It's all right," I said. "He's my partner. Come on in, Meyer."

I closed the door and locked it.

"What are we gonna do, Harry? I don't understand it. How could a thing like this happen, so all of a sudden? Everything looked so all right. What are we gonna do?"

"Don't worry about it," I said, pushing him into a chair. "Everything is gonna be okay. I just spoke to Golig and he's coming right down. Don't worry about it."

"But Harry, what are we gonna do? What'll we say when—?"

"You don't say anything, Meyer. Let me do all the talking. If they ask you any questions, you don't know from nothing. You were the factory man and I handled all the finances. You don't know a thing. These crazy bastards think they got us up against the ropes, but they haven't. Wait'll the accountants finish with the audit. There's a hundred cents on the dollar here and more. We're solvent and the figures'll show it. You take my word for it, Meyer, the first time this thing comes up for hearing, the petition'll be dismissed. So don't worry about it."

"But Harry—"

"Now, Meyer, please. Don't get excited. And just listen to me carefully. They haven't got a thing on us and they won't find anything, either. Because the figures and the books are absolutely one hundred percent. There's nothing to be afraid of. The only thing they might question you about, is those checks we drew and deposited in your personal account. But don't worry about it. If they ask you any questions, you just say we used it for expenses. For payroll. And for things like that. That's all. If they ask anything else, you just don't know. You were the factory man, that's all. Understand?"

He shook his worried face up and down.

"So don't worry about it so much," I said, patting him on the shoulder. "Just remember those two things. If they ask about the personal account in the Manufacturers, we used the cash to pay bills and payroll. They ask you anything else, you just don't know, that's all. Tell them to ask me. Understand?"

"I understand, Harry."

"All right," I said, "let's go."

I helped him up and unlocked the door. The custodian was standing in the showroom arguing with Golig.

"It's all right, there," I said, walking toward him and moving Babushkin along with me.

"What the hell is *he?*" the custodian said, shaking his head toward Golig, "one of your partners, too?"

"No," I said, "he's my lawyer. He's all right. Let him in."

Golig walked toward me, and I put my hand on Babushkin's shoulder once more.

"So you got that straight, Meyer," I said, "haven't you?"

"Yeah, Harry," he said, shaking his head. "Okay."

"Fine." I turned to Golig. "Come into my private office, Golig," I said.

From my seat between Babushkin and Golig at one side of the medium-sized room, I looked around. A long table stretched down the middle, with chairs all around it. And at the far end, at a desk set at right angles to the table, his back to the windows, a heavy-set, good-looking *goy,* with gray-streaked hair, was bent over, writing busily.

"Is that the Referee?" I asked Golig in a whisper.

"That's him," Golig said. "John E. James in person."

"He looks like a *putz* to me."

"Yeah? Well, don't kid yourself, Harry. He's as smart as they come. Just don't get wise. Answer all questions respectfully, understand?"

I nodded and continued my inspection. The man who sat at the end of the table, to the left of the Referee, was a stenographer. I could tell that by the pens and ruled paper and bell-shaped ink bottle he was laying out. But the little guy who sat facing him across the table, the one that looked like Ben Turpin, had me stopped.

"Who's Handsome Dan?" I asked Golig.

"That's Josh Siegel. He's the attorney for the petitioning creditors."

"You mean he's going to examine?"

Golig nodded.

I began to feel a little better. I had expected a courtroom, with a judge and a jury and what not. Instead, we were in this single room, on the eighteenth floor of an ordinary office building on Pine Street, surrounded by as choice an assortment of heels as you could find anywhere. I felt so relieved, that when I caught McKee's eye, where he sat among other creditors across the room from me, I even smiled at him. He didn't smile back.

At about ten o'clock the Referee stopped writing and looked up.

"What matter is this?" he asked.

"Apex Modes, Inc." the stenographer said. "Twenty-one-A examination."

"All right. Go ahead."

Golig picked up his brief case and moved over to the table, facing Siegel. He spread his papers and sat back.

"Mr. Harry Bogen," Siegel called.

I got up and walked to the chair at the head of the table, to the right of the Referee, facing the stenographer.

"Raise your right hand," the Referee said. I did. "Do you swear to tell the truth in the matter of"—he glanced down at the papers in front of him—"in the matter of Apex Modes, Inc.?"

"Yes," I said.

"Proceed," the Referee said.

I sat down.

"What is your full name, Mr. Bogen?" Siegel asked.

I told him. I didn't like his snotty voice right from the start. But I remembered what Golig had said. I answered respectfully.

"You are an officer of Apex Modes, Inc.?"

"Yes."

"What office do you hold?"

"President."

"You were in constant touch with all the affairs of the business, were you not?"

"I don't quite understand what—"

"I mean, Mr. Bogen, you knew just what was going on all the time, didn't you?"

"I suppose so," I said with a shrug.

"What do you mean, you suppose so? Don't you know?"

"Well, to such a general question, it's a little hard to give a positive—"

"Well, all right," he said, waving his hand. "Let's put it this way, Mr. Bogen. What particular functions, I mean, what were your special duties, Mr. Bogen, in the business?"

"I was the salesman."

"You were the salesman. Were you a salesman exclusively? Did you have any other duties?"

"Oh, I sort of watched over things generally, you know."

"You mean, Mr. Bogen, do you not, that you were sort of the financial man, you—"

Golig jumped up.

"I object, Your Honor. The witness has made no such statement. I object to Mr. Siegel's—"

"Sustained," the Referee said in a bored voice. I looked at him quickly, but he seemed to have his eyes closed.

"All right," Siegel said, rubbing his mustache. "I'll withdraw that. Mr. Bogen, who took care of the finances of the business?"

"Why, what do you mean?"

"Don't you know what the word finances means?"

I opened my mouth to say something, but I caught Golig's eye, so I shut up.

"Sure," I said, "but if you'll be more specific, I'll—"

"Well, who arranged for loans from the bank? Who arranged for lines of credit with the various silk houses? Who—?"

"Oh, I did all that."

"You did." He turned to his papers and looked at them for a moment. "What was Mr. Babushkin's status in the firm? I mean, what were his duties—?"

"I object, Your Honor," Golig said, getting up. "It is not for this witness to say what Mr. Babushkin—"

"Mr. Referee," Siegel said, interrupting him, "this man was the president of the firm. He ought to know what his partner—"

"Overruled," the Referee said in his slow voice. "The witness will answer the question."

Siegel looked at me and I said, "Will you repeat the question, please?"

He waved at the stenographer.

"Read the question to the witness."

"What was Mr. Babushkin's status in the firm?" the stenographer read. "I mean, what were his duties?"

"Answer the question, Mr. Bogen," Siegel said.

"He was the factory man," I said.

"What does that mean?"

"He was the factory man. He took care of the factory. He did the designing, the styling, he supervised the cutters, the contractors, all that stuff."

"Did he have anything at all to do with the finances of the Company?"

"Not to my knowledge."

"What do you mean, not to your knowledge? Don't you know?"

"Well, I—"

"I object, Your Honor," Golig said.

"All right, all right," Siegel said before the Referee could speak. "I'll withdraw that." He turned back to me. "Then I take it that so far as you know, Mr. Babushkin had nothing whatsoever to do with the finances of the Company?"

"That's right."

He questioned me for an hour, about the business and how it was run. Plenty of times I was taking careful aim to see if I could spit right into his eye from where I was sitting, but I remembered Golig's advice and answered respectfully. In a way, I was even enjoying it a little, the way I could control the whole room by what I said. If I answered in a certain way, I could keep the room quiet, but if I wanted to play a little dumb, or answer in another way, I could get them all excited. I began to understand why lawyers have such big cans. They get flattened out from jumping up and down on them to make objections.

Finally, at about eleven-thirty, Siegel picked up a batch of checks from among his papers on the table, and turned to me.

"Mr. Bogen," he said, "I show you now a series of—" Then he stopped. "Never mind that," he said to the stenographer. "I withdraw the question." He turned back to me. "That's all, Mr. Bogen."

"Any questions?" the Referee said, turning to Golig.

"No questions," Golig said.

I got up and walked back to my seat against the wall.

"Mr. Meyer Babushkin," Siegel called.

Babushkin got up and walked to the witness chair like a guy who has lost a bet and is on his way to kiss somebody's behind in Macy's front window on a busy Saturday at noon.

Siegel put him through the paces, the same as he had done to me. The only difference was that from Babushkin he got more respectful answers. Because Babushkin probably didn't even know how to be disrespectful if he wanted to. And even if he did know, right then he was so scared that he never could have remembered how.

Suddenly Siegel turned back to the table, picked up the same batch of checks he had started to show me, and waved them under Babushkin's nose.

"Did you have a personal bank account, Mr. Babushkin? I mean an account other than the firm bank account?"

"Yes, sir."

"What bank was that account in?"

"The Manufacturers."

"Have you still got that account there?"

"I think so. I don't know."

"What do you mean, you don't know?"

Golig jumped up.

"I object, Your Honor, to Mr. Siegel's browbeating the witness. He has answered the question. He said he didn't know. He's never gone through bankruptcy before, and for all he knows, he thinks his personal bank account was seized along with the other assets of the firm. How should he—?"

"Mr. Referee!" Siegel shouted. "I object to my learned adversary leading the witness and putting words in his mouth. If he has any objections, let him state them in the approved lawyer-like way. I ask Your Honor to instruct Mr. Golig to refrain from cleverly putting answers into the mouth of the witness by means of long-winded objections. Let him—"

"That's enough, gentlemen," the Referee said quietly. "We'll have no colloquy between attorneys. If there are any objections to be made, make them in the customary manner. Proceed."

"Read the last question," Siegel said to the stenographer.

"Question: Have you still got that account there? Answer: I think so. I don't know. Question: What do you mean, you don't know?"

"Well, Mr. Babushkin," Siegel said, "what do you mean, you don't know?"

"I thought maybe, I thought maybe they, they took it away from me, like they took, you know, like they took everything else."

Siegel gave Golig a dirty look. Golig smiled at him.

"When did you start this personal account of yours, Mr. Babushkin?"

"About two, three months ago. I don't know."

"Would it refresh your recollection if I were to show you a transcript of your account with the bank?"

"I—I don't know."

"I am reading, if it please the court, from a transcript of the account of Meyer Babushkin with the Manufacturers Banking Company, furnished by the said Manufacturers Banking Company, and indicating that—"

"I object, Your Honor," Golig cried. "I object to Mr. Siegel's reading from any papers that have not been introduced into evidence."

"All right," Siegel said. "I offer the transcript in evidence."

"And I object on the ground that it is incompetent, irrelevant, immaterial, and not binding on the parties."

"Let me see it," the Referee said. Siegel handed it to him. He looked at it for a moment, then handed it back. "Objection overruled," he said. "Mark it in evidence."

"Exception," Golig said and sat down.

The stenographer marked it and handed it back to Siegel.

"I am reading, Mr. Babushkin, from Trustee's Exhibit One of this date. The first entry on this transcript is a deposit of one thousand dollars and it is dated May fourteenth of this year. Is that the date on which this account was started, Mr. Babushkin?"

"I guess so."

"Don't you know?"

"If it says so, it's so."

Siegel put down the transcript and picked up the batch of checks.

"If Your Honor please," he said, "I have here in my hand, and wish to offer in evidence, a series of thirty-one checks, all drawn by Meyer Babushkin on his account in the Manufacturers Banking Company, to the order of Cash, all endorsed by Mr. Babushkin on the back, all running in consecutive numerical order from number one to number thirty-one, indicating that they were taken from the same checkbook, each check drawn in the round sums of five hundred, one thousand, or fifteen hundred dollars, and the entire group of thirty-one checks aggregating a total of thirty-two thousand five hundred dollars. I offer this group of checks in evidence as one exhibit."

"Same objection," Golig repeated.

"I offer them subject to connection, if Your Honor please," Siegel said.

"Same objection," Golig repeated.

"Same ruling," the Referee said.

"Exception," Golig said.

Besides Siegel there were two other people in that room who knew what his next move was going to be. They were Golig and myself. And I had told Golig.

Siegel picked up a second batch of checks and said, "I now offer in evidence, if Your Honor please, a *second* group of thirty-one checks, drawn on the *corporation* bank account of Apex Modes, Inc. to the order of Meyer Babushkin, each one endorsed by Meyer Babushkin, and deposited by him in his *personal* bank account in the Manufacturers Banking Company. These checks are drawn in identical amounts with those in Trustee's Exhibit Two of this date, and total, similarly, an aggregate of thirty-two thousand five hundred dollars. I offer this *second* group of checks in evidence as one exhibit."

"Same objection," Golig said.

"Same ruling," the Referee said. "I'll take it subject to connection."

"Exception," Golig said.

After the stenographer finished marking the checks in evidence, the Referee stood up.

"We will adjourn until two o'clock," he said, and walked out.

Golig and I grabbed Babushkin and hustled him out to a restaurant. He said he wasn't hungry, but I didn't allow myself to be influenced by that. When I'm hungry, I eat.

"Remember, Meyer," we told him before we went back, "he hasn't got a thing on us. He thinks he has, but he hasn't. He's gonna ask you a lot of questions about what you did with the cash you got after you deposited the corporation checks in your personal account, but you just remember what we told you. You used it to pay bills, to pay labor, and things like that. Understand?"

He nodded.

We were right. We? Well, *I* was right.

As soon as Babushkin was back in the witness chair, Siegel picked up the checks.

"Mr. Babushkin," he said. "Trustee's Exhibit Three of this date represents a series of checks issued by Apex Modes, Inc. to you and deposited by you in your personal account. These checks were not your *salary* from the corporation, were they?"

"No."

"What were they for?" Siegel said; then quickly, to the stenographer, "No, strike that out. I withdraw the question." He picked up the second batch of checks. "And Trustee's Exhibit Two of this date, Mr. Babushkin, represents an almost identical series of checks drawn by you on your personal account, to the order of cash, endorsed by you, and obviously cashed. In other words, Mr. Babushkin," he said, choosing his words and wrapping his lips around each one so carefully that his mustache began to do double loops, "to put it more clearly, Mr. Babushkin, in the ten weeks preceding the bankruptcy, between the date you opened your personal account and the date of the bankruptcy, some thirty-two thousand five hundred dollars of corporate funds were withdrawn by you, deposited in your personal account, and almost immediately withdrawn from that personal account practically in the form of cash. Isn't that right?"

"Yes."

Siegel turned away from him for a moment, then, suddenly, he spun around, shot his hand out at him, and barked, "What did you do with that money?"

Babushkin just stared at him, blinking his eyes a little. He was so dumb that he was smart. His mind moved so slowly that tricks like these had no effect on him.

"What did you do with that money, Mr. Babushkin?"

"I—I used it in the business."

"You *what?*"

"I used it in the business."

"How?"

"I used it to pay for labor."

"To pay for *labor?*"

"Yes."

"Why couldn't you pay your labor with corporate checks? Why did it have to be by cash, in this peculiar way?"

"We had trouble with our contractors. The union wanted us to use only union contractors. So we used scab contractors and we had to pay them in cash."

Siegel looked at him with his mouth open. Take my word for it, he wasn't a lovely sight.

"Why couldn't the corporation pay them with cash? Why did it have to go through your personal bank account?"

"We didn't want it to show on the books."

Siegel's mouth dropped another few inches, until I could see what he'd had for lunch. I didn't blame him for looking surprised. The explanation was so cockeyed, that even I, who had invented it, couldn't follow it.

"Do you mean to say, Mr. Babushkin, that you spent thirty-two thousand five hundred dollars on labor in ten weeks?"

"No. We bought goods and things like that, too."

"You bought goods?"

"Yes."

"Why didn't you buy your goods through the regular channels, from your regular creditors, on terms?"

"We made some very high-priced stuff. The ordinary houses, they didn't carry the kind of goods we needed. We needed exclusive imports. We had to go shopping around for them, and pay cash."

Say, he wasn't bad! Or else I was a peach of a coach. Probably the latter.

"Who bought this goods?"

"I did."

Well, *that* was in the record.

Siegel rubbed his mustache, and turned back to the table. He scowled as he shoved his papers around, and for a few moments it was quiet. Then he turned back to Babushkin and asked quietly, with a little smile:

"Would you mind giving us the names of these contractors to whom you say you paid this money?"

"I don't remember."

"You don't remember?"

"No."

"Didn't you keep any kind of a record?"

"We didn't want it should show in the books."

"You mean to say you don't remember the name of a single one?"

"No."

"How did you remember who they were when it came to paying them?"

"I had it written down in a little book."

"Oh, so you *did* have a record."

"Yes."

"Where is that little book now?"

"I lost it."

"You lost it?"

"Yes."

"When?"

"I don't know."

"When did you see this so-called little book last?"

"I don't remember."

Siegel changed the tone of his voice and said, "All right, Mr. Babushkin, now about this goods you say you bought. Give us the names and addresses of some of the people you bought from."

"I don't remember."

"You don't remember a single one?"

"No."

Siegel twisted up his face and said, "It wouldn't be, Mr. Babushkin, that you had their names in this little book of yours, too, would it?"

"That's right."

Siegel smacked his papers down on the table and turned excitedly to the Referee.

"Mr. Referee," he said angrily, "I respectfully submit that this witness is deliberately withholding information. It seems ridiculous that a week or two after the expenditure of such large sums of money the witness should be unable to recall a single name among the many he claims he dealt with. I ask that Your Honor direct the witness to tell the truth or suffer the consequences in a contempt proceeding."

"Just a moment, please," Golig said, hopping up. "Mr. Siegel seems to forget that my client is under oath. I resent Mr. Siegel's innuendo that my client is perjuring himself, and demand an apology on his part. I have refrained from objecting to the unorthodox manner in which Mr. Siegel has

been conducting this 21-A examination, Your Honor, but I simply must draw the line when he says in so many words that my client is lying."

Siegel yelled, "I wouldn't apologize to him if—"

"Quiet!" the Referee said suddenly. He didn't say it loud, but they all shut up. "I will thank you gentlemen to remember that you are in a court of law." He turned to Babushkin. "You understand, Mr. Babushkin," he said, "that you are under oath, do you not?"

Meyer nodded.

"And that if you do not tell the truth while you are under oath, you may be punished by the court?"

Meyer nodded again. It was his only talent.

"You may proceed with the examination," the Referee said to Siegel.

Siegel bit his lip, stared at Babushkin, glared at Golig, rubbed his mustache, and said, "No more questions."

"No questions," Golig said.

"That's all," the Referee said to Babushkin, and he got out of the chair.

There was a stir in the room and both lawyers began to put their papers together and a few people began to get up and walk out.

"May it please the court."

It was Siegel's voice. The room quieted down again.

"May I have a word, Your Honor?"

The Referee nodded.

"I respectfully submit," Siegel said, "that it seems perfectly clear from the evidence taken today, Your Honor, that this business was shockingly milked with the deliberate intention and purpose of defrauding its creditors. I respectfully call Your Honor's attention to the fact that I intend to bring a turnover motion in this court against Mr. Babushkin for thirty-two thousand five hundred dollars."

"The court," the Referee said, "can take no cognizance of your intentions, Mr. Siegel, until such time as the proper papers are filed with it." He picked up his diary. "Do you want an adjourned date, Mr. Siegel, on this 21-A hearing?"

"No, sir," Siegel said. "I shall file my turnover papers with Your Honor tomorrow."

"Very well," the Referee said. "Hearing adjourned."

A Capitalist Triumph

Abraham Cahan was the editor of *The New York Jewish Forward* in its great days of the early-twentieth century, when its Yiddish pages spoke to and on the behalf of three million Eastern European immigrants. His novel, *The Rise of David Levinsky* (1917), written in English, captures the diversity of Jewish experience in America, the immensely varied responses of immigrant Jews to the American environment, and the thoughts and feelings of a successful clothing manufacturer. Above all, Cahan communicates the essential loneliness and alienation of the rich, self-made Jewish businessman, estranged from the American environment while triumphing within it at the same time.

Rembrandt, *The Gold Weigher* (probably Jewish), 1639, Amsterdam.

The road was a great school of business and life to me. I visited scores of cities. I met hundreds of human types. I saw much of the United States. Every time I returned home I felt as though, in comparison with the places which I had just vis-

ited, New York was not an American city at all, and as though my last trip had greatly added to the "real American" quality in me.

Thousands of things reminded me of my promotion in the world. I could not go to bed in a Pullman car, walk over the springy "runner" of a hotel corridor, unfold the immense napkin of a hotel dining-room, or shake down my trousers upon alighting from a boot-black's chair, without being conscious of the difference between my present life and my life in Antomir.

I was full of energy, full of the joy of being alive, but there was usually an undercurrent of sadness to all this. While on the road I would feel homesick for New York, and at the same time I would feel that I had no home anywhere, that my mother was dead and I was all alone in the world.

I missed Dora many months after she made me move from her house. As for Max, the thought of him, his jealousy and the way he groveled before me the last time I had seen him, would give me a bad taste in the mouth. I both pitied and despised him, and I hated my guilty conscience; so I would try to keep him out of my mind. What I missed almost as much as I did Dora was her home. There was no other to take its place. There was not a single family in New York or in any other American town who would invite me to its nest and make me feel at home there. I saw a good deal of Meyer Nodelman, but he never asked me to the house. And so I was forever homesick, not for Antomir—for my native town had become a mere poem—but for a home.

I did some reading on the road. There was always some book in my hand-bag—some volume of Spencer, Emerson, or Schopenhauer (in an English translation), perhaps. I would also read articles in the magazines, not to mention the newspapers. But I would chiefly spend my time in the smoker, talking to the other drummers or listening to their talk. There was a good deal of card-playing in the cars, but that never had any attraction for me. I tried to learn poker, but found it tedious.

The cigarette stumps by which I had sought to counteract my hunger pangs at the period of my dire need had developed the cigarette habit in me. This had subsequently become a cigar habit. I had discovered the psychological significance of smoking "the cigar of peace and good will." I had realized the importance of offering a cigar to some of the people I met. I would watch American smokers and study their ways, as though there were a special American manner of smoking and such a thing as smoking with a foreign accent. I came to the conclusion that the dignity of smoking a cigar lasted only while the cigar was still long and fresh. There seemed to be special elegance in a smoker taking a newly lighted cigar out of his mouth and throwing a glance at its glowing end to see if it was smoking well. Accordingly, I never did so without being conscious of my gestures and trying to make them as "American" as possible.

The other cloak salesmen I met on the road in those days were mostly representatives of much bigger houses than mine. They treated me with ill-concealed contempt, and I would retaliate by overstating my sales. One of the drummers who were fond of taunting me was an American by birth, a fellow named Loeb.

"Well, Levinsky," he would begin. "Had a big day, didn't you?"

"I certainly did," I would retort.

"How much? Twenty-five thousand?"

"Well, it's no use trying to be funny, but I've pulled in five thousand dollars today."

"Is that all?"

"Well, if you don't believe me, what's the use asking? What good would it do me to brag? If I say five thousand, it is five thousand. As a matter of fact, it'll amount to more." Whereupon he would slap his knee and roar.

He was a good-looking, florid-faced man with sparkling black eyes—a gay, boisterous fellow, one of those who are the first to laugh at their own jests. He was connected with the largest house in the cloak trade. Our relations were of a singular character. He was incessantly poking fun at me; nothing seemed to afford him more pleasure than to set a smokerful of passengers laughing at my expense. At the same time he seemed to like me. But then he hated me, too. As for me, I reciprocated both feelings.

One day, on the road, he made me the victim of a practical joke that proved an expensive lesson to me. The incident took place in a hotel in Cincinnati, Ohio. He "confidentially" let me see one of his samples, hinting that it was his "leader," or best seller. He then went to do some telephoning, leaving the garment with me the while. Whereupon I lost no time in making a pencil-sketch of it, with a few notes as to materials, tints, and other details. I subsequently had the garment copied and spent time and money offering it to merchants in New York and on the road. It proved an unmitigated failure.

"You are a nice one, you are," he said to me, with mock gravity, on a subsequent trip. "You copied that garment I showed you in Cincinnati, didn't you?"

"What garment? What on earth are you talking about?" I lied, my face on fire.

"Come, come, Levinsky. You know very well what garment I mean. While I was away telephoning you went to work and made a sketch of it. It was downright robbery. That's what *I* call it. Well, have you sold a lot of them?" And he gave me a merry wink that cut me as with a knife.

One of the things about which he often made fun of me was my Talmud gesticulations, a habit that worried me like a physical defect. It was so distressingly un-American. I struggled hard against it. I had made efforts to speak with my hands in my pockets; I had devised other means for keeping them from participating in my speech. All of no avail. I still gesticulate a great deal, though much less than I used to.

One afternoon, on a west-bound train, Loeb entertained a group of passengers of which I was one with worn-out stories of gesticulating Russian Jews. He told of a man who never opened his mouth when he was out of doors and it was too cold for him to expose his hands; of another man who never spoke when it was so dark that his hands could not be seen. I laughed with the others, but I felt like a cripple who is forced to make fun of his own deformity. It seemed to me as though Loeb, who was a Jew, was holding up our whole race to the ridicule of Gentiles. I could have executed him as a traitor to his people. Presently he turned on me.

"By the way, Levinsky, you never use a telephone, do you?"

"Why? Who says I don't?" I protested, timidly.

"Because it's of no use to you," he replied. "The fellow at the other end of the wire couldn't see your hands, could he?" And he broke into a peal of self-satisfied mirth in which some of his listeners involuntarily joined.

"You think you're awfully smart," I retorted, in abject misery.

"And you think you're *awfully* grammatical." And once more he roared.

"You are making fun of the Jewish people," I said, in a rage. "Aren't you a Jew yourself?"

"Of course I am," he answered, wiping the tears from his laughing black eyes. "And a good one, too. I am a member of a synagogue. But what has that got to do with it? I can speak on the telephone, all right." And again the car rang with his laughter.

I was aching to hurl back some fitting repartee, but could think of none, and to my horror the moments were slipping by, and presently the conversation was changed.

At the request of a gay little Chicagoan who wore a skull-cap a very fat Chicagoan told a story that was rather *risqué.* Loeb went him one better. The man in the skullcap declared that while he could not bring himself to tell a smutty story himself, he was "as good as any man in appreciating one." He then offered a box of cigars for the most daring anecdote, and there ensued an orgy of obscenity that kept us shouting (I could not help thinking of similar talks at the cloak-shops). Loeb suggested that the smoking-room be dubbed "smutty room" and was applauded by the little Chicagoan. The prize was awarded, by a vote, to a man who had told his story in the gravest tone of voice and without a hint of a smile.

Frivolity gave way to a discussion of general business conditions. A lanky man with a gray beard, neatly trimmed, and with the most refined manners in our group, said something about competition in the abstract. I made a remark which seemed to attract attention and then I hastened to refer to the struggle for life and the survival of the fittest. Loeb dared not burlesque me. I was in high feather.

Dinner was announced. To keep my traveling expenses down I was usually very frugal on the road. I had not yet seen the inside of a dining-car (while stopping at a hotel I would not indulge in a dining-room meal unless I deemed it advisable to do so for business considerations). On this occasion, however, when most of our group went to the dining-car I could not help joining them. The lanky man, the little Chicagoan, and the fleshy Chicagoan—the three "stars" of the smoker—went to the same table, and I hastened, with their ready permission, to occupy the remaining seat at that table. I ordered an expensive dinner. At my instance the chat turned on national politics, a subject in which I felt at home, owing to my passion for newspaper editorials. I said something which met with an encouraging reception, and then I entered upon a somewhat elaborate discourse. My listeners seemed to be interested. I was so absorbed in the topic and in the success I was apparently scoring that I was utterly oblivious to the taste of the food in my mouth. But I was aware that it was "aristocratic American" food, that I was in the company of well-dressed American Gentiles, eating and conversing with them, a nobleman among noblemen. I throbbed with love for America.

"Don't be excited," I was saying to myself. "Speak in a calm, low voice, as these Americans do. And for goodness' sake don't gesticulate!"

I went on to speak with exaggerated apathy, my hands so strenuously still that they fairly tingled with the effort, and, of course, I was so conscious of the whole performance that I did not know what I was talking about. This state of my mind soon wore off, however.

Neither the meal nor the appointments of the car contained anything that I had not enjoyed scores of times before—in the hotels at which I stopped or at the restaurants at which I would dine and wine some of my customers; but to eat such a meal amid such surroundings while on the move was a novel experience. The electric lights, the soft red glint of the mahogany walls, the whiteness of the table linen, the silent efficiency of the colored waiters, coupled with the fact that all this was speeding onward through the night, made me feel as though I were partaking of a repast in an enchanted palace. The easy urbanity of the three well-dressed Americans gave me a sense of uncanny gentility and bliss.

"Can it be that I am I?" I seemed to be wondering.

The gaunt, elderly man, who was a member of a wholesale butcher concern, was seated diagonally across the table from me, but my eye was for the most part fixed on him rather than on the fat man who occupied the seat directly opposite mine. He was the most refined-looking man of the three and his vocabulary matched his appearance and manner. He fascinated me. His cultured English and ways conflicted in my mind with the character of his business. I could not help thinking of raw beef, bones, and congealed blood. I said to myself, "It takes a country like America to produce butchers who look and speak like noblemen." The United States was still full of surprises for me. I was still discovering America.

After dinner, when we were in the smoking-room again, it seemed to me that the three Gentiles were tired of me. Had I talked too much? Had I made a nuisance of myself? I was wretched. . . .

My business continued to grow. My consumption of raw material reached gigantic dimensions, so much so that at times, when I liked a pattern, I would buy up the entire output and sell some of it to smaller manufacturers at a profit.

Gradually I abandoned the higher grades of goods, developing my whole business along the lines of popular prices. There are two cloak-and-suit houses that make a specialty of costly garments. These enjoy high reputations for taste and are the real arbiters of fashion in this country, one of the two being known in the trade as Little Paris; but the combined volume of business of both these firms is much smaller than mine.

My deals with one mill alone—the largest in the country and the one whose head had come to my rescue when my affairs were on the brink of a precipice—now exceeded a million dollars at a single purchase to be delivered in seven months. The mills often sell me at a figure considerably lower than the general market price. They do so, first,

because of the enormous quantities I buy, and, second, because of the "boost" a fabric receives from the very fact of being handled by my house. One day, for instance, I said to the president of a certain mill: "I like this cloth of yours. I feel like making a big thing of it, provided you can let me have an inside figure." We came to terms, and I gave him an advance order for nine thousand pieces. When smaller manufacturers and department-store buyers heard that I had bought an immense quantity of that pattern its success was practically established. As a consequence, the mill was in a position to raise the price of the cloth to others, so that it amply made up for the low figure at which it had sold the goods to me.

Judged by the market price of the raw material, my profit on a garment did not exceed fifty cents. But I paid for the raw material seventy-five cents less than the market price, so that my total profit was one dollar and twenty-five cents. Still, there have been instances when I lost seventy-five thousand dollars in one month because goods fell in price or because a certain style failed to move and I had to sell it below cost to get it out of the way. To be sure, cheaper goods are less likely to be affected by the caprices of style than higher grades, which is one of several reasons why I prefer to produce garments of popular prices.

I do not employ my entire capital in my cloak business, half of it, or more, being invested in "quick assets." Should I need more ready cash than I have, I could procure it at a lower rate than what those assets bring me. I can get half a million dollars, from two banks, without rising from my desk—by merely calling those banks up on the telephone. For this I pay, say, three-and-a-half or four percent, for I am a desirable customer at the banks; and, as my quick assets bring me an average of five percent, I make at least one percent on the money.

Another way of making my money breed money is by early payments to the mills. Not only can I do without their credit, but I can afford to pay them six months in advance. This gives me an "anticipation" allowance at the rate of six percent per annum, while money costs me at the banks three or four percent per annum.

All this is good sport.

I own considerable stock in the very mills with which I do business, which has a certain moral effect on their relations with my house. For a similar purpose I am a shareholder in the large mail-order houses that buy cloaks and suits of me. I hold shares of some department stores also, but of late I have grown somewhat shy of this kind of investment, the future of a department store being as uncertain as the future of the neighborhood in which it is located. Mail-order houses, on the other hand, have the whole country before them, and their overwhelming growth during past years was one of the conspicuous phenomena in the business life of the nation. I love to watch their operations spread over the map, and I love to watch the growth of American cities, the shifting of their shopping centers, the consequent vicissitudes, the decline of some houses, the rise of others. American Jews of German origin are playing a foremost part in the retail business of the country, large or small, and our people, Russian and Galician Jews, also are making themselves felt in it, being, in many cases, in partnership with Gentiles or with their own coreligionists of German descent. The king of the great mail-order business, a man with an annual income of many millions, is the son of a Polish Jew. He is one of the two richest Jews in America, having built up his vast fortune in ten or fifteen years. As I have said before, I know hundreds, if not thousands, of merchants, Jews and Gentiles, throughout this country and Canada, so I like to keep track of their careers.

This, too, is good sport.

Of course, it is essential to study the business map in the interests of my own establishment, but I find intellectual excitement in it as well, and, after all, I am essentially an intellectual man, I think.

There are retailers in various sections of the country whom I have helped financially—former buyers, for example, who went into business on their own hook with my assistance. This is good business, for while these merchants must be left free to buy in the open market, they naturally give my house precedence. But here again I must say in fairness to myself that business interest is not the only motive that induces me to do them these favors. Indeed, in some cases I do it without even expecting to get my money back. It gives me moral satisfaction, for which money is no measure of value.

Am I happy?

There are moments when I am overwhelmed by a sense of my success and ease. I become aware that thousands of things which had formerly been forbidden fruit to me are at my command now. I distinctly recall that crushing sense of being debarred from everything, and then I feel as though the whole world were mine. One day I paused in front of an old East Side restaurant that I had often passed in my days of need and despair. The feeling of desolation and envy with which I used to peek in its windows came back to me. It gave me pangs of self-pity for my past and a thrilling sense of my present power. The prices that had once been prohibitive seemed so wretchedly low now. On another occasion I came across a Canal Street merchant of whom I used to buy goods for my push-cart. I said to myself: "There was a time when I used to implore this man for ten dollars' worth of goods, when I regarded him as all-powerful and feared him. Now he would be happy to shake hands with me."

I recalled other people whom I used to fear and before whom I used to humiliate myself because of my poverty. I thought of the time when I had already entered the cloak business, but was struggling and squirming and constantly racking my brains for some way of raising a hundred dollars; when I would cringe with a certain East Side banker and vainly beg him to extend a small note of mine, and come away in a sickening state of despair.

At this moment, as these memories were filing by me, I felt as though now there were nobody in the world who could inspire me with awe or render me a service.

And yet in all such instances I feel a peculiar yearning for the very days when the doors of that restaurant were closed to me and when the Canal Street merchant was a magnate of commerce in my estimation. Somehow, encounters of this kind leave me dejected. The gloomiest past is dearer than the brightest present. In my case there seems to be a special reason for feeling this way. My sense of triumph is coupled with a brooding sense of emptiness and insignificance, of my lack of anything like a great, deep interest.

I am lonely. Amid the pandemonium of my six hundred sewing-machines and the jingle of gold which they pour into my lap I feel the *deadly silence of solitude.*

I spend at least one evening a week at the Benders'. I am fond of their children and I feel pleasantly at home at their house. I am a frequent caller at the Nodelmans', and enjoy their hospitality even more than that of the Benders. I go to the opera, to the theaters, and to concerts, and never alone. There are merry suppers, and some orgies in which I take part, but when I go home I suffer a gnawing aftermath of *loneliness and desolation.*

I have a fine summer home, with servants, automobiles, and horses. I share it with the Bender family and we often have visitors from the city, but, no matter how large and gay the crowd may be, the country makes me sad.

I know bachelors who are thoroughly reconciled to their solitude and even enjoy it. I am not.

No, I am not happy.

In the city I occupy a luxurious suite of rooms in a high-class hotel and keep an excellent chauffeur and valet. I give myself every comfort that money can buy. But there is one thing which I crave and which money cannot buy—happiness.

Many a pretty girl is setting her cap at me, but I know that it is only my dollars they want to marry. Nor do I care for any of them, while the woman to whom my heart is calling—Anna—is married to another man.

I dream of marrying some day. I dread to think of dying a lonely man.

Sometimes I have a spell of morbid amativeness and seem to be falling in love with woman after woman. There are periods when I can scarcely pass a woman in the street without scanning her face and figure. When I see the crowds returning from work in the cloak-and-waist district I often pause to watch the groups of girls as they walk apart from the men. Their keeping together, as if they formed a separate world full of its own interests and secrets, makes a peculiar appeal to me.

Once, in Florida, I thought I was falling in love with a rich Jewish girl whose face had a bashful expression of a peculiar type. There are different sorts of bashfulness. This girl had the bashfulness of sin, as I put it to myself. She looked as if her mind harbored illicit thoughts which she was trying to conceal. Her blushes seemed to be full of sex and her eyes full of secrets. She was not a pretty girl at all, but her "guilty look" disturbed me as long as we were stopping in the same place.

But through all these ephemeral infatuations and interests I am in love with Anna.

From time to time I decide to make a "sensible" marriage, and study this woman or that as a possible candidate, but so far nothing has come of it.

There was one woman whom I might have married if she had not been a Gentile—one of the very few who lived in the family hotel in which I had my apartments. At first I set her down for an adventuress seeking the acquaintance of rich Jews for some sinister purpose. But I was mistaken. She was a woman of high character. Moreover, she and her aged mother, with whom she lived, had settled in that hotel long before it came to be patronized by our people. She was a widow of over forty, with a good, intellectual face, well-read in the better sense of the term, and no fool. Many of our people in the hotel danced attendance upon her because she was a Gentile woman, but all of them were really fond of her. The great point was that she seemed to have a sincere liking for our people. This and the peculiar way her shoulders would shake when she laughed was, in fact, what first drew me to her. We grew chummy and I spent many an hour in her company.

In my soliloquies I often speculated and theorized on the question of proposing to her. I saw clearly that it would be a mistake. It was not the faith of my fathers that was in the way. It was that medieval prejudice against our people which makes so many marriages between Jew and Gentile a failure. It frightened me.

One evening we sat chatting in the bright lobby of the hotel, discussing human nature, and she telling me something of the good novels she had read. After a brief pause I said:

"I enjoy these talks immensely. I don't think there is another person with whom I so love to talk of human beings."

She bowed with a smile that shone of something more than mere appreciation of the compliment. And then I uttered in the simplest possible accents:

"It's really a pity that there is the chasm of race between us. Otherwise I don't see why we couldn't be happy together."

I was in an adventurous mood and ready, even eager, to marry her. But her answer was a laugh, as if she took it for a joke; and, though I seemed to sense intimacy and encouragement in that laugh, it gave me pause. I felt on the brink of a fatal blunder, and I escaped before it was too late.

"But then," I hastened to add, "real happiness in a case like this is perhaps not the rule, but the exception. That chasm continues to yawn throughout the couple's married life, I suppose."

"That's an interesting point of view," she said, a noncommittal smile on her lips.

She tactfully forbore to take up the discussion, and I soon dropped the subject. We remained friends.

It was this woman who got me interested in good, modern fiction. The books she selected for me interested me greatly. Then it was that the remarks I had heard from Moissey Tevkin came to my mind. They were illuminating.

Most of the people at my hotel are German-American Jews. I know other Jews of this class. I contribute to their charity institutions. Though an atheist, I belong to one of their synagogues. Nor can I plead the special feeling which had partly accounted for my visits at the synagogue of the Sons of Antomir while I was engaged to Kaplan's daughter. I am a member of that synagogue chiefly because it is a fashionable synagogue. I often convict myself of currying favor with the German Jews. But then German-American Jews curry favor with Portuguese-American Jews, just as we all curry favor with Gentiles and as American Gentiles curry favor with the aristocracy of Europe.

I often long for a heart-to-heart talk with some of the people of my birthplace. I have tried to revive my old friendships with some of them, but they are mostly poor and my prosperity stands between us in many ways.

Sometimes when I am alone in my beautiful apartments, brooding over these things and nursing my loneliness, I say to myself:

"There are cases when success is a tragedy."

There are moments when I regret my whole career, when my very success seems to be a mistake.

I think that I was born for a life of intellectual interest. I was certainly brought up for one. The day when that accident turned my mind from college to business seems to be the most unfortunate day in my life. I think that I should be much happier as a scientist or writer, perhaps. I should then be in my natural element, and if I were doomed to loneliness I should have comforts to which I am now a stranger. That's the way I feel every time I pass the abandoned old building of the City College.

The business world contains plenty of successful men who have no brains. Why, then, should I ascribe my triumph to special ability? I should probably have made a much better college professor than a cloak-manufacturer, and should probably be a happier man, too. I know people who have made much more money than I and whom I consider my inferiors in every respect.

Many of our immigrants have distinguished themselves in science, music, or art, and these I envy far more than I do a billionaire. As an example of the successes achieved by Russian Jews in America in the last quarter-century it is often pointed out that the man who has built the greatest sky-scrapers in the country, including the Woolworth Building, is a Russian Jew who came here a penniless boy. I cannot boast such distinction, but then I have helped build up one of the great industries of the United States, and this also is something to be proud of. But I should readily change places with the Russian Jew, a former Talmud student like myself, who is the greatest physiologist in the New World, or with the Russian Jew who holds the foremost place among American songwriters and whose soulful compositions are sung in almost every English-speaking house in the world. I love music to madness. I yearn for the world of great singers, violinists, pianists. Several of the greatest of them are of my race and country, and I have met them, but all my acquaintance with them has brought me is a sense of being looked down upon as a money-bag striving to play the Mæcenas. I had a similar experience with a sculptor, also one of our immigrants, an East Side boy who had met with sensational success in Paris and London. I had him make my bust. His demeanor toward me was all that could have been desired. We even cracked Yiddish jokes together and he hummed bits of synagogue music over his work, but I never left his studio without feeling cheap and wretched.

When I think of these things, when I am in this sort of mood, I pity myself for a victim of circumstances.

At the height of my business success I feel that if I had my life to live over again I should never think of a business career.

I don't seem to be able to get accustomed to my luxurious life. I am always more or less conscious of my good clothes, of the high quality of my office furniture, of the power I wield over the men in my pay. As I have said in another connection, I still have a lurking fear of restaurant waiters.

I can never forget the days of my misery. I cannot escape from my old self. My past and my present do not comport well. David, the poor lad swinging over a Talmud volume at the Preacher's Synagogue, seems to have more in common with my inner identity than David Levinsky, the well-known cloak-manufacturer.

The Goldwater Story

Barry Goldwater, a U.S. Senator from Arizona for many years and an unsuccessful Republican candidate for president in 1964, tells his family's story to journalist Howard Simons. What principally comes through in this vivid, circumstantial account is how Jews do their own thing, no matter what.

The reason my family, my father's family, never followed the Jewish faith when they came to Arizona was that there just weren't any synagogues. There were no rabbis.

My grandfather Michael was one of twenty-two children, and he left Poland when the Russians started to give the Jews a bad time. I have been trying ever since the 1930s to trace those twenty-two people, and I haven't had much luck. But Mike's brother Joe left Poland with him, and they went to France. It was a case of fighting in the French army or leaving there, so they went to England. I think this was about 1845.

Well, anyway, my grandfather Mike married an English girl named Sarah Nathan, who lived down in Whitechapel. During the war, one or two times when I was in London, I tried to find the old synagogue there, but it had been bombed. The wedding certificate and the records were destroyed in the bombing. Well, they had two children in London, Elizabeth and my uncle Morris. In 1850, Mike and Joe left London to go to California because of the Gold Rush. My grandmother Sarah and her sister, whom I never knew much about, traveled to Panama and there they rode horses across the Isthmus. They picked up the boat on the other side and went to San Francisco. My grandfather and my great-uncle arrived in San Francisco about 1850, maybe '51, and they went to a little town called Sonora. This is a mining town up in the hills, and there my grandfather established a liquor store. The second floor was the town whorehouse. Well, my grandmother, whom I never knew, objected to the girls' working at night and raising her two children during the day.

At the same time, the two brothers had a business in San Francisco, and that really was their home. The women stayed in San Francisco and the men went back to see them. The women never moved with them, except to Los Angeles, where they opened a store down where the old Union Station was or is now.

Then, in 1860, they heard of gold in Arizona. My grandfather was never a very successful businessman. He sold a lot but he didn't make money. As I say, he maintained his home in San Francisco. He was very, very active in Jewish affairs up there; became a member of a Masonic lodge. But in 1860, he and his brother left Los Angeles and drove two wagons to what is now Yuma, Arizona. Gold had been discovered in several places along the Colorado River. They first took their wagons up to the junction of the Gila River and the Colorado and then moved up to a little town called La Paz. He stayed there until he was convinced the river changes its course so much that he could never depend on the ferry. They had flat-bottomed boats that went up the river. He could never depend on them, so he went downstream about six miles and found a little town called Ehrenberg.

Now the strange thing is, I always thought Herman Ehrenberg was a Jew. One day about

1934, 1935, I drove my old uncle down to Ehrenberg, and all that was left of our store was an adobe wall. I can see it yet. It had a beer stein painted on it: FIVE CENTS. He took me inside and said, "Now over in the corner was where your uncle Henry ran the post office. He didn't believe in delivering the mail. If they didn't come for it, he just threw it away." Well, I dug around in there and I found a letter written in German to the sheriff of San Bernadino County. I had it translated and it was a letter from Ehrenberg's brother inquiring as to the death of Herman Ehrenberg, who my uncle and my grandfather had found murdered at a trading post on one of their trips by horse from Los Angeles to Ehrenberg.

They were very, very close friends. Ehrenberg was a fabulous man—we are working on a history of his life now. But I sent the letter—this is before the war—to the library in Berlin, asking if they could put me in touch with Emil Ehrenberg, which was his brother's name. Well, I never got an answer. I went off to war and when I got back, here was a letter addressed to me from an Ehrenberg. But it was signed "Heil Hitler." I said, Well, he couldn't have been Jewish. Turned out he was a Lutheran.

They kept their business in Ehrenberg, my uncle Morris and my uncle Henry. They had a lot of interesting stories about the family. Where there was gold, the family would go looking for it. They'd never find it, but they'd do something else. They never made money until my father took over the business. My father made money. The other brothers I never knew, except Henry. Once in a blue moon, he would show up. There were two other brothers, Sam and Ben, both of whom died quite young. They were professional gamblers and died of tuberculosis. They were about forty-five or forty-six years old. They lived in Northern California.

The family moved the store from Ehrenberg for a short while to Wickenberg; it's a little resort town. There, my grandfather and his brother ran the Vulture mine. Henry Wickenberg had discovered this fabulous gold mine. Where my uncle learned how to run a stamp mill, God only knows, but he did. Henry sold the mine and he still owed my grandfather and his brother about $90,000. So they just went out and worked the mine; kept their rifles handy. When they got their $90,000, they turned the mine over to the new owner. Well, they took $140 million out of the mine. It's the whole story of my life.

My grandfather opened a store in Phoenix about 1870. It didn't work out. They went bankrupt, but he did establish a freighting business. He hauled freight to the different army camps around that part of the state. They moved to Prescott, Arizona, which became more or less our family home, and there they opened a store. My father, Baron, came over from Los Angeles, where he was born, and my uncle Morris, and occasionally Henry. But Henry was more interested in looking for gold. He was either down in Mexico or up in California, digging for gold, so I never knew him very well.

They bought the store from my grandfather. The three brothers—Henry, Morris, and my father—bought it from Mike in 1882. Mike went back to San Francisco and spent the rest of his life there. I think Sarah died about 1903 and Mike about 1906. I never knew him. At that time, we had stores in Prescott, one each in Wickenberg, Ehrenberg, Bisbee, where there was the famous Bisbee massacre. They held the store up, threatened to kill my grandfather. They put him under the bed and put a gun on him. They killed five people. These were some outlaws. They just came in, held them up, and robbed them. A posse was quickly formed, and they caught them and in about three weeks they hung all five of them over in Tombstone. We had a store in Tombstone; a little one in Benson.

I think we had one in a little station called Fairbanks, where my great-uncle Joe married the Mexican widow of their partner. The store was, in those days, called Castañeda and Goldwater. He died, and Joe married this girl. I think I met Joe once in my life. He was shot by the Indians. He lived. They took him down to a ranch and dug two balls out of his back. He wore those balls as a watch fob until he died. I think they buried him with them on. He was very active in Jewry in Los Angeles. I think he was a big contributor to the Cedars of Lebanon Hospital and some temple. He became a very wealthy man. You are old enough to remember Boss Overalls—you remember, the one with the mule teams pulling? Well, that was his business. He had some children, but I never knew them. As I say, there were twenty-two in that family.

My father, I call him a merchant prince. He was never home a lot. He traveled when we were young, went to New York, went abroad. He'd come back home. We'd see him. He was a very handsome man, extremely well dressed. No interest in politics. He couldn't hit a nail on the head with a hammer. Never learned to drive a car. He had a great philosophy. He said, "Never do anything yourself you can pay somebody else to do." It's all right, but it gets expensive. He was a club man. He liked to play poker; he liked to play bridge and chess, billiards. So he was never a man around whom stories would grow. But my uncle who came to Arizona, he had been born in London, so when he came to Arizona in 1863 or '64, he was fourteen or fifteen years old. He grew up with the territory.

The store in Prescott was a very successful one. My uncle Morris was in politics, he was a Mason, he was selected "Man of the Century" by his city. He was mayor of the town for twenty-seven years. He served in the territorial legislature, in the territorial senate, and was vice-president of the state's constitutional convention. Now, here's a man who never went to school. At this point was he still Jewish, maintaining his Judaism? No. But he never renounced it. He lived with this couple and the husband died, and after twenty years public opinion got the best of him. He married the woman he had been living with. They were married in the Episcopal church, but he never called himself an Episcopalian. And in his Masonic work, he only went up to the thirty-second degree by the Scottish Rite, because going up the York Rite in Masonry, you don't disown God but you don't put the great faith in God that you do in the Scottish Rite. He became Grand Master of the Lodge of Arizona. He gave me my third degree in Masonry, but I can remember on his front door there was a little tin—I don't know [mezuzah]—and in it was a little piece of paper. When he died he had a Masonic funeral.

When my father was married, he married a Gentile and they were married by an Episcopal minister, mainly because there were no rabbis. I don't think it was a case of the men in my family *wanting* to leave the faith.

There were many Jews in the early territorial days of Arizona: Zeckendorf and Steinfeld. Oh, any number of them. The Mormons had a very wide habit of establishing a town, but they always found a Jew to run the bank. That's where Zeckendorf came from. Solomonsville, a Mormon town. His family was there to run the bank. But my grandfather was always Jewish. My aunts, there were three of them. One of them stayed in San Francisco and was never married. That was

Elizabeth. The other two moved to New York, and they were always Orthodox Jews. One was Lieberman and one was Butler. They are all dead. In fact, the last child, who was my age, died about three months ago, and I remember that when she married a Gentile, her father and mother disowned her; they were that Orthodox. And they used to give me hell all the time because I was an Episcopalian. I said, "I can't help it." That's just about the whole story of the family.

Did they all come to the United States? I don't know. I've started in London and I wrote or telephoned every Goldwasser, Gildwasser, Goldwater—never found a one. I found a man in Australia who I'm pretty well convinced is one of the brothers. And then the mayor of Bulawayo, Zimbabwe. I remember one day this woman came into my office, after I was senator, and she said, "You know, I think we are related. I think my husband is related to your father." And she showed me a picture, and my God, he was a spitting image of my father. So I went to Zimbabwe—then Rhodesia—and went over to the town and looked the fellow up. The father had died. But the son was the spitting image. So we became pretty fast friends, and the last I heard of him, they were looking for him because he had absconded with about a quarter of a million dollars.

I never found any more.

I remember Dr. Monroe Goldwater in New York. We were not related and he was a very, very strong Democrat. I had several pleasant meetings with him. The fire chief of Cleveland, Ohio, was Goldwater. We could never establish a relationship. There's a Catholic priest in Saint Louis named Goldwater. I've been working on this family history now since 1939, and I finally just gave up. Every once in a while I'll get a letter from somebody saying, "My mother was Goldwater," and I'll get in touch with them, but they didn't come from that part of Poland. But I have to think that we're all related.

I never knew of any anti-Semitic feelings in Arizona. But even then, when I was a boy, we had one synagogue and one rabbi. I think there are now fifty-odd rabbis in the city and a very big Jewish population. There was never any problem with joining the country club, joining the social clubs. That just didn't exist in Arizona. And it didn't exist very much in the whole West. But it was never any handicap in Arizona. It was never even brought up. You know, the West was never liberal. We were a territory of the Confederacy before we were a territory of the Union, so politically we inherited the conservatism of the Democratic South. You know, I've never given it much thought. My best friend, Harry Rosenzweig, and I have touched occasionally on the subject of why wasn't there discrimination? It just didn't exist. I think now there probably is some. But it never has been a factor in my life or the life of Harry or any of the Jewish families, and Lord knows that most of my old friends are Jewish.

Today, once in a while, if I don't vote right on a matter affecting Israel, I'll hear. But I vote just the way I want, and people know it, so they don't bother me much. One of my best friends out there is the top rabbi; we were in the reserve forces together and we used to serve together.

My being half-Jewish led to a joke during the campaign in 1964. But it wasn't me; it was my brother. He was playing golf with Bob Hope. They went up to some course on the Hudson River and brother Bob signed his name and the pro said, "Oh, I'm sorry, Mr. Goldwater, but you can't play here. We don't allow Jews to play." Bob reportedly said, "Well, can I play nine holes? I'm only half-Jewish." I knew my brother wasn't that smart. This fellow used to be on the radio—he had a show, "Can You Top This?" He knew the origin of every joke. So I met him once and we were talking and he said, "You know, there are only seven basic jokes." I said, "All right, did you ever hear this story?" And I told it to him. He said, "Yeah. That was first heard when they were building the Temple of Solomon. And the Gentiles would come over with their aprons on and say, 'Can I work? I'm half Jewish.'" I don't know where my brother heard it, because I get credit for it and he's the one who told it. I still hear it. People will kid me. Even today I'll go out to dinner with good friends of mine and they'll have ham and they'll say, "Go ahead, Goldie, you can eat it; just eat half of it." It's all kidding.

Tel Aviv, 1939

The Zionist experiment, particularly its socialist kibbutz (agricultural collective) component, was supposed to change Jewish character, to eradicate alienation and a sense of living on the edge. This selection from his 1946 novel, *Thieves in the Night*—written after the author lived for several months on a kibbutz—shows that Arthur Koestler believed that the Jewish ethos hadn't actually changed in Palestine, but had only taken on new shapes and colors. In the Tel Aviv of 1939, there was a hesitancy, an uncertainty, a lack of confidence, a shortfall in full commitment. There was something missing.

Koestler was a Budapest Jew, originally a Zionist, who became a Communist and a Soviet agent in Berlin and Paris before breaking with the Bolsheviks and publishing in wartime London the seminal anti-Communist novel, *Darkness at Noon*, a devastatingly realistic portrayal of the Stalinist purge trials of the mid-thirties. His equally realistic novel about Jewish Palestine was poorly received in Jewish circles and has since been forgotten. Koestler went on to become one of the most successful and influential political novelists and commentators of his generation.

Having finished with this week's business in Haifa, Joseph early the next morning took the autobus to Tel Aviv. He slept for most of the three hours' journey through the orange and lemon groves of the Maritime Plain of Samaria of which the strip along the coast was in Hebrew, the next, parallel inland belt in Arab possession. Whenever Joseph, waking, looked through the window, he saw not the landscape but an unprotected flank. When they arrived in Tel Aviv, the khamsin had just reached its peak.

Each time Joseph came to Tel Aviv he was torn between his contrasting emotions of tenderness and revulsion. Tenderness for the one and only purely Hebrew town in the world with the lyrical name of Hill of Spring and the jostling vitality of its hundred and fifty thousand citizens; revulsion from the dreadful mess they had made of it. It was a frantic, touching, maddening city which gripped the traveler by his buttonhole as soon as he entered it, tugged and dragged him round like a whirlpool, and left him after a few days faint and limp, not knowing whether he should love or hate it, laugh or scorn.

The whole adventure had started less than a generation ago, when the handful of native Jewish families in Arab Jaffa decided to build a residential suburb of their own, on what they imagined to be modern European lines. Accordingly they left the molehill of the Arab port with its labyrinthine bazaars, exotic smells and furtive daggers, and started building on the yellow sand of the Mediterranean dunes the city of their dreams: an exact imitation of the ghetto suburbs of Warsaw, Cracow and Lodz. There was a main street named after Dr. Herzl with two rows of exquisitely ugly houses each of which gave the impression of an orphanage or Police barracks, covered for beauty with pink, green and lemon-coloured stucco which after the first rains looked as if the house had contracted smallpox or measles. There was also a multitude of dingy shops, most of which sold lemonade, buttons and flypaper.

In the early 1920s, with the beginnings of Zionist colonisation, the town had begun to spread with increasing speed along the beach. It grew in hectic jumps according to each new wave of immigration—an inland tide of asphalt and concrete advancing over the dunes. There was no time for planning and no willingness; growth was feverish and anarchic like that of tropical weeds. Each newcomer who had brought his savings started to build the house of his dreams; and woe to the municipal authority who tried to interfere. Was this the Promised Land or not? For a decade or so, while the Eastern European element predominated among the immigrants, the source of inspiration of all these petrified daydreams remained the stone warren of the Polish small town. The Hill of Spring became a maze of stucco, with rusty, iron railings along narrow-chested balconies and an Ionic plaster-column or Roman portico for embellishment.

However, life in Tel Aviv in those early days owed its peculiar character not to the people who had houses built, but to the workers who built them. The first Hebrew city was a pioneer city dominated by young workers of both sexes in their teens and twenties. The streets belonged to them; khaki shirts, shorts and dark sun-glasses were the fashionable wear, and ties, nicknamed "herrings," a rarity. In the evening, when the cool breeze from the sea relieved the white glare of the day, they walked arm in arm over the hot asphalt of the new avenues through whose chinks the yellow sand oozed up and which ended abruptly in the dunes. At night, they built bonfires and danced the horra on the beach, and at least once a week they dragged pompous Mayor Dizengoff or old Chief Rabbi Hertz out of their beds and took them down to the sea to dance with them. They were hard-working, sentimental and gay. They were carried by a wave of enthusiasm which had a crest and no trough. They were touchy only on one point, the Hebrew language. They fought a violent and victorious battle against the use in public of any other tongue; the slogan "Hebrews talk Hebrew" was everywhere—on buses, shops, restaurants, hoarding-posts; speakers from abroad who tried to address a meeting in Polish, German or Yiddish were howled down or beaten up. There were few cafés in those days but many workers' clubs; the cheap cafés sold meals on credit and got their supplies on credit; landlords let rooms on credit in their houses which were built on credit; and yet the town, instead of collapsing into the sand on which it was built, waxed and grew. . . .

—Ah, those were the good old times, the legendary days of ten years ago! As Joseph walked through the noisy crowd in Eliezer Ben Yehuda Street, of the two emotions battling in his chest revulsion got the upper hand. This cheap and lurid Levantine fair had ceased to be the pioneer town he had known and loved. One noisy café followed the other with flashy decorations, dance-parquets and microphones and blaring loud-speakers through which crooners from the suburbs of Bucharest and aged artistes from Salonica poured out their Hebrew imitations of American imitations of Cuban serenades. There were beauty parlours and antique shops and interior-decoration shops; and in the harsh white blaze of the sun it all looked like a noontide spook—the oppressive dream of a sybarite who has over-eaten at lunch. This was the newest quarter of the town, built since the recent immigration from Germany and Central Europe had started, and the stucco-idyll of the older parts had been defeated by the aggressive cubism of the functional style. The houses here looked like rows of battleships in concrete; they had flat oval terraces with parapets jutting out like conning towers, and they all seemed to shoot at each other. The streets had no skyline and no perspective; the eye jumped restlessly along the jagged, disconnected contours without ever coming to rest.

Last week Joseph had run into Matthews, and Matthews had asked him for luncheon today at the Café Champignon on the beach. As Joseph crossed the overcrowded terrace in the noise of the orchestra playing the "Merry Widow," people turned their heads to look at him; he was the only person here in the traditional Commune dress. He felt a sudden homesickness for Ezra's Tower; it seemed to him that he had left it not two days, but weeks ago.

Seated at a table near the railing, overlooking the sea, he saw Matthews, who was arguing with a waiter. Joseph felt a sudden relief at the sight of the heavy-jawed face with the squashed boxer's nose—it was so obviously Gentile in these sharp-featured Semitic surroundings.

"Listen," Matthews was explaining to the waiter as Joseph sat down, "I ordered a bottle of Chablis. This is syrup."

The waiter, dressed in a white jacket whose sleeves were too short for him, lifted his shoulders. "But please—it is written on the bottle: Chablis."

"It is muck," said Matthews. "Taste it."

"But please: Here it is written on the bottle. Perhaps it should be sweet—I don't know. I have been a teacher before in Kowno, Lithuania."

"Taste it," said Matthews.

"But I don't drink—ulcers, sir, please."

"Then take this away and get me some beer."

"We have no beer, please, only wine."

"Then call the manager."

"But the manager is busy."

"Listen," said Matthews. "How would you like it if I bashed this bottle on your head?"

The waiter looked at him doubtfully, lifted his shoulders, and carried the bottle away. A minute later he returned with two jugs of iced beer, smiling all over his crumpled face.

"Well, how do you like Tel Aviv?" asked Joseph.

Matthews took a deep draught and put his glass down, sighing with contentment. "Swell," he said. "If you were allowed to punch somebody's nose once a day, it would be the swellest city with the swellest people in the world."

"Particularly the waiters," said Joseph.

"Maybe the poor guy was really a teacher in Kowno, Lithuania, and got his ulcers in a concentration camp."

Joseph looked round the terrace and sighed. The khamsin lay on people's faces like a spasm. The women were plump, heavy-chested, badly and expensively dressed. The men sat with sloping shoulders and hollow chests, thinking of their ulcers. Each couple looked as if they were carrying on a quarrel under cover of the "Merry Widow."

"I can't blame the Gentiles if they dislike us," he said.

"That proves you are a patriot," said Matthews. "Since the days of your prophets, self-hatred has been the Jewish form of patriotism."

Joseph wiped his face. The khamsin hot wind was telling on him. He felt sick of it all: Judaism, Hebraism, the whole cramped effort to make something revive which had been dead for two thousand years.

"It is all very well for you to talk as a benevolent outsider," he said. "The fact is, we are a sick race. Tradition, form, style, have all gone overboard. We are a people with a history but no background. . . . Look around you, and you'll see the heritage of the ghetto. It is there in the wheedling lilt of the women's voices, and in the way the men hold themselves, with that frozen shrug about their shoulders."

"I guess that shrug was their only defense. Otherwise the whole race would have gone crackers."

"I know. That's what I keep repeating to myself. But sometimes one gets fed up and wants to run away to a country with a moderate climate and moderate people, who don't live in absolutes. Here even the sky conforms to the all-or-nothing law: nine months of scorching sun without a drop of rain, and three months of deluge. . . ."

He leant back and drank some beer. "This is nice," he said. "Reminds me of a certain country pub back home. It was dim and smoky and the men said one word each in half an hour."

"It's always the same story," said Matthews. "If you are a dumb ox you want to be a chatty parrot. If you are a parrot, you wish you were a dignified ox. Drink your beer and take it easy with your Dostoevski."

Joseph drained his glass, smiling. "Of course," he said, "the crowd at a dog race at home isn't a much prettier sight than this one. But the flaws in other races are diluted, while with us you get them in concentration. It's the long inbreeding, I suppose. They called us the salt of the earth—but if you heap all the salt on one plate it doesn't make a palatable dish. Sometimes I think that the Dead Sea is the perfect symbol for us. It is the only big inland lake under sea level, stagnant, with no outlet, much denser than normal water with its concentrated minerals and biting alkaloids; over-salted, over-spiced, saturated. . . ."

"They extract a lot of useful chemicals from it," said Matthews.

"Oh—quite. Marx and Freud and Einstein and so on. They are the crystallised products of the brine. But for all that the water doesn't get more palatable. . . ."

"How about some grub?" said Matthews.

"Waiter! The guy won't listen. I guess this one was an opera conductor in Danzig."

"The trouble with this town is," Joseph went on, "that ten years ago the immigrants were mainly volunteers with an ideal in their head, and now they are mainly expatriates with a kick in their pants. Oh, you should have seen it ten years ago! Now it has become a town of refugees—the saltiest stratum of the Dead Sea."

Matthews had at last succeeded in getting hold of the waiter and gave his orders. He seemed bored with the discussion.

"Stop worrying about your Dead Sea," he said. "These ship-wrecked folk don't matter. What matters is your new native generation and they're O.K."

"Yes—but they are on the other extreme. No salt at all. No intellectual passion, no sensitivity."

"Christ—you can't have it both ways. Maybe for fifty years you'll have to stop producing Einsteins and give other people a chance."

Between Two Worlds

The ambivalent status of Jews is articulated by the leading Soviet Jewish poet Itsik Feffer (purged by Stalin in the late-thirties). There are the old Jews and the new Jews; but however different in appearance and behavior, they all exist somewhere on the social margin.

The English version of the poem is by John Hollander.

So what if I've been circumcised
With rituals, as among the Jews?
Field winds have tanned my middle-sized,
Pale, dreaming feet to darker hues.

Some Jews long for tsholnt *a special Sabbath*
     dish yet—
We toughs, for smoke, and flame in motion;
Eight years' embattled meadows, set
Underneath the sky's blue ocean.

I'm a quiet guy and hardly a villain;
My honesty has no great appeal;
I'm never known to put on tfiln, *Philacteries*
I'm never known to wheel and deal.

So what if I've been circumcised
With rituals, as among the Jews?
Field winds have tanned my middle-sized,
Pale, dreaming feet to darker hues.

PART TWO
GROWING UP

A beautiful young Jewish face: The great French actress
Sarah Bernhardt, late nineteenth century.

INTRODUCTION

Jewish literature, stretching from Germany of 1800 through Eastern Europe of 1900, to the United States and Canada of the 1930s to the 1990s, is particularly rich in accounts of growing up—roughly covering the ages of ten to thirty, spanning experiences of schooling, marriage, early job-seeking and business and career pursuits.

This genre of growing-up accounts in the form of fiction, memoirs, and autobiographies is prominent in Jewish literature. Written in a wide variety of languages, the *bildungsroman* (this personal development story) was perhaps the single most popular prose genre in Western literature from the Age of Romanticism down to the last third of the twentieth century—attracting almost every great writer from Goethe to Joyce.

But there is a structural, ideological, and psychological reason for the proliferation of compelling Jewish accounts of growing up. The Jewish child, adolescent, and young adult (at least until the proliferation of so many upper-middle-class Jewish American and Canadian families after 1970, who by their wealth and power could seemingly provide cocoon-like protection for their young) knew how marginal the situation of his family was, both economically and politically. He learned readily from family talk about Jewish vulnerability and suffering. Sometimes he studied or read enough Jewish history to imbibe a view of Jewish history as an endless series of repressions, exiles, and martyrs. Yet the youthful Jew—his psyche impelled by deep biological urges for survival, and often a hopeful view of anticipated favorable environments—usually felt he could overcome adverse circumstances in society at-large, among Jews in general, or a dysfunctional family in particular, and achieve his dreams and ambitions.

While they were young, the Jews could exude determination and retain a high degree of optimism. In spite of the misery of the Jewish past, marginality of the Jewish present, difficulties, obstacles, or even hurts pressing in from their own families, somehow they would find a way to fulfill their humanity and realize the mature adult image of themselves that their better natures signaled.

Later on, the prison house of society, culture, and family, and the rolling tide of historical persecution and traditional deprivation would often begin to close in on them. Perhaps that is why the Jewish literature of growing up is so much more upbeat, even more joyful than the literature of maturing years. Biology heedless of society's cruel restraints created the young Jew; repetitious history bore down on the older ones.

Father and Son

It is commonly agreed today that the greatest Jewish novel of growing up is *Call It Sleep*, written in 1934 by a young New York writer, Henry Roth. It is also perhaps the gloomiest, reflecting the depths of the Depression and probably the author's own bitter experience with an abusive father. Yet despite the extremely adverse circumstance in the novel, with the help of a sacrificing and loving mother, the child David's spirit is not broken by his menacing and violent father. Possibly, father and son are to be seen as symbolic figures—the Jew from the Old Country pitted against the native-born American seeking liberation from the horrors of the past.

Sadly, Roth's obscure publisher went out of business soon after his novel was published. The novel received modest circulation and notice, gaining wide public attention only in the past decade. Roth, in his disappointment, turned from writing to other employment and the sequel to *Call It Sleep* was not published until the early 1990s, when Roth was an old man.

His mother rose, lit the gas lamp. Sudden, blue light condensed the candle flames to irrelevant kernels of yellow. He eyed them sadly, wishing that she hadn't lit the lamp.

"They will be coming soon," she said.

They! He started in dismay. They were coming! Luter. His father. They! Oh! The lull of peace was over. He could feel dread rising within him like a cloud—as though his mother's words had been a stone flung on dusty ground. The hush and the joy were leaving him! Why did Luter have to come? David would be ashamed to look at him, could not look at him. Even thinking of Luter made him feel as he felt that day in school when the boy in the next seat picked his nose and rolled the snot between his fingers, then peered round with a vacant grin and wiped it off under the seat. It made his toes curl in disgust. He shouldn't have seen him, shouldn't have known.

"Is Mr. Luter going to come here too?"

"Of course." She turned to look at him. "Why do you ask?"

"I don't know. I just thought—I—I thought maybe he didn't like the way you cooked."

"The way I—? Oh! I see!" She reddened faintly. "I didn't know you could remember so well." She looked about as though she had forgotten something and then went up the stairs into the front-room.

He stared out of the window into the dark. Rain still beat down. They must be hurrying toward him now in the rain, hurrying because it was raining. If only he could get away before they came, hide till Luter was gone, never come back till Luter had gone away forever. How could he go? He caught his breath. If he ran away now before his mother came back—stole out through the door silently. Like that! Opened the door, crept down the stairs. The cellar! Run by and run away, leaving upstairs an empty kitchen. She would look about, under the table, in the hall; she would call—David! David! Where are you? David! He'd be gone—

In the frontroom, the sound of a window opening, shutting again. His mother came in, bearing a grey covered pot between her hands. Rain drops on its sides, water in the hollow of the lid.

"A fearful night." She emptied the overflowing lid into the sink. "The fish is frozen."

Too late now.

He must stay here now, till the end, till Luter had come and gone. But perhaps his mother was wrong and perhaps Luter wouldn't come, if only he never came again. Why should he come here again? He was here yesterday and there was nobody home. Don't come here, his mind whispered to itself again and again. Please, Mr. Luter, don't come here! Don't come here any more.

The minutes passed, and just at that moment when it seemed to David that he had forgotten about Luter, the familiar tread of feet scraped through the hallway below. Voices on the stair! Luter had come. With one look at his mother's pursed, attentive face, he sidled toward the frontroom, sneaked up the stairs and into the dark. He stood at the window, listening to the sounds behind him. The door was opened. He heard their greetings, Luter's voice and slow speech. They must be taking their coats off now. If only they would forget about him. If only it were possible. But—

"Where's the prayer?" he heard his father ask.

A pause and his mother's voice. "He's in the frontroom I think. David!"

"Yes, mama." A wave of anger and frustration shook him.

"He's there."

Satisfied that he was there, they seemed to forget him for a little while, but again his father and this time with the dangerous accent of annoyance.

"Well, why doesn't he come in? David!"

There could be no more delay. He must go in. Eyes fixed before his feet, he came out of the frontroom, shuffled to his seat and sat down, conscious all the time that the others were gazing at him curiously.

"What's the matter with him?" asked his father sharply.

"I don't quite know. Perhaps his stomach. He has eaten very little today."

"Well, he'll eat now," said his father warningly. "You feed him too many trifles."

"A doubtful stomach is a sad thing," said Luter condoningly, and David hated him for his sympathy.

"Ach," exclaimed his father, "it isn't his stomach, Joe, it's his palate—jaded with delicacies."

His mother set the soup before him. "This will taste good," she coaxed.

He dared not refuse, though the very thought of eating sickened him. Steeling himself against the first mouthful, he dipped the spoon into the shimmering red liquid, lifted it to his lips. Instead of reaching his mouth, the spoon reached only his chin, struck against the hollow under his lower lip, scalded it, fell from his nerveless fingers into the plate. A red fountain splashed out in all directions, staining his blouse, staining the white table cloth. With a feeling of terror David watched the crimson splotches on the cloth widen till they met each other.

His father lowered his spoon angrily into his plate. "Lame as a Turk!" he snapped, rapping the table with his knuckles. "Will you lift your head, or do you want that in the plate too?"

He raised frightened eyes. Luter glanced at him sidewise, sucking his teeth in wary disapproval.

"It's nothing!" exclaimed his mother comfortingly. "That's what table cloths were made for."

"To splash soup on, eh?" retorted her husband sarcastically. "And that's what shirts were made for too! Very fine. Why not the whole plate while he's at it."

Luter chuckled.

Without answering, his mother reached over and stroked his brow with her palm. "Go on and eat, child."

"What are you doing now," demanded his father, "sounding his brow for fever? Child! There's absolutely nothing wrong with the brat, except your pampering him!" He shook his finger at David ominously. "Now you swill your soup like a man, or I'll ladle you out something else instead."

David whimpered, eyed his plate in cowed rebellion.

"Take heed!"

"Perhaps he had better not eat," interposed his mother.

"Don't interfere." And to David, "Are you going to eat?"

Trembling, and almost on the verge of nausea, David picked up the spoon and forcing himself, ate. The sickening spasm passed.

Impatiently, his father turned to Luter. "What were you saying, Joe?"

"I was saying," said Luter in his slow voice, "that you would have to lock up the place after you left—only one door, you see. The rest I will close before I go." He reached into his coat pocket and drawing out a ring of keys, detached one. "This one closes it. And I'll tell you," he handed the key to David's father. "I'm putting it down as four hours. The whole job won't take you more than two—three at most."

"I see."

"You won't get the extra this week though. The bookkeeper—"

"Next week then."

Luter cleared his throat. "You're having one diner less tomorrow evening," he said to David's mother.

"Yes?" she asked in constrained surprise, and turning to David's father, "Will you be so late, Albert?"

"Not I."

"No, not Albert," chuckled Luter, "I."

David's heart leaped in secret joy.

"Then I shan't prepare dinner for you tomorrow night?"

"No, I have something to do tomorrow night," he said vaguely. "Sunday perhaps. No, I'll tell you. If I'm not here by seven o'clock Sunday, don't keep the dinner waiting for me."

"Very well."

"I'll pay for the week in full anyhow."

"If you're not coming—" she objected.

"Oh, that doesn't matter," said Luter, "that's settled." He nodded and picked up his spoon.

During the rest of the meal, David ate cautiously peering up furtively from time to time to see whether anything he did was displeasing his father. At Luter, he never ventured a glance for fear the very sight of the man would confuse him into further blunders. By the time his mother set the dessert before him, he was already casting about for some way to retreat, some place where he could hide and yet be thought present, or at least, be accounted for. He might feign drowsiness and his mother would put him to bed, but he could not do that now. It was too early. What would he do till then? Where could he escape for a little while? The rooms of the house passed before his mind. The frontroom? His father would say, "What is he doing in there in the dark?" The bedroom? No. His father would say the same thing. Where? The bathroom. Yes! He would sit on the toilet-seat. Stay there till he heard some one call, then come out.

He had eaten the last prune, and was just about to slip from his chair when out of the corner of his eye, he saw Luter's hand move toward his vest-pocket and draw out his watch.

"I must go!" He smacked his lips.

He was going! David could have danced for joy. It was too good to be true!

"So soon?" asked his mother.

To David's surprise, his father laughed, and a moment later Luter joined him as if they shared some secret joke.

"I'm somewhat late as it is." Luter pushed his chair back and rose. "But first I must pay you."

David stared at his plate, listening. He could think of only one thing—Luter was going, would be gone in another minute. He glanced up. His father had just gone into the bedroom and in the moment of his absence Luter darted quick eyes at his mother. David shivered with revulsion and hastily looked down. Taking the coat which David's father had just brought out, Luter got into it, and David with all the forces of his mind, tried to hasten the feet that were moving toward the door.

"Well," Luter finally said, "a good week to you all. May the prayer," his hat pointed at David, "recover soon."

"Thank you," said his mother. "Good week."

"Lift your head," snapped his father. David hastily looked up. "Goodnight, Joe, I'll see you tomorrow. Good luck." Both men laughed.

"Goodnight." Luter went out.

With a quiet sigh of relief David uncurled from the tense, inner crouch his body seemed to have assumed, and looking about saw his father gazing at the door. His face had relaxed into a bare smile.

"He's looking for trouble," he said dryly.

"What do you mean?"

His father uttered an amused snort. "Didn't you notice how peculiarly he behaved tonight?"

"I did—" she hesitated, watching his face inquiringly—"at least—Why?"

He turned to her; her eyes swerved back to the dishes.

"Didn't you notice how embarrassed he was?"

"No. Well. Perhaps."

"Then you don't notice very much," he chuckled shortly. "He's off to a marriage-broker."

"Oh!" Her brow cleared.

"Yes. It's a secret. You understand? You know nothing about it."

"I understand," she smiled faintly.

"He's free as air, and he's looking for a stone around his neck."

"Perhaps he does need a wife," she reminded

him. "I mean I have often heard him say he wanted a home and children."

"Ach, children! Fresh grief! It isn't children he's looking for, it's a little money. He wants to open a shop of his own. At least that's what he says."

"I thought you said he was looking for troubles?" she laughed.

"Certainly! He's hurrying things too much. If he waited a few more years he'd have enough money of his own to set up a shop—without a wife. Wait! I said to him. Wait! No, he said. I need a thousand. I want a big place four or five presses. But he'll find out what a Yiddish thousand is. If it melts no further than five hundred the morning after he ducked under the canopy, let none call him unfortunate." He belched quietly, the Adam's apple on his neck jogging, and then looked around with knit brows as though seeking something.

"I heard him ask you to close up the shop," she inquired.

"Yes, he's giving me a little overtime. I won't be home till four or five—perhaps later. Bah!" he burst out impatiently, "The man makes eighteen dollars a week—six more than I do—and he itches to pawn himself to a wife." He paused, looked about again—"Where's The Tageblatt?"

His wife looked up startled. "The Tageblatt," she repeated in dismay, "Oh, where are my wits, I've forgotten to buy it. The rain! I put it off."

He scowled.

Noisily setting the dishes down in the sink, she wiped her hands on a towel. "I'll be only a minute."

"Where are you going?"

"My shawl."

"What's the matter with him, hasn't he feet?"

"But I can do it so much more quickly."

"That's the whole trouble with you," he said curtly. "You do everything for him. Let him go down."

"But it's wet out, Albert."

His face darkened, "Let him go down," he repeated. "Is it any wonder he won't eat. He moulders in the house all day! Get your coat on." His head jerked sharply. "Shudder when I speak to you."

David sprang from his seat, gazed apprehensively at his mother.

"Oh," she protested, "why do you—"

"Be still! Well?"

"Very well," she said, annoyed yet resigned, "I'll get him his coat."

She brought his coat out of the bedroom and helped him into it, his father meanwhile standing above them and muttering, as he always did, that he was big enough to fetch and get into his clothes by himself. Uneasily he tried to take his rubbers from her, but she insisted on helping him.

"It's two cents," she gave him a dime. "Here is ten. Ask for The Tageblatt and wait till they give you change."

"Eight cents change," his father admonished. "And don't forget The Tageblatt."

As David went out, his mother trailed behind him into the hall.

"Are you going down with him too?" his father inquired.

But without making a reply, she leaned over David and whispered. "Hurry down! I'll wait!" And aloud as if giving him the last instruction. "The candy store on the corner."

David went down as quickly as he could. The cellar door was brown in the gaslight. The raw night air met him at the end of the doorway. He went out. Rain, seen only where it blurred the distant lamps, still fell, seeking his face and the nape of his neck with icy fingers. The candy store window glimmered near the corner. His breath an evanescent plume, he hurried toward it, splashing in hidden puddles, his toes curling down against the rising chill. The streets were frightening, seen in loneliness this way, rain-swept, dark and deserted.

He didn't like his father. He never would like him. He hated him.

The candy store at last. He opened the door, hearing overhead the familiar tinny jangle of the bell. Gnawing a frayed chicken bone the half-grown son of the store-keeper came out of the back.

"Waddayuh want?"

"De Tageblatt."

The boy lifted a newspaper out of a small pile on the counter, handed it to David, who having taken it, turned to go.

"Where's your money?" demanded the boy impatiently.

"Oh, hea." David reached up and handed over the dime that he had been clutching in his hand all this time.

Clamping the bone between his teeth the boy made change and returned it, greasy fingers greasing the coins.

He went out, hurried toward the house. Walking was too slow; his mother would be waiting. He began to run. He had only taken a few strides forward when his foot suddenly landed on something that was not pavement. The sound of hollow iron warned him too late—A coal-chute cover. He slipped. With a gasp, he teetered in air, striving, clawing for a moment at a void, and then pitched forward, sprawling in the icy slush. Money and newspaper flew from his hands and now lay scattered in the dark. Frightened, knees and stockings soaked, he pushed himself to his feet, and began wildly looking about for what he had dropped.

He found the newspaper—sopping. Then a penny. More, there was more. He peered frantically in the dark. Another penny. Two cents now. But he had eight before. He plunged his hand here, there into the numbing snow, felt along the rough pavement, retraced, groped. Further ahead! Back! Nothing. Beside the curb maybe! Nothing. He would never find it. Never! He burst into tears, ran toward the house, careless now whether he fell or not. It would be better for him if he fell now, if he were hurt. Sobbing, he entered the hallway. He heard a door open upstairs, and his mother's voice at the top of the stairs.

"Child, I'm here."

He climbed up.

"What is it? What is it? Why, you're soaked through!" She led him in.

"I lost the money." He wailed. "I only have two—two cents."

His father was staring at him angrily, "You've lost it, have you? I had a feeling you would. Paid yourself for your errand, have you?"

"I fell in the snow," he sobbed.

"It's all right," said his mother gently, taking the newspaper and the money away from him. "It's all right."

"All right? Will everything he does be all right always? How long will you tell him that?" His father snatched the paper from her. "Why, it's wringing wet. A handy young man, my son!"

His mother took his coat off. "Come sit near the stove."

"Indulge him! Indulge him!" her husband muttered wrathfully and flung himself into a chair.

"Look at that paper!" He slapped it open on the table. "My way would be a few sound cuffs."

"He couldn't help it," she interposed placatingly. "It's very slippery and he fell."

"Bah! He couldn't help it! That's all I ever hear from you! He has a downright gift for stumbling into every black moment of the year. At night he breaks one's sleep with a squalling about dreams. A little while ago he flings his spoon into his soup. Now—six cents thrown away." He slapped his hand on the paper. "Two cents ruined. Who can read it! Beware!" he shook a menacing finger at David who cowered against his mother's side. "There's a good beating in store for you! I warn you! It's been gathering for years."

"Albert," said his wife reddening, "you are a man without a heart."

"I?" His father drew back, his nostrils curving out in anger. "A plague on you both—I have no heart? And have you any understanding, any knowledge of how to bring up a child?" He thrust his jaw forward.

A moment of silence followed and then "I'm sorry," she said, "I didn't mean it. I meant only—these things happen sometimes—I'm sorry!"

"Oh, you're sorry," he said bitterly. "I have no heart! Woe me, to labor as I labor, for food for the two of you and for a roof over your heads. To labor and to work overtime! In vain! I have no heart! As if I gorged myself upon my earnings, as if I drank them, wallowed in the streets. Have you ever gone without anything? Tell me!"

"No! No!"

"Well?"

"I meant only that you didn't see the child all day as I did—naturally you don't know when anything is wrong with him."

"I see enough of him when I see him. And I know better than you what medicine he needs most."

His mother was silent.

"You'll be saying he needs a doctor next."

"Perhaps he—"

But someone was knocking at the door. She stopped speaking, went over and opened it—Yussie came in; he held a wooden clothes-hanger in his hand.

"My mother wants you to go upstairs," he said in Yiddish.

David's mother shook her head impatiently.

"Have you taken to gadding about?" asked her

husband disgustedly. "Only a few days ago, you had no neighbors at all."

"I've only been there once," she said apologetically. And to Yussie, "Tell your mother I can't come up just now."

"She's waiting for you," he answered without stirring. "She's got a new dress to show you."

"Not now."

"I ain' goin' op," Yussie switched into English as if to avoid any further discussion. "I'm gonna stay hea." And apparently satisfied that his mission had been performed, he approached the uneasy David who was still seated beside the stove. "See wot I got—a bow 'n' arrer." He brandished the clothes-hanger.

"I'll have to go for just a minute," she said hesitantly. "This child—she'll be wondering—"

"Go! Go!" said her husband sullenly. "Am I stopping you?" He picked up the newspaper, plucked a match from the match-box and then stalked up into the frontroom and slammed the door behind him. David heard him fling himself down upon the couch.

"I'll be back in a minute," said his mother wearily, and casting a hopeless glance after her husband, went out.

"Aintcha gonna play?" asked Yussie after a pause.

"I don' wanna," he answered morosely.

"W'yncha wanna?"

"Cause I don' wanna." He eyed the clothes-hanger with disgust. It had been upstairs in a closet; it was tainted.

"Aaa, c'mon!" And when David refused to be persuaded, "Den I'm gonna shootchuh!" he threatened. "Yuh wanna see me?" He lifted the clothes-hanger, pulled back an imaginary string. "Bing! I'm an Innian. If you don' have a bow 'n' arrer, I c'n kill yuh. Bang!" Another shaft flew. "Right innee eye. W'yntcha wanna play?"

"I don' wanna."

"W'yntcha get a bow 'n' arrer?"

"Lemme alone!"

"I'm gonna shootchuh again den," he dropped to the floor. "Bing! Dot one went right inside. Yuh dead!"

"Go 'way!"

"I don' wanna go 'way," he had become cross. "I'm gonna shootcha all I wan'. Yuh a cowid."

David was silent. He was beginning to tremble.

"I c'n even hitcha wit my hatchet," continued Yussie. "Yuh a cowid." He crawled up defiantly.

"Wanna see me hitcha wit my hatchet?" He had grasped the clothes-hanger at one end, "Yuh dare me?"

"Get otta here!" hissed David frantically. "Go in yuh own house!"

"I don' wanna," said Yussie truculently. "I c'n fightchoo. Wanna see me?" He drew back his arm, "Bing!" The point of the clothes-hanger struck David in the knee, sending a flash of pain through his whole leg. He cried out. The next moment, he had kicked at Yussie's face with all the force in his leg.

Yussie fell forward on his hands. He opened his mouth, but uttered no sound. Instead his eyes bulged as if he were strangling, and to David's horror the blood began to trickle from under his pinched white nostrils. For moments that seemed years of agony the blood slowly branched above his lip. He stood that way tranced and rigid. Suddenly he sucked in his breath, the sound was flat, sudden, like the sound of a stone falling into water. With terrified care, he reached up his hand to touch the scarlet bead hanging from his lips, and when he beheld the red smear on his finger tips, his face knitted with fright, and he threw back his head, and uttered the most piercing scream that David had ever heard. So piercing was it that David could feel his own throat contract as though the scream were splitting from his own body and he were trying to stifle it. With the awful realization that his father was in the next room, he sprang to his feet.

"Here, Yussie," he cried frenziedly, trying to force the clothes-hanger into his hands. "Here, hit me Yussie. G'wan hit me Yussie!" And striking himself a sharp blow on the brow, "Look, Yussie, you hoited me. Ow!"

But to no avail. Once more Yussie screamed. And now David knew he was lost.

"Mama!" he moaned in terror. "Mama!" And turned toward the frontroom door as if toward doom.

It opened. His father glared at them in angry surprise. Then his features grew taut when his eyes fixed on Yussie. His nostrils broadened and grew pale.

"What have you done?" His voice was deliberate and incredulous.

"I—I—" David stammered, shrunken with fear.

"He kicked me right in duh nose!" Yussie howled.

Never taking his blazing eyes from David, his father came down the parlor stairs. "What?" he ground, towering above him. "Speak!" Slowly his arm swung toward the sobbing Yussie; it was like a dial measuring his gathering wrath. "Tell me did you do this?" With every word he uttered his lips became thinner and more rigid. His face to David seemed slowly to recede, but recede without diminishing, growing more livid with distance, a white flame bodiless. In the molten features, only the vein upon his brow was clear, pulsing like a dark levin.

Who could bear the white heat of those features? Terror numbed his throat. He gagged. His head waited for his eyes to lower, his eyes for his head. He quivered, and in quivering wrenched free of that awful gaze.

"Answer me!"

Answer me, his words rang out. Answer me, but they meant, Despair! Who could answer his father? In that dread summons the judgment was already sealed. Like a cornered thing, he shrank within himself, deadened his mind because the body would not deaden and waited. Nothing existed any longer except his father's right hand— the hand that hung down into the electric circle of his vision. Terrific clarity was given him. Terrific leisure. Transfixed, timeless, he studied the curling fingers that twitched spasmodically, studied the printer's ink ingrained upon the finger tips, pondered, as if all there were in the world, the nail of the smallest finger, nipped by a press, that climbed in a jagged little stair to the hangnail. Terrific absorption.

The hammer in that hand when he stood! The hammer!

Suddenly he cringed. His eyelids blotted out the light like a shutter. The open hand struck him full against the cheek and temple, splintering the brain into fragments of light. Spheres, mercuric, splattered, condensed and roared. He fell to the floor. The next moment his father had snatched up the clothes-hanger, and in that awful pause before it descended upon his shoulders, he saw with that accelerated vision of agony, how mute and open mouthed Yussie stood now, with what useless silence.

"You won't answer!" The voice that snarled was the voice of the clothes-hanger biting like flame into his flesh. "A curse on your vicious heart! Wild beast! Here, then! Here! Here! Now

I'll tame you! I've a free hand now! I warned you! I warned you! Would you heed!"

The chopping strokes of the clothes-hanger flayed his wrists, his hands, his back, his breast. There was always a place for it to land no matter where he ducked or writhed or groveled. He screamed, screamed, and still the blows fell.

"Please papa! Please! No more! No more! Darling papa! Darling papa!" He knew that in another moment he would thrust his head beneath that rain of blows. Anguish! Anguish! He must escape!

"Now bawl!" the voice raged. "Now scream! But I pleaded with you! Pleaded as I would with death! You were stubborn were you! Silent were you! Secret—"

The door was thrown open. With a wild cry, his mother rushed in, flung herself between them.

"Mama!" he screamed, clutching at her dress. "Mama!"

"Oh, God!" she cried in terror and swooped him into her arms. "Stop! Stop! Albert! What have you done to him!"

"Let him go!" he snarled. "Let him go I tell you!"

"Mama!" David clung to her frenziedly. "Don't let him! Don't let him!"

"With that!" she screamed hoarsely, trying to snatch the clothes-hanger from him. "With that to strike a child. Woe to you! Heart of stone! how could you!"

"I haven't struck him before!" The voice was strangled. "What I did he deserved! You've been protecting him from me long enough! It's been coming to him for a long time!"

"Your only son!" she wailed, pressing David convulsively to her. "Your only son!"

"Don't tell me that! I don't want to hear it! He's no son of mine! Would he were dead at my feet!"

"Oh, David, David beloved!" In her anguish over her child, she seemed to forget everyone else, even her husband. "What has he done to you! Hush! Hush!" She brushed his tears away with frantic hand, sat down and rocked him back and forth. "Hush, my beloved! My beautiful! Oh, look at his hand!"

"I'm harboring a fiend!" the implacable voice raged. "A butcher! And you're protecting him! Those hands of his will beat me yet! I know! My blood warns me of this son! This son! Look at this child! Look what he's done! He'll shed human blood like water!"

"You're stark, raving mad!" She turned upon him angrily. "The butcher is yourself! I'll tell you that to your face! Where he's in danger I won't yield, do you understand? With everything else have your way, but not with him!"

"Hanh! you have your reasons! But I'll beat him while I can."

"You won't touch him!"

"No? We'll see about that!"

"You won't touch him, do you hear?" Her voice had become as quiet and as menacing as a trigger that, locked and at rest, held back by a hair incredible will, incredible passion. "Never!"

"You tell me that?" His voice seemed amazed. "Do you know to whom you speak?"

"It doesn't matter! And now leave us!"

"I?" Again that immense surprise. As though one had dared to question a volcanic and incalculable force, and by questioning made it question itself. "To me? You speak to me?"

"To you. Indeed to you. Go out. Or I shall go."

"You?"

"Yes, both of us."

With terrified, tear-blurred eyes, David watched his father's body shake as if some awful strife were going on within him, saw his head lunge forward, his mouth open to speak, once, again, then grow pale and twitch, and finally he turned without a word and stumbled up the parlor steps.

His mother sat for a moment without moving, then quivered and burst into tears, but brushed them off.

Yussie was still standing there, mute and frightened, his blood smeared over his chin.

"Sit there a moment." She rose and set David on a chair. "Come here you poor child," she said to Yussie.

"He kicked me righd on de nose!"

"Hush!" She led Yussie to the sink, and wiped his face with the end of a wet towel. "There, now you feel better." And wetting the towel again, came over to David and set him on her lap.

"He hit me first."

"Now hush! We won't say anything more about it." She patted the lacerated wrist with the cold towel. "Oh! my child!" she moaned biting her lips.

"I wanna go opstai's," blubbered Yussie. "I'm gonna tell my modder on you." He snatched up the clothes-hanger from the floor. "Waid'll I tell my modder on you, yuh gonna gid it!" He flung the door open and ran out bawling.

His mother, sighing painfully, shut the door after him, and began undoing David's shirt. There were angry red marks on his breast and shoulders. She touched them. He whimpered with pain.

"Hush!" she murmured again and again. "I know. I know, beloved."

She undressed him, fetched his nightgown and slipped it over him. The cold air on his bruises had stiffened his shoulders and hands. He moved stiffly, whimpering.

"It really hurts now, doesn't it?" she asked.

"Yes." He felt himself wanting to sniffle.

"Poor darling, let me put you to bed." She set him on his feet.

"I have to go now. Numbuh one."

"Yes."

She led him into the bathroom, lifted the toilet-seat. Urination was painful, affording relief only as a mournful sigh affords relief. His whole body shuddered as his bladder relaxed. A new sense of shyness invaded him; he crept furtively around to stand with his back to her, contracted when she pulled the chain above his head. He went out into the bright kitchen again, into the dark bedroom, and got into bed. There was a lingering, weary sadness in the first chill of the covers.

"And now sleep," she urged, bending down and kissing him. "And a better day."

"Stay here."

"Yes. Of course." She sat down and gave him her hand.

He curled his fingers around her thumb and lay staring up at her, his eyes drawing her features out of deep shadow. From time to time a sudden gasp would shake him, as though the waves of grief and pain had run his being's length and were returning now from some remote shore.

Mottel Gets a Job

Of much sunnier disposition in describing growing up in the Old Country was the work of the prolific writer we know as Sholem Aleichem. In the dozen years before his death in 1916 he poured out a huge volume of fiction about life in the impoverished Eastern European shtetl, while actually living in New York as an affluent immigrant and producing comic material by the yard for Yiddish newspapers.

Obviously, Sholem Aleichem was looking at the Old Country through sentimentally filtered glasses, an attitude he knew his immigrant readers wanted him to take. Today Aleichem is best known for his stories about Tevya the Milkman, which were further sentimentalized in the highly successful treacly musical comedy of the 1960s, *Fiddler on the Roof*. His best book by far, however, is his account of the growing up of Mottel, the Cantor Peissi's orphaned son, from which this is taken. Here the honey is slightly cut with vinegar.

Mama just told me a good piece of news—I've got a job. And not at a plain workingman's shop, either, God forbid. Mama said that her enemies won't live to see the day when Mottel, the son of the late Peissi the Cantor, becomes a common workingman. My job, she said, was simply grand and easy as pie. All day long I'd be in school—that is, in the Talmud Torah—and at night I'd sleep over at Old Man Lurie's house.

"Old Man Lurie is a wealthy man," Mama said. "The only trouble is that he's not a healthy man. I mean generally he feels quite well—he eats, drinks, and sleeps. Except at night. That's when he can't sleep a wink. Lies awake all night long. So his children are afraid of leaving him alone at night. They just need another human being in the room with him. Even a youngster would do, as long as he's human. Putting another old man into the room doesn't seem proper. But a child doesn't matter. It's just like having a little cat around. They're offering five rubles per week and supper when you come back from Talmud Torah. And the supper's going to be first-class, as befits a rich house. What they throw away there would be enough for all of us. Now off to school, Mottel, and when you come home this evening, I'll bring you over to Old Man Lurie's. You won't have to do a bit of work. You'll have a royal dinner and a fine place to sleep. Plus five rubles a week. That will buy you some new clothes and a pair of boots."

Sounds good, huh? So why the tears? But with Mama it can't be helped. She's simply got to have a good cry. At Talmud Torah I only take up space. I don't learn a thing. There's no grade for my age level. So I help the teacher's wife around the house and play with the pussycat. Working for the teacher's wife isn't hard at all. I sweep the house, bring in the firewood, do anything she tells me to. It's a snap. You can't even call it work. Just so long as I don't have to study. Studying—there's nothing worse!

But best of all is the pussycat. People say a cat is an unclean beast. I say that's a lie. A cat is a clean animal. People say a cat is a mischievous little devil. I say that's a lie, too. A cat is a kind, cuddly creature. A dog is a tail-wagging cringer. A cat plays up to you. When you pat her head, she shuts her eyes and begins to purr. I love cats—but so what? Talk to my pals and they'll tell you thousands of fairy tales. That when you touch a cat you have to wash your hands. That touching a cat affects your memory. They don't know what else to dream up.

They've got a funny habit—if a cat comes up to them, they give it a swift kick in the ribs. Me, I can't bear to see a cat beaten. But my friends laugh at me. They don't feel sorry for animals at all. I'm talking about the kids who go to Talmud Torah with me. They're a bunch of murderers. They make fun of me. On account of my stiff, coarse pants they call me "Wooden Pantaloony," and my mother "Mrs. Sniffles," because she's always crying.

"Here comes your ma, Mrs. Sniffles," they yelled. She had come to call for me and take me to my job—a job as easy as pie. On the way, Mama complained about her sad and bitter lot (sad alone was not enough). God had given her two children, but now she was widowed and alone.

"Knock wood," she said, "at least your brother Eli made a good marriage. He fell into a bed of clover. The only trouble is that his father-in-law is a boor. Ah me, a baker, alas! What can you expect of a baker?" Mama complained as we made our way to the Lurie house.

"Old Man Lurie's room is like a royal palace," Mama whispered. Which was just the place I was dying to see. But meanwhile we were still in the kitchen, Mama and I. But the kitchen wasn't half bad, either. The oven was gleaming and white. The pots shone. Everything sparkled. We were asked to be seated. A lady appeared, dressed like a rich noblewoman. She talked to Mama and pointed at me. Mama nodded in agreement, continually wiped her lips, and refused to sit down. But me, I took a seat. As Mama was leaving, she told me to mind my manners and be a good boy, and managed to sniffle a bit and wipe her eyes. Tomorrow she would call for me and take me to school.

They gave me supper. Soup and white-loaf (imagine, white bread in the middle of the week!). And meat, heaps of it. After supper, they told me to go upstairs. Since I didn't know what they meant by "upstairs," Khana the cook, a swarthy woman with a long nose, took me by the hand and showed me. I followed her. It was a pleasure to walk barefoot up the carpeted stairs. It wasn't quite dark yet, but already the lamps were lit. Dozens of them. There were all sort of designs and pictures pasted on the walls. The chairs were covered with leather. Even the ceiling

was painted like—forgive the comparison—the one in the synagogue. Even nicer.

I was brought into a large room. It was so huge that had I been alone, I would have raced from one wall to another, or even rolled around on the velvet quilt spread over the entire floor. Turning somersaults on such a quilt must be loads of fun. Even sleeping on it wouldn't be half bad, either.

Old Man Lurie was a tall, handsome man with a gray beard and a broad forehead. He wore a skull-cap made of pure velvet; his slippers, stitched with heavy thread, were of velvet, too. He sat poring over a huge thick book. He didn't say a word as he studied, but merely chewed the tip of his beard, jiggling his leg and grumbling softly to himself.

Old Man Lurie was a queer duck. I stared at him and asked myself: Does he see me or doesn't he? Apparently he didn't see me, for he didn't even look my way, and no one said anything to him about me. They just placed me in the room and locked the door behind me. Suddenly Old Man Lurie, still not looking at me, began to speak:

"Come here, sir, and I'll show you what Rambam has to say."

Who was he addressing? Me? Calling *me* sir? I looked around. There was no one else in the room.

"Come here, sir," Old Man Lurie bellowed once again in his gruff voice, "and you'll see what Rambam says."

By now I was afraid to approach.

"Are you calling me?"

"Yes, you, sir, who else?" said Old Man Lurie, gazing into the book.

He took me by the hand, pointed out the passage, and explained what Rambam Maimonides had to say. As he proceeded, his voice grew shriller and he became increasingly wrought up. Finally, he worked himself into such a dither that he turned beet-red. He kept gesticulating with his thumb and frequently treated me to an elbow jab in the ribs.

"Well, sir, what do you say to that? That was good, huh?"

Even if it were top-notch, I couldn't make heads or tails of it. So I kept quiet. I was silent and he seethed. He seethed and I was silent. Then I heard the jangle of keys on the other side of the door.

The door opened and in came the lady dressed

like a rich noblewoman. She approached Old Man Lurie and shouted right into his ear. Apparently he was deaf. If not, why did she have to shout? She told him to leave me alone, for it was time for me to go to sleep. She took me away from the old man and bedded me down on a cot with springs. The linen was white as snow. The silken quilt was soft. I was in Paradise. The nobly dressed lady covered me and left the room, locking the door.

Hands behind his back, Old Man Lurie began pacing in the room, looking down at his fine slippers. He muttered and grumbled to himself, moving his eyebrows most peculiarly. But I was so drowsy I couldn't keep my eyes open any longer.

Suddenly Old Man Lurie came up to me and said: "You know what? I'm going to eat you up."

I stared at him. I didn't know what he was driving at.

"Get up. I'm going to eat you up."

"Who? Me?"

"Yes, you. I have to eat you up. And no ifs and buts about it."

Old Man Lurie kept talking and pacing in the room, his head down, his hands at his side, his forehead wrinkled. But little by little he lowered his voice. Soon he was whispering to himself. I followed every word, scarcely able to catch my breath. He asked himself questions and then answered them.

"Rambam states that the universe is not eternal. How is that inferred? By the fact that every effect must have a cause. How can I demonstrate this? By asserting my own will. How? If I want to eat him up, I eat him up. But what about compassion? Compassion has nothing to do with it. I assert my will. The will is the ultimate purpose. I eat him up. I want to eat him up. I must eat him up."

That Old Man Lurie certainly brought me a fine piece of news. He must eat me up. What would Mama say? Suddenly I became scared. A shiver ran over me. The cot I was lying on was not quite up to the wall. Little by little I moved closer to the wall and slipped to the floor. My teeth began to chatter. I listened, waiting for him to come and eat me up. How did I pass the time? I quietly called to Mama and felt the wet drops rolling down my cheeks into my mouth. The drops were salty. Never before did I long for Mama as I did then. I also longed for my brother Eli, but not that much. And I also recalled my father, after whom I am saying the Mourner's Prayer. Who would say

the Mourner's Prayer after me if Old Man Lurie gobbled me up?

Apparently I had fallen asleep. For when I suddenly woke up, I looked around, anxious to know where I was. I touched the wall and the cot. I raised my head and saw a huge, bright room. Velvet quilts were on the floor. Pictures were pasted on the walls. The ceiling like—forgive the comparison—the one in the synagogue. Old Man Lurie was still sitting over his huge book which he called "Rambam." I liked the name "Rambam" because it sounded like "Bimbam." Suddenly I recalled that only last night Old Man Lurie had wanted to eat me up. I was afraid that if he saw me he'd try the same trick again. So once more I hid between the cot and the wall and remained absolutely still.

The door opened up with a clatter. The nobly dressed lady entered, followed by Khana carrying a big tray filled with pitchers of coffee and hot milk, and a platter of freshly baked butter rolls.

"Where's the lad?" said Khana. She looked around and spotted me in my hiding place.

"You're some little devil, aren't you? What are you doing down there? Come down to the kitchen with me. Your mother's waiting for you."

I jumped up and dashed barefoot down the padded stairs, singing rhythmically, "Rambam, Bimbam. Bimbam, Rambam," until I came to the kitchen.

"What's the rush?" Khana said to Mama. "Let him at least have a cup of coffee and a butter roll. You also ought to have a cup of coffee. It's no skin off their back. They got plenty."

Mama thanked her and sat down. Khana served coffee and fresh butter rolls.

Did you ever eat sugar cakes made with fresh eggs? Well, that's what a rich man's butter rolls taste like. They're even better than cake. I can't even begin to describe the taste of the coffee. It was sheer delight. Mama held the cup and sipped the coffee, enjoying every drop. She gave me most of her butter roll. Seeing this, Khana raised a fuss, as though we had insulted her.

"What are you doing? Eat. Eat. There's plenty."

Khana gave me another butter roll. That made two and a half. I listened to their conversation, one I was already familiar with. Mama complained about her bad fortune. A widow left with two children, one in a bed of clover, the other, poor fellow, not. I would like to know just what a bed of clover really is. Is it a bed filled with clover leaves? Always green and grassy?

Khana listened to Mama and shook her head. Then Khana began to talk and complain about *her* bad fortune. She stemmed from a fine, respectable family, yet now she had to cater to others. Her father had been a well-to-do house-holder, but a fire ruined him. Then he fell sick. After that he died. If her father were to get up and see his Khana standing in front of someone else's oven . . . ! But thank God she had no cause for complaint. She had a good job. The only trouble was that the old man was a bit. . .

A bit what? I didn't know. Khana made little circles around her ear with her finger. Mama listened to Khana and shook her head. Then Mama began to talk again. Now Khana listened and shook *her* head. As we left Khana gave me another butter roll and I showed it to the kids in Talmud Torah. They crowded around me, gaping at me as I ate it. Apparently it was a rare delicacy for them. I gave each of them a little piece. They licked their fingers.

"Where'd you get a treat like that?"

I puffed out both my cheeks and stood before them with my hands deep in the pockets of my stiff, coarse pants. I chewed slowly, swallowed and did a silent little jig with my bare feet, as though to say: "Tsk, tsk, you poor beggars. Some treat, butter rolls! Ha, ha. You ought to try it with coffee, and then you'd know what heaven is really like."

The eternal conundrum of devout Jewish parent and child: Mizrahi, *The Binding of Isaac*, 1888.

A Writer's Beginning

Isaac Leib Peretz was a prominent Yiddish writer of the Odessa Renaissance at the end of the nineteenth century. His retelling of Hasidic tales (one of which is presented in part three) gained him an enormous readership in the Yiddish-speaking world. Even more important was his influence as an editor and lecturer and ideological proponent of Yiddishkeit—a largely secular but still historically-minded Yiddish culture. Yiddishkeit was an intellectual movement that was unfortunately undermined by the Palestinian Zionists' choice of modernized Hebrew as their community's language and by the very rapid, somewhat unanticipated transition from Yiddish to English on the part of the first generation of immigrant Jews born in New York. By 1925 Peretz's dream of Yiddishkeit was defeated.

In this selection from his memoirs, Peretz writes of the psychological and cultural context out of which the ambitions and motifs of his literary ethos emerged. It convincingly communicated the complexity of the Odessa Renaissance's kind of Yiddish culture of the late-nineteenth century—the cross-currents of the parochial and the universal, the traditionally Jewish and the secular European.

The argument could be made that this culture was too heterogeneous in it derivations to survive in an integrated and stable form beyond Peretz's own generation. Once the Zionists had opted for Hebrew and the great immigration to magnetic America was underway, it was doomed. Peretz's nostalgia is an oblique recognition of this fragile situation.

I suffered for the exile of the Shekhina, of God's Divine Presence. Why does falsehood triumph over truth? Why do mistakes determine fate? And why does the Redeemer—as it says in Lamentations—"keep ashes in his mouth and remain silent?"

Then there was the problem of being in exile for real.

In gala uniforms, with musical instruments that glittered in the sunlight, a division of troops paraded one gala day from the officers' quarters at the castle down the length of the cobblestone street to the barracks at the Shebreshin gate. They were accompanied all the way by a gang of kids. Except for the druggist and his three dark ladies, everyone ran to their windows, or to the doors of their shops. As the band exploded in a tri-umphant, joyful march, I felt stricken: "Where is my army, my martial music?" Tears rose in my eyes.

In my mind's eye, I already owned a large part of the world, all of ancient Israel, that land flowing with milk and honey where every man sat under his vine and his fig tree. True, it was a mistaken geography. Just recently, when I wrote the story "Devotion unto Death," I had Lake Kinneret lapping the shores of the holy city of Safed. But what a piece of the world that was! A land with cities (including Jerusalem), villages, rivers and seas (the Dead Sea in their center), mountains covered with vineyards. All I actually saw with my own eyes on the other side of the fortress was Stabrow, the village I mentioned earlier.

I don't remember just when it was, but once I

was filled with a powerful desire to climb to the balcony of the clock tower. So I stole away from my parents' house, climbed the slippery, narrow, dizzying tower stairs, and emerged on the balcony, from where I could suddenly see two or three miles of unimpressive, flat land around the city, "buildings like houses of cards, people like grasshoppers," and a few scattered dwarf trees. To my intense dismay, I concluded that the higher you are, the farther you see—but not necessarily the better.

Gradually, my little world began to expand. It reached out beyond the city and annexed the engineers' garden, from which the ladies with blossoms on their skirts came into town to stroll about the castle.

Here is the story of that garden: For many years the fortress had not served its purpose. The ramparts were no longer awesome, the cannons and piles of ammunition had been removed, the water had dried in the moats, and the frogs had moved to the swamps in the meadow. The garrison was gone, and it had been replaced in the barracks with uhlans and Cossacks. The major general with his bristly mustache had said farewell to the city, drunk a toast, taken his gift, and gone. There was no trace of the three drawbridges, and the moats had been filled in to serve as roads to the highway. The supervisor stayed on to keep Jewish boys from swimming, and everyone forgot about the engineers who lived in the garden outside town. They were still doing the calculations for the proper dismantling of the fortress, and in the meantime, the garden where they lived in a large white house that shone through the trees was a locked Gentile paradise.

Sometimes, walking along the highway, I would get down into the ditch near the engineers' garden and look in with longing. I would stick my head as far as it would go between the fence posts and stare. There were lots of trees and garden paths and the gleaming white house among the green trees, and the fluttering white dresses, bedecked with flowers, of the engineers' wives. On a side path I sometimes saw an angelic little girl on a swing. Her laughter rang aloud. Her golden locks flew in the wind as her father the general pushed the swing himself.

In the festive evenings brightly colored Chinese lanterns swayed in the leaves over the length of the main path to the house, casting strips of rainbow light on the ground below. The regimental band would play in front of the house. New guests kept arriving from the officers' quarters. There was dancing and drinking, and the occasional echo of a toast before it was swallowed up in the music of the brass.

Sometimes on quiet evenings you could hear piano music inside the house. Mikhl, the leader of our Jewish band of musicians, who later served as the model for one of my stories, would stumble through the ditch—he was seldom fully sober—and thirstily strain to hear the music. From these melodies he was said to improvise moralistic songs for the veiling of the bride, processionals to the wedding canopy, and other dance music for Jewish weddings. Boys who loved music, among them members of the synagogue choir, gaped with their heads between the posts. When we were noticed, we were chased away—why should Jewish children be permitted to enjoy themselves? The guard dogs would be unleashed against us, and in tearing our heads from between the fence posts to flee we would leave behind pieces of our skin.

Then suddenly someone remembered the engineers, and they were summoned to begin their work. The paradise opened up, and my child's world expanded. Much later, when I fashioned my fictional garden for the wealthy Jew of Safed, I joined it to sections of Saxony Park in Warsaw and the Rabbinic gardens of Strukov and Biala. But on that first occasion when I entered the garden, my heart was pounding as if I were one of the four great sages of the Talmud entering that mysterious orchard from which only one of them would emerge intact. I had entered the garden whole. But having already begun to "cut the plants in the garden of faith," I wondered whether I would emerge unscathed.

I walked along the long, dark garden path thinking about death.

Why did God create death, and what happens afterward? The soul flies to heaven or to hell. Maimonides maintains that something of the dead person's mind continues to exist at the highest level to which his soul had been educated on earth. But what of my little brother who died so young that his reason had no time to develop? What about infants in the cradle or stillbirths? The Baal Shem Tov tells us that we will continue to lead the same life that we led here on earth, but pleasurably or miserably according to our merits. The rich landowner remains a rich landowner and the teamster a teamster—a kind of reward and punishment of the imagination, a chimerical settling of accounts, as if the Almighty were deceiving us. There was a crazy middle-aged woman in town who had been divorced or thrown out by her husband, along with her clothes and jewelry. All day long she wandered around the streets with her bundle. I don't know where she spent the nights. She would stop in the market, open her bundle to spread out her things, look them over and smile, try on her jewelry, one piece at a time. She took off one wig and put on another. She also tried to change her clothes in the middle of the market, as though this were a holiday in the middle of the week. Her emaciated face and her eyes beamed with joy. Does another such paradise await her? Here the police came and dragged her off to jail. Up there, in the imaginary world, where there are no police, she may be able to change her clothes ten times a day.

As for the body, it was but dust and ashes. "The spirits speak" was only a symbolic expression, whereas "The dead don't know that they are dead" was literal truth. But I could not imagine how anyone lies in the grave without feeling the confinement, the dampness, the dark, and the worms eating his body. What if there remains a bit of awareness, a touch of feeling, God help us? All my limbs went icy.

And why die at all? Where was the justice in that? Because Adam sinned by eating of the Tree of Knowledge. Was knowledge sinful, or the fact that God forbade it? And if eating of it were a sin, did it merit eternal punishment for all subsequent generations? "I will visit the sins of the fathers on the children to the third and the fourth generations," says the Bible, but it doesn't say forever! And why was the fruit of the Tree of Life forbidden? "Lest he live forever." Well, why not? "They will be equal to me." What's wrong with that? Later He did demand just that—"I am Holy, thou must be Holy too," and "Be thou merciful also." He wanted us to be like Him after all.

And then how very harsh and terrifying was the punishment, the agony of death.

Now comes Maimonides again, the wise and profound philosopher who divides the world thus: Everything from the earth to the heavenly spheres is subject to the law of Aristotle; everything above the spheres is subject to the law of Moses—"He is true and His Torah is true."

Maimonides says it's all a textual error. There is no pain, no suffering, no agony, no death. None of it exists, just as the darkness doesn't exist. There is only light. "He formed light and created darkness" is only a figure of speech in prayer. It was light that God created! Darkness is only the absence of light, what remains when God takes the light away. And He has the right to take it away because He didn't have to give it to us in the first place. By the same reasoning, there is no illness, only health. Health is real, the gift of God. Its absence is called illness, but the word doesn't signify anything real.

God created life, and when He takes it back, there is death. We cannot complain. He does not bring death, He takes back only what is His. Beruria, wife of Rabbi Meir, was right when she told her husband not to weep. "Our two sons haven't died, Meir. The Almighty has taken back only what He entrusted to us." "The Lord gives and the Lord takes." Job understood it, and so clearly! I have this same sense from the words that Leah speaks in my play *The Golden Chain*: "Snow is clear, ice is clear, everything is clear—everything but life."

But my young heart resisted this cold logic, and pumped the hot, rebellious blood through my veins until my temples throbbed: "What is death? Why do we die?"

You might be interested to hear of my own brushes with death.

When I was still a child, I barely missed meeting the Angel of Death face-to-face. One day I was on my way to my grandmother's store to get my weekly allowance of six groschen. As I entered the shop, I felt weak and dizzy. I tried to lean on the wall, but my hand wouldn't hold. I fell, and felt myself falling into a deep chasm.

When I regained consciousness, I was in the big room of my grandmother's house, in a big bed, and it was before dawn. I heard a soft, pious chanting. Slowly, I opened my eyes. My uncle Shmuel was studying in a corner of the room by a lamp, his face obscured by a holy book. I could hear the chanting, but I couldn't make out the words. In order to hear better I tried to move to the edge of the bed, but my body would not obey me. My bones ached. I was frightened, and realized I must be sick. I didn't want to ask about it lest I interrupt his learning. My illness might have been the reason my uncle Shmuel Leybush was chanting in such a heartfelt way, so that the merit of his study would help me. I lay there motionless. My head felt heavy. I touched it, and found it wrapped in a kerchief. There was a sour smell in my nostrils—the kerchief had been soaked in vinegar. I glanced toward the window. A white night shone into the room and bottles of medicine stood on the windowsill. What was wrong with me? When did I get sick, and why was I here? I plied my weak head with questions and remembered how I had gone to my grandmother's store and collapsed there. I must be seriously ill. That was why my uncle was so absorbed in his studying. In the marketplace, which the windows faced, a wagon drove by, and dogs began to bark. "Dogs bark; the Angel of Death has come to town." Things were grim. But no, the dogs must have barked because of the wagon that passed. Meanwhile, I was getting hotter and hotter with fever. I was bathed in sweat and my body seemed to be on fire.

When I woke again—I think it was the same day—before I opened my eyes, I heard voices around my bed:

"He is *ours*"—the voice of my grandmother.

"The yellow bottle . . . "—my aunt Yente.

"And I say it was the cupping"—my aunt Temma.

My mother only laid her hand on my forehead.

"Back from the other side, really from the other side!" This was a man's voice that I didn't recognize. I heard his footsteps as he left the room and closed the door behind him.

"A close call—a very close call," I thought.

But I had an even more frightening brush with death at the well. In the middle of one corner of the market there is a well under a wooden roof supported by four heavy posts. The well is surrounded by a wooden railing about as high as a grown man's chest. The water is drawn in buckets on a rotating iron chain that winds around a roller when you turn a gigantic, spiked wheel.

It sounds like your ordinary town well. But it was very, very deep, and when you pressed up against the railing (children had to stand on tiptoe) to look down inside, you could see a little wheel of light flashing over the black surface of the water—a liquid smile is how I might describe it

today. If you looked into the well long enough, your head began to spin and you were seized by a marvelous attraction to that smile. It drew you so magnetically that you had to hold on tight to keep yourself from jumping in. There was magic in the black well water and its liquid smile.

That's not all. Boys and girls said that on really dark nights when all the lights went out in the houses, and the city was asleep, cats would gather at the well, white cats and black cats, and arranging themselves along the points of the wheel in alternating fashion—black cat beside white cat— they would yowl in unison. As they yowled, their motion along the wheel would set it turning, until the buckets would come up and down, faster and faster. The night watchman who patrolled the marketplace, a Gentile said to be in his nineties, would hear the yowling of the cats and the creaking of the wheel, and the buckets going down, slapping the water, spurting back with a little laugh, and then the buckets rising again, turning over by themselves, and splashing the water back into the well. He would shudder and make the sign of the cross, over and over again. The old women said that the cats were not really cats at all but wandering souls, seeking their redemption in the water. The black cats were men who had scorned the ritual bath; the white cats were wives who had not attended scrupulously to the Jewish laws of modesty and ritual immersion.

It was no ordinary well, as you can see.

One Friday as I was running across the marketplace, I saw workmen taking down the railing, which was rotting with age, and blocking the approach to the well with boards. With my own ears I heard them say, "We'll put up the new railing on Monday." Then I forgot all about it. Friday night after dinner—it was a hot summer evening—I grabbed the copper jug and ran to the well for fresh water. I ran right over and tried to lean over the railing to check if you could see the water smile at night.

As I've already recalled, an old woman grabbed me and pulled me back. This was Raggedy Freydl, the tar seller who figures in my story "The Cellar Room." She saved me from certain death.

She saved me, that is, for day! But death and its terrors claimed me at night. In contrast to my love of life by day, every night for a long, long time I fell into the same deep well. It got to the point where it wasn't death that frightened me but its brother sleep. I would try to keep my eyes wide open all night so as not to fall into a chasm, as I had done in my grandmother's shop. I didn't want to sink into oblivion and be torn from life.

The heavier my eyelids grew from the lead of sleep, the greater my terror and my desire to hold on to life. I would tear open the window or run outside into the marketplace. The market slept in the blue darkness of the night, its houses frozen, and the windows black. Inside, there were people breathing, animate, yet I had no sense of their lives. Why was that? Why were there walls between us, between my life and theirs?

This feeling came over me recently when I passed through a quiet, remote Swiss village at night. Suddenly, I was seized by the pain of being cut off from the life behind the shutters. People were breathing, yearning, grieving, complaining, or rejoicing there, enjoying their happiness in the silent night, while I had no knowledge, no experience, no share of it. Yet I was a person, like them. I had a tremendous urge to stand up and shout so loud that all the people would wake up and throw open the shutters, and thrust their heads out through the open windows. It was the same feeling I had when I was a boy.

The Three-Star Canadian Bar Mitzvah

In 1959, Mordechai Richler's *The Apprenticeship of Duddy Kravitz* fell like a bomb on the staid Jewish establishment of Canada (who were soon even more embarrassed and outraged when a good Hollywood film was made from the book). Mordechai Richler grew up in Montreal and although he spent twenty years residing in London, his best books are set among the then-large Montreal Jewish community. Everything that Richler, with vivacious and biting humor, says about Montreal Jews can be repeated with small variation about Jews in Toronto and in New York, Los Angeles, and other large American cities.

Early on, Richler was an unflinching portrayer of the new affluence-driven and media-inspired vulgarity of the Canadian/American Jewish middle class. His picture is one of high accuracy, and contrary to carping at the time, is no more hostile to this subculture than Sholem Aleichem was to the world of the Shtetl. Now the Jews have affluence and security, and are deeply immersed in popular media culture. That is the difference for the bar mitzvah boy in Richler's world as compared to Aleichem's.

The Cohen boy's *bar mitzvah* was a big affair in a modern synagogue. The synagogue in fact was so modern that it was not called a synagogue any more. It was called a Temple. Duddy had never seen anything like it in his life. There was a choir and an organ and a parking lot next door. The men not only did not wear hats but they sat together with the women. All these things were forbidden by traditional Jewish law, but those who attended the Temple were so-called reform Jews and they had modernized the law to suit life in America. The Temple prayer services were conducted in English by Rabbi Harvey Goldstone, M.A., and Cantor "Sonny" Brown. Aside from his weekly sermon, the marriage clinic, the Sunday school, and so on, the Rabbi, a most energetic man, was very active in the community at large. He was a fervent supporter of Jewish and Gentile

Brotherhood, and a man who unfailingly offered his time to radio stations as a spokesman for the Jewish point of view on subjects that ranged from "Does Israel Mean Divided Loyalties?" to "The Jewish Attitude to Household Pets." He also wrote articles for magazines and a weekly column of religious comfort for the *Tely*. There was a big demand for Rabbi Goldstone as a public speaker and he always made sure to send copies of his speeches to all the newspapers and radio stations.

Mr. Cohen, who was on the Temple executive, was one of the Rabbi's most enthusiastic supporters, but there were some who did not approve. He was, as one magazine writer had put it, a controversial figure.

"The few times I stepped inside there," Dingleman once said. "I felt like a Jesuit in a whorehouse."

But Mr. Cohen, Farber, and other leaders of the community all took seats at the temple for the High Holidays on, as Mr. Cohen said, the forty-yard line. The Rabbi was extremely popular with the young-marrieds and that, their parents felt, was important. Otherwise, some said with justice, the children would never learn about their Jewish heritage.

Another dissenter was Uncle Benjy. "There used to be," he said, "some dignity in being against the synagogue. With a severe orthodox rabbi there were things to quarrel about. There was some pleasure. But this cream-puff of a synagogue, this religious drugstore, you might as well spend your life being against the *Reader's Digest*. They've taken all the mystery out of religion."

At the *bar mitzvah* Mr. Cohen had trouble with his father. The old rag peddler was, he feared, stumbling on the edge of senility. He still clung to his cold-water flat on St. Dominique Street and was a fierce follower of a Chassidic rabbi there. He had never been to the Temple before. Naturally he would not drive on the Sabbath and so that morning he had got up at six and walked more than five miles to make sure to be on time for the first prayers. As Mr. Friar stood by with his camera to get the three generations together Mr. Cohen and his son came down the outside steps to greet the old man. The old man stumbled. "Where's the synagogue?" he asked.

"This is it, Paw. This is the Temple."

The old man looked up at the oak doors and the magnificent stained glass windows. "It's a church," he said, retreating.

"It's the Temple, Paw. This is where Bernie is going to be *bar mitzvah*."

"Would the old chap lead him up the steps by the hand?" Mr. Friar asked.

"Shettup," Duddy said.

The old man retreated down another step.

"This is the *shul*, Paw. Come on."

"It's a church."

Mr. Cohen laughed nervously. "Paw, for Christ's sake!" And he led the old man forcefully up the steps. "Stop sniffling. This isn't a funeral."

Inside, the services began. "Turn to page forty-one in your prayer books, please," Rabbi Goldstone said. "Blessed is the Lord, Our Father. . . ."

The elder Cohen began to sniffle again.

"Isn't he sweet," somebody said.

"Bernie's the only grandchild."

Following the *bar mitzvah* ceremony, Rabbi Goldstone began his sermon. "This," he said, "is National Sports Week." He spoke on Jewish Athletes—From Bar Kochva to Hank Greenberg. Afterwards he had some announcements to make. He reminded the congregation that if they took a look at the race horse chart displayed in the hall they would see that "Jewish History" was trailing "Dramatics Night" by five lengths. He hoped that more people would attend the next lecture. The concealed organ began to play and the Rabbi, his voice quivering, read off an anniversary list of members of the congregation who over the years had departed for the great beyond. He began to read the Mourner's Prayer as Mr. Friar, his camera held to his eye, tip-toed nearer for a medium close shot.

The elder Cohen had begun to weep again when the first chord had been struck on the organ and Mr. Cohen had had to take him outside. "You lied to me," he said to his son. "It is a church."

Duddy approached with a glass of water. "You go inside," he said to Mr. Cohen. Mr. Cohen hesitated. "Go ahead," Duddy said. "I'll stay with him."

"Thanks."

Duddy spoke Yiddish to the old man. "I'm Simcha Kravitz's grandson," he said.

"Simcha's grandson and you come here?"

"Some circus, isn't it? Come," he said, "we'll go and sit in the sun for a bit."

Linda Rubin came to the *bar mitzvah*. So did Irwin. "Well," he said, "look who's here. Sammy Glick."

"All right," Linda said sharply.

Duddy introduced Cuckoo Kaplan to Mr. Friar and Cuckoo did some clowning for the camera. "You've got a natural talent," Mr. Friar said.

Duddy apologized to Cuckoo because he couldn't pay him for being in the movie.

"That's show biz," Cuckoo said.

At the reception that night Duddy danced with Linda once. "If Yvette knew she'd be jealous," Linda said.

"Aw."

"Am I going to be invited to see your movie?"

"Sure."

But in the days that followed Duddy began to doubt that there ever would be a movie. Mr. Friar was depressed. His best roll of film had been over-exposed. It was useless. The light in the Temple was, he said, a disaster. "I say, old chap, couldn't we restage the *haftorah* sequence?" he asked.

"You're crazy," Duddy said.

Mr. Friar went to Ottawa to develop the film at the National Film Board and when Duddy met him at the station three days later Mr. Friar was very happy indeed. "John thinks this is my greatest film," he said. "You ought to see the rushes, Kravitz. Splendid!" But Duddy was not allowed to see the rushes. Night and day Mr. Friar worked in secret on the cutting and editing. Duddy pleaded with him. "Can't I see something? One reel. A half of a reel, even." But Mr. Friar was adamant. "If I was Eisenstein you wouldn't talk to me like that. You'd have confidence. You must be fair to me, Kravitz. Wait for the finished product."

Meanwhile Mr. Cohen phoned every morning. "Well?" he asked.

"Soon, Mr. Cohen. Very soon."

Duddy, still trying to meet the Brault property deadline, was out early every day pushing liquid soap and toilet supplies. He began to drive his father's taxi during off-hours again. Then he had a stroke of luck. Brault accepted a further payment of a thousand dollars and agreed to wait one more month for the final payment. "Everything," Duddy told Yvette, "depends on Mr. Friar. If the movie's O.K. we're in. If not. . . ."

"Duddy, you look terrible. Look at the circles under your eyes. You've got to stop driving that taxi and get some sleep at night."

Three weeks after the *bar mitzvah* Mr. Friar was ready. He arranged a private screening for Duddy and Yvette. "I'm beginning to think we'd be making a grave error if we sold this film to Mr. Cohen. It's a prize-winner, Kravitz. I'm sure we could get distribution for it."

"Will you turn out the goddam lights and let me see it, please?"

Duddy didn't say a word all through the screening, but afterwards he was sick to his stomach.

"It's not that bad," Yvette said. "Things could be done to it."

"You think we'd be making a mistake?" Duddy said. "Jeez. I could sell Mr. Cohen a dead horse easier than this pile of—"

"If you so much as cut it by one single frame," Mr. Friar said, "then my name goes off the film."

Duddy began to laugh. So did Yvette.

"Timothy suggested we try it at Cannes."

"Jeez," Duddy said. "Everyone's going to be there. But everyone. The invitations are all out."

Duddy took to his bed for two days. He refused to see anyone.

"I'm so worried," Yvette said.

Mr. Friar kissed her hand. "You have a Renaissance profile," he said.

"He won't even answer the phone. Oh, Mr. Friar, please!" she said, removing his hand.

"If there were only world enough and time, my love. . . ."

"I'm going to try his number once more," Yvette said.

But Duddy was out. On the third day he had decided that he could no longer put off seeing Mr. Cohen. He went to his house this time. "Ah," Mr. Cohen said, "the producer is here."

"Have you got the movie with you?" Bernie asked.

Mrs. Cohen poured him a glass of plum brandy. "If you don't mind," she said, "there are a few more names I'd like to add to the guest list."

"I've got some bad news for you. I'm canceling the screening. Tomorrow morning my secretary will call everyone to tell them the show's off."

"Aw, gee whiz."

"Is it that bad?" Mr. Cohen asked.

"It's great. We're going to enter it in the Cannes Festival."

"I don't understand," Mrs. Cohen said.

"You won't like it. It's what we call *avant-garde*."

"Watch it," Mr. Cohen said, "this is where he begins to lie. Right before your eyes the price is going up."

Duddy smiled at Mrs. Cohen. "I suppose what you expected was an ordinary movie with shots of all the relatives and friends . . . well, you know what I mean. But Mr. Friar is an artist. His creation is something else entirely."

"Can't we see it, Maw?"

"Aren't you taking a lot for granted, young man? Don't you think my husband and I can appreciate artistic quality when we see it?"

"Don't fall into his trap," Mr. Cohen said.

Duddy turned to Mr. Cohen. "I'll let you in on a secret," he said. He told him that Mr. Friar had been a big director, but he had had to leave Hollywood because of the witch-hunt. That's the only reason why he was in Montreal fiddling with small films. He wanted to make his name and get in on the ground floor of the Canadian film industry, so to speak. Turning to Mrs. Cohen, he added, "Please don't repeat this, but if not for Senator McCarthy I wouldn't have been able to hire a man as big as Friar for less than five thousand dollars. Not that he isn't costing me plenty as it is."

Mr. Cohen started to say something, but his wife glared at him. She smiled at Duddy. "But why can't we see the movie? I don't understand."

"It's different. It's shocking."

"Oh, really now!"

"Mr. Friar has produced a small screen gem in the tradition of *Citizen Kane* and Franju's *Sang des Bêtes.*"

"How can we cancel all the invitations at this late date? We insist on seeing it."

Duddy hesitated. He stared reflectively at the floor. "All right," he said, "but don't say I didn't warn you first."

Mr. Cohen laughed. "Don't believe a word he says, Gertie. It's good. It must be very good. Otherwise he wouldn't be here talking it down. But, listen here, Kravitz, not a penny more than I promised. Wow! What a liar!"

Duddy gulped down his plum brandy. "I'm not selling," he said. "That's something else. You can see it, but. . . "

"Hey," Mr. Cohen said, "hey there. Are you getting tough with an old friend?"

"I want it, Daddy. I want the movie! Gee whiz, Maw."

"You outsmarted yourself, Mr. Cohen. You wouldn't give me an advance or put anything in writing."

"Sam, what's the boy saying?'

"You gave me your word, Kravitz. A gentleman doesn't go back on his word."

Bernie began to cry.

"You can't blame him, Mrs. Cohen. He didn't want to take too big a chance on a young boy just starting out."

"Alright," Mr. Cohen said hoarsely, "just how much do you want for the film?"

"Money isn't the question."

"Such a liar! My God, never in my life—Will you stop crying please? Take him out of here, Gertie."

"I'm not going."

"Well, Kravitz, I'm waiting to hear your price. Gangster!"

Duddy hesitated.

"Please," Mrs. Cohen said.

"I can't sell outright. I'd still want to enter it in the festival."

"Of course," Mrs. Cohen said warmly.

"We can't talk here," Mr. Cohen said. "Come up to my bedroom."

But Duddy wouldn't budge. "For fifteen hundred dollars," he said, "I'll give you an excellent colour print. But you'd have to sign away all rights to a percentage of the profits on Canadian theatre distribution."

"What's that? Come again, please?"

"We're going to distribute it as a short to Canadian theatres."

"Gee whiz."

"For twenty-five hundred dollars in all I'll make you a silent partner. I'd cut you in for twenty per cent of the net theatre profits. My lawyers could draw up the agreement. But remember, it's a gamble. This is an art film, not one of those crassly commercial items."

"Would my husband's name appear anywhere?"

"We could list him in the credits as a coproducer with Dudley Kane Enterprises."

Mr. Cohen smiled for the first time. "A boy from the boys," he said, "that's what you are."

"Maybe you'd like to think it over first."

"Sam."

"Alright. O.K. I'll write him a cheque right now." Mr. Cohen looked at Duddy and laughed. "Look at him. He's shaking."

After Duddy had left with the cheque Mr. Cohen said, "I could have got it for less if you and Bernie hadn't been here."

"Then why are you smiling?"

"Because yesterday I spoke to Dave in Toronto. He's with Columbia of Canada now and he told me a screen short is worth up to twenty thousand dollars. I could have got it for less, it's true, but in the end it still won't have cost me a cent for the colour print. And think of the publicity. It must be terrific, you know. Otherwise he wouldn't have talked it down like that. He's still got a lot to learn, that boy."

Duddy met Yvette at a quarter to ten the next morning. He told her what had happened while they waited for the bank to open. "But that's wonderful," she said.

"Yeah, sure, until they see the damn thing. Then the lawsuits start. And nobody in town will ever want me to make a movie for them again."

"Maybe they'll like it."

"Are you kidding? Listen, I'm taking cash for this cheque. Pay Brault and put the rest in your account. If they sue I'll go into bankruptcy."

"All right."

"I hope the cheque's still good. Maybe he's stopped payment on it."

THE SCREENING . . .

NARRATOR:

They came with tributes for the boy who had come of age.

22. Camera pans over a table laden with gifts. Revealed are four Parker 51 sets, an electric razor, a portable record player. . .

"Murray got the player wholesale through his brother-in-law."

. . . three toilet sets, two copies of *Tom Sawyer*, five subscriptions to the *National Geographic* magazine, a movie projector, a fishing rod and other angling equipment, three cameras, a season's ticket to hockey games at the Forum, a set of phylacteries and a prayer shawl, a rubber dinghy, a savings account book open at a first deposit of five hundred dollars, six sport shirts, an elaborate chemistry set, a pile of fifty silver dollars in a velvet-lined box, at least ten credit slips (worth from twenty to a hundred dollars each) for Eaton's and Morgan's, two sets of H. G. Wells's *Outline of History*.

As choir sings "Happy birthday, Bernie!"

23. Hold a shot of numerous cheques pinned to a board. Spin it.

"Dave's cheque is only for twenty-five bucks. Do you know how much business he gets out of Cohen every year?"

"If it had been Lou you would have said he had a bad year. Admit it."

"Hey, Bernie," Arnie yelled, "how many of those cheques bounced? You can tell us."

"I was grateful for all of them," Bernie said, "large or small. It's the thought that counts with me."

"Isn't he sweet?"

"Sure," Arnie said, "but he could have told me that before."

24. A shot of Rabbi Goldstone's study. Bernard sits in an enormous leather chair and the Rabbi paces up and down, talking to him.

NARRATOR:

But that afternoon, in the good Rabbi's study, the young Hebrew learns that there are more exalted things in this world besides material possessions, he is told something of the tragic history of his race, how they were exploited by the ancient Egyptian imperialists, how reactionary dictators from Nehru to Hitler persecuted them in order to divert the working-classes from the true cause of their sorrows, he learns—like Candide—that all is not for the best in the best of all possible worlds.

As Al Jolson sings "Eli, Eli"

25. Rabbi Goldstone leads Bernard to the window and stands behind him, his hands resting on the lad's shoulders.

"Five'll get you ten that right now he's asking Bernie to remind his father that the Temple building campaign is lagging behind schedule."

Rabbi Goldstone coughed loudly.

NARRATOR (RECITES):

"I am a Jew: hath not a Jew eyes? Hath not a Jew hands, organs, dimensions, senses, affections, passions, fed with the same food, hurt with the same weapons, subject to the same diseases, healed by the same oils, warmed and cooled by the same winter and summer as a Christian is? If you prick him does he not bleed?"

26. Rabbi Goldstone autographs a copy of his book, *Why I'm Glad To Be A Jew*, and hands it to Bernard.

27. Hold a close-shot of the book.

From there the movie went on to record the merry-making and odd touching interludes at the dinner and dance. Relatives and friends saw themselves eating, drinking, and dancing. Uncles and aunts at the tables waved at the camera, the kids made funny faces, and the old people sat stonily. Cuckoo Kaplan did a soft-shoe dance on the head table. As the camera closed in on the dancers Henry pretended to be seducing Morrie Applebaum's wife. Mr. Cohen had a word with the band leader and the first *kazatchka* was played. Timidly the old people joined hands and began to dance around in a circle. Mr. Cohen and some spirited others joined in the second one. Duddy noticed some intruders at the sandwich table. He did not know them by name or sight, but remembering, he recognized that they were FFHS boys and he smiled a little. The camera panned lovingly about fish and jugs and animals modelled out of ice. It closed in and swallowed the bursting trumpeter. Guests were picked up again, some reeling and others bad-tempered, waiting for taxis and husbands to come round with the car outside the temple.

Sex and Money in Newark

In 1959, the very year that Richler upset Canadian Jews, Philip Roth did the same for the infinitely larger number of Jews in the New York metropolitan area with *Goodbye, Columbus* (which was also made into a Hollywood film). Roth chronicles the lessons in sex and money given to a young Jew of modest means and less sexual experience by the dynamic Brenda, the daughter of a Newark bathroom fixtures magnate. (Jews do not live in Newark anymore, having moved to the New Jersey exurbs and abandoned the old city to the African Americans).

Richler's portrayal of Brenda's mores, attitudes and talk is a very accurate rendering of what was then called a JAP (Jewish American Princess)—a product of the postwar boom and weakening of family bonds and abandonment of traditional Jewish values. That is why it hurt and resulted in tedious condemnation of Roth's book from sundry pulpits in metropolitan New York.

Roth's work has always been characterized by his capacity to connect money, sex, and power within a family. This connection was obvious to the new suburban generation of the 1950s. Rabbinical bromides could not wish it away.

"Goddam her!" Brenda said to me as she paced up and down my room.

"Bren, do you think I should go—"

"Shhh . . ." She went to the door of my room and listened. "They're going visiting, thank God."

"Brenda—"

"Shhh . . . They've gone."

"Julie too?"

"Yes," she said. "Is Ron in his room? His door is closed."

"He went out."

"You can't hear anybody move around here. They all creep around in *sneakers*. Oh, Neil."

"Bren, I asked you, maybe I should just stay through tomorrow and then go."

"Oh, it isn't you she's angry about."

"I'm not helping any."

"It's Ron, really. That he's getting married just has her flipped. And me. Now with that goody-good Harriet around she'll just forget I ever exist."

"Isn't that okay with you?"

She walked off to the window and looked outside. It was dark and cool; the trees rustled and flapped as though they were sheets that had been hung out to dry. Everything outside hinted at September, and for the first time I realized how close we were to Brenda's departure for school.

"Is it, Bren?" but she was not listening to me.

She walked across the room to a door at the far end of the room. She opened it.

"I thought that was a closet," I said.

"Come here."

She held the door back and we leaned into the darkness and could hear the strange wind hissing in the eaves of the house.

"What's in here?" I said.

"Money."

Brenda went into the room. When the puny sixty-watt bulb was twisted on, I saw that the place was full of old furniture—two wing chairs with hair-oil lines at the back, a sofa with a paunch in its middle, a bridge table, two bridge chairs with their stuffing showing, a mirror whose backing had peeled off, shadeless lamps, lampless shades, a coffee table with a cracked glass top, and a pile of rolled up shades.

"What is this?" I said.

"A storeroom. Our old furniture."

"How old?"

"From Newark," she said. "Come here." She was on her hands and knees in front of the sofa and was holding up its paunch to peek beneath.

"Brenda, what the hell are we doing here? You're getting filthy."

"It's not here."

"*What?*"

"The money. I told you."

I sat down on a wing chair, raising some dust. It had begun to rain outside, and we could smell the fall dampness coming through the vent that was outlined at the far end of the storeroom. Brenda got up from the floor and sat down on the sofa. Her knees and Bermudas were dirty and when she pushed her hair back she dirtied her forehead.

There among the disarrangement and dirt I had the strange experience of seeing us, *both* of us, placed among disarrangement and dirt: we looked like a young couple who had just moved into a new apartment; we had suddenly taken stock of our furniture, finances, and future, and all we could feel any pleasure about was the clean smell of outside, which reminded us we were alive, but which, in a pinch, would not feed us.

"What money?" I said again.

"The hundred-dollar bills. From when I was a little girl . . ." and she breathed deeply. "When I was little and we'd just moved from Newark, my father took me up here one day. He took me into this room and told me that if anything should ever happen to him, he wanted me to know where there was some money that I should have. He said it wasn't for anybody else but me, and that I should never tell anyone about it, not even Ron. Or my mother."

"How much was it?"

"Three hundred-dollar bills. I'd never seen them before. I was nine, around Julie's age. I don't think we'd been living here a month. I remember I used to come up here about once a week, when no one was home but Carlota, and crawl under the sofa and make sure it was still here. And it always was. He never mentioned it once again. Never."

"Where is it? Maybe someone stole it."

"I don't know, Neil. I suppose he took it back."

"When it was gone," I said, "my God, didn't you tell him? Maybe Carlota—"

"I never knew it was gone, until just now. I guess I stopped looking at one time or another . . . And then I forgot about it. Or just didn't think about it. I mean I always had enough, I didn't need this. I guess one day *he* figured I wouldn't need it."

Brenda paced up to the narrow, dust-covered window and drew her initials on it.

"Why did you want it now?" I said.

"I don't know . . ." she said and went over and twisted the bulb off.

I didn't move from the chair and Brenda, in her tight shorts and shirt, seemed naked standing there a few feet away. Then I saw her shoulders shaking. "I wanted to find it and tear it up in little pieces and put the goddam pieces in her purse! If it was there, I swear it, I would have done it."

"I wouldn't have let you, Bren."

"Wouldn't you have?"

"No."

"Make love to me, Neil. Right now."

"Where?"

"Do it! *Here.* On this cruddy cruddy cruddy sofa."

And I obeyed her.

The next morning Brenda made breakfast for the two of us. Ron had gone off to his first day of work—I'd heard him singing in the shower only an hour after I'd returned to my own room; in fact, I had still been awake when the Chrysler had pulled out of the garage, carrying boss and son down to the Patimkin works in Newark. Mrs. Patimkin wasn't home either; she had taken her car and had gone off to the Temple to talk to Rabbi Kranitz about the wedding. Julie was on the back lawn playing at helping Carlota hang the clothes.

"You know what I want to do this morning?" Brenda said. We were eating a grapefruit, sharing it rather sloppily, for Brenda couldn't find a paring knife, and so we'd decided to peel it down like an orange and eat the segments separately.

"What?" I said.

"Run," she said. "Do you ever run?"

"You mean on a track? God, yes. In high school we had to run a mile every month. So we wouldn't be Momma's boys. I think the bigger your lungs get the more you're supposed to hate your mother."

"I want to run," she said, "and I want you to run. Okay?"

"Oh, Brenda . . . "

But an hour later, after a breakfast that consisted of another grapefruit, which apparently is all a runner is supposed to eat in the morning, we had driven the Volkswagen over to the high school, behind which was a quarter-mile track. Some kids were playing with a dog out in the grassy center of the track, and at the far end, near the woods, a figure in white shorts with slits in the side, and no shirt, was twirling, twirling, and then flinging a shot put as far as he could. After it left his hand he did a little eagle-eyed tap dance while he watched it arch and bend and land in the distance.

"You know," Brenda said, "you look like me. Except bigger."

We were dressed similarly, sneakers, sweat socks, khaki Bermudas, and sweat shirts, but I had the feeling that Brenda was not talking about the accidents of our dress—if they were accidents. She meant, I was sure, that I was somehow beginning to look the way she wanted me to. Like herself.

"Let's see who's faster," she said, and then we started along the track. Within the first eighth of a mile the three little boys and their dog were following us. As we passed the corner where the shot putter was, he waved at us; Brenda called "Hi!" and I smiled, which, as you may or may not know, makes one engaged in serious running feel inordinately silly. At the quarter mile the kids dropped off and retired to the grass, the dog turned and started the other way, and I had a tiny knife in my side. Still I was abreast of Brenda, who as we started on the second lap, called "Hi!" once again to the lucky shot putter, who was reclining on the grass now, watching us, and rubbing his shot like a crystal ball. Ah, I thought, there's the sport.

"How about us throwing the shot put?" I panted.

"After," she said, and I saw beads of sweat clinging to the last strands of hair that shagged off her ear. When we approached the half mile Brenda suddenly swerved off the track onto the grass and tumbled down; her departure surprised me and I was still running.

"Hey, Bob Mathias," she called, "let's lie in the sun . . . "

But I acted as though I didn't hear her and though my heart pounded in my throat and my mouth was dry as a drought, I made my legs move, and swore I would not stop until I'd finished one more lap. As I passed the shot putter for the third time, I called "Hi!"

She was excited when I finally pulled up alongside of her. "You're good," she said. My hands were on my hips and I was looking at the ground and sucking air—rather, air was sucking me, I didn't have much to say about it.

"Uh-huh," I breathed.

"Let's do this every morning," she said. "We'll get up and have two grapefruit, and then you'll come out here and run. I'll time you. In two weeks you'll break four minutes, won't you, sweetie? I'll get Ron's stop watch." She was so excited—she'd slid over on the grass and was pushing my socks up against my wet ankles and calves. She bit my kneecap.

"Okay," I said.

"Then we'll go back and have a real breakfast."

"Okay."

"You drive back," she said, and suddenly she was up and running ahead of me, and then we were headed back in the car.

And the next morning, my mouth still edgy from the grapefruit segments, we were at the track. We had Ron's stop watch and a towel for me, for when I was finished.

"My legs are a little sore," I said.

"Do some exercises," Brenda said. "I'll do them with you." She heaped the towel on the grass and together we did deep knee bends, and sit-ups, and push-ups, and some high-knee raising in place. I felt overwhelmingly happy.

"I'm just going to run a half today, Bren. We'll see what I do . . ." and I heard Brenda click the watch, and then when I was on the far side of the track, the clouds trailing above me like my own white, fleecy tail, I saw that Brenda was on the ground, hugging her knees, and alternately checking the watch and looking out at me. We were the only ones there, and it all reminded me of one of those scenes in race-horse movies, where an old trainer like Walter Brennan and a young handsome man clock the beautiful girl's horse in the early Kentucky morning, to see if it really is the fastest two-year-old alive. There were differences all right—one being simply that at the quarter mile Brenda shouted out to me, "A minute and fourteen seconds," but it was pleasant and exciting and clean and when I was finished Brenda was standing up and waiting for me. Instead of a tape to break I had Brenda's sweet flesh to meet, and I did, and it was the first time she said that she loved me.

We ran—I ran—every morning, and by the end of the week I was running a 7:02 mile, and always at the end there was the little click of the watch and Brenda's arms.

At night, I would read in my pajamas, while Brenda, in her room, read, and we would wait for Ron to go to sleep. Some nights we had to wait longer than others, and I would hear the leaves swishing outside, for it had grown cooler at the end of August, and the air-conditioning was turned off at night and we were all allowed to open our windows. Finally Ron would be ready for bed. He would stomp around his room and then he would come to the door in his shorts and

T-shirt and go into the bathroom where he would urinate loudly and brush his teeth. After he brushed his teeth I would go in to brush mine. We would pass in the hall and I would give him a hearty and sincere "Goodnight." Once in the bathroom, I would spend a moment admiring my tan in the mirror; behind me I could see Ron's jock straps hanging out to dry on the Hot and Cold knobs of the shower. Nobody ever questioned their tastefulness as adornment, and after a few nights I didn't even notice them.

While Ron brushed his teeth and I waited in my bed for my turn, I could hear the record player going in his room. Generally, after coming in from basketball, he would call Harriet—who was now only a few days away from us—and then would lock himself up with *Sports Illustrated* and Mantovani; however, when he emerged from his room for his evening toilet, it was not a Mantovani record I would hear playing, but something else, apparently what he'd once referred to as his Columbus record. I *imagined* that was what I heard, for I could not tell much from the last moments of sound. All I heard were bells moaning evenly and soft patriotic music behind them, and riding over it all, a deep kind of Edward R. Murrow gloomy voice: "*And so goodbye, Columbus,*" the voice intoned, "*. . . goodbye, Columbus . . . goodbye . . .*" Then there would be silence and Ron would be back in his room; the light would switch off and in only a few minutes I would hear him rumbling down into that exhilarating, restorative, vitamin-packed sleep that I imagined athletes to enjoy.

One morning near sneaking-away time I had a dream and when I awakened from it, there was just enough dawn coming into the room for me to see the color of Brenda's hair. I touched her in her sleep, for the dream had unsettled me: it had taken place on a ship, an old sailing ship like those you see in pirate movies. With me on the ship was the little colored kid from the library—I was the captain and he my mate, and we were the only crew members. For a while it was a pleasant dream; we were anchored in the harbor of an island in the Pacific and it was very sunny. Up on the beach there were beautiful bare-skinned Negresses, and none of them moved; but suddenly *we* were moving, our ship, out of the harbor, and the Negresses moved slowly down to the shore and began to throw leis at us and say

"Goodbye, Columbus . . . goodbye, Columbus . . . goodbye . . ." and though we did not want to go, the little boy and I, the boat was moving and there was nothing we could do about it, and he shouted at me that it was my fault and I shouted it was his for not having a library card, but we were wasting our breath, for we were further and further from the island, and soon the natives were nothing at all. Space was all out of proportion in the dream, and things were sized and squared in no way I'd ever seen before, and I think it was that more than anything else that steered me into consciousness. I did not want to leave Brenda's side that morning, and for a while I played with the little point at the nape of her neck, where she'd had her hair cut. I stayed longer than I should have, and when finally I returned to my room I almost ran into Ron who was preparing for his day at Patimkin Kitchen and Bathroom Sinks.

Happy memories of a Jewish childhood: Friday night, the Jewish family at home. Cologne, Germany, 1860.

Marriage in Medieval Cairo

The pivotal point in growing up among Jews has always been marriage. Talmudic Judaism put no stock in celibacy. On the contrary, the ancient rabbis taught that a man who was not married was only half a man. Furthermore, for reasons of mental health, early marriage was prescribed. Because marriage was regarded as a normal and necessary stage in life, the legalities and ceremonies connected to marriage were kept simple, as can be seen in the following documents relating to betrothal. They are from Old Cairo (Fusat), Egypt in the tenth and eleventh century, from the synagogue *geniza* (archive), as translated by S. D. Goitein.

A New York Jewish family at the Seder table, 1924 (posed studio portrait).

. . . So-and-so declared before us: I wish to betroth and take as wife So-and-so, and here are the "gratifications" which I shall give her. He produced three rings, one of plaited gold and two of silver. We asked him: "What is the marriage gift?" [meaning the one given in addition to the formal, betrothal gift] He replied: "Twenty good gold pieces, ten for the early and ten for the late installment." We asked: "Where are the first ten?" He said: "I do not have them at present. I shall give them to her, or to a representative of hers, as soon as God has them ready for me." We betook ourselves to her, and, after her identity was established by two trustworthy witnesses, she legally appointed So-and-so as her representative. Having done this, we betrothed him to her in a definite marriage bond and gave the "gratifications" to her representative. . . .

This is our local custom with regard to marriage. If she has come of age, she empowers her father to receive her betrothal gift; if she is a minor, he does so on his own, as approved by the sages. The congregation assembles in the synagogue which the father attends and he receives there the betrothal gift for his daughter. This Reuben [meaning the father of the daughters] was a scholar and an old man, and scholars and others gathered in the house of study. [The old scholar prayed in a *beth midrāsh,* or house of study.] Simeon [the groom] stood up from his seat and gave the betrothal gift to Reuben, while the scholars from the school of the late R. Nathan were seated around. Simeon spoke up and said: "May your daughter be married to me by this ring."

The Story of a Marriage

Around 1800, it was customary among Polish Jews to marry very young—as early as the age of eleven. Usually the young couple worked things out, but the results could be difficult and unfortunate. This candid account of such a rocky marriage is from the remarkable autobiography of Solomon Maimon, who like many Polish Jews at the time migrated westward into Germany. Maimon became a successful businessman and scholar, but his unhappy early marriage was something he thought deeply and unhappily about many decades later.

In my youth I was very lively, and my nature had much that was agreeable. In my passions I was violent and impatient. Till about my eleventh year, as my upbringing was very strict and I was kept from all contact with women, I felt no special inclination towards the fair sex. But an incident produced a great change in me in this respect.

A poor but very pretty girl about my own age was taken into our house as a servant. She charmed me uncommonly. Desires began to stir in me, which I had previously never known. But in accordance with the strict rabbinical morality, I was obliged to guard against casting an attentive eye on the girl, and still more against speaking with her; only now and then was I able to throw a stolen glance.

Our landlord neighbor had two sons and three daughters. The eldest daughter, Deborah, was already married. The second, Pessel, was about my age; the local peasantry professed to find a certain resemblance in our features, and therefore conjectured that by all the laws of probability there would be a match between us. We two also had an inclination towards one another. But by ill luck the youngest daughter, Rachel, fell down a cellar and dislocated a leg. The girl recovered completely, but her leg remained somewhat crooked. The landlord then started a hunt after me; he was altogether determined to have me for son-in-law. My father was quite agreeable to the relationship but wished to have as his daughter-in-law the straight-legged Pessel rather than Rachel of the crooked leg. The landlord, however, declared that this was impossible, inasmuch as he had fixed on a rich husband for the elder, while the younger was destined for me; and as my father was unable to give me anything, he was willing to provide for her richly out of his own fortune. Besides a considerable sum which he agreed to give as a portion, he was willing in addition to make me joint heir of his fortune, and to provide me with all necessaries the whole of my life. Moreover, he promised to pay my father a fixed sum immediately after the betrothal, and not only to leave him undisturbed in his rights, but also to seek to promote his domestic prosperity in every way possible.

Had my father heeded these representations, he would without doubt have established the fortune of his house, and I should have lived with a spouse, who, it is true, had a crooked leg, but (as I found out some time afterwards when I was tutor in her family) was in other respects an amiable woman. I should thus havé been freed from all cares and in the lap of fortune, and I should have been able to apply myself to my studies without hindrance. But unhappily my father scorned this proposal. He was absolutely determined to have Pessel for his daughter-in-law; and since this was impossible, the two families began to feud. But as the landlord was rich and my father poor, he naturally drew the short end of the stick.

Some time afterwards another matrimonial proposal for me turned up. Mr. L. . . . of Schmilowitz, a learned and at the same time a rich man, who had an only daughter, was so enchanted with my fame, that he chose me for his son-in-law without having set eyes upon me. He began by entering into correspondence with my father on the subject, and left it to him to stipulate the conditions. My father answered his letter in lofty style, compounded of biblical verses and passages from the Talmud, in which he expressed the conditions briefly by means of the following verse from the Canticles (8:12): "Thou, O Solomon, shalt have the thousand, and those that keep the fruit thereof two hundred." Consent was given on all points.

My father accordingly journeyed to Schmilowitz, saw his future daughter-in-law, and had the marriage contract drawn in accordance with the terms agreed upon. Two hundred gulden were paid to him on the spot. He was not content with this sum, however, but insisted that in his letter he had been obliged to limit himself to two hundred gulden merely for the sake of the beautiful verse which he did not wish to spoil: he would not enter into the transaction at all unless he received for himself twice two hundred gulden (fifty thalers in Polish money). They had therefore to pay him two hundred gulden more, and to hand over to him the "little presents" for me, namely, a cap of black velvet trimmed with gold lace, a Bible bound in green velvet with silver clasps, and similar gifts. With these things he came home rejoicing, gave me the presents, and told me that I was to prepare myself for a disputation to be held on my marriage day, which would fall two months hence.

Already my mother had begun to bake the cakes she was expected to take with her to the wedding, and to prepare all manner of preserves; and I began to think about the disputation I was to hold, when suddenly the mournful news arrived that my bride had died of smallpox. My father could easily reconcile himself to this loss, by reflecting that he had made fifty thalers by his son in an honorable way, and might now receive another fifty thalers for him. Neither could I, never having seen my bride, particularly mourn her loss; I thought to myself, "The cap and the silver-clasped Bible are already mine, and a bride will also not be long awanting; as for my disputation, it can serve me another time." My mother alone was disconsolate over the loss. Cakes and preserves are of a perishable nature and will not keep long. The labor which my mother had expended was therefore rendered fruitless by the fatal mishap. Furthermore, she could find no safe place to keep the delicacies from my secret attacks. . . .

On the first evening of my marriage my father was not present. He had told me at my departure that he still had certain details to settle on my account, and that I must therefore await his arrival. Accordingly, I refused to appear that evening despite all pressure brought to bear upon me. The marriage festivities went on notwithstanding. We waited the next day for my father, but still he did not come. Then they threatened to bring a party of soldiers to drag me to the marriage ceremony; but I replied that if this were done it would avail them little, for the ceremony would not be lawful except as a voluntary act. At last, to the joy of all concerned, my father arrived towards evening, the details in question were amended, and the marriage ceremony was performed.

Here I must mention a little anecdote. I had read in a Hebrew book of an approved plan by which one spouse might secure lordship over the other for life. One was to tread on the other's foot at the marriage ceremony; and if both hit on the stratagem, the first to succeed would retain the upper hand. Accordingly, when my bride and I were placed side by side at the ceremony, this trick occurred to me, and I said to myself, "Now you must not let the opportunity pass of securing lordship over your wife for your whole lifetime." I was just going to tread on her foot, but a certain *je ne sais quoi,* whether fear, or shame, or love, held me back. While I was in this irresolute state, I suddenly felt my wife's slipper on my foot with such force that I should almost have screamed aloud if shame had not restrained me. I took this for a bad omen, and said to myself, "Providence has destined you to be the slave of your wife; you must not try to slip out of her fetters." From my faint-heartedness and the heroic mettle of my wife the reader may easily conceive why this prophecy had in fact to be realized.

But I was not only under the slipper of my wife, but—what was very much worse—under the lash of my mother-in-law. Nothing of all that she had promised was fulfilled. Her house, which she had settled on her daughter as a dowry, was burdened with debt. Of the six years' board which she had promised me I enjoyed scarcely half a year's, and this amid constant brawls and squabbles. Confident by reason of my youth and want of spirit, she even ventured now and again to lay hands on me, but this I repaid not infrequently with compound interest. Scarcely a meal passed during which we did not fling bowls, plates, spoons, and similar furniture at each other's head.

Once I came home from the academy ravenously hungry. As my mother-in-law and wife were occupied with the business of the tavern, I went myself where the milk was kept, and finding a dish of curds and cream, I fell upon it, and began to eat. My mother-in-law came as I was thus occupied, and shrieked in rage, "You are not going to devour the milk with the cream!" The more cream the better, thought I, and went on eating, without allowing myself to be disturbed by her screams. She was going to wrest the dish forcibly

from my hands, beat me with her fists, and let me feel all her ill-will. Exasperated by such treatment, I thrust her from me, seized the dish, and smashed it on her head. That was a sight! The curds ran down all over her. In her rage she seized a scantling of wood, and if I had not speedily cleared out, she would certainly have beaten me to death.

Scenes like this were of frequent occurrence. At such skirmishes, of course, my wife had to remain neutral, and whichever party gained the upper hand, it touched her very closely. "Oh!" she often complained, "if only the one or the other of you had a little more patience!"

Tired of a ceaseless open war I once hit upon a stratagem, which had good effect, at least for a short time. I rose about midnight, took a large earthenware vessel, crept with it under my mother-in-law's bed, and began to speak aloud into the vessel after the following fashion: "O Rissia, Rissia, you ungodly woman, why do you treat my beloved son so ill? If you do not mend your ways, your end is near, and you will be damned to all eternity." Then I crept out again, and began to pinch her cruelly; and after a while I slipped silently back to bed.

The following morning she got up in consternation and told my wife that my mother had appeared to her in a dream and had threatened and pinched her on my account. In confirmation she showed the blue marks on her arm. When I came from the synagogue, my mother-in-law was not at home, but I found my wife in tears. I asked the reason, but she would tell me nothing. My mother-in-law returned with a dejected look, her eyes red with weeping. She had gone, as I afterwards learned, to the Jewish burial ground, had thrown herself on my mother's grave, and had begged forgiveness of her fault. She then had the burial place measured, and ordered a wax taper as long as its circumference for burning in the synagogue. She also fasted the whole day, and towards me she showed herself extremely amiable.

I knew what was the cause of the transformation, of course, but pretended not to observe it, and rejoiced in secret over the success of my stratagem. In this way I obtained peace for some time, but unfortunately not for long. The whole was soon forgotten again, and on the slightest occasion the dance would go on as before. In short, I was soon afterwards obliged to leave the house altogether, and accept a position as a private tutor. I would come home only for the great feast days.

In my fourteenth year my eldest son, David, was born to me. At my marriage I was only eleven years old, and owing to the retired life common among people of our nation in those regions, as well as the want of social contact between the sexes, I had no idea of the essential duties of marriage, but looked on a pretty girl as on any other work of nature or art. It was therefore natural that for a considerable time after marriage I could have no thought about its consummation. I used to approach my wife with trembling as an object of mystery. It was therefore supposed that I had been bewitched during the wedding; and under this supposition I was brought to a witch to be cured. She set on foot all sorts of operations, which of course had a good effect, although indirectly, by stimulating the imagination.

My life in Poland from my marriage to my emigration, which period embraces the springtime of my existence, was a series of manifold miseries. All means for the promotion of my development were wanting, and as a necessary corollary, my potentialities were aimlessly dissipated. The description of my then state causes my pen to drop from my hand, and I strive to stifle my painful memories.

The general constitution of Poland at the time; the condition of our people in it, who, like the poor ass with double burden, are oppressed by their own ignorance and the religious prejudices connected therewith, as well as by the ignorance and prejudices of the ruling classes; the misfortunes of my own family—all these causes combined to hinder the course of my progress, and to check the effect of my natural inclination.

By dint of instruction received from my father, but still more by my own industry, I had got on so well, that in my eleventh year I was able to pass as a full rabbi. I possessed besides some disconnected knowledge in history, astronomy, and other mathematical sciences. I burned with desire to acquire more knowledge, but how was this to be accomplished with the want of guidance, of scientific books, and of all other requisites? I was obliged to content myself with making use of any help that chance offered, without plan or method.

In order to gratify my desire of scientific knowledge, the only means available was to learn foreign languages. But how was I to begin? To study Polish or Latin with a Catholic teacher was for me impossible, on the one hand, because the prejudices of my own people prohibited all languages but Hebrew and all sciences but the Talmud and the vast array of its commentators, and on the other hand, because the I attended his medical lectures for some time. But after all I could not overcome my dislike for the art, and accordingly gave up the lectures. By and by I became acquainted with other Christian scholars, especially with the late Herr Lieberkühn, who was so justly esteemed on account of his abilities as well as for his warm interest in the welfare of mankind. I also made the acquaintance of some teachers of merit in the Jesuits' College at Breslau.

At last my situation in Breslau also grew precarious. The children of Herr Zadig, in pursuance of the occupations to which they were destined in life, entered into commercial situations, and therefore required teachers no longer. Other means of support also gradually failed. As I was thus obliged to seek subsistence in some other way, I devoted myself to giving lessons. I taught Euler's *Algebra* to a young man, gave two children instruction in the rudiments of German and Latin, and had other pupils. But even this did not last long, and I found myself in a sorrowful plight.

Meanwhile, my wife and eldest son arrived from Poland. A woman of rude education and manners but of great good sense and the courage of an Amazon, she demanded that I should at once return home with her, not seeing that what she asked was impossible. I had now lived in Germany some years, had happily emancipated myself from the fetters of superstition and religious prejudice, had abandoned the rude manner of life in which I had been brought up, and had extended my knowledge in many directions. I could not return to my former barbarous and miserable condition, deprive myself of all the advantages I had gained, and expose myself to rabbinical rage at the slightest deviation from the ceremonial law or the utterance of a liberal opinion. I represented to her that I could not go at once, that I should require first of all to make my situation known to my friends here as well as in Berlin and solicit from them the assistance of two or three hundred thalers, so that I might be able to live in Poland independent of my religious associates. But she would listen to nothing of all this, and declared her resolution to obtain a divorce if I would not go with her immediately. I could only choose the lesser of two evils, and I consented to the divorce.

Meanwhile, however, I was obliged to provide for the lodging and board of these guests, and to introduce them to my friends in Breslau. Both of these duties I performed, and I pointed out, especially to my son, the difference between the manner of life one leads here and that in Poland. I sought to convince my son by several passages in the *Moreh Nebukhim* that enlightenment of the understanding and refinement of manners are rather favorable to religion than otherwise. I went further, and sought to convince him that he ought to remain with me. I assured him that with my direction and the support of my friends he would find opportunities of developing the good abilities with which Nature had endowed him, and would obtain for them some suitable employment. These representations made some impression upon him; but my wife went with my son to consult some orthodox Jews in whose advice she thought she could thoroughly confide, and they urged her to press at once for a divorce, and on no account to let my son be induced to remain with me. This resolution, however, she was not to disclose till she had received from me a sufficient sum of money for household purposes. She might then separate from me forever, and start for home with her booty.

This pretty plan was faithfully followed. By and by I had succeeded in collecting some score of ducats from my friends. I gave them to my wife, and explained to her that to complete the required sum it would be necessary for us to go to Berlin. She then began to raise difficulties and declared point-blank that for us a divorce was best, as neither could I live happily with her in Poland, nor she with me in Germany. In my opinion she was perfectly right. But it still made me

sorry to lose a wife for whom I had once entertained affection, and I could not let the affair be dealt with lightheartedly. I told her, therefore, that I should consent to a divorce only if it were enjoined by the courts.

This was done. I was summoned before the court. My wife stated the grounds on which she claimed a divorce. The president of the court then said, "Under these circumstances we can do nothing but advise a divorce." "Herr President," I replied, "we came here, not to ask advice, but to receive a judicial sentence." There upon the chief rabbi rose from his seat (that what he said might not have the force of a judicial decision), approached me with the codex in his hand, and pointed to the following passage: "A vagabond who abandons his wife for years, and does not write to her or send her money, shall, when he is found, be obliged to grant a divorce." "It is not my part," I replied, "to institute a comparison between this case and mine. That duty falls to you, as judge. Take your seat again, therefore, and pronounce your judicial sentence on the case."

The president became pale and red by turns, rose and sat down again, while the rest of the judges looked at one another. At last the presiding judge became furious, began to call me names, pronounced me a damnable heretic, and cursed me in the name of the Lord. I left him to storm, however, and went away. Thus ended this strange suit, and things remained as they were before.

My wife now saw that nothing was to be done by means of force, and therefore she took to entreaty. I also yielded at last, but only on condition that at the judicial divorce the judge who had shown himself such a master of cursing should not preside in the court. After the divorce my wife returned to Poland with my son. I remained in Breslau for some time; but as my circumstances became worse and worse, I resolved to return to Berlin.

Jack and Sadie

In the 1920s expanding fields of American popular entertainment—vaudeville, film, and then radio—offered clear avenues of economic opportunity and upward social mobility for young Jews, who still suffered heavy discrimination in the corporate and professional world. The most successful American radio comedian of his generation was Jack Benny, originally from the Chicago area. Benny specialized in playing the old stock character of ghetto humor, the amiable miser. Here is his memoir of how he met and married Mary Livingstone, his lifelong companion and collaborator; she was originally Sadie.

I didn't hear love knocking. Like every turning point in my life it came accidentally without fanfares. I didn't realize that here, at last, was my dream girl. I was just going to a party in Vancouver, in British Columbia, a party I didn't really want to go to. It was 1921. I was still a struggling violin act with jokes. I was tired of being compared to Ben Bernie and had just changed my name to Jack Benny. I was twenty-seven years old. I was shy with girls and had never been in love. Lust, yes; love, no. I was playing the Orpheum in Vancouver, working in the deuce spot on a bill that included the Marx Brothers. From their crazy singing act, the Four Nightingales, that had broken me up in Waukegan back in 1910, they had become one of the outstanding rip-and-tear farcical acts in vaudeville. They closed the show—because nobody could follow them. It was about twenty minutes of total insanity.

Zeppo, the youngest brother, talked me into going to this party. He said he knew some fascinating Vancouver girls and it would be wild, with Canadian ale, Canadian rye, Canadian women and Canadian whoopee. I told him I didn't like wild parties and I didn't like wild women. He talked me into going with him.

We drove to a large frame house on the outskirts of the city. When we entered, much to my relief, we were in a nice family home. Zeppo's wild party was just in his imagination. It was his idea of a put-on—I would expect a wild evening and be disappointed. Instead it was Zeppo who was disappointed at my reaction. We were guests at the home of Henry Marks, a distant relative of the Marx Brothers. He was a well-to-do dealer in scrap metals and, like my father, a strict orthodox Jew.

Tonight was the first night of Passover and we had been invited to the family seder. I was introduced to Mrs. Marks, their older daughter, Ethel, who was about twenty, her younger sister, Sadie, and a little boy, Hilliard. Sadie was fourteen with long black curly hair tied in a red ribbon. She was trying to act grown up. She had borrowed her sister's dress and high-heeled shoes on which she wobbled. She hung on my every word. She thought I was a suave handsome Prince Charming. Though I was thirteen years older, she made up her mind she was going to marry me someday. I didn't take her seriously—she was just a cute kid.

The seder was a traditional one and gave me a warm feeling of being at home. During dinner little Hilliard asked the four traditional questions, the first of which I should have heeded: "Why is this night different from all other nights?" It was the most important night of my life, but I didn't know it.

There was the reading of the Haggadah, the long story of the persecution of the Jews in Egypt and their exodus, under the leadership of Moses, to the promised land of Israel. We sang the old songs and then Papa Marks proposed that since I was a violinist myself, he would like me to hear his daughter Sadie play a piece by Bach. To make a confession—I didn't listen. I'd always hated auditioning girl violinists and I whispered to Zeppo to make some excuse so we could get out of there before we had a whole evening of amateur fiddling. Sadie heard me. She finished the piece but her eyes were flashing with anger.

She paid me back. The next day at the matinee she brought three of her friends. The four girls sat in the first row at the Orpheum. During my whole act they stared up with vacant expressions. They didn't laugh once. I didn't recognize Sadie Marks—I had already forgotten her. But I was very upset by four girls in the front row not laughing.

Two years later Sadie moved to San Francisco with her family. I was playing the Pantages. She came to see the show and afterward went to the stage door to say hello. She said, "Hello, Mr. Benny, I'm—"

"Hello," I said, and walked right by her.

In 1926 in Los Angeles I went out on a double date with a fellow vaudevillian, Al Bernovici, his new wife, Ethel, and Ethel's younger sister. Ethel looked vaguely familiar, but I couldn't place her. The sister, my blind date, was a smashing brunette with a vivacious smile and sparkling brown eyes. I remember she wore a simple black dress with a pearl choker and a white cloche hat. I made no connection between this smartly dressed, poised woman and the little girl who played Bach on that first night of Passover. She didn't let on that I had not only ignored her the first time we met, but was even ruder later in San Francisco.

This time it was love. Love at *third* sight.

The four of us had dinner at Musso Frank's in Hollywood. I don't remember many of the details except that I kept staring at her and she kept smiling and I wanted desperately to say clever and provocative things, but I was tongue-tied and embarrassed. Later I learned that Sadie hadn't wanted to go on this date because she was seriously seeing someone else and also because she distrusted actors. At that time Ethel was not having a happy time with Al, and Sadie blamed it on his being a performer. Like my parents, Sadie thought all actors were happy-go-unlucky. Yet she liked me. She didn't know why, but she liked me.

I know why I liked *her*. She was different from most other women I met in show business. She

had manners, she listened politely when others spoke, she dressed with style and simplicity. She was exquisitely lovely. She had a way of laughing—like the music of a rippling arpeggio of silvery notes.

I asked her for a date the following evening. She said no. The evening after that? No. Any evening? No.

Well, I just couldn't get her out of my mind. I thought about her and thought about her all through the night. The next morning I went to the Hollywood Boulevard branch of the May Company where I knew she was working in ladies hosiery. I couldn't think of a convincing reason why I should be at a ladies hosiery counter, but I went there anyway. "Well, it's a small world," was my brilliant opening line. And then I just stood there looking dumb.

"Can I show you some silk stockings, Mr. Benny?" she asked.

I nodded. I would have given a million dollars right then to have had a fiddle in my hands.

"These beige imports from Paris are quite nice," she said, opening a box. She made a little fist and burrowed it into the stocking. "You'll notice how sheer they are, Mr. Benny."

"I'll say they are," I agreed, still gazing at her face.

"Then we have this number in a flesh tone suitable for evening," she said. "I'm sure any woman would love them."

"I'll take a dozen of these and a dozen of those," I said hoarsely. I was in a trance.

"What size does she wear?"

"The same as you."

She wrapped the hosiery. I asked her to lunch. She accepted. I went to her counter every day, bought stockings and then we went for lunch. I bought enough French hosiery to restock the May Company. Sadie later told me that she had broken all sales records for that department in the history of the store. It was the only way I could think of as an excuse to be near her. It never occurred to me to simply tell her that I was crazy about her, that I was in love with her and wanted to spend the rest of my life with her. I was too shy and afraid. So instead I bought silk stockings in gross lots.

Sadie broke up with her boyfriend, and although I had to go back on tour, I telephoned her often.

It was around this time I first heard of some crazy new invention—wireless radio. My friend Goodman Ace, who would have a wonderful radio show, *Easy Aces,* told me millions of people were putting earphones on their ears and scratching around with crystal sets so they could listen to bands playing and people talking and it didn't cost a nickel. I told him such people were nuts. The next time I played Kansas City, where Goody lived, he told me even more people were buying "radios." He thought this would finish vaudeville entertainment and I had better get out of vaudeville and into radio. I didn't listen to him. Not then. I was sure it would all blow over. He was already doing an hour show every week on a local Kansas City station making jokes and talking about movies, shows and books. I told him he was wasting his time. I thought he should become a full-time comedy writer. He was the best comedy writer of that time. I bought material from him whenever I could afford it.

In 1926 there was this new thing called a network. It was the National Broadcasting Company of the RCA Corporation. I gave them six months. Will Rogers said at the time, "Radio is too big a thing to be out of." What did a cowboy know, anyway?

I admit I was a little stunned when I heard about the money Sam 'n' Henry were getting paid in the theaters that played movies in combination with stage shows. They had been a small-time vaudeville act at a top salary of $200 a week. Then they concocted a silly little fifteen-minute radio program about a taxi cab company with characters named the Kingfish, Amos and Andy. They even had Pepsodent Toothpaste for a sponsor. They were on five nights a week. I remember you could walk down a street on a warm evening when the windows were open and hear their voices. When the blackface team of Sam 'n' Henry returned to the theaters they changed the name of the act to Amos 'n' Andy and got $5,000 a week. Their listeners were in the millions and these fans wanted to see Amos 'n' Andy in person.

I still thought it would blow over as soon as people got tired of the novelty. Who would want to hear disembodied voices from a speaker when you could see real entertainers in the flesh on a stage?

Besides, I had other things on my mind.

I was in love. I was dying to marry Sadie, but I was afraid of marriage. I couldn't live without her, but I was afraid of marriage.

For about a year our romance was of great value to the stockholders of AT&T. I telephoned Sadie three or four times a day. Sometimes we talked for an hour. At the end of the tour I rushed back to Los Angeles to resume buying hosiery. Now we went for dinner and drives as well as lunch.

Then I returned to New York and a show called *The Great Temptations* in which my aim was to prove to Jake Shubert that I was a comedian and not a fiddler. The phone calls resumed. I still could not muster the courage to tell her I loved her. Not only was I shy, but my reservations about the responsibilities of marriage continued. I took marriage seriously, as a lifetime proposition. I didn't share the easy come, easy go marital attitude of many people in and out of show business.

Meanwhile Sadie decided that since I had never mentioned love or marriage to her, I probably wasn't serious after all. While visiting in Vancouver she met a young real estate man who fell in love with her and proposed marriage. They got engaged. She didn't break the news to me. Her sister did. I ran into Ethel (by now and evermore called Babe) in Chicago when *The Great Temptations* moved there.

"You can't let her do this. She'll ruin her life. She's too young to get married," I told Babe.

Babe said, "You tell her yourself."

She called her sister and put me on the phone.

"Listen," I cried, now so worked up I forgot I was shy, "what's this I hear about you getting married? YOU'RE TOO YOUNG TO GET MARRIED! Come to Chicago and talk to your older sister . . . and me."

Sadie came to Chicago to talk it over. First she talked it over with Babe and on Sunday we drove out to Lake Forest, where my father was then living. She talked it over with my father. We drove to Waukegan and I showed her the sights. Later that evening she talked it over with me.

"Are you really in love with this man?" I asked.

"I thought I was," she replied, looking me straight in the eye, "but now I'm not so sure."

"Are you really going to marry him?"

"Yes."

I hesitated. I cleared my throat. "Well," I said nervously, "I wasn't planning to get married. I mean—never in all my life, but if I ever were to get m-m-married, I certainly would plan to marry you and if you should say you would marry *me,* I would marry *you.*"

"I don't know what you mean, Jack."

"I think we ought to get married."

"Why?"

"My father likes you."

"Really?"

"You could join my act."

"That's a silly reason to get married."

"I'm going to use a girl in the act. Look at George Burns and Gracie Allen. They're married. They work together."

"I'm not an actress."

"You could be."

"Oh, Jack," she said.

I finally blurted out, "What I mean is, I love you and I want you to be my wife."

"You said I was too young to get married."

"To him maybe, but not to me."

She accepted.

An Intellectual Couple Starts Out

In the 1920s, it was much harder for young Jews to find a place in the literary and academic world of New York than in the entertainment business. One who did gain success, becoming the first Jewish tenured professor of English at Columbia University, and a model and mentor for many others, was Lionel Trilling. His wife, Diana Trilling, in time also became a prominent writer. Here is a subtle, frank, and poignant account of the meeting and early years of marriage of this remarkable and influential couple, from her autobiographical *The Beginning of the Journey* (1993). It is an exceptional work of American Jewish *bildungsroman*, recalling a strange and difficult time and place.

Diana Trilling highlights a common pattern of experience among the New York Jewish intellectuals of the 1930s and 1940s. Later on, in the 1960s and 1970s, these same people appeared to be cultural power brokers and pillars of the establishment. But the pillars were once pebbles.

My mother had died a year before I met Lionel, and I lived with my father and unmarried sister—unless a young woman was without family, it was unheard of for her to have her own apartment. As I recall the strictness of my upbringing and its deference to the proprieties which were in the service of morality, I am at a loss to explain my father's tolerance of my going to speakeasies; in fact, the attitude of both my parents toward their children and drinking. It was not consistent with their usual rules for us. Both my parents came from Poland but they came from very different backgrounds. My father had been raised in a Yiddish-speaking home in the Warsaw ghetto. My mother grew up in the native Polish countryside, close to the land and its old habits of thinking and feeling. They were also of widely different temperaments and might have been expected to bring conflicting views to the rearing of their children. But, as parents, they were indissolubly one. While they lived for our well-being—this is indisputable—they belonged to a generation of Eastern European Jews (or at least my father did and my mother unquestioningly took his moral and intellectual guidance) for whom there was an intimate relation between happiness in the young and wrongdoing or, at any rate, between happiness and injudiciousness of a kind which leads to harm.

Orthodox Judaism's comforting symbol for devout young people: Torah mantle, Germany, 1876.

Pleasure was not the principle of our home. We were abstemious with laughter; I learned early in life that to laugh before breakfast was to cry before dinner. Yet so far as drinking was concerned, my parents were incongruously, even irresponsibly, relaxed. Even when I was a very small child, if beer or whiskey was being served to a guest, I was given my token drink, and as a young woman when I traveled with my father I always had cocktails before dinner. Perhaps my parents had heard that the best way to curb a taste for alcohol was through early and long familiarity with it. I remember getting a food parcel

from my mother at college in which, along with a roast chicken, she had included a flask of whiskey. I was carelessly unwrapping the package in front of several dormitory neighbors when it suddenly came to me that drinking was punishable by expulsion. "Oh! Gravy," I exclaimed and threw the bottle into my underwear drawer. My mother died in 1926, a year after I graduated. Living with my father in New York, I often came home drunk from speakeasies or parties where we had been drinking bootleg liquor. My father would come to my room the next morning to wake me. On the floor lay the clothes which I had unsteadily stepped out of the night before. He would shake his head and say quietly, "Drunk again, young lady?" When my father addressed me as "young lady," it usually meant that he was displeased. But he said no more than this. He went to the bathroom and drew a tub for me. Until Lionel and I decided to marry, we were never wholly sober in each other's company and until I became gravely ill a year after our marriage, I doubt that I left any social gathering without being more than a little drunk. Even after the repeal of Prohibition—in fact, until we were well into middle age—the people Lionel and I knew continued to drink too much; unrecognized alcoholism is the ruling pathology among writers and intellectuals. I have the impression that the way in which people behave under the influence of liquor has considerably changed over the years. In our younger life, people got drunk faster and tended to become either belligerent or giggly when they had been drinking. Drunkenness had its touch of theater. It was not unusual to become sick to one's stomach. We had a friend who was so squeamish that he would refuse a sandwich which had been garnished with a pickle or olive yet he made it his unofficial duty to hold the heads of sick young women at parties; he found it a useful strategy for initiating a seduction. No doubt much of our youthful drunkenness, especially our sick stomachs, was due to the poor quality of Prohibition liquor and to the strange combinations in which we drank it. At Mario's, Lionel's and my favorite drink was something called a Bullfrog, made of gin, apricot brandy, and grenadine. We alternated our Bullfrogs with Alexanders; these were made, I think, of brandy, crème de cacao, and heavy cream. Alexanders were liquid desserts but we drank them not only before dinner but through long evenings of conversation.

On Bullfrogs and Alexanders, Lionel and I got to know each other well enough to decide to marry. We did not become lovers until six months before we married. It was of the utmost urgency that this violation of the conventions not be known to our families. Even four or five years later, in the mid-30s, when Lionel's mother discovered that a college friend of Lionel's sister, Harriet, had asked Harriet to go to bed with him, she expected Lionel (in her quaint phrase) to horsewhip him. Of our friends at the time of our marriage, we knew only one other couple that engaged in so irregular a form of courtship, and I am still convinced that if my father had found us out, he would have—he would have what? There was no talk of sin in my family or, for that matter, of virtue, whether maintained or sacrificed. I was never taught that I would burn in hell for my misdeeds. But I had my own scorching hell of the imagination, a terrible unmanned place to which I would be remanded in punishment for any major infringement of family law, and as I thought of my father's discovering that Lionel and I had gone to bed together, I could hear the creaking of its gates. Surely, going to bed with a man before marriage was the most courageous act of my life. No light penetrated the darkness of my sexual upbringing. The only teaching about sex which I received from my parents, if anything this retrograde and ugly can be called teaching, came from a sexology by one of the Kellogg brothers of cold-cereal fame—in my early childhood my father spent a brief holiday at their diet-and-exercise retreat in Battle Creek, Michigan. The volume he brought home to us from this Eden of wholesomeness opened up for at least one of his children an unrelieved vista of doom and degradation as a consequence of virtually any sexual activity—when in adult life I showed the book to a psychiatrist friend, he pleaded with me to burn it lest it fall into the hands of yet another young reader. In my high school, the girls were during one term temporarily separated from the boys and given a home-nursing course. With no apparent logic, it included a lecture on what was called sex hygiene. We were told about menstruation and that we must not allow boys to touch us lest it excite them dangerously in ways which girls did not know about—the responsibility was then ours

if they went to prostitutes and contracted a venereal disease. At seventeen, I overheard my mother talking to a woman of a younger and more progressive generation than her own; she was explaining that the sexual ignorance—"innocence" was the word she used—in which she and her contemporaries reared their daughters was designed to preserve their illusions. Was she, I wonder, being honest? And if so, how extreme must have been her own disillusionment from which she hoped to shield my sister and me. At parties which I went to with Lionel when we were not yet married, we often played a game called Truth. It had the unadmitted purpose of allowing *the* question to be asked of a girl: Was she or was she not a virgin? Virgins we all were supposed to be while we waited for marriage to rescue us and, with few exceptions, virgins we all were. This was the world as I knew it, my world and Lionel's world, the world into which we and our friends had graduated from college. It was not everyone's world. It was obviously not the world of Mary McCarthy, who was only seven years younger than I. The memoir of Mary McCarthy's young womanhood is a heavy calendar of sexual adventure: She reports of herself that she went to bed with a different man virtually every day during her early years in New York, soon after she graduated from Vassar. There is of course no such thing as a single unchallenged tendency of culture, no one response to the laws which may at any moment seem to govern our society. Mine was the corner of the world and of my generation for which necking was the chief premarital sexual activity. Neither Lionel nor I knew how to drive a car. If we wished to go to a country restaurant—and there were then many charming restaurants on the outskirts of New York—we went in my father's car, driven by his chauffeur. I am still embarrassed to remember that stolid young Dutchman; he had much to be grateful for in his phlegmatic nature. One night in the summer of 1928, the summer after Lionel and I met, as we drove home from dinner at a restaurant on the Hudson near Croton, Lionel complained of a sore throat. He had contracted scarlet fever and was critically ill for many weeks. The illness is recreated in his novel, *The Middle of the Journey,* and includes his love affair with a rose. He was not permitted visitors and I sent him a gift of Talisman roses. They were then newly bred and very beautiful; their basic color was a gentle shade of peach but they could veer to a sudden fierce bronze.

We drank too much but we and our friends, especially those of us who were Jewish—and that was most of us—are not to be confused with characters in a Hemingway novel. No Jew I knew drank with the abandon and virtuosity of the people in Hemingway. Indeed, Jewish men were at that time said to be free not only of alcoholism but also of schizophrenia; Jewish women were thought to be immune to cancer of the cervix. The author of *The Sun Also Rises,* though only a decade older than we, was of a different moral generation than ours: He was separated from us by the First World War. We were old enough to go to speakeasies and even to marry but there was an important sense in which we were still children, good Jewish children within quick and decisive call of our parents. At whatever geographic remove from our homes, we carried our mothers and fathers with us. Other than in the early Nick Adams stories, no Hemingway character has a mother or father. The lack of family and social roots in the people of whom Hemingway writes is perhaps not unconnected with whatever it is that robs him of the literary stature of Proust or Joyce or Thomas Mann or D. H. Lawrence. We and our friends were passionately in search of lives unlike those of our parents. Our parents were nonetheless always with us as we made our journeys of self-creation. . . .

I have known few men who would have tolerated as Lionel did the intrusion, however useful, of their wives into their work or who would have welcomed them into their own professions as Lionel later welcomed me into criticism. We were married twelve years before I launched my writing career. Lionel took the greatest pleasure in it; it obviously posed no threat to him. He said that he had always wanted to belong to a literary "line;" now people could think that Diana Trilling was his mother. He never condescended to me or derided me. Had he been less generous, it would have taken more than the magic of my father's communication to me as a child to fortify me against self-doubt. He was not being magnanimous on principle; he had no ideological commitment to the equality of the sexes—the issue of women's rights did not especially interest him. In the actual conduct of our lives, the two of us, in fact, silently accepted the premise that my first responsibility was to my home and family. Had this been put in words, I daresay that even as far back as the 30s and 40s I would have protested it. But so long as it was not formulated, I was able to deceive myself that it was as a matter of free will and competence that I took on the tasks of the home—they were easier for me to do than they would have been for Lionel and I was better at them. We were married for forty-six years when Lionel died and for all of those years, whether or not I had work to do, I looked upon the discharge of my household obligations as my first duty. But although Lionel took my domestic role for granted, he had no wish to limit me to it; he was happy for me to branch out in any direction which appealed to me. That the addition of a professional job to a woman's home-making occupations demands the expenditure of double energies was not a subject which was much discussed in my generation. Lionel wanted as much for me in self-realization—but how he would have hated that word!—as he wanted for himself. I wanted as much for him as he wanted for himself and more than I wanted for myself. There was nothing special about this. It was the way that nice girls were raised.

PART THREE

MATURING AND DYING

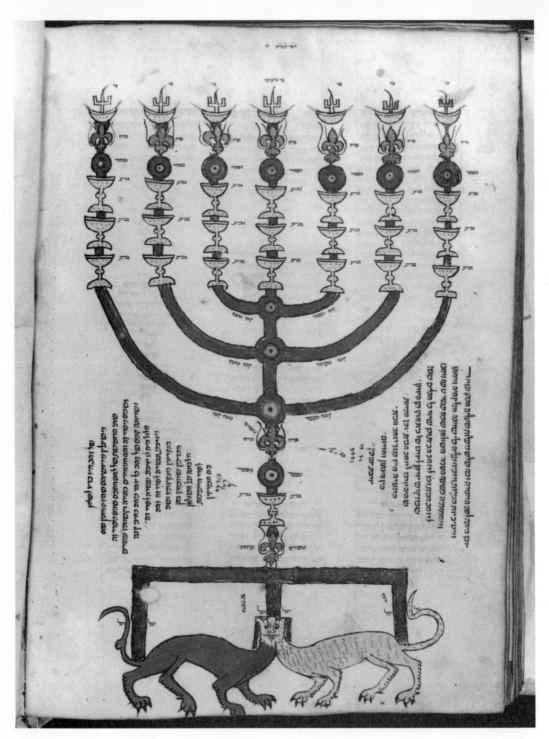

The responsibilities of adulthood: Menorah page from Mishneh Torah: medieval manuscript of treatise on Talmudic law by Maimonides, c. A.D.1180.

INTRODUCTION

The buoyancy, optimism, and naive expectations of the young Jew slowly dissipate as he grows older. Growing up is a relatively sunny time for the Jew; middle age becomes much more difficult and frustrating, lapsing for many Jews into a bitter, defeated old age.

Although immortality was not originally part of Biblical Judaism and resurrection of the dead is mentioned only in passing in one Biblical work, the Book of Daniel, written around 300 B.C., with the idea of personal immortality then imported from Mesopotamia, and resurrection not being made an article of Jewish faith until the twelfth century, Jews have an elaborate procedure of marking death by collective mourning. A week of "sitting Shiva"—the family mourning ritual—is prescribed and the close relative of the deceased must commemorate his or her "yahrzeit" (anniversary of death) by praying in the synagogue and lighting a special candle.

This focus on the death ritual is compensation for the disappointment of old age that afflicts so many Jews. This frustration is due not only to the widespread disappointment of unfulfilled ambitions and the erosion of the early joys of youth's good health and naive expectations: This is a condition generic to human nature. Jewish maturing and aging has characteristically been further adversely affected by the realization of so many Jews that they are not much wanted in the world, that they have grown up as an underprivileged and often despised minority, and that their intelligence, talents, and hard work will not be fairly rewarded in this world.

The Rattle of a Simple Man

I. L. Peretz's "Bontsha the Silent," a retelling of an old Hasidic folktale, is the single best known and most often anthologized story in Yiddish literature. In its original Hasidic form, the story celebrates the goodness rising from the piety and unadorned pleasure in ordinary things reflected in the life of a simple, pious man. The simple life, the plain mentality, unswerving faith and piety, are blessed by God. In Peretz's telling, there is a faint but perceptible subtext of derisory questioning of faith in such a common man's mentality and lifestyle. The translation is by Hilde Abel.

Here on earth the death of Bontsha the Silent made no impression at all. Ask anyone: Who was Bontsha, how did he live, and how did he die? Did his strength slowly fade, did his heart slowly give out—or did the very marrow of his bones melt under the weight of his burdens? Who knows? Perhaps he just died from not eating—starvation, it's called.

If a horse, dragging a cart through the streets, should fall, people would run from blocks around to stare, newspapers would write about this fascinating event, a monument would be put up to mark the very spot where the horse had fallen. Had the horse belonged to a race as numerous as that of human beings, he wouldn't have been paid this honor. How many horses are there, after all? But human beings—there must be a thousand million of them!

Bontsha was a human being; he lived unknown, in silence, and in silence he died. He passed through our world like a shadow. When Bontsha was born no one took a drink of wine; there was no sound of glasses clinking. When he was confirmed, he made no speech of celebration. He existed like a grain of sand at the rim of a vast ocean, amid millions of other grains of sand exactly similar, and when the wind at last lifted him up and carried him across to the other shore of that ocean, no one noticed, no one at all.

During his lifetime his feet left no mark upon the dust of the streets; after his death the wind blew away the board that marked his grave. The wife of the gravedigger came upon that bit of wood, lying far off from the grave, and she picked it up and used it to make a fire under the potatoes she was cooking; it was just right. Three days after Bontsha's death no one knew where he lay, neither the gravedigger nor anyone else. If Bontsha had had a headstone, someone, even after a hundred years, might have come across it, might still have been able to read the carved words, and his name, Bontsha the Silent, might not have vanished from this earth.

His likeness remained in no one's memory, in no one's heart. A shadow! Nothing! Finished!

In loneliness he lived, and in loneliness he died. Had it not been for the infernal human racket someone or other might have heard the sound of Bontsha's bones cracking under the weight of his burdens; someone might have glanced around and seen that Bontsha was also a human being, that he had two frightened eyes and a silent trembling mouth; someone might have noticed how, even when he bore no actual load upon his back, he still walked with his head bowed down to earth, as though while living he was already searching for his grave.

When Bontsha was brought to the hospital ten people were waiting for him to die and leave them his narrow little cot; when he was brought from the hospital to the morgue twenty were waiting to occupy his pall; when he was taken out of the morgue forty were waiting to lie where he would lie forever. Who knows how many are now waiting to snatch from him that bit of earth?

In silence he was born, in silence he lived, in silence he died—and in an even vaster silence he was put into the ground.

Ah, but in the other world it was not so! No! In paradise the death of Bontsha was an overwhelming event. The great trumpet of the Messiah announced through the seven heavens: Bontsha the Silent is dead! The most exalted angels, with the most imposing wings, hurried, flew, to tell one another, "Do you know who has died? Bontsha! Bontsha the Silent!"

And the new, the young little angels with brilliant eyes, with golden wings and silver shoes, ran to greet Bontsha, laughing in their joy. The sound of their wings, the sound of their silver shoes, as they ran to meet him, and the bubbling of their laughter, filled all paradise with jubilation, and God Himself knew that Bontsha the Silent was at last here.

In the great gateway to heaven Abraham our Father stretched out his arms in welcome and benediction: "Peace be with you!" And on his old face a deep sweet smile appeared.

What, exactly, was going on up there in paradise?

There, in paradise, two angels came bearing a golden throne for Bontsha to sit upon, and for his head a golden crown with glittering jewels.

"But why the throne, the crown, already?" two important saints asked. "He hasn't even been tried before the heavenly court of justice to which each new arrival must submit." Their voices were touched with envy. "What's going on here, anyway?"

And the angels answered the two important saints that, yes, Bontsha's trial hadn't started yet, but it would only be a formality, even the prosecutor wouldn't dare open his mouth. Why, the whole thing wouldn't take five minutes!

"What's the matter with you?" the angels asked. "Don't you know whom you're dealing with? You're dealing with Bontsha, Bontsha the Silent!"

When the young, the singing angels encircled Bontsha in love, when Abraham our Father embraced him again and again, as a very old friend, when Bontsha heard that a throne waited for him, and for his head a crown, and that when he would stand trial in the court of heaven no one would say a word against him—when he heard all this, Bontsha, exactly as in the other world, was silent. He was silent with fear. His heart shook, in his veins ran ice, and he knew this must all be a dream or simply a mistake.

He was used to both, to dreams and mistakes. How often, in that other world, had he not dreamed that he was wildly shoveling up money from the street, that whole fortunes lay there on the street beneath his hands—and then he would wake and find himself a beggar again, more miserable than before the dream.

How often in that other world had someone smiled at him, said a pleasant word—and then, passing and turning back for another look, had seen his mistake and spat at Bontsha.

Wouldn't that be just my luck, he thought now, and he was afraid to lift his eyes, lest the dream end, lest he awake and find himself again on earth, lying somewhere in a pit of snakes and loathsome vipers, and he was afraid to make the smallest sound, to move so much as an eyelash; he trembled and he could not hear the paeans of the angels; he could not see them as they danced in stately celebration about him; he could not answer the loving greeting of Abraham our Father, "Peace be with you!" And when at last he was led into the great court of justice in paradise he couldn't even say "Good morning." He was paralyzed with fear.

And when his shrinking eyes beheld the floor of the courtroom of justice, his fear, if possible, increased. The floor was of purest alabaster, embedded with glittering diamonds. On such a floor stand my feet, thought Bontsha. My feet! He was beside himself with fear. Who knows, he thought, for what very rich man, or great learned rabbi, or even saint, this whole thing's meant? The rich man will arrive, and then it will all be over. He lowered his eyes; he closed them.

In his fear he did not hear when his name was called out in the pure angelic voice: "Bontsha the Silent!" Through the ringing in his ears he could make out no words, only the sound of that voice like the sound of music, of a violin.

Yet did he, perhaps, after all, catch the sound of his own name, "Bontsha the Silent?" And then the voice added, "To him that name is as becoming as a frock coat to a rich man."

What's that? What's he saying? Bontsha wondered, and then he heard an impatient voice interrupting the speech of his defending angel. "Rich man! Frock coat! No metaphors, please! And no sarcasm!"

"He never," began the defending angel again, "complained, not against God, not against man; his eye never grew red with hatred, he never raised a protest against heaven."

Bontsha couldn't understand a word, and the harsh voice of the prosecuting angel broke in once more. "Never mind the rhetoric, please!"

"His sufferings were unspeakable. Here, look upon a man who was more tormented than Job!"

Who? Bontsha wondered. Who is this man?

"Facts! Facts! Never mind the flowery business and stick to the facts, please!" the judge called out.

"When he was eight days old he was circumcised—"

"Such realistic details are unnecessary—"

"The knife slipped, and he did not even try to staunch the flow of blood—"

"—are distasteful. Simply give us the important facts."

"Even then, an infant, he was silent, he did not cry out his pain," Bontsha's defender continued. "He kept his silence, even when his mother died, and he was handed over, a boy of thirteen, to a snake, a viper—a stepmother!"

Hm, Bontsha thought, could they mean me?

"She begrudged him every bite of food, even the moldy rotten bread and the gristle of meat that she threw at him, while she herself drank coffee with cream."

"Irrelevant and immaterial," said the judge.

"For all that, she didn't begrudge him her pointed nails in his flesh—flesh that showed black and blue through the rags he wore. In winter, in the bitterest cold, she made him chop wood in the yard, barefoot! More than once were his feet frozen, and his hands, that were too young, too tender, to lift the heavy logs and chop them. But he was always silent, he never complained, not even to his father—"

"Complain! To that drunkard!" The voice of the prosecuting angel rose derisively, and Bontsha's body grew cold with the memory of fear.

"He never complained," the defender continued, "and he was always lonely. He never had a friend, never was sent to school, never was given a new suit of clothes, never knew one moment of freedom."

"Objection! Objection!" the prosecutor cried out angrily. "He's only trying to appeal to the emotions with these flights of rhetoric!"

"He was silent even when his father, raving drunk, dragged him out of the house by the hair and flung him into the winter night, into the snowy, frozen night. He picked himself up quietly from the snow and wandered into the distance where his eyes led him.

"During his wanderings he was always silent; during his agony of hunger he begged only with his eyes. And at last, on a damp spring night, he drifted to a great city, drifted there like a leaf before the wind, and on his very first night, scarcely seen, scarcely heard, he was thrown into jail. He remained silent, he never protested, he never asked, Why, what for? The doors of the jail were opened again, and, free, he looked for the most lowly filthy work, and still he remained silent.

"More terrible even than the work itself was the search for work. Tormented and ground down by pain, by the cramp of pain in an empty stomach, he never protested, he always kept silent.

"Soiled by the filth of a strange city, spat upon by unknown mouths, driven from the streets into the roadway, where, a human beast of burden, he pursued his work, a porter, carrying the heaviest loads upon his back, scurrying between carriages, carts, and horses, staring death in the eyes every moment, he still kept silent.

"He never reckoned up how many pounds he must haul to earn a penny; how many times, with each step, he stumbled and fell for that penny. He never reckoned up how many times he almost vomited out his very soul, begging for his earnings. He never reckoned up his bad luck, the other's good luck. No, never. He remained silent. He never even demanded his own earnings; like a beggar, he waited at the door for what was rightfully his, and only in the depths of his eyes was there an unspoken longing. 'Come back later!' they'd order him; and, like a shadow, he would vanish, and then, like a shadow, would return and stand waiting, his eyes begging, imploring, for

what was his. He remained silent even when they cheated him, keeping back, with one excuse or another, most of his earnings, or giving him bad money. Yes, he never protested, he always remained silent.

"Once," the defending angel went on, "Bontsha crossed the roadway to the fountain for a drink, and in that moment his whole life was miraculously changed. What miracle happened to change his whole life? A splendid coach, with tires of rubber, plunged past, dragged by runaway horses; the coachman, fallen, lay in the street, his head split open. From the mouths of the frightened horses spilled foam, and in their wild eyes sparks struck like fire in a dark night, and inside the carriage sat a man, half alive, half dead, and Bontsha caught at the reins and held the horses. The man who sat inside and whose life was saved, a Jew, a philanthropist, never forgot what Bontsha had done for him. He handed him the whip of the dead driver, and Bontsha, then and there, became a coachman—no longer a common porter! And what's more, his great benefactor married him off, and what's still more, this great philanthropist himself provided a child for Bontsha to look after.

"And still Bontsha never said a word, never protested."

They mean me, I really do believe they mean me, Bontsha encouraged himself, but still he didn't have the gall to open his eyes, to look up at his judge.

"He never protested. He remained silent even when that great philanthropist shortly thereafter went into bankruptcy without ever having paid Bontsha one cent of his wages.

"He was silent even when his wife ran off and left him with her helpless infant. He was silent when, fifteen years later, that same helpless infant had grown up and become strong enough to throw Bontsha out of the house."

They mean me, Bontsha rejoiced, they really mean me.

"He even remained silent," continued the defending angel, "when that same benefactor and philanthropist went out of bankruptcy, as suddenly as he'd gone into it, and still didn't pay Bontsha one cent of what he owed him. No, more than that. This person, as befits a fine gentleman who has gone through bankruptcy, again went driving the great coach with the tires of rubber, and now, now he had a new coachman, and

Bontsha, again a porter in the roadway, was run over by coachman, carriage, horses. And still, in his agony, Bontsha did not cry out; he remained silent. He did not even tell the police who had done this to him. Even in the hospital, where everyone is allowed to scream, he remained silent. He lay in utter loneliness on his cot, abandoned by the doctor, by the nurse; he had not the few pennies to pay them—and he made no murmur. He was silent in that awful moment just before he was about to die, and he was silent in that very moment when he did die. And never one murmur of protest against man, never one murmur of protest against God!"

Now Bontsha begins to tremble again. He senses that after his defender has finished, his prosecutor will rise to state the case against him. Who knows of what he will be accused? Bontsha, in that other world on earth, forgot each present moment as it slipped behind him to become the past. Now the defending angel has brought everything back to his mind again—but who knows what forgotten sins the prosecutor will bring to mind?

The prosecutor rises. "Gentlemen!" he begins in a harsh and bitter voice, and then he stops. "Gentlemen—" he begins again, and now his voice is less harsh, and again he stops. And finally, in a very soft voice, that same prosecutor says, "Gentlemen, he was always silent—and now I too will be silent."

The great court of justice grows very still, and at last from the judge's chair a new voice rises, loving, tender. "Bontsha my child, Bontsha"—the voice swells like a great harp—"my heart's child . . ."

Within Bontsha his very soul begins to weep. He would like to open his eyes, to raise them, but they are darkened with tears. It is so sweet to cry. Never until now has it been sweet to cry.

"My child, my Bontsha . . . "

Not since his mother died has he heard such words, and spoken in such a voice.

"My child," the judge begins again, "you have always suffered, and you have always kept silent.

There isn't one secret place in your body without its bleeding wound; there isn't one secret place in your soul without its wound and blood. And you never protested. You always were silent.

"There, in that other world, no one understood you. You never understood yourself. You never understood that you need not have been silent, that you could have cried out and that your outcries would have brought down the world itself and ended it. You never understood your sleeping strength. There in that other world, that world of lies, your silence was never rewarded, but here in paradise is the world of truth, here in paradise you will be rewarded. You, the judge can neither condemn nor pass sentence upon. For you there is not only one little portion of paradise, one little share. No, for you there is everything! Whatever you want! Everything is yours!"

Now for the first time Bontsha lifts his eyes. He is blinded by light. The splendor of light lies everywhere, upon the walls, upon the vast ceiling, the angels blaze with light, the judge. He drops his weary eyes.

"Really?" he asks, doubtful, and a little embarrassed.

"Really!" the judge answers. "Really! I tell you, everything is yours. Everything in paradise is yours. Choose! Take! Whatever you want! You will only take what is yours!"

"Really?" Bontsha asks again, and now his voice is stronger, more assured.

And the judge and all the heavenly host answer, "Really! Really! Really!"

"Well then"—and Bontsha smiles for the first time—"well then, what I would like, Your Excellency, is to have, every morning for breakfast, a hot roll with fresh butter."

A silence falls upon the great hall, and it is more terrible than Bontsha's has ever been, and slowly the judge and the angels bend their heads in shame at this unending meekness they have created on earth.

Then the silence is shattered. The prosecutor laughs aloud, a bitter laugh.

The Struggle for Survival

The Russian Yiddish novelist of the nineteenth century, who wrote under the name of Mendele Mokher Seforim (Mendele the Bookseller) was the Jewish Emile Zola, and a realistic portrayer of life in the shtetl and villages of Eastern Europe. It was a life constantly threatened by poverty and insecurity. But something more universal is implied in Mendele's novels and short stories, such as the tremendous exertions of the maturing, aging Jew, desperate in his efforts against the odds of bad circumstances and doomed in the outcome.

The old Jew tastes the bitter bread of loneliness and failure. The translation is by Raymond Sheinolin.

Shloymele's path up to this time may not have been strewn with roses, but neither was it unduly hard: a straight road at least, without obstacles or pitfalls. But from this point on, the road became ever more crooked and bumpy, and thick with brambles. It led up steep hills, down deep valleys, and across many a dangerous chasm. The first stumbling blocks were communal troubles, a series of disasters that plagued the town of Kapulye.

The economic mainstay of Kapulye, the source of its renown among the Jewish villages of Lithuania, was its "Astrakhan" industry, and particularly its manufacture of cloth for women's kerchiefs. Astrakhan was a heavy material of a dark green color, sold by the *arshin*. It was used mainly for lining, and for making caftans for the poor. The archives of Kapulye nowhere explain how it came to be called Astrakhan. The kerchief material was a thin, bleached linen, in length and breadth about the size of a handkerchief, and it too was produced by the local weavers. The women would wrap this white turban over their hairnet in such a way that two corners fell over the nape of the neck, where they looked like a pair of blintzes, with a second, smaller "fan" alongside each fold. Around their turbaned head a kerchief would then be wound like hoops of a barrel, twisted into a knot on the forehead and the ends drawn back and tucked in on either side near the ears. On the heads of pious old ladies,

this knot stood right in the middle of the forehead, like a man's phylactery; younger women wore it modishly off to one side. Wives of well-to-do men wore silk, cashmere, or Turkish kerchiefs on the Sabbath and holidays, and printed wool kerchiefs, known as apple-kerchiefs, on weekdays. A bridegroom's parents would send both kinds of kerchief to the bride before the wedding, while the bride's parents sent the groom a fur hat.

Such was the finery of our grandmothers!

The kerchief was always kept starched and ironed. The work of smoothing and ironing a kerchief was performed by two women working together, thus: The women would stand as far apart as the length of the kerchief allowed, holding an edge in each hand so that the kerchief was stretched out lengthwise between them. Into the hollow thus formed, a large, smooth ball of glass or iron was placed. One of the women lifted her arms a bit and the ball rolled down from her side to her partner's; the second woman repeated the motion, sending the ball right back. In this way, the ball rolled back and forth until the kerchief was smooth.

It was the greatest fun in the world to watch two women smoothing kerchiefs. They stood so seriously facing one another, raising their arms with a jerk of the shoulders, their stomachs protruding, and their heads cocked to one side; they would make faces and glare, exchange poisonous smiles and sarcastic cracks. Anyone who had the chance to watch them in action had no need of theater.

The kerchiefs were finished by Gentile weavers in their own homes, and local Jewish businessmen would buy them up for cash and spools of new thread, each businessman dealing regularly with his group of weavers. These businessmen were generally young husbands who were still living with their in-laws or who still had some cash left over from the dowry. Reb Khayim's married sons supported themselves in this way. The kerchiefs were then sold to the great merchants, who distributed them throughout the cities of Lithuania. They were very popular and sold well, providing a good income for the many Jews of Kapulye whose livelihood they were.

Business went on in the same way for generations, until a government ordinance, the Clothing Decree, forbade Jewish women to shave their heads, and required that Jews, including Jewish women, dress like Germans.

Mercifully, the decree had not yet come into force in Kapulye, where men still wore sidelocks and fur hats, and women still shaved and covered their heads with kerchiefs as before. But in other towns the situation was shameful. Jewish men were donning hats! Jewish women were replacing their kerchiefs with "Lithuanian bonnets"—a kind of rag, if you will. No kerchiefs meant no business; and no business meant nothing to eat. Kapulye was laid flat by the blow. Spinners, weavers, small and big businessmen—all were hit by the decree. The tavernkeepers suffered, because if the weaver can't afford bread, he can't afford a drink either. And if spinners, weavers, tradesmen and tavernkeepers can't make a living, then the storekeepers, craftsmen and laborers are also in trouble, because who can afford to give them business? A new crop of paupers and beggars came into being. Bankrupt householders became *kheyder*-teachers to support their children, and *kheyder*-teachers proliferated like weeds. Soon there were more teachers than pupils. Times were very bad, and when things go badly, people become ill-tempered too, bickering and fighting, each one trying to snatch a morsel out of the other's mouth. The erstwhile peace and quiet of Kapulye was now gone.

Reb Khayim was also affected by the collapse of the kerchief market, for his married sons lost their means of support. Then, a brother-in-law who dealt in linen thread went bankrupt and fled, abandoning wife and child, and leaving Reb Khayim no choice but to support them, though this put a great strain on his resources. His own business fell off too. He had been farming the meat tax, but since the townspeople were now eating much less meat, he suffered enormous losses. His family was no longer as comfortable as it had been, nor as amicable. Shloymele began to taste the bitterness in life. The peacefulness of childhood was at an end.

Once trouble comes, it pours in from all sides. One fine summer day, during the dry season, a terrible fire broke out in Kapulye, destroying over half the houses in town, including the one that belonged to Freydl's family. Heaps of ashes lined the street, and sooty chimneys protruded like gravestones in a cemetery. Hungry, ragged and homeless, people wandered about the streets like living corpses. Some rummaged through the heaps of rubble of their ruined homes looking for mementos of better times. The joy they displayed over a nail or a pot or some roasted potatoes found among the ashes was more depressing than the dumb misery of those other poor souls who merely sat about mournfully, hanging their heads.

Reb Khayim took Freydl's family into his own home. There wasn't enough room for them, and the crowding caused great inconvenience, but in the emergency the change was accepted by everyone, out of pity.

The only one who did not suffer was Shloymele; in fact, the situation rather pleased him. He was together with Freydl under one roof, and the less room there was, the better for him. Each day brought unlimited opportunities of meeting her, of gazing at her face, hearing her sweet voice, watching her bare arms while she worked, and all without any fear of discovery. Shloymele went out of his way to give Freydl's parents a hand however he could, fetching and carrying things simply to curry their favor. In hopes of pleasing them, he went every day with a wheelbarrow to their burnt down house just when Freydl was scavenging there. Silently he dug and searched, putting whatever he found in his wheelbarrow; and whatever Freydl found, he quietly took from her hand and added to the haul. When the wheelbarrow was full he pulled it home, flushed red as a beet and sweating with exertion, while Freydl helped by pushing from behind. In this way he dismantled a whole chimney and oven and carried the bricks home. The joy of a warrior returning triumphant from battle with booty of silver and gold did not surpass Shloymele's joy as he and Freydl reached home, pulling the wheelbarrow laden with bricks, bits of iron, and other odds and ends salvaged from the fire. The truth is bitter, but it must be told: This fire, this terrible affliction that caused suffering to so many people, brought Shloymele a good deal of pleasure. He was like an heir who makes a show of weeping at his father's death, but who secretly feels great satisfaction.

It was only later, when Shloymele himself got burned, so to speak, that he felt the pangs of sorrow. Freydl's parents, who had lost all hope of restoring their fortunes in Kapulye, moved to a distant town, taking their children with them. Shloymele was badly hurt by the separation. His very life seemed ruined.

Like tidal waves, trials and sorrows of all kinds now swept over Kapulye. Luckily, its unlimited experience with all forms of disaster has taught tiny, pliant Israel how to bend like a reed when the great breakers sweep over, and how to raise its head upright once they have passed, Blessed is He who said: "Fear not, Israel . . . when thou passest through rivers, they will not sweep you away, and when thou walkest through fire, thou shalt not be burnt." A decree is enacted prohibiting the wearing of kerchiefs—no one would deny its disastrous consequences. But Jews can adapt to anything. They pull in their belts a bit, go hungry a bit, eat their hearts out a bit, and make do with a little less. A fire breaks out—true, a terrible misfortune. But God is our Father, and Jews are merciful people. They write letters, send out messengers, wait hopefully, and what happens?—Nothing. The messengers, after all, are also flesh and blood; they too have wives and children; they too have to eat. When autumn comes, bringing cold and rain, making the outdoor life impossible, the homeless slowly move into other people's homes wherever a place can be found. And if there's not enough room for everybody—no matter! At least all are together. An epidemic breaks out and people die—so the rabbis proclaim a fast, and the people recite Psalms. The poverty gets worse—so whoever is able, takes his walking stick and knapsack and leaves. There's plenty of room in God's world, in the region of Volhinia, for example, where teaching is a good business. Jews pick themselves up and move. Does everything then seem to be going well?—A "papers" decree is enacted, prohibiting anyone from teaching Toyre unless he has a government permit, a piece of paper. Terrible! But Jews do what is necessary under the circumstances, and God is merciful, and the teaching goes on.

Thus did the people of Kapulye weather that bitter time.

Why Do Jews Like Chinese Food?

The University of Toronto Anthropologist Ivan Kalmar examines American/ Canadian Jewish folkways at the end of the twentieth century, using the ethnographer's favorite route of analyzing eating habits.

Most anthropologists would probably agree that their discipline has a number of moral agendas. One of them is to convince people that what we think of as "good" and "bad" is not thought of the same way in other cultures, and, more importantly, that there is no solid reason for saying that our way of looking at it is better than theirs. Lévi-Strauss points out that before eating quietly became a universal value in Europe, eating with your mouth open was quite acceptable in some countries, including France. Indeed, the French viewed with some amusement the Germans, who ate with their mouths closed. What goes for food goes for many other habits of behaviour and even of thought, that is to say, it goes for culture in general. There are, most anthropologists agree, no objective grounds for viewing one culture as "better" than another. This attitude has been called "cultural relativism." The term "relativism" has fallen into disfavour, because it can be taken to denote the extreme position that *everything* in the world of values and of thought is relative (to culture in this case). Such extreme relativism leads to obvious pitfalls. For example, it would result in our having to agree that human sacrifice is not "bad" if done within the traditions of a culture. And if someone could convince us that Nazi anti-Semitism was integral to German culture, then we might have to accept the Holocaust as not "bad," either. So I must make it clear that here I am using the term "relativism" in a milder, less extreme sense. A relativist in this weaker sense might concede that there are *some* absolute values or truths. But he or she will challenge vehemently and wherever possible the idea that anything is good or true simply because habit, tradition, or authority maintains that it is. In this sense, anthropologists are mostly relativist, and all eji are anthropologists—particularly those enjoying their meal in a Chinese restaurant.

Except for those who are worried about MSG, almost every eji [Adult Secular Jew] could be said to love Chinese food. Often when I am eating Chinese with a mostly Jewish crowd, the Jewish predilection for the cuisines of Canton, Peking, and Szechwan becomes a topic of light-hearted discussion. Indeed, it appears the Jews don't just love dipping into a bowl of hot-and-sour soup, they also love talking about the fact that they love doing so. Yet the puzzle of why Jews like Chinese food still remains, I believe, to be solved.

To start with, one might note that we Jews like both to talk and to eat. We will leave it to the psychoanalysts to decide whether we are an "oral people." What is certain is that eating has nearly as central a place in the life of the eji as in that of the traditionalist, who anchors much of his or her Jewish identity in eating kosher. "A good bowl of chicken soup never hurt nobody" is probably as important a slogan of Ashkenazi Jewishness as any quotation from the Bible or Talmud.

Non-Jews have always found Jewish eating habits peculiar. Shakespeare presents Shylock as eager to interact with the Gentiles, but refusing to eat with them: "I will buy with you, sell with you, talk with you, walk with you, and so following; but I will not eat with you, drink with you, nor pray with you." Of course, the reference here is to traditional religious rules of diet. But the completely nonreligious eat "different," too. Back in the sixteenth century, Spanish satirists loved to lampoon the peculiar eating habits of the most "assimilated" of Jews, those who had converted to the Christian faith. More recently in the cosmopolitan cities of the West, the Jews have been in the forefront of the public experimenting with exotic foods. All New York professors are prone to eating Ethiopian or Jamaican food, but the Jewish ones more so than the rest. The less sophisticated Jew will stick to Chinese. The average uptown lower-middle-class Jew, whose Gentile neighbours (if there are any) consider chow mein an adventure, will delight in mushu pork and bird's nest soup.

The eji wants to say to the non-Jew: "Don't think that your food is superior." But it would seem too self-interested to add, "Jewish food is just as good." So the Jew says, "Chinese food is just as good." Exotic Chinese cuisine can be just as fine as the "dignified" cuisines of the West! It follows, of course, that Jewish cuisine can also be just as good, but the eji need not say so.

The Jewish diner in Chinatown is making a relativist statement similar to that of the anthropologist in his or her exotic "field." The diner is saying that no cuisine is inherently better than any other. The anthropologist is saying that no culture is inherently superior to any other. Both relativist statements can serve indirectly to validate the eji's self-respect as a member of a cultural minority.

I will go even further. The attitude of the Jewish guest in a Chinese restaurant has its parallels not only in anthropology but even in physical science. The diner who says that hot-and-sour soup can be just as good as Yorkshire pudding, depending on your culinary preferences, is saying that there is no privileged cuisine. The anthropologist who says that spirit possession among the Comoro Islanders can be just as meaningful as psychoanalysis, depending on your cultural background, is saying that there is no privileged culture. And the nuclear physicist *à la* Albert Einstein, who says that objects have different dimensions and that time passes at a different pace, depending on where we observe them from, is saying that there is no privileged point of observation in the universe—that in addition to our vantage point as slow-moving objects on the surface of a single planet, other points of observation yielding other views of things are conceivable.

All three attitudes, of the diner, of the anthropologist, and of the physicist, can be summed up under the one relativist proposition: "There is no single truth." It is true that Chinese food is good, but it is also true that Western food is good. In the world of cuisine, there are multiple truths. It is true that spirit possession can offer valuable knowledge if you are a Comoro Islander, but it is not true if you are an average Westerner. And in physics, under some conditions the "true" length of a rocket is less if you're looking at it from a "stationary" position on Earth than its equally "true" length would be if you observed it from another extremely fast-moving rocket. There are multiple truths in anthropology and in physics, as in cuisine. Indeed, what I am claiming is that, to the eji, there are multiple truths everywhere.

This relativist attitude to the truth is exemplified by the rabbi in the following anecdote:

A man comes to the Rabbi, complaining about his marriage. "All our problems are my wife's fault. She doesn't look after the children. She doesn't cook. She doesn't clean." "You know what," answers the Rabbi, "you're right." The man's wife comes in, and grumbles, "My husband doesn't work. He doesn't go to the synagogue. He doesn't study. It's all his fault." "You know what," the Rabbi replies again, "you're right, too." A rabbinical student, a *yeshiva bokher,* who has been observing the proceedings, can no longer hold his peace. "But, Rabbi," he exclaims, "you said the husband is right, and the wife is right, too. They can't both be right!" The Rabbi reflects for a while, scratches his beard, and then says to the *yeshiva bokher,* "You know what, you're right, too!"

It is typical for the early-twentieth-century jokers who made this up to locate the scene in a traditional rabbi's quarters. There is every reason to believe, however, that it was told by the "assimilated" eji rather than by the old-fashioned

Orthodox. I heard it from my father, who has had little contact with *yeshiva bokhers.* European Jews of his generation tell such jokes with an attitude of benign contempt, like the Americans who tell Polish jokes, or the French and Dutch who tell jokes about the Belgians. It would be worth exploring the extent to which jokes about rabbis and their disciples served to project the eji's own insecurities onto the "real Jews," the "backward" traditionalists from whom the eji attempted to distance themselves.

The joker who tells the anecdote does not—need it be said—consciously aim to make a statement about plural truths. The eji who dips his shrimp in black bean sauce is even less aware of any significance the act may have beyond giving pleasure to the palate. But our daily actions carry a multiplicity of meanings we do not always perceive ourselves. In the case of the Jewish diner in a Chinese restaurant, for example, we are dealing not only with an unconscious statement in support of relativism, but also with an interesting symbolic relationship between the Jew and the Chinese. . . . much as they trembled before the prospect of Jewish world domination. In both cases, they perceived a secretive cabal plotting to rule everyone. It might be said that the fear of the Chinese has something to do with their enormously large numbers, while the Jews are only a small group. However, there has always been in anti-Semitism a streak that claims that there are many more Jews than are visible. Recently in Poland, anti-Semites have been claiming, despite all the statistical evidence, that the country still has hundreds of thousands of Jews. There is a curious parallel here. The Chinese multitudes, so feared by the racists, are out of sight in far-away China; while it is purported that huge numbers of Jews are out of sight right here because the Jews hide their true numbers by suppressing the relevant figures—and by exaggerating their losses during the Holocaust.

The Jews themselves, however, draw a parallel of another sort between themselves and the Chinese. It is common for Jews to interpret anti-Chinese prejudice, particularly in Asia itself, as paralleling anti-Jewish prejudice here. When the defeat of South Vietnam occasioned a largely Chinese exodus from the country, Jewish communities everywhere adopted "boat people" and participated enthusiastically in charitable events.

Israel instituted its first refugee assistance program for non-Jews, among other things bringing into the country its first genuine Chinese restaurateurs, and making the Chinese food craze an Israeli as well as a general Jewish phenomenon.

The appearance of Chinese restaurant owners in Israel, by the way, added to Israelis' feelings of being "a normal country just like others" (as had the arrival of Filipino guest workers). Similarly, eji diners in the Diaspora feel more like everybody else in a Chinese restaurant, because they believe that the Chinese probably cannot tell a Jew from a non-Jew (nor would they care to), so that they "mistake" the Jew for a "normal" American, Canadian, etc. A popular New York Jewish anecdote speaks of a Chinese waiter in Brooklyn, who goes back to China and means to show off his English. He is devastated when he is told that he has learned Yiddish instead.

Add some little things. Older Jewish women are famous for their love of the Chinese gambling game mah-jong. And older Jewish couples were conspicuous among the first North American visitors to China when that country opened its borders to tourists following the demise of the cultural revolution.

Among younger Jews, especially professionals, a certain amount of animosity against the Chinese has developed as a result of recent competition from highly educated immigrants from Hong Kong, and one can detect a corresponding rise in anti-Jewish sentiment among the Chinese. However, on the whole, relations between the two communities are pleasant, if not close. So the choice of Chinese food as the favoured exotic food of relativism-bent Jews is not purely the result of its greater availability or superior taste; the choice is reinforced by the symbolism that makes a parallel between Chinese and Jews. . . .

In the symbolism of our visit to the Chinese restaurant, what matters is not only *what* we eat, but also *how* we eat it: with our mouths open, some of us. The Chinese restaurateur may confuse us with WASPs. The guests at the neighbouring table might, on the other hand, be very much aware that they're sitting next to Jews. As some of the Jewish guests wolf up their orange duck, they make no effort to hide their culinary ecstasy. Those who can, fence triumphantly with their chopsticks. The adults never stop tormenting the waiter for more rice or more water. The children

express without restraint their contempt for some of the parents' culinary choices. To many a Gentile onlooker, the Jewish diners exemplify the lack of manners said to be characteristic of their "race."

Naturally, many, and probably most, Jews dine with perfectly genteel restraint. Yet it is an easily observed fact that many don't. Unrestrained gluttony is proverbially associated by not a few Jews with Jewish celebrations. Some overly sensitive Jews complain when Jewish novelists draw pictures of oral barbarism at a bar mitzvah or other function. They call the authors anti-Semitic. They deny that some Jews are loud eaters, contradicting themselves the next minute by pointing out that others (Italians!) can be loud eaters, too. Yet the same Jews may complain about bar or bat mitzvahs where they themselves witnessed such behaviour.

Everyone but the most hardened anti-Semite must agree that some Jews are among the most polished ladies and gentlemen. So was Monsieur Haas, the French socialite on whom Proust based his Swann character in *Remembrance of Things Past*. In more recent times, so is Henry Kissinger. But it is doubtful that even such elegant individuals place the same value on good manners that some Gentiles do. It is not likely that Kissinger remembers his youth in the way Joseph Alsop, a well-known journalist and self-declared WASP, does:

If you were sufficiently unfortunate as to have to wear a white tie, a whole series of other strict rules came into severe force. First and foremost, the waistcoat could not show a white line beneath the two side-wings of the coat, yet it must not be too short to cover amply the top of the trousers. For an evening suit a double line of braid on the trousers was required, whereas a mere single line of broader braid was needed for a dinner jacket. . . . (It was highly desirable for the stiff shirt and collar, which were absolutely essential with evening dress, to be washed in such a way that when ironed, the starched line was glossy.)

This excerpt from a much longer discourse given by Alsop on the informal dress code of the WASP of yore is remarkable not so much in its detail as in its importance to the culture of the WASP. Alsop devotes to clothes more space than to anything else in his depiction of what it felt like to be a WASP. But he dwells also on linen, table habits, and the pronunciation of certain words. In short, he associates WASPdom with the loving observance of exacting rules of manners.

There is, to be sure, no greater ritualist of food and attire than the Orthodox Jew. Among Jews, the traditional men can be distinguished by their garb and hairdo and the women by their shaved heads covered by a wig, and their diet is regimented by the laws of *kashruth.* But observing tradition is never thought of as a sign of good taste, any more than kosher food is an example of fine cuisine.

Among the Jews, the equivalent of the WASP preacher or schoolmaster sternly admonishing children on their manners simply does not exist. "It is noisy here like in a Jewish school," an international simile we have mentioned earlier, captures the difference. Even the most liberal WASP schoolmaster must find it a struggle to fight the feeling that some of his Jewish pupils are culturally predisposed to bad manners.

Some Gentiles do not even make the effort. They equate Jewishness with bad manners, period. It is debatable if "mild" versions of anti-Semitism exist, but if they do, one of them is the sort that does not necessarily blame the Jews for any religious or economic crimes. It simply complains that they are too loud.

The more sympathetic non-Jews would not put it that way, however. They say, instead, that they are impressed with the honesty of Jewish feeling. Jews appear to be less "uptight" about protocol, they express their likes and dislikes, they joke freely about embarrassing topics, they are less fazed by authority and protocol. And it is not only the North American Gentiles, long accustomed to the Italian Jew as a figure of their popular culture, who think that way. If Sartre is any indication, the French share this view. In the Jew, writes Sartre,

the rationalist is constantly overwhelmed by a fresh and powerful mass of passions and emotions. He joins crude sensibility to the refinements of intellectual culture. There is a sincerity, a youth, a warmth in the manifestations of friendship of a Jew that one will rarely find in a Christian, hardened as the latter is by tradition and ceremony.

Typically for a non-Jew, Sartre considers Jewish sensibility to be refreshing, but crude.

Jewish tactlessness was the central topic of John Cuddihy's brilliant book, *The Ordeal of Civility.* To the New York sociologist, the work of Marx, Freud, and Lévi-Strauss derived largely from a Jewish inability to cope with Gentile society's emphasis on "good manners." The Jews, says Cuddihy, were late to modernize, and when finally they entered the secular world, they brought with them the "crude" manners of a closely knit, patriarchal society.

But the basis of Jewish hostility to "good manners" is not, or not essentially, a kind of sour-grapes feeling in those whose upbringing did not prepare them for the best of society. Jewish "crudeness" is not so much a survival from before modernization as it is a half-conscious response to what many Jews see as Gentile snobbery.

Sartre came closer to the point when he remarked that the Jew "has as much natural tact as anybody, if by that is understood a basic comprehension of others, but he doesn't seek to have it." The Jew does not seek to "have manners" because, as a cultural outsider, he or she knows that the idea of "good manners" is a relative one.

One attraction that Chinese food has for many Jews is that eating it does not seem to require the strict, WASP-derived table manners that some associate with "fancy" restaurants serving Western food. In choosing a Chinese dish, the eji are making a statement: There is no privileged point of view on food, there is no privileged point of view on etiquette. In their personal lives, these eji display the same relativism and the same equation of cuisine, table manners, and culture that have been characteristic of the thinking of Lévi-Strauss and other great anthropologists, many of them from the ranks of the eji.

We have said, however, that eji relativism reaches beyond anthropology. Relativism has pervaded eji creativity throughout the arts and sciences. Paul Simon's "world music," which incorporates elements of many musical traditions (a style not of his own invention but which he helped to popularize), is an example that is relatively close to anthropology itself. In the past there have been some bizarre manifestations of eji artistic relativism, such as the films of Dziga Vertov. Vertov was a Soviet Jewish cineaste of the 1920s, who filmed indiscriminately anything the camera saw, without editing. The point was an ideological one: There were no grounds for preferring one visual experience to another. The boldness of such ultimate relativism hides a fear of making a solid choice and standing behind it. It follows from it, that (since *everything* is essentially just like everything else) the Jews are just like everyone else; but it robs all things and people totally of their individual distinctiveness. Predictably, Vertov's films excited some other avant-garde artists, but bored most viewers to death.

A more sophisticated approach to relativism would have been to recognize that although there are no grounds for preferring one thing (a cultural practice, a cuisine, a race) to another *in general,* there are distinctive contexts in which each is more appropriate than the other. Christmas turkey and *gefilte* fish are inherently of equal worth; equally tasty if equally well made. But the turkey is more suitable for Christmas and the fish for the Jewish Sabbath meal; moreover, through each meal's association with culturally distinctive festivities, the Christian may have developed a special taste for the turkey and the Jew for the fish. In other words, the two kinds of food are equally "good," not because there is no difference between them at all, but because on some occasions, the turkey is more appropriate, and in others, the fish.

Why I Did Not Become a Professor

As the Jew ages, no matter how successful in career or business, he wonders if he should have followed a different route in life. It is the universal condition of Jewish angst. Here Bernard Berenson, the great authority on Florentine art in the first half of the twentieth century, looks back in his autobiography on his career and justifies why in spite of his great learning in the field of Renaissance Italian art, and the important books he wrote on the subject (in collaboration with his Gentile wife), he chose not to be an academic but instead what he calls "an archaeologist." In practice this meant that Berenson worked as a connoisseur and certifier for the leading trafficker in Renaissance art of his day, Lord Duveen (from an Anglo-Dutch Jewish family), authenticating paintings and sculptures, usually accurately, that Duveen's agents found in shops and storerooms in northern Italy.

As Berenson suggests, he made a lot of money out of this job and left his grand villa outside Florence to Harvard University as an institute for Renaissance studies. Berenson was a poor Jewish immigrant from the slums of Boston who won a scholarship to Harvard, and shortly after graduation became the European art agent for the Boston collector Isabel Gardner (the result of their collaboration can be seen today in the Gardner Museum on the Fenway in Boston). This is taken from Berenson's autobiography published in 1949.

Returning to self, I must speak of still another illusion I have not succeeded in dispelling. It is that I might have made more of it. Not in a worldly way, not by way of power or place, or recognition—none of these and kindred things.

What I fear is that I have not borne the fruit that as a plant I should have brought to full ripeness. Of all careers suitable to my make-up, have I pursued the one that got the best out of me? In the career I have followed, have I always chosen the

The angst of the Jewish intellectual: A medallion depicting the early nineteenth century German Jewish poet Heinrich Heine, who converted to Christianity.

most spiritually profitable fields? I fear not. I cannot rid myself of the insistent inner voice that keeps whispering and at times hissing, "You should not have competed with the learned nor let yourself become that equivocal thing, an 'expert.' You should have developed and clarified your notions about the enjoyment of the work of art. These notions were your own. They were exhalations of your own vital experience. They were no echo or sediment of what you had heard and what you had read. You should have elaborated these notions, using your previously published but undefended statements as themes for exposition and discussion, rather than to leave them the way you did, thrown down as axioms. Having done which, you should have applied these notions now bodied forth as theories, you should have tried to treat the other arts in the same way, not only the visual but the verbal and musical."

The inner voice goes on to say: "Recall the summer of 1895. You had the *Florentine Painters* behind you. You were a wanderer in Germany. You were alone, you had no company but your thoughts. You wanted no other, for these thoughts made you happy with what they revealed, with what they penetrated, with what they irradiated. Your mind worked as never before and, shame, never since. You had visions, clear, detailed visions of what you should do for years and years to come—a lifetime, in fact. Remember, you mapped out one book on ideated sensations, and another on life-enhancement, and a third on the portrait. Instead of accepting this revelation as the light to guide you for the rest of your days, as the Pisgah sight of your promise, you let yourself be seduced into undertaking a work on the Drawings of the Florentine Painters. How could you be so easily lured away from the path that divine guidance had opened and lit up for you?"

Yes, I remember. My brain was teeming with ideas. One was that if we were only gifted enough we should not want to perpetuate a work of art, unless it was necessary for daily life, like the houses we lived in, the buildings we worked in and the gardens and parks we breathed in. If we were as sure of producing each day a painting, a sculpture, a poem, a piece of music as satisfactory to our minds and hearts as our daily food was to our bodies, we should want it, so to speak, fresh from the oven. The day's leisure would be filled with the enjoyment of the day's masterpieces with no time, energy, or desire to look backward to what had been created the day before and all the days before that day. I was fascinated by the idea and was spinning it out and embroidering it till it flashed upon me that we should then be but instinctive animals, exercising gifts superior to those of bird and beaver, singing and weaving and constructing, but as unconscious of past and future. I recalled that it was the ever present sense of the past, of what mankind had already achieved, that distinguished us from the rest of creation. The least advanced of our species have regard for their immediate forebears, and as they get more civilized they acquire more and more interest in what their clan and tribe and people have been before them. Many stop short at their family trees, far branched enough to necessitate much memory, and at the doughty deeds of their ancestors, the warrior classes down to the armigerous of this day. Others try to embrace, and if they cannot embrace long to know, the autobiography of the entire race from the first dawn of consciousness, its many sorrows and compensating joys, its achievements, its constructions, its dreams, its yearnings, its triumphs and defeats as embodied in its stories, its songs, its temples, its palaces, its country seats, its town dwellings, its music, its dancing. In a word the completest human being, as distinct from no matter how superior a mere animal, is the man of culture, and he is that because he has the fullest and most cheering and most inspiring sense of what man has been and therefore still may be.

I could retort to the voice, "All about me, ever since I left Harvard, it was said that I was loafing, that I was wasting my best years in mere amusement, that the little I had published was no proof that I could or did work. I dared not resist the chance offered of proving that I could toil and plod and pedantize and bore with the best of them."

Ten years (if I include both editions) were spent on this task. I cannot say wasted. This book, to my limited knowledge, started the relatively new, if not entirely new, approaches to the study of an artist's drawings, apart from their intrinsic value as creations, to which also more attention was given than ever before perhaps. Moreover, it was the first time that the attempt was made to study what drawings remained out of the entire output of a school of painters. The two chief novelties referred to were, first, the inclusion of the drawings as an integral part of the artist's creativeness, and valued at least as much as his finished work; the other, the light the sketches for a given picture throw on the creative process of the artist as well as upon his individual gifts. Was he, for instance, a born painter like, say, Titian, or a born draughtsman like Michelangelo?

Today no monograph on an artist is published that does not take into account his drawings as much as his completed works. That it is so may be partly the result of my approach to the subject in *The Drawings of the Florentine Painters*.

The same result might not have followed had I written the few pages in which I could have stated and explained how to study drawings and left it at that. The mind, it has often been remarked, seems as unable to live on extracts only as the body. Both require mere bulk. The difference is that nature has made tolerable provisions for elimination from intestines, and medicine supplies purges. Neither God nor man has yet invented a way of ridding the mind of useless and false knowledge. Hence the famous phrase of Josh Billings: "The trouble with people is not that they don't know but that they know so much that ain't so."

And yet it is a pity that I spent so many years on a task which others might have done as well once the path was laid out. The little satisfaction that accrued from the completion of the work could not quiet a gnawing conviction that I should have spent ten years to better purpose than to prove that one could be a systematic worker.

This book, in two folios too heavy to lift, has never been seriously reviewed either in the first edition or in the second, but with the public estimation it established my reputation as an authority. That reputation alone would have cost me the friendship of some of my close adherents, no small sacrifice. One of them came to me during my annual visit to London and told me with a choking voice that in Bond Street my word was law, and that it stood in the way of his career. To me at the moment it meant nothing, nor could I conceive that this fellow student would turn not into an adversary but an out and out enemy. Perhaps I did not reflect that I, too, might hanker after authority if I had not possessed it. And having had it for three decades at least may be the reason why I do not miss it, now that it has vanished.

It cost even more. My authority soon sank to something less distinguished, less respectable even. I soon discovered that I ranked with fortune-tellers, chiromancists, astrologers and not even with the self-deluded of these, but rather with the deliberate charlatans. At first I was supposed to have invented a trick by which one could infallibly tell the authorship of an Italian picture. A famous writer on the Renaissance, Vernon Lee, thought it was close and even mean of me not to let her share the secret. Finally it degenerated into a widespread belief that if only I could be approached the right way I could order this or that American millionaire to pay thousands upon thousands and hundreds of thousands for any daub that I was bribed by the seller to attribute to a great master. Proposals of this nature, no matter how decorously veiled, became a nuisance and a burden; and in the end I was compelled in self-defense to refuse to see people unless I was sure that they brought no "great masters" with them. Needless to say that every person I would not receive, every owner whose picture I would not ascribe to Raphael or Michelangelo, or Giorgione, Titian or Tintoretto, etc., etc., turned into an enemy.

Perhaps much if not all of this would have been avoided if I had let myself be solicited to write on other subjects than Italian Renaissance painting. Convinced on the one hand that to know all that at a given moment could be discovered in the exploration of this field, to know enough to be sure one was not humbugging, was a whole-time job; and on the other hand, fully aware of how limited was my capacity for concentrated work, I refused to write, let alone to play the expert, on any question outside my own parish, and refrained from publishing anything on contemporary art. The one exception I can recall to mind confirmed the resolution. It was this: In the *New York Nation* early in this century I happened to read a letter from Paris in which the correspondent spoke of Matisse as a *fumiste* whose only object was to *épater les bourgeois*. It was too much. I took up my pen and sent a short note of protest to set the readers of my favourite and revered weekly to rights. The attention aroused by these few lines of print made me aware of the authority I could wield as a critic of modern art. The entire Stein family, Michael, Sally, Leo, Gertrude, who at the time arrogated to themselves the office of High Protectors of newness in painting, began to prod me to leave all I had and to dedicate myself to expounding the merits of the new school. When I would not, they sadly put me down as having made the great refusal. Other artists approached me from every side. Years later, as the first World War was nearing its chequered end, a lady of fashion insisted on taking me to a studio. She would not tell me whose. Nor would it have enlightened me if she had, never having heard the artist's name before. I was treated to a private show of daubs and absurdities which I enjoyed but moderately. The lady who had brought me tried to stir me to utter some words of appreciation. Finally the painter himself spoke up and said, "You made Matisse. Can't you do the same for me?" He could no more realize than the people who came to have their *croûtes* or forgeries baptized as great masters that there was any "damned merit" in the case, a matter of quality to be considered. Happily this aspirant soon deserted painting for apostolic journalism in book form.

I dreaded the personal element in my job, and that was a contributing and perhaps chief reason why I would not write on contemporary art. My standards were based on what survived of the greatest and best in fifty centuries of creative genius. It would not be fair to measure up against it the product of any single day, not even this day. Yet I had no other balances in which to weigh the artist. Besides I could not forget what one successful painter told me. Critics, he said, who spoke ill of him were malignant charlatans, and braying asses when they praised him. His adjectives were perhaps excessive but his substantives not far from the truth. From us critics, the painter cannot ask for the only observations that interest him, helpful technical ones. He despises our amateurishness and studio gossip. He wants nothing but our help in building up his reputation and selling his pictures.

Among the indigent and most unappreciated of the painters whom the Steins took up and treated with almost maternal solicitude was Picasso. Lest I forget it I record now, as it comes back to my memory: Meeting this most protean and acrobatic of painters, the most ready to take any jump, to put on any motley or mask, to twist himself into any shape and always with dazzling dexterity—meeting him after he had become the sovereign idol of the public that writes, that "turtle-eats," that buys, he condescended to recall that he had known me at the Steins' and added, "Ah, those Steins, how they did exploit me!"

It would not be fair to deny that being an authority brought material advantages. Not only did it enable me to pay for assistance in any work, for comfort at home and abroad, and for expensive journeys, but it gave me the means to acquire the books and photographs that my study and research required. The only boast I feel like making is that the library I have accumulated item by item during the last fifty years will enable those who come after me to continue my kind of work for generations to come. It will require relatively little outlay to keep it up to date.

All that. Yet I repeat that I took the wrong turn when I swerved from more purely intellectual pursuits to one like the archæological study of art, gaining thereby a troublesome reputation as an "expert." My only excuse is, if the comparison is not blasphemous, that like Saint Paul with his tent-making and Spinoza with his glass-polishing, I too needed a means of livelihood. Mine did not take up more of my time but very much more of my energy. Those men of genius were not hampered in their careers by their trades. Mine took up what creative talent there was in me, with the result that this trade made my reputation and the rest of me scarcely counted. The spiritual loss was great and in consequence I have never regarded myself as other than a failure. This sense of failure, a guilty sense, makes me squirm when I hear myself spoken of as a "successful man" and as having made "a success of my life." I used to protest but gave it up at last, for nobody would believe that my vehement negatives were more than polite modesty or indeed the conceit of an ambition that had not yet been satisfied. So I now put up with being admired as a success just as after

years and years of correcting people for doing so, I put up with being addressed as "Dr." or "Professor," titles I have no right to as I have never had a doctor's degree and still less have I ever occupied a university chair.

On the other hand fairness compels me to say that this absorption in archæological study and research was far from a mere slavery imposed by ambition, or even need. I enjoyed it too much. Indeed I venture to doubt whether anybody has passed through life with so much freedom from forced labour as I have. I was blessed from early years with a knack for throwing myself head over heels into the task before me. There was a moment in my twenties when it looked as if I should have to leave Europe and return to teach in some Western college. The prospect was scarcely pleasing but I recall cheering myself with the confidence that I should end by enjoying it.

And so it was with the *Florentine Drawings*. I was carried on the wings of curiosity. The zest for the work made me beat the pavement with pleasure as I walked from Fiesole to and from the Uffizi, and I was almost ecstatic as I pored over the portfolios in the icy-cold printroom pervaded by the keeper's rank and stale cigar smoke.

Dying and Burial

In Bernard Malamud's 1957 novel *The Assistant*, the death, burial, and mourning of a Harlem Jewish storekeeper is seen through the eyes of his African-American employee.

Morris died in the hospital, three days later, and was buried the day after in an enormous cemetery—it went on for miles—in Queens. He had been a member of a burial society since coming to America and the services took place in the Society's funeral parlor on the Lower East Side, where the grocer had lived as a young man. At noon in the chapel's antechamber, Ida, gray-faced and in mourning, every minute on the edge of fainting, sat in a high-backed tapestried chair, rocking her head. At her side, wasted, red-eyed from

weeping, sat Helen. Landsleit, old friends, drawn by funeral notices in the Jewish morning papers, lamented aloud as they bent to kiss her, dropping pulpy tears on her hands. They sat on folding chairs facing the bereaved and talked in whispers. Frank Alpine stood for a moment, his hat uncomfortably on, in a corner of the room. When the place grew crowded he left and seated himself among the handful of mourners already assembled in the long narrow chapel, dimly lit by thick, yellow wall lamps. The rows of benches were dark

Respect for the dead: Jewish burial plaque. Rome, second–third century A.D.

handwritten paper praise for Morris Bober and lamentation for his loss. When he announced the body could be seen, the undertaker and his assistant, a man in a chauffeur's cap, lifted the coffin lid and a few people came forward. Helen wept profusely at her father's waxen, berouged image, the head wrapped in a prayer shawl, the thin mouth slightly twisted.

Ida flung up both arms, crying in Yiddish at the corpse, "Morris, why didn't you listen to me? You went away and left me with a child, alone in the world. Why did you do it?" She broke into racking sobs and was gently escorted by Helen and the breathless undertaker to her seat, where she pressed her wet face against her daughter's shoulder. Frank went up last. He could see, where the prayer shawl fell back a little, the scar on the grocer's head, but outside of that it wasn't Morris. He felt a loss but it was an old one.

The rabbi then prayed, a stocky man with a pointed black beard. He stood on the podium near the coffin, wearing an old Homburg, a faded black frock coat over brown trousers, and bulbous shoes. After his prayer in Hebrew, when the mourners were seated, in a voice laden with sorrow he spoke of the dead man.

"My dear friends, I never had the pleasure to meet this good grocery man that he now lays in his coffin. He lived in a neighborhood where I didn't come in. Still and all I talked this morning to people that knew him and I am now sorry I didn't know him also. I would enjoy to speak to such a man. I talked to the bereaved widow, who lost her dear husband. I talked to his poor beloved daughter Helen, who is now without a father to guide her. To them I talked, also to landsleit and old friends, and each and all told me the same, that Morris Bober, who passed away so untimely—he caught double pneumonia from shoveling snow in front of his place of business so people could pass by on the sidewalk—was a man who couldn't be more honest. Such a person I am sorry I didn't meet sometime in my life. If I met him somewhere, maybe when he went to visit in a Jewish neighborhood—maybe at Rosh Hashana or Pesach—I would say to him, 'God bless you, Morris Bober.' Helen, his dear daughter, remembers from when she was a small girl that her father ran two blocks in the snow to give back to a poor Italian lady a nickel that she forgot on the counter. Who runs in wintertime without hat or

and heavy. In the front of the chapel, on a metal stand, lay the grocer's plain wooden coffin.

At one P.M., the gray-haired undertaker, breathing heavily, escorted the widow and her daughter to the front row on the left, not far from the coffin. A wailing began among the mourners. The chapel was a little more than half-full of old friends of the grocer, a few distant relatives, burial society acquaintances, and one or two customers. Breitbart, the bulb peddler, sat, stricken, against the right wall. Charlie Sobeloff, grown heavy-faced and stout, appeared, with Florida tan and sad crossed eye, together with his stylish wife, who sat staring at Ida. The entire Pearl family was present, Betty with her new husband, and Nat, sober, concerned for Helen, wearing a black skull cap. A few rows behind them was Louis Karp, alone and ill at ease among strangers. Also Witzig, the baker, who had served Morris bread and rolls for twenty years. And Mr. Giannola, the barber, and Nick and Tessie Fuso, behind whom Frank Alpine sat. When the bearded rabbi entered the chapel through a side door, Frank took off his hat but quickly put it on again.

The secretary of the Society appeared, a soft-voiced man with little hair, his glasses lit with reflections of the wall lamps, and read from a coat, without rubbers to protect his feet, two blocks in the snow to give back five cents that a customer forgot? Couldn't he wait till she comes in tomorrow? Not Morris Bober, let him rest in peace. He didn't want the poor woman to worry, so he ran after her in the snow. This is why the grocer had so many friends who admired him."

The rabbi paused and gazed over the heads of the mourners.

"He was also a very hard worker, a man that never stopped working. How many mornings he got up in the dark and dressed himself in the cold, I can't count. After, he went downstairs to stay all day in the grocery. He worked long long hours. Six o'clock every morning he opened and he closed after ten every night, sometimes later. Fifteen, sixteen hours a day he was in the store, seven days a week, to make a living for his family. His dear wife Ida told me she will never forget his steps going down the stairs each morning, and also in the night when he came up so tired for his few hours' sleep before he will open again the next day the store. This went on for twenty-two years in this store alone, day after day, except the few days when he was too sick. And for this reason that he worked so hard and bitter, in his house, on his table, was always something to eat. So besides honest he was a good provider."

The rabbi gazed down at his prayer book, then looked up.

"When a Jew dies, who asks if he is a Jew? He is a Jew, we don't ask. There are many ways to be a Jew. So if somebody comes to me and says, 'Rabbi, shall we call such a man Jewish who lived and worked among the Gentiles and sold them pig meat, trayfe, that we don't eat it, and not once in twenty years comes inside a synagogue, is such a man a Jew, rabbi?' To him I will say, 'Yes, Morris Bober was to me a true Jew because he lived in the Jewish experience, which he remembered, and with the Jewish heart.' Maybe not to our formal tradition—for this I don't excuse him—but he was true to the spirit of our life—to want for others that which he wants also for himself. He followed the Law which God gave to Moses on Sinai and told him to bring to the people. He suffered, he endured, but with hope. Who told me this? I know. He asked for himself little—nothing, but he wanted for his beloved child a better existence than he had. For such reasons he was a Jew. What more does our sweet God ask his poor people? So

let Him now take care of the widow, to comfort and protect her, and give to the fatherless child what her father wanted her to have. 'Yaskadal v'yiskadash shmey, rabo. B'olmo divro . . . '"

The mourners rose and prayed with the rabbi.

Helen, in her grief, grew restless. He's overdone it, she thought. I said Papa was honest but what was the good of such honesty if he couldn't exist in this world? Yes, he ran after this poor woman to give her back a nickel but he also trusted cheaters who took away what belonged to him. Poor Papa; being naturally honest, he didn't believe that others come by their dishonesty naturally. And he couldn't hold onto those things he had worked so hard to get. He gave away, in a sense, more than he owned. He was no saint; he was in a way weak, his only true strength in his sweet nature and his understanding. He knew, at least, what was good. And I didn't say he had many friends who admired him. That's the rabbi's invention. People liked him, but who can admire a man passing his life in such a store? He buried himself in it; he didn't have the imagination to know what he was missing. He made himself a victim. He could, with a little more courage, have been more than he was.

Helen prayed for peace on the soul of her dead father.

Ida, holding a wet handkerchief to her eyes, thought, So what if we had to eat? When you eat you don't want to worry whose money you are eating—yours or the wholesalers'. If he had money he had bills; and when he had more money he had more bills. A person doesn't always want to worry if she will be in the street tomorrow. She wants sometimes a minute's peace. But maybe it's my fault, because I didn't let him be a druggist.

She wept because her judgment of the grocer was harsh although she loved him. Helen, she thought, must marry a professional.

When the prayer was done the rabbi left the chapel through the side door, and the coffin was lifted by some of the Society members and the undertaker's assistant, carried on their shoulders outside, and placed in the hearse. The people in the chapel filed out and went home, except Frank Alpine, who sat alone in the funeral parlor.

Suffering, he thought, is like a piece of goods. I bet the Jews could make a suit of clothes out of it. The other funny thing is that there are more of them around than anybody knows about.

The Laws of Mourning

The sixteenth-century handbook for Orthodox behavior, *Shulchan Orech*, sets down how mourning should be conducted. Its central importance in Jewish life is indicated.

1. One should not grieve excessively for the dead, and whosoever grieves excessively for him, will weep for another [dead] save that three days [are designated] for weeping, seven for lamenting, thirty [to abstain from] cutting the hair and wearing laundried garments.

2. This applies to the rest of the people, but [as to] scholars [who died], everything is according to their wisdom; and one does not weep for them more than thirty days, nor does one make a lamentation for them more than twelve months, and likewise, a Sage whose [death] report was received after twelve months, is not lamented.

3. One may go out to the cemetery and visit the dead until three days [after being placed in the sepulchral chamber], for perhaps he is still alive.

4. During the first three days [of mourning], the mourner should look upon himself as if a sword is resting between his shoulders; from the third to the seventh, as if it is standing in the corner facing him; from the seventh to the thirtieth, as if it is passing before him in the market place; and throughout the entire year, the judgment is aimed against that family. But if a male child is born in that family, the entire family becomes healed.

5. When one [member] of a company dies, the whole company should feel troubled.

6. Whosoever does not observe mourning rites as the Sages commanded is a cruel person, but one should fear and be troubled and investigate his conduct and repent.

Sitting Shiva

Mordechai Richler, in his 1971 novel, *St. Urbain's Horseman,* brilliantly uses the occasion of sitting shiva—the mandatory seven days of family mourning— to communicate not only all the cross-currents of love and hate that affect a family over time, but also the whole recent social history of Montreal Jews. The mood here, in contrast with his earlier novel of growing up, *The Apprenticeship of Duddy Kravitz* (an excerpt of which can be found in part two), captures the diversity of the Jewish experience of maturing, for some successful, for others failing bitterly, but overall covered with a wistfulness, regret, and disappointment. This is a marvelous piece of social history.

A glass of water, with a swab of absorbent cotton resting on the rim, was perched on top of the faulty, whirring air conditioner. Jake's grandmother freshened the water each morning. It was there to slake her first-born son's soul, in the event that it returned thirsty or feverish. The late Issy Hersh's small, modest apartment was stifling. Overflowing. It reeked of Hersh sweat, decaying Hersh bodies, the rumpled men received visitors in the little box of a living room. While Jake's grandmother, Fanny, his sister Rifka, his aunts, accepted mourners like dues in the master bedroom, where cancer, lodging in Issy Hersh's kidney, had taken root and spread tentacles throughout his body.

Earlier, when Jake had emerged from the airplane at Dorval, the worse for six hours of gin, he had discovered Herky pacing up and down in front of the customs barrier.

"Good flight?" Herky barked.

Jake shrugged.

"How's the family?"

"Well."

"And the wife, keeping her looks?"

Fuck you.

"He died peacefully. I want you to know that." Once inside his air-conditioned Buick, Herky demanded, "That a good tie?"

"*What?*"

"We're going straight to Paperman's." The funeral parlor. "They'll have to cut it with a razor blade. That's the law, you know." Go to hell, Herky.

Jake's big-booted, leathery-faced grandmother, the belly that had swelled for fourteen children hanging useless now, an empty pouch—foolish Fanny determined to out-quake Rifka—his dour girdled aunts—all combined to send up a counterpoint of sobs and moans throughout the rabbi's eulogy at the funeral parlor. The solemn menfolk, the brothers and cousins next in line, glared at the coffin, this one tolerating what he had been assured was a stomach ulcer and another awaiting the results of a biopsy.

All his life Issy Hersh had worn forced-to-clear suits and fire sale shoes and now even his casket seemed too large. His last bargain.

The rabbi was brief.

"Words fail me to adequately express the sorrow I share with you. Even as Jewish law limits the topics of discussion for those who mourn, I find my speech curtailed because I mourn with you for Isaac Hersh, who all his years exuded and emanated Jewishness, real *yiddishkeit;* affluent in the rich symbolism of his people, which he readily spread amongst us. May the fond memories we have of a fine, outpouring Jewish soul inspire us to emulate all that was good in him . . . "

The women, subsiding into limousines, caught their second wind at the cemetery and began to lament anew, wailing with abandon. Poor Fanny, whose perch within the family hierarchy was exceedingly rocky now, the tolerated second wife of an underinsured, all but penniless husband, with a stepdaughter who abominated her and a stranger for a stepson, necessarily outbid all the others. Even Aunt Sophie, over whom her son, twenty-two-year-old Irwin, obese, his face florid, held a parasol. Irwin, who wore a straw hat with a tartan band, was staring at Jake. Jake shot him a piercing look, and Irwin, flushing a deeper red, wiggled his eyebrows pleadingly and averted his eyes.

The older generation of Hersh menfolk, brothers and cousins to Issy, filed past the grave dutifully but truculent, appealingly truculent, each taking up the workman's spade in turn to shovel wet clay onto the coffin. Smack, smack. The Hershes, all of them, seemingly one cherished decomposing body to Jake now. Like him, susceptible to germs. Wasting. Shivering together in spite of the blistering heat. Diminished by one.

Suddenly, the enveloping black birds began to twitter. All manner of rabbis, young and old, blackbearded and cleanshaven, rocked in prayer, heads bobbing, competing in piety. For each Hersh buried paid dividends above ground. Every expired Hersh was bound to be commemorated by a rabbi's study or additional classroom for the yeshiva, a *sefer torah* donated here or an ark paid for there, a parochial-school library or a fully equipped kindergarten. In Everlasting Memory of . . .

"*Oy, oy,*" Rifka wailed.

"Issy! My Issy!" Fanny put in, outreaching her.

Jake couldn't even coax a tear out of himself; he felt altogether too drained and fearful of the wailing to come.

But once back in the widow's apartment, a veritable oven that day, their hands washed and stomachs biting with hunger, the men shed their jackets and loosened their ties and belts, the women unbuckled and unzipped. Everybody was talking at once, positioning themselves by the table, as plates of hard-boiled eggs, bagels, and onion rolls were followed by platters of lox, roast chicken, and steaming potato varenikes, apple cake and chocolate chip cookies, peaches and plums, bottles of Tab and diet Pepsi. Once more Jake sensed the immense Irwin gaping at him. Caught out, Irwin wiggled his eyebrows again, blushed, and spit a plum pit into his hand.

Uncle Sam switched on his transistor radio and the sated Hershes gathered around to hear the ram's horn blown at the wailing wall in Jerusalem.

"If only Issy could have lived," Jake's grandmother said, crumpling, "to hear the *shofar* blown in Jerusalem."

An interloping rabbi squeezed the old lady's mottled hand. "You mustn't question the Almighty," he cautioned her, "or He might call you up for an answer."

Exactly what Rabbi Meltzer had told the Horseman. Did they subscribe, Jake wondered, to the same chief rabbi of platitudes? Had they been issued with similar condolence kits on graduation from yeshiva?

Now the men, slippered and unshaven (except for Jake, who scorned that ritual), staked claims, according to their need, to a place on the sofa or a chair by the balcony door, the seat handiest to the kitchen or the one nearest the toilet. As Uncle Jack emerged from the toilet, Irwin asked, "Everything come out all right?" his shoulders heaving with laughter. Then he caught Jake's reproving glance, shrugged, and retreated.

"Did you notice that Sugarman, the *chazer*, wasn't even at Paperman's?"

"It wasn't overcrowded with your in-laws either."

Uncle Abe rubbed his unshaven chin and complained of the first day's stiffness.

"After a few days it gets soft," he was assured.

"That's my trouble too," Uncle Lou said.

Uncle Sam figured the rabbi's speech was a washout, but Uncle Morrie didn't agree. "A rabbi's speech," he said, "should be like a miniskirt. Eh, Yankele?"

Jake saluted the reference to London.

"Long enough to cover the subject, short enough to make it interesting."

Herky, encouraged, pitched in with a convoluted story about a cracker, a Jew, and a Negro, all delivered in an Amos 'n' Andy accent, and culminating with the Negro saying, "I've got foah inches. Is that all? the hebe asks. *Foah inches from the ground, baby.*"

Uncle Morrie laughed and wiped the corners of his eyes with a handkerchief. "You guys," he said.

Jake's ponderous silence was taken for disapprobation.

"Listen here, Yankele," Uncle Lou said, clapping him on the back. "If it was your Uncle Morrie here we had just buried—"

Which earned him a poisonous look.

"—and your father, may he rest in peace, was still with us, he would be leading with the jokes."

"You're absolutely right," Jake said, sorry that they had misunderstood him.

"Then here's one for you, by jove, with a Limey twist. 'Ow do you get six elephants into a Vauxhall?"

"I wouldn't know."

"Blimey, old thing. Three in the front, three in the back."

Jake mustered a smile and raised his glass to Uncle Lou.

"And 'ow would you get six giraffes into the same car?" A pause. "You remove the elephants," Lou exploded.

"Clever."

"Yankel, you should never lose your stench of humor. That's a philosophy that's never failed me."

"I remember," Jake said, and he drifted onto the balcony where Irwin towered over a brood of younger cousins, a transistor clapped to his ear.

"Mays just homered," he said. "They're going to walk McCovey," and seeing Jake, he gulped, and turned his back to him.

Jake decided to seek out Fanny before he had drunk himself into incoherence. She was in the small bedroom.

"Anything I can do for you?" Jake asked.

"Sit."

So he sat.

"You know, one night—after we were married, you understand—your father and I, well . . ." She blushed. ". . . We were fooling around, you know. You know what I mean?"

"You were what?"

"Well, you know. I got pregnant. But he made me see somebody."

"Why?"

"He thought his brothers would laugh at him. At his age, a baby."

"I'm sorry."

"You're a very thoughtful person. I'd come to visit you in London, if I could afford it."

Which drove Jake back into the hall, where he could see Irwin, alone on the balcony now, waddling over to the railing. He thrust a finger into his nostril, dug fiercely, and slowly, slowly, extracted a winding worm of snot. Irwin contemplated it, sleepy-eyed, before he wiped it on the railing.

Uncle Jack was holding forth, dribbling cigar ash.

"Hey, did you hear the one about the two Australian fairies? One of them went back to Sydney."

Herky clapped Jake on the back. "Got to talk to you." He ushered Jake into the toilet ahead of him. "How are you fixed money-wise kid?"

"I'd love to help you, Herky," Jake replied, swaying, "but it's all tied up."

"You don't understand. I don't need your money. You've got kids now. I'm sure you want to invest for the future. You're my one and only brother-in-law and . . . well, I'd like to put you on to something good."

"I read you."

Herky lit up, exuding self-satisfaction. "What do you think is the most valuable thing in the world today?"

"The Jewish tradition."

"Where will boozing get you? Nowhere." Herky plucked Jake's glass out of his hand. "I'm serious, for Chrissake."

"All right, then. Not having cancer."

"I mean a natural resource."

"Gold?"

"Guess again."

"Oil?"

Herky spilled over with secret knowledge. "Give up?"

Don't you know you're going to die, Herky? But he didn't say it.

"Water."

"*What?*"

"H_2O. Watch this." With a flick of the wrist, Herky flushed the toilet. "It's going on everywhere, day and night. Now you take the Fraser River, for instance. More than once a day the untreated contents of one hundred thousand toilet bowls empty into it."

"That's a lot of shit, Herky."

"Flush, flush, flush. Canada's got more clean water than any other country in the Free World, but even so, there's a limit, you know."

Jake retrieved his drink.

"You project ten years ahead and there will be container tankers, fleets of them, carrying not oil or iron ore, but pure Canadian water, to polluted American cities."

"So?"

"Watch closely now." Herky flushed the toilet again. "All over the city, people are doing the same, but—but—this toilet, like any other, *flushes the same amount of water no matter what the need*. You read me?"

"Loud and clear."

"I call them mindless, these toilets, I mean."

"I'm tired, Herky. Come to the point."

"The average person urinates maybe four times a day, but defecates only once, yet this toilet is mindless, it is adjusted to provide enough power to flush a stool down the drain each time. Millions of gallons daily are being wasted in the Montreal area alone. Which is where I come in. We are developing a cistern that will give you all the zoom you need for defecation, but will release only what's necessary to wash urine away. In other words, a toilet with a mind. The biggest breakthrough since Thomas Crapper's Niagara. Once we get costs down and go into production, I expect our unit to become mandatory equipment in all new buildings. I'm offering you a chance to come in on the ground floor. Well?"

"You certainly are thinking big, Herky."

"You've got to move with the times."

"Let me sleep on it, O.K.?"

"O.K., but meanwhile, mum's the word."

A half hour before the first evening star, the rabbis trooped into the insufferably hot apartment in shiny black frock coats. The local yeshiva's Mafia. Ranging from tall spade-bearded men in broad-brimmed black hats to pimply, wispy-bearded boys in oversize Homburgs. Finally, there came the leader, the fragile Rabbi Polsky himself, who led the men in the evening prayer.

Immediately behind Jake, prayerbook in hand, stood flat-footed Irwin, breathing with effort. As Jake stumbled self-consciously through the prayer for the dead, Irwin's troubled breathing quickened—it raced—stopped—and suddenly he sneezed, and sneezed again, pelting Jake's neck with what seemed like shrapnel. As Jake whirled around, Irwin seemed to draw his neck into his body. Bulging eyes and a sweaty red face rising over a succession of chins were all that confronted Jake. But as he resumed his prayers, he was conscious of Irwin, biting back his laughter, threatening to explode. The moment prayers were over, Irwin shot out onto the balcony, heaving, a soggy hand clamped to his nose.

Rabbi Polsky, holy man to the Hershes, was thin and round-shouldered, his skin gray as gum, with watery blue eyes and a scraggly yellow beard. He padded on slippered feet to a place on the sofa. A cunning field mouse. Accusingly impecunious amid Hersh affluence. His shirt collar curling and soiled, his cuffs frayed, Rabbi Polsky came nightly, wiped his mouth with an enormous damp handkerchief, and preached to the Hershes, all of whom virtually glowed in his presence.

"There came to me once a man to ask me to go to the Rebbe in New York to ask him what he should do for his father who was dying. He paid for me the air ticket, I went to Brooklyn, I spoke with the Rebbe, and I came back and said to the man the Rebbe says pray, you must pray every morning. Pray, the man asked? Every morning. So he went away and every morning before going to the office he said his prayers after years of not doing it. Then one morning he had an appointment with a *goy*, a financier, from out of town, at the Mount Royal Hotel. He had to see the *goy* to make a loan for his business. The *goy* said you be here nine o'clock sharp, I'll try to fit you in, I'm very busy. All right. But the man overslept and in the morning he realized if he takes time to say his prayers he will be late. He will lose his loan. All the same he prayed, and when he got to the Mount Royal Hotel and went to the man's room, the *goy* was in a rage, shouting, hollering, *you* keep *me* waiting. You need me and you keep me waiting? So the man said his father was dying and his rabbi had told him he must pray every morning, and that's why he was late. You mean to say, the *goy* asked, even though if I deny you this loan your business is ruined, you were late so as not to miss one morning's prayers for your father? Yes. In that case, the *goy* said, let me shake your hand, put it there, you are a fella I can trust. To lend money to such a man will be a genuine pleasure."

Euphoria filled the Hershes. Only Jake protested, nudging Uncle Lou. "We now know

that praying is good for credit, but what happened to the man's father?"

"You know what your trouble is? You don't believe in anything."

Rabbi Polsky, possibly with Jake in mind, continued:

"Sometimes young people question the law. There's no reason for this . . . that's a superstition . . . You know the type, I'm sure. Why, for example, they ask, should we not eat seafood?"

Uncle Lou poked Jake. "Your sister Rifka is on a seafood diet."

"What?"

"Every time she sees food she wants it."

"Why," the rabbi asked, "shouldn't we eat crab or lobster? To which I would answer you with the question why is there such madness among the *goyim*, they run to the psychiatrist every morning? Why? It is now scientifically revealed in an article in *Time* magazine that eating seafood can drive you crazy. It promotes insanity."

"Jake, it's for you," Uncle Jack said, holding out the kitchen phone.

"Who is it?"

"The boss," he replied with a big wink.

"Would you mind shutting the door after you, please?" Jake asked, before taking the call.

It was Nancy, enormously concerned for his sake. "I thought you would phone last night."

"Honestly, I'm all right."

"There's no need to pretend."

"The embarrassing thing is," Jake said, "it's like a family party. I'm not grieving. I'm having a wonderful time."

Sitting with the Hershes, day and night, a bottle of Remy Martin parked between his feet, such was Jake's astonishment, commingled with pleasure, in their responses, that he could not properly mourn for his father. He felt cradled, not deprived. He also felt like Rip Van Winkle returned to an innocent and ordered world he had mistakenly believed long extinct. Where God watched over all, doing His sums. Where everything fit. Even the holocaust which, after all, had yielded the state of Israel. Where to say, "Gentlemen, the Queen," was to offer the obligatory toast to Elizabeth II at an affair, not to begin a discussion on Andy Warhol. Where smack was not habit-forming, but what a disrespectful child deserved; pot was what you simmered the chicken soup in; and camp was where you sent the boys for the summer. It was astounding, Jake was incredulous, that after so many years and fevers, after Dachau, after Hiroshima, revolution, rockets in space, DNA, bestiality in the streets, assassinations in and out of season, there were still brides with shining faces who were married in white gowns, posing for the *Star* social pages with their prizes, pear-shaped boys in evening clothes. There were aunts who sold raffles and uncles who swore by the *Reader's Digest*. French Canadians, like overflying airplanes distorting the TV picture, were only tolerated. DO NOT ADJUST YOUR SET, THE TROUBLE IS TEMPORARY. Aunts still phoned each other every morning to say what sort of cake they were baking. Who had passed this exam, who had survived that operation. A scandal was when a first cousin was invited to the bar mitzvah *kiddush*, but not the dinner. Eloquence was the rabbi's sermon. They were ignorant of the arts, they were overdressed, they were overstuffed, and their taste was appallingly bad. But within their self-contained world, there was order. It worked.

As nobody bothered to honor them, they very sensibly celebrated each other at fund-raising synagogue dinners, taking turns at being Man-of-the-Year, awarding each other ornate plaques to hang over the bar in the rumpus room. Furthermore, God was interested in the fate of the Hershes, with time and consideration for each one. To pray was to be heard. There was not even death, only an interlude below ground. For one day, as Rabbi Polsky assured them, the Messiah would blow his horn, they would rise as one and return to Zion. Buried with twigs in their coffins, as Baruch had once said, to dig their way to him before the neighbors.

Phoning Hanna, in Toronto, Jake had to cope with Jenny first.

"Sitting *shiva* with the hypocrites, are you?"

Oh, God.

"I suppose whenever my name's mentioned they cross themselves, so to speak," she said, giggling at her own joke.

He hadn't the heart to say her name had not been mentioned once, and next thing he knew Doug was on the line.

"I want you to know why I didn't send flowers."

"You're not supposed to," Jake said wearily.

"It's not that. You know I'm beyond such ethnic taboos. Instead of flowers, I've sent a check in memory of your dad to SUPPORT in Hanoi."

"You did?"

"It goes toward buying artificial limbs for children maimed in the air raids."

"I knew you'd always come through in a crunch, Doug. Now may I please speak to Hanna?"

"So, Yankel?"

"Hanna, how are you?"

"I'm sorry. You know we were never friendly in the old days, but, after all, he's your paw, and I'm sorry." She inquired about Nancy and the baby and demanded photographs of Sammy and Molly. "I wanted to come to Montreal, but you know how Jenny feels about the Hershes. She wouldn't give me the fare. Big deal. I'll hitchhike, I said, like the hippies . . . "

"I'd send you the fare, Hanna, you know that, but . . ." He feared the family would treat her shabbily.

"I know. Don't explain. Couldn't you come here for a day?"

"There's the new baby, Hanna. Really, I . . . "

"It's O.K. Next time, yes?"

"We'll go to a hockey game together."

"Hey, Red Kelly's in parliament. He's an M.P."

"Who?"

"What do you mean, who? The Maple Leafs' defenseman. You remember, Imlach traded with Detroit for him."

"And he's in parliament now?"

"*Aquí está nada.*"

"*Aquí está Hanna.*"

"Yes, sir. Alive and kicking. A living testimonial to Carling's beer. How's Luke?"

"The same."

"You two; you give me a royal pain in the ass. When will you make it up?"

His mother made Jake lunch in her apartment. She said how sad she was his father had died. He was not to blame if he had not been intelligent enough for her and she was certain he would have been a good husband for a simple woman. And that done, she asked, "How's my new baby?"

"Nancy's baby is fine," Jake replied.

Again and again he was driven back to St. Urbain to linger before the dilapidated flat that had once held Hanna, Arty, Jenny, and, briefly, the Horseman. More than once he strolled around the corner and into the lane. To look up at the rear bedroom window, Jenny's window, that had used to be lit into the small hours as she applied herself with such ardor to her studies, the books that were to liberate her from St. Urbain, the offices of Laurel Knitwear, and all the oppressive Hershes.

"You know what she's plugging away at in there?" Issy Hersh had said. "Latin. A dead language."

Through a hole in the fence, Jake contemplated the backyard where the Horseman had once set up a makeshift gym, doing his stuff for admiring girls, high-quality girls. He and Arty, Jake recalled, had used to watch from the bedroom window and once they had seen Joey, his eyes shooting hatred, strike a stranger ferociously in the stomach.

Suddenly, a dark-eyed, olive-skinned boy appeared in the yard, ran to the fence, and confronted Jake. "Fuck off, mister."

Duddy, he remembered, Arty, Gas, and me.

Everything happened so quickly. One day Arty, Duddy, Stan, Gas, and Jake were collecting salvage, practicing aircraft recognition, and the next, it seemed, the war was over. Neighbors' sons came home.

"What was it like over there?"

"An education."

Is Hitler really dead? was what concerned everybody. That, and an end to wartime shortages and ration books. One stingingly cold Saturday afternoon a man came to the door. Leather cap, rheumy eyes, an intricately veined nose. Battle ribbons riding his lapel. One arm was no more than a butt, the sleeve clasped by a giant safety pin, and with the other arm, the good arm, the man offered a Veteran's calendar, the Karsh portrait of Churchill encased in a gold foil V. "They're only fifty cents each."

"No, thanks," Mr. Hersh said.

Reproachfully, the man's bloodshot gaze fastened on his battle ribbons. "Ever hear of Dieppe?" he growled, flapping his butt.

Jake looked up at his father imploringly.

"And did you ever hear of the Better Business Bureau," Mr. Hersh demanded, "because it so happens they have broadcast a warning for law-abiding citizens not to buy combs from cripples *who just claim to be war veterans.*"

"Jew bastard."

Mr. Hersh slammed the door. "You see what they're like, all of them, underneath. You see, Jake."

"But did you see his arm? He lost it at Dieppe maybe."

"And did *you* see his schnozz? He's a boozer. The only battle he ever fought was with Johnny Walker. You've got to get up early in the morning to put one over on Issy Hersh."

Or, Jake thought—remembering Tom the gardener with a chill of shame, Sammy watching, all eyes—or his first-born son Jacob.

The old friends Jake sought out, were, to his dismay, churlish or resentful.

"What's the famous director doing here, back on the farm?" Ginsburg demanded. Arty's enthusiasm for Jake's film iced over with three drinks. "If you had asked me when we were kids, I never would have picked you to make it. Stan maybe." Witty, corrosive Stan Tannenbaum, with whom Jake had sat in Room Forty-one, at Fletcher's Field High. Stan was a professor now, his long greasy hair bound by a Cree headband, a pendant riding his barrel belly. "I'm the leading authority on Shakespeare in this country and I adore teaching it, but it humbles a man, you know. I don't flatter myself into thinking I have anything to add. There's so much crap being written today. Take your buddy, Luke Scott, for instance."

Gordie Rothman, another old schoolmate, who had forsaken teaching for corporation law, insisted they meet for a drink at Bourgatel's. "The truth is the money's rolling in . . ." He was happily married with two children, a house in Westmount, and what he called a shack in Vermont, just in case the French Canadian business got out of hand. "There's only one thing." Gordie slid a plastic-covered, leather-bound folio out of his attaché case. "I'd like to get my screenplay produced."

"You mean to say you've written a . . ."

"What the fuck, don't come on with me. Before you were well known who ever heard of you?"

"Nobody."

"I've sent the script to agents in New York and even London, but naturally they couldn't care less about anything set in Canada. You've got to have connections in this game, I realize that, and somebody like you . . ."

"I'll read it, Gordie. But I've got high standards, you know."

"Listen here, me too. But not everybody is James Joyce. I mean I'm sure you'd like to be able to direct as well as Hitchcock or . . . or Fellini . . ." Suddenly agitated, he glared at Jake. "I knew you when you were nothing. Nobody ever thought that much of you here. How in the hell did you ever get into films?"

"Sleeping with the right people," Jake said, winking.

After prayers each evening, the comforters streamed into the apartment. Dimly remembered second cousins, old neighbors, business associates. They compared Miami hotels for price and rabbis for oomph, but, above all, they marveled at the miracle of the Six-Day War and followed, with apprehension, the debate over the ceasefire continuing at the U.N. One rabbi, a suburban mod, wanted the Israeli victory enshrined by a new holiday, a latter-day Passover.

Uncle Lou accosted each visitor with the same question. "What kind of tanks were the Egyptians using in Sinai?"

"Russian."

"Wrong. Not rushin'. Standin' still."

Whenever guests celebrated the feats of the Israeli air force, Lou taunted them with the impending Bond drive. "Never before in the history of man," he was fond of saying, "will so few owe so much to so many."

Jack assured all comers that the Egyptians had used gas in Yemen only to test it for the Jews.

"But the Israelis were using napalm," Jake protested.

"By Jake here, whatever we do is rotten. Whatever they do is A-1. Do you know they had ovens ready in Cairo for our people?"

Only Uncle Sam was not surprised by the Israeli victory. He reminded everybody that it was the Jews who had turned the tide against the Nazis in World War II. At Tobruk.

"They stood against five Arab nations," Uncle Abe said again and again, "all alone. It has to be the fulfillment of divine intervention, even the most skeptical man must accept it was God's fulfillment to Abraham . . . "

One evening Max Kravitz drifted in, holding his taxi cap in his gnarled hands. Max's hair was white, his face grizzly. "Do you remember me," he demanded, driving Jake against a wall.

"Yes."

"What? You mean to say you remember me after all these years?"

"Yes, Of course I do."

"Well, I don't remember you," Max replied triumphantly.

Arty, long established as a dentist, came to pay his respects. Arty had become a joker. Such a joker, they said. He told wonderful stories; then, as you laughed, Arty's head would shoot forward to within inches of your gaping mouth, his eyes scrutinizing, his nose sniffing tentatively, appalled by what they perceived and smelled, his smile abruptly transformed into a pitying headshake. The next morning you found yourself sprawled, gagging and struggling, in his chair. Joking, cunning Arty had drilled his way through Hersh family molars, shoving in an upper plate here and striking a buck-tooth bonanza there, working his passage into a split-level in Ville St. Laurent.

They mourned the passing of Issy Hersh for a week, the truculent rabbis surging in nightly to be followed by prayers and more guests. The sweetest time for Jake was the early afternoon, when, riding a leaden lunch, the drooping Hershes wrestled sleep by reminiscing about their shared childhood and schools, their first jobs, all on a French Canadian street.

"They're so dumb," Aunt Malka said, shaking her head with wonder. "There's one I used to tell a joke to on Friday and on Sunday in the middle of church service she would finally get it and begin to laugh."

What about the Separatists?

For them, birth control would be a better policy. They breed like rabbits.

Suddenly, the apartment darkened. Irwin's body filled the screen door to the balcony to overflowing, the transistor held to his ear. "Arnie's just shot a birdie on the fifteenth. That puts him only two down on Casper."

"That Arnie. Wow!"

"Where's Nicklaus?"

"Hold it."

Artfully, Jake brought the conversation around to Cousin Joey and Baruch.

"When they brought Baruch over, you know, the nut, he had never seen a banana before. Paw gave him a banana and he ate it with the peel."

Uncle Abe, chuckling with fond remembrance, said, "On the ship that gangster came over on, another Jew was robbed of his wallet. They searched high and low and couldn't find it. Two special cops were waiting at the foot of the gangway, looking into all the hand luggage. Baruch comes sailing down the gangway with his satchel already open for inspection. He is eating an apple and whistling. Inside the apple is the money from the wallet."

"That Baruch. Boy!"

And all at once, Jake, come to sit with the Hershes in mourning for his father, feeling closer to them than he had in years, felt obliged to honor the Horseman in his absence. Without preamble, he turned on Uncle Abe, reminding him of Joey's last visit to Montreal, the men waiting in the car outside the house on St. Urbain, the gutted MG in the woods, and Jenny's abiding hatred. "You turned him in, didn't you, Uncle Abe?"

Uncle Abe's face flamed red. "What are you talking about, you drunken fool?"

"All I want is a straight answer."

"Here it is, then," and he slapped Jake hard across the cheek, stomping out of the living room.

"Well," Jake said, startled, trying to smile into hostile faces, faces all saying you deserved it.

The room was choked in silence.

"Hey," Uncle Lou said, "have you heard the one about the girl who wouldn't wear a diaphragm because she didn't want a picture window in her play room?"

"I've had enough of your puerile jokes, Uncle Lou."

"Well, pip pip, old bloke. And up yours with a pineapple."

Rifka shook a fist at him. "You come here once a year maybe and you booze from morning until night and stir up trouble. Then you fly off again. Who needs you anyway?"

Herky, roused, demanded, "What ever happened to that James Bond film you were supposed to direct? Big shot."

"Flush, flush, flush," was the most dazzling retort Jake could come up with before he fled indignantly to the balcony, lugging his brandy bottle with him.

Unfortunately Cousin Irwin was already there. Mountainous Irwin, huffing, as he clipped his fingernails. Irwin, having once peered into Jake's hot indignant face, retreated, wiggling his eyebrows ingratiatingly.

"Say something, you prick. Say something to me."

"Can do."

"Well. Go ahead."

Irwin pondered, he screwed his eyes. Briefly, he contemplated a gasoline pool in the Esso service station opposite. He scratched his head and studied his fingernails. Finally, as if pouncing on the words, he demanded, "Got many irons in the fire?"

Oh, my God, Jake thought, and he bounded back into the living room, where heads bent together to whisper leaped apart.

"Look here," Jake pleaded, "we're all going to die—"

"What have you got?" Sam asked.

"—sit down, you fool, it's not contagious. Oh, hell, what am I sitting *shiva* for anyway. I don't believe in it. Why should I try to please any of you?"

"Out of respect for your father."

"I never respected my father."

"Whoa, boy."

I loved him, Jake added to himself, unwilling to say as much to them.

"He's not dead a week," Rifka howled, "and he doesn't respect him. You hear, do you all hear?"

"He didn't leave any money, dear. There's no need to come on."

"Rotten thing. Animal. The day you married that *shiksa* you broke his heart."

Uncle Abe was back, his slippers flapping.

"I shouldn't have slapped you. I'm sorry, Jake."

"No. You bloody well shouldn't have slapped me. You should have given me a straight answer to my question."

"Can you not," Abe asked wearily, "take an apology like a gentleman?"

"Did you tell them where they could find Joey?"

Sighing, Uncle Abe led him into the kitchen, shutting the door after them.

"Do you see Joey in London?"

"I think he's in South America now. I haven't seen him since I was a boy."

Uncle Abe's eyes flickered with relief. Or so it seemed to Jake.

"You're lucky, then. Because he's rotten."

"Tell me why."

"You think the world of your cousin. Is that right?"

"Maybe."

"Joey did fight in the International Brigade in the Spanish Civil War, I'll grant him that—"

"And in Israel in forty-eight. He rode in the last convoy into Jerusalem."

"Good. Fine," Uncle Abe said, his smile dubious. "And if that's enough to make him a hero for you, let's leave it at that, shall we?"

"No. Let's not."

"Tough guy. O.K. He came crawling back to us, in 1943, with his tail between his legs, because he was in trouble with gangsters. He drove all the way from Las Vegas, without daring to look back."

"What sort of trouble was he in?"

"Nothing grand, Jake, nothing stylish. Squalid trouble. With bookmakers, mostly. He gambled, O.K., so do a lot of people. He didn't pay his debts. O.K., he's not the first. But he was also a gigolo. He was a blackmailer. He squeezed women for money, sometimes even marrying them. Do you remember the women who used to come to the house on St. Urbain?"

Jack nodded.

"Well, to begin with they were fast types, bar flies, with husbands overseas in the army. Then there was a young Westmount girl, he met her at a horse show, I think, and that led to more society types, looking for kicks. After all, Joey was a colorful fellow. He'd been a stuntman in the movies. He'd played professional baseball. And when it came to horses, he could ride with the best of them. But he was also a roughneck, you know. No education. He got too ambitious for his own good, he got beyond himself. He began to hang out at the Maritime Bar, in the Ritz, you know, making time with married women. They bought him clothes, they gave him money, and when he didn't have enough he signed for credit, using me as a reference. I must have settled more than two thousand dollars in debts after he skipped town."

"You put the men on to him after the trouble at the Palais d'Or. You betrayed him."

"Cock-and-bull, that's what you're talking. It wasn't like that, Jake. Your cousin suffered from a swelled head. He got involved with the wife of somebody important here, a man of real quality and position, with an influential family. The wife had a drinking problem and hot pants for Joey. She was most indiscreet, to say the least. When the husband was out of town, Joey stayed in the house. Right on top of the hill. He didn't leave with empty pockets. Jewels disappeared, so did some of the family plates. The husband came to see Joey. He offered him money, but it wasn't enough. They quarreled. Joey hit him. Then your hero got cold feet, but it was too late to run. The woman's husband wanted him taught a lesson. What could he do, he had become a laughingstock. So he hired some ruffians to give Joey what for."

"I've been to see Joey's wife in Israel," Jake said, hoping to startle him.

"Joey's wife. One of them, you mean. There are others."

"He told her the family was responsible for his father's death and his, almost."

"His words. Golden words. The man is a congenital liar."

Jake told Uncle Abe about the Mengele papers he had discovered on the kibbutz. He told him about Deir Yassin, the Kastner trial, and how, after seeking the Horseman in Munich and Frankfurt, he had become convinced that Joey was trying to track down Josef Mengele in South America. To his immediate regret, he also told him about Ruthy.

Uncle Abe shook his head, amazed. He guffawed. "De la Hirsch," he said, "that's a hot one."

"I am not amused. Neither am I convinced by your tales of Joey's philandering. You turned him in, Uncle Abe."

"I wish I had. I could have done it without batting an eyelash."

"In God's name, why?"

"You have no idea how close we were to a race riot here. Those days weren't these days. Those days they were painting *à bas les juifs* on the highways, the young men were hiding in the woods, they weren't going to fight in the Jews' war. We could all be shoveled into a furnace, as far as they were concerned. And now, they have the *chutzpah* to say how much they admire the Zionists. The Separatists say they are no more than Zionists in their own country and the Jews should support them. Over my dead body, Yankel. They get their independence today and tomorrow there's a run on the banks. Why? Because of the Jews; and it will be hot for us here again. Listen, you don't live here. In your rarefied world, film people, writers, directors, actors, it hardly matters this one's a Jew, that one's black. God help me, I almost said Negro. You lead a sheltered life, my young friend. We live here in the real world, and let me tell you it's a lot better today than it was when I was a youngster. I rejoice, I celebrate it, but I remember. And how, I remember. And I'm on guard. Your *zeyda*, my father, came here steerage to be a peddler. He couldn't speak English and trod in fear of the *goyim*. I was an exception, one of the first of my generation to go to McGill, and it was no pleasure to be a Jew-boy on campus in my time. Those days weren't these days. In my time we were afraid too, you know. We couldn't buy property in the town of Mount Royal, we smelled bad. Hotels were restricted, country clubs, and there were quotas on Jews at the universities. I can remember to this day driving to the mountains with Sophie, she was four months pregnant, a young bride, I got a flat tire on the road and walked two miles to a hotel to phone a garage. No Jews, No Dogs, it said on the fence. I close my eyes, Yankel, and I can see the sign before me now. But today, I'm a Q.C. I serve on the school board. The mayor has come to an anniversary dinner at our synagogue, he wore a skullcap. Ministers from Ottawa, the same. There are Jews sitting on the bench. Why, today we even have Jews who are actually members of the University Club. Three members already."

"And you're flattered, are you?"

"Flattered, no, pleased, yes. My Irwin hardly knows anything of anti-Semitism. He's a fine boy, you know, you should have a chat with him. He's serious, and he's got respect for his elders, not like some of them, his age, they're on drugs now. I lectured at McGill, you know. The peddler's boy, how about that? I spoke on Talmudic law, and those kids, my God, my God, Jewish children, I see them, they're taller than we were, big, healthy, the girls a pleasure to look at, dressed like American princesses, the boys with cars, and I think to myself, we've got reason to be proud, we've done a fine job here. The struggle was worth it. And what do they want, our Jewish children? They want to be black. LeRoi Jones, or whatever his name is, and this Cleaver nut tell them the Jews are rotten to the core, and they clap hands. It's a *mechaieh*. Not that they know a Yiddish word; French, that's what's groovy. Their hearts are breaking for the downtrodden French Canadians. Well, only two generations earlier, these same French Canadians wanted only to break their heads. And if it's not the blacks, or the French Canadians, it's the Eskimos. They can't sleep, they feel guilty about the Indians. So there they are, our Jewish children, wearing Indian headbands. Smoking pot. It's the burden of being white, it bugs them. How long have we even been white? Only two generations ago, who was white? We were kikes, that's all."

A Good Mother Remembered

An eleventh-century Jewish merchant in the Arabic Mediterranean world comforts his sister on the death of their mother. The sentiments are standard among pious, affluent Jews. The translation from a document in the Cairo Geniza archive is by S. D. Goitein.

To appreciate our letter, observe the extreme attachment and devotion of a middle-aged woman to her old mother—as is often found in traditional communities. The letter combines phrases normally used in letters of condolence with others betraying special features. Our writer could be so intimate, because his sister was literate. He calls her learned, advises her to read certain books of the Bible, and sends her a "Book of Comfort" written in Arabic to keep her busy in her mourning. The script of the letter is pleasant, but not that of a trained scribe.

As one whom his mother comforts, so I shall comfort you; and you will be comforted through Jerusalem.

From her brother Barakat—may he be granted that no evil should anymore befall her.

My most noble, prudent and learned sister. I wish to comfort you over our loss of that precious pearl, our lady, our mother—may God place her in the Garden of Eden. With her, all our happiness has gone and our joy has passed away; the crowns have fallen from our heads, for we have always lived by her *merit* and prayed to God on the strength of her good deeds. She was taken from our midst because of our sins—may God have mercy upon her and compensate us for her loss.

Now, dear sister, you know and understand better than anyone that no one is spared this cup of sorrow. She is a saint wherever she is. Our sages have said of a pious person like our mother: "She is like a pearl that is lost; wherever she may be, she remains a pearl; only those who have lost her have become poorer."

I entreat you, Rayyisa, fortify yourself as much as you can. For were you to weep even a thousand years, it would be of no avail. You will only become ill and you yourself will perish. I implore you, dear sister, be composed for God's sake, and he will richly reward you. Read, sister, the book of Ecclesiastes, the words of our lord Solomon; this will improve your faith. In addition, I am sending you the book *Relief after Adversity*; please study it.

I, myself, am writing this note after having soaked my eyes with tears over the loss of our mother and her motherly love. However, what can we do against God's decree, "and who may say to Him: What are you doing?" (Ecclesiastes 8:4) May God strengthen our hearts; your being alive consoles us; a woman who has left behind a daughter like you is not dead.

Again, dear sister, do not do harm to yourself by useless excess. Remember that others lost their mother, father, and children, and still accepted God's judgment with resignation. No one need

teach you, for you know well what happened to the prophets and others, and take good care of yourself, so that you do not perish. Attend to the words of the prophet: "Do not weep for the dead, nor bemoan him; weep sore for him that goes away." Read the books of Ecclesiastes and Proverbs and submit to the judgment of your Creator, the True one.

Remember that our lamented mother had always wished and prayed to die in your arms and those of your brothers. Now she has died, with her eyes resting upon you and full of joy that you were there. May God replace the grief for her [with something better]. Now, dear sister, know that I revered our mother, although I was far away from her, but despite my being so far away, this separation by death caused me unsurpassable grief. How far more you, poor woman, must have been affected, you, who have never had a happy day in your life, and had revered her so much. Now, you have lost her company and the blessings of her merits—may God keep you company in his mercy and help you with his might and may he not make you lonely separated from your only (son), nor may he cause you shame from him; but may he guide him and me to his holy law. And may he let us die like her: *after a life of piety and good deeds.*

Please excuse me for not coming in person to comfort you. We all need comfort after this loss, and I in particular. May God help and guide you, and may he grant you and me the blessings of her merits; for she is in a state of beatitude. Finally, may he fulfill all the joyous hopes which I entertain for you and support you. *And peace upon you.*

This unassuming and straightforward letter is a good introduction to the thinking of the Geniza people about the enigma of spiritual contact with our beloved after they have been separated from us by death. The loss is absolute; we no longer enjoy the feeling that we are protected by their presence. Yet, a relationship continues, which may be compared with the mutual responsibility of relatives, as far as material possessions are concerned. Relatives (and, to a certain extent, the members of the community) share mutual responsibilities. They are usually helpful to one another during lifetime and inherit from one another after death has occurred. In a period when "the dead provided for the daily needs of the living," inheritance played a more general and tangible role than seems to be so in our own society. Inner life was structured in a similar way. Our letter, which opens with the outcry that with the death of the mother her children have lost the protection enjoyed by her good deeds, can no longer dare to pray to God, that is, to approach him, concludes with the wish that God may grant them the blessings of her "merits", while they themselves would try to emulate her. Even more so: Her worthy daughter embodies the mother as if she were still alive.

PART FOUR
DIVINE INTOXICATION

INTRODUCTION

Not later than the first half of the first millennium B.C., the Jews became intoxicated with their God, Yahweh, and until the rise of secular Jewish European and American culture in the late-nineteenth century, the Jews were willing and happy victims of divine substance abuse.

Even today, somewhere around 20 percent of the Jews in the world are persistently consumed by their relationship with God, both individually and in light of their membership in a holy community and perhaps another 40 percent of ethnic Jews still think about God occasionally—at Bar Mitzvahs, funerals, and on the Day of Atonement.

This God was Yahweh, very much a Jewish deity. But he was also God of all peoples, who would call the Gentiles to account. The Jews, so went the traditional belief, were bound to God by a contract, but it was one they had not freely entered into (the first requirement of a legal contract!). God had in fact imposed His covenant on them.

The covenant held Jews to a higher ethical standard than other peoples; the Jews would be rewarded for observing the covenant, punished if they violated it. Yet following rigorously the moral and behavioral code inscribed in the divine covenant did not assure that the Jews, collectively or individually, would not suffer, because at times God made the Jews sacrificial lambs to prevent the divine punishment of the Gentiles.

God was omniscient and omnipotent but He did not always intervene in human affairs to protect his Chosen People, the Light Unto the Nations. God demanded frequent daily prayer but did not necessarily listen to these prayers.

Eventually God would send a Messiah (Redeemer) to heal the Jews and restore them in triumph to their ancestral land. This Messiah would be a human prince, a scion of the House of David, or perhaps something more metaphysical.

Goodness in this life would be rewarded in an afterlife and by a bodily resurrection at the end of time, but such things were not to be closely discussed. The Talmudic rabbis merely said that all Jews, except heretics, had a place "in the world to come," whatever that might mean.

This is the theology and theodicy (justification of God to man) that developed in Ancient Judaism, certainly between 700 and 200 B.C., perhaps earlier, mostly in Judea but some of it probably in Mesopotamia.

A hundred and fifty years of recent historical and archaeological research cannot say much more about the formative period of this Jewish divine intoxication. But that it stayed with the Jews, that it became central to rabbinical, Orthodox Judaism, as both a joy and a burden to the people, as both a revelation and a mystification, cannot be doubted.

In the Late Middle Ages and in the nineteenth and early twentieth centuries, powerful creative minds played with this intoxicating vision, combined it with other cultures and philosophies, and attempted innovative explication and extrapolation. Since 1940 there have been no significant additions or amendments to Jewish religious thinking. You lived with it or you did not. You drank deeply from the divine bottle or you went cold turkey—well, maybe a little nip now and then.

The Essentials of Biblical Judaism

Here are the key proof-texts of the Jewish faith, drawn respectively from (1) the Book of Deuteronomy, which describes the covenant; (2) the Book of Isaiah, with its image of Israel as the suffering servant (what scholars call Deutero-Isaiah, probably written in Mesopotamia); (3) the Book of Job, which describes the problem of bad things happening to good men and bad people prospering; and (4) the Book of Psalms, which describes God's comfort and majesty.

The translation is the now standard text from the 1988 edition of the Jewish Publication Society.

FROM THE BOOK OF DEUTERONOMY

At the end of those forty days and forty nights, the LORD gave me [Moses] the two tablets of stone, the Tablets of the Covenant. And the LORD said to me, "Hurry, go down from here at once, for the people whom you brought out of Egypt have acted wickedly; they have been quick to stray from the path that I enjoined upon them; they have made themselves a molten image." The LORD further said to me, "I see that this is a stiff-necked people. Let Me alone and I will destroy them and blot out their name from under heaven,

The symbol of ancient Judaism: The seven-branch candelabra. Rome, second century A.D.

and I will make you a nation far more numerous than they." . . .

And now, O Israel, what does the LORD your God demand of you? Only this: to revere the LORD your God, to walk only in His paths, to love Him, and to serve the LORD your God with all your heart and soul, keeping the LORD's commandments and laws, which I enjoin upon you today, for your good. Mark, the heavens to their uttermost reaches belong to the LORD your God, the earth and all that is on it! Yet it was to your fathers that the LORD was drawn in His love for them, so that He chose you, their lineal descendants, from among all peoples—as is now the case. Cut away, therefore, the thickening about your hearts and stiffen your necks no more. For the LORD your God is God supreme and Lord supreme, the great, the mighty, and the awesome God, who shows no favor and takes no bribe, but upholds the cause of the fatherless and the widow, and befriends the stranger, providing him with food and clothing. You too must befriend the stranger, for you were strangers in the land of Egypt.

You must revere the LORD your God: Only Him shall you worship, to Him shall you hold fast, and by His name shall you swear. He is your glory and He is your God, who wrought for you those marvelous, awesome deeds that you saw with your own eyes. Your ancestors went down to Egypt seventy persons in all; and now the LORD your God has made you as numerous as the stars of heaven. . . .

Therefore impress these My words upon your very heart: Bind them as a sign on your hand and let them serve as a symbol on your forehead, and teach them to your children—reciting them when you stay at home and when you are away, when you lie down and when you get up; and inscribe them on the doorposts of your house and on your gates—to the end that you and your children may endure, in the land that the LORD swore to your fathers to assign to them, as long as there is a heaven over the earth. . . .

See, this day I set before you blessing and curse: Blessing, if you obey the commandments of the LORD your God that I enjoin upon you this day; and curse, if you do not obey the commandments of the LORD your God, but turn away from the path that I enjoin upon you this day and follow other gods.

FROM THE BOOK OF ISAIAH

He was despised, shunned by men,
A man of suffering, familiar with disease.
As one who hid his face from us,
He was despised, we held him of no account.
Yet it was our sickness that he was bearing,

Our suffering that he endured.
We accounted him plagued,
Smitten and afflicted by God;
But he was wounded because of our sins,
Crushed because of our iniquities.
He bore the chastisement that made us whole,
And by his bruises we were healed.
We all went astray like sheep,
Each going his own way;
And the LORD visited upon him
The guilt of all of us.

He was maltreated, yet he was submissive,
He did not open his mouth;
Like a sheep being led to slaughter,
Like a ewe, dumb before those who shear her,
He did not open his mouth.
By oppressive judgment he was taken away,
Who could describe his abode?
For he was cut off from the land of the living
Through the sin of my people, who deserved the
*   punishment.*
And his grave was set among the wicked,
And with the rich, in his death—
Though he had done no injustice
And had spoken no falsehood.
But the LORD chose to crush him by disease,
That, if he made himself an offering for guilt,
He might see offspring and have long life,
And that through him the LORD's purpose might
*   prosper. . . .*
And was numbered among the sinners,
Whereas he bore the guilt of the many
And made intercession for sinners.

FROM THE BOOK OF JOB

Why do the wicked live on,
Prosper and grow wealthy?
Their children are with them always,
And they see their children's children.
Their homes are secure, without fear;
They do not feel the rod of God.
Their bull breeds and does not fail;

Their cow calves and never miscarries;
They let their infants run loose like sheep,
And their children skip about.

They sing to the music of timbrel and lute,
And revel to the tune of the pipe;
They spend their days in happiness,
And go down to Sheol in peace.
They say to God, "Leave us alone,
We do not want to learn Your ways;
What is Shaddai that we should serve Him?
What will we gain by praying to Him?"
Their happiness is not their own doing.
(The thoughts of the wicked are beyond me!)
How seldom does the lamp of the wicked fail,
Does the calamity they deserve befall them,
Does He apportion [their] lot in anger!
Let them become like straw in the wind,
Like chaff carried off by a storm.
[You say,] "God is reserving his punishment for
    his sons;"
Let it be paid back to him that he may feel it,
Let his eyes see his ruin,
And let him drink the wrath of Shaddai!
For what does he care about the fate of his
    family,
When his number of months runs out?
Can God be instructed in knowledge,
He who judges from such heights?
One man dies in robust health,
All tranquil and untroubled;
His pails are full of milk;
The marrow of his bones is juicy.
Another dies embittered,
Never having tasted happiness.
They both lie in the dust
And are covered with worms. . . .

I cry out to You, but You do not answer me;
I wait, but You do [not] consider me.
You have become cruel to me;
With Your powerful hand You harass me.
You lift me up and mount me on the wind;
You make my courage melt.
I know You will bring me to death,
The house assigned for all the living.
Surely He would not strike at a ruin
If, in calamity, one cried out to Him.
Did I not weep for the unfortunate?
Did I not grieve for the needy?

I looked forward to good fortune, but evil came;
I hoped for light, but darkness came.

My bowels are in turmoil without respite;
Days of misery confront me.
I walk about in sunless gloom;
I rise in the assembly and cry out.
I have become a brother to jackals,
A companion to ostriches.
My skin, blackened, is peeling off me;
My bones are charred by the heat.
So my lyre is given over to mourning,
My pipe, to accompany weepers.

FROM THE BOOK OF PSALMS

The LORD is my shepherd;
I lack nothing.
He makes me lie down in green pastures;
He leads me to water in places of repose;
He renews my life;
He guides me in right paths
as befits His name.
Though I walk through a valley of deepest dark-
    ness,
I fear no harm, for You are with me;
Your rod and Your staff—they comfort me.

You spread a table for me in full view of my ene-
    mies;
You anoint my head with oil;
my drink is abundant.
Only goodness and steadfast love shall pursue
    me
all the days of my life,
and I shall dwell in the house of the LORD
for many long years. . . .

Sing to the LORD a new song,
sing to the LORD, all the earth.
Sing to the LORD, bless His name,
proclaim His victory day after day.
Tell of His glory among the nations,
His wondrous deeds, among all peoples.
For the LORD is great and much acclaimed,
He is held in awe by all divine beings.
All the gods of the peoples are mere idols,
but the LORD made the heavens.
Glory and majesty are before Him;
strength and splendor are in His temple.

Ascribe to the LORD, O families of the peoples,
ascribe to the LORD glory and strength.
Ascribe to the LORD the glory of His name,
bring tribute and enter His courts.
Bow down to the LORD majestic in holiness;
tremble in His presence, all the earth!

Declare among the nations, "The LORD is king!"
the world stands firm; it cannot be shaken;
He judges the peoples with equity.
Let the heavens rejoice and the earth exult;
let the sea and all within it thunder,
the fields and everything in them exult;

The Exile from Eden

The story in the Book of Genesis of the exile of Adam and Eve from Eden is paradigmatic of man's fall from a state of bliss and a central motif in Christianity as well as Judaism. Here is the story of the fall—summarized here by folklorists Robert Graves and Raphael Patai—as it appears in Genesis and was further developed in Jewish Haggadah (Legend). The fall of man is a myth deeply etched in the Jewish collective unconscious.

The awesome figure of the medieval rabbi holding the Torah Scroll. Illustration from Maimonides' *Mishneh Torah,* medieval manuscript.

A. God permitted Adam and Eve, his wife, to eat fruit from every tree in Eden except the Tree of Knowledge of Good and Evil, which it would be death to taste or even touch. The Serpent who was there subtly asked Eve: "Has God not forbidden you to eat any fruit whatsoever?" She answered: "No, but he warned us on pain of death to abstain from a certain tree in the middle of this garden." The Serpent cried: "Then God has deceived you! Its fruit does not cause death, but only confers wisdom: He is keeping you in ignorance." Thus Eve was persuaded to taste the fruit, and made Adam do likewise.

B. When they had eaten, Adam and Eve looked at each other and, suddenly understanding that they were naked, plucked fig-leaves and sewed them into aprons. They heard God walking through the garden at dusk, and hid among the trees. God called: "Adam!", and again: "Adam, where are you?" Adam looked out from his hiding-place and said: "I heard Your approach, Lord, and hid my nakedness for shame." God asked: "Who told you of nakedness? Have you then eaten fruit of the forbidden tree?" Adam answered: "Eve gave me fruit from the tree, and I ate it." God turned to Eve: "Alas, woman, what have you done?" She sighed, saying: "The Serpent tricked me." God cursed the

Serpent: "You shall lose your legs, and writhe upon your belly for ever, eating dust! I set a lasting enmity between you and woman. Her children will stamp on your children's heads until their heels are bruised."

Then He cursed Eve: "I will multiply your labour and sorrow; you shall bear children in pain; you shall yearn for your husband, and be ruled by him!"

C. His next curse fell upon Adam: "Because you have listened to Eve rather than to Me, I curse the soil that you must now till all the days of your life, eating bread in the sweat of your brow, struggling to uproot thorns and thistles. And at length death shall return your body to the dust from which I formed it!"

D. Since aprons of fig-leaves were too fragile for such hard labour, God mercifully made Adam and Eve garments of skin. But He said to Himself: "This man has become like a god in his knowledge of good and evil! What if he were to pluck the fruit hanging on the Tree of Life, and live eternally?" With that, He drove Adam out of Eden, posting at its East Gate certain cherubim called "the Flame of Whirling Swords," to bar his way.

E. The Serpent had rudely thrust Eve against the Tree of Knowledge, saying: "You have not died after touching this tree; neither will you die after eating its fruit!" He also said: "All former beings are ruled by the latest beings. You and Adam, created last of all, rule the world; eat therefore and be wise, lest God send new beings to usurp your rule!" As Eve's shoulders touched the tree, she saw Death approaching. "Now I must die," she groaned, "and God will give Adam a new wife! Let me persuade him to eat as I do, so that if we must both die, we shall die together; but if not, we shall live together." She plucked a fruit and ate, then tearfully pleaded with Adam until he agreed to share it.

F. Eve later persuaded all beasts and birds to taste the fruit—or all except the prudent phoenix, which has remained immortal ever since.

G. Adam wondered at Eve's nakedness: because her glorious outer skin, a sheet of light smooth as a finger-nail, had fallen away. Yet though the beauty of her inner body, shining like a white pearl, entranced him, he fought for three hours against the temptation to eat and become as she was; holding the fruit in his hand meanwhile. At last he said: "Eve, I would rather die than outlive you. If Death were to claim your spirit, God could never console me with another woman equaling your loveliness!" So saying, he tasted the fruit, and the outer skin of light fell away from him also.

H. Some hold that Adam, by eating the fruit, won the gift of prophecy; but that, when he tried to pluck leaves for an apron, the trees drove him off, crying: "Begone, thief, who disobeyed your Creator! You shall have nothing from us!" Nevertheless, the Tree of Knowledge let him take what he wished—they were fig-leaves—approving his preference of wisdom to immortality.

I. Others make the Tree of Knowledge an immense wheat stalk, taller than a cedar; or a vinestock; or a citron-tree, whose fruit is used in celebration of Tabernacles. But Enoch reports that it was a date-palm.

J. According to some, the garments God gave Adam and Eve resembled fine Egyptian linens from Beth Shean, that mould themselves to the body; according to others they were of goat-skin, or coney-skin, or Circassian wool, or camel's hair, or of the Serpent's slough. Others again say that Adam's garment was a High-priestly robe, bequeathed by him to Seth; who bequeathed it to Methuselah; whose heir was Father Noah. Although his first-born son, Japheth, should have inherited this robe, Noah foresaw that the Children of Israel would spring from Shem, to whom therefore he entrusted it. Shem gave the robe to Abraham who, as God's beloved servant, could claim the first-born's right; Abraham to Isaac; Isaac to Jacob. It then passed to Reuben, Jacob's first-born son; and so the legacy continued, generation after generation, until the privilege of offering up sacrifices was taken by Moses from the first-born of Reuben's house, and given to Aaron the Levite.

K. Adam and Eve were driven out of Eden on the First Friday, the day in which they had both been created and had sinned. On the First Sabbath, Adam rested and prayed God for mercy. At its close he went to the Upper Gihon, strongest of rivers, and there did seven weeks' penance, standing in midstream with water to the chin, until his body turned soft as a sponge.

L. Afterwards an angel came to Adam's comfort, and taught him the use of fire-tongs and a smith's hammer; also how to manage oxen, so that he should not fall behindhand in his ploughing.

M. This view of Eden continues to be shared in the Middle East, not only by the nomads who regard fellahin as "slaves of the soil," but by most of the agricultural population itself. It was held, even before the Creation story received its final shape, by a bitter Greek farmer, Hesiod, who was the first writer to regard agriculture as an evil laid upon mankind by ruthless gods. An entirely different view is expressed by the Greek myth of Triptolemus: whom Demeter rewards for his father's sake by initiating him into the mysteries of agriculture, which he rides out through the world to teach, mounted on a serpent-drawn chariot.

N. Eden as a peaceful rural retreat, where man lives at his ease among wild animals, occurs not only in the story of Enkidu but in Greek and Latin legends of the Golden Age, and must be distinguished from the jeweled paradise which Gilgamesh and Isaiah's Helel visited. The terrestrial paradise represents a jaded city-dweller's nostalgia for simple country joys, or a dispirited labourer's for the fruit-eating innocence of childhood; the celestial paradise is enjoyed in a schizophrenic trance, induced either by asceticism, by glandular disturbance, or by use of hallucinogenic drugs.

O. It is not always possible to judge which of these causes produced the mystic visions of, say, Ezekiel, "Enoch," Jacob Boehme, Thomas Traherne, and William Blake. Yet jeweled gardens of delight are commonly connected in myth with the eating of an ambrosia forbidden to mortals; and this points to a hallucinogenic drug reserved for a small circle of adepts, which gives them sensations of divine glory and wisdom. The Gilgamesh reference to buckthorn must be a blind, however—buckthorn was eaten by ancient mystics not as an illuminant but as a preliminary purgative. Soma, the Indian ambrosia, is said to be still in secret use among Brahmans.

P. All gardens of delight are originally ruled by goddesses; at the change from matriarchy to patriarchy, male gods usurp them. A serpent is almost always present. Thus, in Greek myth, the Garden of the Hesperides, whose apple-trees bore golden fruit, was guarded by the Serpent Ladon, and had been Hera's demesne before she married Zeus, though her enemy Heracles eventually destroyed Ladon with Zeus's approval. The jeweled Sumerian paradise to which Gilgamesh went, was owned by Siduri, Goddess of Wisdom, who had made the Sun-god Shamash its guardian; in later versions of the epic, Shamash has degraded Siduri to a mere "ale-wife" serving at a near-by tavern. Indra, the leading Aryan god, appears to have borrowed a new form of soma from the variously named Indian Mothergoddess.

Q. A paradise whose secrets have lately been revealed is the Mexican Tlalócan—a picture of which Heim and Wasson reproduce from the Tepantitla fresco in *Les Champignons Hallucinogènes du Mexique*. It shows a spirit, branch in hand, weeping for joy on entering an orchard of fantastically bright fruit-trees and flowers, watered by a river, full of fish, flowing from the mouth of a divine toad. This is the God Tlalóc, who corresponds closely with the Greek Dionysus, and whom his sister Chalcioluthlicue has made coruler of her paradise. In the foreground lie irrigation canals over which four mushrooms meet to form a cross denoting the cardinal points of the compass. Behind the spirit rises a spotted serpent—Tlalóc in another aspect; a flowery dragon and huge coloured butterflies hover aloft. The hallucinogenic drug inducing this vision was a toxic mushroom, still ritually eaten in several provinces of Mexico. *Psilocybin,* the active agent, is now ranked by psychiatrists with lysergic acid and mescaline as among the leading psychodelotics—"revealers of man's inner self."

R. Hallucinogenic mushrooms are common throughout Europe and Asia. Some varieties, which do not lose their toxic qualities when cooked, seem to have been introduced into sacred cakes eaten at Greek Mysteries; and also at Arabian Mysteries, since the Arabic root *ftr* occurs in words meaning "toadstool," "sacrificial bread," and "divine ecstasy." Perseus went to the jeweled Garden of the Hesperides aided by Athene, goddess of Wisdom and, according to Pausanias, later built and named Mycenae in honour of a mushroom found growing on the site, from which flowed a pool of water. That the Indian paradise closely resembles these others suggests that soma is a sacred mushroom disguised in food or drink—not, as most authorities hold, a variety of milkweed; and the ancient Chinese reverence for a "Mushroom of Wisdom" may have its origin in a similar cult.

S. The fervent love between Enkidu and the priestess, though omitted from the *Genesis* story, has been preserved by a Talmudic scholiast who makes Adam wish for death rather than be parted from Eve. Yet the myth of the Fall licenses man to blame woman for all his ills, make her labour for him, exclude her from religious office and refuse her advice on moral problems.

T. Ambrosia-eaters often enjoy a sense of perfect wisdom, resulting from a close coordination of their mental powers. Since "knowledge of good and evil," in Hebrew, means "knowledge of all things, both good and evil," and does not refer to

the gift of moral choice, the "Tree of Life" may have once been the host-tree of a particular hallucinogenic mushroom. For example, the birch is host to the *amanita muscaria* sacramentally eaten by certain Palaeo-Siberian and Mogol tribes.

U. An addition to the story of Adam's penance occurs in the tenth-century Irish *Saltair na Rann*, based on an earlier Syrian *Life of Adam and Eve* evidently drawn from Hebrew sources: He fasts in Jordan, not Gihon, with water to his chin and, as a reward, God lets Raphael give him certain mystical secrets. According to this text, God created Adam at Hebron; which may be a pre-Exilic version of the myth. Some Byzantine writers make Adam repent only in his 600th year.

V. The Serpent is widely regarded as an enemy of man, and of woman.

The Day of Atonement

Yom Kippur, the day of awesome atonement for transgressions is the most important holy day in the Jewish calendar and it goes back a long way, at least to the sixth century B.C. The Jewish sages have, over time, contemplated deeply the meaning of Yom Kippur; and their wisdom on this subject is here summarized in a book published in 1948 by Shmuel Yosef Agnon, Israel's greatest novelist and Nobel laureate in literature. In it, he stresses the necessity of reaching peace and forgiveness with other humans: Peace with God is not enough.

"Yom Kippur does not make atonement for transgressions committed in men's relationships with one another." Our teacher, Rabbi Samuel Garmison [eighteenth century], wrote that the Omnipresent shares in the transgressions that men commit in their relationships with one another which are also in part transgressions against the Omnipresent. For example, if a man insults his fellow, lo, he has transgressed against the commandment, "Thou shalt love thy neighbor as thyself" (Lev. 19:18). There are many such

examples. So long as a man has not appeased his fellow, even that part of the transgression which is a transgression in his relationship with God is not atoned for. [Birke Yosef]

The Kabbalists wrote: "The prayer of him who does not banish hatred on Yom Kippur is not heard." [Kaf ha-Hay-yim, Jerusalem]

Let not this matter be light in the eyes of any man in Israel, for it is the cornerstone of atonement on Yom Kippur, and of the acceptance of prayers, and of our own speedy redemption. The

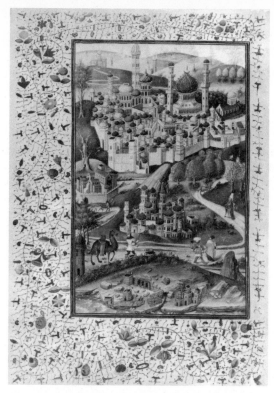

Dreams of the Holy City: Jerusalem, fifteenth century.

the stubbornness of his own heart and does what is right in his own eyes, the righteous and the wicked, the great and the small alike. The divisions and cleavages that exist among us are public and well known.

For we do not behave like members of one nation, having one tongue, as we should; for indeed do we not all have one Father, and did not one God create us all? Then why are we not united, all the seed of Israel? How much more ought we to be one, dwelling as we do in the land of our foes, literally like one lamb among thousands and tens of thousands of wolves! Is it not enough that all the peoples hate us—why should we hate one another too? Now a fire doth issue from the rock of our division, and there is none to extinguish. On the contrary; every man hastens to add fuel to it until it grows into a great consuming fire. May God who is good make atonement for us and remove our heart of stone and renew a steadfast spirit in our midst and remove hatred and contention from us, until we be united in the land. [Hemdat Yamim]

It is the custom to go to visit one's friends on the eve of Yom Kippur to beseech their forgiveness, though there is generally no need to do so, for one has not sinned against one's friends, and even if one has sinned against them, it was unintentional, and love covers all sins; their enmity must certainly have left them already. Yet being an ancient custom, it is worthy of respect, for there is no knowing what feelings are stored up in the hearts of one's friends.

I do not say that one ought not to go to visit one's friends, but rather that people ought not to neglect an act that is both proper and an obligation, to wit, that of visiting the person whom one knows for a certainty one has sinned against. And if he will not do so, you ought to send many friends to plead with him. Even if it is the other person who has sinned, one ought to go to that person and make peace with him.

But people who turn what is nonessential into the essential, and repudiate the essential, the forgiving and being forgiven by one's enemies, are, I think, in the wrong.

same is true of its opposite, God keep us from it, enmity, that is, which is like gall and wormwood. For, there is no doubt that this quality, enmity, hinders the coming of our Messiah, and is the reason why our prayers are not accepted, while we remain in exile, where there is no peace in our midst. For in truth, it is because of our iniquities which are great that many evils and misfortunes daily fall on our heads, there being none who seek to know why God acted thus to his preferred people whom he chose for his inheritance. It is because of this that we pass from downfall to downfall, and every day is more accursed than that which comes before it. There is no doubt that God is righteous and it is we who have done wickedly; our sufferings proceed from our own hand, and not God's. For every man walks after

Talmudic Angelology

The Babylonian Talmud, completed in Iraq in the sixth century A.D., became the authorized commentary on the Bible and behavioral code for believing Jews and it remains the authoritative text for Orthodox Jews. The Talmud, running to six thousand folio pages, is more like a library than a book. Almost any subject can be found treated in its pages, including discussion of the nature of angels. The Talmudic view of angels is here summarized by Abraham Cohen.

The underlying motive of Rabbinic angelology was certainly not to invent intermediaries between God and the world, as is sometimes alleged. What has been said on the subject of divine immanence proves that there was neither need of, nor place for, such go-betweens. The true purpose was the glorification of God. In their daily experience the people saw the sovereign of their country accorded the highest honours and held in the profoundest reverence. The more magnificent the surroundings of the monarch and the larger his retinue, the greater was the admiration extended to him. . . .

God was the King of kings, the Sovereign of the whole Universe; and in his imagination he pictured "earthly kingship as being like the Kingship of heaven," only on an infinitely reduced scale. As the ruler of so vast a kingdom, God provided Himself with an enormous host of ministers to carry out His behests.

The angels, as beings worthy to stand in proximity to the Throne of Glory, necessarily were more perfect creatures than man. Nevertheless, they too were created and could never attain the perfection of God. . . .

The general belief was that angels were immortal and did not propagate their species (Gen. R. viii. ii). On occasion, however, God may destroy numbers of them when they withstand His will. They require no physical nourishment being sustained by the lustre of the *Shechinah* [Divine Spirit]. They are not troubled by the *Jetzer Hara*, the evil impulse, which means that they are not subject to normal human passions (Gen. R. xlviii. ii).

Human beings are akin to the angels in three respects: "They have knowledge like the ministering angels; they have an erect stature like the ministering angels; they converse in the Holy Tongue (i.e. Hebrew) like the ministering angels." On the point of language, with the exception of Gabriel, who was acquainted with every mode of speech, the angels were said to be ignorant of Aramaic; and for that reason one should not offer petitions for his needs in that language, since it was an angelic duty to carry the prayers which were uttered to the Throne of God. It has been suggested that there was a practical purpose behind that assertion, viz. the desire to preserve Hebrew as at least the language of prayer, although it had been displaced by Aramaic as the vernacular of the Jews. . . .

Angels are delegated special duties, and one of them is appointed to function in connection with prayer. It was said: "After all the places of worship have completed their services, the angel who is appointed over prayer gathers up all the devotions which had been offered in all the places of worship, forms them into crowns and sets them upon the head of the Holy One, blessed be He."

A practice grew up among the people of invoking angels. That it was deprecated by the Rabbis is evident from the words they put into the mouth of God: "If trouble befall a man, let him not cry to Michael or Gabriel; but let him cry to Me and I will answer him at once."

Kabbalah

The Talmud and the Bible were supplemented in the Later Middle Ages by the wisdom of the Kabbalah, a pastiche of Neoplatonic mysticism and Hellenistic astrology and demonology that appears to be ultimately derived from the Gnostic movement of the first century A.D. Kabbalism first existed as an esoteric, underground religion among some of the more mystic-minded rabbis. It became more public in southern France in the early-thirteenth century and took definitive form among the rabbis in Christian Spain in the fourteenth century. In the latter location was written the main Kabbalistic text, the Zohar, from which these selections are taken. All but the last extract below was edited by Abraham E. Millgram; the final extract is a summary paraphrase made by A. E. Waite.

The Kabbalah represented an antirationalist movement among European Jewry, resisting the efforts made by Maimonides in the late-twelfth century to achieve an integration of Judaism and Aristotelian science. It can therefore be regarded as something of a demotic cultural tendency, trying to keep rabbinical Judaism within the thought-world of ordinary people, for whom Aristotelian science was inaccessible.

The Kabbalistic texts were closely studied by Christian scholars of the Renaissance, and were also a source for both the Jewish messianic movement of the seventeenth century as well as the common man's democratic religious movement of Hasidism in the eighteenth century.

As the last extract below indicates, the Kabbalists were fascinated by heterosexual copulation, partly because it was parallel to God's union with Israel, partly because the sexual act brought new souls into the world.

R. Hiya adduced the following text: "And God saw their works that they turned from their evil way" (Jonah III, 10). "See now," he said, "when the sons of men are righteous and observe the commands of the Torah, the earth becomes invigorated, and a fullness of joy pervades it, because then the *Shekinah* [Divine Spirit, Divine Image] rests upon the earth, and there is thus gladness above as well as below. But when mankind corrupt their way and do not observe the commands of the Torah, and sin before their Master, they, as it were, thrust the *Shekinah* out of the world, and the earth is thus left in a corrupt state. For the *Shekinah* being thrust out, another spirit comes and hovers over the world, bringing with it corruption. It is in this sense that we say that Israel 'gives strength unto God,' that is, to the *Shekinah*, and thereby makes the world more secure. Should, however, Israel—God forbid—prove sinful, then, in the words of the Scripture, 'God withdraws himself above the heavens'" (Ps. LVII, 6).

When the righteous are afflicted by illness or sufferings . . . it is that all the sinners of their generation may receive redemption. How is this proven? By all the members of the human body. At the time when all the members of the human body, suffer through an evil illness, then one member must be operated upon, so that all the remaining members may recover. Which member? The arm. It is operated upon and the blood is drawn from it, and from this results the convales-

Kabbalah. Page from the Zohar. Printed version, Mantua, Italy, 1558–1560.

the scrutiny of angelic supervisors. These abide in ethereal space on the four sides of the world. On the eastern side there is the chief supervisor . . . who is attended by a number of other chieftains, all awaiting the word of prayer that is about to ascend to the ethereal realm on that side. The moment it does so the supervisor takes it up. If it be fitly uttered, he, together with all the other chieftains, kisses that utterance and carries it aloft into the supernal firmament, where other chieftains are awaiting it. When kissing the utterance of prayer they say: "Happy are ye; O Israel, who know how to crown your Master with holy crowns. Happy is the mouth from which issued this utterance, this crown." Then the letters of the Divine Name that abide in the ethereal space soar upwards . . . with the prayer utterance until Heaven is reached, where the prayer is taken in charge by another chief to carry it still higher. . . .

When the Holy One, praised be He, was about to create the world, the universe was already present in His thought. He then formed also the souls which were eventually to belong to man; these souls presented themselves to Him in exactly the same form which they were to take later in the human body. God examined them one by one, and found several which were to corrupt their ways (morals) in this world. When the time came each of the souls was summoned before God, Who said: "Go to that part of the earth and animate such and such a body." The soul replied: "O, Master of the universe, I am happy in this world and do not want to leave it for another where I shall be subjected and exposed to all kinds of contamination." The Holy One, blessed be He, then said: "From the day you were created you had no other destination but the world to which I send you." Seeing that it must obey, the soul sorrowfully took the earthly path and descended among us. . . .

Do not think that man is but flesh, skin, bones and veins; far from it! That which really constitutes man, is his soul; and the things we call skin, flesh, bones and veins are for us but a garment, a cloak, but they do not constitute man. When man departs (this earth), he divests himself of all the cloaks that cover him. Yet, the different parts of the body conform to the secrets of the supreme wisdom. The skin represents the firmament which extends everywhere and which covers everything, like a cloak. The flesh reminds us of the evil side of

cence of all the other members of the body. So it is with the children of the world, its members stand towards each other equally, like members of the human body each to the other. At the time that the Holy, blessed be He, desires to give health (sanctification) to the world, He afflicts a just (pious) one from the midst of the world with sickness and pain, and through him He gives health to all the world. . . .

Prayer is spiritual worship. Deep mysteries are attached to it, for men know not that a man's prayer cleaves the ethereal spaces, cleaves the firmament, opens doors and ascends on high. At the moment of daybreak, when light emerges from darkness, . . . the *Shekinah* descends whilst Israel enter the Synagogue to offer praise to their Master in song and hymn. It behooves, then, every man, after equipping himself with emblems of holiness, to attune his heart and his inner being for that act of worship and to say his prayers with devotion. For the words that he utters ascend on high, for the universe (that is, as we have said above, the purely external and sensual element). The bones and the veins represent the celestial chariot, the forces that exist within the servants of God. However, all this is but a cloak; for the deep mystery of Celestial Man is within. All is as mysterious below as it is above. Therefore it is written: And God created Man in His image. The mystery of terrestrial man is according to the mystery of the Celestial Adam. Yet, as we see in the all-covering firmament stars and planets which form different figures that contain hidden things and profound mysteries, so there are on the skin that covers our body certain figures and lines which are the planets and stars of our body. All these signs have a hidden meaning and attract the attention of the wise who can read the face of man. . . ."

R. Simeon was once on a journey in company with his son R. Eleazar and R. Abba and R. Judah. As they were going along, R. Simeon said: "I marvel how indifferent men are to the words of the Torah and the problem of their own existence!" He proceeded to discourse on the text.

R. Hiya said: "I have often wondered at the words, 'For the Lord heareth the poor' (Ps. LXIX, 34). Does He then hear only the poor?" R. Simeon replied: "These words signify that the poor are indeed nearer to the King than all others, for it is written, 'A broken and a contrite heart, O God, thou wilt not despise' (Ps. LI, 18), and no one in the world is so broken in heart as the poor man. Mark this! Most human beings appear before the Holy One in body and in soul, but the poor man presents himself before the Throne of the Most High in soul only, and the Holy One is nearer to the soul than to the body."

There are however two classes whose respective duties differ with the degrees of their election; there are those who are termed ordinary mortals, meaning the rank and file of the chosen people, but there are also the Sons of the Doctrine, chosen among the chosen out of thousands. The counsel imposed on the first class is to sanctify their conjugal relations in respect of the time thereof, which is fixed at midnight, or forward from that hour, the reason being that God descends then into Paradise and the offices of sanctity are operating in the plenary sense. But this is the time when the counsel to the Sons of the Doctrine is that they should arise for the study of the Law, for union thereby with the Community of Israel above and for the praise of the Sacred Name of God.

The Sons of the Doctrine are described as reserving conjugal relations for the night of the Sabbath, being the moment when the Holy One is united to the Community of Israel. The thesis is that God is One and as such it is agreeable to Him that He should be concerned with a single people. Out of this arises the question as to when man may be called one, and the answer is that this comes about when the male is united to the female in a holy purpose: It is then that man is complete, is one and is without blemish. It is of this that the man and the woman must think at the moment of their union; it is in uniting bodies and souls that the two become one; man in particular is termed one and perfect; he draws down the Holy Spirit upon him and is called the Son of the Holy One, blessed be He. . . .

Whosoever has intercourse with his spouse, on what day soever, must obtain her consent beforehand with words of affection and tenderness; failing consent, he should proceed no further, for the act of union must be willing and not constrained. Nuptial intercourse is interdicted during the day because of the words: "And he lighted upon a certain place, and tarried there all night, because the sun was set."

Making a Golem

A prominent theme in Kabbalistic lore was the making of a *golem,* an android. The purpose was not to create a servant—although the golem was frequently set to work—but rather to imitate God's creation of Adam. Here are two accounts of golem-making (translated by Gershom Scholem), the first from thirteenth-century Spain and the second from seventeenth-century Germany, describing golem activity among Polish Jews.

Then take a bowl full of pure water and a small spoon, fill it with earth–but he must know the exact weight of the earth before he stirs it and also the exact measurement of the spoon with which he is to measure [but this information is not imparted in writing.] When he has filled it, he should scatter it and slowly blow it over the water. While beginning to blow the first spoonful of earth, he should utter a consonant of the Name in a loud voice and pronounce it in a single breath, until he can blow no longer. While he is doing this, his face should be turned downward. And so, beginning with the combinations that constitute the parts of the head, he should form all the members in a definite order, until a figure emerges.

After saying certain prayers and holding certain fast days, they make the figure of a man from clay. . . . And although the image itself cannot speak, it understands what is said to it and commanded; among the Polish Jews it does all kinds of housework, but is not allowed to leave the house. On the forehead of the image, they write: *emeth,* that is, truth. But an image of this kind grows each day; though very small at first, it ends by becoming larger than all those in the house. In order to take away his strength, which ultimately becomes a threat to all those in the house, they quickly erase the first letter *aleph* from the word *emeth* on his forehead, so that there remains only the word *meth,* that is, dead. When this is done, the golem collapses and dissolves into the clay or mud that he was . . . They say that a *baal shem* [Faith healer] in Poland, by the name of Rabbi Elias, made a golem who became so large that the rabbi could no longer reach his forehead to erase the letter *e.* He thought up a trick, namely that the golem, being his servant, should remove his boots, supposing that when the golem bent over, he would erase the letters. And so it happened, but when the golem became mud again, his whole weight fell on the rabbi, who was sitting on the bench, and crushed him.

Sectarian Conflict

Sectarian religious conflict existed among Jews as well as among Christians and Muslims. In the later days of the Second Temple it was the Pharisees, from whom the Talmudic and Orthodox rabbinical tradition descended, against the Sadducees. The Pharisees claimed that Moses received an oral as well as a written law from Yahweh on Mt. Sinai and it was the Pharisaic rabbis who had the authority to disseminate and interpret this oral law. The Sadducees were Biblical fundamentalists—they recognized only the authority of the Tanach, the written law. After the destruction of the Second Temple, the high priests of the Temple, with whom the aristocratic Sadducees were affiliated, vanished and the Sadducee party also rapidly disappeared, leaving the Pharisaic rabbis and their direct successors in control by default.

But in the ninth century, the same dispute erupted again, initially in Mesopotamia. This time those who rejected the oral law and rabbinical authority were called Karaites, led by a certain Anan, the loser, it is believed, in a struggle over succession to leadership of the Jewish community in Iraq.

In this selection a twelfth-century Spanish rabbi, Abraham Ibn Daud, castigates the Karaites as hellish heretics and upholds the rabbinate party. There is no charity here, only implacable hatred. Today in Israel there are still a few hundred Karaites, immigrants after 1950 from Egypt, where they held out through the centuries against the dominant rabbinates. The translation is by Gerson D. Cohen.

Thus there were ten generations from the prophets Haggai, Zechariah and Malachi until Rabban Johanan B. Zakkai, five generations of tannaim and seven generations of amoraim, giving a total of twenty-two generations until the end of the amoraic period. Then there were five generations of saboraic rabbis, eight generations of the gaonate and three generations of the rabbinate. . . .

All of them were trustworthy witnesses, who received [the tradition] on the testimony of trustworthy witnesses, and their sacred chain of tradition has never been broken.

Such is not the case with the heretics. The fact is that Anan the wicked and his son Saul, may the name of the wicked rot, were disciples of R. Jehudai, who broke with him and his tradition without any substantive ground whatever, but only out of the envy that overcame them. Hence, they cannot possibly say: "Thus have we received on the testimony of So-and-So [who received] from the prophets."

Instead, they fabricate things out of their own hearts.

What is more, they are disqualified by the sheer meagerness of their number. . . .

Moreover, there is [a mother] characteristic [of the heretics] which you ought to bear in mind. That is that they never did anything of benefit for Israel, nor produced a book demonstrating the cogency of the Torah or work of general knowledge or even a single poem, hymn or verse of consolation. "They are all dumb dogs who cannot even bark." If one of them finally did produce a book, he reviled, blasphemed and spoke insolently against Heaven. . . .

[On the other side of the fence,] in the case of the rabbis, you can note the sacred chain [of transmission] which we have recounted. Besides those [listed one hundred forty herein], there were a million saintly scholars [whose names we have not recorded], since we have listed only the heads of academies.

Wisdom Derives from Many Sources

Sharply contrasting with the dogmatic sectarianism of the preceding selection is this passage in a mid-thirteenth-century homily on education in which a rabbi, Jacob Anatoli, communicates a spirit of tolerance and claims that wisdom can be learned from adherents to other religions and from heretics. The translation is by Marc Saperstein.

This is the definition of a wise man, according to the rabbis: "Who is wise? He who learns from everyone, as the Bible says, *From all my teachers I have gained insight, for Your decrees are my study*" (Ps. 119:99). Their proof from this verse shows that they understood it to mean not that the speaker was praising himself for having greater wisdom and insight than his teachers, but that he learned and acquired wisdom from everyone he found capable of teaching him, even if that person was not of his faith, which can be a cause of hatred. But since he relies upon the Torah and applies himself to know it fully, learning from an adherent of a different religion can bring nothing but great benefit. This is the meaning of *for Your decrees are my study*.

This same idea is the subject of the preceding verse, which says, *Your commandment enables me to gain wisdom from my enemies, for it always stands by me* (Ps. 119:98). Because he relies and depends upon the Torah, because the commandments are an enduring support, it will benefit him to learn from everyone. This is the desired diligence with regard to wisdom: to seek it from everyone, whether esteemed or scorned, whether a believer or a heretic. An intelligent person who finds a nut breaks it open, eats the kernel, and throws away the shell.

The Messiah Has Come!

Late-seventeenth- and eighteenth-century Jews were periodically stirred by momentary belief that the Messiah had come. The most widely acclaimed of these "false messiahs" was a certain young man from Turkey named Sabbatai Zevi. In 1672, Zevi's publicist, the self-proclaimed prophet, Nathan of Gaza, sent the following circular letter to Jewish communities all over the Mediterranean in Western Europe and Poland and gained an instantaneous fervid response. Even some wealthy and learned Jews participated in messianic rituals, standing on the roofs of houses with bodies of disinterred and potentially resurrectable relatives and ready to be transported by angels to the Holy Land.

The mania stopped almost as quickly as it started when Zevi was given by the Sultan of Turkey the choice of death or conversion to Islam, and chose the latter. Even then some followers of Zevi persisted as a Muslim sect in Greece and the Levant until modern times.

Historians attribute the messianic craze to a variety of factors: the widespread influence of a particularly apocalyptic form of Kabbalistic doctrine taught by the esteemed rabbi Isaac Luria, who wrote on the Golan Heights in the early-sixteenth century; the general economic depression that hit Western Europe badly in the early-seventeenth century, hurting and worrying Jewish mercantile families; and the Cossack rebellion and pogroms against Jews in the Ukraine and Poland in 1648. The following translation of part of Nathan of Gaza's remarkable letter is by Gerschom Scholem from his magisterial 1973 biography of Sabatai Zevi.

Know for certain that at the present time there are no more sparks of the Shekhinah [Divine Presence] left in the demonic realm. . . .

Hence we must no longer perform actions of *tiqqun* [Healing], but merely adorn the bride [that is, the Shekhinah] and make her face the bridegroom. . . . All these things require lengthy explanations, and time does not permit me to disclose them. But what I want to say is this: the meditations (*kawwanoth*) which the great master Isaac Luria had revealed are no longer applicable in our days, since all the worlds are now [on a] different [mystical level].. . .

At the present time, too, there are opposing forces, but they are merely harming themselves. They cannot oppose [the progress of the messiah] because now it is surely [the preordained time of] the last end. Do not ask how our generation has merited this. For because of the great and infinite sufferings—more than any mind can comprehend—which the rabbi Sabbatai Sevi has suffered, it is in his power to do as he pleases with the Israelite nation, to declare them righteous or—God forfend—guilty. He can justify the greatest sinner, and even if he be [as sinful] as Jesus he may justify him. And whoever entertains any doubts about him, though he be the most righteous man in the world, he [that is, the messiah] may punish him with great afflictions. In short, you must take it for absolutely certain that Israel will have no life unless they believe all these things without a sign or miracle. It is by a divine dispensation that they who are worthy in this generation have been allowed to see the beginning of redemption. Do not mind them that do not believe, even if it was your dearest friend.

The Messiah rules: Sabbatai Zevi as King of the Jews. Amsterdam, 1666.

And now I shall disclose the course of events. A year and a few months from today, he [Sabbatai] will take the dominion from the Turkish king without war, for by [the power of] the hymns and praises which he shall utter, all nations shall submit to his rule. He will take the Turkish king alone to the countries which he will conquer, and all the kings shall be tributary unto him, but only the Turkish king will be his servant. There will be no slaughter among the uncircumcised [that is, Christians], except in the German lands. The ingathering of the exiles will not yet take place at that time, though the Jews shall have great honor, each in his place. Also the Temple will not yet be rebuilt, but the aforementioned rabbi [Sabbatai Sevi] will discover the exact site of the altar as well as the ashes of the red heifer, and he will perform sacrifices. This will continue for four or five years. Thereafter the aforementioned rabbi will proceed to the river Sambatyon, leaving his kingdom in the charge of the Turkish king [who would act as the messiah's viceroy or Great Vizier] and charging him [especially] with regard to the Jews. . . .

At the end of this period the signs foretold in the Zohar will come to pass, and they will continue until the next sabbatical year [that is, 1672]. This is the meaning of the Talmudic saying, "In the seventh year the son of David will come." The seventh year, that is the Sabbath, signifying King Sabbatai. At that time the aforementioned rabbi will return from the river Sambatyon, together with his predestined mate, the daughter of Moses.

In the same year he will return from the river Sambatyon, mounted on a celestial lion; his bridle will be a seven-headed serpent and "fire out of his mouth devoured." At this sight all the nations and all the kings shall bow before him to the ground. On that day the ingathering of the dispersed shall take place, and he shall behold the sanctuary all ready built descending from above. There will be seven thousand Jews in Palestine at that time, and on that day there will be the resurrection of the dead that have died in Palestine. Those that are not worthy [to rise at the first resurrection] will be cast out from the Holy Land. The [general] resurrection outside the Holy Land will take place forty years later.

The Essentials of Hasidism

Martin Buber was the most influential Jewish religious thinker of the twentieth century. Working first in his native Germany and after 1937 in Jerusalem (where he was not much admired by the faculty of the Hebrew University), he tried to explicate the essentials of eighteenth-century Hasidism and to revive it by expounding its doctrines in light of Kierkegaard, Hindu theology, and existential philosophy, as he does here, in his 1948 book on Hasidism.

For Buber the key words in Hasidism are *love* and *unity*. While some have seen Hasidism as part of the late-eighteenth-century European Romantic revolt against reason, learning, and authority, and others have seen it as a religious expression of social revolt among the poor in the villages of Eastern Europe, Buber perceived Hasidism as a great spiritual upheaval with a message central to the needs of twentieth-century people.

Historically, it is very difficult to establish the actual origins and early purposes of Hasidism because the life of the founder of the movement, the Besht (the Bal Shem Tov, the Master of the Holy Name, who lived in an impoverished province of Poland and the Ukraine, and died in 1760) is shrouded in

We start from the view which we found in the above mentioned parable of Rabbi Shmelke about the man who strikes himself. It is a principle of identification worthy of being placed beside the Indian "Tat twam asi." A saying dating back to the Baalshem himself as again related to the commandment to love the neighbour "as thyself": "For every man in Israel has a root in the Unity, and therefore we may not reject him 'with both hands,' for whoever rejects his companion rejects himself; to reject the minutest particle of the Unity is to reject it all." For the sake of clearness I put beside this saying a robust and popular parable derived from the school of Rabbi Yechiel-Michal of Zlotchov. Once more, a man comes complaining before a Zaddik—this time the Zaddik is a somewhat rude jester who even clothes his exhortations in a jest, Rabbi Meir of Pshemyslany—that someone is depriving him of his livelihood. "Have you ever seen," said the Zaddik, "a horse drinking from a brook? It kicks with its hoofs, does it not? Why? Well, it sees its reflection and takes it for another horse trying to drink away its water. But you ought to know that it is you all the time: You are standing in your own way."

The high-strung postulate of identification is entirely reconcilable, in Hasidism, with the insight into the special character of the relation of every man to himself, but even the problematics peculiar to this relationship is clearly recognized. It is just out of this problematics that new aspects of the commandment of love are gained. I quote two sayings which appear to be mutually contradictory, but which actually complement each other. The Baalshem explains the commandment as follows. "It is up to you to love your neighbour as much as you love yourself, and who is to know your many shortcomings as well as you yourself? As you still manage to love yourself, so you must love your neighbour despite all the shortcomings you may find in him." And a Zaddik of the fifth generation said of himself: "How can I fulfil the commandment of love, if I do not love myself and cannot even bear to look at myself? What can I do? I practise repentance until I can bear to look

at myself again. Even so I must do to my neighbours." Here two men of varying grades face each other. The one does not permit knowledge of his inward defects to prevent him from paying his person the loving attention apparently natural to men; to the other, the aspect of his own soul as it happens to be is an insurmountable obstacle against loving himself, he can only overcome it by purifying, changing himself—by "turning"—incidentally, a concept in Jewish tradition highly characteristic of the fusion of the ethical with the religious element. Does this mean that he cannot in any circumstance contrive to love the imperfect and so not even his fellowmen, until they too have done repentance? But surely, it is evident that just by love he can assist the others to repent, teach and advise them. The deeper significance of the saying is that the Zaddik, who, by truthful turning to God attains a stage where he loves himself in God, i.e. in perfection, can help a man who confides in him to love himself even so, that is, truthfully, instead of the deceptive perspective of egoism.

At this point already the love factor begins to penetrate from the realm of individual relationship between man and man in the relationship with the community. Whatever the Zaddik accomplishes in each individual he accomplishes in the coherence of the Whole. "And this is the work of the candlestick," quotes a hero of suffering and master of prayer in the fourth generation, the Maggid of Koznitz, from the instructions for the preparation of the vessels in the holy tent "a solid work of gold from its shaft to its flower," and Israel including the apostates, "'that no rejected person be rejected by him'—from the beginning to the end down to the very lowest, all one solid work and complete unity, and the rectification should be made on all, for they are all divine particles from above." Each rectification which the Zaddik achieves on the individual, he achieves on the whole of Israel, which is the true candlestick that beams up unto Heaven and lightens the earth.

Out of this conception of the whole, which recurs in Hasidic literature in innumerable teach-

The Zenith of Old Orthodoxy: The Vilna Goan, late eighteenth century. The greatest Talmudic scholar of his day and opponent of early Hasidism.

ings, parables and examples of individual cases, a peculiar outlook can be detected, which occurs clearly enough even in the first generations and has not been further elaborated since. It is the idea of the "loving more." Originating from the Baalshem, it gained a foothold in Rabbi Pinhas of Koretz and his school. It is reported of the Baalshem, that he ordered a Hasid whose son had fallen among the disbelievers, to love him more than hitherto, and this surplus of love is said to have returned the young man to the community. The following teaching originates from Rabbi Pinhas. "If someone despises and harms you, you should fortify yourself and love him more than before. By such love you make him turn to God. Therefore the wicked must also be loved, only their doings are to be hated." And the most genuine pupil of Rabbi Pinhas (of whom the story is related that death came over him one night as he lay on the ground being unable to decide concerning a man whether to give him away before court, or to tell a falsehood, and saw no other way out than death), Rabbi Raphael of Bershad used to teach: "If a man notices that his neighbour hates him, he should love him the more; and the mean-

ing of it is: The whole of Israel is a vehicle of holiness, and if love and unity prevail among them, then the Shekhinah and the holiness rest upon them; if, however, there is, which God forbid, a split, then a rent is formed and an opening, and the holiness falls down into the shells." So where too little loving is done in one place, it becomes necessary to love all the more in another place in order to effect a leveling and thus restore the entirety of the "vehicle." The world below bears the Divine only when it coheres as an entirety and every man for his own part can contribute to the preservation of this entirety. And the same principle of "loving more" operates right into the intimacy of interpersonal life. A pupil of Rabbi Raphael relates: "During the summer-journey the Rabbi called me and asked me to come and sit beside him in his carriage. I said: 'I fear, I may leave you little room;' then he said to me in a particularly affectionate manner: 'Let us love each other more, and then there will be plenty of room for both of us.'" The feeling of being cramped in the human world is derived from inadequate love.

What is important is not a general, impersonal sort of love; it has to be quite concrete, direct and effective. No example shows so clearly what is wanted as that well known and popular tale, passed on from the mouth of a great lover and helper, Rabbi Moshe Leyb of Sasov. He is supposed to have himself related (I have chosen the most popular and complete of all the current versions), how he sat among a crowd of peasants in a village inn and overheard their conversation; he heard one asking the other: "Do you like me?" and the other replying: "Why, certainly, I like you very much." But the former looked at him gloomily and rebuked him for such words. "How can you say you like me? Do you know my shortcomings?" The other was silent, and thus they sat facing each other in silence, as there was nothing left to be said. He who loves truly, knows from the depth of his identity with his neighbour, from the very foundations of his neighbour's being he knows, wherein his friend is wanting. That alone is love.

And how is this attained? One must, taught the Baalshem in a badly preserved parable commenting on the verse of the Proverbs "As in water face to face, so the heart of man to man"—bow down low towards one's neighbour as when someone wants to approach his reflection in the water and bows down low so that it comes towards him until his head touches the water and he sees nothing more because both have become the one that they really are; so does man's heart come to man, and not just this one to that one, but all to all. So is the "humble" Moses said to have bowed down to the "earth's surface" and mutual love to have inspired the whole of Israel. The same truth is presented from a different angle and with a similar reference to the humility of Moses, by an early Zaddik of the third generation. Every man, he taught, was more important to Moses than he himself, "and this was his service, to bring Israel also to the stage where everyone should love his neighbour by being inferior in his own eyes, and his neighbour superior to him. . . . And this is the meaning of what is written: 'When Moses held up his hand,' that is his power and rank which was the quality of true humility; then the quality of humility also prevailed throughout Israel and then every man thought of the preference of the other and of his own lowliness and loved his neighbour with perfect love, and thereby did they vanquish Amalek," that is, the force of evil.

And again the ethical wholly penetrates the religious. The "holy Yehudi" and his friends were fond of drawing an analogy between the association of two Jews standing side by side on an equal footing, drinking each other's health with cheer and love, and that of two "yoods" which are the smallest letters in the Alphabet, no more than tiny dots, though when placed side by side they express the name of God; if, however, two little dots are placed one above the other, then they merely signify a pause. Where two are side by side on an equal footing and are fond of each other without any reservation, there is God.

In the face of this great significance of being on an equal footing with one another the differences in value between men fade away. Not only is there in everybody a divine particle, but there is in everybody one peculiar to him, to be found nowhere else. "In every man," says Rabbi Pinhas, "there is a precious substance, which is in nobody else." The individuality and irreplaceability of every human soul is a basic teaching of Hasidism. In His Creation God has in mind an infinitude of unique entities, and within it He has in mind every single one, without exception, as endowed with a particular faculty, a value which none other possesses; everyone has in the eyes of God a specific importance in the fulfillment of which

none can compete with him, and to everyone He is devoted with a particular love, having regard to the treasurable value hidden in him. There are, of course, men great and small, in wisdom rich and poor, adorned by virtues and seemingly lacking in virtues, some devoted to God and others wrapped up in themselves, but God never withholds His grace even from those who are decried as being foolish or wanton. Rabbi Pinhas compares this with a prince who, in addition to his magnificent palaces, also owns all kinds of tiny cottages, each hidden away in some wood or village, where he calls occasionally when hunting or in order to take recreation. And it is not pertinent to say that the large palaces should rightly be there, and not the little cottages, because, as the saying goes, "The purpose served by the unimportant one cannot be served by the important. . . . This also holds true for the righteous man. Certainly his virtue and his service are immeasurably great, and yet he cannot accomplish what the wicked man accomplishes." So the man who wishes to tread in the path of God must not turn relative differences into absolute ones. The Maggid of Koznitz, quoting the above parable of Rabbi Pinhas, extends the maxim of the Mishnah "despise no man" not only to the ignorant but also to the wicked and mean. For, as the Mishnah says: "There is no man who has not his own hour. . . . Even the wicked man has his own hour, when he devotes himself to the Creator," though he may only speak "one word" to Him "in perfection, . . . for not as chaos did He create him." Were there no such moment in the life of the most wicked, he would not have been created at all. And it is to this moment, this single holy word, this single holy act, that God looks forward. How could man forget this! He must not be fastidious where God is not so. It is related of the Rabbi of Sassow that at midnight, when he was deep in the study of the Law, a drunken peasant rapped at his window and demanded admittance. At first the Rabbi was annoyed at the interruption, but then he remembered: "If God suffers him in His world, then he must needs be there; therefore I too must suffer him in my world." He let him in and prepared a bed for him. On another occasion he was reproached with having given some infamous person all the money he possessed. "I also am not good," he said, "and yet God gives me whatever I need."

God wastes His love even on the most wicked; how then may man manage his own with rigid accounting according to honour and merit! The Polish Rabbis once came together in order to sit in judgment over those who had become disloyal to Jewish customs. But before they promulgated the judgment severing the "breakers of the yoke" from the loyal, they decided to ask Rabbi Wolf of Zbaraz, also one of the great lovers, for his assent. "But do I love you any more than I love them?" was his reply. The proceedings were not continued.

"The perfect Zaddik," teaches the Baalshem, "in whom there is no evil, sees evil in no one." Similarly, the story goes of Rabbi Susya, the great ecstatic and "fool of God," that even when someone committed an evil in his presence he would only see the good side of the man. According to legend he achieved this stage because, on one occasion, when in the presence of his teacher, the Maggid of Mezritch, he attacked a habitual sinner asking how he was not ashamed to confront the holy man, the latter blessed him that he might thereafter see only the good in everyone. According to another account his attitude was to perceive the sins of others as being his own and to reproach himself with them.

For him who is not a perfect Zaddik, the Baalshem expounds the following complementary teaching: "If someone happens to see something sinful or to hear about it, let him mark well that there is in him a minute quantity of that sin and let him set about putting himself right. . . . Then the sinner too will, if you draw him into the same unity with you, since all are One Human Being. Thus do you effect the accomplishment of the saying: 'Forsake the evil and do (make) good,' as you are making good out of evil." Here the Jewish religious wisdom coincides, from an entirely different angle, with an ancient Chinese one: Whosoever brings himself into unison with the Sense of Being, also brings the world into unison with it; but the Hasidic saying states what is lacking in all Taoism: You must draw the next man into the unity, and so exercise on him an influence for good.

What we must beware of is this persistent discrimination between ourselves and our neighbour, the conceit of discrimination, the deception of discrimination—indeed, this entire triumphal world of illusion, based upon a self-satisfying discrimination. Nothing disturbs the unity of God's work, the foretaste of Eternity, as much as this overbearing discrimination between myself and my neighbour, as if indeed I excelled in one way or another above somebody else. The most extreme manifestation, in the scope of language, ever expounded in Hasidism against this overflow of false differentiation, is what Rabbi Raphael of Bershad said in the last summer before his death: "We must now lay aside all pious deeds, so that there be no more estrangement of the heart from any other Jew."

There is, however, yet another category of people whom we find it particularly hard to love; they are our enemies. This relationship has been described by the saying of another great Zaddik, also one of the first, Rabbi Yehiel-Michal of Zloczov, likewise a short time before his death. He ordered his sons to pray for the well-being of their enemies. "And do you think," he added, "that this is not divine service? It is a service greater than all prayer." Here the integration of the ethical into the religious has reached its climax.

Hasidism is one of the great religious movements, which show directly that the human soul can, as a whole, united within itself, live in communication with the wholeness of Being—not only isolated solitary souls, but a community-bound multitude of souls. The realms which have been separated from each other through apparent necessity recognize, in the sublime moments of such movements, the unjustness of their mutual demarcation and merge into one. The lucid flame of human unity embraces all the forces and ascends to the Unity Divine.

The unification of the ethical and religious domains, as it has been accomplished in so exemplary a manner by Hasidism, if only in short-lived blossom, brings forth what we, in our human world, call Holiness. We can hardly have knowledge of Holiness as human property by any way other than through such unification. It is important to learn to know it.

Many of the "free" can learn from Hasidism that there is such a thing as Holiness; many of the "pious" can learn what it is.

The Sayings of Rabbi Nachman

We appear to have authentic writings of the Besht's great-grandson, Rabbi Nachman of Bratislava, who died at the age of forty in 1810. What is remarkable in Nachman's sayings is not the Kabbalistic imagery or traditional rabbinical urging to draw near to God, but the concern about heartbreak and depression. The strength of the religious thought in Nachman is on a psychological level.

The world is a rotating wheel.

It is like a Dreidle [Spinning top used at Hanukah], where everything goes in cycles. Man becomes angel, and angel becomes man. Head becomes foot, and foot becomes head. Everything goes in cycles, revolving and alternating. All things interchange, one from another and one to another, elevating the low and lowering the high.

All things have one root.

There are transcendental beings such as angels, which have no connection with the material.

There is the celestial world, whose essence is very tenuous.

Finally, there is the world below, which is completely physical.

All three come from different realms, but all have the same root.

All creation is like a rotating wheel, revolving and oscillating.

At one time something can be on top like a head with another on bottom like a foot.

Then the situation is reversed. Head becomes foot, and foot becomes head. Man becomes angel, and angel becomes man.

Our sages teach us that angels were cast down from heaven. They entered physical bodies and were subject to all worldly lusts. Other angels were sent on missions to our world and had to clothe themselves in physical bodies. We also find cases where human beings literally became angels.

For the world is like a rotating wheel. It spins like a Dreidle, with all things emanating from one root.

This is why we play with a Dreidle on Chanukah.

Chanukah is an aspect of the Holy Temple.

The primary concept of the Temple is the revolving wheel.

The Temple was in the category of "the superior below and the inferior above." G-d lowered His presence into the Temple and this is "the superior below." The Temple's pattern was engraved on high, "the inferior above."

The Temple is therefore like a Dreidle, a rotating wheel, where everything revolves and is reversed.

The Temple refutes philosophical logic.

G-d is above every transcendental concept, and it is beyond all logic that He should constrict Himself into the vessels of the Temple. "Behold the heaven, and the heaven of heaven cannot contain You, how much less this Temple."

But G-d brought His presence into the Temple, and so destroyed all philosophical logic.

Philosophy cannot explain how man can have any influence on high. It cannot say how a mere animal can be sacrificed and rise as a sweet savor giving pleasure to G-d. They explain that this pleasure is the fulfillment of His will, but how can we even apply the concept of desire to G-d?

But G-d placed His presence in the Temple and accepts the animal as a sweet savor.

He made the fact contradict philosophical logic.

After all this we can return to our original discussion. We have no need of philosophy, which is anyway strongly forbidden. We must have faith in

G-d, that He created, sustains, and will eventually renew all worlds.

Heartbreak is in no way related to sadness and depression.

Heartbreak involves the heart, while depression involves the spleen.

Depression comes from the Other Side and is hated by G-d. But a broken heart is very dear and precious to G-d.

It would be very good to be brokenhearted all day. But for the average person, this can easily degenerate into depression.

You should therefore set aside some time each day for heartbreak. You should isolate yourself with a broken heart before G-d for a given time. But the rest of the day should be joyful.

The Rebbe emphasized this many times telling us not to be brokenhearted except for a fixed time each day. He said that we should always be joyful and never depressed.

Depression is like anger and rage. It is like a complaint against G-d for not fulfilling one's wishes.

But one with a broken heart is like a child pleading before his father. He is like a baby crying and complaining because his father is far away.

Depression can cause one to forget his name.

Once the Rebbe spoke in a light vein about the dead, who are asked their name by an angel and cannot remember it. He said that the name is forgotten because of the dead person's great sadness and depression.

Always be joyful, no matter what you are. Even if you feel far from G-d, be happy and praise him, "for not making me a heathen."

For deeds done against G-d's will, set aside a time every day to isolate yourself with a broken heart, before G-d. Be heartbroken—but not depressed—even during this hour. The rest of the day should then be spent in happiness.

With happiness you can give a person life.

A person might be in terrible agony and not be able to express what is in his heart. There is no one to whom he can unburden his heart, so he remains deeply pained and worried.

If you come to such a person with a happy face, you can cheer him and literally give him life. This is a great thing and by no means an empty gesture. The Talmud teaches us that two merri-makers were worthy of unusual merit merely because they made others happy. . . .

You must be very worthy to be able to meditate for a given time each day and regret what you must.

Not every one can have such mental tranquillity each day. The days pass and are gone, and one finds that he never once had time to really think.

You must therefore make sure—to set aside a specific time each day to calmly review your life. Consider what you are doing and ponder whether it is worthy that you devote your life to it.

One who does not meditate cannot have wisdom.

He may occasionally be able to concentrate, but not for any length of time. His power of concentration remains weak, and cannot be maintained.

One who does not meditate also does not realize the foolishness of the world. But one who has a relaxed and penetrating mind can see that it is all vanity.

Many desire to travel widely and become famous and powerful. They do not have enough perception to realize that this is vanity and striving after the wind. It is all the more foolish because it does not actually result in pleasure even in this world. The main result of such fame is suffering and insults. . . .

The Rebbe often spoke about his childhood piety. He said that he began anew many times each day. He would begin the day with deep devotion, resolving that from then on he would be a true servant of G-d. Then the temptation of a tasty meal or such would get the better of him, and he would fall from his high level of devotion. But on that same day he would begin again, with new resolve toward true devotion.

The Rebbe would thus fall and begin anew several times each day. He often told us how he continually began serving G-d anew.

This is an important rule in devotion.

Never let yourself fall completely.

There are many ways you can fall. At times your prayer and devotion may seem utterly without meaning. Strengthen yourself and begin anew. Act as if you were just beginning to serve G-d. No matter how many times you fall, rise up and start again. Do this again and again, for otherwise you will never come close to G-d.

Draw yourself toward G-d with all your might.

Remain strong, no matter how low you fall. Whether you go up or down, always yearn to come close to G-d. You may be brought low, but cry out to G-d and do everything you can to serve Him in joy. For without this inner strength, you will never be able to truly approach G-d.

Keep pushing until you can do nothing else but serve G-d all your life. Be ready to do so even without a promise of reward.

You may imagine that you are so far from G-d that you have no Future Reward. You must still serve Him as you can, even without such promise. It may seem that you are damned, but your responsibility is still there. Continue serving G-d as best you can. Snatch a good deed, a lesson, a prayer, and G-d will do what is good in his eyes.

It is told that the Baal Shem Tov once became very dejected. He could find no inspiration and was sure he no longer merited the Future Reward. But then he said, "I love G-d—even without reward."

This is the only path to G-d, and no matter how lowly you are, you can still follow it. Strengthen yourself and begin anew, even many times each day. As time passes, you will then find yourself on the road leading to G-d. Amen.

Reform Judaism

Reform or Liberal Judaism was established in Germany in the mid-nineteenth century and it moved to the U.S.A. with the substantial German Jewish immigration of the middle decades of the century. A Reform seminary was established in Cincinnati, the prime midwestern center of German Jewry, and it produced many distinguished rabbinical graduates. By the 1920s, Reform Judaism had gained many adherents in New York and other cities.

Here is the essence of Reform Judaism as articulated by Rabbi Isaac Mayer Wise, its founder, in 1860. What this faith consists of is a blending of the less radical side of prophetic Judaism with the German liberal universalistic Enlightenment tradition of Immanuel Kant, as propounded at the end of the eighteenth century by Moses Mendelsohn. The content is rational ethics, not a specific Halachic code of behavior; that is left up to individual choice. God is just, and man with his free will can live by His moral precepts and be rewarded.

Along with departing from the Orthodox tradition, the pessimistic view of traditional Christianity that man's nature is depraved is also explicitly rejected by Mayer Wise. Israel is still the light to all the nations, but the coming of the Messiah is turned into a metaphor for universal acceptance of prophetic ethics. Perhaps a million Jews in the U.S.A. and Canada still belong to (but rarely attend) Reform synagogues, often very large and handsome ones, where this Kantian Judaism is preached.

As a son or daughter of the divine covenant, it is furthermore expected of you that you truly believe in the justice and grace of our God. You cannot and shall not for one moment believe that an original sin rests upon man, for it would be unjust for God to punish all unborn generations for the sin of the first parents of the human race. Nor shall you believe that there is a devil, and much less that the devil or unclean spirits exercise any influence on man; for God is absolutely good, He cannot have created anything absolutely evil. Nor shall you believe the doctrine of universal depravity, i.e., that evil propensities predominate in most men; for this would be an unjust charge against our Creator. On the contrary, you shall believe that man was made in the image of God, that he was gifted with all the qualities to be good, just, righteous, pious and happy. God in His infinite goodness bestowed upon us intellect, moral freedom, respect for justice, truth and magnanimity, aversion to injustice and meanness, and the desire to worship the Most High. Sin is the consequence of ignorance or error, therefore the Lord revealed to us the Law and truth. As a son or daughter of the divine covenant you are required to regard every human being as the image of God, and to love your neighbor as yourself. You are required to instruct the ignorant, enlighten the erring, pity him who goes astray, protect the weak, feed the hungry, clothe the naked and give shelter to the homeless, because each of these is the image of God. If you can look upon man from this exalted point of view and do to every one as love dictates, if thus you behold man as God's noblest work, His image, His reflex on earth, "His son," then you will do as God's redeemed ones are required to do, then you fulfill the stipulations of the divine covenant. . . .

You yourself must appear and do appear every moment before the judgment seat of God. Your righteousness is your advocate and your wickedness is your adversary. You are responsible to your God for all you do or omit; for to your intellect and free will the divine laws are addressed. If you are prepared to meet your God at His judgment seat, if you, the child, require no advocate before your Father, then come to us and be of the divine covenant; then with us appear as children of the house before the Father, and His paternal love will receive you.

Again, we must admonish you not to believe for a moment that God is unjust or unkind. Laws in themselves imply the possibility that they might be violated. In fact, virtue is the triumph of our good nature. God in ordaining the Law must have known that we might transgress it. Just and gracious as He is, He must have enabled the prodigal son to return to the father. So he has done. Sin does not estrange God from us, for God is not affected by our actions; but it estranges us from God, for we forget him when we disregard His laws. Cease to sin, be rebellious no more, improve your heart, obey again the laws of God; the cause of estrangement between God and yourself will then be removed, and you will have made atonement for your sins. . . .

The antecedents of Reform Judaism. Moses Mendelssohn, 1787, Berlin, founder of the Haskala (Jewish Enlightment) and forerunner of Reform Judaism.

■ ■ ■

There is but one truth and this was revealed to Israel; therefore Israel is the mountain of the Lord which all nations must finally ascend, there to learn of God's ways and to walk in His paths. As God revealed His nature and will to Israel, even so He will ultimately be known to humanity. As He revealed his name to Israel, so He shall be called the nameless great first cause of all, Jehovah, blessed forever be His glorious name. Whenever the nations will know God in truth and light, they will also know that they learned Him from Israel, and they shall call him Jehovah, as we claim him, not Allah, not Jupiter, not Jesus, not Messiah, but Jehovah, the God of all, the cause and governor of all; then "His name will be one." The knowledge and fear of God will invite all men to know and observe His laws; this is redemption, there is the fountain-head of salvation. This is our Messiah for whom we wait.

Neo-Orthodoxy

The most widely respected spokesman for resurgent Orthodox Judaism in the 1980s was Rabbi Joseph B. Soloveitchik of Boston. Here he offers a sophisticated attack upon Reform Judaism as subjectivist and lacking in religious content. Any defensiveness about the Halachic-Kabbalistic-Hasidic tradition is gone from this statement. Here is the aggressive voice of neo-Orthodoxy—convinced that the complex heritage of the Talmudic and post-Talmudic tradition is integral with modern psychology and comparative religion, whereas Reform Judaism is a weak, empty faith that cannot endure. The downside of Soloveitchik's militant attitude is its effect of enhanced divisiveness among believing Jews.

The basic error of religious liberalism is to be discerned less in its ideology than in its methodical approach. Liberalism has traveled in the wrong direction—from subjectivity to objectivity—and in so doing his misconstrued both. Religious liberalism is based upon a very "simple" methodological principle. Subjective religiosity, the moderns say, is subordinated to the omnipotent authority of time and change. It is impossible therefore to consider any set of religious norms and dogmas as immutable, for the objective order moving parallel to the subjective undergoes the same metamorphoses. Let us admit that modern religious subjectivism is indeed incommensurable with the objective order sanctioned by tradition. One is still tempted to ask how the fathers of contemporary liberalism intend to mould a modern religious act out of the "new" chaotic mass of subjectivity? The method of objectification is, of course, at their disposal. They may project subjective flux upon externality and create a new, artificial objective order. But this very method is fallacious. If, for example, a certain school of liberal thought asserts that the traditional dogmas pertaining to the essence and attributes of God are not acceptable to the scientific mind, then the question arises: What type of divinity is to be offered as a substitute for the traditional God? In other words,

what method of construction is to be applied in forming a modern theology? We know that such a school will always begin with the subjective domain. It will perhaps claim to have analyzed the deepest strata of the religious consciousness and to have examined the God-thirsty soul with all its conflicting emotions and paradoxical sentiments. Out of such hylitic matter liberalism attempts to mould a new deity which is half pantheistic and half moralistic. The ultramodern God is both a metaphysical *élan vital* and a cosmic moral *telos*.

The fallacy of this movement lies in its utter lack of methodology. Where is the assurance that these philosophers, while exploring modern religious subjectivism, have not erred and strayed? Columbus of old, sailing an uncharted sea, mistook the American continent for the "Indies." The liberals of today, instead of religious subjectivity, plunge mistakenly into some other subjective "order"—the moral or aesthetic. There being no boundary lines in the subjective sphere, trespasses upon the territory of ethics and aesthetics occur unwittingly. When viewed from any other aspect but the objective, subjectivity does not present separate realism. It is only the act of a retrospective analysis that classifies religiosity. Religious subjectivity is synonymous with the subjective "order" surveyed from the premises of objectivity. If one seeks primordial subjectivity he would find an evanescent flux, neither religious nor mundane, but, similar to Aristotelian matter, unregulated and chaotic. If an objective compass be lacking, the final port of landing is uncertain.

Liberalism has approached its subject matter with bias. It has boldly declared traditional dogmas to be incongruous with modern subjectivism. Actually, they have neither examined that ancient order of subjectivity out of which these "old-fashioned" concepts of God have evolved, nor have they investigated the religiosity of modern man. This being the case, the abandonment of certain traditional concepts in favor of more modern ones is nothing but sheer whimsicality if not foolhardy iconoclasm.

If the commensurability of traditional beliefs with modern religious experience is to be investigated, the method of retrospective exploration—the regressive movement from objective religious symbols to subjective flux—must be applied.

For were we to analyze the mystery of the God-man relation as reflected in the Jewish religious consciousness from both traditional and modern aspects, it would be necessary that we first gather all objectified data at our disposal: passages in the Holy Writ pertaining to divinity and divine attributes; the norms regulating the God-man contact such as the norm of love and fear of God; moments of tension between God and man, as in the case of Job; many Halakhic problems where certain attitudes of man towards Divinity have found their expression; all forms of cult, liturgy, prayer, Jewish mysticism, rational philosophy, religious movements, etc. Out of this enormous mass of objectified constructs, the underlying subjective aspects could gradually be reconstructed. The latter, in turn, should be compared to central structural facts of modern psychology, typology and the philosophy of religion. It is not too far fetched to anticipate the result of such an inquiry and predict that the traditional intimate God-man communion would not be as simple and naive as the moderns would have us imagine.

Although the method of reconstruction can be adopted and utilized by any theistic religion, it is of immense importance in the field of Jewish philosophy. One of the most perplexing problems that has confused the methodological error at the root of reform ideology is clear.

Creative Life-Force Among Jews

The most original Jewish religious thinker of the twentieth century was the German theologian Franz Rosenzweig. The following selection is translated from the 1930 second edition of Rosenzweig's *The Star of Redemption* by William W. Hallo.

The source of Rosenzweig's theory lies in the widely adhered-to kind of liberal Darwinism the flourished momentarily in the 1920s, such as the doctrine of *élan vital* expounded by the French Jewish philosopher, Henri Bergson.

There is an evolving creative force in the universe and among species—a vital biological force that shapes itself macrocosmically into redemptive love, and micrcosmically into the driving force of Jewish blood down through the generations.

That is what Rosenszweig is saying. A difficult doctrine, and one never acceptable to the rabbis of any persuasion, it was seemingly made obsolete by Hitlerian race theory and by political Zionism.

Redemption originates with God, and man knows neither the day nor the hour. He only knows that he is to love, and to love always the nighest and the neighbor. And as for the world, it grows in itself, apparently according to its own law. And whether world and man find each other today or tomorrow or whenever—the times are incalculable; neither man nor world knows them. Only He knows the hour who at every moment redeems the Today unto eternity.

There is only one community in which such a linked sequence of everlasting life goes from grandfather to grandson, only one which cannot utter the "we" of its unity without hearing deep within a voice that adds "are eternal." It must be a blood-community, because only blood gives present warrant to the hope for a future. If some other community, one that does not propagate itself from its own blood, desires to claim eternity for its "we," the only way open to it is to secure a place in the future. All eternity not based on blood must be based on the will and on hope. Only a community based on common blood feels the warrant of eternity warm in its veins even now. For such a community only, time is not a foe that must be tamed, a foe it may or may not defeat—though it hopes it may!—but its child and the child of its child. It alone regards as the present what, for other communities, is the future, or, at any rate, something outside the present. For it alone the future is not something alien but something of its own, something it carries in its womb and which might be born any day. While every other community that lays claim to eternity must take measures to pass the torch of the present on to the future, the blood-community does not have to resort to such measures. It does not have to hire the services of the spirit; the natural propagation of the body guarantees it eternity.

What holds generally for peoples as groups united through blood relationship over against communities of the spirit, holds for our people in particular. Among the peoples of the earth, the Jewish people is "the one people," as it calls itself on the high rung of its life, which it ascends Sabbath after Sabbath. The peoples of the world are not content with the bonds of blood. They sink their roots into the night of earth, lifeless in itself but the spender of life, and from the lastingness of earth they conclude that they themselves

will last. Their will to eternity clings to the soil and to the reign over the soil, to the land. The earth of their homeland is watered by the blood of their sons, for they do not trust in the life of a community of blood, in a community that can dispense with anchorage in solid earth. We were the only ones who trusted in blood and abandoned the land; and so we preserved the priceless sap of life which pledged us that it would be eternal. Among the peoples of the world, we were the only ones who separated what lived within us from all community with what is dead. For while the earth nourishes, it also binds. Whenever a people loves the soil of its native land more than its own life, it is in danger—as all the peoples of the world are—that, though nine times out of ten this love will save the native soil from the foe and, along with it, the life of the people, in the end the soil will persist as that which was loved more strongly, and the people will leave their lifeblood upon it. In the final analysis, the people belong to him who conquers the land. It cannot be otherwise, because people cling to the soil more than to their life as a people. Thus the earth betrays a people that entrusted its permanence to earth. The soil endures, the peoples who live on it pass.

And so, in contrast to the history of other peoples, the earliest legends about the tribe of the eternal people are not based on indigenousness. Only the father of mankind sprang from the earth itself, and even he only in a physical sense. But the father of Israel came from the outside. His story, as it is told in the holy books, begins with God's command to leave the land of his birth and go to a land God will point out to him. Thus in the dawn of its earliest beginnings, as well as later in the bright light of history, this people is a people in exile, in the Egyptian exile and subsequently in that of Babylonia. To the eternal people, home never is home in the sense of land, as it is to the peoples of the world who plough the land and live and thrive on it, until they have all but forgotten that being a people means something besides being rooted in a land. The eternal people has not been permitted to while away time in any home. It never loses the untrammeled freedom of a wanderer who is more faithful a knight to his country when he roams abroad, craving adventure and yearning for the land he has left behind, than when he lives in that land. In the most profound sense possible, this people has a land of its own only in that it has a land it yearns for—a holy land. And so even when it has a home, this people, in recurrent contrast to all other peoples on earth, is not allowed full possession of that home. It is only "a stranger and a sojourner." God tells it: "The land is mine." The holiness of the land removed it from the people's spontaneous reach while it could still reach out for it. This holiness increases the longing for what is lost, to infinity, and so the people can never be entirely at home in any other land. This longing compels it to concentrate the full force of its will on a thing which, for other peoples, is only one among others yet which to it is essential and vital: the community of blood. In doing this, the will to be a people dares not cling to any mechanical means; the will can realize its end only through the people itself.

Transactional Theology

The most frequently-cited (if not read) work of Jewish religious thought of the twentieth century is Martin Buber's *I and Thou*, from whose 1958 second edition this translation by Ronald Gregor Smity is taken.

Buber's approach is that of transactional or existential psychology. By our relationship with another person we develop a consciousness and fulfillment of our own personality. The good life is one of constant interaction. And through the course of this discovery of the *Thou* of another person, we also enter into discovery and communication with the *Thou* of God. To be a fully interacting person is also to be a believer and communicator with God.

It could be claimed that this is only an updated twentieth-century version of the old pharisaic coda, love your neighbor as yourself. But it is a little more sophisticated than that.

Burber was influenced by the vanguard philosophical movement in Germany of the 1920s, that of phenomenology. Its proponents were Edmund Husserl, who was Jewish, and Martin Heidegger who became a big Nazi. The tremendous popularity of Buber's *I and Thou* in recent decades is partly attributable to its concordance with phenomenology and with the American school of New Age psychology founded by Carl Rogers and Abraham Maslow in the 1960s.

There is an obvious affinity between Buber's enthusiasm for Hasidism and his transactional, phenomenological theology. A group of Hasidics holding hands and dancing in a circle, not only relating emotionally to one another, but also preparing a way to communicate with God—this neoromantic idea did not go over very well with Buber's colleagues at the Hebrew University in the 1950s. At a California college today, Buber would be idolized as a New Age guru. *I and Thou* is written in an elliptical, mystical style of German and is very difficult to transpose into readable English.

Pure relation can only be raised to constancy in space and time by being embodied in the whole stuff of life. It cannot be preserved, but only proved true, only done, only done up into life. Man can do justice to the relation with God in which he has come to share only if he realises

Portrait, 1962, by Eugene Spiro, of Martin Buber, most influential Jewish religious thinker of the twentieth century.

Only when these two arise—the binding up of time in a relational life of salvation and the binding up of space in the community that is made one by its Centre—and only so long as they exist, does there arise and exist, round about the invisible altar, a human cosmos with bounds and form, grasped with the spirit out of the universal stuff of the æon, a world that is house and home, a dwelling for man in the universe.

Meeting with God does not come to man in order that he may concern himself with God, but in order that he may confirm that there is meaning in the world. All revelation is summons and sending. . . .

God remains present to you when you have been sent forth; he who goes on a mission has always God before him: the truer the fulfillment the stronger and more constant His nearness.

Subjectivism empties God of soul, objectivism makes Him into an object—the latter is a false fixing down, the former a false setting free; both are diversions from the way of reality, both are attempts to replace reality. . . .

History is a mysterious approach. Every spiral of its way leads us both into profounder perversion and more fundamental turning. But the event that from the side of the world is called turning is called from God's side redemption.

God anew in the world according to his strength and to the measure of each day. In this lies the only authentic assurance of continuity . . .

The Meaning of the Covenant

A much-cited and hysterically admired American Jewish thinker is Rabbi Abraham Joshua Heschel, who taught at a Conservative rabbinical seminary, the Jewish Theological Seminary in New York, for three decades after World War II. Heschel's interpretation of the covenant became the theme of countless Conservative sermons. It owes much to the American pragmatist thinker, William James, who wrote in the first decade of the twentieth century at Harvard.

Pragmatism, as propounded by William James or John Dewey, was extremely popular with American Jewish Conservative and Reform rabbis in the 1930s and 1940s. It seemed easily compatible with FDR's brand of democratic liberalism, which the great majority of American Jews espoused.

There is only one way to define Jewish religion. It is the *awareness of God's interest in man,* the awareness of a *covenant,* of a responsibility that lies on Him as well as on us. Our task is to concur with His interest, to carry out His vision of our task. God is in need of man for the attainment of His ends, and religion, as Jewish tradition understands it, is a way of serving these ends, of which we are in need, even though we may not be aware of them, ends which we must learn to feel the need of.

Some people think that religion comes about as a perception of an answer to a prayer, while in truth it comes about in our knowing that God shares our prayer. The essence of Judaism is the awareness of the *reciprocity* of God and man, of man's *togetherness* with Him who abides in eternal otherness. For the task of living is His and ours, and so is the responsibility. We have rights, not only obligations; our ultimate commitment is our ultimate privilege. . . .

The God of the philosophers is all indifference, too sublime to possess a heart or to cast a glance at our world. His wisdom consists in being conscious of Himself and oblivious to the world. In contrast, the God of the prophets is all concern, too merciful to remain aloof to His creation. He not only rules the world in the majesty of His might: He is personally concerned and even stirred by the conduct and fate of man. "His mercy is upon all His works" (Psalms 145:9).

These are the two poles of prophetic thinking: The idea that God is one, holy, different and apart from all that exists, and the idea of the inexhaustible concern of God for man, at times brightened by His mercy, at times darkened by His anger. He is both transcendent, beyond human understanding, and full of love, compassion, grief or anger.

God does not judge the deeds of man impassively, in a spirit of cool detachment. His judgment is imbued with a feeling of intimate concern. He is the father of all men, not only a judge; He is a lover engaged to His people, not only a king. God stands in a passionate relationship to man. His love or anger, His mercy or disappointment is an expression of His profound participation in the history of Israel and all men.

Prophecy, then, consists in the proclamation of the divine *pathos,* expressed in the language of the prophets as love, mercy or anger. Behind the various manifestations of His pathos is one motive, one need: The divine need for human righteousness.

The pagan gods had animal passions, carnal desires, they were more fitful, licentious than men; the God of Israel has a passion for righteousness. The pagan gods had selfish needs, while the God of Israel is only in need of man's integrity. The need of Moloch was the death of man, the need of the Lord is the life of man. The divine pathos, which the prophets tried to express in many ways, was not a name for His essence but rather for the modes of His reaction to Israel's conduct which would change if Israel modified its ways.

The surge of divine pathos, which came to the souls of the prophets like a fierce passion, startling, shaking, burning, led them forth to the perilous defiance of people's self-assurance and contentment. Beneath all songs and sermons they held conference with God's concern for the people, with the well, out of which the tides of anger raged.

The Bible is not a history of the Jewish people, but the story of God's quest of the righteous man. Because of the failure of the human species as a whole to follow in the path of righteousness, it is an individual—Noah, Abraham—a people: Israel—or a remnant of the people, on which the task is bestowed to satisfy that quest by making every man a righteous man.

There is an eternal cry in the world: God is beseeching man. Some are startled; others remain deaf. We are all looked for. An air of expectancy hovers over life. Something is asked of man, of all men.

PART FIVE

VICTIMS AND MARTYRS

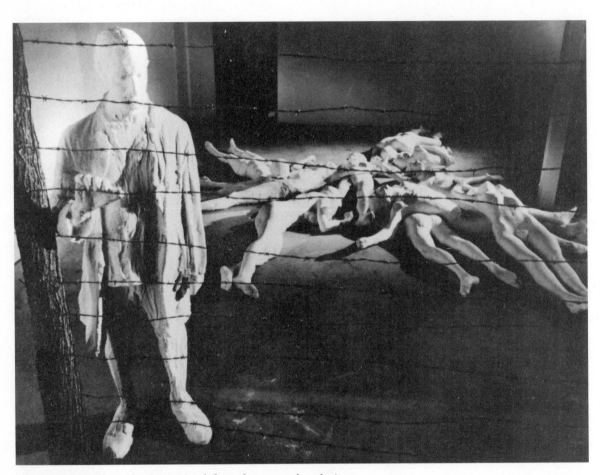

The Holocaust, sculpture by George Segal, from plaster, wood, and wire.

INTRODUCTION

Through much of their history, Jews have expected to be victims and martyrs. The Pentateuch told them they were the people of the covenant, witnesses of God's light to the nations, so the Gentiles, who did not share this privileged status, would be jealous of them and hate them. The prophet Deutero-Isaiah, writing in exile in Iraq in the sixth century B.C., designated the Jew as God's Suffering Servant, as the Man of Sorrows.

After their intense competition for converts with the Christian Church of the Roman Empire, and after the political triumph of the Church in A.D. 312, the Jews could expect to suffer, and did. The Islamic Koran was almost as hard on the Jews as the Christian Gospels, so sooner or later Muslim fundamentalists would come down on them, and did. In Poland, Russia, and the Ukraine, the Jews felt the seething envy and resentment of the peasant masses as well as their village priests: they knew they were living on borrowed time, and they were. In the nineteenth and twentieth centuries, the Jews were prey to violence in wartime, and to fanatical nationalist and racial propaganda at all times.

Yet all this lugubrious history paled before the Holocaust of the 1940s—the worst genocide in world history, during which the best nations stood by and allowed the worst to reduce the Jewish world population by more than one-third in four years, during which indescribable cruelty and carnage fell upon all segments of the Jewish population under Nazi rule, the young and old, the rich and poor.

How much suffering does Yahweh want his Suffering Servant to endure? How much sorrow shall fall upon the Man of Sorrows? The rabbis were struck dumb, at least those who were not themselves exterminated. No Jewish theologian has ever given a comforting or reasonable explanation of the Holocaust.

Jew, in your very long history you have been victim and martyr. You have been the prey of religious fanaticism, racial hatred, political ambition, and social jealousy. You have cringed in terror. You have fled in desperation. You have been swallowed up in mass killing. You have suffered abnegation, deprivation, discrimination, exile, and elimination.

And why? No one knows why. God knows why, but He is silent. Over everything else the Jew does and feels, there is the numbing noise in the background, there is the darkness lying low on the noon's horizon, there is the threat of victimization, oppression, and martyrdom. For what? For God's Holy Name—al Kiddish-hashem, said the rabbis. For the very young, for the very old and sick, and for the nonbeliever, not even this bleak and remote satisfaction existed. Jew you were the victim then, Jew you are the martyr now. Is it over? Has suffering run its course? Has sorrow expended its resources? Has blood flowed beyond supply?

Is this a thing of history—a condition of time and place, of many times and places—or will it come again, the darkness and the terror springing from the damp and rancid earth? No one knows . . .

The Poets' Laments

Here are dirges for Jewish suffering by three twentieth-century poets. The first is from Chaim Nachman Bialik's *City of Slaughter*, a lengthy dirge written after witnessing the results of the pogroms in 1904 in Kishinev in Russian-ruled Rumania. Bialik, who died in Israel in 1934, is generally regarded as the greatest Jewish poet, in both Yiddish and Hebrew, of modern times. The translation is by Steven L. Jacobs.

The second selection is by Perets Markish, regarded as the leading Soviet Jewish poet; he was eliminated in a Stalinist purge in 1939. The poem is dated 11 Tishrei 5681—the day after Yom Kippur, September 23, 1920—and is a response to pogroms in the Ukraine. The translation is by Leonard Wolf.

The third poem was written in the Vilna ghetto in 1943 by Abraham Sutzkever. The translation is by Seymour Mayne.

And I will harden your heart and a sigh will not come out.
Behold the calves of slaughter, they are lying there all of them—
Is there reward for their death—Speak, with what will it be paid?
Forgive me, eternally wretched, your God is poor like you,
Poor is He in your life, so much the more so in your death,
When tomorrow will you come for your reward and knock upon My door—
I will say to you, come and see: I have become impoverished!
I grieve for you, my children, and my heart, my heart, grieves for you:
Your slain—they have been slain for nought, and I and you
Do not know why you died, for whom, and because of what you died,
There was no reason for your deaths just as there is no reason for your lives.
And the Shechina, what does she say?—She hides her head in the cloud
And withdraws and is ashamed because of oppression, pain, and disgrace . . .
I, too, night after night, go down to the graves,
Stand looking at the slain, shamed secretly—

However, as I live, saith the Lord, I will let no tear descend.
Terror, terror round about . . . it wanders in the stable,
It rests upon the walls and is pressed within the silence.
And from underneath the heaps of wheels, from between the holes and fissures,
Skin you will feel like the spasm of crushed limbs,
Shifting the wheels heaped high upon their backs,
Twisting in their agony and rolling in their blood;
A last muffled groan—a tortured faint sound
Above your head is still suspended as if congealed,
Like troubled sorrow, eternal sorrow, excited there and afraid.
It is the very spirit of contrition, much-afflicted and greatly chastised, that
Imprisons itself here within this prison-house and
Is thrusted here into eternal wretchedness and no longer desirous of leaving,
And one black Shechina, tired of sorrow and exhausted,
Wanders about here in every corner but finds no rest for itself,

*Wanting to weep—but not able, desiring to
 groan—but keeping silent,*
*Silently would she perish in her mourning and
 secretly be strangled,*
*Spreading forth her wings over the shadows of
 the martyrs, her head beneath her wing,*
*Shadowing over her tears and weeping without
 speech—*

*And you, you too, son of man, close the gate
 behind you*
*So that you will be shut up here in the dark and
 direct your eyes to the ground*
*And stand here a long time and become one
 with the sorrow*
*And fill your heart with it for all the days of
 your life,*
*And when your soul is destroyed and all its
 strength ceases—*
It will be an escape for you and a poison fount,
*Crouched in you like a curse, waiting to destroy
 you like an evil spirit.*
*Embracing you and oppressing you like the
 oppression of a nightmare;*
*And in your bosom you will carry it to the four
 winds of the heavens,*
*And you will seek but not find for it an expres-
 sion.*

*And you will go to the outside of the city and
 come to the cemetery,*
*No man will see you in your journey and alone
 will you come there,*
*And you will visit the graves of the martyrs from
 the youngest of them to the eldest,*
*And you will stand by their crumbling dust and
 I will let silence rule over you;*
*And your heart will melt within you from
 oppression, pain, and disgrace—*
And I will close your eyes; there will be no tears,
*And you will know that it is a time to low like
 an ox bound for the slaughtering-place—*
*The pain is very great and very great is the dis-
 grace—*
*And which of the two is greater?—Speak, son of
 man!*
Or better—Be silent! Be my silent witness,
*For you have found Me in My disgrace and have
 seen Me on the day of My calamity;*
*And when you return to the children of your
 people—do not return to them empty-handed,*

*But take with you the chastisement of My dis-
 grace and bring it down upon their head*
*And take My pain with you and set it to their
 bosom.*

*And you turn to go from the graves of the dead,
 and the carpet*
*Of grass surrounding delays your eyes for one
 moment,*
*The grass is tender and juicy, like it should be at
 the beginning of Spring:*
*The buds of death and grass of graves you see
 with your eyes;*
*And you pluck from them a handful and scatter
 them behind you,*
*Saying: Uprooted grass is the people—is there
 hope for the uprooted?*
*And you close your eyes from seeing them; then
 will I take you and cause you to return*
*From the cemetery to your brothers who sur-
 vived the slaughter,*
*And you will go with them on their fast-day to
 their Houses of Prayer*
*And you will hear the cry of their destruction
 and be swept away by their tears;*
*And the House will be full of wailing, crying,
 and wild groaning,*
*And the hair of your flesh will stand on end and
 fear will call out to you and trembling—*
*Thus will groan a nation which has surely per-
 ished . . .*
*You will look into their heart—behold desert and
 wilderness,*
*And if a wrath of vengeance will grow in it— no
 seed will survive,*
*Not even a single potent curse will it bring forth
 from their lips.*
*Are their wounds then not true—why is their
 prayer deceit?*
*Why do they lie to Me on the day of their
 calamity, and what profit is there in their
 lies?*
Behold, yea behold: Still they rot in their agony,
*All of them steeped in tears, raising lamentation
 in their wailing,*
*And behold they are beating their breasts, con-
 fessing their sin*
*Saying: "We have trespassed, we have dealt
 treacherously"—And their hearts will not
 believe their mouths.*
Can a shattered idol sin, can potsherds be guilty?

Why then do they make supplication to Me?—
  Speak to them and let them roar!
Let them raise a fist against Me; let them
  demand satisfaction for their humiliation,
The humiliation of every generation from the
  first unto the last,
Let them break asunder the Heavens and My
  throne with their fist.

After you, the killed of the Ukraine;
After you, butchered
In a mound in Gorodishche,
The Dnieper town . . .

KADDISH

No! Heavenly tallow, don't lick my gummy
beards.
Out of my mouth's brown streams of pitch
Sob a brown leaven of blood and sawdust.
No. Don't touch the vomit on the earth's black
  thigh.

Away. I stink. Frogs crawl on me.
Looking for mother-father here? Seeking a
  friend?
They're here. They're here, but taint the air with
  stink.
Away. Awkwardly they delouse themselves with
  hands like warped brass.

From top to bottom, a mound of filthy wash.
Claw, crazed wind. Take what you want; take it.
Before you, the church sits like a polecat beside a
  heap of strangled fowl.

Ah, black thigh. Ah, blazing blood. Out, shirt-
  tails! To the dance; to the dance.

We're laid out here. All. All. A mound. The whole
  town.

Was it from some hunger
or from greater love—
but your mother is a witness to this:
I wanted to swallow you, my child,
when I felt your tiny body losing its heat
in my fingers
as though I were pressing
a warm glass of tea,
feeling its passage to cold.

You're no stranger, no guest,
for on this earth one does not
give birth to aliens.
You reproduce yourself like a ring
and the rings fit into chains.

My child,
what else may I call you but: love.
Even without the word that is who you are,
you—seed of my every dream,
hidden third one,
who came from the world's corner
with the wonder of an unseen storm,
you who brought, rushed two together
to create you and rejoice:—

Why have you darkened creation
with the shutting of your tiny eyes
and left me begging outside
in the snow swept world
to which you have returned?

No cradle gave you pleasure
whose rocking
conceals in itself the pulse of the stars.
Let the sun crumble like glass
since you never beheld its light.
That drop of poison extinguished your faith—
you thought
it was warm sweet milk.

I wanted to swallow you, my child,
to feel the taste
of my anticipated future.
Perhaps in my blood
you will blossom as before.

But I am not worthy to be your grave.
So I bequeath you
to the summoning snow,
the snow—my first respite,
and you will sink
like a splinter of dusk
into its quiet depths
and bear greetings from me
to the frozen grasslands ahead—

VILNA GHETTO
JANUARY 18, 1943

A Novelist's Insight

The Israeli writer Aharon Appelfeld, in a series of novels, captured as no one else has what it meant to educated, middle-class Jews of Central Europe to be pulled into the Nazi maelstrom. Set in 1939 and 1940, as the war threatens and begins, Appelfeld's novels communicate the piercing siren of the looming Holocaust with unequaled sensibility and great literary art.

Like the works of all major fiction writers, Appelfeld's novels transcend their time and place and signal the universal and timeless terror experienced by Jews sensing their doom advancing from the quiet horizon. This selection is from *Badenheim 1939*, translated by Dalya Bilu (1980).

At last the signal was given. Mandelbaum ran lightly down the steps, like an athlete, and stood at the head. Strangely enough, there were no traces of his weeks of strict seclusion left now. The trio stationed themselves next to him, haggard and obedient. After them came the twins, and Sally and Gertie with the yanuka between them. Dr. Langmann stood in a row by himself. The heavy musicians, burdened with their clumsy bundles, hung back, afraid of being in the front rows. The conductor ignored them. He was now completely absorbed in conversation with the half-Jewish waitress. The waitress walked leaning on a wooden cane, holding herself erect.

"It's a pretty view, isn't it?" said the conductor. He had always been a man of few words, and now the ones he wanted seemed to be evading him out of spite.

The wet green fields lay spread around them. A delicate morning mist rose languidly in the air. How easy the transition was—they hardly felt it. The hotel owner pushed the rabbi's wheelchair as if he had been born to the task. No one offered to help him.

In the dull confusion of the last days a strange relationship had grown up between the waitress and the conductor. When she was ill the conductor had been to visit her and they had exchanged a few words. Ever since then they had not stopped thinking of each other. The night before, when everyone was celebrating at Sally and Gertie's, they sat together in the Luxembourg Gardens. He was as shy as a child and she laughed. He told her about his inheritance and savings, all the confidential details that had accumulated in his systematic mind.

"So you're a rich man," she said.

After years of living inside himself, nagging his musicians and balancing his petty accounts, he now felt for the first time that the chains had fallen from his hands. She spoke of the journey, the new way of life. Of her Austrian father she spoke with a kind of contempt, as if he were not a man but a beast.

Now they walked together. The fields rolled away into the distance. There was no sound but the whispering footsteps. The policemen walked a little distance behind, without urging them on. Professor Fussholdt was happy. He had finished proofreading his new book. The pages were tied in a bundle with thick string. Mandelbaum walked by his side and asked him questions. Professor Fussholdt imitated the rhetoric of the Jewish functionaries who imagined that they were bringing the Messiah with their speeches. His hostility to everything considered Jewish culture, Jewish art, was lighter now. The bitterness and mockery had been buried in his book. Mitzi walked behind him like a stranger. The longer they walked the more his eloquence flowed, full of ingenious puns, witticisms, and plays on words. For months he had not spoken to a soul and now the words poured out of him.

The rabbi dozed in his wheelchair. The column of people approached the country cottages. The smell of morning milk and manure mingled in the air. Next to the oak tree the nature lovers had once paused to listen to the bird calls. Here "the Blue-bird" once stood and made his inspiring speeches.

Salo did not seem at home on the open road he was so used to. For years he had traversed these fields with his medium-sized suitcase. The farmers, to tell the truth, did not like him. They always bought on credit and never paid their debts. His nonchalance suddenly deserted him. He huddled up to the musicians. The musicians sheltered him.

"The conductor hates us. What harm have we ever done him?" said the musician Zimbelman.

"Don't pay him any attention," said Salo.

"Even the hotel owner doesn't hate us."

"He'll come round. He won't have any alternative. You're his musicians after all, and he hasn't got any others besides you. By the way, did you get Pappenheim to sign Form 101?"

"No," said Zimbelman, "we forgot."

"That's a pity. Form 101's a good form, it gives you a lot of benefits."

"Dr. Pappenheim's always been very good to us. He even promoted us. We didn't dare ask."

"That's very important," said Salo. "In the end, salary scales are the same everywhere. He promoted you to Musicians, eleventh grade, didn't he? A very decent grade."

"For myself," said Zimbelman, "I would like to work fewer hours. The drums drive me out of my mind. I'd be glad to take a year or two's leave. Believe me, I need it."

"I believe you. But the years on the threshold of retirement are critical. It's better to keep your rights. For my part I'd also take an early pension if it was up to me, but my firm's very strict, they suck the workers dry. I've already collected twenty years of seniority without missing a day. I've got a month's annual leave coming to me. I promised my wife a holiday in Majorca. Believe me, I deserve it."

"Majorca?" said Zimbelman. "I've never heard of it."

"A warm, wonderful island. I owe it to her. She brought the children up. Wonderful children."

"Do you think we'll be able to save something in Poland?" asked Zimbelman.

"Of course. Prices there are much lower, and if we go on getting our salaries in Austrian currency, we'll be able to save a lot."

The fields grew greener and greener. The pasture was cut into squares; they looked as if they had been measured with a ruler. A horse grazed in the field and a farmer's wife stood at her door. That was the way it had always been and that was the way it was now too.

"How strange it is," said the waitress, and tears came into her eyes.

"What do you mean?" said the conductor. "This is only a transition. Soon we'll arrive in Poland. New sights, new people. A man must broaden his horizons, no?"

"And I feel so bad, so like nothing at all."

"It's only a transition, only a transition. Soon we'll reach the station, the kiosk. I'm very partial to the lemonade, it's a local brand, very tasty." The words that had been buried in him for years suddenly blossomed. He wanted to lavish words on her. But the ones that he had in his possession did not seem able, for some reason, to combine into coherent sentences.

The rabbi woke from his slumbers and said aloud: "What do they want? All these years they haven't paid any attention to the Torah. Me they locked away in an old-age home. They didn't want to have anything to do with me. Now they want to go to Poland. There is no atonement without asking forgiveness first."

The rabbi's voice took the column of people by surprise. He spoke in a jumble of Hebrew and Yiddish. The people could not understand a word he said, but his anger was obvious. The hotel owner did not stop pushing the wheelchair. He pushed it as if he had been doing so for years.

Mitzi approached Dr. Langmann, who was walking absorbed in himself, and told him that the night before she had dreamed a very vivid dream. Dr. Langmann, who could not abide idle chatter, averted his long, bald head and said that he too had been unable to sleep because of the dogs. Mitzi told him how when she was still a little girl of five or six her father had taken her to Vienna, to the Prater: It was a wonderful autumn day but her father, a busy, troubled man, only wanted to tire her out before taking her to the hospital to have her tonsils out. When they reached the hospital she sensed the impending catastrophe and tried to escape. All the hospital staff came running. The operation was performed. "And I dreamt it all last night, exactly as it happened."

"The station, the station!" a woman's voice exclaimed. The policemen at the station signaled to the policemen escorting the people.

"We've arrived, we've arrived at last!" cried Mitzi. From the station they could still see Badenheim: A low hill cut like a cone, with the roofs of the houses like little pieces of folded cardboard. Only the hotel and bell tower seemed real. The kiosk owner was delighted to see all the people, and their eyes lit up at the sight of the lemonade, the newspapers, and journals—a testimony to the life that was still going on around them. Dr. Langmann bought the financial weekly and studied it like a man returning to a beloved city after years of absence. His eye fell on some ridiculous item and he laughed out loud. Sally and Gertie equipped themselves with two big parcels—one of cigarettes and one of sweets. The yanuka dirtied his suit and they busied themselves with cleaning it.

The skeptical bitterness did not leave the rabbi's lips. He placed no faith in these delusions. He had seen much in his life and all that was left in him was suspicion, and in this transition too his suspicions did not cease but only grew more intense. The headwaiter bought sausages. The dog liked sausages. The headwaiter's happiness knew no bounds.

The musicians crowded together in a corner, in the shade. Some of the plates had been broken on the way, and they had to unpack their cases and pack them again. This annoying necessity, which gave rise to anger and mutual recriminations, marred the festive atmosphere a little. Strangely enough, Mandelbaum did not despise them. He asked them how they were and inquired about the resorts they played in. His questions relaxed the tension a little.

The people did not forget Samitzky and bought him some bottles of vodka. Samitzky sat on a bench and did not utter a word. "When are we leaving?" asked a woman's voice. Another woman stood next to the closed ticket office and made

herself up. Salo put on his old expression again, his traveling salesman's expression. At any moment, it seemed, he would open his medium-sized suitcase and offer his samples for sale. From here the carriages would pick the people up and there was always the same fragrance in the air, the fragrance of the transition from the town to the country, and from the station to the enchanted Badenheim. There were no carriages now, but the fragrance still lingered in the air, mingled with an intoxicating dampness.

And suddenly the sky opened and light broke out of the heavens. The valley in all its glory and the hills scattered about filled with the abundance, and even the trembling, leafless trees standing wretchedly at the edge of the station seemed to breathe a sigh of relief.

"What did I tell you?" exclaimed Dr. Pappenheim, opening his arms in an expansive gesture that seemed too big for him. Tears of joy came into his eyes. All the misery of the days in confinement suddenly burst inside him.

Sally and Gertie wrapped the yanuka up warmly. Karl took the sweater off the bottle: Two little fish were already dead and the rest floated limply and listlessly in the water. "Can no one help me?" cried Karl despairingly.

The light poured from the low hills directly onto the station platform. There was nowhere to hide. "Come and see, everybody!" Mitzi suddenly cried, in an affected feminine voice. A little distance away, as if on an illuminated tray, a man was walking with two armed policemen behind him. They came closer as if they were being borne on the light.

"Peter, Peter!" shouted the hotel owner in relief.

Peter.

But their amazement was cut short. An engine, an engine coupled to four filthy freight cars, emerged from the hills and stopped at the station. Its appearance was as sudden as if it had risen from a pit in the ground. "Get in!" yelled invisible voices. And the people were sucked in. Even those who were standing with a bottle of lemonade in their hands, a bar of chocolate, the headwaiter with his dog—they were all sucked in as easily as grains of wheat poured into a funnel. Nevertheless Dr. Pappenheim found time to make the following remark: "If the coaches are so dirty it must mean that we have not far to go."

Auschwitz

Of the many Holocaust survivors' memoirs, the outstanding is today generally regarded as Primo Levi's *Survival in Auschwitz* (1960). Primo Levi was a major Italian novelist. The translation is by Stuart Wolf.

The doors had been closed at once, but the train did not move until evening. We had learnt of our destination with relief. Auschwitz: a name without significance for us at that time, but it at least implied some place on this earth.

The train traveled slowly, with long, unnerving halts. Through the slit we saw the tall pale cliffs of the Adige Valley and the names of the last Italian cities disappear behind us. We passed the Brenner at midday of the second day and everyone stood up, but no one said a word. The thought of the return journey stuck in my heart, and I cruelly pictured to myself the inhuman joy of that other journey, with doors open, no one wanting to flee, and the first Italian names . . . and I looked around and wondered how many, among that poor human dust, would be struck by fate. Among the forty-five people in my wagon only four saw their homes again; and it was by far the most fortunate wagon.

We suffered from thirst and cold; at every stop we clamoured for water, or even a handful of snow, but we were rarely heard; the soldiers of the escort drove off anybody who tried to approach the convoy. Two young mothers, nursing their children, groaned night and day, begging for water. Our state of nervous tension made the hunger, exhaustion and lack of sleep seem less of a torment. But the hours of darkness were nightmares without end.

There are few men who know how to go to their deaths with dignity, and often they are not those whom one would expect. Few know how to remain silent and respect the silence of others. Our restless sleep was often interrupted by noisy and futile disputes, by curses, by kicks and blows blindly delivered to ward off some encroaching and inevitable contact. Then someone would light a candle, and its mournful flicker would reveal an obscure agitation, a human mass, extended across the floor, confused and continuous, sluggish and aching, rising here and there in sudden convulsions and immediately collapsing again in exhaustion.

Through the slit, known and unknown names of Austrian cities, Salzburg, Vienna, then Czech, finally Polish names. On the evening of the fourth day the cold became intense: The train ran through interminable black pine forests, climbing perceptibly. The snow was high. It must have been a branch line as the stations were small and almost deserted. During the halts, no one tried any more to communicate with the outside world: We felt ourselves by now "on the other side." There was a long halt in open country. The train started up with extreme slowness, and the convoy stopped for the last time, in the dead of night, in the middle of a dark silent plain.

On both sides of the track rows of red and white lights appeared as far as the eye could see; but there was none of that confusion of sounds which betrays inhabited places even from a distance. By the wretched light of the last candle, with the rhythm of the wheels, with every human sound now silenced, we awaited what was to happen.

Next to me, crushed against me for the whole journey, there had been a woman. We had known each other for many years, and the misfortune had struck us together but we knew little of each other. Now, in the hour of decision, we said to each other things that are never said among the living. We said farewell and it was short; everybody said farewell to life through his neighbour. We had no more fear.

The climax came suddenly. The door opened with a crash, and the dark echoed with outlandish orders in that curt, barbaric barking of Germans in command which seems to give vent to a millennial anger. A vast platform appeared before us, lit up by reflectors. A little beyond it, a row of lorries. Then everything was silent again. Someone translated: We had to climb down with our luggage and deposit it alongside the train. In a moment the platform was swarming with shadows. But we were afraid to break that silence: Everyone busied himself with his luggage, searched for someone else, called to somebody, but timidly, in a whisper.

A dozen SS men stood around, legs akimbo, with an indifferent air. At a certain moment they moved among us, and in a subdued tone of voice, with faces of stone, began to interrogate us rapidly, one by one, in bad Italian. They did not interrogate everybody, only a few: "How old? Healthy or ill?" And on the basis of the reply they pointed in two different directions.

Everything was as silent as an aquarium, or as in certain dream sequences. We had expected something more apocalyptic: They seemed simple police agents. It was disconcerting and disarming. Someone dared to ask for his luggage: They replied, "luggage afterwards." Someone else did not want to leave his wife: They said, "together again afterwards." Many mothers did not want to be separated from their children: They said "good, good, stay with child." They behaved with the calm assurance of people doing their normal duty of every day. But Renzo stayed an instant too long to say goodbye to Francesca, his fiancée, and with a single blow they knocked him to the ground. It was their everyday duty.

In less than ten minutes all the fit men had been collected together in a group. What happened to the others, to the women, to the children, to the old men, we could establish neither then nor later: The night swallowed them up, purely and simply. Today, however, we know that in that rapid and summary choice each one of us had been judged capable or not of working usefully for the Reich; we know that of our convoy no more than ninety-six men and twenty-nine women entered the respective camps of Monowitz-Buna and Birkenau, and that of all the others, more than five hundred in number, not one was living two days later. We also know that

not even this tenuous principle of discrimination between fit and unfit was always followed, and that later the simpler method was often adopted of merely opening both the doors of the wagon without warning or instructions to the new arrivals. Those who by chance climbed down on one side of the convoy entered the camp; the others went to the gas chamber.

This is the reason why three-year-old Emilia died: The historical necessity of killing the children of Jews was self-demonstrative to the Germans. Emilia, daughter of Aldo Levi of Milan, was a curious, ambitious, cheerful, intelligent child; her parents had succeeded in washing her during the journey in the packed car in a tub with tepid water which the degenerate German engineer had allowed them to draw from the engine that was dragging us all to death.

Thus, in an instant, our women, our parents, our children disappeared. We saw them for a short while as an obscure mass at the other end of the platform; then we saw nothing more.

Instead, two groups of strange individuals emerged into the light of the lamps. They walked in squads, in rows of three, with an odd, embarrassed step, head dangling in front, arms rigid. On their heads they wore comic berets and were all dressed in long striped overcoats, which even by night and from a distance looked filthy and in rags. They walked in a large circle around us, never drawing near, and in silence began to busy themselves with our luggage and to climb in and out of the empty wagons.

We looked at each other without a word. It was all incomprehensible and mad, but one thing we had understood. This was the metamorphosis that awaited us. Tomorrow we would be like them.

Without knowing how I found myself loaded on to a lorry with thirty others; the lorry sped into the night at full speed. It was covered and we could not see outside, but by the shaking we could tell that the road had many curves and bumps. Are we unguarded? Throw ourselves down? It is too late, too late, we are all "down." In any case we are soon aware that we are not without guard. He is a strange guard, a German soldier bristling with arms. We do not see him because of the thick darkness, but we feel the hard contact every time that a lurch of the lorry throws us all in a heap. At a certain point he switches on a pocket torch and instead of shouting threats of damnation at us, he asks us courteously, one by one, in German and in pidgin language, if we have any money or watches to give him, seeing that they will not be useful to us any more. This is no order, no regulation: It is obvious that it is a small private initiative of our Charon. The matter stirs us to anger and laughter and brings relief.

What we have so far said and will say concerns the ambiguous life of the Lager. In our days many men have lived in this cruel manner, crushed against the bottom, but each for a relatively short period; so that we can perhaps ask ourselves if it is necessary or good to retain any memory of this exceptional human state.

To this question we feel that we have to reply in the affirmative. We are in fact convinced that no human experience is without meaning or unworthy of analysis, and that fundamental values, even if they are not positive, can be deduced from this particular world which we are describing. We would also like to consider that the Lager was preeminently a gigantic biological and social experiment.

Thousands of individuals, differing in age, condition, origin, language, culture and customs, are enclosed within barbed wire: There they live a regular, controlled life which is identical for all and inadequate to all needs, and which is more rigorous than any experimenter could have set up to establish what is essential and what adventitious to the conduct of the human animal in the struggle for life.

We do not believe in the most obvious and facile deduction: that man is fundamentally brutal, egoistic and stupid in his conduct once every civilized institution is taken away, and that the Häftling is consequently nothing but a man without inhibitions. We believe, rather, that the only conclusion to be drawn is that in the face of driving necessity and physical disabilities many social habits and instincts are reduced to silence.

But another fact seems to us worthy of attention: There comes to light the existence of two particularly well differentiated categories among men—the saved and the drowned. Other pairs of opposites (the good and the bad, the wise and the foolish, the cowards and the courageous, the unlucky and the fortunate) are considerably less distinct, they seem less essential, and above all

they allow for more numerous and complex intermediary gradations.

This division is much less evident in ordinary life; for there it rarely happens that a man loses himself. A man is normally not alone, and in his rise or fall is tied to the destinies of his neighbours; so that it is exceptional for anyone to acquire unlimited power, or to fall by a succession of defeats into utter ruin. Moreover, everyone is normally in possession of such spiritual, physical and even financial resources that the probabilities of a shipwreck, of total inadequacy in the face of life, are relatively small. And one must take into account a definite cushioning effect exercised both by the law, and by the moral sense which constitutes a self-imposed law; for a country is considered the more civilized the more the wisdom and efficiency of its laws hinder a weak man from becoming too weak or a powerful one too powerful.

But in the Lager things are different: here the struggle to survive is without respite, because everyone is desperately and ferociously alone. If some Null Achtzehn vacillates, he will find no one to extend a helping hand; on the contrary, someone will knock him aside, because it is in no one's interest that there will be one more "musselman" dragging himself to work every day; and if someone, by a miracle of savage patience and cunning, finds a new method of avoiding the hardest work, a new art which yields him an ounce of bread, he will try to keep his method secret, and he will be esteemed and respected for this, and will derive from it an exclusive, personal benefit; he will become stronger and so will be feared, and who is feared is, ipso facto, a candidate for survival.

In history and in life one sometimes seems to glimpse a ferocious law which states: "To he that has, will be given; from he that has not, will be taken away." In the Lager, where man is alone and where the struggle for life is reduced to its primordial mechanism, this unjust law is openly in force, is recognized by all. With the adaptable, the strong and astute individuals, even the leaders willingly keep contact, sometimes even friendly contact, because they hope later to perhaps derive some benefit. But with the musselmans, the men in decay, it is not even worth speaking, because one knows already that they will complain and will speak about what they used to eat at home. Even less worthwhile is it to make friends with them, because they have no distinguished acquaintances in camp, they do not gain any extra rations, they do not work in profitable Kommandos and they know no secret method of organizing. And in any case, one knows that they are only here on a visit, that in a few weeks nothing will remain of them but a handful of ashes in some nearby field and a crossed-out number on a register. Although engulfed and swept along without rest by the innumerable crowd of those similar to them, they suffer and drag themselves along in an opaque intimate solitude, and in solitude they die or disappear, without leaving a trace in anyone's memory.

The result of this pitiless process of natural selection could be read in the statistics of Lager population movements. At Auschwitz, in 1944, of the old Jewish prisoners (we will not speak of the others here, as their condition was different), *"kleine Nummer,"* low numbers less than fifteen thousand, only a few hundred had survived; not one was an ordinary Häftling, vegetating in the ordinary Kommandos, and subsisting on the normal ration. There remained only the doctors, tailors, shoemakers, musicians, cooks, young attractive homosexuals, friends or compatriots of some authority in the camp; or they were particularly pitiless, vigorous and inhuman individuals, installed (following an investiture by the SS command, which showed itself in such choices to possess satanic knowledge of human beings) in the posts of Kapos, *Blockältester,* etc.; or finally, those who, without fulfilling particular functions, had always succeeded through their astuteness and energy in successfully organizing, gaining in this way, besides material advantages and reputation, the indulgence and esteem of the powerful people in the camp. Whosoever does not know how to become an "Organisator," "Kombinator," "Prominent" (the savage eloquence of these words!) soon becomes a "musselman." In life, a third way exists, and is in fact the rule; it does not exist in the concentration camp.

To sink is the easiest of matters; it is enough to carry out all the orders one receives, to eat only the ration, to observe the discipline of the work and the camp. Experience showed that only exceptionally could one survive more than three months in this way. All the musselmans who finished in the gas chambers have the same story, or more exactly, have no story; they followed the slope down to the bottom, like streams that run down to the sea. On their entry into the camp, through basic incapacity, or by misfortune, or through some banal incident, they are overcome before they can adapt themselves; they are beaten by time, they do not begin to learn German, to disentangle the infernal knot of laws and prohibitions until their body is already in decay, and nothing can save them from selections or from death by exhaustion. Their life is short, but their number is endless; they, the *Muselmänner,* the drowned, form the backbone of the camp, an anonymous mass, continually renewed and always identical, of nonmen who march and labour in silence, the divine spark dead within them, already too empty to really suffer. One hesitates to call them living: One hesitates to call their death death, in the face of which they have no fear, as they are too tired to understand.

They crowd my memory with their faceless presences, and if I could enclose all the evil of our time in one image, I would choose this image which is familiar to me: an emaciated man, with head dropped and shoulders curved, on whose face and in whose eyes not a trace of a thought is to be seen.

If the drowned have no story, and single and broad is the path to perdition, the paths to salvation are many, difficult and improbable.

The most traveled road, as we have stated, is the *"Prominenz." "Prominenten"* is the name for the camp officials, from the Häftling-director *(Lagerältester)* to the Kapos, the cooks, the nurses, the night-guards, even to the hut-sweepers and to the *Scheissminister* and *Bademeister* (superintendents of the latrines and showers). We are more particularly interested in the Jewish prominents, because while the others are automatically invested with offices as they enter the camp in virtue of their natural supremacy, the Jews have to plot and struggle hard to gain them.

The Jewish prominents form a sad and notable human phenomenon. In them converge present, past and atavistic sufferings, and the tradition of hostility towards the stranger makes of them monsters of asociality and insensitivity.

They are the typical product of the structure of the German Lager: If one offers a position of privilege to a few individuals in a state of slavery, exacting in exchange the betrayal of a natural solidarity with their comrades, there will certainly be someone who will accept. He will be withdrawn from the common law and will become untouchable; the more power that he is given, the more he will be consequently hateful and hated. When he is given the command of a group of unfortunates, with the right of life or death over them, he will be cruel and tyrannical, because he will understand that if he is not sufficiently so, someone else, judged more suitable, will take over his post. Moreover, his capacity for hatred, unfulfilled in the direction of the oppressors, will double back, beyond all reason, on the oppressed; and he will only be satisfied when he has unloaded on to his underlings the injury received from above.

We are aware that this is very distant from the picture that is usually given of the oppressed who unite, if not in resistance, at least in suffering. We do not deny that this may be possible when oppression does not pass a certain limit, or perhaps when the oppressor, through inexperience or magnanimity, tolerates or favours it. But we state that in our days, in all countries in which a foreign people have set foot as invaders, an analogous position of rivalry and hatred among the subjected has been brought about; and this, like many other human characteristics, could be experienced in the Lager in the light of particularly cruel evidence.

The Final Solution

Leni Yahl, the Israeli historian of the Holocaust, summarizes Hitler's speeches against the Jews in late 1941 and early 1942 as it became clear that the war in Russia was not going well. The planning for the Final Solution of the Jewish question was undertaken at the Wannsee Conference in January 1942, in a Berlin suburb, by Adolf Eichmann and other senior Nazi officials.

Some historians have seen the Final Solution of systematic extermination of the Jews as a response to the onset of German military failure in Russia. In Yahl's version, Hitler's long-term hatred of Jews was given a sharper edge by the Russian military situation and the Wannsee Conference, and implementation of the Final Solution arose from this moment but also from roots in the Nazi past. If Hitler had taken Moscow and Leningrad in December 1942, instead of being stopped at the approaches to the city, would he have been more generous to the Jews? There is no reason to think so.

This was a time of problems, tensions, and even apprehension for the Nazi regime. The campaign against Russia had been stalled before Moscow and Leningrad and the rigors of the Russian winter had inflicted a heavy blow on the unprepared German army. Not only were the troops inadequately clothed but the equipment was unsuited to the harsh climatic conditions; supplies were often cut off because of the collapse of the railway network. The Japanese attack on Pearl Harbor had changed the war situation. After the U.S. declaration of war on Japan. Hitler had no alternative but to declare war on the United States, though he could have been in no doubt as to the dangers that now faced him. On December 11 he convened the Reichstag, as was his wont at fateful moments, particularly in the international arena, and delivered a speech in which he tried to answer various urgent questions while declaring war on the United States.

Analysis of this speech suggests that Hitler felt a strong urge to explain and justify his actions and to bolster the confidence of his followers. As always, he claimed that his only desire was peace

Medieval caricature of Jews. From a Passover Haggadah.

and that his enemies had forced war on him. At the same time he proclaimed that "a historical correction of unique proportions has been imposed on us by the Creator," meaning the salvation of Europe. He described the triumphs of the German army in all the war arenas, but felt the need to cite climatic conditions as the reason for his postponement of the attack on Russia from May to June 1941. He had launched the war, he said, because otherwise the Russians would have attacked first and conquered all of Europe.

Hitler's main verbal onslaught, however, was directed against Roosevelt, whom he described as a slave to the Jewish warmongers, eager to enter the war because of his economic debacles in the United States. He accused the U.S. president of violating international law and of having, in contravention of all concepts of justice and law, restricted the freedom of movement of German nationals living in the United States. In fact, he accused Roosevelt of all those acts of deception and aggression of which he himself was guilty. Thus he spoke of "the deliberate incitement by this man who plays the peace lover and all the time is inciting to war." Roosevelt, Hitler claimed, together with Great Britain, was aiming at "untrammelled dictatorial rule over the world," and to achieve this aim would stop at no crime. The force behind him was the "eternal Jew." According to Hitler's political calculations, the confrontation with the United States was essential, but he certainly had had no

intention of launching this battle before he had triumphed over Russia. Now he knew only too well that the Russian *Blitzkrieg* had failed and that for the first time he had not been the initiator of an additional move but had been forced to adopt it as a result of the initiative of others.

Hitler's speech on the anniversary of his rise to power, January 30, 1942, can be seen as the continuation of his diatribe against his adversaries. This time he was not addressing the Reichstag, as was the tradition, but a popular meeting in the largest auditorium in the Berlin Sports Palace. He felt the need to appeal to the people directly in order to instill new spirit in them and strengthen their faith in him and in the future of the Reich. Again, he spoke of "international Jewry" that backed the misdeeds of all his enemies, but the main brunt of his attack this time was leveled at Great Britain. Then he reiterated his well-known interpretation of the history of Germany after World War I, whose collapse was brought about by the "eternal Jew." The greatest catastrophe at the time was class war which the Jews had encouraged since they "had interests in both camps. On the one hand, they directed capital and, on the other hand, they controlled the anti-Capitalists. Sometimes, in one family there were two brothers, one in each camp."

His main theme was the war, which had been brought about, so he asserted, by the hatred of others, mainly the British and the Americans. In contrast to the creative projects he had initiated, the leaders of those countries—"the chatterer and drunk, Churchill, and the madman, Roosevelt"—were not capable of creating anything, only of destroying. And since they hated the Germans, the Germans were obliged to hate them in return; and he went straight on to identify this hatred with the hatred of the Jews, "It is evident to us that this war can end only in the elimination of the Aryan peoples or the disappearance of Jewry from Europe." He then repeated his "prophesy" of January 30, 1939:

> This war will not end as the Jews imagine, namely, in the liquidation of all the European and Aryan peoples: The outcome of this war will be the extermination of Jewry. For the first time it will not be other nations who will bleed to death. For the first time we will practice the ancient Jewish law: an eye for an eye, a tooth for a tooth!

The wider the struggle, he said, the more anti-Semitism would spread!

> It will find fertile soil in every prison camp, in every family to whom we explain why, in the end, they must make sacrifices. And this world enemy, the wickedest of all times, will play his role no longer, at least for one thousand years.

Hitler went on to rant and boast, but again felt the need to justify the fact that the attack on Russia had been checked not, he claimed, by the Russians, but by the winter cold. At the end of the speech, he promised that the coming year would again be one of great victories, although he did not promise that it would bring the end of the war.

Hitler delivered this address ten days after the Wannsee Conference. Just as his speech of January 30, 1939, had provided the official sanction for the appointment of [Reinhard] Heydrich to run the Emigration Center [Transport Jews to Concentration Camps], he now endorsed the Final Solution as an integral part of his war policies and even set it up as the yardstick for success. Now that new difficulties faced him and new dangers threatened, Hitler attributed great significance to the plan for the extermination of the Jews, as if their destruc-

tion would confound his enemies and their death would symbolize his triumph.

The Wannsee Conference marked the beginning of the full-scale, comprehensive extermination operation and laid the foundations for its organization, which started immediately after the conference ended. According to the plans, the Jews of the Reich were to be deported first, and as noted before, Himmler intended the operation to encompass 150,000 victims. Eichmann immediately set to work. On January 31, 1942, he sent an express letter *(Schnellbrief)* marked "secret" to all the state police stations *(Stapoleitstellen)* in the Greater Reich that opened, "The evacuation of the Jews to the East, recently carried out in several areas, is the beginning of the final solution of the Jewish problem in the original Reich, in Ostmark, and in the Protectorate of Bohemia and Moravia."

He went on to explain that the operation had initially encompassed only isolated places and that only partial operations had been carried out, but now a full-scale operation was in preparation. He, therefore, requested precise data on the location of Jews in the Reich and gave instructions for compiling the data. He also specified which categories were to be excluded from the deportations—Jews who were partners in mixed marriages, foreign nationals, Jews employed in industry working for the war effort, and those over fifty-five who were *"particularly* weak and, hence, cannot be transferred." Also to be excluded were those over sixty-five. The number of people in the various categories, including, of course, those who were to be deported, should be determined. He ordered this information to be submitted within ten days. Next, Eichmann's office sent out "directives for the technical implementation of the evacuation of Jews to the General gouvernement." These directives listed the categories already noted in the express letter; in addition, they provided detailed instructions for the organization of the transports that were more or less identical with those familiar to us from the wave of deportations organized in the autumn of 1941. They stressed the need to include all tools and equipment of any kind in the possession of the evacuees.

The instructions were conveyed not only in writing. On March 4, 1942, Eichmann convened all his representatives from the territories outside the Reich in his office to discuss the organizational problems of the deportations. The participants were by now all well versed in the resolutions of the Wannsee Conference. Moreover, at the beginning of January instructions had already been sent in Himmler's name to stop further emigration of former German Jews from the occupied territories. At an additional meeting on March 6, the representatives were shown the plan for the evacuation of fifty-five thousand Jews from the Greater Reich, among them twenty thousand from Prague and eighteen thousand from Vienna.

The Elimination of Hungarian Jewry

The Budapest Jews had prospered under Hapsburg rule in the late-nineteenth and early-twentieth centuries. They were a highly educated group, prominent in business and the learned professions, especially in law. The Jews did less well in the rightist Hungarian republic that succeeded Hapsburg rule in 1918. They suffered severely during the early years of the war when Hungary was a German puppet state. But in 1944 there were still close to a million Jews in Budapest and a few other centers when Adolf Eichmann undertook their elimination—and half were exterminated before the war came to an end.

In 1962 Eichmann was captured by Israeli agents in Argentina, secretly taken to Jerusalem, put on public trial, and executed. The New Yorker magazine sent Hannah Arendt to report on the trial and her reports were collected in a best-selling book *Eichmann in Jerusalem* that aroused much criticism among American Jewish community leaders. In reading Arendt's account, it is not easy to see what they were so excited about.

Arendt mentioned how Eichmann made use of wealthy Hungarian Jewish community leaders in rounding up Jews for extermination. This may have been a shock at the time to many, but it was even then a well-known fact. Indeed a prominent Hungarian Jewish community leader who had collaborated with Eichmann and survived the war—the "Dr. Kastner" mentioned in Arendt's account—was shot dead with impunity on the streets of Jerusalem by a Holocaust survivor. In the early 1960s, American Jews' understanding of how the Holocaust operated was extremely naive, and remains so to this day in some quarters.

Hannah Arendt was a German Jewish émigré—first in the 1930s to Paris and then to New York—who was one of the leading academic political philosophers of her generation. As a graduate student in Germany in the late 1920s, she was a disciple and also mistress of Martin Heidegger, the eminent phenomenological philosopher who became a big Nazi. It appears that there was a long correspondence between Arendt and Heidegger, resuming after the War, some of which was made public in a book published in 1995. She remained devoted to him.

Hungary, mentioned earlier in connection with the troublesome question of Eichmann's conscience, was constitutionally a kingdom without a king. The country, though without access to the sea and possessing neither navy nor merchant fleet, was ruled—or, rather, held in trust for the nonexistent king—by an admiral, Regent or *Reichsverweser* Nikolaus von Horthy. The only visible sign of royalty was an abundance of *Hofräte*, councilors to the nonexistent court. Once upon a time, the Holy Roman Emperor had been King of Hungary, and more recently, after 1806, the *kaiserlichkönigliche Monarchie* on the Danube had been precariously held together by the Hapsburgs, who were emperors *(Kaiser)* of Austria and kings of Hungary. In 1918, the Hapsburg Empire had been dissolved into Successor States, and Austria was now a republic, hoping for *Anschluss*, for union with Germany. Otto von Hapsburg was in exile, and he would never have been accepted as King of Hungary by the fiercely nationalistic Magyars; an authentically Hungarian royalty, on the other hand, did not even exist as a historical memory. So what Hungary was, in terms of recognized forms of government, only Admiral Horthy knew.

Behind the delusions of royal grandeur was an inherited feudal structure, with greater misery among the landless peasants and greater luxury among the few aristocratic families who literally owned the country than anywhere else in these poverty-stricken territories, the homeland of Europe's stepchildren. It was this background of unsolved social questions and general backwardness that gave Budapest society its specific flavor, as though Hungarians were a group of illusionists who had fed so long on self-deception that they had lost any sense of incongruity. Early in the 30s, under the influence of Italian Fascism, they had produced a strong Fascist movement, the so-called Arrow Cross men, and in 1938 they followed Italy by passing their first anti-Jewish legislation; despite the strong influence of the Catholic Church in the country, the rulings applied to baptized Jews who had been converted after 1919, and even those converted before that date were included three years later. And yet, when an all-inclusive anti-Semitism, based on race, had become official government policy, eleven Jews continued to sit in the upper chamber of the Parliament, and Hungary was the only Axis country to send Jewish troops—a hundred and thirty thousand of them, in auxiliary service, but in Hungarian uniform—to the Eastern front. The explanation of these inconsistencies is that the Hungarians, their official policy notwithstanding, were even more emphatic than other countries in distinguishing between native Jews and *Ostjuden*, between the "Magyarized" Jews of "Trianon Hungary" (established, like the other Successor States, by the Treaty of Trianon) and those of recently annexed territories. Hungary's sovereignty was respected by the Nazi government until March, 1944, with the result that for Jews the country became an island of safety in "an ocean of destruction." While it is understandable enough that—with the Red Army approaching through the Carpathian Mountains and the Hungarian government desperately trying to follow the example of Italy and conclude a separate armistice—the German government should have decided to occupy the country, it is almost incredible that at this stage of the game it should still have been "the order of the day to come to grips with the Jewish problem," the "liquidation" of which was "a prerequisite for involving Hungary in the war," as Veesenmayer put it in a report to the Foreign Office in December, 1943. For the "liquidation" of this "problem" involved the evacuation of eight hundred thousand Jews, plus an estimated hundred or hundred and fifty thousand converted Jews.

Be that as it may, as I have said earlier, because of the greatness and the urgency of the task Eichmann arrived in Budapest in March, 1944, with his whole staff, which he could easily assemble, since the job had been finished everywhere else. He called Wisliceny and Burner from Slovak and Greece, Abromeit from Yugoslavia, Dannecker from Paris and Bulgaria, Siegfried Seidl from his post as Commander of Theresienstadt, and, from Vienna, Hermann Krumey, who became his deputy in Hungary. From Berlin, he brought all the more important members of his office staff: Rolf Günther, who had been his chief deputy; Franz Novak, his deportation officer; and Otto Hunsche, his legal expert. Thus, the *Sondereinsatzkommando* Eichmann (Eichmann Special Operation Unit) consisted of about ten men, plus some clerical assistants, when it set up its headquarters in Budapest. On the very evening of their arrival, Eichmann and his men invited the

Jewish leaders to a conference, to persuade them to form a Jewish Council, through which they could issue their orders and to which they would give, in return, absolute jurisdiction over all Jews in Hungary. This was no easy trick at this moment and in that place. It was a time when, in the words of the Papal Nuncio, "the whole world knew what deportation meant in practice;" in Budapest, moreover, the Jews had "had a unique opportunity to follow the fate of European Jewry. We knew very well about the work of the *Einsatzgruppen.* We knew more than was necessary about Auschwitz," as Dr. Kastner was to testify at Nuremberg. Clearly, more than Eichmann's allegedly "hypnotic powers" was needed to convince anyone that the Nazis would recognize the sacred distinction between "Magyarized" and Eastern Jews; self-deception had to have been developed to a high art to allow Hungarian Jewish leaders to believe at this moment that "it can't happen here"—"How can they send the Jews of Hungary outside Hungary?"—and to keep believing it even when the realities contradicted this belief every day of the week. How this was achieved came to light in one of the most remarkable non sequiturs uttered on the witness stand: The future members of the Central Jewish Committee (as the Jewish Council was called in Hungary) had heard from neighboring Slovak that Wisliceny, who was now negotiating with them, accepted money readily, and they also knew that despite all bribes he "had deported all the Jews in Slovak. . . ." From which Mr. Freudiger concluded: "I understood that it was necessary to find ways and means to establish relationships with Wisliceny."

Eichmann's cleverest trick in these difficult negotiations was to see to it that he and his men acted as though they were corrupt. The president of the Jewish community, Hofrat Samuel Stern, a member of Horthy's Privy Council, was treated with exquisite courtesy and agreed to be head of the Jewish Council. He and the other members of the Council felt reassured when they were asked to supply typewriters and mirrors, women's lingerie and eau de cologne, original Watteaus and eight pianos—even though seven of these were gracefully returned by Hauptsturmführer Novak, who remarked, "But, gentlemen, I don't want to open a piano store. I only want to play the piano." Eichmann himself visited the Jewish Library and the Jewish Museum, and assured everybody that

all measures would be temporary. And corruption, first simulated as a trick, soon turned out to be real enough, though it did not take the form the Jews had hoped. Nowhere else did Jews spend so much money without any results whatever. In the words of the strange Mr. Kastner, "A Jew who trembles for his life and that of his family loses all sense of money." *(Sic!)* This was confirmed during the trial through testimony given by Philip von Freudiger, mentioned above, as well as through the testimony of Joel Brand, who had represented a rival Jewish body in Hungary, the Zionist Relief and Rescue Committee. Krumey received no less than two hundred and fifty thousand dollars from Freudiger in April, 1944, and the Rescue Committee paid twenty thousand dollars merely for the privilege of meeting with Wisliceny and some men of the SS Counterintelligence service. At this meeting, each of those present received an additional tip of a thousand dollars, and Wisliceny brought up again the so-called Europe Plan, which he had proposed in vain in 1942 and according to which Himmler supposedly would be prepared to spare all Jews except those in Poland for a ransom of two or three million dollars. On the strength of this proposal, which had been shelved long before, the Jews now started paying installments to Wisliceny. Even Eichmann's "idealism" broke down in this land of unheard-of abundance. The prosecution, though it could not prove that Eichmann had profited financially while on the job, stressed rightly his high standard of living in Budapest, where he could afford to stay at one of the best hotels, was driven around by a chauffeur in an amphibious car, an unforgettable gift from his later enemy Kurt Becher, went hunting and horseback riding, and enjoyed all sorts of previously unknown luxuries under the tutelage of his new friends in the Hungarian government.

There existed, however, a sizable group of Jews in the country whose leaders, at least, indulged less in self-deception. The Zionist movement had always been particularly strong in Hungary, and it now had its own representation in the recently formed Relief and Rescue Committee (the *Vaadat Ezra va Hazalah*), which, maintaining close contact with the Palestine Office, had helped refugees from Poland and Slovak, from Yugoslavia and Rumania; the committee was in constant communication with the

American Joint Distribution Committee, which financed their work, and they had also been able to get a few Jews into Palestine, legally or illegally. Now that catastrophe had come to their own country, they turned to forging "Christian papers," certificates of baptism, whose bearers found it easier to go underground. Whatever else they might have been, the Zionist leaders knew they were outlaws, and they acted accordingly. Joel Brand, the unlucky emissary who was to present to the Allies, in the midst of the war, Himmler's proposal to give them a million Jewish lives in exchange for ten thousand trucks, was one of the leading officials of the Relief and Rescue Committee, and he came to Jerusalem to testify about his dealings with Eichmann, as did his former rival in Hungary, Philip von Freudiger. While Freudiger, whom Eichmann, incidentally, did not remember at all, recalled the rudeness with which he had been treated at these interviews, Brand's testimony actually substantiated much of Eichmann's own account of how he had negotiated with the Zionists. Brand had been told that "an idealistic German" was now talking to him, "an idealistic Jew"—two honorable enemies meeting as equals during a lull in the battle. Eichmann had said to him: "Tomorrow perhaps we shall again be on the battlefield." It was, of course, a horrible comedy, but it did go to show that Eichmann's weakness for uplifting phrases with no real meaning was not a pose fabricated expressly for the Jerusalem trial. What is more interesting, one cannot fail to note that in meeting with the Zionists neither Eichmann nor any other member of the *Sondereinsatzkommando* employed the tactics of sheer lying that they had used for the benefit of the gentlemen of the Jewish Council. Even "language rules" were suspended, and most of the time a spade was called a spade. Moreover, when it was a question of serious negotiations—over the amount of money that might buy an exit permit, over the Europe Plan, over the exchange of lives for trucks—not only Eichmann but everybody concerned: Wisliceny, Becher, the gentlemen of the Counterintelligence service whom Joel Brand used to meet every morning in a coffee house, turned to the Zionists as a matter of course. The reason for this was that the Relief and Rescue Committee possessed the required international connections and could

more easily produce foreign currency, whereas the members of the Jewish Council had nothing behind them but the more than dubious protection of Regent Horthy. It also became clear that the Zionist functionaries in Hungary had received greater privileges than the usual temporary immunity to arrest and deportation granted the members of the Jewish Council. The Zionists were free to come and go practically as they pleased, they were exempt from wearing the yellow star, they received permits to visit concentration camps in Hungary, and, somewhat later, Dr. Kastner, the original founder of the Relief and Rescue Committee, could even travel about Nazi Germany without any identification papers showing he was a Jew.

The organization of a Jewish Council was for Eichmann, with all his experience in Vienna, Prague, and Berlin, a routine matter that took no more than two weeks. The question now was whether he himself would be able to enlist the help of Hungarian officials for an operation of this magnitude. For him this was something new. In the ordinary course of events, it would have been handled for him by the Foreign Office and its representatives, in this instance, by the newly appointed Reich plenipotentiary, Dr. Edmund Veesenmayer, to whom Eichmann would have sent a "Jewish adviser." Eichmann himself clearly had no inclination for playing the role of adviser, a post that had nowhere carried a rank higher than *Hauptsturmführer,* or captain, whereas he was an *Obersturmbannführer,* or lieutenant colonel, two ranks higher. His greatest triumph in Hungary was that he could establish his own contacts. Three men were primarily concerned—Lászlo Endre, who because of an anti-Semitism that even Horthy had called "insane" had recently been appointed State Secretary in Charge of Political (Jewish) Affairs in the Ministry of the Interior; Lászlo Baky, also an undersecretary in the Ministry of the Interior, who was in charge of the *Gendarmerie,* the Hungarian police; and the police officer Lieutenant Colonel Ferenczy, who was directly in charge of deportations. With their help, Eichmann could be sure that everything, the issuance of the necessary decrees and the concentration of the Jews in the provinces, would proceed with "lightning speed." In Vienna, a special conference was held with the German State

Railroad officials, since this matter involved the transportation of nearly half a million people. Höss, at Auschwitz, was informed of the plans through his own superior, General Richard Glücks of the W.V.H.A., and ordered a new branch line of the railway built, to bring the cars within a few yards of the crematoria; the number of death commandos manning the gas chambers was increased from 224 to 860, so that everything was ready for killing between 6,000 and 1,200 people a day. When the trains began arriving, in May, 1944, very few "able-bodied men" were selected for labor, and these few worked in Krupp's fuse factory at Auschwitz. (Krupp's newly built factory near Breslau, in Germany, the Berthawerk, collected Jewish manpower wherever it could find it and kept those men in conditions that were unsurpassed even among the labor gangs in the death camps.)

The whole operation in Hungary lasted less than two months and came to a sudden stop at the beginning of July. Thanks chiefly to the Zionists, it had been better publicized than any other phase of the Jewish catastrophe, and Horthy had been deluged with protests from neutral countries and from the Vatican. The Papal Nuncio, though, deemed it appropriate to explain that the Vatican's protest did not spring "from a false sense of compassion"—a phrase that is likely to be a lasting monument to what the continued dealings with, and the desire to compromise with, the men who preached the gospel of "ruthless toughness" had done to the mentality of the highest dignitaries of the Church. Sweden once more led the way with regard to practical measures, by distributing entry permits, and Switzerland, Spain, and Portugal followed her example, so that finally about thirty-three thousand Jews were living in special houses in Budapest under the protection of neutral countries. The Allies had received and made public a list of seventy men whom they knew to be the chief culprits, and Roosevelt had sent an ultimatum threatening that "Hungary's fate will not be like any other civilized nation . . . unless the deportations are stopped." The point was driven home by an unusually heavy air raid on Budapest on July 2. Thus pressed from all sides, Horthy gave the order to stop the deportations, and one of the most damning pieces of evidence against Eichmann was the rather obvious

fact that he had not obeyed "the old fool's" order but, in mid-July, deported another fifteen hundred Jews who were at hand in a concentration camp near Budapest. To prevent the Jewish officials from informing Horthy, he assembled the members of the two representative bodies in his office, where Dr. Hunsche detained them, on various pretexts, until he learned that the train had left Hungarian territory. Eichmann remembered nothing of this episode, in Jerusalem, and although the judges were "convinced that the accused remembers his victory over Horthy very well," this is doubtful, since to Eichmann Horthy was not such a great personage.

This seems to have been the last train that left Hungary for Auschwitz. In August, 1944, the Red Army was in Rumania, and Eichmann was sent there on his wild-goose chase. When he came back, the Horthy regime had gathered sufficient courage to demand the withdrawal of the Eichmann commando, and Eichmann himself asked Berlin to let him and his men return, since they "had become superfluous." But Berlin did nothing of the sort, and was proved right, for in mid-October the situation once more changed abruptly. With the Russians no more than a hundred miles from Budapest, the Nazis succeeded in overthrowing the Horthy government and in appointing the leader of the Arrow Cross men, Ferenc Szalasi, head of state. No more transports could be sent to Auschwitz, since the extermination facilities were about to be dismantled, while at the same time the German shortage of labor had grown even more desperate. Now it was Veesenmayer, the Reich plenipotentiary, who negotiated with the Hungarian Ministry of the Interior for permission to ship fifty thousand Jews—men between sixteen and sixty, and women under forty—to the Reich; he added in his report that Eichmann hoped to send fifty thousand more. Since railroad facilities no longer existed, this led to the foot marches of November, 1944, which were stopped only by an order from Himmler. The Jews who were sent on the marches had been arrested at random by the Hungarian police, regardless of exemptions, to which by now many were entitled, regardless also of the age limits specified in the original directives. The marchers were escorted by Arrow Cross men, who robbed them and treated them with the utmost brutality. And that was the end. Of an original Jewish population of eight hundred thousand, some hundred and sixty thousand must still have remained in the Budapest ghetto—the countryside was *judenrein*—and of these tens of thousands became victims of spontaneous pogroms.

On February 13, 1945, the country surrendered to the Red Army.

The chief Hungarian culprits in the massacre were all put on trial, condemned to death, and executed. None of the German initiators, except Eichmann, paid with more than a few years in prison.

Jewish Collaborators with the Germans

Arendt's account of Hungarian Jewish community leaders' collaboration with Eichmann looks pretty mild compared to the following general assessment of European Jewish leaders' involvement with the German Jewish policy, written in 1992 by Raul Hilberg, the leading American historian of the Holocaust.

Hilberg's calm but devastating indictment passed with no controversy whatsoever. Is that because American Jewish community leaders have become more sophisticated since the days of the Arendt controversy three decades ago, or because they have wisely learned that on some subjects connected to Jewish victimization it is best to be silent?

A ubiquitous feature of Nazi domination of the Jewish communities was the system of *Judenräte,* or Jewish councils. These governing bodies were established under law or decree, or simply in pursuance of oral instructions. The councils were designed to serve two purposes. Primarily they were to be conduits for regulations imposed upon the Jews, but they were also intended to be the principal or exclusive channel for petitions or appeals from the captive victims to the perpetrators. The Germans did not want to deal with the Jews individually.

The role of the councils was consequently different from the activity of their peacetime predecessors. In prewar times, the various Jewish community organizations were essentially caretakers of synagogues, cemeteries, religious schools, and hospitals. The councils, on the other hand, were faced with massive Jewish unemployment, crowding, hunger, and epidemics. Long before Hitler came to power, Jewish leaders were concerned about improving the Jewish situation; now they pleaded for mitigations or postponements of

harsh restrictions and impositions. In earlier days, the Jewish communities would employ administrators, bookkeepers, and clerks to run community institutions; the new councils also established a regulatory bureaucracy, and in the east, where they were ghetto governments, they maintained a standing Jewish police force as well. Once, the Jewish leaders had carried out only a Jewish mission, but as members or functionaries of councils they were expected to enforce a multitude of peremptory demands of "the authorities," be it the supply of statistical information, the surrender of Jewish belongings, the recruitment of forced laborers, or the seizure of people for deportation. As one German official summarized the new system, "Jews who disobey instructions of the Jewish council are to be treated as saboteurs."

The aggregate membership of the councils is numbered in the many thousands. The principal reason for this high figure is geographic. Only in Central and Western Europe were councils set up on a country by country basis. In the east they were placed in charge of local communities city by city and town by town. It is true that there were more Jews in the Warsaw Ghetto than in France, more in the Lodz Ghetto than in Belgium, but most of the hundreds of ghettos in the east had relatively small populations, and in each of these communities there was a council burdened with problems as crushing as any. The size of the councils could vary. Twenty-four members was the rule for countries or cities, twelve or fewer for towns. In some regions or localities no councils were formed. They were dispensed with where killing began immediately, as in Croatia and Serbia or the cities of Dnepropetrovsk and Kiev in the occupied U.S.S.R. Councils were absent also in Denmark and Italy, two countries that had resisted German pressure. No council came into being in Athens, after local Jewish leaders decided with Greek backing to disappear in the mountains. By and large, however, councils covered the German-dominated continent.

Ordinarily, German agencies made no attempt to find out who was who in a Jewish community. The appointment process in a newly occupied city would often consist of a short search for a recognizable Jewish leader who would be told to fill a council with the requisite number of men. There were no specific rules for eligibility. Typically, an order by Security Police Chief Reinhard Heydrich to his mobile units operating behind the lines of German armies invading Poland in 1939 stated that councils were made up "so far as possible" of the "remaining suitable personalities" and rabbis. Not stated but self-explanatory was the requirement that council chairmen and key council members would be fluent in German.

Who then served on the councils? The appointments were overwhelmingly conventional. Choices had to be made quickly and the candidates were people who could be called upon on short notice. In the main, they were businessmen, professionals, religious figures, or prewar Jewish community officials. Younger men were elevated primarily in smaller towns. Women in leadership positions were rare. It would not have occurred to anyone to suggest a Communist or, for that matter, an ultrareligious Jew, whose garments and earlocks would have given offense to the Germans.

The first chairman of a Jewish council was Rabbi Leo Baeck. By background and appearance he was ideal for the post. The son of a rabbi who had written books, Baeck himself became a rabbi who wrote books. He belonged to the liberal branch of Judaism, while remaining traditional in his practice of the religion. Not a Zionist, he did not condemn the Zionist movement. When the First World War broke out, he volunteered to be "field rabbi," a position that did not make him a chaplain, inasmuch as the German army accorded this status only to Protestant and Catholic clergymen, but that did allow him to wear a German uniform and to pray publicly for the Emperor and for Germany.

Tall and bearded, Baeck was married to a rabbi's daughter, who was his perfect wife until her death in 1937. He had a pulpit and a teaching position in a liberal Jewish seminary. At home his private library was located in a room equipped with a ladder on wheels running along the bookshelves. During the 1920s Baeck was also active in Jewish community politics, and in 1933 he was hoisted by his supporters into the top position of the newly formed Reich Representation of Jewish Land Federations.

Between 1933 and 1939, the Nazi regime gradually impoverished the Jews and called for their emigration. At this point the Jewish community organizations increased their welfare work and tried to facilitate the departure of families, children, and adolescents. By 1938 this machinery was taken over by the Gestapo. Baeck, still at the helm, was sixty-five years old. Having turned down all opportunities for emigration, he was determined to stay at his post as long as ten Jews were left in Germany. Baeck projected reliability and respectability to the remaining Jews, and together with his associates he also presented to the community a constellation of reassuring familiar faces.

After the outbreak of war, however, the Reichsvereingung, as the Jewish council was called in Germany, was drawn into such activities as pushing Jewish families into Jewish apartment houses and preparing victims for transport to the east. Under orders of the Gestapo, Baeck's subordinates assigned space, resources, and personnel for the efficient conduct of the deportations. Baeck himself presided at meetings of the Reichsvereingung during these twilight hours of German Jewry, but the protocols reveal only a shadowy figure who did not speak. In January 1943, Baeck was sent to the "Old People's Ghetto" of Theresiendstadt. More than ten Jews were left in Germany, but they were a small fraction of the Jewish population before 1933.

In Austria, which was annexed in March 1938, almost all the Jews lived in Vienna. The Jewish community leaders in the city were immediately placed under arrest, and the SS brought in a "practitioner" who would know what to do with them. The practitioner was Adolf Eichmann. His first move was to reject the president of the Jewish community, Dr. Desider Friedmann, perhaps because Friedmann had been a member of a lodge or because he had accompanied the last Austrian chancellor on an economic mission. Instead Eichmann selected Dr. Josef Löwenherz, who was the vice president of the prewar community and also a veteran Zionist, but who was managerial and considered nonpartisan in intra-Jewish politics. At the first meeting of Eichmann and Löwenherz, the thirty-two-year-old SS lieutenant slapped the stately Jewish leader, who was twenty years his senior, and gave him his instructions. As Eichmann wrote to a friend in the SS: He had the Jewish leaders trotting along and working diligently. Löwenherz in fact worked in Vienna until the Red Army occupied the city seven years later. Most of Austria's Jews emigrated in 1938 and 1939, but the large majority of the remainder were deported in 1941 and 1942, with the diligent assistance of the community machinery.

Continuity was also common in occupied Poland. The Lublin Judenrat was virtually in its entirety the prewar Jewish leadership. In Warsaw, the peacetime president of the Jewish community had fled and his place was taken by his fifty-nine-year-old deputy, Adam Czerniakow. An engineer, Czerniakow had been trained in Germany before the First World War and had held administrative posts in Poland between the wars. As chairman of the Warsaw Jewish Council he had harsh words for Jewish leaders who had fled or emigrated right after the German invasion. He considered them deserters.

A deputy of another kind was Chaim Rumkowski, the Jewish "Elder" of Lodz. In that city, the prewar president was also gone, the vice president moved to the top post, and Rumkowski became the new vice president. Early during the occupation most of the new council members were shot and Rumkowski was chosen as the Jewish leader by the German overlords. Tall, blue-eyed, silver-haired, and clean-shaven, he was sixty-two years old. He did not have much education, and as a merchant before and after the First World War he experienced one or two business failures, but he attempted to discharge his debts. A Zionist, he involved himself in community affairs and managed several orphanages with devotion. Widowed and childless, he became a dedicated autocrat in the ghetto. He was able to act alone, because the fear-stricken men who had replaced the murdered councilmen were merely his advisory board.

Increasingly self-assured, Rumkowski accustomed himself to power. Now he could reward friends and intimidate adversaries. With every step he focused attention on his unique position. When he married again, he chose a woman less than half his age. When bank notes were printed in the ghetto, they bore his likeness. Frequently he made speeches with phrases like "I do not like to waste words," "My plan is based on sound logic," "I have decided," "I ordered," "I forbid," and "My Jews." Rumkowski presided over his community through periods of starvation and deportations for almost five years.

In Bialystok, power was given by the council to an engineer, Ephraim Barasz, because the council chairman, Rabbi Gedalia Rosenman, was too feeble to hold the office in more than a titular way. Barasz, like many major Jewish leaders in Poland, was a Zionist. Born in a smaller town nearby, he moved to Bialystok in 1934 and became the genuine manager of the community organization. Between 1939 and 1941 the city was under Soviet rule. When the Germans occupied Bialystok, Barasz became the vice chairman of the council. He was forty-nine. Although the council met periodically under Rosenman, Barasz was clearly the man in charge. At a meeting of June 29, 1942, a council member effusively praised Barasz. The council, he said, had become a government and Barasz its prime minister, "as well as the minister of the interior, minister of industry, because in the ghetto everything must be concentrated in one hand."

Control was also solidified in one man in Vilnius, but there the process took longer and it was the outcome of massive upheavals and dire insecurity in the Jewish community. Like Bialystok, Vilnius was incorporated to the U.S.S.R. from 1939 to 1941, but unlike the Bialystok Jews, the community in Vilnius lost more than half of its residents in several waves of shootings during the initial months of the German occupation. A Judenrat was formed immediately upon orders of the military commander, but most of its members, including the chairman, were killed after a brief period. Following this massacre, two ghettos were established, each with its own Judenrat. Soon there was a partial exchange of population. Old people, the ill, orphans, and the unemployed were sent to Ghetto No. 2. Artisans and holders of work permits were moved to Ghetto No. 1. Ghetto No. 2 was doomed and during the following year, Ghetto No. 1 became a disciplined, tightly run community. The prime mover of this militarization was the ghetto's police chief, Jacob Gens. By the middle of 1942, he was named by the German overseers as the "Ghetto Representa-tive," and the Judenrat chairman, Anatol Fried, became his deputy in an outright switch of positions.

Gens was thirty-nine nears old when he took over the reins of the Vilnius ghetto. In his youth he pursued academic studies, which he interrupted to join the newly formed Lithuanian army at the age of sixteen. There he rose to the rank of Senior Lieutenant and married a non-Jewish Lithuanian woman who was also well educated. He wanted a transfer from the infantry to the nascent Lithuanian air force, but the air arm accepted only bachelors. Gens then continued his studies at the university, remaining a reserve officer. He taught languages, literature, and physical education in a Jewish high school, moved to Kaunas with his wife and baby daughter, and eventually worked for the Shell Oil Corporation. Gens was a Lithuanian patriot who made anti-Soviet speeches, but he was also a conscious Jew who followed the right-wing militant Zionist movement, known as the Revisionists and led by Vladimir Jabotinsky. This man, who died in 1940, had preached that if Jews would not liquidate the Diaspora, the Diaspora would liquidate the Jews. Gens, working hard, stayed in Lithuania. Under the gathering war clouds of the late 1930s he was called back into the army, attended staff officers school, and was promoted to captain. When the Soviets arrived, he lost his job and was in danger of being purged. He found refuge in Vilnius.

As police chief of Ghetto No. 1, Gens appointed several Revisionists to key positions in his department. When some of the inhabitants of Ghetto No. 2 tried to slip into his ghetto, he opposed the infiltration on the ground that the ill, the old, and the unskilled would add to the vulnerability of people who were healthier, younger, and more capable. Later, as Representative, he mobilized all the resources of the ghetto to make it a workshop, staking everything on its survivability until the moment of liberation. Like all Jews, Gens was subject to ghettoization, but as a practical matter, he did not have to be in the ghetto at all. He probably could have found refuge with the help of former Lithuanian army associates, and that of his wife, who was living at his insistence outside the ghetto. Alternatively he might have escaped to fight with Jewish partisans, who would have welcomed him as a trained military officer. But he chose to remain and be judged by history.

In emphasizing a policy of accommodation and production, Gens did not differ from other ghetto potentates. The Vilnius Ghetto, however, had a Jewish resistance movement, which he tolerated, but with which he was in competition. He was going to join it if all else failed; in the meantime he held it in check. Gens, sure of himself, persisted in his course, even while the resisters were in a quandary over the question of risking severe German retaliation for a chance to fight. In this contest Gens prevailed. He drove a wedge between the organizers of resistance and the ghetto community. The people followed *him*. From the examples of Baeck, Löwenherz, Czerniakow, Rumkowski, Barasz, and Gens, one can see a spectrum of leaders and types of leadership, from old officeholders to emerging crisis managers, and from a traditional superintendency to the aggressive and internally unhampered decision making of a dictator. What had not occurred in Germany, Austria, or the principal cities in Poland was a major argument about whether there should be a Jewish council at all. Such debates did take place in the Netherlands, France, and Romania.

The discussion in the Netherlands was relatively short. A suspended Supreme Court judge, Lodewijk Ernst Visser, opposed the council, and a classics professor, David Cohen, asserted that idealists like Visser could always look down on those who adopted a realistic path, but that realism was inevitable. Visser died very soon after expressing his view, and Cohen, together with the diamond merchant Abraham Asscher, served in the council as cochairmen.

In France and Romania the outcome was not the clear ascendancy of one faction over another, but a divided power center, with challenges and tensions. The Jewish council in France (the Union générale des Israelites de France, abbreviated UGIF) was formed after a lengthy deliberation at the end of 1941. Its creation was a demand of the French Vichy regime, and thus the UGIF was to be answerable to a government that was itself subject to German control, completely so in the occupied north, and after November 1942 also in the south. Those who by reason of their activities or prominence had been suggested by Vichy to become members of the new body had a choice. They could accept or refuse, although in the latter case someone else might be named.

One who dropped out was René Mayer, born in 1895, veteran of the First World War, lawyer, chef-de-cabinet of a minister, Pierre Laval, in 1925, and active in management positions involving transportation and utilities. When France faced defeat in 1940, he was in London but made his way back to Paris. Early in 1941, he wanted the Vichy government to urge foreign Jews to leave France. His reservations about the UGIF were based not only on the fact that it was going to be a Judenrat but also on the fear that it would be a device to reduce the rights of French Jews to the level of Jewish immigrants. After his refusal to join the UGIF, he escaped to North Africa and joined Free French forces on the side of Britain.

One of the candidates who did accept an appointment to the UGIF was Raymond-Raoul Lambert, born in 1894, veteran of the First World War, *chevalier de la légion d'honneur,* editor of a French Jewish weekly, and administrator of a committee assisting Jewish refugees from Germany. When the Second World War broke out, he returned to the army with the rank of captain. After his demobilization, he toyed with the idea of leaving France with his family, if only to spare his children the painful experience of discrimination against Jews, but he remained and took over the UGIF in the Southern Zone.

Unlike Germany and other countries, where an old Jewish community organization was not allowed to coexist with a new Judenrat, France still had its peacetime Jewish Consistoire Central. In 1940, it was headed by the sixty-seven-year-old elder statesman Jacques-Edouard Helbronner, holder of the *croix de guerre* and cousin of two Rothschilds. He went to law school with Paul Gerlier (later a cardinal), served on the staff of War Minister Paul Painlevé in the First World War, and knew Marshal Philippe Pétain. When the UGIF was formed, he declined to accept its presidency or serve it as a member. He is reported to have opposed the idea of a protest by Cardinal Gerlier against the treatment of foreign Jews, lest French Jews be endangered. After German forces entered the Southern Zone, Lambert asked Helbronner to make an appeal to Premier Laval. Helbronner refused.

In Romania the contrasting figures were Wilhelm Filderman and Nandor Gingold. Filderman, born in 1882, was an attorney. During the First World War he had been an officer in the Romanian army and by 1923 he became the president of the Romanian Jewish community organization, which in the 1930s became the Federation of Romanian Jews. The dangers facing the Jews of Romania prompted Filderman to address persistent appeals and protests to Romanian authorities. He wrote to Marshal Antonescu after the Jews of Bessarabia and Bukovina were pushed across the Dnestr. He went to the Marshal to have the Jewish star decree voided in Romania, and later he asked for mitigations in the exaction of special taxes and forced loans. For the deportees languishing in ghettos under Romanian control between the Dnestr and Bug rivers, he pledged his personal funds, albeit with the condition that American or other foreign Jewish organizations deposit in Swiss banks an equivalent sum for his personal use after the war. The Romanian government was annoyed with Filderman, and once it arrested him, but the Romanians wavered enough to give him answers or even concessions.

Filderman and Gingold were opposites in almost every respect, but they were not opponents. As the de facto head of Romania's Judenrat, the Centrala, Gingold was insecure enough to meet with Filderman on occasion and to recruit a variety of assistants, including some Filderman supporters. Gingold did accept responsibility for publishing anti-Jewish regulations and handing over Jewish assets to the Romanian government. He was in his mid-thirties when he took the helm of the Centrala. Trained as a physician and a recent convert to Catholicism, he remained a patriotic Romanian even while Romanian army and gendarmerie units killed Bessarabian,

Bukovinian, and Ukrainian Jews en masse. The Jews of Old Romania, he reasoned, did not have to fight at the front for Romania. Their contributions of property and labor were a substitute under the circumstances for the sacrifices demanded of a nation in a war. The government for its part was not impressed with Gingold, even though he did its work. He labored, unloved by Jews and unappreciated by the Romanians, in his Bucharest ivory tower, cut off from the world.

The large majority of the Jewish leaders were convinced that on their own they could not reverse the process of destruction. Their single objective was stability. Change, which was welcomed at one time as a step toward betterment, was dreaded now, because it meant deterioration and harm. That is why these leaders tried to retard the downward trend, to save at least some people, or as a last resort to make the lot of everyone more bearable. In this struggle for postponements, exceptions, and mitigations, any pause was a respite, and even a new low would be turned into a foundation for new hope. The crowded disease-ridden ghetto as such had become the promise of a haven, and the imposition of forced labor a lifeline to survival.

In making their appeals, the Jewish leaders varied only in style. When Filderman addressed Antonescu in protest against the deportations of the Bessarabian and Bukovinian Jews, he wrote the words: "This is death, death, death." Seldom, however, was the Jewish leadership so blunt. One did not mention the unmentionable, and most often petitions were designed to achieve limited goals. Czerniakow in Warsaw appealed for the privilege of buying unrationed foodstuffs for the ghetto. The Jewish leaders in Berlin asked for milk to be sent along with children about to be deported. Barasz in Bialystok tried to lower a deportation quota, and the Hungarian Jewish council, accepting deportation as a given, wanted it only to be carried out in a humane spirit. All of these particular petitions were unsuccessful, as were most of the others, but pleas could never be dispensed with. For the Jewish leadership, they were the only conceivable mode of dealing with the perpetrators.

In their internal deliberations, the leaders had two watchwords. One was preserving the substance, the other salvation through work. In Helbronner's mind, the substance was the old established French Jewry. For Gens, it was the young and healthy part of the Jewish population. In a crisis it did not include the elderly, the incapacitated, or the "criminals." Once, when Gens sent his police from Vilnius to the neighboring small ghetto of Oszmiania, he sacrificed people who could not work anymore, preserving the remainder. Gens made it a principle not to surrender young women and children. He did not in any case have many of the latter.

The exhortation to work had its basis in a fundamental principle. Inasmuch as the ghettos were economic units, they had to trade something for the meager supply of food and fuel, and to the extent that ghetto production was essential to the Germans, it might save the inmates from destruction. Not surprisingly, therefore, Rumkowski and Gens strove to turn their ghettos into factories, while Barasz voiced concern that the number of Jews working in the Bialystok Ghetto was too small. This is what Barasz said in an extraordinary session of the Jewish council on October 11, 1942:

Today we have called into the meeting all those who share with us the heavy burden of the ghetto in order to state quite openly where we stand in the world. Most recently the danger to the district and city of Bialystok has come palpably close. That is why we must try to avert it or push it into the future or at least reduce its extent. Unfortunately, Bialystok had recently become the second-largest ghetto after Lodz and therein lies the big danger. The gaze of our enemies bores through us and only exceptional circumstances can preserve us from disaster. The fire is lapping from east to west and has almost reached our district. In order that this fire does not spread further, we have to take exceptional measures in Bialystok itself. . . .

The crux of the danger lies in the percentage of fourteen thousand workers among the thirty-five thousand ghetto inhabitants. Even if the authorities did not ask us for labor, we would have to attempt with all our strength to penetrate the economy; so that, if one wished to annihilate us, a gap would be created in the economy, and for this reason we would be spared. Only then is there any hope for us; we cannot expect mercy. . . .

The Jewish leaders were in the cauldron themselves. They too were victims. How, in these circumstances, did they judge their own positions? The fewest of them would speak of wielding power, although they were conscious of knowing more than the Jewish multitude and of making decisions for the whole community. They did not think that they enjoyed undeserved privileges, even though they were aware that they ate better and were housed more spaciously than most other Jews. They believed that their service was an obligation, and they were convinced with absolute certainty that they carried the entire burden of caring for the Jewish population. In this respect, even Rumkowski fits the mold. As he said at one time, "I am no politician but just a work horse in heavy harness, pulling a wagon loaded with seventeen thousand human lives."

The Jewish leaders were, in short, remarkably similar in their self-perception to rulers all over the world, but their role was not normal and for most of them neither was their fate. The survivors among them came mainly from the west. Leo Baeck of Berlin was found in 1945, a prominent inmate of Theresienstadt. Remembered by a large number of refugees who had left Germany before the war, he was repeatedly honored and an institute was named after him.

His counterpart in Vienna, Josef Löwenherz, quietly took up residence in New York. He received no adulation at all. Löwenherz had an efficient assistant in Vienna, Rabbi Benjamin Murmelstein, who was heavily involved in deportations and who finally presided as the Elder in the Theresiendstadt Ghetto. Murmelstein prudently chose a life of anonymity in Rome, where he was engaged in business activity. After his death in 1989, the Jewish Community of Rome refused to bury him near his wife, but allowed him a plot at the edge of the cemetery. The proconsuls of the Netherlands Community, Cohen and Asscher, were placed on trial before a Jewish court of honor, at which Asscher refused to appear. He died shortly afterward. Cohen was indicted by the Dutch government, but the charges were dropped. In Romania, Filderman resumed his old post as chief of the Jewish community but later left, pursued by the Communist government. Nandor Gingold of the Centrala had resigned his post before Romania's surrender upon his promotion to the status of an assimilated Romanian in 1944. In 1945, he was placed on trial for spoliation, sentenced to life imprisonment, but released to practice medicine for many years in a Bucharest clinic. René Mayer, who did not want to join the UGIF, became a cabinet member and premier in postwar France. Raymond-Raoul Lambert, the leader of the UGIF in the Southern Zone, was seized in 1942 and transported to Auschwitz, where he was gassed with his family. Lambert's opponent, the old, distinguished Jacques Helbronner, was arrested a few months later. He too was killed in Auschwitz. In Poland, the overwhelming majority of the Jewish leaders died with their communities. Adam Czerniakow in Warsaw committed suicide when the deportations began and when he realized that he could not save the Jewish orphans. Jacob Gens lost his battle for the survival of the Vilnius Ghetto. Called by the Germans one day and probably suspecting that this was his end, he went anyway and was greeted by a bullet. Barasz was killed in 1943 when the Bialystok Ghetto was liquidated, and Rumkowski boarded one of the last trains from Lodz to Auschwitz.

Decline and Fall in Lodz

It is perhaps not sufficiently realized that the Holocaust of the early 1940s was but the final and most horrible chapter of the decline and fall of Ukrainian and Polish Jews that began with the First World War.

The chronicler of the decline and fall of the high Jewish bourgeoisie in the great community of Lodz, Poland was I. J. Singer in his panoramic novel, *The Brothers Ashkenazi*. I. J. Singer is commonly referred to today as the relatively obscure elder brother of Isaac Bashevis Singer, but in the 1940s the degree of fame was reversed. While I. B. Singer in New York was struggling to get a reputation and audience, I. J. Singer, who died in New York in 1944, was regarded by the rapidly diminishing circle of Yiddish readers as the greatest Jewish novelist of his generation.

The Brothers Ashkenazi, of which an excellent English translation by Joseph Singer was published in 1980, and is now available in a Penguin paperback, is a novel of Tolstoyan ambition and proportion about a Jewish capitalist family in Lodz from the early 1900s into the 1920s. The leading character, Max Ashkenazi, is meant to stand for the grand Jewish bourgeoisie of eastern Europe overcome by war and revolution. Singer is not very good at character development: His people are more symbols than real individuals. But as a social historian Singer was first rate. He began writing his magnum opus in Warsaw in 1933 and completed it in New York in 1935. By the time he died in 1944, the Germans had wiped the once large and prosperous Lodz Jewish community off the face of the earth. Here is the concluding section of the novel, set in the period immediately after World War I.

Like a glutton released from an enforced diet, the long-starved city went wild, trying to make up for its years of deprivation. Again the police chased pedestrians congregating on Piotrkow Street, and again they were ignored. The jobbers, brokers, and agents were back in their element—scribbling, bickering, haggling, gripping each other's lapels, testing thread over match flames, unraveling fabrics, shouting, jostling, gesticulating—as if nothing had intervened.

Lodz was Lodz again. The cafés and restaurants were crowded with patrons buying, selling, bragging, telling smutty jokes. Cabbies whipped starved nags to rush merchants to banks, stock exchanges, countinghouses. Newsboys screamed headlines. Loaded drays rumbled over cobblestoned streets. Chimneys draped a heavy veil of stinking smoke over every house and courtyard. The hobbled soles of workers' shoes echoed against the cracked sidewalks, and whistles and sirens rent the air with their deranged shrieks.

The poorly printed marks issued by the fledgling Polish treasury dropped in value from day to day, even from morning to evening of the same day. People couldn't wait to rid themselves of them as if they were tainted. Housewives tried to shop as early as possible before their money grew even more worthless. Merchants changed prices even as they weighed out the goods. Some closed altogether to open later when their goods brought higher prices. Peasants wouldn't sell the food they brought in from the country, preferring to let it rot before accepting worthless cash for products they had sweated to grow.

The factories worked around the clock, and everything they turned out was snatched up by merchants the moment it came off the line. The city and the nation were overcome by a fever of consumption. Manufacturers took loans from banks regardless of the rate of interest. By the time these loans fell due their actual value was a hundredth of what it had been at their inception. Customers lined up at stores to buy valuable goods for worthless money. Bank officials were on the phone all day, taking quotations. Curbstone brokers raced around, buying and selling money.

The newspapers put out edition after edition listing the latest currency rates. The treasury issued new money, simply tacking on new zeros to the banknotes. Beggars flung bills in denominations of hundreds of thousands into the faces of their benefactors. Professors and economists wrote doomsday articles predicting the coming crash. Anti-Semitic newspapers blamed the inflation on the Jews. On walls, in marketplaces and bazaars, placards sprang up depicting hook-nosed, blubber-lipped Jewish bankers trampling on Polish currency. Here and there a Jewish second-hand clothes dealer paid with a cracked skull for the perfidy of his coreligionists. Policemen did their bit for the economy by chasing money lenders, who tossed the worthless bills into the gutter to avoid arrest. The landed gentry, the ministers, and the deputies of the Polish parliament, the Sejm, took enormous loans from the State Bank to buy up land, tracts of forests and estates.

In the meantime, people went on with their lives. They married, had children, married off their offspring. Like flies caught in spider webs, the men, women, and children of Balut sat glued to their looms, working until they dropped. But all the millions they earned weren't enough to prepare for the Sabbath.

The chimneys of Ashkenazi's plant belched black smoke into the sky, and its whistles blew shriller than ever as the English machines spit out goods at a blinding rate. But none of this brought Max any satisfaction. He saw the direction in which Lodz and the nation were heading. He knew that the paper chain holding everything together must soon break. And who would suffer from the tragedy? Not the profiteers and speculators, but the innocent, the ethical. Soon the suppliers would demand payment for their raw materials not with the Polish mark, but with stable foreign currency. But there was no foreign currency available in Lodz.

His own position was precarious. He had gone into heavy debt on the basis of expectations fashioned of logic. But in a time of madness, logic became absurdity, and absurdity, logic.

He sat in his large office surrounded by turmoil and excitement but unable to shake off his melancholy. He knew that the best solution would be to withdraw from the collective madness and shut down the factory, which now drifted like a rudderless ship toward its own destruction.

The best course in such instance was to drop anchor and wait for the storm to subside, but this he could not do. If he threw his thousands of employees out of work now, they would blow up the factory with him in it. Nor would Panczewski do anything to protect him. He would catch it from all sides—from the unions, from the press, even from the Jewish revolutionaries, although he employed no Jews. The government might even decide to seize his factory on some pretext or other. There was no such thing as justice anymore under the new regime. A man was no more a master of his own property here than he was across the border under the Soviets. But rather than steal from *everybody*, as the Soviets did, the Poles stole only from the Jews. They only awaited the slightest excuse to rob him blind. Even though the law was on his side, by the time he was through with the lawyers and judges they would have picked his holdings to pieces.

No, he could do nothing to avert the coming calamity. He would let his ship drift until it struck a rock and sank.

The men with whom he did business tried to comfort him. "Let the madness go on, Mr. President. Maybe it will all turn out for the best. For now, things are booming, and everyone is getting by. Let tomorrow be God's sorrow. . . ."

But Ashkenazi wouldn't let himself be lulled by such easy optimism. That was what had brought down his father-in-law, Haim Alter. That was for idlers, dreamers, utopians. The catastrophe was coming, and no blind, silly faith would avert it. . . .

Just as in the past the clatter of machinery had represented cash falling into his pocket, now it symbolized yet another nail being hammered into his coffin.

Still, he rose each morning at dawn to go to his office, and he stayed there late into the nights. His sickly, half-paralyzed wife remonstrated with him: "Max, get more rest. The 'golden' business won't run away, God help us. Think of your health first."

"I can't stay in bed while the factory is operating," he explained, and dressed hurriedly to get to the plant in time with the first worker.

The servant brought him a magnificent breakfast on a silver platter, but all he could get down was a crust of bread and a half glass of milk, the meal of the lowliest beggar. The only things that kept him alive now were his work and his premonitions of the future.

Just as he had miscalculated in business, Max Ashkenazi also miscarried in his effort to straighten out his personal life.

He did everything he could to begin a new existence, one that would make up for his previous mistakes. He had sworn to do this in Petrograd, then in the prison dungeon, and finally during the seven days of mourning for his brother. It was because of him, Max, that his daughter had been left a widow, and he resolved to pay her back for all the grief he had caused her both intentionally and unintentionally. He had also determined to bring back his son from abroad in order to be a father and a protector to him. And lastly, he was anxious to do right by Dinele, to make up for all his sins against her so that her final years, at least, would be serene and untroubled. But the house that he had so mercilessly destroyed would not let itself be put together again. The glue that would cement the broken shards simply didn't exist.

The moment the palace was his again, he insisted that his daughter move in with him. He didn't need such a huge place just for himself and his wife. More than ever he was appalled by the vastness of the rooms, the emptiness of the unused wings. Loneliest of all was the huge table in the dining hall where the couple dined in morose solitude.

Ashkenazi yearned for the warmth and friendliness his daughter and granddaughter would introduce to the glacial rooms. Priveshe's laughter rang like the bell of a merry sleigh when she raced through the spacious halls. But even though both Max and his wife begged her to move in with them, Gertrud declined.

Max suspected that her reason was that she didn't want to leave Dinele alone. He discussed the matter with his wife, and she agreed to apportion a separate wing of the palace to the two women. The present Madam Ashkenazi had nothing against her husband's first wife. They were all of an age when such things as jealousy were forgotten, and all that remained was the easy camaraderie of birds seeking to flock together. But Dinele, too, refused the offer.

Deeply disappointed, Max sent his ex-wife and daughter large amounts of money so that they would lack for nothing. He also saw to his brother's estate so that Gertrud would suffer no financial worries in the future. But for all that, she wouldn't move into his palace or get close to him.

She pitied her father now and sympathized with his loneliness, but she felt no love for him. The years of estrangement wouldn't allow themselves to be erased overnight. She even nursed hidden resentments against him. It was because of him that she had lost her husband. All her father had ever brought her had been anguish and misery. She wasn't religious, but she *was* superstitious, and she believed that her father had always been a jinx to her. She didn't reprove him, for she saw how miserable he was. Life had paid him back for all his sins. Apparently there was such a thing as justice and retribution in the world.

Her mother urged her to take little Priveh to visit her grandfather. "He is still your father," she reminded her. "He keeps calling. He even sent his car around for you."

When, on rare occasions, Gertrud did come to visit, her father put all his business affairs aside. He gave her presents and embraced her. He took little Priveh on his scrawny lap, crawled on all fours on the rug for her, and barked like a dog. That which he had neglected to give his own children, he now gave to his grandchild in excess. His elderly wife hugged the little girl in her half-paralyzed arms, kissed her plump little hands and every ringlet on her head.

After she and her mother left, the palace seemed lonelier than ever.

Next, Max launched a vigorous effort to bring his son home. He sent money, letters. After lengthy urging, Ignatz came. Max didn't recognize him. Before him stood a burly, mature man with nothing of the boy he remembered. His voice was grating and deep, coarsened by the years of military service. Max had to stand on tiptoe to kiss him. Ignatz barely responded to the greeting. He spoke mostly French, which his father didn't understand. He was the quintessential soldier. A deep scar ran down his face, emphasizing his tough, un-Jewish appearance. "Caught this at the front," he explained with a laugh, as if recalling some happy memory. "The bastard sliced me good and proper. . . ."

Ashkenazi recoiled from the brutal stranger. He felt even more alienated around the woman his son had brought with him. She was swarthy with high cheekbones and black eyes lacking even a trace of Jewish origin. She wore long earrings and lots of bracelets over her brown wrists and revealed thin, shapely legs beneath her short skirt. She understood nothing but French. Ashkenazi suspected that she was a native of one of the French African colonies. He flushed when she kissed his cheek with a passionate *Mon père! Mon père!"*

She carried around a tiny dog, constantly kissed his black button nose, and addressed him in fervent endearments spoken in some strange tongue. She was totally without inhibition. She would rush up to Ignatz, shower him with kisses, whisper endearments, and generally carry on in an indecent manner. Knowing his son's violent temper, Max avoided asking Ignatz any questions about her.

After a few days Max began to discuss practical matters with his son. He offered to take him in, teach him the textile business so that there would be someone to carry on the House of Ashkenazi after he, Max, was gone. But Ignatz refused to set foot inside the factory. He spent his days fencing, swimming, playing with the dog, and squabbling with the woman. During their frequent, violent quarrels she screamed until the window-panes rattled. Max didn't understand a word of the flood of invective that escaped her, but he sensed the passion behind it. Normally Ignatz didn't answer. But when her voice grew too shrill and she flew at him with her nails, he knocked her down like any Gentile laborer.

Max's blood ran cold. He felt deeply embarrassed before his wife and servants. But the dusky woman didn't seem to mind too much. The moment she finished sobbing, she powdered her face, applied lipstick and mascara, and began to kiss and fondle Ignatz with the same fervor with which she had attacked him minutes before.

At mealtimes she wolfed her food and drank glass after glass of wine. Ignatz often borrowed his father's car and raced it through the countryside, terrifying peasants and livestock alike. The police kept charging him, and whenever Max needed the car, it wasn't available.

Worst of all were Ignatz's insatiable demands for money. He consorted with all kinds of unsavory characters, gambled heavily, frequented cabarets, ran around with officers, and got drunk. Night after night he was brought home senseless. He also abused the servants and threw magnificent tantrums.

When Max tried to remonstrate with him, Ignatz threatened to leave for Paris.

"What will you do there?" his father asked.

"I'll join the Foreign Legion," Ignatz grunted, glaring with hate at his father. "I'm sick of everything anyhow. . . ."

But Max wouldn't let him go. Again and again he gave him money and bailed him out of trouble, hoping for some change in his son's attitude. But nothing pleased Ignatz. He detested the meals served him; he despised Lodz, its people, its language. He talked only of Paris. His woman skulked about even surlier than he. Once in a while a cloud seemed to lift from Ignatz's eyes. He was pleasant to his father and brought Dinele to the palace, where he clung to her like a child. Max looked on befuddled while Dinele blushed like a schoolgirl.

Ignatz shoved his parents together roughly. "Well, kiss and make up!" he growled, as if issuing an order to a corporal. "Enough feuding already!" And he beamed with pride over his accomplishment.

The swarthy woman clapped her hands. "Bravo! Bravo!" she cried, laughing insanely.

The parents assumed at those times that their son had changed, that he was now ready to settle down, take up a decent existence and provide them some pleasure for all the past grief he had brought them.

But he quickly reverted to his wild, sullen ways, went to Warsaw for days at a time without letting anyone know where he was, and returned in a foul mood. One day he announced that he could no longer remain in the city that stuck like a bone in his craw. He left with his woman and his things right then and there. A week later a curt telegram arrived, informing Max that he was back in Paris and requesting money to be forwarded to his hotel.

Max telephoned Dinele to tell her about the telegram, knowing how she worried about their son. "At least we know he's alive, the bargain . . ." he reassured her.

There was no hope for Ignatz, he knew. He would never amount to anything. He, Max, had wanted an heir to perpetuate the House of Ashkenazi, but this wasn't to be. His only fear now was that his son would convert, if he hadn't already done so, God forbid. . . .

"What did I do to deserve this?" Max wondered. He had worked like a horse all his life, abjured all pleasures. For whom had he worked, after all? Certainly not for himself. He had never needed anything then, and he didn't need anything now. His entire daily food intake amounted to a few groschen. For whose sake had he begun everything anew? Only for them, his children. And what was the result? His daughter avoided him; his son was a wastrel who despised him. . . .

Following the days of worry and heartache at the factory, he had nothing to come home to but his gnawing loneliness and his sickly wife's groaning. At work he could still achieve a measure of forgetfulness, but the nights were long and unbearable. All kinds of brooding thoughts came to the surface. Hidden ailments of all sorts erupted. His bones ached; he suffered heartburn, stitches in the side. There was pressure on his heart. He had suffered these complaints even before the war, but he had never bothered to consult a doctor—there simply had been no time for it. His work had kept him too busy to think about such things. Doctors had warned him to guard his health, but he had ignored them. He had no patience with illness. He had even neglected his teeth, unwilling to spare the time for the dentist's chair. He would swallow bicarbonate of soda to still the burning in his chest and apply hot-water bottles to ease the pains in his sides and back. He had refused to go to the spas to which the doctors had directed him. Now the ailments came back all together. His wasted body was racked with cramps, aches, pains. His wife urged him to see doctors, brought in the biggest specialists to examine him, but he refused their services. He knew beforehand what they would tell him—to get plenty of rest, to go to resorts, to cease all worry, to get plenty of sleep, and generally to take care of himself.

He wasn't able to follow a single one of these advices. His plant was in terrible trouble. His wife was sick. His house was like a mausoleum. His daughter was estranged; Ignatz wrote or wired only when one of his checks was late. Nor could Max stop thinking about his brother. He still pictured him as he had seen him last—his body stretched out on the ground, with the trickle of blood running down into his beard and coagulating there. As much as he tried to chase this image, it wouldn't go away. He took all kinds of sleeping pills and potions, but to no avail. His system grew quickly accustomed to each one so that they had no effect upon him.

He had failed miserably in his attempt to rebuild the shattered House of Ashkenazi. The shards lay irrevocably scattered, and as he padded through the dark palace in his bathrobe and slippers, the bronze Mephistopheles bared his teeth at him in a malicious, sinister smile.

The paper chain holding Lodz together burst into a million pieces. The poorly printed marks were taken out of circulation to be replaced by silver guilders complete with the inevitable reliefs of Poland's saviors. Along with the worthless marks also vanished all the work in the city, all hustle and bustle, all trade, the whole paper existence.

The warehouses were saturated with goods for which there were no buyers. The stores no longer sold a groschen's worth of merchandise. The jammed sidewalks grew deserted. In the cafés and restaurants waiters stood around swatting idly at flies. The agents, brokers, moneychangers, commission men, and traveling salesmen sat at tables, scribbling away, but they didn't order so much as a cup of coffee. They only chain-smoked, lighting their cigarettes with million-mark notes.

Lodz had come full circle. The speculators, profiteers, idlers, and various dreamers and hangers-on had managed to land on their feet, while solid businessmen, shrewd investors, insiders, and so-called experts ended up stuck with mounds of the worthless marks.

Just as Max had predicted, representatives of foreign wool and cotton suppliers came to demand payment for their raw goods. But all their customers had to offer were excuses. A rash of bankruptcies erupted. The courts and lawyers worked overtime. The musty, dim offices of notaries filled with husbands putting all their worldly goods in their wives' names.

All factories stood idle. Not a wisp of smoke rose from the sooty chimneys. Workers by the thousands milled in the streets. Huge mobs lined up before labor exchanges, waiting for announcement of jobs that never materialized. Help was needed in France to dig coal, and the men surged forward to sign up. Agents of shipping lines tantalized the people with tales of life in the Americas and urged them to buy tickets and emigrate. Elegant flimflam artists posed as foreign consuls and issued counterfeit visas and passports on the spot. Anti-Semitic agitators vilified Jews for conspiring to ship good Christians out of the country in order to take over Poland for themselves. Priests and monks took up collections for the construction of a new church in the city. Revolutionaries issued proclamations urging a revolt of the oppressed. Secret agents, policemen, patriotic housewives, and students set upon these agitators and hustled them off, beaten and bloody, to the police stations.

"Hang the Trotskyites!" they bellowed. "Send them back to Palestine!"

In Balut, malnourished children peered out from behind grimy windows at the deserted streets. Secondhand clothes dealers walked about with empty sacks, their gloomy eyes cast heavenward but bereft of all hope. Real and pretend cripples crawled and slithered through courtyards, parroting beggars' laments.

The people of Balut had nothing more to hope for. The mills had already destroyed their livelihoods even before the collapse. The Polish and German workers wouldn't allow them into the factories, not even into those owned by Jews. They couldn't collect workmen's compensation since Magistrate Panczewski bent the law so that only employees of large factories were eligible for such payment.

Young and healthy Jewish youths applied at the labor exchanges for the filthiest jobs—digging sewers and building roads—but even this the Gentiles denied them. "Beat it, Moshes!" they hooted. "Starve to death!"

All that was left them was charity and the soup kitchens set up by the Jewish community. The storekeepers dozed the days away without taking in so much as a groschen.

All the activity now centered on the railroad stations. Men, women, and children carrying bundles of bedding and Sabbath candelabra filled all the wagons as Jewish Lodz raced to escape. Wives went to their husbands in America, fathers to their children, children to their parents. Farmers anxious to go back to the land emigrated to Argentina.

Jewish boys and girls carrying military knapsacks and blue and white flags set out to colonize Palestine. They sang their Hebrew songs and danced their horas. Those who came to see them off shouted, "Next year in Jerusalem!"

Affluent Jews, accompanied by their bejeweled wives and daughters, took trains to Italian ports; from there they would sail on luxury liners to Palestine. They weren't going there to till the soil and dry the marshes like the pioneers, but to buy and develop real estate, build plants and factories, and restore their fortunes.

Lodz was in a crisis. You couldn't earn a groschen in a city glutted with goods for years to come. Like hyenas, tax collectors descended upon the city to grab what they could for the national treasury. The only people seen in the deserted streets were soldiers and civilian officials in gorgeous uniforms replete with braid and insignia. They confiscated machinery from cellars, stripped bedding from beds, removed food from shops, and took everything away to be sold for taxes. Jewish housewives trailed after the wagons, lamenting as if hearses were removing their loved ones to their final rest.

Business establishments were sealed; jewelry was plucked from women's necks and wrists; men's watches and wallets were seized. The wealthier Jews fled the city, salvaging whatever they could in order to resettle in the Land of Israel and build a new Poland, a new Piotrkow Street in the Land of the Ancestors, in North or South America.

The city Gentiles stood before the gates of their houses, watching the exodus of Jews from the land their ancestors had occupied for a millennium. They didn't know whether to cheer or mourn.

Peasants shielded their eyes to watch the crowded trains rush by. Their wives listened to the exotic songs chanted by the Jewish pioneers, and their flaxen-haired children ran out from behind thatched fences with their dogs to scream and bark at the trains and hurl rocks at the windows.

Lodz was like a limb torn from a body that no longer sustained it. It quivered momentarily in its death throes as maggots crawled over it, draining its remaining juices.

And as the city succumbed, so did its king, Max Ashkenazi. Without the smoky air to breathe, without the hum of machinery to lull him, he languished. He lay awake nights, reviewing his life. The images of those he had known and wronged passed before his eyes—his parents, his in-laws, but especially Jacob Bunem. He could see the trickle of blood run down into the beard and congeal there, and his own blood chilled. He put on his robe and slippers and wandered through the palace. He went to the window and looked out at the deserted factory, at the stacks looking like huge extended tongues thrust into the sky.

He went to the bookcase and glanced over the books. He stopped where the Jewish holy volumes were kept somewhat out of sight and took down a worn copy of the Scriptures. He took it back to bed and switched on his night lamp. He leafed through the pages, scanning the moralistic exhortations in Ecclesiastes and Proverbs. They no longer struck him as preposterous ravings of fatuous dotards but as observations rife with truth and perception. He came to a folded page. It was the Book of Job, which he had been reading during the period of mourning for his brother. Eagerly he began to read half aloud:

So Satan went forth from the presence of the Lord, and smote Job with sore boils from the sole of his foot even unto his crown. And he took him a potsherd to scrape himself therewith; and he sat among the ashes. . . . Now when Job's three friends heard of all this evil that was come upon him, they came every one from his own place, Eliphaz the Temanite, and Bildad the Shuhite, and Zophar the Naamathite; and they made an appointment together to come to bemoan him and to comfort him. And when they lifted up their eyes afar off,

and knew him not, they lifted up their voice, and wept; and they rent every one his mantle, and threw dust upon their heads toward heaven. So they sat down with him upon the ground seven days and seven nights, and none spoke a word unto him; for they saw that his grief was very great. After this opened Job his mouth and cursed his day—

From the adjoining rooms the clocks tolled the hour. Max Ashkenazi put down the book to listen. Just then he felt his chest tighten as if gripped by steel pincers. He cried and reached for the bellpull, but by the time the servant came his master was already dead. His head had fallen upon the opened Bible, and his fingers still clutched the cord.

All Lodz turned out for the funeral of Max Ashkenazi. Piotrkow Street was black with people, droshkies, carriages, and cars. Wild-bearded Hasidim walked next to top-hatted bankers, grimy vendors, clerks, brokers, heder students, beggars, thieves, workers. In Max Ashkenazi's passing they saw the demise of Lodz itself. His funeral was its funeral. And they trudged along, mourning not his passing, but that of their own existence.

Three women in black walked just behind the coffin, one widow supporting the other.

The gravediggers had already prepared a grave small enough for a child for the King of Lodz. A stranger recited the mourner's prayer. Men stooped to throw handfuls of dirt upon the coffin.

"Dust thou art and unto dust shalt thou return," they mumbled over their shoulders.

A dense cloud settled overhead. The wind blew dust into the people's faces. With feet as heavy as the leaden sky, they turned back to the sullen, desolate city.

"Sand," they complained, shielding their eyes from the pursuing dust. "Everything we built here we built on sand. . . ."

In the swiftly falling dusk, a flock of birds formed in the shape of a crescent and cawed against the ominous sky.

Exile from Alexandria

Parallel to the decline and fall of the grand Jewish bourgeoisie of Central Europe, as described by Appelfeld, and of Poland, as chronicled by I. J. Singer, was the loss of wealth and place by the small but very old and sophisticated Jewish mercantile class of the Eastern Mediterranean's Arab countries. After the creation of Israel they were almost all driven out within a few years by militant Arab dictators, such as Nasser in Egypt. Some went to Israel where they suffered tremendous economic and status declension and were regarded as second-class "Orientals." Others spread all over Western Europe and the United States.

The most sensitive account of the victimization of the Jewish bourgeoisie in the Eastern Mediterranean is by Andre Aciman in his widely acclaimed 1994 family memoir *Out of Egypt*. Aciman, who now teaches French literature at Princeton University, comes from an old Alexandrian family who conversed in French and sometimes in old Ladino (a Spanish dialect written in Hebrew characters going back to the late Middle Ages) but barely knew enough Arabic to communicate with their Arab servants and workers. They took long vacations in Italy and were part of the Mediterranean cosmopolitan intelligentsia and international business class. Here is Anciman's painful description of his family's expulsion from Nasser's Egypt.

A Jewish bourgeoisie had prospered in Alexandria since the city was founded in the fourth century B.C. In the first century A.D., one-third of Alexandria's population was Jewish. Now the Jews were evicted.

Two days later the third blow fell.

My father telephoned in the morning. "They don't want us anymore," he said in English. I didn't understand him. "They don't want us in Egypt." . . .

Despite the frantic packing and last-minute sale of all the furniture, my mother, my grandmother, and Aunt Elsa had decided we should hold a Passover seder on the eve of our departure. For this occasion, two giant candelabra would be brought in from the living room, and it was decided that the old sculptured candles should be used as well. No point in giving them away. Aunt Elsa wanted to clean house, to remove all traces of bread, as Jews traditionally do in preparation for Passover. But with the suitcases all over the place and everything upside down, nobody was eager to undertake such a task, and the idea was abandoned. "Then why have a seder?" she asked with embittered sarcasm. "Be glad we're having one at all," replied my father. I watched her fume. "If that's going to be your attitude, let's *not* have one, see if I care." "Now don't get all worked up over a silly seder, Elsa. Please!"

My mother and my grandmother began pleading with him, and for a good portion of the afternoon, busy embassies shuttled back and forth between Aunt Elsa's room and my father's study. Finally, he said he had to go out but would be back for dinner. That was his way of conceding. Abdou, who knew exactly what to prepare for the seder, needed no further inducements and immediately began boiling the eggs and preparing the cheese-and-potato *buñuelos*.

Meanwhile, Aunt Elsa began imploring me to help read the Haggadah that evening. Each time I refused, she would remind me that it was the last time this dining room would ever see a seder and that I should read in memory of Uncle Nessim. "His seat will stay empty unless somebody reads." Again I refused. "Are you ashamed of being Jewish? Is that it? What kind of Jews are we, then?" she kept asking. "The kind who don't celebrate leaving Egypt when it's the last thing they want to do," I said. "But that's so childish. We've never not had a seder. Your mother will be crushed. Is that what you want?" "What I want is to have no part of it. I don't want to cross the Red Sea. And I don't want to be in Jerusalem next year. As far as I'm concerned, all of this is just worship of repetition and nothing more." And I stormed out of the room, extremely pleased with my *bon mot*. "But it's our last evening in Egypt," she said, as though that would change my mind.

For all my resistance, however, I decided to wear one of my new ties, a blazer, and a newly made pair of pointed black shoes. My mother, who joined me in the living room around half past seven, was wearing a dark-blue dress and her favorite jewelry. In the next room, I could hear the two sisters putting the final touches to the table, stowing away the unused silverware, which Abdou had just polished. Then my grandmother came in, making a face that meant Aunt Elsa was truly impossible. "It's always what she wants, never what others want." She sat down, inspected her skirt absentmindedly, spreading its pleats, then began searching through the bowl of peanuts until she found a roasted almond. We looked outside and in the window caught our own reflections. Three more characters, I thought, and we'll be ready for Pirandello.

Aunt Elsa walked in, dressed in purple lace that dated back at least three generations. She seemed to notice that I had decided to wear a tie. "Much better than those trousers with the snaps on them," she said, throwing her sister a significant glance. We decided to have vermouth, and Aunt Elsa said she would smoke. My mother also smoked. Then, gradually, as always happened during such gatherings, the sisters began to reminisce. Aunt Elsa told us about the little icon shop she had kept in Lourdes before the Second World War. She had sold such large quantities of religious objects to Christian pilgrims that no one

would have guessed she was Jewish. But then, at Passover, not knowing where to buy unleavened bread, she had gone to a local baker and inquired about the various qualities of flour he used in his shop, claiming her husband had a terrible ulcer and needed special bread. The man said he did not understand what she wanted, and Elsa, distraught, continued to ask about a very light type of bread, maybe even unleavened bread, if such a thing existed. The man replied that surely there was an epidemic spreading around Lourdes, for many were suffering from similar gastric disorders and had been coming to his shop for the past few days asking the same question. "Many?" she asked. "Many, many," he replied, smiling, then whispered, "*Bonne pâque,* happy Passover," and sold her the unleavened bread.

"*Se non è vero, è ben trovato,* if it isn't true, you've made it up well," said my father, who had just walked in. "So, are we all ready?" "Yes, we were waiting for you," said my mother, "did you want some scotch?" "No, already had some."

Then, as we made toward the dining room, I saw that my father's right cheek was covered with pink, livid streaks, like nail scratches. My grandmother immediately pinched her cheek when she saw his face but said nothing. My mother too cast stealthy glances in his direction but was silent.

"So what exactly is it you want us to do now?" he asked Aunt Elsa, mildly scoffing at the ceremonial air she adopted on these occasions.

"I want you to read," she said, indicating Uncle Nessim's seat. My mother stood up and showed him where to start, pained and shaking her head silently the more she looked at his face. He began to recite in French, without irony, without flourishes, even meekly. But as soon as he began to feel comfortable with the text, he started to fumble, reading the instructions out loud, then correcting himself, or skipping lines unintentionally only to find himself reading the same line twice. At one point, wishing to facilitate his task, my grandmother said, "Skip that portion." He read some more and she interrupted again. "Skip that too."

"No," said Elsa, "either we read everything or nothing at all." An argument was about to erupt. "Where is Nessim now that we need him," said Elsa with that doleful tone in her voice that explained her success at Lourdes. "As far away from you as he can be," muttered my father under his breath, which immediately made me giggle. My mother, catching my attempt to stifle a laugh, began to smile; she knew exactly what my father had said though she had not heard it. My father, too, was infected by the giggling, which he smothered as best as he could, until my grandmother caught sight of him, which sent her laughing uncontrollably. No one had any idea what to do, what to read, or when to stop. "Some Jews we are," said Aunt Elsa, who had also started to laugh and whose eyes were tearing. "Shall we eat, then?" asked my father. "Good idea," I said. "But we've only just begun," protested Aunt Elsa, recovering her composure. "It's the very last time. How could you? We'll never be together again, I can just feel it." She was on the verge of tears, but my grandmother warned her that she, too, would start crying if we kept on like this. "This is the last year," said Elsa, reaching out and touching my hand. "It's just that I can remember so many seders held in this very room, for fifty years, year after year after year. And I'll tell you something," she said, turning to my father. "Had I known fifty years ago that it would end like this, had I known I'd be among the last in this room, with everyone buried or gone away, it would have been better to die, better to have died back then than to be left alone like this." "Calm yourself, Elsica," said my father, "otherwise we'll all be in mourning here."

At that point, Abdou walked in and, approaching my father, said there was someone on the telephone asking for him. "Tell them we are praying," said my father. "But sir—" He seemed troubled and began to speak softly. "So?" "She said she wanted to apologize." No one said anything. "Tell her not now." "Very well."

We heard the hurried patter of Abdou's steps up the corridor, heard him pick up the receiver and mumble something. Then, with relief, we heard him hang up and go back into the kitchen. It meant she had not insisted or argued. It meant he would be with us tonight. "Shall we eat, then?" said my mother. "Good idea," I repeated. "Yes, I'm starving," said Aunt Elsa. "An angel you married," murmured my grandmother to my father.

After dinner, everyone moved into the smaller living room, and, as was her habit on special gatherings, Aunt Elsa asked my father to play the record she loved so much. It was a very old recording by the Busch Quartet, and Aunt Elsa always kept it in her room, fearing someone might ruin it. I had noticed it earlier in the day lying next to the radio. It meant she had been planning the music all along. "Here," she said, gingerly removing the warped record from its blanched dust jacket with her arthritic fingers. It was Beethoven's "Song of Thanksgiving." Everyone sat down, and the adagio started.

The old 78 hissed, the static louder than the music, though no one seemed to notice, for my grandmother began humming, softly, with a plangent, faraway whine in her voice, and my father shut his eyes, and Aunt Elsa began shaking her head in rapt wonder, as she did sometimes when tasting Swiss chocolate purchased on the black market, as if to say, "How could anyone have created such beauty?"

And there, I thought, was my entire world: The two old ones writhing in a silent stupor, my father probably wishing he was elsewhere, and my mother, whose thoughts, as she leafed through a French fashion magazine, were everywhere and nowhere, but mostly on her husband, who knew that she would say nothing that evening and would probably let the matter pass quietly and never speak of it again.

I motioned to my mother that I was going out for a walk. She nodded. Without saying anything, my father put his hand in his pocket and slipped me a few bills.

Outside, Rue Delta was brimming with people. It was the first night of Ramadan and the guns marking the end of the fast had gone off three hours earlier. There was unusual bustle and clamor, with people gathered in groups, standing in the way of traffic, making things noisier and livelier still, the scent of holiday pastries and fried treats filling the air. I looked up at our building: On our floor, all the lights were out except for Abdou's and those in the living room. Such weak lights, and so scant in comparison to the gaudy, colored bulbs that hung from all the lampposts and trees—as if the electricity in our home were being sapped and might die out at any moment. It was an Old World, old-people's light.

As I neared the seafront, the night air grew cooler, saltier, freed from the din of lights and the milling crowd. Traffic became sparse, and whenever cars stopped for the traffic signal, everything grew still: Then, only the waves could be heard, thudding in the dark, spraying the air along the darkened Corniche with a thin mist that hung upon the night, dousing the streetlights and the signposts and the distant floodlights by the guns of Petrou, spreading a light clammy film upon the pebbled stone wall overlooking the city's coastline. Quietly, an empty bus splashed along the road, trailing murky stains of light on the gleaming pavement. From somewhere, in scattered snatches, came the faint lilt of music, perhaps from one of those dance halls where students used to flock at night. Or maybe just a muted radio somewhere on the beach nearby, where abandoned nets gave off a pungent smell of seaweed and fish.

At the corner of the street, from a sidewalk stall, came the smell of fresh dough and of angel-hair being fried on top of a large copper stand—a common sight throughout the city every Ramadan. People would fold the pancakes and stuff them with almonds, syrup, and raisins. The vendor caught me eyeing the cakes that were neatly spread on a black tray. He smiled and said, "*Etfaddal,* help yourself."

I thought of Aunt Elsa's chiding eyes. "But it's Pesah," I imagined her saying. My grandmother would disapprove too—eating food fried by Arabs on the street, unconscionable. The Egyptian didn't want any money. "It's for you," he said, handing me the delicacy on a torn sheet of newspaper.

I wished him a good evening and took the soggy pancake out onto the seafront. There, heaving myself up on the stone wall, I sat with my back to the city, facing the sea, holding the delicacy I was about to devour. Abdou would have called this a real *mazag,* accompanying the word, as all Egyptians do, with a gesture of the hand—a flattened palm brought to the side of the head—signifying blissful plenitude and the prolonged, cultivated consumption of everyday pleasures.

Facing the night, I looked out at the stars and thought to myself, over there is Spain, then France, to the right Italy, and, straight ahead, the land of Solon and Pericles. The world is timeless and boundless, and I thought of all the ship-wrecked, homeless mariners who had strayed to this very land and for years had tinkered away at their damaged boats, praying for a wind, only to grow soft and reluctant when their time came.

I stared at the flicker of little fishing boats far out in the offing, always there at night, and watched a group of children scampering about on the beach below, waving little Ramadan lanterns, the girls wearing loud pink-and-fuchsia dresses, locking hands as they wove themselves into the dark again, followed by another group of child revelers who were flocking along the jetty past the sand dunes, some even waving up to me from below. I waved back with a familiar gesture of street fellowship and wiped the light spray that had moistened my face.

And suddenly I knew, as I touched the damp, grainy surface of the seawall, that I would always remember this night, that in years to come I would remember sitting here, swept with confused longing as I listened to the water lapping the giant boulders beneath the promenade and watched the children head toward the shore in a winding, lambent procession. I wanted to come back tomorrow night, and the night after, and the one after that as well, sensing that what made leaving so fiercely painful was the knowledge that there would never be another night like this, that I would never eat soggy cakes along the coast road in the evening, not this year or any other year, nor feel the baffling, sudden beauty of that moment when, if only for an instant, I had caught myself longing for a city I never knew I loved.

Exactly a year from now, I vowed, I would sit outside at night wherever I was, somewhere in Europe, or in America, and turn my face to Egypt, as Moslems do when they pray and face Mecca, and remember this very night, and how I had thought these things and made this vow.

The Martyrdom of Colonel Marcus

The Israeli War of Independence of 1948 has in retrospect assumed mythic proportions as a great Israeli triumph. In a sense this is true because the war confirmed the establishment of the State of Israel within borders more extended than the proposed U.N. partition of Palestine had allocated.

But Israelis suffered casualties almost equal to one percent of their population and the brave but poorly trained and badly equipped Israeli army failed in its highest mission of taking East Jerusalem from the British-trained and -led Jordanese army, the only organized professional Arab army it came up against. The Israelis were greatly helped by volunteers from abroad. Most of the pilots in the Israeli air force were from abroad, most but not all Jews.

The Israeli army was helped by the strategic leadership offered by the West-Point-trained American Colonel Mickey Marcus. His death by "friendly fire" was a severe blow to Israeli military leadership. Twenty-two years later, in his excellent book on the War of Independence, the American writer Dan Kurzman for the first time revealed in detail the circumstances of Marcus' death.

Have all guard units been put on special alert?" asked Mickey Marcus, just returned from Jerusalem headquarters to central front headquarters near Abu Ghosh.

Yigal Allon, his face gray with fatigue, said: "Yes, there's nothing to worry about."

Marcus glanced at his watch. It was about 1 A.M., June 11.

"Well, I'm going to bed," Marcus said. "I'm beat."

The American had had an active day, and now he could rest. The long-negotiated truce was fixed for 10 A.M., just a few hours away, and it appeared that fighting would be over for its duration. Since the Arabs might make a last-minute effort to improve their positions before the deadline, he had ordered a special alert in the command area, but he guessed they had already exhausted themselves—just as his own men had.

Little more than twelve hours before, an Arab Legion unit, following up its third victory at Latrun, had attacked the settlement of Gezer near the main Israeli regional base of Hulda. After a fierce battle, it succeeded in breaking in and capturing the surviving defenders. Marcus immediately dispatched a Yiftach unit to counterattack and toward evening it recaptured the settlement, now reduced to cinders.

Despite this ultimate hard-won victory, Marcus felt that his exhausted troops had reached the limits of endurance and he stalled off GHQ pleas for a new Israeli attack on Latrun. Upon learning that Gezer had been recaptured, Marcus and his commanders, in a surge of relief and good cheer, had gathered late in the afternoon of June 10 round a campfire to consume their first real meal in weeks. Ingenious aides had managed to forage from the countryside a lamb, a variety of fruit, *arak,* and even black caviar—found in the kitchen of Jerusalem's King David Hotel. As the impromptu banquet was ending, Alex Broida (Marcus's aide) approached, his slender, distinguished face reflecting his pique at not having been invited, and reminded Marcus, happily groggy with *arak,* that he was expected in Jerusalem shortly.

Now, several hours later, on their return to central front headquarters, they could enjoy the luxury of a good sleep for the first time in days. It seemed a fitting way to usher in the truce. And what more fitting place was there than atop the hill where the Holy Ark of the Covenant, containing the tablets dictated to Moses on Mount Sinai, was brought in 1100 B.C. after being recovered from the Philistines?

Marcus and his commanders were billeted in the monks' quarters of the abandoned Monastère Notre Dame de la Nouvelle Alliance, built on the spot where more than two thousand years ago an ancient synagogue marked the holy place. Broida, still disturbed by his omission from the list for the feast, was further agitated when he learned he was not to share a room with the commander he revered, but had been assigned to the room next door. Marcus was to stay with Mulah Cohen, Allon's deputy.

As they entered their respective quarters, Marcus grinned at Broida.

"See you in the morning," he said cheerfully . . .

Eighteen-year-old Eliezer Linski, a one-year veteran of the Palmach, glanced at his watch; only twenty more minutes to go.

It was 3:40 A.M. At 4 A.M., his hour on guard would be up. Another man would replace him and he could go back to sleep. He wouldn't get much more sleep, for he would be awakened early to take part in the squad leaders' course that was being conducted in the monastery area. But every minute he could squeeze in somehow seemed important. Besides, guard duty that night was more harrowing than usual, and his post, facing west, was one of the most dangerous since it crowned a gentle terraced slope on which local Arabs cultivated wheat. It would be far easier for Arabs to attack there than to climb the steep grades isolating the camp on the other three sides.

As Linsky stood with his Czech rifle slung over his shoulder in the humid, moonless night, he wondered whether the cease-fire due to start in a few hours would permit him to take some leave with his family in the village of Rishpon near Tel Aviv.

He looked at his watch again. Only fifteen min-

utes to go. Perhaps it would be quiet that night after all.

Suddenly (according to Linski's later testimony) he heard the sound of stones rolling about thirty yards away. Nervously, he removed his rifle from his shoulder, advanced about five yards, and cried:

"Mi sham?" "Who is there?"

He waited hopefully for the password, *"Haderech shelanu"* ("The road is ours"), but no reply came. He recalled the verbal orders that had been given all Palmach guards. If someone did not answer the first challenge, the guard was to fire a shot in the air. If the person continued to advance, the guard was to act according to circumstances. In peacetime, he would try to avoid shooting at the trespasser regardless. At a time of alert, he was normally to fire.

As Linski waited anxiously for an answer, he saw a figure in a white garment standing on the low, broken wall that surrounded the monastery area.

Once more, the guard shouted: "Who is there?"

When again he received no reply, he fired a shot into the air, and the figure jumped from the wall and ran toward the monastery, mumbling incoherently in what sounded to Linski like English; the guard had learned some English in elementary school, but his knowledge of the language was very poor. What Israeli in the camp would be speaking English, he wondered in alarm. He did not know of any American or Englishman there, but his battalion had often fought Arab Legion forces led by British officers and had even captured some. The intruder might be an Arab masquerading as a Briton. Perhaps a saboteur!

Linski, sweating profusely, yelled: "Halt or I'll shoot!"

But when the figure went on running, the young guard maintained in his testimony, "I fired a non-direct shot from the hip, an instinctive shot, a shot that was not aimed by sight with the intention of hitting, but only of stopping."

At the same moment, Linski testified, "they fired from the other position also. The figure ran a few meters and fell. I shouted to the other position to stop firing and they stopped."

Linski ran to the figure sprawled on the ground and found a man clad only in shorts and undershirt, wrapped in a white blanket. He turned his pocket flashlight onto the face. The man looked dead. Linski then felt his pulse and was sure that he was. Another guard from a position about twenty yards to the north of Linski's post, the position from where Linski testified he had heard firing, then joined him.

"Go get Menachem!" Linski exclaimed (referring to Menachem Kupinski, who was in charge of the guards).

Kupinski, who had been sleeping in his clothes and boots with a weapon at his side, was awakened by the shout: "There's an Arab in the camp and he's probably dead!"

Dashing to the scene, he sent his men away and examined the body with his flashlight. From the clothes and blanket he doubted that the victim was an Arab. Soon the camp commanders were surrounding the body.

Colonel Michael David Marcus lay with a bullet hole in his chest, one of the last fighters for Israel to die before the truce . . .

Alex Broida had been turning restlessly in bed unable to sleep when, about the time of the killing, he heard several shots nearby—he did not remember afterwards how many—with a pause of a few seconds between them. Some minutes later, he heard Mulah Cohen's voice in the garden and then someone replying: ". . . He answered in English."

Broida, feeling instinctively that something had happened to Marcus, went down to the garden and asked a soldier if anything was wrong.

"Nothing as far as I know," the soldier replied.

Broida, though still uneasy, went back upstairs and finally fell into a fitful sleep. At 5 A.M., he was awakened by Yosef Tabenkin, the commander of the Harel Brigade's fourth battalion.

"Alex, get up! Yigal wants to speak to you."

Broida jumped out of bed and into the corridor, where he met Yigal Allon. He could tell what had happened from Allon's eyes before the Palmach commander spoke.

Broida was silent. They hadn't even bothered to tell him until more than an hour after it happened . . .

Later that morning, Dr. Issachar of the Palmach wrote in a deposition:

At 0400 on June 11, I was called to the wounded man Stone [Marcus] who was brought to Abu Ghosh. I examined his wounds and declared that the wounds he suffered caused his immediate death. As far as could be seen, he was wounded by a *Sten* bullet . . . [The bullet was apparently never found.]

Eliezer Linski testified that he had fired a Czech rifle.

Awakened at his home when a radio message from Allon arrived, Ben-Gurion, in his pajamas, stood rigid with shock as he read the news of Marcus's death. Of all the men to die! A man of such heart . . . and the one real military expert in Israel. As he sat on his bed, his despair turned swiftly to bitterness and suspicion. The message said Marcus had been killed accidentally by a guard. That certainly seemed odd—and just when he had been appointed commander of the Jerusalem front. He began to wonder just how far some Palmach men would go to make sure the Palmach would determine strategy.

Later that day, he summoned Yaacov S. Shapiro—an old lawyer friend whom he intended to appoint Attorney General in the Israeli Ministry of Justice—to his office.

"Yaacov," he said, "I want all the facts in the Marcus case. I want you to make a thorough investigation and then report to me."

Shapiro agreed and immediately set out to work. However, he later wrote in his report:

I didn't find it necessary to visit the Abu Ghosh monastery since I am well acquainted with the monastery and the surrounding area from past visits. . . . The sketch prepared for me . . . gave me a good idea of the area and the surroundings.

Shapiro also considered it unnecessary to question personally most of the witnesses, requesting only signed statements. He did not attempt to square Dr. Issachar's declaration that "as far as can be seen" Marcus was killed by a Sten bullet with Linski's testimony that he fired a Czech rifle; nor did he even refer in his summary to this discrepancy. The exit hole left by a 9-caliber Sten bullet is usually considerably larger than that left by a 7.92-caliber Czech rifle bullet, though the size of the aperture may be influenced by the proximity of the gun (Linski was about ten yards from Marcus when he fired), or by obstacles the projectile strikes. Ignored also was a statement by the doctor that there were "two surface wounds" on Marcus's right arm. What might have caused these wounds?

These unanswered questions are related to still another omission in Shapiro's report: reference to Linski's testimony that he had heard other shots fired almost simultaneously with his own, and to Broida's statement that he, too, heard a series of shots.

Significantly, Linski stated: "I think that the man fell from my shot, but I heard that others think that he might have fallen from shots from the other post."

Moreover, the guard at the other post, who carried a Sten gun, was never questioned, at least for the record, or even identified in the report—possibly because the fatal bullet appeared to have entered Marcus's body from the side nearest Linski.

But perhaps the chief mystery was what Marcus was doing at all outside the perimeter of the camp, particularly in the most dangerous zone. Having had a good deal of liquor before going to bed, he might have gotten lost trying to find the latrine, which was located to the west but within the camp itself. And "the general assumption," Shapiro wrote in his report,

. . . is that he went . . . to attend to his needs. But if this assumption is correct, a few problems arise: The deceased was well acquainted with the camp. He was there two days a week, and for two days before the incident. He walked around there quite often (he even took sun baths). It is difficult to believe that he lost his way. . . . The deceased knew that the camp was on the alert and the guards had been told to keep especially on their toes. As an experienced soldier, he certainly knew of the danger entailed by leaving the camp at such an hour, beyond the border of the camp and a guard post. He was acquainted with the Palmach soldier and he undoubtedly knew that it is difficult to identify oneself in English to a Palmach guard.

At any rate, Shapiro concluded flatly that "Commander Marcus was killed by a shot fired upon him by Private Eliezer Linski" in the line of duty.

No evidence came to light that anyone might have deliberately tried to kill Marcus, who was well liked even by those who disagreed with his tactics and might have resented the appointment of an "outsider" to the highest field command. Eliezer Linski, as he himself conceded, may well have fired the fatal bullet. But though the investigation report, kept secret for twenty years, expressed this conclusion unreservedly, no real attempt was ever made to prove it.

1492

Of the many disasters in Jewish history none has burned more searingly into Jewish memory than the Sephardi expulsion from Christian Spain in 1492. Much about this event remains in dispute, particularly the number of Jews who actually departed the country rather than accept conversion. The traditional figure of three hundred thousand was devised by Isaac Barbanel, one of the top Sephardi leaders. He went into exile (and a successful new political career in Italy) and wrote an account of the expulsion of 1492. Because he chose to leave rather than to stay, as the other most prominent Sephardi Jew, Abraham Senior, did, it was in Barbanel's interest to make the exile from Spain as tremendous a turning-point and as massive an atrocity as possible.

Research in Spanish archives in recent years has reduced the number of Jews who departed rather than convert to forty thousand, the figure offered by the distinguished British historian Henry Kamen, or one hundred thousand, the total estimated by the Israeli scholar Haim Beinart. Yet a recent book on Sephardi history by Jane S. Gerber, who teaches Jewish history at the City University of New York, sticks with the traditional figure of three hundred thousand. Jewish history has a tendency to stay with traditional tropes and be impervious to empirical research, to vehement rabbinical approval.

In this selection from the book *The Spanish Inquisition*, Henry Kamen explains how and why the expulsion of 1492 came about. The current Spanish monarch after half a millennium has apologized for 1492—better late than never.

"The kings and lords of Castile have had this advantage, that their Jewish subjects, reflecting the magnificence of their lords, have been the most learned, the most distinguished Jews that there have been in all the realms of the dispersion; they are distinguished in four ways: in lineage, in wealth, in virtues, in science." Such was the fully justified boast of a fifteenth-century Castilian rabbi. Where all other countries in Europe could consider the Jews as a troublesome minority alien to their history, in the Iberian peninsula alone were they intimately and anciently connected with the mainstream of the country's history. The Jewish problem is our direct concern, for without it there would have been no Spanish Inquisition.

At the heart of racial and religious persecution in mediaeval Spain lay the problem of coexistence between the three great faiths of the peninsula: Muslim, Christian and Jewish. The first great persecution of the Jews occurred in the seventh century, and made them look with relief to the Moorish invasions and the establishment of the Muslim Caliphate at Córdoba. Under the liberal Caliphate the Jews prospered socially and economically. This came to an end in the twelfth century with the overthrow of the Caliphate by a new wave of Moorish invaders, the Almorávides, who persecuted Christians and Jews alike and destroyed their places of worship. The Jews fled to Christian territory and, under the tolerant eye of Christian rulers, continued to prosper in their new surroundings. Thus although intermittent persecution did occur, some degree of tolerance

Auto-da-fé: Execution of alleged crypto-Jews (Marranos) by the Spanish Crown at the Behest of the Inquisition. Spain, around 1530.

was the general rule. "In the commercial sphere, no visible barriers separated Jewish, Christian and Saracen merchants during the major period of Jewish life in Spain. Christian contractors built Jewish houses and Jewish craftsmen worked for Christian employers. Jewish advocates represented Gentile clients in the secular courts. Jewish brokers acted as intermediaries between Christian and Moorish principals. As a by-product, such continuous daily contacts inevitably fostered tolerance and friendly relationships, despite the irritations kept alive in the name of religion."

Political factiousness and economic jealousy soon helped to break down the security of this prosperous minority. From the thirteenth century onward, anti-Jewish legislation, first called for in the Fourth Lateran Council at Rome in 1215, became commonplace. It was the Council of Arles which first in 1235 ordered all Jews to wear a round yellow patch, four fingers in circumference, over their hearts as a mark of identification. Such legislation was never properly enforced in Spain because of powerful Jewish opposition, but the Cortes of Castile did approve of it in 1371 at the Cortes of Toro and again in 1405 at the Cortes of Madrid, with little success. This new anti-Jewish trend was accompanied by popular riots and occasional slaughter. Finally the whole question erupted in 1391 into the worst series of massacres ever suffered by the Jews in the peninsula. Religious fanaticism was clearly the driving force but, as a contemporary chronicler observed, "all this was more out of a thirst for robbery than out of devotion." In June 1391 over four thousand Jews were murdered in Seville alone. The pogroms of this year occurred in all the largest cities of Spain, and the ghettos or *aljamas* of Seville, Barcelona, Valencia, Toledo and other cities were totally wiped out. Those who were not murdered were compelled to accept baptism. It is from this time, the age of forcible mass conversions after pogroms, that the conversos came into existence on a grand scale.

The converso was not simply a convert. Christian society was all too conscious that converted Jews had in reality been forced unwillingly into their new faith: The converso was from the first, therefore, regarded with suspicion as a false Christian and a secret judaizer or practiser of Jewish rites. The conversos or New Christians soon came to be distrusted even more than the Jews, for they were considered to be a fifth column within the body of the Church. New words were coined to describe them, the most common being *marranos,* a word which probably derived either from the Hebrew *maranatha* (the Lord comes) or from a description of the Jews as those who "marran," or mar, the true faith. The conversos were thus resented by the body of Old Christians, who distrusted the sincerity of their faith and objected to the prominent part they played in Christian society. Although no longer Jews in religion, they now began to be subjected to all the rigours of anti-Semitism.

The roots of anti-Semitism are universal in character and as incomprehensible as they are deeply ingrained. The nature of the problem in Spain did not perhaps differ fundamentally from its nature in any other place or time. But we can begin to understand some of the reasons for anti-Semitism in Spain, and for the foundation of the Inquisition, by outlining the important role played by the Jews in Spanish society. In Christian Spain the first great era of the Jews was the thirteenth century, when their science and influence reached heights great enough to justify the claim of Mosé Arragel with which this chapter opens. Jewish scientists and writers distinguished themselves at the Court of Alfonso X of Castile. The medical profession was virtually monopolised by Jews, and royal and aristocratic circles relied heavily on this race for physicians: As one historian observes of the kingdom of Aragon, "there was not a noble or prelate in the land who did not keep a Jewish physician," and a similar situation also existed in Castile. The unfortunate sequel in any critical period was that Jewish doctors were accused of poisoning their patients. This was given as a contemporary reason for the expulsion of the Jews in 1492, the royal physician, a Jew, being accused of having poisoned the Infante Don Juan, son of Ferdinand and Isabella. For the next two centuries converso doctors carried on the work of their Jewish forebears, many of them suffering at the hands of the Inquisition because of prejudice or ignorance.

The most important cause of hostility to Jews, however, lay in their financial activities. In the first place they acted as tax-gatherers and fiscal officials to the crown and aristocracy. In answer to a protest of the Cortes of Burgos against this practice in 1367, Henry II claimed that "we farmed out the collection of the revenue to Jews because we found no others to bid for it;" and in 1469 the Cortes of Ocaña complained to Henry IV that "many prelates and other ecclesiastics farm to Jews and Moors the revenue and tithes that belong to them; and they enter churches to apportion the tithe among the contributors, to the great offense and injury of the Church." A direct result of hostility to this situation may be seen in the serious rioting at Toledo in 1449, when murders and sackings marked the resentment of the population against converso tax-gatherers employed by the royal minister Alvaro de Luna. Right up to the time of the expulsion, moreover, Jews held prominent official positions in the financial service of the crown. "From the beginning of the Reconquest till the capitulation of the last Moorish fortress on the peninsula in 1492, Jews were to be found in the Spanish states, especially in Castile, in key positions as ministers, royal counsellors, farmers of state revenue, financiers of military enterprises and as majordomos of the estates of the crown and of the higher nobility." Thus in the thirteenth century, under Jaime I of Aragon, the bailiffs or controllers of royal revenue in Barcelona, Gerona, Saragossa, Tarazona, Tortosa, Lérida, Valencia and other cities, were all Jews. In 1369 a Jew, Joseph Pichon, was "chief treasurer and manager of the revenues of the realm" under Henry II, just as over a century later a Jew, Gerónimo Pérez, was one of the principal treasurers of the Catholic monarchs. Needless to say, the Catholic monarchs could hardly have financed their campaign against Granada without the help of the two great Jewish financiers Abraham Senior and Isaac Abarbanel.

The chronicler of the Catholic monarchs, Andrés Bernáldez, summed up the hold of Jewish finance on the nation in this way; the Jewish exiles, he said, had been:

merchants, salesmen, tax-gatherers, retailers, stewards of nobility, officials, tailors, shoemakers, tanners, weavers, grocers, pedlars, silk-mercers, smiths, jewellers, and other like trades; none broke the earth, or became a farmer, carpenter or builder, but all sought after comfortable posts and ways of making profits without much labour.

One particular example is illuminating. In Saragossa, the capital of Aragon, the *aljama* had become by the fifteenth century a virtual bank, controlling the greater part of the capital of the Christian population. Municipalities in Aragon used to resort to the *aljama* for loans and credit, and so great was the dependence of all social classes in Saragossa on it that when it was open for business "there appeared . . . nobles, gentry, clergy, friars from all the religious orders, representatives of nunneries, and parish officials." In fact, so identified were the Jews with fiscal administration that at the end of the seventeenth century a writer complained:

Formerly all who applied themselves to the gathering of taxes were Jews and people of low origin; yet now, when they are not so, people look on them as Hebrews, even though they be Old Christians and of noble descent.

Besides their financial role in the state, however, the Jews offended the Christians by their social position. They were not only a powerful middle class: They also had dangerously close links with the aristocracy, into which several conversos had married; both these factors constituted a threat to the predominance of the nobility. It is not at first obvious why this threat should be considered a serious one. If, for instance, we adopt the very general figure of a population of nine millions for Castile and Aragon in about 1482, within this figure we can identify a middle class of over half a million persons. Of this latter figure, by far the greater part represents the Jewish population of Spain. This limitation of the Jews to one social class alone is a recognizable feature of the community. It is also a probable indication of the basic weakness of the community, in not having any roots among the mass of the population. Jews were also despised for their unwillingness to take part in manual labour. As Andrés Bernáldez put it:

They never wanted to take jobs in ploughing or digging, nor would they go through the fields tending cattle, nor would they teach their children to do so; all their wish was a job in the town, and earning their living without much labour while sitting on their bottoms.

This belief that the Jew refused to put his hand to hard manual work and preferred to make easy profits while others sweated, was to become a basic factor in popular anti-Semitism. The popular belief did, however, have some basis in reality. Jewish farmers and peasants are all but unknown in available documentation. Even in the lists of *autos de fe* of the Inquisition, the farmer is virtually nonexistent and the financier continuously present. This shows that the Jews were essentially an urban population, with the *aljamas* as their focus and the towns as their field of activity. The example of Badajoz, in agricultural Extremadura, shows that all the 231 conversos punished by the Inquisition between 1493 and 1599 came from the professional and commercial classes. They held posts ranging from that of mayor and municipal official to the lesser occupations of physicians, lawyers, traders, shopkeepers and manufacturers. The same is true for Saragossa and other principal cities of which we have details. The fact that these examples come from cities need not be misleading, for the inquisitorial tribunal sitting in the city also took cognisance of the rural areas. Against this evidence we can cite the case of Aguilar de la Frontera, near Córdoba. Of the sixty *sanbenitos* or penitential garments hung up in churches in this region in the late-sixteenth century, about nineteen belonged to *labradores,* that is, to peasant farmers. This proportion is perhaps unrepresentative, but should be kept in mind as a modification to the general picture. If Jews were largely cut off from the land, however, they were not cut off from the aristocracy. Despised for their religion, they could still become converts to Christianity and, as conversos, penetrate into the upper reaches of the nobility of the realm. In this lay the threat to the noble caste and to true religion, a threat which several modern writers have categorised as "the converso danger." Because of this danger, they argue, it became necessary to bring the Inquisition into existence. What is not clear, however, is whether the danger is represented as one to the purity of religion or to the purity of the nobility. For the latter alternative, at least, a great deal of evidence is available.

The class of conversos had grown enormously in the course of the fifteenth century, and the number of Jews had correspondingly diminished through conversion and emigration. The massacres of 1391 were followed throughout the next century by sporadic pogroms and the inevitable conversions. But the height of anti-Semitic legislation was reached in 1412 when, on the advice of the zealous Valencian saint, Vincent Ferrer (who shares some responsibility for the events of 1391), and the converso Chancellor of Castile, bishop Pablo de Santa María, it was decreed that Jews and Moors should wear distinguishing badges, be deprived of the right to hold office or possess titles, and should not change their domicile. In addition they were excluded from various trades such as those of grocers, carpenters, tailors and butchers; could not bear arms or hire Christians to work for them; were not allowed to eat, drink, bathe or even talk with Christians; and were forbidden to wear any but coarse clothes. This savage legislation, which was meant to speed up the rate of conversions, forced the minority races into misery and mourning. One of the victims lamented:

> They forced strange clothing upon us. They kept us from trade, farming and the crafts. They compelled us to grow our beards and our hair long. Instead of silken apparel, we were obliged to wear wretched clothes which drew contempt upon us. Unshaved, we appeared like mourners. Starvation stared everyone in the face.

Yet of course this proved to be an effective way of converting the Jews. By the mid-fifteenth century the growing numbers of conversos represented an open challenge to the old aristocracy. Marriage alliances had carried many formerly Jewish families into the heart of the Castilian and Aragonese nobility. In 1449 a petition to the bishop of Cuenca stated that all the noblest families of Spain were now of Jewish blood, and among them the Henríquez, from whom Ferdinand the Catholic descended through his mother. In Aragon nearly every noble house had Jewish blood in it, and half the important offices at the Aragonese court were held by conversos. In Castile the highest ranks of the clergy were contaminated. Under Isabella the Catholic at least four prominent bishops were conversos; as well as Cardinal Juan de Torquemada, uncle of the first Inquisitor General (himself, of course, of Jewish descent); Diego Deza, the second Inquisitor General; and the pious archbishop of Granada

Hernando de Talavera. Three secretaries of the crown, Fernando Álvarez, Alfonso de Avila, and Hernando del Pulgar, were all New Christians. Individual conversos founded powerful families of their own which contributed not only to the unease of the aristocracy but also to the dismay of the Jews. In Aragon the powerful converso family of De la Caballería "contributed, besides a few prominent clerics, the Vice-Chancellor of the kingdom of Aragon, the Comptroller General of the royal household, a Treasurer of the kingdom of Navarre, an Admiral, a Vice-Principal of the University of Saragossa, and a prominent antisemitic writer. Don Juan Pacheco, Marquis of Villena and Grand Master of the Order of Santiago, was a descendant on both sides of the former Jew, Ruy Capon. His brother, Don Pedro Giron, was Grand Master of the Order of Calatrava, while the archbishop of Toledo was his uncle. Seven at least of the principal prelates of the kingdom were of Jewish extraction, as well as the Treasurer." Among the most distinguished of Castilian converts was Salomón Ha Levi, chief rabbi of Burgos, who was opportunely converted along with his brothers in 1390, adopted the name Pablo de Santa María, entered the Church, and eventually became in turn bishop of Cartagena, bishop of Burgos, tutor to the son of Henry III of Castile, and papal legate. His eldest son Gonzalo became Spanish delegate to the Council of Constance, bishop successively of Astorga, Plasencia, and Sigüenza, and also attended the Council of Basel. His second son, Alonso de Cartagena, succeeded his father in the see of Burgos.

Further citation of individual cases would be superfluous. It was accepted by all contemporaries that the blood of the aristocracy had been gravely compromised by the Jewish converts. In Aragon an assessor of the Inquisition of Saragossa drew up what became known as the *Libro verde de Aragón,* a genealogical table tracing the origins of the nobility, from which it became clear that the most prominent families in the kingdom had not escaped converso infiltration. This document, which was set down in manuscript in the first decade of the sixteenth century, was soon to become a source of major scandal, for copies were passed from hand to hand, added to and distorted, until the government could no longer tolerate so vicious a slander against the leading nobles of the realm. In 1623, therefore, the extreme measure was taken of ordering all available copies of these *libros verdes* to be burnt. But already a far more powerful libel had been circulating in secret. In 1560 the Cardinal Francisco Mendoza y Bobadilla, angered by a refusal to admit two members of his family into a military order, presented to Philip II a memorandum, later to be known as *Tizón de la Nobleza de España,* or *Blot on the Nobility of Spain,* in which he claimed to prove that virtually the whole of the nobility was of Jewish descent. The proofs he offered were so incontrovertible that the *Tizón* was reprinted many times down to the nineteenth century, almost always as a tract against the power and influence of the nobility. At no time was even the slightest attempt at a rejoinder to these two publications made. The implications for a social class that affected to despise the Jews and conversos could not fail to be serious. On the one hand the nobility was claiming for itself a privileged position in return for its long services to the crown, and on the other it was being morally undermined by a racial dilution which tended to bring it into contempt. If the nobles were no longer truly Old Christians, they then had no right to true nobility. The dangerous point was obviously approaching at which membership of the nobility was in itself suspicion of debased blood, and only membership of nonnoble classes provided any guarantee against Jewish descent. In an important memoir upon the royal council presented by the historian Lorenzo Galíndez de Carvajal to the emperor Charles V, it was significantly reported that several of the most important members were of converso origin; among the exceptions, however, was doctor Palacios Rubios, "a man of pure blood because he is of labouring descent." In that "because" lay the ultimate threat to the interests and ideals of Reconquest Spain, and to the position of the aristocratic classes. The struggle against the minorities of the realm now became a struggle for their own existence, and for the maintenance of their name as Old Christians. The apparently negligible "converso danger" had ultimately developed into a threat to the whole social order.

Over and above this was the religious problem. Of the thousands of Jews who in the course of the preceding century had been forced by persecution and massacre to accept baptism, very few embraced Catholicism sincerely. Many, if not most, of them continued to practise the Jewish rites in secret as well as openly, so that the authorities were faced with a large minority of pseudo-Christians who had neither respect nor love for their new faith. Throughout the provinces of Toledo, Extremadura, Andalucia and Murcia, according to a polemic written in 1488, of all the conversos "hardly any are true Christians, as is well known in all Spain." The chronicler and royal secretary Hernando del Pulgar, himself a prominent converso, vouched for the existence of numerous secret judaizers among the New Christians of Toledo. The phenomenon was widespread enough to be commonplace. Understandably then, the ecclesiastical authorities took alarm at the large numbers of false Christians who were mocking God and the true religion. What is surprising is that the bishops of Spain seem never to have realized that the blame for this sad situation rested immediately on the shoulders of those who had provoked the forcible conversion of Jews, and that the false Christians should be made the object of missionary preaching rather than persecution.

Within Spanish Catholicism there thus existed a vast secret core of those who had never reconciled themselves to baptism. The life they led, which was to be substantially the same during all the centuries of their stay in Spain, was a furtive underground one, liable to sudden discovery or betrayal, and cut off from the religious practices of the Jewish community as a whole. Despised by the Old Christians for their race, and scorned by the Jews for their apostasy, the conversos lived for the most part in a social atmosphere they had never willingly chosen. After the foundation of the Inquisition their lot became even more difficult, for the tribunal regularly published instructions showing how judaizers could be detected. Distinctive food and clothes were therefore increasingly done without, in an attempt to throw off suspicion, and few judaizing households even dared to keep books of prayer in Hebrew or any other language, lest a servant should by chance come upon them. The result of these attempts to do without any of the outward detectable signs of Judaism, and to exist only on the internal inspiration of faith, led inevitably to a gradual decay in the Jewish forms of converso religion.

Consequently, as we shall see, the later conversos possessed little or no religion, and they became a nameless community, replenished only now and then by immigrant Portuguese judaizers, but otherwise sorry remnants of a great and martyred race.

In the earlier period, however, their questionable Catholicism made them an obvious target for popular resentment; to this were often added political and other reasons. The disturbances in Toledo in 1449, to which we have already referred, aroused different political factions in the city and led to an alignment of Old Christians against New Christians. The same division of parties arose in the city in 1467, and led to the final confirmation of a notorious statute excluding conversos from any public office in Toledo. There were racial riots in 1470 in Valladolid, and three years later in 1473 the conversos were expelled from Córdoba after a murderous struggle which opened the way for further killings throughout Andalucia, one of the victims being the converso Constable of Castile, who was killed before the altar of a church at Jaén. Though the direct instrument of persecution and massacre in all these cases was the populace in town and countryside we must go beyond the populace to get at the real culprits—the Old Christians with a prominent part in both municipal and ecclesiastical administration, who resented sharing power with men of mixed race and doubtful Orthodoxy. Because of them, racial antagonism and anti-Semitism had come to stay.

Worse, anti-Semitism was made official. The legislation of 1412, which had stipulated among other things that Jews were to wear distinctive badges, was reaffirmed by the Castilian Cortes at Toledo in 1480. Ferdinand enforced this and other measures with due strictness in his realm of Aragon. The Catholic monarchs now began a policy of systematic expulsion. In April 1481 Jews throughout the monarchy were ordered to be confined to their ghettos and not to live outside them. At the end of 1482 a partial expulsion of the Jewish population from Andalucia was ordered. The following year Jews were expelled from the bishoprics of Seville and Córdoba. In 1486 all Jews were expelled from the dioceses of Saragossa, Albarracin and Teruel. The process was piecemeal but efficient. After the fall of Granada, to which Jewish gold (supplied principally by Isaac Abarbanel and Abraham Senior) had contributed, the Catholic monarchs decided to complete their work by ridding Spain of the Jews. On 31 March 1492 an edict of expulsion was issued, giving the Jews of Spain until 31 July to accept baptism or leave the country.

Among those faced with this choice was the great financier Abraham Senior. His services to his queen had been so great that as late as March 1492, when the government ordered its debts to him to be paid, the sum in question came to fifteen million *maravedis*. In addition he was one of the few to receive official permission to take with him out of the country personal possessions in the form of gold and silver, should he wish to accompany his brethren into exile. But, for reasons that we can neither question nor condemn, Senior preferred to stay and accept baptism, adopting for himself and his family the new surname of Coronel. His friend and colleague Isaac Abarbanel went with his people out of the country.

Masada

No event in Jewish history symbolizes Jewish victimization as much as the destruction of the Second Temple at the hands of the Romans in A.D 70. Orthodox Jews still observe a day of mournful fasting at Tisha B'ab in the month of August to commemorate this *churben* (destruction).

Yet little is known as to how and why the great rebellion against Rome that began in A.D. 66 came about. How could the Zealot party that led to uprising ever hope to overcome the collective might of the Roman Empire? What was so bad about the Roman rule, in spite of the occasional incompetent governor? Roman rule over Jews was generally benign in Judea and generous outside of it—Judaism was a legal religion in the Roman Empire, while Christianity for its first three centuries was not.

The only circumstantial account of "the Jewish War" is from a tainted source, Josephus Flavius, an aristocrat who was initially the Jewish commander in the Galilee, who then betrayed his countrymen, went over to the Romans, served as military adviser at the siege of Jerusalem, and returned to Rome to live in a villa provided by the imperial Flavian family and write his partisan memoirs. There was a traditional story that even while Jerusalem was burning, the leading pharisaic rabbi Joachanan Ben Zakkai cut a deal with the enemy which allowed the rabbis to quietly leave the city and reestablish their training school in the north of the country.

One incident that comes through clearly in Josephus' often confused account is the story of Masada. Three years after Jerusalem fell, eight hundred resisting Jews had barricaded themselves on the hill at Masada, forty miles south of Jerusalem, where was located the winter palace of the Roman puppet King Herod. In A.D. 73, after a long and difficult siege, the Roman army finally made its way to the top of Masada, to discover that nearly all the defenders, including women and children, had committed mass suicide. Josephus here imagines the rallying speech of Eleazor, the Zealot commander at Masada.

The Masada story came to be a prominent image in the Zionist and Israeli mind. Until recently all recruits into the Israeli Defense Forces, after completing basic training, camped out over night on top of Masada and as dawn broke took their military oath of allegiance there. Characteristically, the Israelis have turned Masada into a tourist site. You can get to the top in a few minutes by cable car and there is a refreshment stand at the bottom of the hill. Somehow the Israelis see no irony—or humor—in this.

"We, therefore, who have been brought up in a discipline of our own, ought to become an example to others of our readiness to die; yet if we do not stand in need of foreigners to support us in this manner, let us regard those Indians who profess the exercise of philosophy; for these good men do but unwillingly undergo the time of life, and look upon it as a necessary servitude, and make haste to let their souls loose from their bodies; nay, when no misfortune presses them to it nor drives them upon it, these have such a desire of a life of immortality that they tell other men

The ultimate sacrifice: Rembrandt, *Abraham and Isaac,* 1655.

beforehand that they are about to depart; and nobody prevents them, but every one thinks them happy men and gives them messages to be carried to their familiar friends that are dead; so firmly and certainly do they believe that souls converse with one another in the other world. So when these men have heard all such commands that were to be given them, they deliver their body to the fire; and, in order to get a separation of their soul from the body in the greatest purity, they die in the midst of hymns of commendations made to them; for their dearest friends conduct them to their death more readily than do any of the rest of mankind conduct their fellow citizens when they are going a very long journey, who, at the same time, weep for themselves, but look upon the others as happy persons, so soon to be made partakers of the immortal order of beings. Are we not, therefore, ashamed to have lower notions than the Indians? and by our own cowardice to lay a base reproach upon the laws of our country, which are so much desired and imitated by all mankind?

"But put the case that we had been brought up under another persuasion, and taught that life is the greatest good which men are capable of, and that death is a calamity; however, our present circumstances ought to be an inducement to us to bear such calamity courageously, since it is by the will of God, and by necessity, that we are to die; for it now appears that God has made a decree against the whole Jewish nation that we are to be deprived of this life which we would not make a due use of; for do not ascribe your present condition to yourselves, nor think the Romans the true reason that this war we have had with them has become so destructive to us all: These things have not come to pass by their power, but a more powerful cause has intervened and made us offer them an occasion for their appearing to be conquerors over us. What Roman weapons, I pray you, were those by which the Jews of Caesarea were slain? On the contrary, when they were no way disposed to rebel but were all the while keeping their seventh day festival and did not so much as lift up their hands against the citizens of Caesarea, yet did those citizens run upon them in great mobs, and cut their throats and the throats of their wives and children, and this without any regard to the Romans themselves, who never took us for their enemies till we revolted from them. But some may be ready to say that truly the people of Caesarea always had a quarrel against those that lived among them, and that when an opportunity offered itself, they only satisfied their old rancor. What then shall we say to those of Scythopolis, who ventured to wage war with us on account of the Greeks? they were slain, they and their whole families, in the most inhumane manner, which was all the requital made them for the assistance they had offered the others; for that very same destruction which they had prevented from falling upon the others, they suffered themselves from them, as if they had been ready to be the actors against them.

"It would be too long for me to speak at this time of every destruction brought upon us: You must know that there was not a single Syrian city which did not slay its Jewish inhabitants and were not more bitter enemies to us than the Romans themselves: Nay, even those of Damascus, once they were able to allege no tolerable crime against us, filled their city with the most barbarous slaughter of our people and cut the throats of eighteen thousand Jews, along with their wives and children. And as to the multitude of those slain in Egypt, and that by torture also, we have been informed they were more than sixty thousand; indeed, being in a foreign country and so naturally having nothing with which to oppose their enemies, they were killed in the aforementioned manner.

"As for all those of us who have waged war against the Romans in our own country, had we not sufficient reason to have sure hopes of victory? For we had arms, and walls, and fortresses so prepared as not to be easily captured, and courage not to be moved by any dangers in the cause of liberty, which encouraged us all to revolt

from the Romans. But then these advantages sufficed us but for a short time and only raised our hopes, while they really appeared to be the origin of our miseries; for all we had has been taken from us, and all has fallen under our enemies, as if these advantages were only to render their victory over us the more glorious and not disposed to preserve those by whom these preparations had been made.

"And as for those already dead in the war, it is reasonable we should esteem them blessed, for they are dead in defending and not in betraying their liberty; but as to the multitude of those now under the Romans, who would not pity their condition? and who would not make haste to die before suffering the same miseries with them? Some were put upon the rack and tortured with fire and whippings, and so died. Some were half devoured by wild beasts, and yet were preserved alive to be devoured by them a second time, in order to afford laughter and sport to our enemies; and such of those as are still alive are to be looked on as the most miserable, who, being so desirous of death, could not achieve it.

"And where is now that great city, the metropolis of the Jewish nation, which was fortified by so many walls, which had so many fortresses and large towers to defend it, which could hardly contain the instruments prepared for war, and which had so many ten thousands of men to fight for it? Where is this city that was believed to have God Himself inhabiting therein? It is now demolished to its very foundations, and has nothing but that monument of it preserved, I mean the camp of those that destroyed it which still dwells upon its ruins; some unfortunate old men also lie upon the ashes of the Temple, and a few women are there preserved alive by the enemy, to our bitter shame and reproach. Now, who is there that revolves these things in his mind and yet is able to bear the sight of the sun, though he might live out of danger? Who is there so much his country's enemy or so unmanly and so desirous of living as not to repent that he is still alive? And I cannot but wish that we had all died before we had seen that holy city demolished by the hands of our enemies, or the foundations of our holy Temple dug up in so profane a manner.

"But since we had a generous hope that deluded us, that we might perhaps have been able to avenge ourselves on our enemies, though it has now become vanity and has left us alone in this distress, let us make haste to die bravely. Let us take pity on ourselves, our children, and our wives, while it is in our power to show pity to them; for we are born to die, as well as those whom we have begotten; nor is it in the power even of the most happy to avoid it. But for abuses and slavery, and the sight of our wives led away in an ignominious manner, with their children, these are not such evils as are natural and necessary among men; although such as do not prefer death to those miseries when it is in their power so to do, must undergo even them, on account of their own cowardice. We revolted from the Romans with great pretensions to courage; and when, at the very last, they invited us to preserve ourselves, we would not comply with them. Who will not, therefore, believe that they will certainly be in a rage against us, in case they take us alive? Miserable will then be the young men strong enough in their bodies to sustain many tortures! Miserable also will be those of elder years who will not be able to bear those calamities which young men might sustain! A man will be obliged to hear the voice of his son imploring the help of his father, when his hands are bound! But certainly our hands are still at liberty, and have a sword in them! Let them be subservient to us in our glorious design; let us die before we become slaves under our enemies, and let us go out of the world, together with our children and our wives, in a state of freedom.

"This it is that our laws command us to do; this it is that our wives and children desire at our hands; nay, God Himself has brought this necessity upon us; while the Romans desire the contrary, and are afraid lest any of us die before we are captured. Let us therefore make haste, and instead of affording them so much pleasure as they hope for in getting us under their power, let us leave them an example which shall at once cause their astonishment at our death, and their admiration of our hardiness therein."

The defenders of the fortress are persuaded by Eleazar; they kill one another. Only two women and five children survive.

PART SIX

HOPING AND COPING

INTRODUCTION

Whatever the impact of their religious tradition upon individual Jews—whether they scrupulously obey it, are inspired by its principles generally, treat it lightly, or are simply unaffected by it; whatever the threat of victimization and martyrdom that looms close or far on the horizon—from Bishop, Cossack, Nazi, or Arab—or seems so remote as to be rarely thought about, the daily life of Jews goes on.

Perhaps the most distinguishing characteristic of the history of Jewish society is that, within the movably narrow or infinitely wide margins of divinity and persecution, they make the best life they can for themselves. They draw upon tradition, or ignore it; they incorporate much from the ambient culture or little of it. But somehow, outside of intervening moments of collective internal spiritual upheaval or externally generated terror, they live lives of quiet hope within their families and cope effectively, sometimes brilliantly, with the circumstances that time, chance, and Yahweh have given them.

Hoping in the face of potential upheaval and danger, coping with limitation and deprivation and instability: That has been the Jewish way, through the centuries in the myriad of Diaspora environments, and back home in Zion recently and today.

It is these qualities of resilience, ingenuity, and adaptation that have so enraged anti-Semites, whether in ancient Alexandria, modern Russia, or the contemporary Middle East. It is not so much the Jewish God who offends (indeed the Gods of Christianity and Islam both have a Jewish origin) nor the stern moral code that rabbinical Judaism taught, but the ability of Jews to find the cracks and the crevices in the social and economic order wherever they lived and make a go of it: "to Jew it." That is why the Jew-haters have had to resort to expelling and killing Jews. In the end, even when Jews were deprived and confined to ghettos, they could survive and raise their families, and sooner or later attain a piece of the world of learning, a slot in the professions, and a series of business triumphs. So the Jews had to go—to other countries or the death camps.

But when the Jews could make a life for themselves, even in relatively insalubrious ambiances, their hopeful disposition and skillful coping allowed them to prevail and not infrequently to flourish. This is perhaps the central theme of Jewish history. Off the narrow corridors of struggling for survival ran the rooms of Jewish comforts and success, or at least making do.

The Alexandrian Sage

In the second quarter of the first century A.D., among the millions of Greek-speaking Jews in the Eastern Mediterranean, were two brilliant and highly articulate rabbis—Saul of Tarsus in Turkey, who, as St. Paul, became the founder of the Christian Church, and his exact contemporary "Philo the Jew" of Alexandria, Egypt.

Philo was both a philosopher seeking to integrate Judaism and Platonism and an active rabbinical leader of the Alexandrian Jewish community—numbering three hundred thousand in his day. Philo's surviving writings, in Greek, take up twelve volumes. They were preserved by the Christian intellectuals of Alexandria who were greatly influenced by his ideas. But as a rabbinical community leader, Philo spent a lot of time giving advice on daily living to Alexandria's Jews. Not surprisingly, he felt compelled to give much attention to sexual matters. The translation is by Roland Williamson.

The most holy Moses, who was a lover of virtue and goodness and especially of his fellow men, expects all men everywhere to be zealous for piety and justice, offering to penitent sinners, as conquerors, the great reward of participation in the best of all communal life found in the best of cities, and the enjoyment of those blessings, large and small, which it confers. Now these blessings, which are of the greatest importance in connection with the body, are health free from disease, on board ship travel free from danger, and in souls the memory, without forgetfulness, of things worth remembering. But second to these blessings are those which consist of recovery or rectification, recovery from illness, a long-desired escape from great dangers on a sea-voyage and subsequent safety, and the recollection which follows on forgetfulness. This has as its brother and close relative repentance and, although it is not in the first rank of blessings, it comes immediately after the first class and takes the second prize. For absolutely not to sin is a property of God alone, or perhaps of a divine man. But the conversion of a sinful man to a blameless life is the attribute of a wise man who has not been entirely ignorant of what is good for his life. And so when Moses

assembles such people and initiates them into his mysteries, he addresses to them precepts which are conciliatory and friendly, urging them to practise sincerity and to reject pride, and to cling to truth and simplicity as vitally necessary virtues and the source of happiness, and to forsake the fictions of the myths impressed on their tender souls from their infancy by parents and nannies and tutors and numerous of their circle of familiars, influencing them into endless error concerning the knowledge of the best. And what can this best of all things be but God, whose honours they have attributed to those who were not gods at all and glorified them beyond measure, while those empty-minded men forget him altogether? Therefore, all those who did not at first acknowledge their duty to revere the Creator and Father of the universe, yet afterwards embraced monotheism, belief in the rule of one, in place of polytheism, belief in the rule of many, we should accept as our dearest friends and closest kinsmen, since they displayed the nature which God loves, which is the greatest of all bonds in cementing friendship and intimacy; and we ought therefore to rejoice with them: Even if, as men might say, they were previously blind, they have now recovered their sight, are capable now of seeing the most brilliant lights, having escaped from the profoundest darkness. We have now described the first and most important form of repentance, but let a man repent not only of the errors by which he was for a long time deceived when he revered created things before the uncreated Being who is their Maker, but also in the other important things in life, by forsaking that worst of all forms of bad government, mob-rule, for democracy, the form of government which possesses the best laws. This involves passing from ignorance to a knowledge of those things which it is disgraceful not to know, from folly to wisdom, from lack of self-control to self-control, from injustice to justice, from cowardice to courage. For it is excellent and expedient to desert, without looking back, to the ranks of virtue and to abandon vice, that wicked mistress. And as surely as in sunshine the shadow follows the body, so also where honour is given to the God who IS, the whole fellowship of virtues must follow. The proselytes immediately become temperate, masters of themselves, modest, gentle, kind, humane, reverent, just, magnanimous, lovers of truth, superior to all considerations of money and pleasure. Conversely, those who rebel against the holy laws of God are ill-disciplined, shameless, unjust, irreverent, companions of falsehood and false witness, who have sold their freedom for good food, good wine, delicacies and the beauty of the opposite sex, in pursuit of the pleasures of the stomach and the organs below the stomach, which in the end cause serious damage both to the body and the soul. Admirable exhortations to repentance are also given, by which we are taught to change the shape of our life from an irregular and disorderly course into a better state. He says that this task is not too onerous nor removed to a distant place, neither in the air far above us, nor at the ends of the earth, nor beyond the great sea, so that we are rendered incapable of accepting it; but very near, residing in three parts of us, mouth, heart and hands, symbolic respectively of our words, our wills and our actions, for the mouth is the symbol of speech, the heart of intentions and the hands of actions, and in these three happiness consists. For whenever our thoughts match our words and our actions match our intentions, life is praiseworthy and perfect, but whenever they are in conflict, it is imperfect and blame-worthy. If anyone

The old foundation: Torah mantle and scroll from Germany, 1876.

does not forget to maintain this harmony, he will be well pleasing to God and will be at once God-loving and God-beloved. . . .

Again, a prostitute is not accepted within the commonwealth of Moses, since she is a stranger to decency, modesty and chastity, and all other virtues. She contaminates the souls of both men and women with her lewdness. She pollutes the immortal beauty of the mind and honours before it the ephemeral attractiveness of the body. She flings herself at the first man she meets, and sells her beauty like some commodity in the marketplace, prepared to say anything with a view to ensnaring the young men, while at the same time she incites her lovers against one another, offering herself as the disgusting prize for the one offering the most. Let her be put to death by stoning, for she is a disgrace, a plague, a pollution of the common life, corrupting the graces bestowed by nature, instead of adorning them further, as she ought, by her own nobility of life. Flagrant acts of adultery detected on the spot or proved by clear evidence are condemned by law. But in cases in which the guilt is merely suspected, the Law did not think it a good thing to have the cases investigated by men, but rather brought before the tribunal of nature. For men can arbitrate in the case of what is visible, but God can judge also in the case of what is unseen, since to him alone belongs the power to see the soul clearly. So the Law says to the husband who suspects his wife, "Write a formal accusation, and go up to the holy city with your wife and standing before the judges lay bare the suspicious feeling which troubles you, not like a false accuser or a malicious schemer trying to win at all costs, but as one seeking to ascertain the truth accurately without sophistry." The woman, who confronts a double danger—the first of losing her life, the second of bringing shame on her past life (something altogether more terrible than death)—must judge the matter in her own mind, and if she is pure, then she must defend herself boldly, but if she is convicted by her own conscience, let her wash her face with her tears and cover her sins with the evil of her shame. For to refuse to the bitter end to be ashamed is the height of wickedness. But if the evidence is indecisive and does not incline definitely to one side or the other, then let them go to the Temple and let them stand opposite each other, in the presence of the priest for that day, and let the husband explain his suspicions, and let him offer some barley-flour as a kind of sacrifice, to show that his accusation is not made vindictively but that his intentions are honest and that he entertains a reasonable doubt. The priest receives the offering and hands it to the woman and removes her head-scarf, in order that she may be judged with her head bare and minus the symbol of modesty which women usually wear when they are wholly innocent. . . .

The act of adultery is symbolised by the earthen vessel because of its fragility, for death is the penalty required in the case of the adulterous; innocence of the charge is symbolised by the earth and water, since both of them are involved in the birth, growth and maturation of all things. Therefore with the two terms used the lawgiver makes a not irrelevant contribution to the picture.

The water, he says, must be "pure" and "living," since if the woman is innocent her conduct is pure and she deserves to live; the earth is taken not from any clean place but from the "holy" ground of the Temple, which is necessarily fertile, as also must be the chaste wife. When these preliminaries are completed, the woman is to go forward with her head uncovered, carrying with her the sacrifice of barley-meal, as has been described, and the priest, holding the earthen vessel with the water in it, stands facing her and pronounces the following words: "If you have not transgressed the laws of marriage, if no other man has had intercourse with you, so that you have not violated the rights of the man who is joined to you by law, be exonerated and free from the punishment. But if you have neglected your husband and burned with ardent passions, succumbing to the love of another or overcome by love for another, betraying and debasing the closest connections, do not be ignorant of the fact that you are deservedly liable to every kind of curse, the signs of which you will display on your body. Come, then, and drink the drink of testing which will reveal and lay bare what is now hidden and secret." Having written these words on a piece of paper he will wipe them off in the water in the earthenware vessel and give it to the woman. When she has drunk the water she will depart, expecting either the reward for her chastity or the extreme punishment for her immorality. For if she has been falsely accused she may hope to conceive and become pregnant, ignoring all fears of infertility and childlessness. But if she is guilty, she should know that there is awaiting her a swelling of the abdomen, which becomes distended and inflamed, and at the same time a horrible infection in the regions around the womb, which she did not keep pure for the man with whom she had entered into a marriage contract according to ancestral customs. The Law takes such care to prevent the introduction of any innovations into the institution of marriage, that even a husband and wife who have intercourse in accordance with the legitimate practices of married life are forbidden, when they get out of bed, to touch anything as long as they have not bathed or made their ablutions, keeping them at a respectable distance from adultery or from any accusations of adultery.

Medieval Merchants

Corporations of medieval Jewish merchants, organized usually along family lines, not only served economic exchange between the European and Muslim worlds but extended their trade to Sind (India) and China. These Rhadanites, as they were called, were already in the tenth and eleventh centuries finding ways to conduct international commerce that Iberian, Dutch, and English merchants did not attempt until the sixteenth and seventeenth centuries. This description, from a medieval Arabic source, is translated by Norman A. Stillman.

They speak Arabic, Persian, Greek, Frankish, Andalusian, and Slavonic. They travel from East to West and from West to East by both land and sea. From the West, they bring adult slaves, girls and boys, brocade, beaver pelts, assorted furs, sables, and swords. They sail from the Land of the Franks on the Western Sea (the Mediterranean) [Southern Italy] and set out for al-Faramä (Pelusium) [near Portsaio in Egypt]. There they transport their merchandise by pack animal to al-Qulzum [on the Red Sea]. At al-Qulzum they set sail for al-Jär and Jidda, [on the coast of Arabia] after which they proceed to Sind, India, and China. From China they bring musk, aloeswood, camphor, cinnamon, and other products obtained from those regions, as they make their way back to al-Qulzum. Then they transport it overland to al-Faramä, there setting sail on the Western Sea once again. Some go straight to Constantinople to sell their merchandise to the Byzantines, while others go to the capital of the king of the Franks and sell their goods there.

Sometimes they choose to take their merchandise from the Land of the Franks across the Western Sea to Antioch, and thence overland on a three-day journey to al-Jābiya [near Damascus] from which they sail down the Euphrates to Baghdad, then down the Tigris to Ubulla [near Basra]. From Ubulla they sail to Oman, Sind, India, and China—in that order.

The Jewish Town

In the Pale of Settlement—a vast territory comprising the Ukraine, Eastern Poland, Belerus, and Lithuania—in the early years of the century lived between three and four million Jews, a like number having departed for America. Novelists and social scientists have tried to reconstruct the social world in the Pale, and get beneath the piety and sentimentality with which partisan sources have covered it in retrospect.

Here is one of the best efforts of fiction to describe the old Jewish small town. It was written in the late 1920s, when this world was rapidly disappearing, by the Yiddish writer who used the name of Der Nister (the Hidden One). Der Nister's cool yet sympathetic description did not easily coincide with hostile Communist dialectics. Also it doesn't fit too well with the sentimental gurgles issued nowadays from Judaic Studies programs in American universities. It is sharp, clear-eyed, probing, and sensitive. The translation is by Leonard Wolf.

The city of N. is built in three rings. First ring: the marketplace at the very center. Second: surrounding the market, the great city proper with its many houses, streets, byways, back streets where most of the populace lives. Third: suburbs.

Should a stranger find himself in N. for the first time, he would at once be drawn, willy-nilly, to the city's center. That's where the hubbub is, the seething, the essential essence, the heart and pulse of the city.

His nose would be assailed immediately by smells: the smell of half-raw, rough or fine leather of all kinds; the acrid sweetness of baked goods; of groceries; of the salt smell of various dried fish; smells of kerosene, pitch, machine oil; of cooking and lubricating oils; of the smell of new paper. Of scruffy, shabby, dusty humid things: down-at-heels shoes; old clothes; worn-out brass; rusted iron—and anything else that refuses to be useless; that is, determined, via this petty buying and selling to serve someone, somehow.

There in the marketplace are shop after shop, squeezed narrowly together like boxes on a shelf. If one doesn't have a shop in the upper district, then he owns a warehouse in the lower. If he doesn't own a warehouse, then he has at least a covered booth outside a shop. If no booth, then he spreads his goods out on the ground, or depending on what he sells, holds his wares in his hands.

There, in the marketplace, it's a permanent fair. Wagons from nearby (or from distant) settlements arrive to pick up goods, and wagons from the railway depot endlessly discharge their loads—everything fresh, everything new.

Packing and unpacking!

Jewish tenant farmers, village merchants, come in from Andrushivkeh, Paradek, Yampole. They come from Zvill and Korets and even from the more distant Polesia. In summer, they wear their light coats and hoods. In winter, cloaks or fur coats with well-worn collars. They come to buy goods for cash or on credit. Some are decent and honorable—others are something else: Their scheme is to buy on credit, then sell at a profit, then buy on credit again—then declare themselves bankrupt.

Wagons arrive empty and leave fully packed, covered with sacks, tarpaulins, rags—all of them tied down with cords. The wagons drive off at evening; others arrive at dawn.

"*Sholom aleichem.*" A storekeeper hurries down the steps of his shop to greet a newly arrived old customer, to lead him from the wagon directly into his shop lest some other merchant get at him. "*Sholom aleichem,* and how are things in Andrushivkeh?" he says with a show of familiarity, then he gets right to business. "Ah, it's good you're here. I have just what you're looking for. A marvelous this . . . a splendid that . . . "

Rival storekeepers endeavor to strike up conversations with one's customer, to entice him away from his usual shop. They inveigle him in by offering lower prices or better credit terms. Often enough this can lead to real battles. Shopkeepers against shopkeepers, clerks against clerks. Only the porters and errand boys, who occasionally earn something from one or another of the shops, keep aloof, refusing to mix in, to choose sides.

Sometimes it's the market women who quarrel. Then women's cries are heard. Blows are exchanged.

But that happens rarely. For the most part, everyone is much too busy. Morning and night, there's work to be done to meet the needs of hordes of customers—and there's enough profit for all.

Clerks do the heavy work: weighing, measuring, carrying things out, setting them in place and so on. The shopkeepers do the bargaining: the persuading, cajoling, displaying of goods, arriving at prices.

It is, as has been said, a permanent fair. Wholesale and retail. In the more successful shops, the owners carry home bundles of hundred-and-fifty-ruble notes. The less successful tradesmen take home coins in their linen pouches and not much paper money. But they make a greater racket than their richer competitors. Endless contentions, quarrels, shouts, cries. They fight over a groschen or a pound of soap, over the sale of a little starch, the price of a dried fish. And curse each other unsparingly with the same vehemence over small matters as over large:

"Break a bone!"

"Go to hell . . . "

"Drop dead."

"See you at your funeral."

But they make up quickly, too. The stallkeepers drink tea frequently with each other; they dart into each other's booths to arrange a free loan, to borrow a weight for a scale. They club together the money needed to take advantage of an opportune bargain offered by a Gentile. Or they play tricks on each other, or shout to each other across five stalls, across ten. Everyone shouting at once.

That's how it is normally on market days. On special days, the crowding is more intense. There's a greater press of wagons, of unharnessed horses munching hay. Those still harnessed have their noses deep in their feed bags. Colts nuzzle between the legs of mares. A stallion whinnies, making a horsey racket that resounds throughout the market. And along with the horses and people—dirt, filth. In winter, snow that is not snow. In winter and summer, cow flops, horse piss, puddles of kerosene, hay, straw, barrel hoops, barrels, boxes—rarely cleared away.

During important market days, like those during Lent, there's hardly room to move. A mob of varicolored peasant pelts; brown coats; yellow furs; men's coarse-haired beaver jackets; headscarfs, neckcloths, hats, fur caps, felt boots, knitted leggings for landowners and peasants, for men and women.

Well-to-do folk coming to town shop seriously. The poor search for some trifle or other—something that might easily enough be bought at home. But the yearning to come to town is great.

The hunger to wander about the shops, to haggle over baubles. To haggle! To spend as much time as possible over a purchase. For the sheer pleasure of buying.

Those with money move about prudently. They know what they want and where to look for it. The shopkeepers make them welcome, greet them courteously, respectfully. Throughout the bargaining sessions, they take great pains to be accommodating, to keep them from leaving the shop. Naturally, given the press of the crowds, the poorer customers are not very welcome. They are instantly recognizable as they wander confusedly about, their eyes searching every shelf and corner of the shop. It's clear that they have more enthusiasm than cash and are therefore greeted with suspicion or driven away. Their diffident, poverty-stricken questions are not answered, and if a shopkeeper notices that one of his clerks is spending too long with such a customer he passes his clerk a note: "Don't waste time on this one. Can't you see what he wants, the damn thief?"

And, during the Great Market days, thefts are not infrequent. Occasionally it is a peasant who steals something from a shopkeeper, but more usually it is the other way around. There are certain specialists, well known in the market, who weigh with ten-pound weights instead of half a *pood* (twenty pounds). It's done quickly, skillfully. On the scale and off! And the peasant has no inkling of what's happened. Until later, when he comes back complaining bitterly. But then, those specialists, those *half-pooders* as they are called, don't recognize their customer. Often slaps are exchanged, blows. Until the red-faced, drunken policeman, the *buddoshnik*, meddles in the matter, blows his whistle and parts the combatants, and hauls off to jail precisely the one who ought not to be hauled off.

Or it may happen that a peasant slips some trifle into his breast pocket. If he's caught, he's tried unceremoniously on the spot. The shop clerk strikes the blows. If the clerks in the nearby shops get wind of the matter (and if they have the time), they too get into the action. Bringing with them whatever implements are available, they lend a hand at the beating. Male peasants are struck around the head and neck, a woman, whether old or young, is hardly beaten at all. But she is disgraced. Her shawl and babushka are torn off and she is made to stand, disheveled and ashamed, exposed to the scorn of the entire marketplace.

However, such things happen rarely. Now and then. For the most part, customers buy and are satisfied with their purchases, and sellers are pleased with their gains. Everyone's busy, everyone glows.

Whatever the weather—wind, frost, snow, blizzard—no one pays the slightest attention. The market goes on. Profit warms the merchants.

In the course of those busy days, people eat very little. Whatever was eaten in the morning at home before leaving for the market suffices until evening, until dark, until, red-faced, swollen, exhausted, one gets home.

One ignores everything. Trembling hands, freezing faces, noses, ears. Blows are overlooked, and splinters. Never mind. In the evening at home where it's warm, the splinters can be removed.

All of this takes place in the "Rough Market," but similar things happen in the "Noble Market" on a parallel street. There, too, there's no way to get through the press of wagons, though there are no peasants here and generally no retail buyers. Only wholesale.

There, the important cloth merchants and the major ready-made shoe and clothing dealers are. Dealers in all sorts of goods from Lodz, Warsaw, and Bialystok. From distant Polish towns and from others as far away as White Russia.

There, the customers are landowners, rich nobility, prosperous small-town Jews. There, the clerks are more neatly dressed. There, too, customers are received and treated differently. There, flattery and chicanery are of a higher order. There the shopkeepers move about before their shops in skunk coats, forming little clusters in which they carry on serious business conversations, while inside the shops, the sly-tongued, persuasive chief clerks bustle about displaying their goods so skillfully that it is a rare customer who can escape them.

Outside, the shopkeepers talk endlessly about the money market, exchange rates, bankruptcies, trips to Lodz or Kharkov, of rising or falling prices. Inside the windowless shops, where the only light filters in from the street door, there is a perpetual half-light, even by day. The customers stand at counters behind which the clerks display yard goods: linens, woolens, silks, cottons with English, German, Russian labels. Lying labels, false seals. And in the course of displaying and measuring the goods and persuading the buyers, one does—what one does. As the clerks put it, "You steal the suckers blind."

In the Noble Market there is the same busyness during the Great Market days described above. Here, too, wagons are packed, boxes torn open; goods are moved. Porters carrying loads in bump into clerks carrying bundles out of the shops. Shelves are emptied, cash registers filled. These are good days for the shopkeepers, who beam at the flow of money. Good days for the clerks to whom the customers "give a little something." And of course they get a commission on their sales. These are good days for the brokers, for the middlemen who, for a fee, introduce new customers, or who, for a fee, serve as consultants to regular customers in making their deals.

During those Great Market days, the shopkeepers, their wives and even their children are all in the shops. No matter how many employees one has, they are not enough. So one brings in family members. Those who can do real tasks, do them. Others who can only look on serve as lookouts. But no one thinks of leaving the shop, of going home until evening, until night, until very late when the shops are locked and chained, when the shutters, with an iron shriek, are lowered. Then, the contented shopkeepers, their cashboxes full, are accompanied home by their clerks and the members of their family.

And that's how it is in the market before the winter holidays. A little less noisy, but the market always is and remains the market, with its deals, its money hunger, its devotion to profit. And once in it, one is entirely swallowed up by it and becomes unable to understand or to welcome anyone who is not part of it. There's no time for such intruders. And in the eternally established organization of the market, no place for them.

So true is this that if, rarely, some nonmarket person—a clergyman or a child—should appear there (one does not count people who are merely passing through), their presence would be felt as a violation. Children are immediately shooed away by their parents: "What are you doing here? Get on home." A synagogue caretaker, or a cantor, may show up, but only to go from shop to shop to remind someone of a mourning anniversary, or to call shopkeepers to a circumcision or a wedding. But such an intruder must not linger. He must perform his errand quickly and leave. Because he is superfluous.

Even habitually insolent beggars, perpetual tramps, rarely receive alms in the market, but are turned away everywhere with the same sullen phrase: "Go. Go in good health. We don't give in the market. At home." Even the town's mad folk avoid the market, as if they knew that there was no place and no one to care for them there.

Market people are an earnest folk, worrying constantly. Those who don't have much money worry about where to get it. How to borrow a little. Those who have money worry about where to get it, how to borrow more. The prosperous merchants do their business with brokers and rack their brains for the means to pay them, and struggling shopkeepers worry about the weekly ruble they need to pay the interest to the loan sharks. But everyone is busy, heads whirring over profit when there *is* profit, or when there is none, over ways and means to meet expenses.

The clerks are less serious. More carefree. Since their time is not their own, they can be frivolous. The young ones who even at the busiest times are given to practical jokes turn especially silly when there is little to do. This is particularly true in the summer before the harvest, when the market quiets down and hardly anyone from the nearby villages (never mind those from the outlying districts) comes to town. Then, whole days go by with nothing to do.

Except hang around outdoors taking the sun, or cooling off inside the shops or cellars. And when things get particularly dreary, one thanks God for the occasional groschen in the till with which one can slip off to a nearby soda water shop for a drink and a snack. And when things get truly boring, one is grateful to the crazy noblewoman, the Panyi Akoto, notorious throughout the town, if suddenly she shows up in her old-fashioned cloak (from the time of King Sobieski) with its tassels and fringes, her hat with its many ribbons, beads and dangling baubles.

The clerks rush to greet her, as if they meant to welcome her into their shops. One of the clerks outdistances the others and speaking to her in the most respectful, sidelong manner, as one does to the rich—says, "What does *kometz tsaddik* spell?"

"Tso?"

The clerks crack up because the Hebrew letters *kometz tsaddik* actually spell *Tso,* "What" in Russian. And so they have trapped her in their joke, and they laugh, pinch each other, go berserk until their game ends with a crowd gathering, outrage, shouting, swearing, and the cursing of Jews and Gentiles until even the older clerks, even the shopkeepers are involved.

Or another time the clerks may entice the feeble-minded Monish in from a nearby street. Monish, whose blond Jesus-beard frames the deep pallor of his face, is a sickly, gentle, usually silent boy who stutters.

The clerks press him into a corner where he is promised anything he wants if he will only answer, for the thousandth time, the question which, a thousand times before, they have put to him.

"Monish, why do you want to get married?"

"Three reasons," he says, smiling.

"What are they?"

"To c . . . c . . . cuddle. To k . . . k . . . kiss. And to t . . . t . . . tickle."

"And nothing more?"

"Wh . . . wh . . . what else is there?"

Thus the market in its off-season. The shops are opened just for the sake of appearances. There is a weary wait each day for the sun to move across the sky. Then lock-up time and home, only to return the next day for another round of wasted time. To stand in the doorway expecting no customers—because there are none.

And so pass the several weeks of the dead season before harvest-time.

Those who belong, those who are part of the market—shopkeepers, brokers, merchants who derive their livelihood from it, as their parents and grandparents derived theirs—have neither the time nor the inclination to wonder about its composition, or to doubt its permanence.

On the contrary, they take it for granted that the mezuzahs nailed to the doorjambs of the shops and the rusty horseshoes nailed to the thresholds of the meaner little stores are the guardians of their bit of luck. As the bat, killed with a gold coin and buried under the thresholds of the more prosperous shops, is the guardian of their prosperity. That's how it's supposed to be, how it has always been, from the beginning of eternity, and how it will be to the end of time, so ordered by God's law from generation to generation, a heritage decreed by fathers for their children.

Should a stranger come to the market, and should he stay for a while, he would very soon get a whiff of dissolution, the first hint that very soon the full stink of death would rise from the whole shebang: the buying and selling, the hullabaloo of wheeling and dealing, the entire giddiness of all those whirling there.

And especially if he came at night when the market, together with its main and side streets, was asleep, its shops barred, its booths and stalls closed down, its rows of dark warehouses behind heavy iron gates—locked and chained. And if he were to see the bored, yawning night watchmen sitting or standing about in clusters, or singly on various street corners, looking like dark, fur-clad manifestations of the wandering god Mercury, who, long delayed, has finally arrived here out of ancient times. If a stranger did show up, we say, and if he saw all this, if he was not already a prophet, he would not in truth become one. And yet, if he were a man with somewhat refined sensibilities, he would feel grief at his heart; he would sense that the thresholds on which the night watchmen sat were already mourning thresholds, that the sealed doors, chains and locks would never be replaced, and that to enlarge the picture, to frame it truly, one would need to hang a death lamp to burn quietly here in the middle of the market to be a memorial to the place itself.

That then is the market section of the city of N. The first ring. The second section: the city itself.

If on that same night a stranger leaving the market had turned toward the nearest houses, what would first catch his eye would be a series of one-, two- or many-storyed structures built in an old-fashioned way, and in a crazy style. Or better, in no style at all. He would know at once that these were not residences, but were destined for some other purpose. And if at first glance he was not able to tell that purpose, a second look would make everything clear. They were built by the religious community of the city of N. for their God and according to His requirements. He is a wandering and an exiled God, and does not ask much of them: no columns or airy spaces, no superfluous cleanliness. No exterior decor. Only that the guttering light of an economical kerosene lamp should reveal itself through a filthy window at night, that there be silence, and that a wounded spirit may rest on the threshold of the

place, in its windows and on its roof. And that an old, somewhat slovenly bachelor sexton—a not particularly diligent servant of God—sleep in one of the buildings; and in others, let whole groups of homeless beggars lie sleeping on benches, on mountains of rags. Looking themselves like mountains of rags as they snore away there. And in other buildings, on the other hand, let all twelve of the windows that tradition requires in that God's structures be ablaze at midnight with the light of candles and burning lamps; and let there frequently be heard the warm singing of boyish voices which, as they study His laws and His commandments, serve Him, and are so accounted, as sacrifices such as in the days of His glory He received—and to which for a long time now He has been unaccustomed.

Here you have such a building.

Its front faces on a small, empty square. On the lower level, it is surrounded by shops and a few homes, meat and cereal stores and others producing income for the synagogue. On the second story, the synagogue itself, looking out at the square through the many windows of its entry corridor. The other three sides, each with three windows, look out on various little streets.

It is called the Open Synagogue.

Why?

In its builder's will more than a hundred years ago, it was specified in writing that the synagogue door must never close. Neither by day nor night, not in summer or in winter. Never. So long as the building remains standing—till the coming of the Messiah, it is hoped.

And so its door is always open to the town's inhabitants who come to say their prayers and to study there. Open also to those who in summer come in to cool off, and to those who in winter come to warm themselves. Open also to dealers, shopkeepers, porters and others who slip away from the empty tumult of the market so that they may breathe a bit of consoling air. It is a refuge for those poor wanderers for whom it is a pausing point in their arrivals or departures. Wanderers who sometimes stay for weeks, or even months. And nobody, according to the terms of the will, may prevent them.

In that synagogue, prayers are said from early morning to well past midday. Sometimes there are full quorums of ten men, at other times people pray alone. At night there is Torah study to which middle-aged and elderly men come in the evening, and who go home after their studies. Late at night there are sleepless young people.

It is rare then that one finds the Open Synagogue empty. The door swings in and out. Is never closed.

It is a gathering place for various interests. Here, there is a cluster of people talking about their workaday concerns. There, a young man, or an older one, is engrossed in a complex study problem that has no relationship to anything going on around him.

Those studying are of various sorts. Some of them are local young bachelors, wealthy or semi-wealthy, whose parents support them. But for the most part, the scholars are from out of town, looked after by people who think it a benevolent act to provide them with their most urgent necessities. Among these young people are those who come from nearby villages as well as from more distant communities: from Volhynia and the Podolia borders—even from as far away as Poland: each with his accent, mannerisms, songs and gestures.

Now for the congregation. Very poor, tattered, carelessly or badly dressed—and therefore devoted to the impulse that brought them here; a congregation so inspired, so committed, so engulfed by the desire to reach the goal in which they believe that the days are not long enough and they stay up much of the night.

Then the synagogue is brightly lighted. A lamp from the ceiling or from one of the wall brackets hangs above each of the young scholars' heads. Those sitting in the farther corners hold candles above the books they are studying. The accumulated light illuminates not only the synagogue, but it also spills out-of-doors. And a pious passerby, or an inhabitant looking out of one of the nearby low houses, seeing the synagogue so brightly lighted on all sides might get the feeling that he was looking at a lighthouse set in the midst of the city's darkness. The sense that the lighted synagogue is the sleepy town's brilliant representative before heaven, and heaven's directors.

Especially if a pious passerby hears the young voices shouting or humming the famished, ascetic, yearning melodies brought here from the mullah and dervish schools of the godforsaken distant East. These young people, who have voluntarily immured themselves here, utter ecstatic yells, and express by means of those melodies their discontent with corporeality. Creating, we say again, the feeling in a pious passerby that he is watching young victims sacrificing themselves for somebody else's sins.

There you have one synagogue.

And here is another one nearby. The "hot-headed" synagogue, so called because hotheads, half-mad, fanatically pious Hasidic sects like the Kotzkers, the Carliners pray there, wildly climbing the walls, running about cooling their interior religious fervor with the sounds of their own voices.

Facing the "hotheaded" synagogue, the "cold" one.

A building in which, even if you enter it in summer, a cold breeze chills your bones. This, too, is a two-story building. Again, with shops on the first level. On the second story, the synagogue itself.

Highly polished railings, which over the years have been rubbed by many hands holding to them on the way up, lead to a vestibule like a cold-storage vault, then there are several steps up to the synagogue's entryway.

A high, broken ceiling divided into five parts. Beneath the fifth, the middle section, the Torah-reading podium on tall pillars. Chandeliers suspended from ropes make one think that neither the candles in their sockets nor the gas in the lamps could illuminate or warm anything.

Those praying are cold, those studying are dry—Lithuanians. A sense of withered life, an emptiness, emanates from their songs, their prayers. They are called the Ibn-Ezraniks, after the early medieval Spanish poet and philosopher whose rational spirit has found a place like a chilly, abandoned nest among this thicket of synagogues.

If it were not for the synagogue furnishings—the Torah-reading pulpit, the Ark of the Covenant, the podiums, bookcases and books—both the interior and the exterior of this building would be easily taken for some sort of burial structure, or tomb.

Now for the "old one."

The oldest synagogue of all.

As you approach it, you notice how dilapidated the entryway is, worn away by dark and unhappy generations over centuries. If you go in, you sense at once that all those centuries have left behind their despised and desolate breath.

The path to the door, and all along the facade of the building, is paved with flat, well-trodden river stones that have worn thin.

An iron door, broad as a gate and studded with huge round-headed nails, can be opened with a long, old-fashioned, very heavy key—an ancient masterwork with short, chiseled teeth whose like it would be hard to find anywhere. It is a key that needs to be turned several times in its keyhole, and no one except the synagogue's regular sexton knows how to put the key into its proper position.

Inside the gate you come to the synagogue vestibule. Dark, poorly illuminated by an exterior light, and even less by the light that filters through the varicolored panes of glass high up in the second door that leads to the synagogue.

If you open that door and cross the threshold, you will, willy-nilly, raise your head. It would seem that the architects designed the place for that express purpose so that the pious visitor must lift his eyes the moment he crosses the lintel. To make him think that someone higher than himself exists. Above him, and beyond his fate. Inducing in him the first religious tremor.

The ceiling is high and spacious, and if one looks closely at its center—amazing! A ceiling above a ceiling. An intensification not visible at first.

The synagogue: The east wall, and especially the broad pillar that reaches to the highest heights, are covered with gold-painted animals, birds, angels, fruits, flowers, musical instruments and woven branches.

The walls and ceiling are painted in oil. Folk painters, primitive masters, have lavished all of their devout skill, their naïveté and childish simplicity here. They have painted stories of myths, the lives of the Patriarchs. Abraham, for example, bringing Isaac to the sacrifice. Moses on Mount Sinai with the Ten Commandments; Isaac lying bound on the woodpile, and Abraham ready with his knife. And the angel appearing to keep him from killing his only son. Moses with the stone tablets, and around him the smoking mountain and bolts of streaking fire. Then the golden calf, and the shrine of the covenant and so on. And the same for the other walls, and the ceilings, too, decorated with such pictures.

The Torah-reading podium, with its many steps up, is screened on all four sides by artificial trees.

Trees from which children cannot tear away their gaze, and even the hearts of devout adults beat faster at the sight of that tree-screened podium. From its height, the Great Ban used to be read against those who had merited it. At specified times, the appropriate sound of the ram's horn was blown from that podium: whether to announce heaven's decree or the news of a calamitous law of the state. From it, the deaths of great leaders of the people were mourned. From it, new ordinances and laws, whether of the community or the czar, were promulgated.

The synagogue is not very large, in fact, but on a holiday or a festivity, it has been known to absorb the entire population of N., with, naturally, some few left outside. First, the middle section was filled up, then the two side aisles, left and right. The people squeezed together so astutely; they filled every space so closely that it was hard to find space for so much as a pin. The press of bodies and the heated breathing of the multitude were so intense the walls perspired, and streams ran down the smooth oil-painted surfaces. That breathing could be sensed in the synagogue even when it was empty. The breathing of masses of people experiencing their lives on remarkable occasions.

The synagogue is especially for men. But there is a large, screened gallery running along three walls built so that men and women can be kept strictly apart.

But there have been times when the women were permitted to come down to the main floor. But even when they were not permitted, they sometimes seized permission for themselves. They came down an inflamed, angry, hysterical mob and opened the Holy of Holies and flung themselves on it with the sort of passionate outcries men are incapable of—on the occasion of a recruiting decree and the threat of draftee "catchers." Or when there was some other disaster in the town: a plague, an epidemic—cholera, for example.

This synagogue was not used only for the usual prayers. A quorum of men for morning or evening prayers rarely assembled there. There was no Torah study either. Sleeping overnight—strictly forbidden. And yet, essentially, this was the synagogue of synagogues, the only one of God's houses to which the townspeople attributed legendary holiness because it was the site of the martyrdom of a holy man who had suffered for his faith and shown great heroism there. This is why the place is held in such high esteem, why it is enfolded in legend and why the people have kept it closed at all times, opening its great doors only on the most exceptional occasions. And this is why, to repeat, it is closed during the day, and why at night, according to popular belief, it is a gathering place for the souls of the dead; and this is why those who need to pass that synagogue at night keep their distance from it, and this is why even the sexton knocks at the door first before he opens the synagogue in the morning. To alert the gathered souls to his coming.

This synagogue is the tallest building in N. According to decree, no other structure may be built higher. Only the church is taller, but it is not considered a building for comparison since it belongs to a foreign people, a foreign regime. And one has to yield to foreign power, especially when it has superior strength.

Then there are the workingmen's and trades-men's synagogues according to their kind, those of the pious and charitable societies and insti-tutes: shoemakers', tailors', smiths', wheel-wrights', butchers' synagogues. Synagogues of grain brokers, fruit vendors. Of Don men, who travel on the Don River; of Muscovites, Danzigers, hospital workers; of Hasidic sects and other soci-eties—and so on. And all clustered together in one place, cheek by jowl, above, beside, beneath each other.

And now, at night, in one of the synagogues a candle is lighted, in another, no light at all, in a third there are many candles burning. In the first, no Torah students, in the second, there are one or two, in the third, a number of scholars are study-ing. And overshadowing them all, standing guard over them all is the Old Synagogue, tall and som-nolent, with its concrete walk and its mute doors.

A stranger—we say—a stranger who should chance to find his way from the market to this place at night would grasp at once the structure and the style of community life in N. Would per-ceive that the market is the town's living center, and that its God guards its pocketbook. That the people themselves live shunted into the nearby side streets and that they, the streets and their sleeping inhabitants, are not themselves of the essence—rather they are an excrescence on the essence, which is the market. The market which

nourished them yesterday and which tomorrow will feed them again. And to keep from losing the restlessness of yesterday's market, to keep it from dissipating entirely, and as a way of recalling it in tomorrow's tumult, they have, during these quiet hours, set watchmen out, along with their God as well, who is permitted neither to doze nor to sleep; and to that end they have left their youngest children awake in the synagogues, with instructions to rouse Him to His old age and to His duties.

And we will add further that if that stranger, whether in summer or winter, should spend the night in one of those synagogues and should choose to wait there for dawn, he would observe that when it was time for day to open its eye above those places, he would see that when the eye did indeed open, it closed again almost at once, not only because it was not especially clean there, nor even because the houses are clustered as haphazard as in a Gypsy camp. No. The essen-tial reason had to do with the sense of doom, of foreseen disaster, hanging over the place . . . over everything: Over the market, and especially over those synagogue structures which, though they would appear to be the guardians, would appear to be the lookouts, the caretakers of the commu-nity—were, if the truth be told, already a sight to occasion pity. And later, who could tell? Perhaps they would be hung about with the rusted locks of memory; perhaps they would be sold at auc-tion. Or (in the event that nobody bought them) . . . they would collapse from sheer age; or to imagine the best case possible, they would, with the changing times, be renewed and put to other, quite other, uses.

Everything's possible. The day, however, as it opens its eye, sees:

A large city divided in two by a river. Along its banks, the river is screened by rotting old tree trunks, by the dense tops of willow trees. The trees, with their feet in the water, turn it dark green, and in that darkened water live fish, frogs, snakes and all sorts of plants and swarming other things.

Early in the morning a few old fishermen in small boats wait beside nets or beside the fishing rods whose lines they have cast out, hoping to be rewarded for their early morning patience with small river fish.

Flocks of ducks and geese, each flock led by its

respective drake or gander paddling in advance of the flock, quietly swim the breadth of the river from one bank to the other.

Occasional washerwomen, early in the morning, are already doing their laundry at the river's edge, and the sound of rinsing and beating is so insignificant it does not even disturb the fish swimming nearby.

There's a presunrise light on the river, with trees bending over it, and the shadows of night still on the water.

Not far above the level of the river there are meadows which, here and there, are still moist with water left by the spring floods: green meadows, tinged with mildew, covered with the myriad heads of yellow dandelions.

At this time of day there is seldom anybody stirring in those fields, except for an occasional suspicious-looking cluster of people who have come there to conduct their secretive discussions or to divide up the loot of an already achieved theft.

Higher than those meadows, on both sides of the river, the town whose two sides are united first, downstream at the point where the river narrows, by an old-fashioned footbridge that can accommodate three or four people walking abreast; and farther upstream where the river is wide, by a modern bridge made of wood and set on numerous timbers, but broad and handsome with room for two sets of wagons coming and going as well as sidewalks (with handrails) for pedestrians.

Government and Law in the Shtetl

While the Eastern European shtetl is often portrayed in roseate colors as a good-hearted democracy, in fact the shtetl's government and law reflected its polarizing class structure. How power was exercised in the shtetl is here described by social scientists Diane K. and David G. Roskies.

The important point is that shtetl government was not based on democratic principles. It was designed to provide effective institutions of law and administration—to allow the community to cope effectively with its problems. While out of place in today's American Jewish suburbia, in its time and place the shtetl power system did its job.

Folklore and literature alone cannot provide an accurate picture of the inner workings of the shtetl. For if they were our only source, it would seem that each town was made up of a mindless mob of Jews who dutifully followed their leader—the rabbi. In difficult matters, perhaps, Fayvl the Genius would come to bail them out. In fact, nothing could be further from the truth. A shtetl was not run by the *rov* nor by the masses but rather by an elite group of well-to-do householders who controlled the town council called kahal.

The power structure of the shtetl can be summed up by the three K's:

1. Kahal, the central authority.

2. *Khevres*, the real action on the grass-roots level. A *khevre* is a voluntary association organized around work, study or charitable functions.

3. *Kley-koydesh*, which means literally, "the holy vessels." These were the only paid officials of the community, and indispensable for the religious work they performed: rabbi, *shames*, *gabe*, *shoykhet*, *khazn*, watchman, scribe.

The only source of information we now have on the civic affairs of a shtetl is the *pinkes*, a register in which the minutes of the Kahal and *khevre* meetings were recorded. Through the pages of a *pinkes* we can see how the town was run, how the various groups related to each other, how one community related to the next, and how the Jews related to the surrounding Gentile world.

The *pinkes* was always considered and kept as a holy object. There were even some people who believed that a house in which a *pinkes* was kept would always be preserved from fire and that the women of the house would never have trouble giving birth. Until recently, there was a custom in the *shtetlekh* of the Ukraine, to place a *pinkes* under the pillow of a woman who was having great labor pains.

Almost all of the old *pinkeysim* were made of parchment and were bound in fine leather with gold lettering. The size was that of a Talmud. Most were written by a professional scribe, in the same script as a Torah scroll. The title page of a *pinkes* as well as the first letters of each paragraph in the regulations were illuminated with exceptionally fine ornamentation and drawings. Sometimes each page of a *pinkes* was enclosed in a beautiful, colorful frame.

There were three types of *pinkeysim:*

1. The community registers which recorded the decisions and regulations of kahal.

2. The registers of the social and educational *khevres* such as: Visiting the Sick, the Burial Society,Ï Welcoming Visitors, Welcoming the Bride, the Godfather Society, the Great Charity, Free-Loan Association and Redeeming the Captives.

3. The registers of the workers' *khevres:* tailors, cobblers, hatmakers, tanners, and so on.

From the *pinkeysim* of the *khevres* we learn that it was no easy matter getting accepted to any one of them. One had to pass through several stages before qualifying as a full-fledged member. Even after achieving the preliminary qualifications, there was often a waiting period of a few years before being accepted, because new admissions to the *khevre* were very limited. In some cases, the limitations were so great that the *khevre* admitted no more than two new members a year! In other *khevres*, a deadline was set for the

fifteenth of Kislev (late November, early December) for all new admissions.

We could not always find the registers for the workers' *khevres* in the smaller towns of the Ukraine. Nevertheless, our historical-ethnographic expedition did manage to locate a few of these valuable documents.

The title page of these workers' registers usually bore an appropriate biblical or Rabbinic quotation which emphasized the importance of work: "For you shall eat the labor of your hands: Happy shall you be and it shall be well with you" (Psalms 128:2) or "Blessed are you in this world and it will be well with you in the world to come" (Berakhot 8). On the combined *pinkes* of the shoemakers, tanners, and hatmakers of Mikolayev (which was famous for its leather goods) the title-page had the following motto: "Greater is man's pleasure from his labor than from worshipping the Lord" (Berakhot 8).

These registers contain three types of regulations:

1. Matters pertaining to their profession: price control, labor disputes between workers and employers.

2. Matters of internal organization and leadership.

3. Religious affairs.

Elections for the workers' *khevres* took place once a year during the intermediate days of *peysekh*, just like all other elections in the shtetl. New members were chosen either through an "electoral college" or directly by ballot box.

Besides the regular positions that were held in every *khevre* such as chairmen and trustees, the workers' *khevres* would also elect a special seven-man board who were given absolute jurisdiction to represent all the member workers. These seven drew up and signed the contracts; they controlled prices; they granted permission for a worker to go into business for himself; they punished law-breakers and even had the right of excommunication. All their decisions were duly recorded in the *pinkes*.

Working hours were also regulated in quite a modern way. In the tailors' *pinkes* of Loytsk (1721) the following was recorded: "No one, not even a self-employed tailor can work late into the night. On the eve of the Sabbath and holidays, all work must be laid aside at two P.M." If, however, someone was forced to work overtime—because of a wedding or because the local *porets* badly needed the garment—that someone must pay two groschen to charity for each hour of overtime and must also pay his own workers extra.

To avoid competition, the seven-member council enforced price control. From time to time they would issue a price list which would be posted in all the synagogues and houses of study. These lists were very detailed and stated exactly how much should be paid for a new piece of work and how much to repair an old garment.

The council of seven was also responsible for watching over the apprentices. They decided how many years the apprenticeship should last, what type of household chores they had to perform for their boss and what salary they would receive. The contracts drawn up between the apprentice and his employer were approved by the council and recorded in the *pinkes.*

Religious matters take up a large part of the workers' *pinkes.* Almost every workers' *khevre* had its own house of prayer or study, its own *gabe, shames* and *khazn.* When hiring a *khazn,* each *khevre* made sure to chose a *khazn* who was one of them. Cobblers chose a cobbler; tailors, a tailor. Only the Burial Society could not have a *khazn* from its own ranks, in accordance with the age-old principle: "It is forbidden for someone who takes care of burials or for a doctor to pray in front of the ark, because they cannot in all honesty represent the congregation when reciting the prayer 'Heal us, oh Lord,' for they make a living from the dead and the sick."

Workers handled the distribution of synagogue honors quite differently than other groups. Each worker was of equal standing before God. In their *khevres,* no *alies* were ever sold, so as not to allow the richer members to outclass the poorer ones. Instead, members were called up to recite the blessing on the Torah in alphabetical order. Exceptions were only made in special cases: a man who had *yortsayt,* a mourner, a groom, a father celebrating a *bris,* and so on. The same egalitarian system was used in deciding who should carry the Torah around the ark on *shmini atseres* and *simkhes-toyre.*

The money for the upkeep of their *shul* was collected from all on an equal basis. From the *pinkes* of Loytsk we learn that each member had to contribute one groschen every Sabbath eve and two groschen on the eve of a new moon. Each week a collector made the rounds of all the members' houses to collect the dues. If anyone was unable to pay up, the sum was recorded and had to be collected before the yearly elections. For failure to repay such a debt, the council of seven had the right to confiscate something from the individual and pawn it. That year he would not be eligible to run for office in the *khevre.*

The individual *khevres* did not always have their own *shul.* In this case the practice was that in the main synagogue the *alies* on a given Sabbath were reserved for a particular *khevre.* For instance, on the Sabbath after *simkhestoyre,* when the Torah reading starts from the beginning, the Talmud study group was called up to recite the blessings. On the Sabbath of "Lekh-Lekho" when the passage "And you shall circumcise the flesh of your foreskin" (Genesis 17:11) is read, the circumcisers were called up. The story of Abraham inviting the three angels belonged to the Welcoming the Visitors Society. The portion of Mishpotim concerning money-lending was reserved for the Free Loan association. The *khevre* that supplied Jewish soldiers with kosher meat was called up on the Sabbath which included the passage: "These are the beasts which you shall eat among all the beasts that are on the earth" (Leviticus 11:2). Likewise, the passage "The Lord removed from you all illness" was reserved for the Association of Visiting the Sick.

Kahal elections took place on the intermediate days of *peysekh.* The chairman-for-the-month called the election and the majority of eligible electors had to participate. The election results and the names of the new appointees were recorded each year in the community *pinkes* and the outgoing members had to sign their names. The list always read the same way: "In a joyous hour did election take place on _____, the __th day of the intermediate days of *peysekh* in the year ____, as is customary in all the communities."

First, four "heads" were chosen, then three treasurers and finally seven elders. Then the rotating chairmen were elected, a bookkeeper, heads of the various communal institutions such as the

Talmud Torah School, the hospital, the charities, a keeper of the *pinkes*, and a special scribe.

The four kahal heads were the managers of the community. They were responsible for all religious institutions: the synagogues, houses of study, *yeshives*, the ritual bath. They decided on the budgets, hired a doctor, a bathhouse attendant, and the like. When necessary, they also negotiated with other communities.

The treasurers took care of finances. They would submit proposals to raise funds, to economize; they supervised tax collecting. The elders were advisers to kahal. Whenever a new project was undertaken, say the building of a new *besmedresh*, the heads would consult with these elders before reaching a decision.

The community registers are full of entries describing various lawsuits of one individual against another, of the individual against the community, and the community against an individual or a group. A whole range of complaints was recorded: One witness reports that so-and-so tore up books in the *besmedresh;* another testifies that someone was spreading false rumors about a Jewish girl; a third person is called up for breaking the laws of his *khevre.*

The usual punishment was to expel the guilty party from his *khevre* or to deprive him of community privileges—forever, or for a specified amount of time. Kahal was able to enforce the law in almost every case, and this without any Jewish police force or prisons. Some of the penalties that kahal could impose were the following:

1. No honors in the *shul.*

2. No participation in town celebrations.

3. No one is allowed to rent the criminal an apartment or a store.

4. A woman or the wife of a criminal may not use the *mikve*, the ritual bathhouse.

5. No one may give him work.

6. No marriage arrangements with his family are allowed.

7. No one may sell him kosher meat.

8. His children can be expelled from school.

9. He must pay more taxes.

There were even instances in which kahal imposed the death sentence on a Jew and carried it out. This was for the most despicable crime of all—that of informing against Jews to the government.

It seems that the fabulous wealth of the Ukrainian landowners eventually began to rub off on those Jews who did business with them. These Jews began to imitate the life of the *porets:* fancy furniture, horse-drawn carriages, and especially lavish celebrations. These celebrations would last several days and did more harm than good.

First, this would arouse the envy of the non-Jews. They couldn't help but wonder: Where in the world did those Jews get such fancy clothes? They're just a bunch of crooks!

Secondly, it caused a split among Jews themselves. The poorer people, not wanting to fall behind the richer ones, also arranged for magnificent feasts which they could really not afford and which dragged them into new debts and new sorrows.

Thirdly, these long celebrations often led to drunkenness and to general loud behavior.

The spiritual leaders of the Jewish communities in the Ukraine began an all-out campaign to stop these excesses. There is hardly a community register that we managed to find that did not have some sort of ruling to stem the tide of this easy life. The following regulations were recorded in the *pinkes* of Bar:

A. At a reception for the groom, whether a local fellow or a stranger, and at the celebration on the day after the wedding, preserves should not be given to anyone except the very closest relatives.

B. At a wedding feast: If the person sponsoring the feast is a wealthy man (the status to be determined by how much a man paid in taxes each year), he may invite no more than twenty guests not counting relatives, religious leaders, and poor people.

C. If the sponsor is a middle-class householder, he may not invite any strangers, but only religious leaders, poor people, and the closest relatives.

D. If the sponsor is not well-to-do, he may invite only the religious leaders and his closest relatives.

E. At the feast of a circumcision, a wealthy man may invite twenty guests, relatives included, but excluding the religious leaders and poor people.

F. A middle-class householder may invite only ten guests including his relatives, with the same exceptions.

G. Someone who is not well-to-do is forbidden to have a circumcision feast. He may only serve preserves, honey cake, and whiskey.

Of the *kley-koydesh* the rabbi was first on the list. But there was more than one type of rabbi. First, the *rov*. He was closest to "rabbi" in the English sense. He is an authority on Jewish law. Even if more learned men could be found in town, people still consulted the *rov* for advice. The plural is *rabonim*.

Second, *reb*. This is a title for any male Jew who is older or wiser. When a stranger came to town, he was addressed as "Reb Yid"—Reb Jew. The name *reb* can also be used in a sarcastic way, to make fun of the person: "Listen, Reb Yid, are you gonna pay up or not?"

Third, *rebe*. Meaning, a teacher of children. Students always referred to their teacher as *rebe*, and the word carries more respect than *melamed*. A *rov* could also be addressed as *rebe*. Sometimes both terms could be used together. In the shtetl of Orinin, province of Podolia, an especially popular and talented teacher was called "Rebe reb Meyer the melamed." The plural form of *rebe*, used mostly by children, is *rebes*.

Rebe also means a Khasidic leader. A *rebe* is considered to be a holy man by his followers even if he isn't as learned as the local *rov*. He commands authority not because of his scholarship but because of his qualities as a leader, because until 1835 *rabonim* could only serve a community if they were appointed by kahal. They received a salary, usually for life—unless they moved on to another shtetl. The *rov* had two functions: (1) to be an expert in ritual law, advise people on kosher meat, *matse* baking, the employment of non-Jews on *shabes*, and so on; (2) to be an arbiter and counselor in civil and family disputes. In other words, his job was highly specialized, and would not include decisions on how to lay a synagogue floor, sick calls, teaching or leading the prayer service.

Next in line of the *kley-koydesh* was the *shames* who in day-to-day life was even more important than the *rov*. A *shames* often had to serve as bailiff, policeman, notary, recorder, clerk, stove lighter in the *shul*, charity collector, the leader of prayer services, and even Torah reader. The smaller the town, the more a *shames* had to serve as Jack-of-all-trades.

Shtetl Derivatives

Maurice Samuel points out how much of the lifestyle of Shtetl and ghetto in Eastern Europe was derived from the surrounding culture and is not originally Jewish at all.

The episodic is so intimately the garb of the permanent. It is quite fantastic to note how the Yiddish-speaking civilization took elements from the surrounding world and turned them to its peculiar use. The Yiddish language itself is the most striking instance, but it is certainly not the only one. There are folk-religious customs that the naïve Eastern European Jew regarded as having the same sanctity as the law from Sinai, which nevertheless were of local Gentile origin. The *kaftan* and *shtreimel* (gabardine and flat, circular fur headgear) of the Polish Jewish pietist were the national dress of the Poles before the coming of the Jews. The Jews adopted them, the Poles dropped them. Among the Jews that long *kaftan*, that round *shtreimel*, became sacrosanct symbols of Jewishness. If a wayward son threw off the *kaftan* and put on a short coat, his father was as like as not to count him as dead and mourn for him in the prescribed ritual of death.

There was the wearing of the *sheitel*, or wig, obligatory for married women. Every pious Jewish bride had to crop her head before marriage, and the tragic theme has been woven into a thousand Jewish stories. But there is absolutely no mention of such a law in Talmudic literature; nor is the practice known to non-European Jews. Dubnow (I believe) traces it to the practice of cutting off the hair of a bride—and not only of a Jewish bride—so that she might sell it to the wigmaker, and with the money buy herself out from the *jus primæ noctis* of the medieval lord. The Jews retained the symbolic gesture long after the necessity had disappeared, and they made it so Jewish that the refusal of a pious Jewish daughter to sacrifice her hair before marriage was considered the equivalent of apostasy.

The *gefilte* fish of the Friday-evening meal is of Christian (and pre-Christian) origin; the *Chassidic* melodies are Ukrainian and Moldavian; and just as these have become completely and tacitly Jewish in the Yiddish-speaking civilization, so certain Eastern European places like Vilna, Medzibozh,

Volozhin, Belz, Zhitomir have become sanctified in Jewish memory. You say "Vilna" to a non-Jew, and his response is: "The capital of Lithuania." Say it to an Eastern European Jew, his response is—or would have been a little while ago: "The Jerusalem of Lithuania." Volozhin is for everyone else an obscure village in Russia; for the Jew it was a glorious center of scholarship, a name precious to him and to the Almighty, whose sacred word was studied in its famous Talmudic Academy.

All this is the episodic, which cannot be recaptured. In its day it created its proper illusion of permanence, so that even some Jews were misled; they thought it would endure until the coming of the Messiah. Certainly Peretz, though not a Messianist, believed that it would endure along with the rest of the world. He was, as we have seen, confident of a time, close at hand, when anti-Semitism would disappear; he kept on hoping that the Jews by changing their way of life would win the good opinion of the world. And carried along in these illusions, he could never have guessed what in him was episodic and what permanent. He did not know that his essential concern was with the moral being of the Jew, according to the tradition, which he wanted purified whatever the world would think of the Jews. He could not know that if he was to survive beyond Yiddish it would have to be as the traditional Jewish folk moralist.

The Lower East Side

The Jews who left the dangerous and impoverished world of Eastern Europe at the end of the nineteenth century faced impoverishment and deprivation in New York City's Lower East Side of Manhattan. They lived in foul and congested conditions until the first and second decade of the century, when the building of the subway system to Brooklyn and the Bronx and the slowly developing prosperity allowed most of them to escape the hell-holes of Orchard and Delancey Streets.

What life was like on the Lower East Side, how millions coped with poverty, bad housing, and terrible conditions of public health and created new and promising lives in America for their families was described by many contemporary observers. These descriptions were subtly brought together in

Irving Howe's 1976 bestseller, *The World of Our Fathers*. Howe's work leans more heavily on sentimentality than depiction of the criminality and disease that prevailed on the Lower East Side, but its portrayal endures and cannot be improved upon.

Just north of Canal Street and extending from Mott to Elizabeth stood the "Big Flat," an enormous tenement occupying six city lots. Water was supplied to tenants from one tap on each floor, set over a sink outside the north wall. These sinks, serving as the only receptacles for refuse, were loathsome, especially in the winter, when the traps beneath them would freeze. Each apartment had three rooms and drew its light from a single window in the "living room." The two inner rooms were always dark and without ventilation, since the space allotted each resident averaged out to 428 cubic feet per head, far below the legal limit of 600. The annual death rate per 1,000 for the years 1883, 1884, 1885, and the first nine months of 1886 came to 42.40, as compared with 25.72 for the city as a whole; nearly sixty-two percent of the deaths in the "Big Flat" were of children under five years of age, while in the city as a whole the percentage was a bit more than forty-two.

The Jews (also some Italians) living in the "Big Flat," reported an investigator of the New York Association for Improving the Conditions of the Poor, "are locked in the rooms like sardines in a box. . . . On the first floor are rooms for fourteen families, and they are mostly occupied by low women and street walkers. . . . While I was there I saw a family getting put out on the sidewalk. . . . The halls are about ten feet wide, and the smell is something awful."

Meticulous in accumulating detail, this investigator continued: "The rents of rooms are as follows: first floor, $9.50 per month for three rooms; second floor, $9.25; third and fourth floors, $9; fifth and sixth, $8.50 and $8.75."

The investigator visited the top floor, inhabited entirely by "Polish Jews":

In No. 76 a peddler lives, with his wife and four small children. The rooms, like the rest of this floor, are very dirty. In a corner next to these rooms a pile of garbage about two feet high lies, right at the head of the stairs as you go up. The children on this floor are very poorly clad . . . nothing but a loose gown, and no underclothing at all.

Rooms 77, 78, and 79 are crowded with men and women sewing on machines. The men generally work the machines, and the women sew the buttons on and make button-holes. They work for large clothing firms.

Rooms 86, 87, and 88 are full of dirty bedding. The women were sitting out in the hallway sewing on children's knee-pants for some store, and there were no men around.

In room 91 I saw five small children and the mother, but no men. The rooms were full of bedding, but I could see no bedsteads. I heard that it is a lodging-place for Jewish peddlers.

Is there any reason to suppose that the "Big Flat" was spectacularly worse than the surrounding, smaller tenements into which the immigrants were packed? Not really. Some tenements had slightly better physical appointments, and on the East Side as a whole health conditions were somewhat better during the '80s and '90s than in non-Jewish districts, perhaps because of the discipline that the Jewish family was still able to exact. From every available source—contemporary journalism, memoirs, government reports, sociological studies—the evidence seems conclusive: Living conditions in the Jewish quarter during the last decades of the nineteenth century were quite as ghastly as those of early-nineteenth century London.

An immigrant remembers a two-room apartment on Allen Street containing parents, six children, and six boarders. On Saturdays, since the father was a cantor, the apartment was turned

The New Land: Turo synagogue, Newport, Rhode Island, oldest synagogue in the United States.

into a synagogue. Two daughters took in dresses to sew at home. One boarder, a shoemaker, worked in the apartment. "The cantor rehearses, a train passes, the shoemaker bangs, ten brats run around like goats, the wife putters in her 'kosher restaurant.' At night we all try to get some sleep in the stifling roach-infested two rooms."

Poverty has its shadings, wretchedness its refinements:

Not everyone was equally poor. When an immigrant family could occupy a two- or three-room apartment without several boarders, they were considered lucky. Boarders were a natural institution, particularly in the early years when most immigrants came without their families. But even the privilege of being a boarder was not enjoyed by every greenhorn. There were various categories of boarders. A star

boarder slept on a folding bed. But I knew a printer who every night unscrewed a door, put it on two chairs; he couldn't pay as much as the one who had the bed.

Even an unscrewed door made into a bed could seem attractive to those who had no roof. During the '90s, especially in the summers, there were homeless immigrants who found shelter at night in the "expresses" or coaches that were left on the streets after their horses were taken to the stables.

In *Ner Hamaaravi*, a New York Hebrew periodical started in 1895, there is a story called "Breach of Promise" in which a Lithuanian Jew is shown marrying a girl for her money. "At one o'clock in the afternoon the ceremony is performed in the 'American Star Hall,' in the evening two *roomkes* [little rooms] are rented, on the following day furniture is purchased, and in the evening the couple already has three boarders and three *borderkes* [female boarders]. On the third day the husband goes back to work and the wife runs away with one of the boarders to Paterson."

Lawrence Veiller, a splendid human being who devoted himself to tenement reform, organized in 1900 an exhibit in the Sherry Building at 404 Fifth Avenue to prove that in New York "the working man is housed worse than in any other city in the civilized world, notwithstanding the fact that he pays more money for such accommodations than is paid elsewhere." At this exhibit Veiller set up a cardboard model of an entire tenement block, bounded by Chrystie, Forsyth, Canal, and Bayard streets, in the heart of the East Side. With thirty-nine tenements, the block contained 2,781 people, who among them had only 264 water closets and lacked access to even one stationary bathtub. Only forty apartments had hot running water; and on this block, over the past five years, thirty-two cases of tuberculosis had been reported. Veiller, an amateur sociologist before the age of sociology, insisted that even if the block he had chosen was somewhat worse than others, it revealed the truth about the whole of the East Side.

Throughout the '80s and '90s *The New York Times* kept sending reporters to the Jewish quarter, who sniffed about, recoiled from the clamor and stench, yet had to acknowledge the plight of its "half-starved" inhabitants. An explorer in this world "will find no richly-fed men, extravagantly attired, gleaming with diamonds, fat as Jeshurun, rubbing their hands and computing their tremendous and illicit gains with an oily satisfaction." On the contrary, he will see "attenuated creatures, clad in old, faded, greasy, often tattered clothing . . . men and youths whose cheeks are pinched and pale and hollow, whose lungs yield to the first advance of the Autumn cold and fill the air with incessant coughing; whose sad, lustrous eyes look at him pitifully, like the eyes of hunted and captured animals that press up to the bars of their cages." And then, as if to reassure his readers, the *Times* reporter added: "None of them has any jewelry."

Whatever the indignation of reformers and reporters, the problem during the 80s and 90s was less how to escape from the tenements than how to remain in them. Key terms of anxiety have survived the experience of the immigrants, echoing still in the memories of grandsons and granddaughters, and one of the most terrible among these is "dispossess." Only sickness could raise more fright than the prospect of being thrown out on the street. In the depression year ending September 1892, the district of Judge Alfred Steckler, covering the East Side, issued a total of 5,450 dispossess notices. A man of some feeling, Judge Steckler said: "Hundreds of cases full of the most pathetic disclosures are constantly cropping up in my court. . . . I rarely set the machinery of the law in motion without first making an effort to have the landlord give a little further period of grace. . . . Perhaps the granting of a week's grace will give them a chance to get on their feet, and resume their struggle against a poverty that is as hopeless as it is cruel."

No act of individual kindness could change immigrant life as it needed to be changed, yet such acts, when they occurred, were received with a warmth, almost an excess of gratitude. Lillian Wald (1867–1940), the nurse who founded the Henry Street Settlement, grew within her lifetime into a figure of legend, known and adored on every street.

She came to the East Side in 1893, a German-Jewish young woman of twenty-six who had been raised in a comfortable bourgeois family, a "spoiled child" as she later kept insisting, still largely innocent of the sufferings of life. Her father had been an optical dealer in Rochester, New York, and Lillian had gone to "Miss Cruttenden's English-French Boarding and Day School for Young Ladies." She had wanted to enter Vassar at sixteen, but someone at the college ruled that she was too young. If Vassar didn't want her, she would go elsewhere—to another life.

Several years later, Lillian Wald entered the New York Hospital's School of Nursing, learning there what she needed to learn, not least an unflinching and unsentimental capacity for living near pain. In 1893, after a frustrating interval at an orphan asylum where the children were ill-treated, she began running a class in home nursing for East Side women. One day a little girl came up to Miss Wald, asking that she visit someone sick at home. Lillian Wald followed the child to a dismal two-room apartment that housed a family of seven plus a few boarders. "Within half an hour" she had made the central decision of her life: She would move to the East Side, there to give her life as nurse, settlement-house leader, and companion to the afflicted.

There are two kinds of fastidious people, those who recoil from messes and those who stay to clean them up. Lillian Wald stayed, not out of exalted sentiments or angelic temperament, but because there was work to be done responded to primal experiences with candor and directness. It cut through to the essentials of life: the imperative to do right and the comfort of social bonds. Torn apart, as it soon would be, by insoluble conflicts of value, it lived out its inner struggles and confusions to the very brim of its energy.

An old man remembering his East Side childhood would say that on coming home from school he had a recurrent fear that his cot in the dining room would again be occupied by a relative just off the boat from Europe and given shelter by his parents. How many other Americans could share, even grasp, this order of experience? Space was the stuff of desire; a room to oneself, a luxury beyond reach. "Privacy in the home was practically unknown. The average apartment consisted of three rooms: a kitchen, a parlor, and a doorless and windowless bedroom between. The parlor became a sleeping-room at night. So did the kitchen when families were unusually large. . . . Made comparatively presentable after a long day of cooking, eating and washing of dishes and laundry, the kitchen was the scene of formal calls at our house and of the visits of friends and prospective suitors." Cramming everything into the kitchen during the evenings had a practical purpose: It saved money on gas and electricity. During the 1890s desperate families had put "three boarders in the front room and two *borderkes* [female boarders] in the kitchen, but today the rooms are too small," noted the *Forward* in 1904. Once boarders could be assigned separate rooms and neither kitchen nor dining room needed to be let, a major advance had been registered in domestic economy.

Only in the kitchen could the family come together in an approximation of community. On most days everyone ate helter-skelter, whenever he could, but on Friday nights, in the mild glow of the Sabbath, the whole family would eat together. Decorum reigned again, the pleasure of doing things as everyone knew they should be done. When a son failed to show up for Friday-night dinners, that was a signal of serious estrangement— not the least use of rules being that they lend clear meaning to violations.

Sitting around the wooden kitchen table that was covered with a white or checkered oilcloth, fathers read newspapers, mothers prepared food, children did homework, boarders gobbled meals. The father's eyes "often fell on the youth at the table who is studying 'Virgil' or on the girl seated in the rocking chair with the big geography on her lap serving as a desk. The atmosphere of the room was not altogether pleasant . . . due to the pail of refuse under the burning stove, which must remain in the house over night by an edict of the janitor." When families took in work, perhaps "finishing" dresses, it was done in the kitchen. Night after night *landslayt* from the old country, recalls Sophie Ruskay, would come to sit in the kitchen, "waiting uncomplainingly until Mama was at leisure. . . . In Yiddish and with eloquent gestures they told the stories of their hardships." For the kitchen was the one place where immigrants might recall to themselves that they were not mere creatures of toil and circumstances, but also human beings defined by their sociability. The kitchen testified to the utterly plebeian character of immigrant Jewish life; the kitchen was warm, close, and bound all to the matrix of family; sometimes of course it could also be maddeningly noisy and crowded—"my own private Coney Island," Zero Mostel has remembered—and then the sole escape was behind the locked door of a toilet or down the steps and into the streets.

In the kitchen the Jewish mother was sovereign. "My mother," recalls Alfred Kazin in his lyrical memoir,

worked [in the kitchen] all day long, we ate in it almost all meals except the Passover *seder*. . . . The kitchen gave a special character to our lives; my mother's character. All my memories of that kitchen are dominated by the nearness of my mother sitting all day long at her sewing machine, by the clacking of the treadle against the linoleum floor, by the patient twist of her right shoulder as she automatically pushed at the wheel with one hand or lifted her foot to free the needle. . . . The kitchen was her life. Year by year, as I began to take in her fantastic

Jewish immigrant workers, New York, around 1900.

capacity for labor and her anxious zeal, I realized it was ourselves she kept stitching together.

Every recollection of Jewish immigrant life that is concerned with more than the trivia of "local color" notices that as soon as the Jews moved from Eastern Europe to America there followed a serious dislocation of the family. Patterns of the family had been firmly set, indeed, had been allowed to become rigid in the old country: the moral authority of the father, the formal submission of the wife together with her frequent dominance in practical affairs, the obedience of children softened by parental indulgences. . . .

Jewish folklore had elevated the mother to a figure of sanctioned tenderness, and now, together with a somewhat abrasive capacity for battling whatever might threaten her family, she became an object of sentimental veneration. By certain readings, the Oedipal romance was peculiarly Jewish, perhaps even a Jewish invention. Seldom has maternal adoration found so lyrical an expression as in *Call It Sleep*, Henry Roth's novel about the East Side. The mother, Genya, talks to her little boy, David:

"It is summer," she pointed to the window, "the weather grows warm. Whom will you refresh with the icy lips the water lent you?"

"Oh!" he lifted his smiling face.

"You remember nothing," she reproached him, and with a throaty chuckle, lifted him in her arms. . . .

"There!" she laughed, muzzling his cheek, "but you've waited too long; the sweet chill has dulled. Lips for me," she reminded him, "must always be as cool as the water that wet them."

Open sensuality of this kind was no doubt rare in the immigrant milieu, as in any other of the time, but what Roth rendered could be found elsewhere, muffled and shamefaced. More characteristic perhaps is a recollection of Samuel Chotzinoff in which his mother comes through as a shrewd manager whose

resourcefulness in moments of economic crisis appeared unlimited. Some situations, like the purchase of clothes, seemed to demand the brashest of tactics. Others, like the ever-recurring crisis of the gas meter when there wasn't a quarter in the house, called for quiet diplomacy. Of an evening one of my sisters might be entertaining a gentleman who would, perhaps soon, we hoped, reveal himself as a suitor, when suddenly the gas would begin to flicker and go out. At such moments my mother would strike a match, reach for her purse, open it with her free hand, peer in it closely, and announce laughingly that she could find nothing but bills. The gentleman, hastily fumbling in his pocket, would produce a quarter, and the light would come on.

Time brought changes. Learning to relish the privileges of suffering, the Jewish mother could become absurdly, outrageously protective. From that condition, especially if linked, as it well might be, with contempt for her husband, she could decline into a brassy scourge, with her grating bark or soul-destroying whine, silver-blue hair, and unfocused aggression. Nor was it unusual for her to employ ingenuity in order to keep her brood in a state of prolonged dependence, as she grew expert at groaning, cajoling, intimidating. Daughters paled, sons fled.

Yet even behind the most insufferable ways of the Jewish mother there was almost always a hard-earned perception of reality. Did she overfeed? Her mind was haunted by memories of a hungry childhood. Did she fuss about health? Infant mortality had been a plague in the old country and the horror of diphtheria overwhelming in this country. Did she dominate everyone within reach? A disarranged family structure endowed her with powers she had never known before, and burdens too; it was to be expected that she should abuse the powers and find advantage in the burdens. The weight of centuries bore down. In her bones, the Jewish mother knew that she and hers, simply by being Jewish, had always to live with a sense of precariousness. When she worried about her little boy going down to play, it was not merely the dangers of Rivington or Cherry Street that she saw—though there *were* dangers on such streets; it was the streets of Kishinev and Bialystok and other towns in which the blood of Jewish children had been spilled.

Later, such memories would fade among those she had meant to shield and it would become customary to regard her as a grotesque figure of excess.

Venerated to absurdity, assaulted with a venom that testifies obliquely to her continuing moral and emotional power, the immigrant mother cut her path through the perils and entanglements of American life. Everyone spoke about her, against her, to her, but she herself has left no word to posterity, certainly none in her own voice, perhaps because all the talk about her "role" seemed to her finally trivial, the indulgence of those who had escaped life's primal tasks. Talk was a luxury that her labor would enable her sons to taste.

A Reconstituted Life

Isaac Bashevis Singer, the younger brother of the would-be Tolstoyan novelist, I. J. Singer, and eventual winner of the Nobel Prize for Literature, was an extremely prolific, and commercially successful writer who wrote about two distinctive, although at times, overlapping worlds. One of his genres was the somewhat sentimental tale of good-hearted and wise Eastern European rabbis (*In My Father's House*), which essentially continued the literary tradition of Sholem Aleichem and I. L. Peretz. Singer's other focus was on Jewish immigrants in New York in the 1930s and 1940s—a bleak, but at times amusing, world of refugees struggling daily for survival and constantly drenched in sex. This work of I. B. Singer is closer to the quasi-realistic work of his brother and includes some of his best writing.

Of these Manhattan stories perhaps the best is *Enemies, A Love Story* (1972), set in the 1940s. The plot revolves around how the protagonist, Herman, gets involved with three women simultaneously: the first and second to whom he is married, and the third who claims to be pregnant by him. As a fiction writer, Singer is at the zenith of his art here, managing to interweave the pathetic with the hilarious. The book was made into an excellent Hollywood film. The unforgettable character in the book (played by Lena Olin in the film) is Masha, a beautiful, knocked-about woman who emerges from the shattered wartime world and tries to reconstitute her life. In this scene in a Manhattan cafeteria (Singer's favorite locale) Herman hears one version of Masha's story.

Herman entered the cafeteria and saw Leon Tortshiner sitting at a table next to the wall. He recognized him from a photograph he had seen in Masha's album, though Tortshiner was now considerably older. He was a man of about fifty, large-boned, with a square-shaped head and thick dark hair that one could tell at a glance was dyed. His face was broad, with a prominent chin, high cheekbones, and a wide nose with large nostrils. He had thick eyebrows and his brown eyes were slanted like a Tartar's. There was a scar on his forehead that looked like an old knife wound. His somewhat coarse appearance was softened by the aura of Polish-Jewish affability. "He won't murder me," Herman thought. It seemed unbelievable that this boor had once been Masha's husband. The mere thought of it was ridiculous. But that was the way with facts. They punctured every bubble of conceit, shattered theories, destroyed convictions.

A cup of coffee was set in front of Tortshiner. A cigar with an inch of ash at its tip rested on an ashtray. At his left was a dish holding a partially eaten egg cake. Catching sight of Herman, Tortshiner made as if to rise, but fell back in his chair again.

"Herman Broder?" he asked. He stretched out a large, heavy hand.

"Sholom aleichem."

"Sit down, sit down," said Tortshiner. "I'll bring you some coffee."

"No, thanks."

"Tea?"

"No. Thanks."

"I'll get you some coffee!" Leon Tortshiner said decisively. "Since I invited you, you're my guest. I have to watch my weight, that's why I'm only eating an egg cake, but you can afford to eat a piece of cheesecake."

"Really, it's not necessary."

Tortshiner stood up. Herman watched him as he picked up a tray and took his place in the line at the counter. For his broad build, he was too short, with overly large hands and feet and with the shoulders of a strong man. This was how they grew in Poland: more in breadth than in height. He wore a brown striped suit, obviously chosen in an effort to look younger. He returned with a cup of coffee and a piece of cheesecake. He picked up the almost extinguished cigar quickly, puffed at it vigorously, and blew out a cloud of smoke.

"I pictured you altogether differently," he said. "Masha described you as a regular Don Juan." He obviously didn't intend the description to be derogatory.

Herman lowered his head. "Women's notions."

"I debated whether or not to call you for a long time. One doesn't do a thing like this easily, you know. I have every reason to be your enemy, but I'll tell you right off that I'm here for your sake. Whether you believe me or not—that's, as they say, another matter."

"Yes, I understand."

"No, you don't understand. How can you understand? You are, as Masha told me, something of a writer, but I'm a scientist. Before one can understand, one must have the facts, all the information. *A priori* we know nothing, only that one and one make two."

"What *are* the facts?"

"The facts are that Masha bought the divorce from me at a price that no honest woman should pay, even if her life depended on it." Leon Tortshiner spoke in his deep voice, without hurry, seemingly without anger. "I think you should know this, because if a woman is capable of paying such a price, one can never be altogether sure of her integrity. She had lovers before she knew me and also while she lived with me. That is the absolute truth. That's the reason we separated. I'll be frank with you. Normally, I would have no reason to take this interest in you. But I struck up an acquaintance with a person who knows you. He doesn't know our connection, if you want to call it a connection, and he happened to tell me about you. Why make a secret of it? His name is Rabbi Lampert. He told me that you suffered during the war, that you spent years lying in a loft filled with hay, and all that. I know you do some work for him. He calls it 'research,' but you don't have to draw any diagrams for me. You're a Talmudist, I specialized in bacteriology.

"As you know, Rabbi Lampert is working on a book to prove that all knowledge stems from the Torah and he wanted me to help him with the scientific part. I told him plainly that modern knowledge is not to be found in the Torah and there was no point looking for it there. Moses knew nothing about electricity or vitamins. What's more, I don't want to waste my energy for a few dollars. I'd rather manage with less. The rabbi didn't actually mention your name, but when he spoke of a man who had hidden in a hayloft, I put two and two together, as they say. He praises you to the skies. But naturally he doesn't know what I know. He's a strange character. He immediately called me by my first name and that's not my style. Things must take their natural course. There has to be an evolution even in personal relationships. It's impossible to talk to him, because the telephone keeps ringing. I'll wager he has a thousand deals going on at the same time. Why does he need so much money? But I'll come to the point.

"I want you to know, Masha is a bum. Pure and simple. If you want to marry a bum, that's your privilege, but I thought I should warn you before she catches you in her net. Our meeting will, of course, remain a secret. That is the assumption on

The Lower East Side of Manhattan, around 1900.

which I phoned you." Leon Tortshiner picked up his cigar and drew on it, but it had gone out.

While Tortshiner talked, Herman had been sitting with his head bent over the table. He was hot and wished he could open his collar. He felt a burning sensation behind his ears. A trickle of perspiration ran down his back, along his spine. When Tortshiner started to fuss with his cigar, Herman asked in a choked voice, "What price?"

Leon Tortshiner cupped his ear. "I can't hear. Speak a little louder."

"I said, 'What price?'"

"You know what price. You're not so naïve. You probably think I'm no better than she is and in a sense I can understand that. First of all, you're in love with her and Masha is a woman with whom one can fall in love. She drives men crazy. She almost drove me crazy. As primitive as she is, she has the perceptiveness of a Freud, Adler, and Jung put together, plus a little bit more. She's a brilliant actress too. When she wants to laugh, she

laughs; and when she wants to cry, she cries. I told her straight out that if she stopped wasting her talents on foolishness, she could be a second Sarah Bernhardt. So, you see, it's no surprise to me that you're tangled up with her. I won't try to deny it—I still love her. Even a first-year student in psychology learns that one can love and hate at the same time. You're probably asking yourself, why should I tell you these secrets? What do I owe you? To understand, you'll have to hear me out with patience."

"I'm listening."

"Don't let the coffee get cold. Eat a piece of cheesecake. There. And don't be so upset. After all, the whole world is living through a revolution, a spiritual revolution. Hitler's gas chambers were bad enough, but when people lose all values, it's worse than torture. You undoubtedly come from a religious home. Where else did you learn Gemara? My parents weren't fanatics, but they were believing Jews. My father had one God and one wife, and my mother had one God and one husband.

"Masha probably told you that I studied at Warsaw University. I specialized in biology, worked with Professor Wolkowski, and helped him with an important discovery. Actually I made the discovery myself, though he received the credit. The truth is, they didn't reward him either. People think that thieves are to be found only on Krochmalna Street in Warsaw or the Bowery in New York. There are thieves among professors, artists, among the greatest in all fields. Ordinary thieves generally don't steal from one another, but plenty of scientists literally live by theft. Do you know that Einstein stole his theory from a mathematician who was helping him and no one really knows his name? Freud also stole, and so did Spinoza. This really has no connection with the subject, but I'm a victim of this sort of thievery.

"When the Nazis occupied Warsaw, I could have worked for them because I had letters from the greatest German scientists, and they would even have overlooked the fact that I was Jewish. But I didn't want to take advantage of such privileges and went through the whole Gehenna. Later I escaped to Russia, but our intellectuals there did an about-face and even started informing on one another. That's all the Bolsheviks needed. They sent them away to the camps. I myself had once been sympathetic to Communism, but actually, at the time when it would have paid me to be a Communist, I became fed up with the whole system and told them so openly. You can imagine how they treated me.

"In any case, I lived through the war, the camps, the hunger, the lice, and in 1945 I wound up in Lublin. There I met your Masha. She was the mistress, or the wife, of some Red Army deserter who had become a smuggler and a black marketeer in Poland. She apparently got enough to eat from the smuggler. I don't know exactly what happened between them. He accused her of being unfaithful and God knows what else. I don't have to tell you that she's an attractive woman—a few years ago she was a beauty. I had lost my whole family. When she heard I was a scientist, she became interested in me. The smuggler, I suppose, had another woman or half a dozen others. You must keep in mind that in all walks of life there is more chaff than wheat.

"Masha had found her mother and we all left for Germany. We had no papers and had to smuggle ourselves in. Every step of the way was fraught with peril. If you wanted to live, you had to break the law, because all laws sentenced you to death. You were a victim yourself, so you know how it was, though everyone has a different story to tell. It's impossible to talk sensibly to refugees, because no matter what you have to tell, someone will say that it happened just the other way around.

"But let's get back to Masha. We reached Germany and they 'respectfully' interned us in a camp. Generally, couples lived together without the benefit of a marriage ceremony. Who needed such ceremonies at a time like that? But Masha's mother insisted that we get married according to the laws of Moses and Israel. The smuggler probably gave her a divorce, or she hadn't been married to him in the first place. I couldn't care less. I wanted to get back to my scientific work as soon as I could, and I'm not religious. She wanted a wedding; I agreed to a wedding. Others in the camp started to do business immediately—smuggling. The American Army brought all kinds of goods to Germany and they handled it. Jews did business everywhere, even in Auschwitz. If there is a hell, they'll do business there too. I don't say this with malice. What else could they do? The relief organizations provided barely enough to exist on. After all those years of starvation, people wanted to eat well and to wear decent clothes too.

"But what could I do if by nature I'm not a businessman? I stayed at home and lived on what the 'Joint' rationed out to me. The Germans didn't allow me near a university or laboratory. There were a few other loafers like me around and we read books or played chess. This didn't please Masha. Living with her smuggler, she had grown accustomed to luxury. When she met me, she had been impressed because I was a scientist, but that didn't satisfy her for long. She began to treat me like dirt; she made terrible scenes. Her mother, I must tell you, is a saint. She suffered every hell and remained pure. I loved her mother dearly. How often does one find a holy person? Masha's father had also been a fine man, something of a writer, a Hebraist. Who she takes after, I don't know. She just couldn't resist gaiety wherever it was. The smugglers were always giving parties, dances. In Russia they had gotten used to vodka and all its glories.

"When I met Masha in Lublin, it was my impression that she was faithful to the smuggler. But soon it was obvious that she was having all kinds of affairs. The feeble Jews had been killed off and those who were left had iron constitutions, though, as it turns out, they were broken people too. Their troubles are coming to the surface now. In a hundred years, the ghettos will be idealized and the impression created that they were inhabited only by saints. There could be no greater lie. First of all, how many saints are there in any generation? Second of all, most of the really pious Jews perished. And among those who managed to survive, the great drive was to live at any cost. In some of the ghettos, they even ran cabarets. You can imagine what cabarets! You had to step over dead bodies to get in.

"My theory is that the human species is getting worse, not better. I believe, so to speak, in an evolution in reverse. The last man on earth will be both a criminal and a madman.

"I imagine that Masha told you the worst about me. As a matter of fact, it was she who broke up the marriage. While she was running around, I, like an idiot, sat home with her mother. Her mother suffered from an eye disease, and I would read the Pentateuch and the American-Yiddish newspapers out loud to her. But how long could I lead such a life? I'm not old now, and in those days I was in my prime. I was also beginning to meet people and make contact with the scientific world. Women professors used to visit from America—there are quite a number of educated women here—and they became interested in me. My mother-in-law, Shifrah Puah, told me openly that as long as Masha left me alone all day and half the night, I didn't owe her a thing. Shifrah Puah loves me to this day. Once I met her in the street and she embraced me and kissed me. She still calls me 'my son.'

"When my visa for America came through, all of a sudden Masha made up with me. I was granted the visa not as a refugee but as a scientist. I got the visa, not she. She was supposed to have gone to Palestine. Two famous American universities were competing for me. Later I was pushed out of one and then the other by intrigues. I won't go into that now because it has no bearing on the subject. I established theories and made discoveries that the big companies didn't appreciate. The president of one university told me frankly, 'We

can't afford to have a second Wall Street crash.' What I had discovered was nothing more or less than new sources of energy. Atomic energy? Not exactly atomic. I would call them biological. The atomic bomb would also have been ready years before it was if Rockefeller hadn't butted in.

"American billionaires hired thieves to rob the man you see before you. They were after an apparatus I had spent years building with my own hands. If this apparatus had been put into operation—and it was only one step from it—the American oil companies would have gone bankrupt. But without me the machinery and chemicals were of no value to the thieves. The companies tried to buy me off. I've been having difficulties getting my citizenship, and I'm sure they're behind it. You spit in Uncle Sam's face ten times a day and he'll grin and bear it. But try to touch his investments and he turns into a tiger.

"Where was I? Oh, yes, America. What would Masha have done in Palestine? She would have landed in a refugee camp, which would not have been much better than the camp in Germany. Her mother was sick and the climate there would have finished her. I'm not making myself out to be a saint. Soon after we got here, I became involved with another woman. She wanted me to divorce Masha. She was an American, the widow of a millionaire, and she was prepared to set me up in a laboratory so that I wouldn't have to be dependent on a university. But somehow I wasn't ready for a divorce. Everything must ripen, even a cancer. True, I no longer trusted Masha, and as a matter of fact, no sooner did we get here than she started all over again. But it seems that it is possible to love without trust. I once ran into an old schoolmate who told me openly that his wife was living with other men. When I asked him how he could stand it, he answered simply. 'One can overcome jealousy.' One can overcome anything but death.

"How about another cup of coffee? No? Yes, one can overcome anything. I don't know exactly how she met you and I don't care. What difference does it make? I don't blame you. You never swore any loyalty to me, and besides in this world we grab what we can. I grab from you, you grab from me. That there was someone before you, here in America, I know for sure, because I met him and he didn't make a secret of it. It was after she met you that she started asking me for a divorce, but since she ruined my life I didn't feel that I had any obligation to her. She could easily get a civil divorce, because we've been separated for some time. But no one could force me to give her a Jewish divorce, not even the greatest of rabbis. It's her fault that I'm still at loose ends. After the wreck of our marriage, I tried to pick up the threads of my career, but I was so wound up I couldn't concentrate on serious work. I began to hate her, though it isn't in my nature to hate. I sit here with you as a friend and wish you only well. My reasoning is simple: if it hadn't been you, it would have been someone else. If I were as guilty as Masha tries to make me appear, would her mother send me a New Year's card on Rosh Hashanah with a personal note?

"Now I come to the point. A few weeks ago, Masha called me up and asked me to meet her. 'What's happened?' I asked. She hemmed and hawed until finally I told her to come to my place. She came, all dressed up, fit to kill, as they say. I had heard about you, but she began to tell me the whole story, as if it had only happened yesterday. All the details. She'd fallen in love with you; she was pregnant. She wanted to have the baby. She wanted a rabbi to perform the wedding ceremony because of her mother. 'Since when have you become so concerned about your mother?' I asked. I was in a bitter mood. She sat down and crossed her legs like an actress posing for a photograph. I said to her, 'You behaved like a prostitute when you were with me, now pay the price.' She hardly protested. 'We're still man and wife,' she said. 'I guess it's permitted.' To this day I don't know why I did it. Vanity, perhaps. Then I met Rabbi Lampert and he told me about you, your learning, the years of hiding in that attic, and everything became clear, painfully clear. I realized that she'd caught you in her net just as she had me. Why she's attracted to intellectuals is a good question, though undoubtedly she's been mixed up with roughnecks as well.

"That, in short, is the story. I hesitated a long time before deciding to tell it to you. But I came to the conclusion that you had to be warned. I hope, at least, that the child is yours. It looks as if she really loves you, but with such a creature one never can know."

"I won't marry her," Herman said. He spoke the words so quietly that Leon Tortshiner cupped his ear.

"What? Look, there's one thing I want to make sure. Don't tell her about our meeting. I really should have gotten in touch with you sooner, but as you see I am an impractical person. I do things and get myself into all kinds of trouble. If she knew that I told you what had happened, my life would be in danger."

"I won't tell her."

"You know you're not obliged to marry her. She's just the type to have a bastard. If there's someone to be pitied, it's you. Your wife—did she die?"

"Yes, she died."

"Your children too?"

"Yes."

"The rabbi told me that you live with a friend and that you don't have a telephone, but I remembered seeing your phone number in Masha's little book. She has a habit of outlining important phone numbers with circles and little drawings of flowers and animals. She drew a whole garden of trees and snakes around your number."

"How did you happen to be in Brooklyn today if you live in Manhattan?" Herman asked.

"I have friends here," Leon Tortshiner said, obviously lying.

"Well, I must go now," Herman said. "Thanks very much."

"What's your hurry? Don't go yet. I was only thinking of your own good. In Europe, people were accustomed to live secret lives. Maybe it made some sense there, but this is a free country and you don't have to hide from anyone. Here you can be a Communist, an anarchist, whatever you want. There are certain religious sects who hold venomous snakes when they pray, because of some verse in the Book of Psalms. Others go around naked. Masha, too, carries around a whole pack of secrets. The trouble is that those who have secrets betray themselves. Man is his own betrayer. Masha told me things that she didn't have to tell me and that I never would have found out otherwise."

"What did she tell you?"

"Whatever she told me she'll tell you. It's just a matter of time. People like to show off about everything, even a hernia. I don't need to tell you that she doesn't sleep at night. She smokes and talks. I used to plead with her to let me sleep. But the demon in her won't let her rest. If she had lived in the Middle Ages, she would surely have been a witch and flown a broomstick Saturday night to keep a date with the devil. But the Bronx is one place where the devil would have died of boredom. Her mother is also a witch in her own way, but a good witch: half rebbetzin, half fortuneteller. Every female sits in her own net weaving like a spider. When a fly happens to come along, it's caught. If you don't run away, they'll suck the last drop of life out of you."

"I'll manage to run away. Goodbye."

"We can be friends. The rabbi is a savage, but he loves people. He has unlimited connections and he can be of use to you. He's angry at me because I won't read electronics and television into the first chapter of Genesis. But he'll find someone who will. Basically he's a Yankee, although I think he was born in Poland. His real name isn't Milton but Melech. He writes a check for everything. When he arrives in the next world and has to give an accounting, he'll take out his checkbook. But, as my grandmother Reitze used to say, 'Shrouds don't have pockets.'"

I Never Prayed with My Father

Coping means surviving in adverse physical and economic circumstances. This has been the life problem of many millions of Jews in this century. But suppose you are a comfortable middle-class Jew in an upscale urban environment like New York today, or as in the case of this selection, Prague in the early 1920s. Then coping involves the question of affiliation to Judaism and the extent of religious practice, and often the tensions that can prevail between father and son on this subject—very complex tensions and not always simply that the father is more traditionally devout than this son. The son may have a much deeper feeling for Jewishness than the father. It can be a complicated and bitter dispute that roams far beyond the sensibility of rabbinical leaders to resolve or even understand.

This issue of tension between father and son on the subject of Judaism comes out in this part of an astonishing letter from the novelist Franz Kafka to his father, in which the younger Kafka assesses, as only a great writer can, the nature of their differences. How many thousands of times have debates like this gone on in liberated, quasi-assimilated Jewish families living in comfortable circumstances in sophisticated urban environments? How to cope, how to articulate, how to work it out—Kafka speaks for many much less-articulate than himself. As only a great artist can, he communicates universal issues.

While people keep referring to Kafka as "an insurance clerk," he in fact held an executive position in a large health insurance corporation—an exact equivalent would be a vice presidency at Blue Cross. Kafka's novels, such as *The Trial* can be read in three distinctive but not mutually exclusive ways—as a signal of the fragility of the human condition; as an attack upon the modern bureaucratic state; as an expression of the great fear retained by the German-speaking and cultured Jewish high bourgeoisie of Central Europe that they were about to descend into the technobarbarian maelstrom—anticipating the theme of Appelfeld's novels.

Kafka was not an observant Jew but he was very sensitive to Jewish matters, sympathized with Zionism, and might have migrated to Israel in the 1930s if he had lived longer. The manuscripts of his novels were for the most part deposited in Israel, taken there by his friend and literary executor Max Brod.

I found as little escape from you in Judaism. Here some measure of escape would have been thinkable in principle, moreover, it would have been thinkable that we might both have found each other in Judaism or that we even might have begun from there in harmony. But what sort of Judaism was it that I got from you? In the course of the years, I have taken roughly three different attitudes to it.

As a child I reproached myself, in accord with you, for not going to the synagogue often enough, for not fasting, and so on. I thought that in this way I was doing a wrong not to myself but to you, and I was penetrated by a sense of guilt, which was, of course, always ready to hand.

Later, as a young man, I could not understand how, with the insignificant scrap of Judaism you yourself possessed, you could reproach me for not making an effort (for the sake of piety at least, as you put it) to cling to a similar, insignificant scrap. It was indeed, so far as I could see, a mere nothing, a joke—not even a joke. Four days a year you went to the synagogue, where you were, to say the least, closer to the indifferent than to those who took it seriously, patiently went through the prayers as a formality, sometimes amazed me by being able to show me in the prayer book the passage that was being said at the moment, and for the rest, so long as I was present in the synagogue (and this was the main thing) I was allowed to hang about wherever I liked. And so I yawned and dozed through the many hours (I don't think I was ever again so bored, except later at dancing lessons) and did my best to enjoy the few little bits of variety there were, as for instance when the Ark of the Covenant was opened, which always reminded me of the shooting galleries where a cupboard door would open in the same way whenever one hit a bull's eye; except that there something interesting always came out and here it was always just the same old dolls without heads. Incidentally, it was also very frightening for me there, not only, as goes without saying, because of all the people one came into close contact with, but also because you once mentioned in passing that I too might be called to the Torah. That was something I dreaded for years. But otherwise I was not fundamentally disturbed in my boredom, unless it was by the *bar mitzvah,* but that demanded no more than some ridiculous memorizing, in other words, it led to nothing but

some ridiculous passing of an examination; and, so far as you were concerned, by little, not very significant incidents, as when you were called to the Torah and passed, in what to my way of feeling was a purely social event, or when you stayed on in the synagogue for the prayers for the dead, and I was sent away, which for a long time—obviously because of the being-sent-away and the lack of any deeper interest—aroused in me the more or less unconscious feeling that something indecent was about to take place. That's how it was in the synagogue; at home it was, if possible, even poorer, being confined to the first Seder, which more and more developed into a farce, with fits of hysterical laughter, admittedly under the influence of the growing children. (Why did you have to give way to that influence? Because you had brought it about.) This was the religious material that was handed on to me, to which may be added at most the outstretched hand pointing to "the sons of the millionaire Fuchs," who attended the synagogue with their father on the high holy days. How one could do anything better with that material than get rid of it as fast as possible, I could not understand; precisely the getting rid of it seemed to me to be the devoutest action.

Still later, I did see it again differently and realized why it was possible for you to think that in this respect too I was malevolently betraying you. You really had brought some traces of Judaism with you from the ghetto-like village community; it was not much and it dwindled a little more in the city and during your military service; but still, the impressions and memories of your youth did just about suffice for some sort of Jewish life, especially since you did not need much help of that kind, but came of robust stock and could personally scarcely be shaken by religious scruples unless they were strongly mixed with social scruples. At bottom the faith that ruled your life consisted in your believing in the unconditional rightness of the opinions of a certain class of Jewish society, and hence actually, since these opinions were part and parcel of your own nature, in believing in yourself. Even in this there was still Judaism enough, but it was too little to be handed on to the child; it all dribbled away while you were passing it on. In part, it was youthful memories that could not be passed on to others; in part, it was your dreaded personality. It was also impossible to make a child, overacutely observant from sheer nervousness, understand that the few flimsy gestures you performed in the name of Judaism, and with an indifference in keeping with their flimsiness, could have any higher meaning. For you they had meaning as little souvenirs of earlier times, and that was why you wanted to pass them on to me, but since they no longer had any intrinsic value even for you, you could do this only through persuasion or threat; on the one hand, this could not be successful, and on the other, it had to make you very angry with me on account of my apparent obstinacy, since you did not recognize the weakness of your position in this.

The whole thing is, of course, no isolated phenomenon. It was much the same with a large section of this transitional generation of Jews, which had migrated from the still comparatively devout countryside to the cities. It happened automatically; only, it added to our relationship, which certainly did not lack in acrimony, one more, sufficiently painful source for it. Although you ought to believe, as I do, in your guiltlessness in this matter too, you ought to explain this guiltlessness by your nature and by the conditions of the times, not merely by external circumstances; that is, not by saying, for instance, that you had too much work and too many other worries to be able to bother with such things as well. In this manner you tend to twist your undoubted guiltlessness into an unjust reproach to others. That can be very easily refuted everywhere and here too. It was not a matter of any sort of instruction you ought to have given your children, but of an exemplary life. Had your Judaism been stronger, your example would have been more compelling too; this goes without saying and is, again, by no means a reproach, but only a refutation of your reproaches. You have recently been reading Franklin's memoirs of his youth. I really did purposely give you this book to read, though not, as you ironically commented, because of a little passage on vegetarianism, but because of the relationship between the author and his father, as it is there described, and of the relationship between the author and his son, as it is spontaneously revealed in these memoirs written for that son. I do not wish to dwell here on matters of detail.

I have received a certain retrospective confirmation of this view of your Judaism from your attitude in recent years, when it seemed to you that I was taking more interest in Jewish matters. As you have in advance an aversion to every one of my activities and especially to the nature of my interest, so you have had it here too. But in spite of this, one could have expected that in this case you would make a little exception. It was, after all, Judaism of your Judaism that was here stirring, and with it also the possibility to enter into a new relationship between us. I do not deny that, had you shown interest in them, these things might, for that very reason, have become suspect in my eyes. I do not even dream of asserting that I am in this respect any better than you are. But it never came to the test. Through my intervention Judaism became abhorrent to you, Jewish writings unreadable; they "nauseated" you.

The Return to Zion

By the second decade of the twentieth century there were a couple hundred thousand Jews in Palestine, the desiccated malaria-ridden backwater of the decaying Turkish Empire that had once been the rich and mighty kingdom of Judea. The Israeli writer S. Y. Agnon, who later received the Nobel Prize for Literature, beautifully portrays these early days of the new Zion in his best novel (1939), *A Guest for the Night*.

In these concluding chapters of the book, the Zionist experiment is shown to be shot through with ambiguities and complications, both with respect to *what was happening in Palestine and in Zion's relationship with the Old Country in Eastern Europe. The Jews do not yet feel at home in their ancient homeland; they are still tinged with the sensibility of transients. But somehow they will manage and a new Judea will arise.*

After two days I reached the port of Trieste and found my wife and children, who had arranged to come on the same day so that we should embark together on the same ship and go up together to the Land of Israel. I kissed them and said, "Blessed be the Almighty, blessed be He, who has brought us as far as here." "Well," replied my wife, "so we are going back to the Land of Israel." I nodded but said nothing, for my throat was choked with emotion, like a man who sees that all his hopes are coming true.

The air was pleasant, the sea was calm, and the ship moved gently. With our own eyes we saw the Land of Israel drawing steadily nearer and ourselves approaching the Land. No tongue or pen could describe our joy. The ship was full of Jews, old and young, men and women. Some were returning from the Zionist Congress and some from conferences; some from bathing resorts and some from healing spas; some from East and West and some from North and South; some from traveling in various countries and some from going around the world; some from a holiday trip and some from a pleasure trip; some from an ordinary journey and some from a journey that was ordinary; some were returning to renew their travel documents and some to start traveling again. Some of them spoke Russian or Polish, Hungarian or Rumanian, and some spoke German or Spanish, Yiddish or English; some the English of England, some the English of America, and some the English of the Land of Israel. Some of them even spoke Hebrew. Both these and those lay stretched out on deck chairs and looked at the new immigrants, who danced and sang and rejoiced.

Among the immigrants I found our comrade Zvi, from the training farm. All those days I was in the boat Zvi was happy that he had succeeded in fitting the deed to the thought and was going up to settle in the Land of Israel. He was so happy that he did not stop dancing, as if through the dance he was moving on and getting nearer to the source of his vitality. From time to time Zvi would come to see me and talk about our comrades in the Diaspora, the boys in the fields and the girls in the cowshed. They were still few, but their work was recognized, and even the peasants sang their praises. And if the farmers sometimes held up their pay, the true reward of work is work. While we were talking, Zvi asked me if I was hungry. "What kind of question is this?" I asked, surprised. Zvi laughed and said, "I remember the Shavuot feast, when they stole all our food and we could find nothing to eat."

From our comrades in the village we went on to talk about the other groups in Poland, where young men and women were living to prepare themselves for work in the Land, and thus we came to speak of Hannah, the daughter of that righteous man Reb Hayim, may he rest in peace. She was still living in exile and waiting for Zvi to bring her up to the Land of Israel.

"And who gave you an immigration certificate?" I asked Zvi. He laid his hand on his heart and answered, "I myself am my own certificate." I thought he meant that he kept his certificate over his heart, and asked no more. But the end showed that this was not so.

Let me leave Zvi and go back to myself, and my wife and children. My wife and I also hired two deck chairs, and we sat and talked about everything that came into our heads and onto our tongues. There were many, many things to talk about—no book could contain them.

So we sat and talked about the days we had endured abroad and the days that were in store for us in the Land. There were many, many things to talk about; many books could not contain them.

"I am tired of living abroad," said my wife. "To all appearances, I was short of nothing, for our relatives tried to make our stay pleasant, but I missed the Land of Israel."

New hope in Zion: Orchard and farms below Jerusalem, late-nineteenth century. Today this area is covered by condos.

"What were you short of there?" I asked the children. And since I was in a good mood I spoke up in the defense of that rabbi who did not know the Hebrew for a footstool. "Because his mind was floating among matters of the highest import he did not pay attention to something as low as a footstool," I said to the children. "Children," I said to them, "didn't you hear that rabbi singing the praises of Israel? Didn't you hear him saying that Israel is a light to the Gentiles?" "Father," said my daughter, "what are you talking about? He compared Israel to the Greeks." "What's wrong with comparing Israel to the Greeks?" said I. "The Greeks were a wise and clever people, weren't they?" My daughter laughed and said, "But then they bowed down to idols." "What of it?" said my son. "They used to make dolls and play with them. You make dolls, too, don't you?" "When I was a little child I played with dolls," my daughter answered, "but they did it even when they were big." "Praised be your good sense," I said to my daughter. "Now tell me what you did all the time. Did you finish all the *Tales from the Scriptures?*" "You are laughing at me, Father," said my daughter, "I studied the Bible itself."

Several people had gathered around; they stood listening to the children's conversation and praised them for their cleverness. I said to one of them, "When a child says something clever, you should stop him before he lets slip something foolish." So I stopped the children's conversation and talked with the people in my company about the education of the younger generation and the way they study the Bible, which makes the Holy Scriptures an everyday matter. Some said one thing and some another. I told them the story of that old man from the village who came to the Beit Midrash and heard the story of David and Goliath and the story of Bathsheba. Everyone laughed, until their laughter could be heard from one end of the ship to the other. But, as is usual with most people, they drew no moral from the story.

So we sat and talked. We talked about everything under the sun, about the great world and our little country, about summer and winter, sea and dry land. Finally I turned away from my company and turned to my children. I tested them in the Bible and made the time pass pleasantly with questions, such as: "Where is the place where they threw Jonah into the sea?" And they replied, "Ask the fishes and they will tell you."

My dear friends, it would be a good thing if we could make a good ending to our story, especially as we have arrived at the good Land. But since the day we were exiled from our Land, there is no good without evil. When the ship was approaching Jaffa, Zvi jumped into the sea, because the authorities had not given him a certificate to enter the Land, and he relied on the waves to bring him to the shore. The waves were kind at that time; each wave handed him over to the next, and that one to the next again. But rocks and reefs, whose hearts are hearts of stone, struck him, and his blood flowed from their wounds. And when he escaped from the rocks and reefs, the authorities surrounded him and seized him and took him to their hospital, until he should return to health and they should return him into exile.

Zvi's misfortune abated my joy. After I had brought my wife and children to Jerusalem, I went to a number of men in authority to beg mercy for Zvi. Just as those rocks on which he struck were not softened, neither were the hearts of the men in authority. When I saw that this was useless, I went to the distinguished men of the day. When I saw that they were useless, I went to the leaders of the community. When I saw that they were useless I went to the public benefactors. When I saw that they were useless, I went to the lovers of charity. When I saw that they were useless, I relied on our Father in heaven.

In the meantime I stayed with my family in a certain hotel. The owners of the hotel treated me as a guest and also as a resident. At mealtimes they waited first on the guests from abroad, and when it came to paying the bill they demanded a great deal of money, as is usual with foreign guests.

It is hard to be a guest abroad, and all the more so in the Land of Israel. So we rented a little house and bought a little furniture. I put in the few books the marauders had left me and sent the children to school. I set to and arranged my old

books, while my wife arranged the furniture. When I saw my books arranged in orderly fashion in the bookcase and my things lying in their places, I breathed a sigh of relief. For over a year I had been wandering about in foreign lands, like a guest for the night, and suddenly I was living in my own house, among my belongings and my books, with my wife and children.

Zvi's troubles overclouded my spirits. I tried to put them out of my mind, but I could not succeed in putting them out of my heart. In the meantime I started looking after my own affairs and began to divert my attention from others. That is the way of the world: People are more concerned for their own fingernail than for someone else's whole body. Finally, the story of Zvi slipped out of my mind entirely, and if his name had not been mentioned in the papers among those who were sent back abroad, I should have forgotten him.

As I sat in my own niche and enjoyed the peace of my house I began putting out of my mind all that had happened in Szibucz; I no longer saw before my eyes the hotel, its owners and its guests, and the old Beit Midrash, with all those who had come to pray and those who had not come to pray. If I remembered them, I did so only to put them out of my heart again, like a man who sits tranquilly in his home and pays no attention to other men's troubles.

So I sat in the shadow of sweet tranquillity with my wife and children—that sweet tranquillity which no man savors except when he is sitting in his own home. I occupied myself with my affairs, and my wife with hers. One day she was going through my pieces of luggage and laid them out in the sun. Then she took my satchels to mend them, for through much use the leather inside had been torn and holes had appeared. While she was busy with the satchels she called out to me and asked, "What is this?" I saw she was holding a big key that she had found in the crevices of one of the satchels. I was stunned and astonished. It was the key of our old Beit Midrash. But I had given it as a gift to Yeruham Freeman's son on the day he entered into the Covenant of Abraham, so how had it made its way here? No doubt Yeruham Freeman, who had freed himself from all the commandments, was not pleased that I had made his son the guardian of the old Beit Midrash, and had hidden the key in the satchel so as to give it back to me. As I was feeling angry with Yeruham for returning me the key, my wife handed it to me and I saw that this was not the key the old locksmith had made. It was the key the elders of the old Beit Midrash had handed over to me on the Day of Atonement just before the Closing Service. A thousand times I had sought it, a thousand times I had despaired of it, a thousand times I had sought it again without finding it, and had had another key made, and now, when I had no need of one or the other, it had come back to me. How had it disappeared and how had it appeared again? No doubt one day I had left it in my satchel and it had slipped into a hole so that I could not see it, or perhaps on the day when I put on my new coat I had taken out the key from my summer clothes to put it in my winter clothes and forgotten it. How much sorrow and distress, how much trouble I would have avoided if I had had the key at the right time! But there is no argument against the past. After I had recovered somewhat from my emotions, I told the whole story to my wife, who knew nothing of it, because I had not mentioned it in my letters, for I had wanted to explain the whole matter in detail and had not managed to write before the key was lost, and once it was lost I did not mention it in my letters.

"What are you thinking of doing with the key?" said my wife, "send it to Szibucz?" "The one they have is superfluous," said I, "and you tell me to burden them with a second key!" "Well," said my wife, "what will you do with it?" "There came into my mouth the saying of our sages, of blessed memory: "The synagogues and Batei Midrashot abroad are destined to be established in the Land of Israel." And I said to myself: When they establish themselves in the Land of Israel, this man will have the key in his possession.

So I rose and put the key in a box, and hung the key of the box over my heart. I did not hang the key of the old Beit Midrash over my heart, for it was too heavy for my heart to bear; the early craftsmen used to make their keys too big and heavy for the measure of our hearts.

The key being put away in its place, I returned to my work, and whenever I remembered it, I would repeat to myself: "The synagogues and the Batei Midrashot are destined . . . ," and I would open my window and look outside to see if perhaps they were making their way to establish themselves in the Land of Israel. Alas, the land was desolate and silent, and the sound of the steps of the synagogues and Batei Midrashot was not heard. And still the key lies there, waiting with me for that day. However, it is made of iron and brass, and it can wait, but I, who am flesh and blood, find it hard to endure.

Let us leave the key and turn to the owner of the key. I sit in my house and do my work. People come to visit me and ask me about what I saw over there in the land of exile and I ask them about all that has happened here in the Land of Israel. As we talk, the Holy One, blessed be He, brings Szibucz before my eyes, and I close my eyes for a little while and walk among its ruins. Sometimes I stretch out my hand and wish to talk with someone from there.

After a few days I set aside all my affairs and went up to Ramat Rahel to visit Reb Shlomo Bach. I found him standing in the vegetable garden, busy hoeing. The back of his neck was sunburnt and his movements were measured, like those whose business is with the soil. I greeted him and he returned my greeting. When he recognized me, he put down his tools and sat down with me.

I told him about Daniel his son, and Sara Pearl, Daniel's wife, and Raphael and Erela, as well as about the people from our old Beit Midrash who had gone away, some to America and some elsewhere. I also told him about the other people of Szibucz, whether he asked about them or not. Thus Szibucz was privileged to be recalled in Jerusalem.

"How did you come to work in the garden?" I asked him. "When I came to Ramat Rahel," he replied, "and saw that they were all engaged in settling the Land, I said to myself: Everyone is engaged in settling the Land and I am doing nothing. So I asked them to make me a teacher for the children and a cantor in our little congregation. But the old men have no need for a permanent cantor, because each of them knows how to lead the service, and the children have their own teachers and do not need this old man. When I saw that I was superfluous, I felt as if the world had darkened, so I lightened the gloom with the Torah and immersed myself in the Mishna. When I reached the tractates that deal with the religious duties that are linked to the soil of the Land of Israel, I saw that my learning was rootless. I had studied these matters abroad and found no difficulty in them, but in the Land of Israel a man's mind is renewed and he is not content with his earlier interpretations. Once I said to myself: Let me go and see what is this tree of which the sages spoke, and what is this field that is mentioned in the Mishna. When I went out, I heard the young men talking to each other, and through their words the entire subject became clear. It was not that they were referring to the Mishna, but they spoke as usual about trees and plants. I said to myself, 'Wisdom cries outdoors.' After that, whenever I found a difficulty in the words of the Mishna I would go to one of our comrades. If he did not know, then the gardener knew. If he did not know how to explain in our way, he explained in his own way and showed me every single thing in tangible fashion. I found out from my own experience, 'Better is the sight of the eyes than the wandering of the desire.' I need not say much more; the sages were right when they said, 'There is no Torah like the Torah of the Land of Israel.' Here I am, some seventy years old, and I was not privileged to understand the truth of the Torah until I came to the Land."

And Reb Shlomo continued, "Learning leads to doing. As a result of my meetings with the gardener, I was not sitting idle. When he watered the plants, I filled the vessels with water. When he dug out the thorns, I cleared them from the path. This way, I learned how to water a garden and take out the weeds and make hollows around the vines, how to plow and sow and plant. When our comrades saw this, they gave me a patch to grow vegetables, and if the Almighty grants me the privilege, I shall eat the fruits of my patch."

And Reb Shlomo continued, "Our young comrades are pleased with me and call me comrade, which is a title of honor and a high degree in the scale of workers. Our old comrades are not pleased with me, for since I work they think I am trying to make myself popular with the members of the kvutza. So long as I am engaged in my work, I pay no heed to what they say, but now that I have stopped working for a while I remember them." Before I took my leave of Reb Shlomo, he showed me all the things he had planted, and brought me to the children's house, where he showed me his grandson Amnon. God grant he may be like his father and grandfather.

One more time I went up to Ramat Rahel to visit Reb Shlomo. He was standing in the middle of his patch, while the birds flew over his head and pecked at the trees. "Is it possible that the birds should peck at the trees and the gardener does not drive them away?" said I. "I have many joys in the Land," Reb Shlomo replied, "but above them all I rejoice in the birds, for they are witnesses that our redemption is at hand. We find in the Midrash: 'For fifty-two years no bird was seen flying in the Land of Israel.' Now that the birds have returned to this place it is a sign that Israel will return to their nests." From the birds of heaven, Reb Shlomo went on to domestic fowl.

He took me and brought me to a place where the chickens were kept, and showed me fowl so fat that their fat had weakened their wings, and children were standing throwing them crumbs. He, too, took some scraps from his pocket and gave them to Amnon his grandson, so that he should give them to the birds. "If you think they keep the birds for food," said he, "I must tell you that most of our young comrades eat no meat." And having mentioned his comrades he immediately began to sing their praises.

A few days later Reb Shlomo came to my house to tell me the good news that Hannele his son's daughter (this was Hannah, namely Aniela, otherwise Erela) had become betrothed to a certain doctor called Jacob Milch. I congratulated Reb Shlomo, we drank to their good health, and I told him what a fine man Kuba was. "I am certain," I said to Reb Shlomo, "that the couple will soon come up to the Land of Israel, and it will be a good thing for you to have relatives in the Land. Sometimes they will come to visit you, and sometimes you will go to visit them, especially on festivals, when a man wishes to sit with his family."

So we sat for some time and talked, until evening approached and the time came for the Afternoon Service. Reb Shlomo rose and asked, "Which side is the East?" I showed him from my window the direction of the Holy Temple. He sighed, washed his hands, and prayed. After he had completed his prayer I said to him, "Perhaps you would leave the congregation in Ramat Rahel and pray with me." "There is a quorum there without me, thank God," said Reb Shlomo.

From this the talk turned to the old men in the kvutza, who kept quarreling with each other about every little thing, for each of them believed that the Torah had been given in his town alone, and every custom that he had not seen in his town did not seem to him to be a Jewish custom at all. "Perhaps you would like to go back," I said to Reb Shlomo. "Where?" "To Szibucz," I said. He looked at me like a deaf man who can neither hear nor speak. "If you hurry," I said, "you will arrive in time for Erela's wedding. And if you wish to sit and study there I will give you the key of our old Beit Midrash." I rose, opened the box and showed him the key, telling him the whole story. "Here is the key before you," I said. "You can take the key and go back to Szibucz." Reb Shlomo smiled and said, "If the Almighty helps me I will sit and wait here for the footsteps of the Messiah."

"If so," I said to the key, "you stay here with me." The key was silent and gave no answer, first, because it was an inanimate thing and could not speak, and second, because the people in the Beit Midrash had already discussed that matter on the day they gave it to me.

After some time the old man took his leave of me. I went with him to see him on his way. When we reached the crossroads we parted, he going to his home and I to mine. I turned my head and saw that the birds were flying above his head. The fowl of the heavens, who had returned to the Land of Israel, were flying to accompany the old man who was returning to his nest.

I went into my house, put away the key in the box, locked the box on the outside, and hung the key over my heart. I know that no one is enthusiastic about the key of our old Beit Midrash, but I said to myself: One day our old Beit Midrash is destined to be established in the Land of Israel; better, then, for the key to be in my possession.

Seventy Years Later

In the Land of Israel (1982) by Amos Oz, the most widely-read Israeli writer of his generation, is a kind of sequel to S. Y. Agnon's *A Guest for the Night.* Seven decades have passed since the time-setting of the two books. In Oz's book, a work of slightly fictionalized journalism, Israelis of the older generation, still ambivalent and in disagreement among themselves about some important issues, look back over the long struggle to create their state, recount the troubles they have experienced, acknowledge that the story is far from finished, but still exude an air of confidence and satisfaction at what has been achieved.

The cemetery in Zichron Yaakov was consecrated in 1883. The founders of the settlement, their sons, grandsons, perhaps even their great-grandsons are buried here. Many of those lying here died of childhood diseases or in the prime of life. A few lived to be almost a hundred. And some fell in war. At this early-morning hour, there is no one around: silence, pine trees rustling in the sea breeze, an overcast sky. Several of the gravestones have sunk. Others are so eroded that it is impossible to decipher their engravings. And some I copy into my notebook:

"Here lies a God-fearing woman of valor, Mrs.

Dubish, daughter of Reb Yeshayahu Yosef of blessed memory, sixty-five years old. A charitable woman. Her husband's heart was sure of her, her hands always busy spinning wool and weaving flax."

Not far from this woman of valor lies one of the founders: "Here lies a dear and honored man, one of the builders and settlers of the village of Haderah. He sacrificed his life on the altar of love and the redemption of our holy land. Moshe Izvi, son of Mordecai of blessed memory, Shechkser from the city of Riga in Russland. Cut down and gathered to the bosom of his people in the forty-second year of his life, on the sixth day of Shevat, 1897. May he rest in peace."

And also: "Here lies an honest man, Elchanan, son of Reb David Kalman, of Brisk. Spent ten years in Paris. Died on the second day of Shevat, 1898. May he rest in peace."

"Here lies a man of character and industry, who walked in the ways of truth. The leader of the community of Zichron Yaakov for decades. One of her first builders, who bore her sufferings with love and courage, Reb Mattitiyahu Tamshis, of blessed memory. Settled in Eretz Yisrael in 1882, cherishing every stone, exalting the very dust until his dying day." . . .

Sarah says, "I met Zvi in Haifa when I was barely seventeen and he was twenty. He was a very handsome boy. To tell the truth, he was a little too short, but handsome in spite of it. A policeman, in uniform, with that horse; besides, he had already saved up almost a hundred pounds. So we held the wedding in Safed. Afterward we moved around, because of his service. We lived awhile in Haifa and finally settled in Zichron, where our oldest daughter was born. And then one day a farmstead became available in Bat Shlomo. Zvi wanted to go back to live in the place where he was born. His slogan was, Both feet on the land. To tell the truth, I didn't really want to be a farmer very much. I'm a city type. And there were these flies here that bit all the time—the bites would get infected and swollen and there was no remedy. But the minute they said they wouldn't accept us, I became even more stubborn than Zvi. I might even have been angry. I got on the donkey and rode straight to the Baron Rothschild's clerk in Zichron, Mr. Cohen, who spoke only French and Yiddish. Mr. Cohen ridicules me: 'What nonsense, my dear girl, for you suddenly to become farmers! Ridiculous! Your husband the constable knows nothing beyond polishing buttons, and as for you, why, I've been told you were seen wearing silk stockings. What sort of farmers would you make?' But I made a bit of a scandal there and finally I left with a document, a letter. And that's how we got accepted into Bat Shlomo. Bit by bit we built the farm and renovated the house a little. Zvi worked very hard, while I raised the children and helped him out in his work. There was poverty and want and all kinds of mishaps and troubles, but I learned how to be a farmer, all right. The farm was a real farm and the house was a warm nest for

the whole family. And for visitors. In the time of the English, we received the most honored guests—the mayor of Tel Aviv, Zionist leaders, Jewish Agency notables, and plenty of English officers, Zvi's friends. I always made sure there was cold beer on the table for them. Later on, during the Arab riots in '36, when Zvi was a corporal in the mounted police guards, we girls polished everything that was hidden in the 'cache.' We even polished the bullets. When the boys went out on patrol, we would stand on the roof until two in the morning to keep watch. They signaled us with a green lantern if everything was quiet, or, God forbid, with a red one to get the first aid ready."

Zvi continues: "This house has been standing for ninety years now. I took it more than fifty years ago, and we lived in it along with the cows and the horse—one room for the family and one for the livestock. For twenty-three years I raised children and animals under this roof. Piece by piece I built a barn, I built a stable, added onto the house, and all of it with my own two hands. Nothing came from the Jewish Agency. Nothing from the government. Nothing from the banks or the stock exchange. I'm one of the nuts. The property I got was bare and rocky, and by myself I cleared it and revived it and planted it with vineyards and olive groves, and plums and loquats. Sarah helped me. The children would help with the farm work from the time they could walk. And I had faith in the future: I believed that the future would be good, that the Jews had learned their lesson and from now on everyone would work for his living. To this day I believe in the future, but not in the near future, only in the far future, which I won't live to see. The Jews still haven't learned their lesson. The immediate future? Very bad. Blacker than black. Fearsome!

"In nineteen-thirty-and-six God had mercy on us and again bloody riots broke out. I was appointed local commander of the militia. Again there were attacks—they stole one of our flocks, burned our crops, uprooted orchards, so we'd know God hadn't forgotten us. But there was no loss of life. In nineteen-thirty-and-seven I was one of sixty-six boys chosen from all over the country to join the constabulary force in the settlements. The British put us through a military course in Natanya. A Jew from the settlement of Avihayil, Avraham Ikkar, was in charge of us, together with

Berl Locker from the Jewish Agency. Later I was military commander in Bat Shlomo, even after the riots subsided, and then straight through until the War of Independence. During the War of Independence they sent us a squadron of forty boys, and by then I had acquired an old pickup truck from the British army and armor-plated it with lead plates with gravel between them. We'd patrol the Faradis-Yokneam road, which was the only contact for several months between Haifa and the north, and Tel Aviv and the south, since the Arabs from the village of Tira had blocked the coast road. I kept that road to Yokneam open day and night. We fought a few battles; we fought the war in this area by ourselves—no one gave us orders. Actually, a hundred smart alecks at the top would issue a hundred different orders every hour, so I simply ignored them all and did what was right. I had a small allowance from the Jewish community defense fund, so I appointed myself general all the way from Zichron up to Yokneam. We held on and the road stayed open. I'm a little overwhelmed today by the nerve I had during those days. But, then again, the entire War of Independence was one big act of nerve. Nerve and audacity. All of Zionism is audacious. Now the audacity is gone, and we've got a generation of practical people. I already told you, this practicality is the worst madness!"

Sarah says, "In the meantime I raised two girls, Carmela and Ofra, and a son for our old age, Chaim. They all live in Zichron, but they can't join us here in Bat Shlomo because the government won't permit any more building here. They want to turn us into a nature preserve. A museum. A national park for tourists. What, are we a museum?"

Zvi reflects, "Maybe we are. Maybe we really are a museum. I'm seventy-eight years old, and every morning at four or five, I go out to work the land. I want you to know: At five o'clock in the morning this is already an Arab country. To the breadth and length of this country, the Arabs are up and working and the Jews are still fast asleep. All in all, I'm a bit disappointed by the Jews. When I was a policeman, I had this dream that when the Hebrew nation got statehood we wouldn't need police. Or prisons. We would be the Chosen People. Chosen People, never mind; I'll forget that, but why have we become a nation of profiteers? Of thieves? Of panhandlers and parasites? Not to mention the murderers and rapists and robbers. What's gone wrong with us? Maybe we lost our morality along the way. No, no, not because of 'ingathering the exiles.' Sephardic Jews are wonderful people! Hard-working! Honest! Maybe it happened because of the wars with the Arabs. The wars brought us the American aid, the easy money, and that easy money rolls around like a plague. The country is poverty-stricken and the public is bursting from the good life, feasting on the future, on our own birthright and that of our children and grandchildren and great-grandchildren! Going into such debt, it's criminal. Everybody's buying and selling, selling and buying all day long. Lots! Stocks! Bonds! Diamonds! The easy money brought us permissiveness, too. They permit themselves everything: Adulteries, divorces; they bring children into the world and dump them on the trash heap so they won't get in the way of going out and having a good time!

"I want you to know, I'm at a loss. Who says riches bring happiness, permissiveness brings joy, easy money gives you health? Who says? They're taking off from here for Los Angeles. Seems they got the same things there, only more so. There's an old saying: A rich man isn't a happy man. Let them leave! Maybe all those practical Jews will finally leave us and it'll be just us madmen here again. Who knows? Don't ask me what to do. I got no advice to give. Maybe, just maybe . . . Sometimes I think . . . a madmen's club ought to be formed. Ought to call themselves just that, 'The Madmen.' And they would work the land. Or they'd work in trades or industry—they could do that, too! People of importance, moral folks, they should start it. They should set a personal example for the people. The politicians should work a couple of hours every morning out in the fields— all of them, from the prime minister on down, at least during the busy season! And the professors will work a few hours each week in a factory. And the poets. And those singers on television, and dancers, and beauty queens. That would inspire the youth! That would be an example! There's a saying, goes like this: Water, drop by drop, will also split a stone!

"The breakdown pretty much began with statehood. We thought we'd reached a time of rest and security, to live a little, to be permissive like the goyim in the West. But the goyim in the West— turns out they're the ones that know what work is. They work hard! To be normal you've got to be a little crazy. The only normal people in Eretz Yisrael are the ones who are crazy as a loon."

Sarah tells me, "Chaim, our youngest, is already forty-four years old, but he just did sixty days of reserve duty in Lebanon, in a reconnaissance unit where they're all kibbutzniks and he's like God to them. He doesn't miss a day of service. But among them, even among the kibbutzniks, there's already talk of leaving the country. Where will it end? My grandson, my oldest girl's son, is thirty years old. Not long ago he bought a farm and settled in a *moshav* in the Tel Mond bloc. He decided to go back to his roots. And what's happened? The government is strangling him! Destroying him! People tell him, Don't be a fool, don't be a jerk—why be a farmer? Go play the stock market, you'll be a millionaire. Go to the occupied territories, you'll be a millionaire. Be a parasite, you'll become a millionaire. Has this country lost its mind?"

"Down near Tel Aviv," says Zvi, "I hardly ever set foot. It's all marble-coated lies. Falsehoods and Formica. Nobody wants to work. Everyone's a big shot. Now's the season here for thinning out the loquats, before they flower. I get up at five and go out to thin them with the little Arab girls. There isn't a Jew these days willing to do seasonal field-work. That's finished. The stock market has ruined the country. Over there, in Zichron, go take a look at the villas they built, the evacuees from Yammit with their compensation money—castles! America! Sick! And they sit down at the bank bankrolling dollars. Go try to take the exile and the Diaspora out of a Jewish heart. It's easier to get crab grass out of a lawn.

"If we go back in history, you'll see that Moses was no fool. He was a real leader. From Egypt to Eretz Yisrael, on foot, with babies and goats and whatnot, is an easy ten-day walk. Maybe two hundred kilometers all together. But he led them around in circles in the desert, on purpose, for forty years, till they'd forget the fleshpots, till they'd stop being slaves. The Diaspora generation shouldn't enter Eretz Yisrael at all. Maybe it's too late now. What'll become of us? What can be done? Maybe you know?"

Sarah cuts in. "Don't be unkind, Zvi. We have a wonderful younger generation! But only in wartime. If there was peace—I don't know, maybe it would be better if you didn't write down the foolishness I'm talking—if there was peace, the Arabs would finish us off like that, God forbid: They'd work and we'd shrivel up. It's already happened to us once here in this country, decay like that, but just then a wave of idealists arrived and saved us. Maybe another wave of idealists will come along? Maybe such a thing could happen? Little fourteen-year-old *shiksas* from the Arab village work in our fields, and Jewish boys are either in the army in Lebanon, or in the secret service, or flitting around the world, or in the stock market, or the-Devil-knows-where, or just hanging around all day, their heads full of soul-searching."

Says Zvi, "And right now the Arabs are raising a new generation, just the opposite of what used to be—educated, quiet, serious, even idealistic. There's a lot of them going back to their religion. Dreaming all day long about a homeland. There's even some willing to sacrifice themselves. And us? Something's gone wrong—very wrong."

Sarah's face, wearing an expression of sad wisdom, is planed, like that of an aged Slavic peasant woman, with shrewdness and generosity. She sets before me a sort of plan. "Look, changing the government won't help much. We've already seen the likes of all of them—there's no big difference. This Begin is a lawyer. He's clever, fancy-talking, well-educated, but he has no roots. Begin's sort of a new immigrant, a bit like the Diaspora: He doesn't have deep roots in this land. Yigal Allon was a fine boy. Delicate, pleasant, but a little weak. Peres is smart! Very smart. I don't care for him much, but he's smart, maybe even a little too smart! Could that be his problem? I don't know. Arik Sharon is a brave boy. A fighter, no denying it. But terribly impulsive, and not very moral, I think. Rabin's decent, that's for sure, very decent, and honest, but—you know what?—he's very cold. A cold fish. You never see a heart in him, or feelings. A leader should have fire in him, not ice. That's what I think. So who's left? Maybe you know of someone else?

"I'm a simple woman without much formal schooling, and maybe you'll laugh at what I'm going to tell you now, but I have to speak my piece because this situation is actually making me ill. I'm not complaining for myself. I have everything in life: I've married off my children; now even my grandson's getting married; everything has turned out the way I wanted. But where do we go from here? How do we become a working people again? I don't object to what Zvi suggested about the big shots working a couple of hours a week, but that's not very realistic many of them aren't used to it any more, they're not healthy. What do I think? I think, first of all, that we have to throw all the televisions right out the window, and the rock-and-roll radio stations, too, so they won't deaden the senses of our youth day and night. Next the government has to issue a labor law: Anyone who is healthy has to work. Really work—in the fields or in a workshop or a factory—with no exceptions. Like martial law. We'll have to give the Arabs something in the West Bank—not the whole thing—and bid them farewell. Simply part ways. Only we have to take care that there are good security arrangements so there won't be infiltrations and attacks again. And you know something? This might work, because they're sick and tired of it, too. They've suffered a lot already, too. But the important thing is to take leave of them. Ali in a place of his own, and us in our country. And he shouldn't come to work for us. So we won't have *Shabbes goyim* on weekdays: We'll just have to roll up our sleeves and get to work.

"The labor law has to be the first condition for everything else: Anyone who doesn't work, really work—with his hands—won't be accepted at the university, won't get housing rights, won't get free public education, or loans. Won't get a permit to go abroad. But, most important, he won't get any office job. No, sir! Office jobs will only be for people over forty, forty-five. Professors? Artists? Diplomats, merchants, entertainers, members of Parliament, reporters? Why not—after the age of forty-five. Until then everyone works with his hands. But everybody! According to the law! With no exceptions, and no string-pulling and no concessions! First of all the duty to work. Everyone who's not sick. You think this is an infringement on freedom? What freedom? What are you talking about? The freedom to live at someone else's expense? To run wild? To run roughshod over one another? I know the goyim don't have a law like this—but most of the goyim work! It's simple: They work! And us? What about us? You can write this down: This is a simple woman from Bat Shlomo talking and she's telling you we've all gone out of our minds."

The old Bat Shlomo, the one to the south of the road, is a very small village, just a handful of old houses set among tall trees. Here and there a tractor is parked under an asbestos lean-to. Chickens wander about freely. A pigeon coop. Bougainvillaea. Citrus trees and ornamental shrubs in the yard. The walls are covered with lush vines. Old agricultural tools have become decorative objects in the front gardens—a rusted plow, an unwieldy rack, a wooden-wheeled harrow. And the village dogs all bark at the stranger wandering in the street. In the shade of the high treetops, masses of chirping birds make their nests. Weeping willows, coral trees, and rose bushes, too, grown wild, higher than a man's head. Somber cypress trees. Behind every house there is a barn or a sheep pen, a chicken coop, storage sheds; beyond them the vineyards, the orchards, and the fields. On one of the porches stands a stone-topped table, surrounded by eight green chairs. There is not a soul in the street at this midday hour. In the evening, with the setting of the sun, it will be good to sit in the garden in the sea breeze, to pass the time with one or two neighbors and stories from the day's work in the field, to drink coffee, to fondle the grandchildren and dogs, to meander in conversation until it is dark and the air turns cool.

This, too, was part of the old dream—not grandiose, but this probably is what those first immigrants intended at the beginning of one hundred years of solitude and pain. It was perhaps about a yard like this, with a barn at its edge, with a stand of fruit trees and a patch of vegetables, that Zvi Bachur's father dreamed eighty years ago—the man from the region of Minsk who, "when they were getting ready to go off to America, got up one morning, had his glass of tea, suddenly slammed his fist on the table, and said, 'We're not going to America. We are going to Palestine.' And there was a great ruckus!" Perhaps for rest and respite such as this did those buried in the cemetery of Zichron Yaakov give their lives: the woman of valor, Mrs. Dubish, who spun wool and wove flax; and Moshe Zvi Shechkser, who came from Riga in Russland and "sacrificed his life on the altar of love and the redemption of our holy land;" Reb Mattityahu Tamshis, who cherished her every stone, exalted "the very dust until his dying day;" and also Shlomo Heller, who "lived in his faith far removed from all petty calculations." In yards like these, in a little village like this, perhaps they strove to heal their lives and to raise their children and their children's children to work the earth "perhaps in suffering, yes, but without disgrace."

Yet that was not how things happened. The attacks came, and the wars, and the avarice, and all the age-old passions of the heart. Came the ancient curses of the Jews. And many new people came whose intentions were altogether different. The sons and grandsons conquered mountains and valleys by force of arms. Afterward they conquered the marketplace. Moved ahead. Got themselves settled. Succeeded. Rebuilt, by the sweat of Arab natives, a garish, tasteless version of the castle of the village squire. And after that got divorced, "dumped the children," lived it up, saw the world, and then went away to faraway places to trade in arms and enter into a tin-mining deal to make in sixteen months "a cool million dollars, just like that."

The ugly Israeli from Zichron Yaakov speaks: "If you scatter the Jews all over the face of the earth, they'll all land on their feet in any place and put a tear on the world. But if you put them all in one place, they'll just tear one another to shreds. . . . That's it. Nothing you can do about it. It's in the blood."

Zvi Bachur speaks: "It's all marble-coated lies. Falsehoods and Formica."

And his wife, Sarah, says, "We've gone out of our minds."

What will become of us? What can be done? Maybe you know?

The Geniza World

The Geniza (archive) of the Jewish synagogue in Cairo, containing a vast depository of documents on social and economic life of Jewish Sephardic Mediterranean families of the tenth through eighteenth centuries, was discovered in the late-nineteenth century. But the Geniza material was not closely studied until the 1930s when Solomon D. Goitein of the Hebrew University, and later of the University of Pennsylvania and the Institute for Advanced Study at Princeton, began his four decades of research, resulting in his monumental five volume work, *A Mediterranean Society*. Most of the Geniza material is now in the Cambridge University Library; some of it is in the library of the Jewish Theological Seminary in New York; the rest is in many different places. The work of Goitein, his students like Norman A. Stillman, and information from many quarters have allowed in recent years the complex world of Middle Eastern and Levantine Jewish life between the later Middle Ages and the mid-twentieth century to be uncovered. After about 1750 there was a widespread economic decline among Mediterranean Jews, so that by the twentieth century most were relatively poor, living as small craftsman, petty retailers, and hard-scrabble farmers. The majority had very little education. But there remained a narrow stratem of a cosmopolitan, well-educated Jewish bourgeois elite in the Arabic and Levantine world that was blown away in the 1950s.

Ammiel Alcalay, an Israeli of Sephardi background here provides a reliable overview of what he rightly calls the Geniza world. It is a story of effective coping within a difficult environment over many centuries.

Jews and Muslims had common court-yards, just as if we were a single family. We grew up together. Our mothers revealed everything to the Muslim women and they, in turn, opened their hearts to our mothers. The Muslim women even learned how to speak Ladino and were adept in its sayings and proverbs. We didn't live in shelters for the needy like the Ashkenazim and there were no large estates separating our houses from those of the Muslims. The Muslim women used to come down to our places across the roof at dusk to spend the evening in conversation. All the kids played together and if anyone else from the neighborhood bothered us, our Muslim friends would come to our defense. We were allies.

Our mothers would nurse any Muslim children whose mothers had died or were unable to attend to them, just as they would care and watch over them if their mothers were busy or otherwise occupied. And the same was true the other way around. The parents of Muslim boys born after great expectation and long suffering often asked their Jewish friends to arrange for a Jew to perform their circumcision on the eighth day, following Jewish and not Islamic custom. . . . According to Islamic custom, though, a baby nursed by someone other than the mother, was considered a relative. Nissim Franco, son of the *Hacham* Ya'aqob Franco, told me the following story: "Once my brother and I accompanied our father to the train station on the way to Haifa from where he intended to go and visit the saints' tombs in Meron. As we sat in the car a very dignified Muslim sheikh entered and, upon seeing my father, cried out: "*Ya akhi*" (My brother!). They grabbed each other and stood a few moments in a tight embrace. My father asked us to kiss the sheikh's hand. We both got up and kissed his hand after which he blessed us. When my father saw how astonished we were at the whole thing, he turned to us and said: "When I was young we lived with the sheikh's parents in one courtyard. His mother died suddenly and my mother nursed him until he was weaned. So we're brothers."

The space described by Yehoshua also corresponds to that of the *geniza* world. Since Jewish institutions in Palestine were maintained through funds donated by other communities, rabbinical emissaries set out from the four cities—Jerusalem, Hebron, Safed, and Tiberias—to both collect donations and serve for certain periods of time in various functions, most often as rabbis, cantors, teachers, or a combination of all three. Egypt, where Yehoshua's father served on such a mission, was considered the most pleasant post: besides its vicinity to home, many Palestinian, Syrian, and Lebanese Jews lived there. Others went to the "inland west" (Tripoli, Algeria, Tunisia), and the "outer west" (Morocco); still others went to Turkey, Iraq, Bukhara, or India. Those going to Europe adapted themselves by shedding the long cloaks, headwear, and other traditional garb they felt at home in the Levant, and dressing "European," like the *franj*. Besides the official emissaries, businesspeople, families, and individuals also traveled freely and widely, sometimes emigrating for a variety of reasons. The story of Asher Mizrahi, for example, is told: A musician well-known in the Arab cities and villages of Palestine and the composer of many tunes that became standards in the Arab world, he decided to settle in Tunis following the events of 1929, when many Palestinian Jews were killed in the waves of violence that swept the country.

Far from being an unobtrusive, silenced, or submissive minority, the Jewish presence and way of life were not simply tolerated but were always acknowledged and recognized as part of the texture of the Levant itself. While stories about the port of Salonica coming to a complete halt on the Sabbath and Ladino serving as a lingua franca there are well-known, a similar state of affairs—as pervasive, though not as legendary as that prevailing in Salonica—could be found in Baghdad through the 1940s:

It was on Yom Kippur that our community made the full weight of its presence felt in the city. The entire city involuntarily observed our solemn day. With the exception of the theatre whose Muslim owner presented only Egyptian productions, all the movie houses were closed. Rashid Street, the city's main artery, was practically deserted. Muslim passers-by would affect an air of nonchalance which made Baghdad look like an orphaned city. Christian and Muslim businessmen, behind their counters, seemed only to half believe in their work. In the textile bazaar, Shiite shopkeepers gossiped with their neighbours as they sipped on their narghilahs, waiting for their rare customers.

In addition to the more obvious and legal bond of religion, it was to cities that people formed their deepest allegiances. Goitein remarks of the *geniza* world:

The cities preceded the countryside. They were founded and filled with populace immediately after, or even in the course of, the conquest and formed the nuclei of Arabization. Consequently, it was natural that the capital of a country or district be identified in terms of the region it dominated. The region, as it were, was subsumed in its capital. Countries were political complexes, often changing their borders and characters, cities were units of life.

Among Arabs "*al-hanin ila 'l-watan*" ("yearning after one's home") was such a pronounced psychological and social phenomenon that a distinct poetic genre categorized by that expression existed. Medieval geographers such as Yaqut and Ibn Jubayr, astonished at how people could live in certain climates or under certain conditions, finally attributed such irrational predilections to love of one's native city, something that obviously went beyond the dictates of reason and logic. Evidence of one of the ways Jews expressed this throughout the ages can be seen in the names of synagogues founded by new emigrants all over the Levant. Among the many synagogues in Old Cairo were those established by the "Damascenes," "Palestinians," and "Babylonians." After the expulsion of the Jews from Spain in 1492, congregations bearing the names of almost every city in Castile flourished throughout the Ottoman Empire. To this day Sephardi synagogues in Israel carry on the traditions or are named after particular cities. In one neighborhood of Jerusalem alone, the following can be found: the synagogue of the refugees from Hebron; the Ades synagogue of Aram Zoba/Aleppo; the congregations of Manastir, Ionnina, Baghdad, Sa'ana, Aden, Dir Bakr, and Teheran.

A perhaps even more significant expression of this characteristic in the *geniza* world proper was in the precedence one's identification with a native city took over religious affiliation. On the road, Jews had a tendency to feel more comfortable with people from their own city, regardless of their religion. A medieval merchant, the only Jew on the caravan, making his way back to Palestine from Libya, writes: "On this very day a big caravan is setting out for Barqa under the command of Ibn Shibl. I have booked in it for my goods at the price of three dinars, and have already paid the fare. Most of the travelers are [fellow] Barqis. They have promised me to be considerate with regard to the watering places and the keeping of the Sabbath and other matters." Due to the long distances traversed and the frequent and extended periods away from home, the merchants' letters are filled with longing, not just for friends and family but for the specific temper and style of their native or adopted cities. Marriage contracts also attached stipulations assuring the bride-to-be that any move from her native city would have to meet with her approval. In one case, a divorcée from Fustat/Old Cairo "engaged to a divorced man from Alexandria, stipulated that the couple would live in the capital and that she was prepared to accompany him on his visits to his family in Alexandria, but for not more than one month per year." As Goitein adds: "A month, she obviously felt, was the maximum she could stand."

Just as relations between the faiths extended far beyond the "logical minimalizations" that present circumstance and ideology allow, so did the range of possibilities for women. Without trying to construct an apologetic chapter in a book of women's "accomplishments" in which those of men are taken as the sole standard of measurement, Goitein presents the beginnings of a foundation for a more thorough social history of medieval Jewish women, one that could confront and pose a wide range of practical and theoretical questions.

Something as innocuous as naming practices—in which women's names are almost completely "secular" and highly individualized (as opposed to the more standardized Biblical names of men)—

opens the field to inquiries regarding what Goitein refers to as "the chasm between the popular local subculture of women and the worldwide Hebrew book culture of the men." Nevertheless, the basis outlined, the exceptions to the rules (the mention of "the son of the female astrologer;" the world-famous women bankers and merchants along with the more commonplace brokers and agents; the teachers, doctors, and oculists) certainly provide food for thought. Being members of an affluent society, the women of the *geniza* world were freed from many of the more prevalent forms of female bondage. Besides being employed in a variety of vocations, women were engaged in business and were property owners. Marriage contracts not only stipulated the bride's choice of domicile but also provided firm safeguards for economic independence should the marriage break up. Often this provision for independence even preceded marriage and was simply a matter of course in a family's distribution of wealth. Goitein notes: "Women of all classes appear in the Geniza documents as being in possession of immovables. They receive as a gift or donate, inherit or bequeath, buy or sell, rent or lease houses (more often parts of houses), stores, workshops, flour mills, and other types of urban real estate, and also take care of their maintenance."

While clear lines of demarcation between the worlds and activities of men and women certainly existed, women within Jewish society—like Jews within Levantine society—were far from a secluded and submissive minority. Single women traveling overseas—whether for business, pleasure, or religious pilgrimage—were common. It was also an ordinary occurrence for women to initiate judicial actions and then appear in their own defense: "I went to the *qadi* [Muslim judge]," writes a widow from Alexandria quite casually in a letter addressed to the attention of the Jewish Vizier Mevorakh. Despite the chasm between the male-dominated book culture and the generally vernacular literary parameters of women's culture, great attention was paid to both securing and providing for the education of children. This, in fact, was considered a woman's duty. A particularly moving letter written by a woman on her deathbed beseeches her sister to provide for her youngest daughter's *formal* education (*ta'alim*), which would include reading and writing. Whether or not this letter—and others like it—was

actually ever sent, it provides indications as to the prevailing parameters of the possible. This is further buttressed by the fact that, in making the request, the woman refers to the example of their mother, herself an educated and pious person:

This is to inform you, my lady, dear sister— may God accept me as a ransom for you— that I have become seriously ill with little hope for recovery, and I have dreams indicating that my end is near.

My lady, my most urgent request of you, if God, the exalted, indeed decrees my death, is that you take care of my little daughter and make efforts to give her an education, although I know well that I am asking you for something unreasonable, as there is not enough money—by my father— for support, let alone for formal instruction. However, she has a model in our saintly mother.

The affluence of the *geniza* world was reflected not only in the status of women but also in its incredibly rich and diverse material and culinary culture. While the medieval Cairene working class ate lunch out, the middle class usually brought a wide variety of hot, ready-made dishes home from the bazaar. Imported foods were not considered luxury items but basic staples. Highly perishable fruits such as apricots, peaches, and plums came into Egypt from the eastern Mediterranean in a half-dried or glazed state. Almonds, pistachios, walnuts, hazelnuts, and olive oil came in from the east and the west, cheese from Crete, Sicily, and Byzantium, the land of the "Rum." Sugarcane was exported by Iran and southern Iraq, honey by Tunisia, Palestine, and Syria. Spices, as one might well imagine, came from everywhere and formed the ingredients of both the druggist's and perfumer's trades. A relatively simple medicinal mixture could contain as many as twenty different items, each coming from a different corner of the known world.

As the large number and high specialization of occupations testify, the sophistication and variety of commodities readily available was truly astonishing. Local styles and specialties were the pride of many branches of endeavor, among them the metals, glass, pottery, leather, parchment, paper, and furniture industries. One of the major industries, the real "big business" of the time, was the dyeing and textile field, an area embodying, literally, the highly individualized and "exotic" tastes of *geniza* people. Our merchant's "flame-colored robe," mentioned above, was not particularly extraordinary. People ordered every possible nuance and shade of every available color on the spectrum, using highly distinctive epithets like silvery, sandal-colored, clean white, bluish-iridescent, olive green, gazelle-blood, pure violet, musk brown, intensive yellow, sky-blue, crimson, pomegranate red, pearl-colored, ash-grey ("color of bamboo crystals"), basil (brownish-violet), blue-onion, lead-grey, turquoise, gold, indigo, and emerald. Taste was both exquisitely refined and extremely picky. In one letter a trader entreats his supplier: "Please, my lord, the red should be as red as possible, likewise the white and the yellow should be exquisite, I was not satisfied with the yellow. . . . The siglaton robe is of the utmost beauty, but not exactly what I wanted, for it is white and blue, while I wanted to have instead of the latter, onion color, an 'open' color. The lead-colored [bluish-grey] robe is superb, better than all the rest." As if this were not enough, clothing was embellished with numerous kinds of "glitter" and "gloss," iridescence, stripes, waves, and patterns; sleeves often featured calligraphy made to order.

The textile industry, maybe more than any other, fully represented the geographic range and the mobility of the *geniza* world, the intricate network of its cities. Brand names manufactured in Spain but originating in the heart of Asia, the Jurjan dress for instance, indicate the migratory movement of both manufacturers and craftspeople. Often it was difficult to discern whether one was getting the real thing or if the market was flooded with imitation items bearing only the name and the style of the original, such as the clothes named after remote regions of Iran imported to Egypt from Spain or North Africa but actually produced in Palestine. Always up on style, *geniza* people also imported the latest from Europe. One of the most popular items among the brides of Damascus and Fustat/Old Cairo from the tenth to the twelfth century was a *mandil Rumi*, a "European mantilla." This later was embellished by the Yemenites until it could be ordered as a "European mantilla in the Yemenite fashion"; with this modification, it became very popular in Egypt.

Besides serving as a center of wealth and commerce, the city assumed a stature and character much greater than the sum of its parts. Trade and urbanity—the urbanity of trade—formed a nexus of taste, quality, standards, and expectations. . . .

And if we could draw up a list of a person's belongings, all the material objects they had left behind in this world at their departure for the world to come, we would, as well, find concrete traces of all the traders' routes and bits of the varied treasure they had brought back with them. In our case—although the remnants we have been given to examine are not those of a vizier but of a coppersmith who had emigrated from Spain to Egypt—we shall find a clue taking us right back to the palace, its transparent walls and refracting prism. The coppersmith was a craftsman as well as a dealer. The list of his belongings "contains about one hundred and forty brass, bronze and copper vessels of all descriptions, kept on the middle floor of the house where he lived, while, as usual, his workshop was on the ground floor. There, no doubt, he exhibited other products of his art for his customers. The middle floor harbored also his personal belongings, and the third floor was probably occupied by a tenant or by the proprietor of the house." After "three old carpets, a threadbare blue robe, a worn linen robe, a new Spanish robe, a lined chest containing ten Spanish 'raw' [unfulled] robes, an Iraqi *burd* gown, a Nuli turban, a piece of Sicilian cloth, two shrouds in which some china is packed, various pairs of pants and overalls, an Abbadani mat, a woolen curtain and some water jars made of stone," we find "a small chest containing the prayer book of Rabbenu Saadya of blessed memory, a section of the Book of Psalms a Maghrebi prayer book, and a book of poetry in Arabic characters."

The cities, trade routes, bazaars, and houses— the qualitative inner and outer spaces of the *geniza* world—constitute the overall site without yet marking the specific start or duration of the transparent walls/prism metaphor and the poetics of knowledge so accurately refracted by it. This metaphor extends from Benjamin of Tudela's description of the Great Mosque of Damascus, in which the walls both separate people and allow them to see each other, to Jacqueline Kahanoff's prism that reflects light through each of its facets differently. For that, as George Kubler put it, a "cleavage, an inscription in the history of things aiming beyond narration, a cut separating different types of happening to initiate a new collective duration" must be identified, ferreted out of the clues left in the coppersmith's "small chest" and the four books found there. Each of those books channels a possible history of Hebrew and Jewish writing. Together, they can serve as a focal point around which unconventional modes of grouping and a new working order of this history can be proposed. The chronological tags of this proposed new order, for want of better or more exact terms, consist of the biblical/Rabbinic ("premodern"); the Levantine ("modern"); the Enlightenment ("neomodern"); and the New Levantine ("postmodern"). These categories cannot be conceived as inclusive or rigid, defining strict and essential characteristics. They must be considered, rather, as relational scanners, places on a map to refer to for orientation. Thus the Levantine ("modern") category, for instance, would include within it "classical" or "traditional" periods, phases, or writers. Such a proposal corresponds to the two other sets of qualities and distinctions already introduced: those of place, and of social and economic condition.

The first set specifically relates to the actual geographical circumstances of writers: Those who have stayed in a given area, those who left entirely, the newly arrived, others relocated within the wider sphere of the same area but whose work has been realigned by altered conditions, can also be applied to other kinds of "movement." This kind of "movement" would include the ideological ends or uses to which works have been put within the same or another geographical area by different people, groups, political or educational structures and hierarchies.

The Orientals

Goitein did not begin to publish his *Mediterranean Society* until the 1960s. If it had been available in 1949, it might have sensitized many Israeli officials and intellectuals to take a more sympathetic view of the hundreds of thousands of "oriental" (as they were often called) immigrants from Arab countries who inundated the new state of Israel. Perhaps the greatest challenge that Israel faced shortly after independence was absorbing what in time became nearly a million immigrants from the Levant and other Arabic countries, particularly North Africa and Iraq.

In the years following the creation of Israel, in light of Arab resentment and feelings of humiliation over what had happened in 1949, the Arab and Levantine governments took vengeance on their own millennia-old Jewish population and forced them out of just about everywhere. A significant part of the remaining Sephardi Jewish bourgeois elite headed for Western Europe, especially France, and the United States. Israel had to absorb a tidal wave of immigrants who mostly were poor, undereducated, and in some cases disabled and diseased.

The Israeli population, overwhelmingly Ashkenazi, from Eastern and Central Europe, found it much harder to absorb the Orientals than the near million refugees from Hitler's Europe. The Israelis at the time had little understanding of Sephardi history and their ethnic attitudes were suffused with early-twentieth-century prejudices about inferior races. And all this came at a time when the Israeli government's fiscal resources were strained. Not surprisingly, the Orientals generally received rough treatment.

This account of the Sephardi immigration, particularly from North Africa, was published in 1986 by Tom Segev, Israel's leading investigative journalist. It has not been touted at Israeli Bond Dinners. The Western Israelis, some of them, knew at the time they were not doing right by the Orientals; many more would acknowledge that today. Although close to half of the Jewish population of Israel today is Sephardi, less than a quarter of the country's university students are of its background. No Oriental has ever come close to being a candidate for prime minister or president of Israel: The ruling class is overwhelmingly Ashkenazi.

But considering the stressful situation, the cultural dissonance, and the limited resources, the Israelis in 1949 did manage to achieve sufficient integration of the Sephardis into the country so as to maintain social and political stability. By this functional—as compared to ethical—test they managed to cope with a tremendous challenge that could have sunk the new republic.

Itzhak Refael once warned his colleagues on the Jewish Agency Executive that if they insisted on "regulating" the immigration quotas only the immigration from North Africa would remain for it could not be reduced: "everyone agrees that we do not want this to be our only source," he said. He had earlier visited a transit camp in Marseilles where the immigrants from North Africa stayed awaiting their passage to Israel. "The North African human material is not particularly good," he told his colleagues. On his way back he also stopped in the Displaced Persons camps in Germany. He viewed their inmates as also being bad "human material," who were given to a "Diaspora mentality." However, he said he was relieved by the visit: "I must say that the human material (in Germany) is better than I had thought, especially after having visited the North Africans in Marseilles." One of the Mossad's agents in Casablanca reported: "The Moroccans are a very wild people." A few months later the Foreign Ministry prepared a circular for all Israeli representatives overseas, drawing their attention to the fact that at this point most of the immigration was coming from Middle Eastern countries. The percentage of the population that does not belong to the "Ashkenazi community" is steadily growing, and will eventually constitute one third of the

Jewish population of Israel. "This will affect all aspects of life in the country," the Foreign Office warned its diplomats. Its conclusion was that the "preservation of the country's cultural level demands a flow of immigration from the West, and not only from the backward Levantine countries." Israel, which had absorbed with difficulty the waves of immigration from Europe, was even more reluctant to take in newcomers from the Arab countries. They were met with dismay and hostility. "You are familiar with the immigrants from those places," said Shoshana Persits, MK. "You know that we do not have a common language with them. Our cultural level is not theirs. Their way of life is medieval. . . ." Yosef Weitz stated, "While I was talking with Yosef Shprintsak, he expressed anxiety about preserving our cultural standards given the massive immigration from the Orient. There are indeed grounds for anxiety, but what's the use? Can we stop it?" Yaakov Zrubavel, head of the Middle East Department of the Jewish Agency, concurred. "Perhaps these are not the Jews we would like to see coming here, but we can hardly tell them not to come. . . ."

There were agents in North Africa who encouraged emigration to Israel. In some places the Zionist awakening actually worsened the situation

On the edge of the precipice: The Warsaw ghetto, around 1920.

of the Jews, and as things grew worse, their anxious desire to leave increased. Something of this sort happened in several countries. The most characteristic is the case of Iraq. The official version—which many years later was given the legal validity of an Israeli court decision—was that the Jewish immigration from Iraq to Israel, known as "Operation Ezra and Nehemiah," was the outcome of "the longings of Iraq's Jewry for the Holy Land, and the intolerable persecutions of the Iraq authorities, which hunted, imprisoned and hanged Jews."

The exodus from Iraq began during a limited period beginning in the first half of 1950, when the Iraqi parliament resolved to let them leave. In effect, it amounted to an expulsion. Most of the Jews were forced to leave and their property was confiscated. Various sources, including reports of the Mossad for Immigration, indicate that the move of the Iraqi parliament came partly in response to the activities of the Zionist movement

there, aided by the agents of the Mossad who smuggled Jews across the border to Iran. The Mossad's files abound with telegrams reporting the persecution of Jews in Iraq, but almost all of them refer to Jews who had been involved in the activities of the Zionist underground, or who were suspected of belonging to it. There was little harassment of other Jews. In March 1949 the Israeli public was appalled to hear that seven Jews had been hanged in Iraq on charges of Zionist activity. The report was given considerable coverage; there were editorials and public protests, including in the Knesset. But the Mossad's agents in "Berman," i.e., Iraq, telegraphed: "There is no truth in the report about the hanging of Jews on charges of Zionism. A few have been sentenced to death, but they are already out of the country. Many have been tried, but mostly because of letters they received from Israel." However, the heads of the Mossad for Immigration had intentionally fomented worldwide furor against Iraq, in order to hasten the legislation permitting the emigration of Jews. Toward this end they formulated a series of proposed actions, including a statement by the Israeli Foreign Minister in a special meeting with foreign correspondents, agitation in the international press, attempts to block a loan Iraq was seeking to obtain from the World Bank, the incitement of pressure and disturbances around Iraq's Ambassador to the U.N., including demonstrations and booing as he entered and left the U.N. building, as well as an attempt to arrange a face to face meeting with him, an appeal to the U.N., an appeal to Mrs. Eleanor Roosevelt, an "unofficial hint" that Israel might set up an underground movement against the Iraqi ruler, Nuri Said, and an official communication to the U.S., British and French Embassies in Israel that Iraqi Jews in Israel might vent their fury on Israeli Arabs. "It should be emphasized that the Government of Israel is taking steps to ensure the safety of its Arab citizens," the document added, "but it should be hinted that in practice it might not be possible to avoid Arab casualties." It was also proposed to send delegations of Israeli Arabs to the major embassies in Tel Aviv to warn them of the danger they were in as a result of the persecution of Jews in Iraq. All this was meant to force the Iraqi government to expel the Jews, some of whom were Zionists who wanted to go to Israel and some of whom would have preferred to remain in Iraq. Shortly before the Iraqi parliament resolved to let the Jews leave, the Mossad office in Tel Aviv received a telegram from Baghdad, saying: "We are carrying on our usual activity in order to push the law through faster and find out how the Iraqi government proposes to carry it out."

When, after the Declaration of Independence, Israel's gates were opened, the first to be brought over were the thousands of illegal immigrants who had been deported by the British authorities to Cyprus, many of whom were survivors of the Holocaust who, since the war, had been kept in the DP camps in Europe. Their distress was plain to see. The Jews of Morocco, on the other hand, were far away and their distress was not as visible. In October 1948 Itzhak Refael told the Jewish Agency Executive that priority must "of course" be given to the Jews of Eastern Europe, because they might not always be allowed to leave. The Jews of North Africa and "to some extent" those of the Arab countries, would come second and

third. The General Director of the Ministry of Immigration, Y. N. Bahar, thought that the Jews in the Arab countries should be given priority, but his Ministry had little influence on the order of immigration, which was determined by the Jewish Agency, whose members agreed with Refael.

At that time there was still enough room in the abandoned Arab houses, most of which were given to the first arrivals, namely, the Jews from Europe. By the time the Jews from the Arab countries arrived most of those houses were occupied. Thus the priority given to the immigration from Europe intensified the communal inequalities which had existed even under the British Mandate. When Ruth Klieger toured the transit camps on behalf of the Prime Minister, she encountered a group of immigrants from North Africa. This was in the first half of 1949, and though the country and its people were still strange to them, they were already, as Klieger reported, depressed, "seized with a sense of inferiority and of being discriminated against." Many of them brought this feeling with them, and indeed, the discrimination against them had begun even before their arrival.

Most of the immigrants from North Africa received no advance preparation before coming to Israel. The Arab countries remained somehow outside the Zionist movement's sphere of activity, whether on account of the dangers involved, or because its leaders regarded those communities as a primitive fringe. The few Jewish Agency emissaries in North Africa were aware of the dangers of such an attitude and warned against it, but they were ignored. "The work in North Africa may fail for lack of regular agents to deal with escape from there," charged Yosef Barpal. Agent Misha Rabinowitz wrote that "the present immigration, given its makeup and conditions, with its lack of preparation and organization, will place the State of Israel in an intolerable situation. In time to come, we may witness a Moroccan ghetto" in Israel. Another agent wrote, "There is gross discrimination now, and it begins in North Africa." He was referring to the paucity of emissaries and the tiny budget which had been allocated for advance training and preparation in those countries. "This is an Israeli problem," he wrote. "It might result one day in the creation of two racial groups in a single country. . . ." Ben-Gurion tended to blame the leaders of those communities themselves: "For years I have been asking the Sephardis to send gifted young people to the Oriental countries, to work among the Sephardic communities there, especially among the youth, to prepare it for immigration and to look after the immigrants here, and I got no response. . . ." In the Jewish Agency many believed that only Ashkenazi agents should be sent to North Africa. "Three young Sephardic men have just gone there," wrote Ben-Gurion. "Dobkin thinks it's a mistake—they respect only the Ashkenazis."

The travel arrangements were often inefficient and many times the conditions that prevailed were inhumane. Iris Levis, who was sent out by the Jewish Agency to North Africa in February 1949, described the transit camp in Algiers:

In the *Alliance Israelite* building and the little alley behind it live masses of people, crowded like animals. From top to bottom, and even on the stairs, you see people sitting with their belongings. They live, cook, fall ill, give birth and die, men and women, young and old, all of them together. More than fifty people live in one room of four or five square meters.

A physician who worked in one of the transit camps in Marseilles reported to the Immigration Department in Israel:

The immigrants from North Africa arrive here utterly destitute, and almost without clothing. During the passage to Marseilles, which lasts three days, they receive no food. Conditions on board are very bad. The people sleep on the floors without any blankets and are not adequately dressed for the weather. On December 23, 1948, a child died on a ship en route from North Africa, and the French authorities in Marseilles determined the cause of death was exposure and hunger. I am asking you to get in touch at once with the responsible bodies, to improve the situation. . . . In two of the camps there is a great shortage of blankets. People sleep in concrete barracks, on army campbeds, without mattresses, and only a single blanket each. As a result of the bad housing conditions and the recent decline

in nutrition, twelve children have died in these camps. . . . There is a shortage of soap and clothing. . . . I can't understand why in all the European countries the immigrants are provided with clothes while the North African immigrants get nothing. . . .

Hedda Grossmann described the process of moving and migrating from a psychological perspective:

The boys were all from large families and leaving from their native lands either disrupted or broke family ties. Homesickness and disquiet concerning the rest of the family were continually affecting our people and in the beginning caused outbreaks of hysteria, wild behavior, tears and outcries in the night. Some of the boys were generally quieter and more restrained, but their suffering and tension were considerable. . . . In time the boys found various compensations. Casual friends were called brother and sister, and the instructors—parents. There were expressions of physical affection very close to homosexuality, whose origins are easily understood in the context of the relationship between the sexes in this community. . . . This will no doubt cause trouble when they arrive, in view of the fact that there are very few girls and the sexual ratio being so unequal among the Oriental immigrants. In our group, for example, there was not a single girl.

Some parts of Grossmann's report read like an anthropological survey of a remote tribe. It reflects much sympathy and a sincere desire to help, but also a strong sense of alienation. The Jewish Agency emissary in Libya, H. Tsvieli, described the Jews he met there as if he were trading in horses: "They are handsome as far as their physique and outward appearance are concerned, but I found it very difficult to tell them apart from the good quality Arab type."

The poor conditions under which the Jews departed, voyaged to Marseilles and stayed there, led the leaders of the Zionist Federation in Morocco to instruct the Mossad's agents to desist from encouraging the Jews to leave North Africa by all means and all routes. They demanded that the agents devote themselves instead to preparing the immigrants for life in Israel. A year later it was reported that there was a sharp decline in the number of immigrants from North Africa, as a result of the information that reached them concerning the hardships of settling in Israel. "The first thing one notices now is the obvious reluctance to go to Israel," wrote one of the Jewish Agency emissaries after visiting the transit camps in Marseilles. According to him, it had become a widespread attitude: "The people virtually have to be taken aboard the ships by force."

Among the immigrants from North Africa and other Arab countries there were many who did not possess the necessary qualifications which would enable them to have equal status in Israel. Thousands were relegated to the fringes of society even before arrival. In the cities of Morocco there were entire communities which had migrated there from the villages, in order to take economic advantage of the U.S. armed forces landing in Morocco during World War II. Some engaged in peddling, and others in prostitution and crime, and they occupied entire slum quarters. Among the youngsters in her charge, Hedda Grossmann found boys who had grown up in miserable orphanages. There were gangs of thieves and drunks among them. "These will pose a considerable problem for the social services in Israel," she noted. Many of the immigrants came to Israel because they were prompted by relatives, or by the initiative of community leaders, who wished to get rid of them—many were old, sick or welfare cases. The closer they were to French culture, had an education, a profession, or were less religious and traditional in their way, the less they were inclined to go to Israel, preferring instead to settle in France. But even for those who were not sick, aged or destitute, even if they coped well with the process of migration and resettlement, their culture was not the European one which Israel sought to adopt. Many could not read or write in any language. Many had received minimal education, often only a religious one. Almost none had any useful connections in Israel—they found neither relatives nor acquaintances in the Israeli establishment. They knew no Hebrew and were unfamiliar with the bureaucratic system. They brought with them a communal-patriarchal tradition which left little room for individual initiative. Their strangeness reinforced their image as primi-

tives, and their image intensified their alienation. Soon after their arrival they adopted the sense of deprivation felt by those who had come before them. Many of the immigrants from Europe, on the other hand, were helped by relatives and friends who had been in Israel for some time, as well as by families overseas; many would later receive reparations from Germany, which also served to widen the gulf between them and the immigrants from Arab countries.

The North Africans' feeling of deprivation was very intense and painful from the start. "I seem to be a stepson to the Israeli people," wrote Yosef Amoyal, a cobbler from Jaffa, to Prime Minister Ben-Gurion. In years to come it would be argued that it had all been planned that way, that there was an "Ashkenazi conspiracy" to keep them in a state of deprivation and inferiority. There is a remarkable document in the files of the Immigration Department, written in minute capital letters on a sheet of cardboard, whose anonymous author states that he was a doctor who had worked for six months in the North African transit camps in Marseilles. He describes the history of the Jews of North Africa and their present situation, and goes on to provide a highly literary description of the everyday routine in the Marseilles camps. He concludes by stating that the North African immigrants would supply Israel with cheap labor—"coolie labor," as he put it—to replace the Arab workers who did this type of work before Independence. The standard of living of the North African Jew was no higher than that of the Arab farmer, he remarked, and in Israel it would be higher than it was before. The North African immigrants will, therefore, readily adjust to their status, even though it will remain lower than the European standard of Ashkenazi Jews. . . .

The document was not ignored by the Immigration Department—someone ordered it typed and retyped, two and three times over, in many copies. It was subsequently edited, perhaps for publication. The editor polished the text and changed a few words. The passage about the coolie, the Arab farmer and the Moroccan was omitted. Perhaps the editor thought it was nonsensical, or perhaps he feared that it was too offensive to have in print. But the idea was not a new one. There is a record, marked secret, of some remarks made by Berl Locker, Chairman of the Jewish Agency Executive, to the American-Jewish politician, Henry Morgenthau, in October 1948: "In our opinion the Sephardi and Yemenite Jews will play a considerable part in building our country. We have to bring them over in order to save them, but also to obtain the human material needed for building the country."

They were assigned the worst and least profitable part of the country's agriculture—in the mountains, in Galilee and Judea. The rich, easily cultivated, soil in the coastal region and the south was given mainly to immigrants from Europe. There were exceptions, such as the village of Tsrufah on the Carmel coast, which was settled with immigrants from Tunisia, Morocco and Algeria, or Rinthia, near Petah Tikvah, in the center of the country, which was built for Moroccan immigrants, and others. On the other hand, immigrants from Europe were sometimes settled in the mountains of Galilee and in the Negev. The best locations, however, were not allocated to immigrants from the Arab countries. Former immigration official Arye Eliav explained: "This was not an Ashkenazi conspiracy. It happened because the people in charge of the settlement projects, such as Shmuel Dayan, Yaakov Ory, Tsvi Yehuda and others, looked for people who most resembled them, in their general mentality and worldview, and so, inevitably, in their background. They did not have a common language with the others, which is natural enough, as the others were strange to them. They were, of course, well aware of the difference in the quality of various locations, and they fought for the best ones. This was primarily a political struggle, and often a very tough one. . . ."

PART SEVEN

WOMEN

INTRODUCTION

Orthodox Jewish males in their daily morning prayer still thank God not only for not making them Gentiles, but also for not making them women. In order for the minimum number of ten to be attained to constitute a minyon, or synagogue prayer group, only males count. In these circumstances, it is not easy to claim that Judaism has been a faith hospitable to women, but sure enough there are plenty of people who will so claim.

In recent years, however, there have been significant developments that bring women closer to equity and to the empowered center of Jewish life. For more than two decades Reform Judaism has welcomed the ordination of women for the rabbinate and close to half of the rabbinical and cantorial students at Hebrew Union College's Reform seminary in New York are now women. Women chief rabbis in major Reform congregations are still extremely rare, but they are prominent in the ranks of assistant rabbis at large congregations, and in smaller congregations or in a synagogues in outlying cities, women Reform rabbis are now common. Women cantors are evident everywhere in the Reform world.

Only recently has Conservative Judaism allowed the ordination of women, after a fight led by the distinguished medieval historian and chancellor of the Jewish Theological Seminary, Gerson D. Cohen, that went on for several decades. It remains to be seen whether women will ever play a significant leadership role in Conservative Judaism. Orthodox Judaism will not even consider the matter.

Women professors are well represented in the ranks of faculty of the ever-increasing number of Judaic Studies departments and programs, such as at Yale, Princeton, and Binghamton universities.

Jewish women have recently been given a much-enhanced opportunity to enter the top rank of the legal profession because of the way elite law schools have now given admission of women parity with men. Half the students at Harvard, Yale, and New York University law schools are women, and at least a third of these are Jewish women, which means the senior ranks of the major law firms a dozen years from now will be liberally staffed with Jewish women. The lead prosecutor in the O. J. Simpson murder trial, Marcia Clark, was Jewish. There is now for the first time a Jewish woman on the U.S. Supreme Court, Ruth Bader Ginsberg, and the Chief Administrative Judge of New York State, Judith S. Kaye, is Jewish. (When Justice Kaye was a student at New York University Law School in the early 1950s she was relegated to the now defunct and socially downscale night division). Jewish women have come to play an important role in federal politics—both current senators from California are Jewish women.

Jewish women played no role in the first American feminist movement, the suffragette era before 1917. Indeed at least one of the leading feminists of that time, the lesbian president of Bryn Mawr College, was an outspoken anti-Semite. But in the second feminist movement that rose in the late 60s, Jewish women have been in the forefront—such as Betty Friedan, Gloria Steinem, and Erica Jong.

The Talmudic Rabbis Give Sex Lessons

According to Talmudic scholar Daniel Boyarin (1993), these are the key texts offering opinions by the Talmudic rabbis on the matter of sexual intercourse. The missionary position is highly recommended, but a woman should submit to the man's preference for another position, such as anal intercourse. A man should not think about another woman while engaged in sex with his wife. Various adjustments in the time and procedure of intercourse have an impact on the nature of the child born from the union also (a common medieval belief in the Christian world and widely believed in into the twentieth century). A man should not force himself upon his wife but it is a good thing for a wife to arouse her husband.

The Talmudic rabbis' view of sex, whatever their modern apologists may say, is far from an egalitarian attitude to gender. One rabbi says a woman's body is like a piece of meat, subject to her husband's whims; another rabbi says a woman's body is as disposable as a fish. But carnality is recognized much more frankly in the Talmudic literature as compared with medieval (or even modern) Roman Catholicism. Talmudic sexuality is part-way to the playboy philosophy, while Catholicism is no-way.

Jewish wedding ceremony, England, 1769. Plate from a stoneware coffee set.

Why are there lame children? Because they [their fathers] turn over the tables. [Do not use the missionary position in intercourse.]

Why are there dumb children? Because they kiss that place.

Why are there deaf children? Because they talk during intercourse.

Why are there blind children? Because they look at that place. . . .

They asked Imma Shalom [Mother Peace], the wife of Rabbi Eliezer, "Why do you have such beautiful children?" She said to them, "He does not have intercourse with me at the beginning of the night, nor at the end of the night, but at midnight, and when he has intercourse with me, he unveils an inch and veils it again, and appears as if he was driven by a demon." I asked him, "What is the reason [for this strange behavior]?" And he said to me, "In order that I not imagine another woman, and the children will come to be bastards."

Rabbi Yohanan said: The sages say, "Anything that a man wishes to do with his wife, he may do, analogously to meat that comes from the shop. If he wishes to eat it with salt, he may; roasted, he may; boiled, he may; braised, he may. And similarly fish from the store of the fisherman.". . .

A certain woman came before Rabbi. She said to him: Rabbi, I set him the table assumed the missionary position, and he turned it over. He said: How is the case different from fish?

And you shall not wander after your hearts [Num. 16:39]—From hence Rabbi said: Let not a man drink from this cup and have his mind on another cup.

Rabbi Yohanan said: Any man whose wife approaches him sexually will have children such as were unknown even in the generation of Moses. . . .

That refers to a case where she arouses him [but does not explicitly and verbally request sex].. . .

Rami bar Hama said that Rav Asi said: It is forbidden for a man to force his wife in a holy deed, sexual intercourse for it says *One who presses the legs is a sinner* [Prov. 19:2]. And Rabbi Yehoshua ben Levi said: One who forces his wife in a holy deed will have dishonest children. . . .

Can that be? But did not Rava say: If one wants all of his children to be male, he should have intercourse twice in a row.

There is no difficulty: One refers to a case where she does not agree, and one to a case where she does agree.

Sex, Marriage, and Birth Control

In 1974, the British rabbinical scholar and historian, Chaim Bermant, provided this well-informed and plain-spoken account of the traditional Jewish view on sexuality.

Rashi (1040–1105), foremost of all biblical commentators, described sex as a *yetzer hara,* an evil inclination, but added sagely: "If it were not for the evil inclination no man would build a home or marry." This perhaps sums up the difference between the Jewish and Christian attitudes to sex. The one regarded it as an evil to be suppressed, the other as an evil to be harnessed—naturally to the sublime purpose of marriage. But even in marriage it did not mean that a man was free to indulge his sexual appetites to the full. Among Jews this form of bodily pleasure is subject to as many restraints as any other. One was first of all obliged, even in the very depths of passion, to maintain some awareness of its higher purpose. A man, said the *Shulchan Aruch,* the sixteenth-century code of Talmudic Law "should train his mind on pure thoughts and sacred ideas and not be light-headed."

According to some authorities, "a man may do with his wife as he pleases," but only if she so pleases. He cannot approach her against her will and sometimes, as we shall see, not even at her will. The *Shulchan Aruch* itself insists on dignity and modesty in the marital relationship and, to this end, prohibited intercourse by daylight, moonlight or lamplight. The couple had to be alone in a darkened room, and even at such a time a man could not approach his wife "in a spirit of levity, or befoul his mouth with ribald jests." The wife, for her part, was expected to show constant modesty and restraint. On the other hand, she should not be afraid to entice her husband, and the husband should not be averse to being enticed:

It is the duty of one who observes that his wife is trying to please him, and to appear as attractive as possible to gain favour in his eyes, to lie with her even outside the hour set aside for the regular performance of his duties.

A nineteenth century Jewish wedding scene.

But, continued the *Shulchan Aruch,* she must not go too far: "If she approaches him verbally, her behaviour is brazen and his obligation lapses." In this, as in most other matters bearing on family life, the initiative must come from the man, but again it must not come too often. "One should not be too familiar with one's wife except at the times regularly appointed for sexual intercourse." But times—preferably at night—*should* be appointed and, in so far as it lies within one's powers, one should keep to them. One is never at liberty to neglect one's wife, even if she is pregnant or nursing.

Healthy, prosperous men of strong constitution, whose business does not take them away from home, "should perform their duties nightly." The settled labourer has to perform his duty twice a week, itinerant labourers once a week, commercial travelers on short trips, once a week, on distant trips once a month, "while the time appointed for a scholar is from Friday eve to Friday eve." Friday eve, indeed, was a time when the wife had a special claim on the attentions of her husband, and to this end he was required to eat garlic, for, in the words of the Talmud, "garlic promotes love and arouses desire."

But there are times when a man cannot approach or even touch his wife under any circumstances—according to some authorities, he may not even be in the same room with her—and that is during her periods of "impurity," as defined in Leviticus:

And if a woman have an issue, and the issue in her flesh be blood, she shall be in her impurity seven days (15:19).

The sanctions against anyone approaching her during this period were extremely grave:

And if a man shall lie with a woman having her sickness, and he shall uncover her nakedness—he hath made naked her foundation, she hath uncovered the fountain of her blood—both of them shall be cut off from among their people (Leviticus 20:18).

The Rabbis therefore surrounded the scriptural enactments with a whole complex of laws. The seven days of impurity were extended to twelve, and as they felt that one cannot be absolutely sure that bleeding from other causes is not intermingled with menstrual blood, they defined all vaginal bleeding—even though it should leave a stain "no bigger than a mustard seed"—as menstrual; thus, for example, the virgin bride becomes impure from the moment the marriage is consummated and must remain separate from her husband for the next twelve days. (The prospective bride must calculate her wedding date to fall outside her unclean days, otherwise she must keep her distance from her groom even under the *chupah*.) Similarly, a woman is rendered impure by a pregnancy or miscarriage, or indeed through any injury to her reproductive organs that may give rise to bleeding. She must keep a careful record of her periods and should not cohabit on the day she is due in case bleeding should result during intercourse. If her periods are delayed or irregular, one *niddah* period is hardly over before she has to reckon for the onset of another. Women who for one reason or another are prone to frequent or irregular bleeding are unable to cohabit at all and, according to some authorities, their husbands should divorce them. . . .

During her unclean days she should wear special clothes as a reminder that she is a *niddah*. She may prepare food and drink for her husband, but not in his presence, and may not prepare anything for his toilet, nor may he serve her with any beverage. If her husband falls ill and she has no one else to attend to him, she may raise him up or lay him down, or support him, but not with bare hands. And if she should fall ill he may likewise look after her, but only in times of absolute need when there is no one else available.

They should not sit together on the same couch, and if they are at the same table (something which is not really encouraged), they must take care not to pass articles—the salt-cellar, for example—to each other. And of course, however powerful their self-control, they will not sleep in the same bed. Thus the double-bed is unknown in ultra-Orthodox homes, and some Rabbis have written of such beds as symbols of depravity.

After the necessary term of separation is completed, the woman remains prohibited to her husband until she has immersed herself in a *miqvah*, a pool specially constructed for this purpose, though one may also use a spring, river, or bathe in the sea. The main provision is that the waters must be moving and free of any discolouring matter; the *miqvah* must be large enough and deep enough to enable a fully grown woman to immerse herself completely, and it must be leakproof. The immersion laws have nothing to do with physical cleanliness—one is, indeed, required to have a bath before one goes to the *miqvah*. They are entirely a means of spiritual purification and are regarded as so essential to the spiritual well-being of the family that, according to Jewish law, one should not live in a town without a *miqvah*.

The *miqvah*, incidentally, though used largely by women, is not intended exclusively for them. Chassidim use it on the eve of the Sabbath and festivals, and it was customary in some communities of Eastern Europe for the bodies of great rabbis to be immersed in the *miqvah* before they were prepared for burial. This practice stopped only after the local women threatened to boycott the *miqvah*.

A woman must count five days from the beginning of her period, and if by the end of the fifth day she is satisfied that she has no show of blood, she begins to count a further seven during which she must examine herself twice daily to be sure that there has been no further show. "A virtuous woman should not be lax in this matter," writes the *Shulchan Aruch*, "but should examine herself well throughout the entire seven days." If she does not, her immersion is not counted as an immersion, and she remains a *niddah*. If she has found a further show, no matter how slight, during those seven days, she must, even if she found it on the seventh, begin her count anew. If seven consecutive days have passed without a sign of blood, she prepares herself for the immersion by combing her hair, paring her nails and washing herself thoroughly from head to toe. It is imperative before entering the *miqvah* that nothing intervene between her person and the water. If she has make-up, a plaster or dentures, she must remove them; if she has any clot of blood on her skin, she must rub it off; she must pick her teeth—dentists who have ultra-Orthodox women as patients are often kept busy removing temporary fillings; the slightest thing, a touch of paint to the lips, an inkstain on the finger, would be sufficient to make the immersion invalid.

When the woman has finished her necessary preparations, she disrobes and enters the *miqvah* till the water comes over her head. (There is always a female attendant present to make sure it does.) She must stoop slightly to make sure that no part of her body is closed to the water, and when she rises for air, she makes the benediction: "Blessed art Thou O Lord our God, King of the universe, who has sanctified us with Thy commandments and commanded us concerning the laws of immersion," and then goes under twice more. . . .

The performance of a *mitzvah*, a divine commandment, is in itself a source of joy to the devout, and the more demanding the *mitzvah*, the more arduous its performance, the greater the joy. But on a more mundane level, the monthly separations and reunions do introduce a continuous touch of novelty to married life and help to prevent the marital relationship from degenerating into a mere routine. A wife fresh from the *miqvah* often feels like a wife renewed and, by law, has an immediate claim on the attention of her husband—even more pressing than on a Friday night. The husband may stay separate from his wife at a time of famine or hardship, but not on the night of her immersion.

If Judaism has raised the marital relationship to the level of a sacrament, it does not regard sex, even within marriage, as something to be enjoyed for its own sake. Sex is sacred only if sought for the purpose of procreation, and there are authorities who argue that it is wrong to cohabit with a barren woman or even with one who, though once fruitful, is past child-bearing age. Judaism is entirely hostile to birth control, more so, in some ways, than the Catholic Church, for Rabbis do not recognize the "safe period"; if they did, they might have been disposed to ban cohabitation while it lasted. But it is more lenient than Catholicism in its attitude to the life and health of the mother. Thus, abortions are prohibited except if there is a risk to the health of the mother. Then,

in the words of the Talmud, the embryo may "be cut out limb by limb." For the same reason, Judaism is prepared to tolerate some birth-control devices, but never the male sheath, which Jewish law gards as a form of masturbation, a particularly heinous offense.

The female contraceptive is considered less reprehensible, and the pill comes near to finding favour because it does not interfere with the male partner but with the ovular cycle. But in the last analysis, the purpose of every birth-control device is to control birth, something which is not entirely acceptable in Jewish law—except, as was pointed out, if the life of the mother is at stake. There are Orthodox authorities who are prepared to take a more lenient course and also permit birth control where *shalom bayit* (the harmony of the household) is concerned: if the increasing size of the family and the increasing burden on the wife may affect the relationship between her and her husband. One also may limit the size of one's family at times of need, not through birth control, however, but by abstention. But even then, the *Shulchan Aruch* points out, the right to abstain is limited:

If there be a famine, Heaven forbid, or if the land is in distress from any other cause, one may diminish one's conjugal pleasures, except on the night of her immersion, or if they are childless.

Thus, the childless couple after ten years of marriage are regarded by some authorities as living in sin, for the wife is either capable of bearing—in which case she should have borne—or she is not—in which case she should have been divorced. To the ultra-Orthodox, the very thought of resorting to any form of birth control is alien, and families of ten, eleven, or even twelve children are not uncommon.

A Jewish Businesswoman in the Seventeenth Century

The memoirs of Gluckel of Hameln, the matriarch of a prosperous Jewish family in northern Germany in the late-seventeenth century, have survived and this selection is from the translation by Marvin Lowenthal. Gluckel talks about business successes and failures, family matters, and relations with other affluent Jewish families—the subjects that would preoccupy a Jewish matriarch today.

The rabbi of Hildesheim and a *parnas* Elder of the community—I will name no names, for all are now in the Eternal Truth—stood body and soul behind Judah Berlin and tried with all their might to force on my husband a creditor's arrangement, but one that would have borne hard on him. My husband had no mind to accept these terms, and matters were headed for an interminable suit in the civil courts.

But my father-in-law, who was now living in Hildesheim, begged my husband, truly with tears in his eyes, "My dear son," he said, "you see for yourself what passes here; I pray you, for God's sake, let not the matter run into endless litigation; possess your soul in patience and make the best terms you can. The good Lord will bless you again with goods, and in greater plenty."

So, against his will, my husband consented to an arrangement. You can well imagine its terms. This much I know, that when all was said and done, it cost us more than a third of everything we had.

I hold Judah Berlin in less blame than those who abetted him. But we have now forgiven all of them. Nor do we grumble over Judah nor hold ill will against him. He must have thought he was right and asking no more than his due; otherwise he would not—perhaps—have behaved as he did. Yet it went hard on my husband. But who could have helped him? Who prays for what is past, prays in vain.

And the good Lord, who saw our innocence, bestowed on us, e'er four weeks had passed, such excellent business that we close repaired our losses. Later, too, my husband lived with Judah on terms of confidence and understanding. And I will in good time tell you of the honours Judah and his wife paid me when I was in Berlin. He never failed, either, to do a good business turn for my children, so all in all we could not complain of him.

I feel that had our partnership continued with good profits, nothing would have ever come between us. But our falling out, it seems, proved to be a happy stroke for Issachar Cohen. From then on his luck began to bloom.

The whole matter, like everything else in my book, is of no consequence and I have written it down merely to drive away the idle melancholy thoughts that torment me.

Yet you may see from it how all things here below change with the course of time. "God makes us ladders, and one man is given to mount and another to descend." Judah Berlin came to us with nothing; but, with God's help, he would not, I believe, sell out today for one hundred thousand Reichsthalers. Moreover, he has his hand in such business and enjoys such *Aestimation* from the Elector, God increase his glory! that in my opinion, if he continues his march and God be not against him, he will die the richest man in all Germany.

Seder plate. Possibly from England, 1770.

You may also see how many we have helped, with God's aid, to make their way, and how all who have done business for us have become wealthy, but most of them without gratitude, as is the way of the world.

Quite the contrary, many we rendered good have repaid us or our children with evil. But God Almighty is just; and we sinful creatures cannot tell, we do not even know, what is good or bad for us. Many a man, when things go contrary, thinks he is suffering evil, yet the very thing we hold an evil may prove a blessing. If faithful honest Mordecai, God revenge his death! had been spared, many of us would perhaps have escaped a drubbing and doubtless he would himself have become a big man.

We now took on Green Moses; in truth, we did not do a great business with him, yet as I have mentioned we made together a number of tidy deals in seed pearls. He traveled afar, and left his wife and children in Hamburg. We must needs support them, even without knowing whether the profits would cover us. It was a case of casting bread upon the waters. To put it in brief, while we did not profit overmuch, we managed nicely to make both ends meet. We would gladly have continued our dealings together had he not departed from Hamburg and settled in Schottland,

hard by Danzig. Things have not gone badly with him there, and he prospers.

Abraham Cantor of Copenhagen, who served in our house as a lad, did honestly and well by himself. Later, we sent him on a number of occasions to Copenhagen. There he became rich and settled afterwards with wife and children. I am told that today he is a man worth fifteen thousand Reichsthalers and enjoys his good business; he gives his children thousands for dowry.

My kinsman Mordecai Cohen and Loeb Bischere entered into a partnership with my husband. He provided them with money and letters of credit and sent them on to England; but because of the war they failed to reach their destination, and the English trip was abandoned. Nevertheless, they placed a sum of money in Amsterdam against good interest, whereupon my relative Mordecai Cohen traveled through Holland and Brabant and turned very good profits. So this first trip of his laid the foundation of his business and fortune.

My brother-in-law Elias Ries was an inexperienced youth, skilled as yet in no business. My husband, however, advanced him large credits on the spot, and finally sent him with twenty thousand Reichsthalers' credit to Amsterdam.

Many of our Hamburg people, pillars of the community today, have thanked God when we extended them credit. I would fain name more of them, but what good will it do? Where now is the kindness that you, my good and faithful Chayim Hameln, showered on all the world? Gladly gave you this one a helping hand and that one an open heart, and often despite your own distress and again to your own cost. There were times he knew full well no profit could come of it, and his deed was all of loving kindness. And so honourable today are your dear and pious children, that in the face of offense, be it the slightest, they would rather die than seek to harm another.

But of all who took our help, no one seemed to remember it. Yet well they could have given a bit of kindly aid to my dear children, young folks too soon bereft of their good father and lost like "sheep that have no shepherd."

God help us, it was just the contrary. They caused the loss of thousands to my children, and brought it to pass that the money of my son Mordecai fell into base hands. The president of the Council and the entire court agreed it was an honourable deal and that the merchants had no further claim for payment on their wares, for he had openly and honestly bought them. Yet they gave him no peace. On the eve of the Day of Atonement he was compelled to sign away his money and come to such terms with the merchants that, more than aught else, it brought on his ruin. May the great and good God take into account what that meant for him and for me, and let it be an atonement for our sins. They forced my son to it in the "name of God," and may God reward them according to their deeds.

I cannot accuse the man I have in mind for I am ignorant of his thoughts: "Man looketh on the outward appearance, but the Lord looketh on the heart." But this I know full well; my children were young and needed credit, as the rule of business goes; they proposed to sell certain bills of exchange, and merchants took the bills and told them to return after the Bourse was closed. I suspect that the one merchant, meanwhile, made inquiries of a certain Jew he held in high esteem. When my children returned to the merchant, after the Bourse was over, in order to receive cash for their good bills bearing good endorsements, the merchant handed them back the bills. In consequence, they often suffered thereafter for lack of credit.

Great and only God, I implore Thee from the depth of my heart to forgive me my thought. Truly I may have wronged the man I suspected, and well may it be that what he did was done in the "name of God." We must give all into God's hands and remember that this vain world is not for long.

Thou knowest well, Almighty God, how I pass my days in trouble and affliction of heart. I was long a woman who stood high in the esteem of her pious husband, who was like the apple of his eye. But with his passing, passed away my treasure and my honour, which all my days and years I now lament and bemoan.

I know that this complaining and mourning is a weakness of mine and a grievous fault. Far better it would be if every day I fell upon my knees and thanked the Lord for the tender mercies. He has bestowed on my unworthy self. I sit to this day and date at my own table, eat what I relish, stretch myself at night in my own bed, and have even a shilling to waste, so long as the good God pleases. I have my beloved children, and while

things do not always go as well, now with one or the other, as they should, still we are all alive and acknowledge our Creator. How many people there are in this world, finer, better, juster and truer than I, such as I know myself for patterns of piety, who have not bread to put into their mouths! How, then, can I thank and praise my Creator enough for all the goodness He has lavished on us without requital!

If only we poor sinners would acknowledge the everlasting mercy of our God who from the dust of the ground formed us into men, and that we may serve our Creator with all our heart, gave us to know His great and terrible and holy Name!

Behold, my children, all a man will do to gain the favour of a king, flesh and blood that he is, here today and tomorrow in his grave, no one knowing how long may live he who asks or he who gives. And behold the gifts he receives from the transient hand of a king. Honours the king can grant him and put him too in the way of wealth; yet honours and money are but for a space and not for eternity. A man may hoard his honours and his gold until the very last, and then comes bitter Death to make all forgotten; and his honours and his gold are of no avail. Every man, he knows this well and yet he strives loyally to serve a mortal king to gain the passing reward.

How much more, then, should we strive day and night, when we come to serve in duty bound the King of kings who lives and rules forever! For He it is whence come the favours we receive from human kings, and He it is who gives these kings their all and who puts it in their heart to honour whomsoever His holy will decrees, for "the king's heart is in the hand of the Lord." And the gifts of a human monarch stand as naught against the gift of the God of Glory upon those whom He delights to honour: eternity without stain, measure or term.

So, dear children of my heart, be comforted and patient in your sorrows and serve the Almighty God with all your hearts, in your evil days as in your good; for although we often feel we must sink beneath our heavy burdens, our great Lord and Master, we must know, never lays upon His servants more than they can bear. Happy the man who accepts in patience all that God ordains for him or for his children.

Wherefore I, too, beg my Creator give me strength to bear without fret the contrarieties of the world, all of them, be it said, of our own making. "Man is bound to give thanks for the evil as for the good." Let us commend all into the hands of God, and I will now resume my tale.

My daughter Mata was now in her third year, and never was there a lovelier and more charming child. Not only we but everyone who lay eyes on honey, and whoever wishes to learn more of it may read the aforesaid book.

Dear children, fear God with all your heart. What you do not receive in this world, God will bestow upon you manyfold in the world to come, if only you will serve Him with all your soul and might—as I have so often told you and mean to tell you no more. . . .

Somewhile thereafter I betrothed my daughter Freudchen to the son of the rich and eminent Moses ben Loeb.

Meanwhile we were threatened with another blow, which God averted in His mercy. My son Nathan was, as I said, heavily engaged in business with the princely Samuel Oppenheimer of Vienna and his son Mendel. And again he held their notes which were about to fall due. My son, as you know, was accustomed to receive their remittances in time to meet the notes. But now neither remittances nor any word from them came to hand.

At last the sad tidings reached us that Samuel Oppenheimer and his son were flung into prison. As fast as the news spread through Hamburg my son's credit was lost, and whoever held a note in his hands, whether of Oppenheimer or another, pressed my son for instant payment.

So my son had flung at his neck scores of notes, and others followed fast, none of which he dared protest or refuse to honour. The Leipzig Fair was now opening, which he needs must attend. Whereat he paid what he could, pawning all his gold and silver plate, and set out for Leipzig with a heavy heart.

When he parted from me, he said, "Mother dear, I am taking leave of you and God knows how it will be when we meet again. I still have many thousands to pay. Help me, I beg of you, so far as you can—I know the Oppenheimers will not leave me stranded."

My son Nathan rode off with his party of travelers on a Sunday. And Monday my troubles began with the payment of the notes. I did what I could, mortgaged all I had, and went over my head in debt, till I could go no further. When Friday came I still had five hundred thalers to pay, but no means of raising it.

I still possessed bills on a prominent house in Hamburg, which I thought to sell on the Bourse; and I wearily went the rounds of the Bourse, giving them into the brokers' hands. But when the exchange was closed, the brokers brought me back my bills, for no one wished to accept them.

I was in sore distress, but at length God enabled me somehow to pay the five hundred thalers.

On Sabbath I resolved to go to Leipzig, and if I found that the Oppenheimers had sent their remittances to the fair, I would return at once to Hamburg. Otherwise, I determined to go from Leipzig straight to my faithful friend Samson Wertheimer in Vienna, who would surely aid us to regain possession of our own.

I asked my brother Wolf to accompany me. We set forth in a hired wagon, and shortly before reaching Leipzig I halted at a village. Thence I dispatched a messenger to my children in the city, bidding them come to me at once.

They came and told me that the great and rich Oppenheimers were set free, and had sent on remittances to cover all the notes. Quick as I heard this, I sat myself again in the wagon, we wheeled about, and before the Sabbath began I was back in Hamburg. Thus I spent six days to and fro on the road between Hamburg and Leipzig.

Shall I try to tell you the great joy of my children, poor things, above all the joy of my daughter-in-law Miriam, the wife of my son Nathan? We had parted in such distress we never thought to meet again so simply. But God—praise and thanks to the Most High!—had truly helped us in a twinkle.

Even though the rich Oppenheimers paid us for all we had laid out, they could never in all their days repay us for the terror and distress we suffered. May the ever-blessed God continue His mercies toward us and give us to eat our daily bread!

So, praise God, all ended well.

A Hasidic Baby Girl

Esther Singer Kreitman came from a Hasidic family in Poland. In this story, she imagines her birth, and devaluation as a female baby in her Hasidic family, in which the male is valued much more highly than the female. The celebratory attitude toward Hasidic tradition that has been common in recent years ignores the significance of a woman's powerlessness and deprivation in the male-dominated Hasidic society. The translation is by Barbara Harshav.

From the start, I didn't like lying in my mother's belly. Enough! When it got warm, I twisted around, curled up and lay still. . . .

But, five months later, when I felt alive, I was really very unhappy, fed up with the whole thing! It was especially tiresome lying in the dark all the time and I protested. But who heard me? I didn't know how to shout. One day, I wondered if perhaps that wasn't how to do it and I started looking for a way out.

I just wanted to get out.

After pondering a long time, it occurred to me that the best idea would be to start fighting with my Mama. I began throwing myself around, turning cartwheels, often jabbing her in the side; I didn't let up but it didn't do any good. I simply gave myself a bad name so that when, for instance, I'd grow tired of lying on one side and try turning over, just to make myself a little more comfortable, she'd start complaining. In short, why should I lie here cooking up something, it didn't do any good—I had to lie there the whole nine months—understand?—the whole period.

Well (not having any other choice), I consoled myself: I'll simply start later! Just as soon as they let me out into God's world, I'll know what I have to do. . . . Of course, I'll be an honoured guest, I have a lot of reasons to think so. First of all, because of what I often heard my Mama tell some woman who (as I later found out) was my Grandma:

"It does hurt a little but I almost don't feel it," Mama would say. "I'm glad! I was so scared I was barren. A trifle? It's already two years since the wedding and you don't see or hear anything. . . . Minke the barren woman also said she would yet have children. And why should I be surer of it?"

"Well, praised be the one who survives. With God's help, it will come out all right; and God forbid, with no evil eye," Grandma would always answer.

From such conversations, I assumed I would be a welcome guest.

I knew that, here in the other world, where I lived ever since I became a soul, when an important person came, he was supposed to be greeted with great fanfare. First of all, a bright light was to be spread over the whole sky. Angels (waiting for him) were to fly around; merry, beautiful cherubs who spread such holy joy that the person only regretted he hadn't . . . died sooner. It was quite a novelty that I, an honoured, long awaited guest, expected to be born into a big, light home with open windows, where the sun would illuminate everything with a bright light. . . .

Every morning I waited for the birds who were supposed to come greet me, sing me a song. And I was to be born on the first of *Oder*—a month of joy. "When *Oder* begins, people are merry."

But right here "it" comes—the first disappointment.

Mama lay in a tiny room, an "alcove." The bed was hung with dark draperies, which completely screened out the light. The windows were shut tight so no tiny bit of air could get in, God forbid; you shouldn't catch cold. The birds obviously don't like screened out light and closed windows; they looked for a better, freer place to sing.

Wedding ring, nineteenth century.

Meanwhile, no happiness appears either; because I was a girl, everybody in the house, even Mama, was disappointed.

In short, it isn't very happy! I am barely a half hour old but, except for a slap from some woman as I came into the world, nobody looks at me. It is so dreary!

Grandma comes in and smiles at Mama. She looks happy—probably because her daughter has come through it all right. She doesn't even look at me.

"*Mazl tov,* dear daughter!"

"*Mazl tov,* may we enjoy good fortune!"

Mama smiles too but not at me.

"Of course, I would have been happier if it were a boy," says Mama. Grandmother winks roguishly with a half-closed eye and consoles her.

"No problem, boys will also come. . . ."

I listen to all that and it is very sad for me to be alive. How come I was born if all the joy wasn't because of me! I'm already bored to death. Oh, how I want to go back to the other world.

All of a sudden, I feel a strange cold over my body: I am jolted out of my thoughts; I feel myself clamped in two big, plump hands, which pick me up. I shake all over. Could it be—a dreadful idea occurs to me—is she going to stuff me back in for

another nine months? Brrr! I shudder at the very thought.

But my head spins, everything is whirling before my eyes, I feel completely wet, tiny as I am! Am I in a stream? But a stream is cool, pleasant, even nice. But this doesn't interest me as much as the idea of what the two big, clumsy hands want to do with me. I am completely at their mercy.

Thank God, I am soon taken out of the wet. I am brought back to the alcove, already violated, sad. I am carried around the alcove: Everybody looks at me, says something. At last, I am put back to bed. Mama does put a sweet liquid thing in my mouth: I am really hungry for what is in the world.

Mama looks at me with her nice, soft eyes, and my heart warms. A sweet fatigue puts me to sleep and I am blessed with good dreams. . . .

But my happiness didn't last long, a dreadful shout wakes me with a start. I look around. Where did it come from? It's Mama!

People gather round.

"What happened? Where did that shout come from?"

Mama gestures, tries to point, her lips tremble, want to say something and can't. She falls back onto the pillow, almost in a faint.

Seeing they won't get anything out of Mama, they start looking for the reason in the closet, under the bed, in the bed.

All of a sudden, a shout is heard from the nurse, who keeps repeating in a strange voice, "Cats, oh dear God, cats!"

The people look up, can't understand what she's saying. But, except for the word "cats," they can't get anything out of her—so upset is she.

Grandma is also very upset. But she takes heart, makes a thorough search in the bed and, laughing to hide her fear, she calls out, "*Mazl tov,* the cat had kittens. A good sign!"

But apparently, this isn't a good sign. The people are upset.

"On the same day, in the same bed as a cat? Hmmmm, a person and a cat are born the same way," says one brave soul.

They calm Mama. But again, nobody looks at me. Mama falls asleep. And with that, my first day comes to an end. I am, thank God, a whole day old and I have survived quite a bit.

The third day after my birth was the Sabbath.

This time, a big, red Gentile woman puts me in the bath. I wasn't so scared any more, already familiar with the way it smells.

Once again, I lie in bed with Mama. Mama looks at me more affectionately than yesterday. I open my eyes, I would like to look around a bit at the new world. I am already used to the darkness. All of a sudden—it grows darker for me than before.

A gang of women burst into the alcove. I look at them. They're talking, gesturing, picking me up, passing me from one to another, like a precious object. They look at me, they look at Mama, they smile.

Meanwhile, Grandma comes with a tray of treats.

The women make her plead with them, pretend they don't want to try any of the cookies, whiskey, preserves, cherry brandy, berry juice or wine; but, Grandma doesn't give up, so they open their beaks, and finally consent to do her a favour.

Males also stuck their heads into the female alcove. They talked with strange grimaces, gestured, shook their beards, went into a fit of coughing.

With them, Papa succeeded, not Grandma. And I am named Sore Rivke, after some relative of his.

Now they need a wet-nurse. Mama is weak, pale, with such transparent, narrow hands without sinews, she can hardly pick me up. A middle-class woman, she cannot breast-feed me. I am the opposite: A healthy, hearty gal, greedy, I restrain myself from shouting all I want is to eat.

"Not to a *goyish* wet-nurse," says Grandma. Not for all the tea in China. And she can't find a Jewish one. The pharmacist says I should get used to formula, which is better than mother's milk. But I say I don't want to get used to it and I throw up all the time.

This is bitter! Grandma is upset. Mama even more. But Papa consoles them, saying the Holy-One-Blessed-Be-He will help. And He does.

Our neighbour remembers a wet-nurse named Reyzl. She has the voice of a sergeant-major and two red eyes that scare me. She can't come to our home. She has six children of her own but there is no choice.

All the details are worked out, she is given an advance and may everything work out all right.

Reyzl picks me up out of the cradle, takes out a big, white breast, which looks like a piece of puffed up dough and gives it to me to suck, as a test. Well, what should I say? I didn't drown. Even my eyes fill with the taste of a good wet-nurse.

Reyzl looks happily from one to the other.

"Well, what do you say?"

Mama and Grandma glance at each other furtively and are silent. . . .

I have the good fortune to be a tenant at Reyzl's! Not that she needs another tenant because she lives in a flat not much bigger than a large carton. When Reyzl brings me home, her husband comes to greet me carrying their smallest one in his arms and the other five heirs swarming around him. He seems to be pleased with my arrival.

"Well, what do you say about this, eh? Ten gulden a week, my word of honour! Along with old clothes and shoes. Along with the fact that, from now on, they'll give all the repairs only to you! You hear, Beyrish?"

Beyrish is silent. He turns around so his bread-winner won't see his joy.

"You're more of a man than me, I swear. You can earn a gulden faster. . . ," he thinks to himself. But right away he becomes serious. "Where will we put the cradle?" They ponder a long time.

But Reyzl's husband, who is an artist at arranging things in his tiny flat, smacks his low, wrinkled forehead with his hard hand and calls out joyously, "Reyzl, I've got it! Under the table!"

So in a tiny cradle, I am shoved under the table.

With open, astonished eyes, I look at the filthy wood of the table, covered with a host of spider webs, and think sadly, "This is the new world I have come into? And this is its heaven?"

And I weep bitter tears.

Under Hitler's Shadow

The most widely known writing of a Holocaust victim is Anne Frank's first-hand account of the time she and her middle-class Dutch Jewish family spent in hiding from the invading Nazis. Four long years later, they were betrayed and Anne Frank died in the death camps. *The Diary of Anne Frank* and other writings of hers have provided the text for a play and film. What is so compelling in her writing is the clash between the will to live and love of a bright girl in early adolescence and the horrible ambiance in which she lived. Probably centuries from now the writings of Anne Frank will still symbolize the experience of the Holocaust for most people. The Frank family's hidden attic apartment in Amsterdam is now a shrine, visited by hundreds of thousands of people.

Tuesday, 7 March, 1944

Dear Kitty,

If I think now of my life in 1942, it all seems so unreal. It was quite a different Anne who enjoyed that heavenly existence from the Anne who has grown wise within these walls. Yes, it was a heavenly life. Boy friends at every turn, about twenty friends and acquaintances of my own age, the darling of nearly all the teachers, spoiled from top to toe by Mummy and Daddy, lots of sweets, enough pocket money, what more could one want?

You will certainly wonder by what means I got around all these people. Peter's word "attractiveness" is not altogether true. All the teachers were entertained by my cute answers, my amusing remarks, my smiling face, and my questioning looks. That is all I was—a terrible flirt, coquettish and amusing. I had one or two advantages, which kept me rather in favor. I was industrious, honest, and frank. I would never have dreamed of cribbing from anyone else. I shared my sweets generously, and I wasn't conceited.

Wouldn't I have become rather forward with so much admiration? It was a good thing that in the midst of, at the height of, all this gaiety, I suddenly had to face reality, and it took me at least a year to get used to the fact that there was no more admiration forthcoming.

How did I appear at school? The one who thought of new jokes and pranks, always "king of the castle," never in a bad mood, never a crybaby. No wonder everyone liked to cycle with me, and I got their attentions.

Now I look back at that Anne as an amusing, but very superficial girl, who has nothing to do with the Anne of today. Peter said quite rightly about me: "If ever I saw you, you were always surrounded by two or more boys and a whole troupe of girls. You were always laughing and always the center of everything!"

What is left of this girl? Oh, don't worry, I haven't forgotten how to laugh or to answer back readily. I'm just as good, if not better, at criticizing people, and I can still flirt if . . . I wish. That's not it though, I'd like that sort of life again for an evening, a few days, or even a week; the life which seems so carefree and gay. But at the end of that week, I should be dead beat and would be only too thankful to listen to anyone who began to talk about something sensible. I don't want followers, but friends, admirers who fall not for a flattering smile but for what one does and for one's character.

I know quite well that the circle around me would be much smaller. But what does that matter, as long as one still keeps a few sincere friends?

Yet I wasn't entirely happy in 1942 in spite of everything; I often felt deserted, but because I was on the go the whole day long, I didn't think about it and enjoyed myself as much as I could. Consciously or unconsciously, I tried to drive away the emptiness I felt with jokes and pranks. Now I think seriously about life and what I have to do. One period of my life is over forever. The carefree schooldays are gone, never to return.

I don't even long for them any more; I have outgrown them, I can't just only enjoy myself as my serious side is always there.

I look upon my life up till the New Year, as it were, through a powerful magnifying glass. The sunny life at home, then coming here in 1942, the sudden change, the quarrels, the bickerings. I couldn't understand it, I was taken by surprise, and the only way I could keep up some bearing was by being impertinent.

The first half of 1943: my fits of crying, the loneliness, how I slowly began to see all my faults and shortcomings, which are so great and which seemed much greater then. During the day I deliberately talked about anything and everything that was farthest from my thoughts, tried to draw Pim to me; but couldn't. Alone I had to face the difficult task of changing myself, to stop the everlasting reproaches, which were so oppressive and which reduced me to such terrible despondency.

Things improved slightly in the second half of the year, I became a young woman and was treated more like a grownup. I started to think, and write stories, and came to the conclusion that the others no longer had the right to throw me about like an india-rubber ball. I wanted to change in accordance with my own desires. But *one* thing that struck me even more was when I realized that even Daddy would never become my confidant over everything. I didn't want to trust anyone but myself any more.

At the beginning of the New Year: the second great change, my dream. . . . And with it I discovered my longing, not for a girl friend, but for a boy friend. I also discovered my inward happiness and my defensive armor of superficiality and gaiety. In due time I quieted down and discovered my boundless desire for all that is beautiful and good.

And in the evening, when I lie in bed and end my prayers with the words, "I thank you, God, for all that is good and dear and beautiful," I am filled with joy. Then I think about "the good" of going into hiding, of my health and with my whole being of the "dearness" of Peter, of that which is still embryonic and impressionable and which we neither of us dare to name or touch, of that which will come sometime; love, the future, happiness and of "the beauty" which exists in the world; the world, nature, beauty and all, all that is exquisite and fine.

I don't think then of all the misery, but of the beauty that still remains. This is one of the things that Mummy and I are so entirely different about. Her counsel when one feels melancholy is: "Think of all the misery in the world and be thankful that you are not sharing in it!" My advice is: "Go outside, to the fields, enjoy nature and the sunshine, go out and try to recapture happiness in yourself and in God. Think of all the beauty that's still left in and around you and be happy!"

I don't see how Mummy's idea can be right, because then you would have to behave as if you are going through the misery yourself. Then you are lost. On the contrary, I've found that there is always some beauty left—in nature, sunshine, freedom, in yourself; these can all help you. Look at these things, then you find yourself again, and God, and then you regain your balance.

And whoever is happy will make others happy too. He who has courage and faith will never perish in misery!

Yours, Anne

25 March, 1944

It was a terrible time through which I was living. The war raged about us, and nobody knew whether or not he would be alive the next hour. My parents, brothers, sisters, and I made our home in the city, but we expected that we either would be evacuated or have to escape in some other way. By day the sound of cannon and rifle shots was almost continuous, and the nights were mysteriously filled with sparks and sudden explosions that seemed to come from some unknown depth.

I cannot describe it; I don't remember that tumult quite clearly, but I do know that all day long I was in the grip of fear. My parents tried everything to calm me, but it didn't help. I felt nothing, nothing but fear; I could neither eat nor sleep—fear clawed at my mind and body and shook me. That lasted for about a week; then came an evening and a night which I recall as though it had been yesterday.

At half past eight, when the shooting had somewhat died down, I lay in a sort of half doze on a sofa. Suddenly all of us were startled by two violent explosions. As though stuck with knives, we all jumped up and ran into the hall. Even Mother, usually so calm, looked pale. The explosions repeated themselves at pretty regular intervals. Then: a tremendous crash, the noise of much breaking glass, and an ear-splitting chorus of yelling and screaming. I put on what heavy clothes I could find in a hurry, threw some things into a rucksack, and ran. I ran as fast as I could, ran on and on to get away from the fiercely burning mass about me. Everywhere shouting people darted to and fro; the street was alight with a fearsome red glow.

I didn't think of my parents or of my brothers and sisters. I had thoughts only for myself and knew that I must rush, rush, rush! I didn't feel any fatigue; my fear was too strong. I didn't know that I had lost my rucksack. All I felt and knew was that I had to run.

I couldn't possibly say how long I ran on with the image of the burning houses, the desperate people and their distorted faces before me. Then I sensed that it had got more quiet. I looked around and, as if waking up from a nightmare, I saw that there was nothing or no one behind me. No fire, no bombs, no people. I looked a little more closely and found that I stood in a meadow.

Above me the stars glistened and the moon shone; it was brilliant weather, crisp but not cold.

I didn't hear a sound. Exhausted, I sat down on the grass, then spread the blanket I had been carrying on my arm, and stretched out on it.

I looked up into the sky and realized that I was no longer afraid; on the contrary, I felt very peaceful inside. The funny thing was that I didn't think of my family, nor yearn for them; I yearned only for rest, and it wasn't long before I fell asleep there in the grass, under the sky.

When I woke up the sun was just rising. I immediately knew where I was; in the daylight I recognized the houses at the outskirts of our city. I rubbed my eyes and had a good look around. There was no one to be seen; the dandelions and the clover-leaves in the grass were my only company. Lying back on the blanket for a while, I mused about what to do next. But my thoughts wandered off from the subject and returned to the wonderful feeling of the night before, when I sat in the grass and was no longer afraid.

Later I found my parents, and together we moved to another town. Now that the war is over, I know why my fear disappeared under the wide, wide heavens. When I was alone with nature, I realized—realized without actually knowing it— that fear is a sickness for which there is only one remedy. Anyone who is as afraid as I was then should look at nature and see that God is much closer than most people think.

Since that time I have never been afraid again, no matter how many bombs fell near me.

The New American

Mary Antin's 1912 autobiographical novel, *The Promised Land*, is about the daughter of immigrant Russian Jews growing up in Boston in the early years of the century. What American icons meant to her as a way of creating confidence in herself, and her debt to her Gentile public school teachers, are both well developed in this selection.

In the early decades of this century, the public school systems in the large cities of the northeastern U.S.A. were well organized and because school teaching was then regarded as a good career, especially for women, they commanded very good teaching personnel. It was very fortunate for Jewish immigrant families that they needed to use the public schools for their children precisely at a time when the schools' effectiveness was at its height. Public school education thereby became the prime vehicle for social advancement and acculturation of the children of Eastern European Jewish immigrants. Twenty years earlier or fifty years later, the Jewish immigrant families would not have found the schools so benign and effective.

The downside to the routing of Jewish immigrant children through the public schools was the rapid decline of Yiddish as a common language of American Jews—there was of course no concept in those days of state-supported bilingual education.

When the class read, and it came my turn, my voice shook and the book trembled in my hands. I could not pronounce the name of George Washington without a pause. Never had I prayed, never had I chanted the songs of David, never had I called upon the Most Holy, in such utter reverence and worship as I repeated the simple sentences of my child's story of the patriot. I gazed with adoration at the portraits of George and Martha Washington, till I could see them with my eyes shut. And whereas formerly my self-consciousness had bordered on conceit, and I thought myself an uncommon person, parading my schoolbooks through the streets, and swelling with pride when a teacher detained me in conversation, now I grew humble all at once, seeing how insignificant I was beside the Great.

As I read about the noble boy who would not tell a lie to save himself from punishment, I was for the first time truly repentant of my sins. Formerly I had fasted and prayed and made sacrifice on the Day of Atonement, but it was more than half play, in mimicry of my elders. I had no real horror of sin, and I knew so many ways of escaping punishment. I am sure my family, my neighbors, my teachers in Polotzk—all my world, in fact—strove together, by example and precept, to teach me goodness. Saintliness had a new incarnation in about every third person I knew. I did respect the saints, but I could not help seeing that most of them were a little bit stupid, and that mischief was much more fun than piety. Goodness, as I had known it, was respectable, but not necessarily admirable. The people I really admired, like my Uncle Solomon, and Cousin Rachel, were those who preached the least and laughed the most. My sister Frieda was perfectly good, but she did not think the less of me because I played tricks. What I loved in my friends was not inimitable. One could be downright good if one really wanted to. One could be learned if one had books and teachers. One could sing funny songs and tell anecdotes if one traveled about and picked up such things, like one's uncles and cousins. But a human being strictly good, perfectly wise, and unfailingly valiant, all at the same time, I had never heard or dreamed of. This wonderful George Washington was as inimitable as he was irreproachable. Even if I had never, never told a lie. I could not compare myself to George Washington; for I was not brave—I was afraid to go out when snowballs whizzed—and I could never be the First President of the United States.

So I was forced to revise my own estimate of myself. But the twin of my new-born humility, paradoxical as it may seem, was a sense of dignity I had never known before. For if I found that I was a person of small consequence, I discovered at the same time that I was more nobly related than I had ever supposed. I had relatives and friends who were notable people by the old standards—I had never been ashamed of my family—but this George Washington, who died long before I was born, was like a king in greatness, and he and I were Fellow Citizens. There was a great deal about Fellow Citizens in the patriotic literature we read at this time; and I knew from my father how he was a Citizen, through the process of naturalization, and how I also was a citizen, by virtue of my relation to him. Undoubtedly I was a

Fellow Citizen, and George Washington was another. It thrilled me to realize what sudden greatness had fallen on me; and at the same time it sobered me, as with a sense of responsibility. I strove to conduct myself as befitted a Fellow Citizen.

Before books came into my life, I was given to stargazing and daydreaming. When books were given me, I fell upon them as a glutton pounces on his meat after a period of enforced starvation. I lived with my nose in a book, and took no notice of the alternations of the sun and stars. But now, after the advent of George Washington and the American Revolution, I began to dream again. I strayed on the common after school instead of hurrying home to read. I hung on fence rails, my pet book forgotten under my arm, and gazed off to the yellow-streaked February sunset, and beyond, and beyond. I was no longer the central figure of my dreams; the dry weeds in the lane crackled beneath the tread of Heroes.

What more could America give a child? Ah, much more! As I read how the patriots planned the Revolution, and the women gave their sons to die in battle, and the heroes led to victory, and the rejoicing people set up the Republic, it dawned on me gradually what was meant by *my country*. The people all desiring noble things, and striving for them together, defying their oppressors, giving their lives for each other—all this it was that made *my country*. It was not a thing that I *understood*; I could not go home and tell Frieda about it, as I told her other things I learned at school. But I knew one could say "my country" and *feel* it, as one felt "God" or "myself." My teacher, my schoolmates, Miss Dillingham, George Washington himself could not mean more than I when they said "my country," after I had once felt it. For the Country was for all the Citizens, and *I was a Citizen*. And when we stood up to sing "America," I shouted the words with all my might. I was in very earnest proclaiming to the world my love for my new-found country.

I love thy rocks and rills,
Thy woods and templed hills.

Boston Harbor, Crescent Beach, Chelsea Square—all was hallowed ground to me. As the day approached when the school was to hold exercises in honor of Washington's Birthday, the halls resounded at all hours with the strains of patriotic songs; and I, who was a model of the attentive pupil, more than once lost my place in the lesson as I strained to hear, through closed doors, some neighboring class rehearsing "The Star-Spangled Banner." If the doors happened to open, and the chorus broke out unveiled—

O! say, does that Star-Spangled Banner yet wave
O'er the land of the free, and the home of the
brave?—

delicious tremors ran up and down my spine, and I was faint with suppressed enthusiasm.

Where had been my country until now? What flag had I loved? What heroes had I worshipped? The very names of these things had been unknown to me. Well I knew that Polotzk was not my country. It was *goluth*—exile. On many occasions in the year we prayed to God to lead us out of exile. The beautiful Passover service closed with the words, "Next year, may we be in Jerusalem." On childish lips, indeed, those words were no conscious aspiration; we repeated the Hebrew syllables after our elders, but without their hope and longing. Still not a child among us was too young to feel in his own flesh the lash of the oppressor. We knew what it was to be Jews in exile, from the spiteful treatment we suffered at the hands of the smallest urchin who crossed himself; and thence we knew that Israel had good reason to pray for deliverance. But the story of the Exodus was not history to me in the sense that the story of the American Revolution was. It was more like a glorious myth, a belief in which had the effect of cutting me off from the actual world, by linking me with a world of phantoms. Those moments of exaltation which the contemplation of the Biblical past afforded us, allowing us to call ourselves the children of princes, served but to tinge with a more poignant sense of disinheritance the long humdrum stretches of our life. In very truth we were a people without a country. Surrounded by mocking foes and detractors, it was difficult for me to realize the persons of my people's heroes or the events in which they moved. Except in moments of abstraction from the world around me, I scarcely understood that Jerusalem was an actual spot on the earth, where once the Kings of the Bible, real people, like my neighbors in Polotzk, ruled in puissant majesty.

For the conditions of our civil life did not permit us to cultivate a spirit of nationalism. The freedom of worship that was grudgingly granted within the narrow limits of the Pale by no means included the right to set up openly any ideal of a Hebrew State, any hero other than the Czar. What we children picked up of our ancient political history was confused with the miraculous story of the Creation, with the supernatural legends and hazy associations of Bible lore. As to our future, we Jews in Polotzk had no national expectations; only a life-worn dreamer here and there hoped to die in Palestine. If Fetchke and I sang, with my father, first making sure of our audience, "Zion, Zion, Holy Zion, not forever is it lost," we did not really picture to ourselves Judæa restored.

So it came to pass that we did not know what *my country* could mean to a man. And as we had no country, so we had no flag to love. It was by no far-fetched symbolism that the banner of the House of Romanoff became the emblem of our latter-day bondage in our eyes. Even a child would know how to hate the flag that we were forced, on pain of severe penalties, to hoist above our housetops, in celebration of the advent of one of our oppressors. And as it was with country and flag, so it was with heroes of war. We hated the uniform of the soldier, to the last brass button. On the person of a Gentile, it was the symbol of tyranny; on the person of a Jew, it was the emblem of shame.

So a little Jewish girl in Polotzk was apt to grow up hungry-minded and empty-hearted; and if, still in her outreaching youth, she was set down in a land of outspoken patriotism, she was likely to love her new country with a great love, and to embrace its heroes in a great worship. Naturalization, with us Russian Jews, may mean more than the adoption of the immigrant by America. It may mean the adoption of America by the immigrant.

On the day of the Washington celebration I recited a poem that I had composed in my enthusiasm. But "composed" is not the word. The process of putting on paper the sentiments that seethed in my soul was really very discomposing. I dug the words out of my heart, squeezed the rhymes out of my brain, forced the missing syllables out of their hiding-places in the dictionary. May I never again know such travail of the spirit as I endured during the fevered days when I was engaged on the poem. It was not as if I wanted to say that snow was white or grass was green. I could do that without a dictionary. It was a question now of the loftiest sentiments, of the most abstract truths, the names of which were very new in my vocabulary. It was necessary to use polysyllables, and plenty of them; and where to find rhymes for such words as "tyranny," "freedom," and "justice," when you had less than two years' acquaintance with English! The name I wished to celebrate was the most difficult of all. Nothing but "Washington" rhymed with "Washington." It was a most ambitious undertaking, but my heart could find no rest till it had proclaimed itself to the world; so I wrestled with my difficulties, and spared not ink, till inspiration perched on my penpoint, and my soul gave up its best.

When I had done, I was myself impressed with the length, gravity, and nobility of my poem. My father was overcome with emotion as he read it. His hands trembled as he held the paper to the light, and the mist gathered in his eyes. My teacher, Miss Dwight, was plainly astonished at my performance, and said many kind things, and asked many questions; all of which I took very solemnly, like one who had been in the clouds and returned to earth with a sign upon him. When Miss Dwight asked me to read my poem to the class on the day of celebration, I readily consented. It was not in me to refuse a chance to tell my schoolmates what I thought of George Washington.

I was not a heroic figure when I stood up in front of the class to pronounce the praises of the Father of his Country. Thin, pale, and hollow, with a shadow of short black curls on my brow, and the staring look of prominent eyes, I must have looked more frightened than imposing. My dress added no grace to my appearance. "Plaids" were in fashion, and my frock was of a red-and-green "plaid" that had a ghastly effect on my complexion. I hated it when I thought of it, but on the great day I did not know I had any dress on. Heels clapped together, and hands glued to my sides, I lifted up my voice in praise of George Washington. It was not much of a voice; like my hollow cheeks, it suggested consumption. My pronunciation was faulty, my declamation flat. But I had the courage of my convictions. I was face to face with twoscore Fellow Citizens, in clean blouses and extra frills. I must tell them what George Washington had done for their country—for *our* country—for me.

I can laugh now at the impossible metres, the grandiose phrases, the verbose repetitions of my poem. Years ago I must have laughed at it, when I threw my only copy into the wastebasket. The copy I am now turning over was loaned me by Miss Dwight, who faithfully preserved it all these years, for the sake, no doubt, of what I strove to express when I laboriously hitched together those dozen and more ungraceful stanzas. But to the forty Fellow Citizens sitting in rows in front of me it was no laughing matter. Even the bad boys sat in attitudes of attention, hypnotized by the solemnity of my demeanor. If they got any inkling of what the hail of big words was about, it must have been through occult suggestion. I fixed their eighty eyes with my single stare, and gave it to them, stanza after stanza, with such emphasis as the lameness of the lines permitted.

He whose courage, will, amazing bravery,
Did free his land from a despot's rule,
From man's greatest evil, almost slavery,
And all that's taught in tyranny's school,
Who gave his land its liberty,
Who was he?

'T was he who e'er will be our pride,
Immortal Washington,
Who always did in truth confide.
We hail our Washington!

The best of the verses were no better than these, but the children listened. They had to. Presently I gave them news, declaring that Washington

Wrote the famous Constitution; sacred's the
hand
That this blessed guide to man had given, which
says, "One
And all of mankind are alike, excepting none."

This was received in respectful silence, possibly because the other Fellow Citizens were as hazy about historical facts as I at this point. "Hurrah for Washington!" they understood, and "Three cheers for the Red, White, and Blue!" was only to be expected on that occasion. But there ran a special note through my poem—a thought that only Israel Rubinstein or Beckie Aronovitch could have fully understood, besides myself. For I made myself the spokesman of the "luckless sons of Abraham," saying—

Then we weary Hebrew children at last found
rest
In the land where reigned Freedom, and like a
nest
To homeless birds your land proved to us, and
therefore
Will we gratefully sing your praise evermore.

The boys and girls who had never been turned away from any door because of their father's religion sat as if fascinated in their places. But they woke up and applauded heartily when I was done, following the example of Miss Dwight, who wore the happy face which meant that one of her pupils had done well.

The recitation was repeated, by request, before several other classes, and the applause was equally prolonged at each repetition. After the exercises I was surrounded, praised, questioned, and made much of, by teachers as well as pupils. Plainly I had not poured my praise of George Washington into deaf ears. The teachers asked me if anybody had helped me with the poem. The girls invariably asked, "Mary Antin, how could you think of all those words?" None of them thought of the dictionary!

If I had been satisfied with my poem in the first place, the applause with which it was received by my teachers and schoolmates convinced me that I had produced a very fine thing indeed. So the person, whoever it was,—perhaps my father—who suggested that my tribute to Washington ought to be printed, did not find me difficult to persuade. When I had achieved an absolutely perfect copy of my verses, at the expense of a dozen sheets of blue-ruled note paper, I crossed the Mystic River to Boston and boldly invaded Newspaper Row.

It never occurred to me to send my manuscript by mail. In fact, it has never been my way to send a delegate where I could go myself. Consciously or unconsciously, I have always acted on the motto of a wise man who was one of the dearest friends that Boston kept for me until I came. "Personal presence moves the world," said the great Dr. Hale; and I went in person to beard the editor in his armchair.

From the ferry slip to the offices of the "Boston Transcript" the way was long, strange, and full of perils; but I kept resolutely on up Hanover Street, being familiar with that part of my route, till I came to a puzzling corner. There I stopped, utterly bewildered by the tangle of streets, the roar of traffic, the giddy swarm of pedestrians. With the precious manuscript tightly clasped, I balanced myself on the curbstone, afraid to plunge into the boiling vortex of the crossing. Every time I made a start, a clanging street car snatched up the way. I could not even pick out my street; the unobtrusive street signs were lost to my unpracticed sight, in the glaring confusion of store signs and advertisements. If I accosted a pedestrian to ask the way, I had to speak several times before I was heard. Jews, hurrying by with bearded chins on their bosoms and eyes intent, shrugged their shoulders at the name "Transcript," and shrugged till they were out of sight. Italians sauntering behind their fruit carts answered my inquiry with a lift of the head that made their earrings gleam, and a wave of the hand that referred me to all four points of the compass at once. I was trying to catch the eye of the tall policeman who stood grandly in the middle of the crossing, a stout pillar around which the waves of traffic broke, when deliverance bellowed in my ear.

"Herald, Globe, Record, *Tra-avel-er!* Eh? Whatcher want, sis?" The tall newsboy had to stoop to me. "Transcript? Sure!" And in half a twinkling he had picked me out a paper from his bundle. When I explained to him, he good-naturedly tucked the paper in again, piloted me across, unraveled the end of Washington Street for me, and with much pointing out of landmarks, headed me for my destination, my nose seeking the spire of the Old South Church.

I found the "Transcript" building a waste of corridors tunneled by a maze of staircases. On the glazed-glass doors were many signs with the names or nicknames of many persons: "City Editor;" "Beggars and Peddlers not Allowed." The nameless world not included in these categories was warned off, forbidden to be or do: "Private— No Admittance;" "Don't Knock." And the various inhospitable legends on the doors and walls were punctuated by frequent cuspidors on the floor. There was no sign anywhere of the welcome which I, as an author, expected to find in the home of a newspaper.

I was descending from the top story to the street for the seventh time, trying to decide what kind of editor a patriotic poem belonged to, when an untidy boy carrying broad paper streamers and whistling shrilly, in defiance of an express prohibition on the wall, bustled through the corridor and left a door ajar. I slipped in behind him, and found myself in a room full of editors.

I was a little surprised at the appearance of the editors. I had imagined my editor would look like Mr. Jones, the principal of my school, whose coat was always buttoned, and whose finger nails were beautiful. These people were in shirt sleeves, and they smoked, and they didn't politely turn in their revolving chairs when I came in, and ask, "What can I do for you?"

The room was noisy with typewriters, and nobody heard my "Please, can you tell me." At last one of the machines stopped, and the operator thought he heard something in the pause. He looked up through his own smoke. I guess he thought he saw something, for he stared. It troubled me a little to have him stare so. I realized suddenly that the hand in which I carried my manuscript was moist, and I was afraid it would make marks on the paper. I held out the manuscript to the editor, explaining that it was a poem about George Washington, and would he please print it in the "Transcript."

There was something queer about that particular editor. The way he stared and smiled made me feel about eleven inches high, and my voice kept growing smaller and smaller as I neared the end of my speech.

At last he spoke, laying down his pipe, and sitting back at his ease.

"So you have brought us a poem, my child?"

"It's about George Washington," I repeated impressively. "Don't you want to read it?"

"I should be delighted, my dear, but the fact is—"

He did not take my paper. He stood up and called across the room.

"Say, Jack! here is a young lady who has brought us a poem—about George Washington.— Wrote it yourself, my dear?—Wrote it all herself. What shall we do with her?"

Mr. Jack came over, and another man. My editor made me repeat my business, and they all looked interested, but nobody took my paper from me. They put their hands into their pockets, and my hand kept growing clammier all the time. The three seemed to be consulting, but I could not understand what they said, or why Mr. Jack laughed.

A fourth man, who had been writing busily at a desk near by, broke in on the consultation.

"That's enough, boys," he said, "that's enough. Take the young lady to Mr. Hurd."

Mr. Hurd, it was found, was away on a vacation, and of several other editors in several offices, to whom I was referred, none proved to be the proper editor to take charge of a poem about George Washington. At last an elderly editor suggested that as Mr. Hurd would be away for some time, I would do well to give up the "Transcript" and try the "Herald," across the way.

A little tired by my wanderings, and bewildered by the complexity of the editorial system, but still confident about my mission, I picked my way across Washington Street and found the "Herald" offices. Here I had instant good luck. The first editor I addressed took my paper and invited me to a seat. He read my poem much more quickly than I could myself, and said it was very nice, and asked me some questions, and made notes on a slip of paper which he pinned to my manuscript. He said he would have my piece printed very soon, and would send me a copy of the issue in which it appeared. As I was going, I could not help giving the editor my hand, although I had not experienced any handshaking in Newspaper Row. I felt that as author and editor we were on a very pleasant footing, and I gave him my hand in token of comradeship.

I had regained my full stature and something over, during this cordial interview, and when I stepped out into the street and saw the crowd intently studying the bulletin board I swelled out of all proportion. For I told myself that I, Mary Antin, was one of the inspired brotherhood who made newspapers so interesting. I did not know whether my poem would be put upon the bulletin board; but at any rate, it would be in the paper, with my name at the bottom, like my story about "Snow" in Miss Dillingham's school journal. And all these people in the streets, and more, thousands of people—all Boston!—would read my poem, and learn my name, and wonder who I was. I smiled to myself in delicious amusement

when a man deliberately put me out of his path, as I dreamed my way through the jostling crowd; if he only *knew* whom he was treating so unceremoniously!

When the paper with my poem in it arrived, the whole house pounced upon it at once. I was surprised to find that my verses were not all over the front page. The poem was a little hard to find, if anything, being tucked away in the middle of the voluminous sheet. But when we found it, it looked wonderful, just like real poetry, not at all as if somebody we knew had written it. It occupied a gratifying amount of space, and was introduced by a flattering biographical sketch of the author—the *author!*—the material for which the friendly editor had artfully drawn from me during that happy interview. And my name, as I had prophesied, was at the bottom!

When the excitement in the house had subsided, my father took all the change out of the cash drawer and went to buy up the "Herald." He did not count the pennies. He just bought "Heralds," all he could lay his hands on, and distributed them gratis to all our friends, relatives, and acquaintances; to all who could read, and to some who could not. For weeks he carried a clipping from the "Herald" in his breast pocket, and few were the occasions when he did not manage to introduce it into the conversation. He treasured that clipping as for years he had treasured the letters I wrote him from Polotzk.

Although my father bought up most of the issue containing my poem, a few hundred copies were left to circulate among the general public, enough to spread the flame of my patriotic ardor and to enkindle a thousand sluggish hearts. Really, there was something more solemn than vanity in my satisfaction. Pleased as I was with my notoriety—and nobody but I knew how exceedingly pleased—I had a sober feeling about it all. I enjoyed being praised and admired and envied; but what gave a divine flavor to my happiness was the idea that I had publicly borne testimony to the goodness of my exalted hero, to the greatness of my adopted country. I did not discount the homage of Arlington Street, because I did not properly rate the intelligence of its population. I took the admiration of my schoolmates without a grain of salt; it was just so much honey to me. I could not know that what made me great in the eyes of my neighbors was that "there was a piece about me in the paper;" it mattered very little to them what the "piece" was about. I thought they really admired my sentiments. On the street, in the schoolyard, I was pointed out. The people said, "That's Mary Antin. She had her name in the paper." *I* thought they said, "This is she who loves her country and worships George Washington."

To repeat, I was well aware that I was something of a celebrity, and took all possible satisfaction in the fact; yet I gave my schoolmates no occasion to call me "stuck-up." My vanity did not express itself in strutting or wagging the head. I played tag and puss-in-the-corner in the schoolyard, and did everything that was comrade-like. But in the schoolroom I conducted myself gravely, as befitted one who was preparing for the noble career of a poet.

I am forgetting Lizzie McDee. I am trying to give the impression that I behaved with at least outward modesty during my schoolgirl triumphs, whereas Lizzie could testify that she knew Mary Antin as a vain boastful, curly-headed little Jew. For I had a special style of deportment for Lizzie. If there was any girl in the school besides me who could keep near the top of the class all the year through, and give bright answers when the principal or the school committee popped sudden questions, and write rhymes that almost always rhymed, *I* was determined that that ambitious person should not soar unduly in her own estimation. So I took care to show Lizzie all my poetry, and when she showed me hers I did not admire it too warmly. Lizzie, as I have already said, was in a Sunday-school mood even on week days; her verses all had morals. My poems were about the crystal snow, and the ocean blue, and sweet spring, and fleecy clouds; when I tried to drag in a moral it kicked so that the music of my lines went out in a groan. So I had a sweet revenge when Lizzie, one day, volunteered to bolster up the eloquence of Mr. Jones, the principal, who was lecturing the class for bad behavior, by comparing the bad boy in the schoolroom to the rotten apple that spoils the barrelful. The groans, coughs, a-

hem's, feet shufflings, and paper pellets that filled the room as Saint Elizabeth sat down, even in the principal's presence, were sweet balm to my smart of envy; I didn't care if I didn't know how to moralize.

When my teacher had visitors I was aware that I was the show pupil of the class. I was always made to recite, my compositions were passed around, and often I was called up on the platform—oh, climax of exaltation!—to be interviewed by the distinguished strangers; while the class took advantage of the teacher's distraction, to hold forbidden intercourse on matters not prescribed in the curriculum. When I returned to my seat, after such public audience with the great, I looked to see if Lizzie McDee was taking notice; and Lizzie, who was a generous soul, her Sunday-school airs notwithstanding, generally smiled, and I forgave her her rhymes.

I paid a price for my honors. With all my self-possession I had a certain capacity for shyness. Even when I arose to recite before the customary audience of my class I suffered from incipient stage fright, and my voice trembled over the first few words. When visitors were in the room I was even more troubled; and when I was made the special object of their attention my triumph was marred by acute distress. If I was called up to speak to the visitors, forty pairs of eyes pricked me in the back as I went. I stumbled in the aisle, and knocked down things that were not at all in my way; and my awkwardness increasing my embarrassment I would gladly have changed places with Lizzie or the bad boy in the back row; anything, only to be less conspicuous. When I found myself shaking hands with an august School-Committeeman, or a teacher from New York, the remnants of my self-possession vanished in awe; and it was in a very husky voice that I repeated, as I was asked, my name, lineage, and personal history. On the whole, I do not think that the School-Committeeman found a very forward creature in the solemn-faced little girl with the tight curls and the terrible red-and-green "plaid."

The Market

Adele Wiseman won recognition in the 1950s and 1960s in her native Canada with her fiction and memoirs about growing up in the North Main Jewish ghetto in Winnipeg in the 1940s. Subsequently she lived in London for many years and in her later life taught at a midwestern American university. This is Wiseman's recollection of the public market on North Main Street, a center of Jewish life in the 1940s.

Winnipeg then was a city with a population of three hundred thousand, ten percent of which was Jewish. The Jewish population was almost entirely from Eastern Europe. Now the city's population is six hundred thousand and Jews comprise only twenty thousand of them—all living in the affluent South End of the city. In the 1940s, the era that Wiseman remembers, Winnipeg was a distant but flourishing outpost of the Odessa Renaissance, a vibrant center of still-Yiddish literacy. Now the Jewish population is mainly interested in their winter holiday in Palm Springs, California, or buying season tickets to hockey and football games. Yiddish is unknown except to very old people. The market that Wiseman refers to is long gone. Sociologically, Winnipeg Jewish life is as she describes it is as distant as the Age of the Pharaohs.

When we were strangers in the land we made our own welcome and warmed ourselves with our own laughter and created our own belonging. To us the market-place was the least strange of all; there had always been markets.

I was a child then. For me the market was a place of looming backsides, off which we children caromed as off the padded walls of a roller-skating-rink. People were always bending over, searching in barrels, reaching, fingering. There was constant movement, arms and legs shooting out to be bumped into, people carrying things and shouting, "Excuse me," and "Out of the way, little girl!"

From above, odd gifts would come dropping with a benevolent "Here, taste," or drifting unescorted, like the handful of corn-hair, green and damp, that the farmer's wife flung down impatiently as she shucked the corn to prove to her customer that it was really golden bantam. "Here, count yourself. Eight rows. Lovely corn." She turned the golden cob triumphantly while I, watching, wound the cool hair round my fingers and put it to my nose.

To us below, identity smelled loud as voices. The crushed and trodden leaves and over-ripe fruit exhaled vigorous assertions, like echoes of the cries of the stall-keepers above.

"Tomatoes!" cried the man above. "Fresh garden tomatoes! Man-i-toba bee-ooties!"

"Crushed tomato!" echoed the ground around his stall. "I am a crushed tomato!"

"Cucumbers!" cried the farmer. "Firm sweet cucumbers!"

"Leaky!" sang the stench below. "I am a leaky hollow cucumber! Give me a kick and I'll smash apart!"

"Herring! Best schmaltz herring!" the man cajoled, above.

"Herring-barrel drippings; step in and smell worse than a wet and beshitten dog!" sang the world below, to which we children and the wasps and flies and dogs belonged.

Market people smelled too, of many smells, of sour cheese, of hay, of watermelon, of old clothes not for sale. And grandmothers smelled, grandmothers sitting on orange-crates, musty old grandmothers whose faces cracked into a thousand responsive wrinkles when you greeted them with "Hello Bobeh." Sometimes one of them drew you close for a pat on the head. She smelled as a grandmother who sits swathed in dresses and sweaters and coat and shawl and woolen stockings and ankle boots in all weathers can be expected to smell—inoffensively unrefreshing.

Those were the days when I had first heard of "stealers," and, thigh high, I watched keenly, and caught many interesting motions centered on pockets and handbags and thereabouts, though "stealers" usually eluded me. Children invade a thousand privacies, and people, preoccupied with other things, seldom notice the interest that attends their grabbings and their scratchings and their shakings. Movements also cry loud as voices, particularly when they're near and somehow divorced from the heads and voices busy at something else above.

Sometimes I'd see a bigger kid make a grab at something and weave, clamour-hearted, as fast as he could, away from the stall with his fistful of dried cherries jamming the narrow slit of his trouser pocket. "Ha ha!" I'd yell after him, lest he should think the event had gone unnoticed. "Ha ha!" I'd cry, making sure I was safely anchored to my grown-up. "Stealers never prosper!" I'd sing, mostly to myself, but with increasing vigour as he wove further out of sight. "Stealers never prosper!"

At that time my uncle was in the peddling business. He was a cabinet-maker by trade, but because of the Depression he had been forced to get himself a horse and wagon, and buy and sell whatever came to hand. It was a bright moment for me whenever I saw his wagon draw up in the mud lane behind the market. I was quick to let everyone know that this tall man dismounting from the wagon and greeting and being greeted so familiarly was *my* uncle. And, furthermore, I told the other kids who gathered round, his horse Nellie was *my* cousin and they'd better not touch her or she'd take a bite out of them with those big square teeth now ruminating the feedbag. It was well known in the right circles that my uncle treated his horse Nellie better than any other peddler in town treated his horse. Nellie ate well and there were no scars on her. My uncle liked horses. He had come to Canada with the ambition to be a cowboy, and whenever he had time he slipped into one of those Main Street movie-houses to dream away two or three cowboy films.

Sometimes, when he wasn't too busy buying and selling, my uncle actually lifted me onto the horse's back and walked her a few paces, with the wagon rumbling after and my mother uttering little admonitory cries. It is hard to describe the exact sensations of a little girl straddling a tickly, bony old nag while wearing only a cotton dirndl dress and knickers. It was a combination of delight at the idea of what was happening and acute distress at being caught up so intimately in the movement of all that bone and muscle and horsehair machinery. The balance of sensation must have been positive, for I remember protesting loudly when I was lifted off, and wearing the smell of horsiness that clung to me afterwards with deep pride.

All summer, my uncle peddled from the open wagon. In the winter he would transfer to an open sled, load Nellie with a magnificent assortment of protective blankets and furpieces, dress himself up in every warm garment he could find, and spend his days creaking along the snowy streets in the flaming cold. Later, he built himself a caboose that was like a little house on runners, with a tiny window in front through which the reins passed, and with a stove inside and a chimney poking out the roof. Below the rear door there was a step-rung where the kids hooked rides. In the summer he sold fruit and vegetables, chickens, and anything else he could find that might be saleable. In the winter he sold mostly frozen fish and frozen chickens. Such was my pride at seeing my cousin Nellie draw my uncle's chariot along the streets and through the market of our city that I have never been able to get used to the alien idea, first heard when I was quite grown up, that peddling was anything but a superior profession practised by a special breed of men.

In the evening, sometimes, after a day's work, Nellie would draw up in front of our house and Uncle would bring us things—important, valuable things, like a fowl for the Sabbath, or real blood oranges, only partly rotten-ripe. Half a blood orange, gushing red richness, is still pretty good once you've cut away the thick, green hairpiece of mould, and the puddle of stinky brown beneath. Uncle used to save us great packs of orange wrappings too, for in those days nothing went to waste. We were a family of Sunkist bottoms.

If my uncle didn't happen to be dealing in chickens that week, my mother would go down to the market of a Thursday evening, to buy a Sabbath fowl. Some people liked to do their marketing very early in the morning, when the farmers and peddlers were just beginning to set up their stands and the shop-keepers were rubbing the sleep out of their eyes. They claimed that this was the time to get bargains, because merchants are superstitious and believe that if they can make a sale to the first customer who comes along, even a cut-rate sale, it will be a profitable day. Other people preferred to shop at the busiest times on the busiest afternoons of the week. They liked the noise and the argument and the chance of meeting their friends. And they reasoned that the stall men and shop-keepers, anxious to turn over more goods, might give them better prices. Still other people preferred the market in the evening. It was cooler then; the light was softer. It was more like relaxing and enjoying yourself than doing a chore.

A subtle change took place in the relationship between seller and customer in the evening. The customer was no longer in a hurry to get home to make lunch or supper. It was the stall man who was anxious to make his sales and be gone. Limp, picked-over merchandise was offered at drastically reduced prices. You didn't have to haggle so much. "All right, take it, take it. Cut my heart out." The free tragic performance that came with the goods was also a little tired by the time evening came, for sincerity was tempered, on the part of the actor, by the knowledge that he was getting rid of something that would be unfit for sale and a dead loss tomorrow.

There were other reasons why young immigrants liked to stroll through the market in the evening, after work, reasons implied in the stories we heard so often, about how she met him in the market and he bought her a bag of chips and carried home her watermelon.

"Can you eat such a big watermelon all by yourself?"

"No, it's really for my landlady and her family."

"And who's your landlady?"

And it turned out that the landlady's brother-in-law came from the same town in the old country as this young man, which made practically a blood tie, soon to be cemented in a happy marriage, with the landlady's childless brother-in-law helping out the young man to such an extent that they were now practically rich and the watermelon girl hardly spoke to any of her old market acquaintances any more. Success stories often ended in this ambiguous way, but that didn't seem to deter anyone from dreaming.

If we were lucky, we children were taken along to help shop for the weekly chicken. Picking the Sabbath fowl is a serious affair, too serious to be accomplished without much deliberation. First you run your eyes over the clucking coop until they light on an attractive bird. Ask to have a look at her. Take her firmly by the legs. Feel her breast for signs of scrawniness. She must have a good, healthy deposit of white meat. Up-end her and blow into her rear downfeathers to see if the skin beneath reveals a good blush of yellow fat. Give her an extra feel to make sure. Some women even go so far as to insert an expert finger to find out if they'll be getting an egg into the bargain. It's an intricate, intimate business getting to know your fowl, and it is not surprising that the unlucky bird, who has been man-handled, up-ended, and outright violated, lets out a protesting squawk sometimes and madly flaps her wings. But she is soon subdued, and submits in baffled, glaring silence, her red-shot amber eyes fixed in angry resignation.

Once our bird was chosen and paid for she was hauled off to the slaughter shack. Well we children knew that here in this little shack, from which came the desperate squawks of "Help! Help!" the awesome business of the hallowing of the slaughter of food was taking place. As we waited outside we exchanged gory stories about what was going on inside, dared each other to peek in, and wondered whether this was going to be one of those legendary birds who would go on flapping and squawking and jumping around the shack for three hours after its throat had been slit. An uneasy silence fell upon us as we heard from within the shack the ultimate, unavailing cry of tomorrow's boiled chicken hurled into what, but for us, was an indifferent universe.

While we waited for the chicken-plucker to be finished plucking feathers and singeing lice we discussed questions of humane slaughter. Was our way of killing food better than "their" way? Well I should say so! Mostly they just grabbed a chicken by the neck and whirled it round and round to break its neck, poor little thing. Or sometimes they chopped its head off, so there was a red gushy stump left. But even if they only put a bullet in it, it was a pretty messy, unholy way to kill, without even a prayer or anything.

Sometimes, as we grew older, we decided that no way for a chicken to die could be condoned and vowed we wouldn't eat tomorrow's boiled chicken, ever again, not for anything. But there is a magician lurking in the most unassuming mother, who can undo the ardour of even the highest youthful principle. All she has to hear is the trembly, indignant little speech about how you will refuse to eat the meat of this cruelly murdered chicken, and tomorrow, instead of the same old boiled Sabbath fowl you will find a transformation on the table, a metamorphosis, roasted and stuffed and with a salivary allure quite unrelated to the bird whose immolation you swore to remember the day before.

In the evenings, when my aunt and uncle dropped over, I'd get to hear market gossip and peddler's stories, which I was not expected to listen to and forbidden to understand. One story in particular I remember, because I heard so many variations of it, all of them said to have happened to real people, people I could actually recognize on the street. The story always began: "Do you know what happened to so and so last week? You wouldn't believe it. Some men are lucky." After that it would unfold, almost always using the same words, like a culture myth, the dream of peddlers.

One version was about an old man whom I knew well by sight, a meek, unheroic-looking little old fellow. It appears that he was peddling autumn potatoes and onions from door to door one day, when he came across a pretty young widow (young widows were always pretty) with a lot of little children, who told him she didn't have any money for his potatoes, but that she'd trade him something else instead. I knew better than to ask what she'd trade, even though that part baffled me, because if I drew attention to myself I might get sent away again and miss the end of the story. But this old man was a decent sort, my uncle said, and he told her he didn't want to take her trade but he'd give her credit instead. This was very generous of him because he was pretty poor himself, as we all were. But the pretty

widow said that she couldn't stand getting into debt. Clearly she too was decent and proud, like us. So she insisted again that she needed the potatoes to feed her many children and again she offered the old man a trade. Well, he couldn't take it on his conscience to let a whole family starve through a winter in this chilly land just because he was stubborn over a sack of potatoes and she wouldn't take charity. So he was finally forced to accept her terms. And God was good to them both that day.

When my uncle finished with that part about God everybody burst out laughing. My aunt tried to keep a straight face and pursed up her lips and said, "You're all alike, you're all alike," but uncle merely smiled and shrugged his shoulders tolerantly.

Another version of the story had a peddler who wanted to repeat his luck with the pretty young widow. So after he had made his exchange with her in her cellar, he slyly left his galoshes behind. Well, the next day he came driving up with a merry "Giddyap!" and "Ho beck!" and presented himself at her door. She was waiting for him. He got his galoshes all right, right in his face, and a tongue-lashing too. It turned out that this pretty widow had a husband and she'd make sure he'd be waiting if the peddler ever came back again to try to collect twice over on one bargain. And she was right, too, all agreed. There is such a thing as business ethics.

But the ultimate "true trade" story that was clearly everyone's favourite was the one about the local peddler who happened to be selling chickens from door to door. He made the usual bargain with the usual pretty widow, but so well did he keep up his end of the bargain that she even gave him change! This story brought the house down; it seemed to resound to the credit of all peddlers, and when my aunt, blushing, repeated in an exasperated voice, "You're all alike, you're all alike," my uncle's face was a picture of modest acquiescence.

Those were the early years. The time came, one summer, when I went to work in the market myself, to earn my college fees. My boss was a tall, stooping old man who spat a lot. Our tiny hutch was adjacent to the old Winnipeg Farmers' Market. It was a fruit shop, so small you had to pull in your stomach to make room when more than two customers came in at the same time.

The rough, wooden floor was all black and oily from ground-in old gob and squashed fruit-leavings, which it was my job to sweep up in my spare time, when the old man went and sat on a bench outside to gossip with his cronies, and the dim-lit box in which I worked was for a moment free of the squeezers, the hagglers, and the other potential customers, whom he regarded at one and the same time as the providers and despoilers of his livelihood.

All day long—and a long, long day it was—we circled our small domain, checking the boxes and the crates and refilling the cartons and the baskets. Here we nipped a brown leaf, expertly, so it wouldn't show much; there we scraped with deft thumbnail at the first hint of coming mould. From the inside, I got a good close look at the life of anxiety bordering on anguish that is lived by the marginal traders of the perishable goods of the earth. With profit so small, with wastage so high, with the goods he is selling deteriorating by the minute before his very eyes, no wonder the storekeeper gives way sometimes to his gnawing wrath when customer after customer reaches out a greedy hand and in a few short hours a firm, nubile little tomato is turned into a bruised old pro. Every leaf to be discarded was a loss; every fruit or vegetable that a customer criticized was to be defended with peevish and despairing eloquence.

The little fruit shop is gone. The old market on Winnipeg's North Main has given way to a parking-lot and there are rumours of ambitious city plans for the area. The Farmers' Market, what's left of it, has been removed to an arid, antiseptic setting somewhere in the city's outskirts. My uncle doesn't do much business there any more. Nellie, of course, has long since gone where the good nags go, and I suppose it's just as well. Her turd would look out of place on the immaculate asphalt parking semicircle round which the farmers' stalls are neatly ranged.

My uncle now has a roomy, sky-blue, half-ton truck, which is as carefully if not as lovingly groomed as Nellie used to be. He runs a modern business. His cards say POULTRY DEALER. The farmers call him up by phone when they want to sell their fowl, and he's well known to the poultry firms in town that supply the supermarkets. Sometimes he calls me up: "If you'll be ready by six o'clock tomorrow morning I'll take you into the country to pick up some chickens. Dress warm, and be ready. And don't eat any breakfast. We'll stop on the way and you can have what you want."

Whatever I might want, my uncle knows what he wants. The next morning, yawning and white-faced, I follow him into the pancake house on the highway. Shuddering the chill dawn out of my bones, I watch him enjoy his pile of syrup-soaked pancakes as only a man who is not a heavy eater can enjoy something he particularly likes.

But he doesn't waste any time over it. "Noo," he has already risen from the table, as I hastily wipe up the last of my egg, "time to go. The farmer's waiting."

As we hurtle across the spottily creamed prairie of early spring, I watch the sky brightening for day; an immense sweep of unimpeded light pours over us. I watch the sky and feel the peril of the horizon rushing toward us and listen to my uncle reminisce.

"Here's where I got stuck once with the sled and horse. Maybe forty below. I had to tramp to get a farmer and his team steam from their eyes in the day-long heat." "Thank God," remarked one old man, "my sons don't have to make a living this way. Thank God," he repeated, as he stood among the bottles and other junk treasures outside his shop, his hands in his pockets, far from elegantly dressed but nevertheless the picture of a successful man. "You know, every day I thank God," he added, "and especially I thank him for three things. I thank him for my years, for my health, and for my little bit of money in the bank."

We paused at a stall set up in front of an old Toronto house of the kind that it is fashionable for young, artistic people to dream about buying up cheap, and "doing things with," a house decrepit, but with all kinds of "interesting potential if the right people got hold of it." I asked the vendor, an elderly, frail-looking man, "Do you live in that house?"

He was indignant. "You want I should live in a house like that?"

No, they have their own dreams in the marketplace, and you can see them still, the dream-filled eyes of young women brooding over what is to come and the doom-drowned eyes of their grandmothers brooding over where it went to. That old man who looks like the head of the Russian government may be dreaming about the statesman-like qualities he has already discovered in his grandson, or he may be deciding, "Let him own a supermarket if he doesn't want to be a doctor," about that little boy, half-a-hip high, to whom all of life is still a dream to come.

Once, recently, when I was wandering through the limbo of a Montreal supermarket, pushing my cart up and down the long, lonely aisles, picking up packages and putting them down again, calculating sizes of cartons, adding up ounces against conflicting prices, unable to come to any conclusion about who was trying to gyp me more and unable to find a human being who cared enough to fight it out with, I had an odd experience. I was reaching into the milk-products display case which runs along the entire width of the back of the store, when a shopping-cart was driven firmly into the small of my back, pinning me against the refrigerator.

"Would you mind, while you're down there, to reach me a package of cheese?" asked a little old lady, dressed in a fashionable fur coat, with her gloved hands quite firmly maintaining their pressure on the shopping-cart.

When I complied she looked at the neat, glassy package with disgust, and I could see in her eyes the memories of great damp slabs from which the stall women would give you tasters before they cut with a big knife, unerringly, the amount you wanted. But she thanked me politely and I continued on my way. A moment later I was again nudged by the shopping-cart. Again I was asked to reach for something and again I complied. When I had done so she proceeded to drive me along the entire length of the refrigerator, pinned to the front rim of her shopping-cart, as though I were trapped on one of those cow-catchers they used to have on trains. She directed me with a nudge, now on this hip, now on that, now appearing beside, now behind, now with a little racing movement in front, to bar my way and ask me if I'd reach for something, or read the small print on the package because she couldn't see very well. Neither her reflexes nor her eyesight were poor enough to prevent her from spotting any move I made to escape and scotching it with a clever twist of the steering bar. I had the distinct impression that she was surreptitiously putting back everything I dutifully handed her, for all my bending and fetching didn't seem to add much to her cart.

But as she drove me along in front of her I felt a strong conviction that I knew who this old lady was. Her children had peeled off the layers of clothes, of sweaters and skirts and wool stockings and ankle boots. They had bought her a fur coat, through which it is hard to perceive dry-old-lady smell, and exchanged her kerchief for a hat with a feather; they had parked her in an apartment uptown, away from her old friends and the market life that she knew; but I recognized her. And I began to wonder if perhaps she had not recognized something in me, too, in this cold place.

Finally, I turned and put my hand restrainingly on her shopping-cart. "I have to go now," I said, as gently as I could. On an impulse I added, "Good-bye, Bobeh."

For an instant I caught the gleam that precedes the cracking-up of an old lady's face into a thousand smiling wrinkles. Then she glanced round quickly, a puzzled expression gathering up the mobile wrinkles. Her eyes sought my face with an anxious scrutiny. "Do I know you, daughter?" she whispered, finally.

I felt a pang for having upset her. "I used to know you in the market," I lied.

The wrinkles righted themselves slowly to a smile. "Rachel Street?" she said. "That's a market. There at least you can say a word to someone. Not like this." Her gesture took in the whole new world of supermarkets and shopping centres.

"Yes," I agreed. "Yes."

"Still," she added thoughtfully. "It's a good business." And she sighed.

The Activist

Henrietta Szold was the daughter of a Baltimore rabbi. Never married, and influenced by the women's movement for helping the downtrodden and unfortunate that prevailed in the late-nineteenth century, she did social welfare work among immigrant Eastern European Jews in Baltimore. She also in effect ran the Jewish Publication Society and edited its books for two decades. Finally as an active Zionist and prime founder of Hadassah, Szold raised millions of dollars for medical services in Israel. The Hadassah Hospital in Jerusalem, Israel's finest, is her monument. She was never a politician and always retained independent judgment, as her letters from Israel in the critical days of the late-1930s reveal.

Baltimore, 1938

I am literally afraid of what will meet me in Palestine. The economic conditions prevailing there are the worst we have known since the beginning of our adventure. The organization is being disrupted by the various opinions held more or less honestly. And in my thoughts this central interest and responsibility of mine is veiled and darkened and in a measure buried by China-Japan, by Spain, by Germany, by Italy, by the fascistic tendencies manifested by the smaller European states, by misery and lack of vision everywhere. England talks armament, Paris is stupefied, dead, Italy bristles with arms, hope nonexistent, fear and anxiety prevalent. Personally, a mountain of accumulated problems awaits me. Isn't it clear that it would be easier to remain in America, to return to America? But one has a conscience.

When my mood is apprehensive to the point of pain, there arises before my eyes your little white house set in green shaded by elms, and its warm cozy interior, and my conscience almost vanishes. They were idyllic weeks in Connecticut.

Jerusalem, April 1, 1938

I am writing at the end of what has been perhaps the most murderous week since the beginning of the disturbances all but two years ago. I have lost count of the victims, young men, old men, women, and children, with practically not a word of condemnation of the outrages in the Arab press. Last Sunday I felt closer to the ruffianism than ever before. I traveled up to Haifa in a taxi. At less than twenty minutes' distance from the end of our journey, we had a puncture. It delayed us by over a half-hour. Less than an hour later—at five-thirty—two taxis were attacked by armed bands on that very spot. It happened that one of the cars was driven by an Arab chauffeur. All the passengers were wounded, the chauffeur was killed. It's gruesome. And there seems to be no end to it—or to the funds with which the gunmen are kept supplied.

And all this is happening in a country poignantly beautiful and peaceful-looking. Such a riot of bloom, such verdure, such blue skies (but not zephyr winds; winter refuses to depart from the temperature), such rich promise of crops, with oranges gleaming from the trees, in heaps under the trees and on the roadside waiting to be carried to the packing-houses, from the lorries filled to the brim.

Today cables came from Hadassah: Eddie Cantor collected $32,000 for the Austrian Youth Aliyah. Meantime it seems certain that we shall have to tackle Rumania, too. There should be many Eddie Cantors unless the Hitlers and the Francos can be made innocuous.

Jerusalem, August 27, 1938

On Friday a bomb exploded in the Jaffa market-place killing as many persons as are killed, according to the newspaper reports, in a regular pitched battle in the Chinese or the Spanish war. Nevertheless, we are having "disturbances"—not a war—in Palestine!

In the afternoon my associate in the Aliyah, Mr. Hans Beyth, met a friend of his in the streets of Jerusalem. The friend had just arrived in town, his taxi having managed to escape from Ramleh. Ramleh is on the road between Jaffa and Jerusalem. As soon as the news of the bomb explosion in Jaffa reached Ramleh, the hoodlums there jumped to the conclusion that the dastardly deed was perpetrated by the Jews; and they stoned and shot at every taxi carrying Jews. Mr. Beyth's friend was covered with blood from top to toe, but not his own. He escaped unhurt, but the woman who sat next to him in the taxi was wounded in the cheek and her blood ran profusely.

And who was the woman? One of the Burgenlanders, the Austrians, seventy in number, who for months had been living on a raft in the Danube, not permitted to land in Austria (their home for centuries) or to take refuge in Czechoslovakia or Hungary on which their Danubian perch abutted, scourged daily by the Nazis who boarded the raft for the purpose, stung by swarms of mosquitoes by day and plagued by rats at night, their clothing dropping from them, undernourished by the food other Jews managed to get to them. For months all sorts of efforts were made to secure for them United States affidavits or Palestinian certificates. Two weeks ago some certificates were obtained; and she, this bleeding woman in the taxi, had been among the first to be released from her Danubian open-air prison, and promptly she dropped from the frying-pan of the Nazis into the fire of the Arabs.

It's no use warning me not to overwork; it's no use telling anybody in Palestine to take care. One has to grit one's teeth and take a chance.

Jerusalem, October 11, 1938

[To Mrs. David B. Greenberg]

As for my health, it is completely restored. But the warning administered to me was impressive, and I find I must heed it. I cannot work as I used to. I must give myself more sleep; and I do, with the result that I fall behind more and more each day in my work. I cannot keep up with the procession. The march is too rapid. As it is, I am actually at work twelve hours daily. To do what is required calls for at least eighteen, and at that I should not be responding to the demand for personal contacts, not to mention articles, etc., that should be written and visits that should be paid to institutions—*kvuzot*, social service bureaus, and all the rest. As you see, it is not a question of more secretarial help. I have no doubt that others could work faster than I do.

What was the warning? The doctors said "a tired heart." I said "a heart that has been beating for seventy-eight years." He agreed and then said more technically: "A cardiac-vascular disturbance." So that's that.

Jerusalem, October 21, 1938

This week taught me what I could never make myself understand when I read history or a description of a war in the daily papers. I have not been able to imagine how ordinary people went on living in Spain throughout the frightful upheavals in city after city. This week I have been living in a beleaguered city with airplanes whizzing and buzzing through the air, and the reverberations of shots assailing my ears. And what did I and thousands of others in the city do? We picked up the circulars dropped by the planes, we read almost with equanimity that the military commander whose troops had taken possession of the Old City advised us not to leave our houses, we gobbled up all the details of the beleaguerment of the Old City by the soldiery—and we went about our business.

My business the morning of the beginning of the siege was to get out of the city and travel by auto to Haifa via Tel Aviv and from Haifa to Kfar Yeheskiah near Nahalal to attend a meeting of the teachers of the Youth Aliyah.

And again I was struck by the sang-froid with which we accept war, for latterly it has been war. There was a reference in the opening address to the difficulties under which we are carrying on and to our sorrow over the loss of some of our forces—almost a formal reference to the situation— and then on to the thing we had come for. And who were the teachers who had assembled there?

For the most part young men who work in the fields in the morning, teach our youth in the afternoon, and stand guard all night.

If a war breaks out, I am afraid I shall not get back to America. Your analysis of my attitude about leaving my responsibilities is correct. In any case, however, I am working unceasingly toward the end of relieving myself of public responsibilities. I keep saying that I always knew it was hard to get a job, but I never knew it was so hard to get out of a job as I am finding it.

Jerusalem, January 6, 1939

Though I extricated myself from the Vaad Leumi, that is, the Social Service job, a day plus a week ago, the week was as full as usual. In the first place, I must clean up in the Vaad Leumi. I had fallen behind in my work rather considerably, and in the second place a number of really involved problems had arisen in connection with the refugees' plight.

We are having a large illegal immigration. Shiploads arrive on Greek vessels from Austria and Czechoslovakia—twenty four hundred during December. They come naked, hungry, sick. Their voyage, instead of taking four days from Europe, takes four to six weeks. They have to land in the darkness of night, with signal lights from government airplanes playing on them; and they land, not at a port, but at any place along the shore that offers security. Many of them must swim ashore, holding a child and their clothes over their heads (they have no clothes but those on their person).

And on shore begin new troubles—no employment! It's ghastly. The Jewish Agency, for political reasons, cannot deal with them as it deals with legal immigrants. As the director of the Social Service, I took it upon myself to treat them as if they had come in by the front door, with a passport, a visa, and a certificate. But the money! There is none. This morning we had a four hours' meeting with the Agency on the subject. Result: much talk, little planning, no money! I was not a little plagued by my conscience when I considered that it was my last official act in the Social Service. Has one the right to protect oneself?

That is the dragnet which caught me up on my return from my birthday vacation in Nataniah. I stopped over in Tel Aviv on my return in order to meet people interested in the problem. They all had heaps of advice and no one had money. If I had money, I'd need no advice. There is one heartening feature. Last week, six hundred arrived on one of these illegal transports and spilled themselves into Tel Aviv. By evening hundreds of families had volunteered to take them in and in large part feed them.

Jerusalem, June 14–17, 1940

In spite of all my resolutions to "jump off the band-wagon," I am traveling on it faster than ever. Emergency organization is the order of the day; and protest as I will, I am drawn into the hurly-burly. Italy's entry into the war was depressing, but not half as depressing as the peril of Paris.

I had a gardener—Perles, the grandson of our father's best friend!—repot my window plants. Most of them are now ranged on the table on my porch. The fuchsias bloomed, but wanly. There is too much sun, too little moisture for them; they are now standing *under* the table for protection. Mr. Perles insists upon my keeping the begonias and the amaryllis indoors. Do you remember the begonia that bloomed so incessantly? It is still blooming. The other one, from Ayanot, is gorgeous as to leaf and bloom. The aralia did not survive the winter well. The cacti are flourishing. The maidenhair fern could not be resuscitated. The most luxuriant pot next to the Ayanot begonia is the one planted with a little slip by Adele from the Ehrlich garden. Your enumeration of the spring blossoms in Eva Leah's woods made me homesick beyond words. But it was right for me to stay here!

. . . We who get together and discuss the news of the day—and how we discuss it!—are heartsick over France. I feel, foolishly I admit, that I am being treated badly in particular. It is the second time in my life that I am experiencing a German victory over France. I remember well the war of 1870 and the Commune in Paris.

Apart from the world situation, and my constant brooding over Adele's going from us, and over your having to settle so much of what by right is my business, a huge unanswered personal correspondence stares me in the face and all my papers still lying on the shelves as you deposited them. Nor do I ever "catch up to myself" in my work—the old, old story.

Jerusalem, November 20, 1940

[To Mrs. Rose Jacobs]

My working days are far shorter than they used to be. I can't any more extend them far into the night and until the morning after. And my Youth Aliyah and Kehillah obligations fill my working day, such as it is, to repleteness. Yet honesty compels me to confess that not lack of leisure alone is the explanation of my silence. There are so many reasons for not pouring out one's soul on paper these days, again for both external and internal considerations, that words of all kinds dry up on one's lips and in one's pen. . . .

Jerusalem, December 7, 1940

I wonder whether I shall survive those eightieth-anniversary celebrations of which rumors reach me day after day. One of them at least I scotched and I succeeded, I hope, in influencing its character. There was to be a public meeting at which speakers were to tell the Palestinian world—or perhaps they were to tell me—who and what I am. I have attended one funeral like that. It was in celebration of my seventy-fifth birthday. I cannot stand another. So, when an occasion presented itself, I suggested a program: The Developments in Jewish Life during the Last Eighty Years: (a) in Zionism, (b) in Palestine, (c) in America. The suggestion was accepted with alacrity. In what spirit and with what vim, honesty of purpose, and analytical ability the speakers will execute it remains to be seen. They probably will introduce me as the heroine, because they won't believe that eulogies are distasteful to a person who has never considered herself (and never will consider herself) as a public character, and who knows her own shortcomings as a simple member of a community—whose eighty years have served primarily to teach her that years alone are not important. Well, we shall see.

A Neo-Orthodox Feminist

Irving and Blu Greenberg are an exemplary couple. A sometime history professor at Yeshiva University, and for many years a rabbi of the Orthodox synagogue in upscale Riverdale, the Bronx, Irving Greenberg founded a neo-Orthodox institute and is generally regarded, along with Rabbi Joseph Soloveitchik of Boston, as the leading American Orthodox thinker of his generation.

Blu Greenberg is the prime spokeswoman for combining Orthodoxy and feminism. In 1981 she articulated her views as follows:

On occasion I have been asked: How can one so rooted in Jewish tradition, so at home with Halakhic prescriptions and proscriptions, have such strong feminist leanings? Are the two not mutually exclusive, anomalous, contradictory? To the extent that one's worldview is shaped by small incidents, special encounters, and chance events, as much as it is by environment, endowment, and formal education, I would like to share with the reader some of those points along the route of a transition woman.

I was born into a strongly traditional family. With all the structure this entails, it was quite natural to be socialized early into the proper roles. I knew my place and I liked it—the warmth, the rituals, the solid, tight parameters. I never gave a thought as to what responsibilities I did or didn't have as a female growing up in the Orthodox Jewish community. It was just the way things were—the most natural order in the world.

My friends and I shared the same world of expectation. I remember the year of the bar mitz-

Before feminism: Jewish woman waiting for the Sabbath, Vienna, 1920.

vahs of our eighth-grade male friends. We girls sat up in the women's section of the synagogue and took great pride in "our boys." If we thought about ourselves at all, it was along the lines of "thank God we are females and don't have to go through this public ordeal." Quite remarkably, there never was any envy of what the boys were doing, never a thought of "why not us?" Perhaps it was because we knew that our big moment would come: As proper young ladies growing up in the modern Orthodox community in the 1950s, *our* puberty rite was the Sweet Sixteen.

My short-lived encounter with daily prayer ended when I was fourteen. I had graduated from a local yeshiva in Far Rockaway, New York, and had begun commuting to a girls' yeshiva high school in Brooklyn. This meant getting up an hour earlier to catch the 7:18 Long Island train, so prayer was the first thing to go. I had it down to a science: If I laid out my clothes in exactly the

right order the night before, I could set the alarm for 6:52, get up, wash, dress, eat the hot breakfast without which, my mother insisted, a person could not face the world each day, and still have time to walk briskly to the train. I would reserve a four-seater in the same car each day. Just as the train started to pull out, my friends who were attending the boys' yeshiva would come dashing down the platform and fling themselves onto the slowly moving train. I knew that they had been up since six o'clock to allow enough time for *sha-harit,* the mandatory morning prayers. There they were, a little bleary-eyed, already spent at 7:18, with just a package of Sen-Sen for breakfast. Those were wonderful, funny trips. Though I laughed with the boys each morning, I certainly didn't envy their more rigorous regimen.

I also relished the tale told about my cousin Tzvi, then thirteen. He was on his way from Seattle to the Telshe Yeshiva in Cleveland. It was a night flight, and because of a delay and the change of time zones, the plane was still in the air as it neared time for the morning devotions. A no-nonsense thirteen-year-old when it came to religious obligation, Tzvi went to the back of the plane, strapped on his tefillin, and began to pray. In the 1950s, it took a lot of guts to be so conspicuous; many Americans, especially in the West, genuinely believed that Jews had horns. The Northwest Airlines stewardess, however, was not one of them. She gently put her arm around Tzvi and said, "What's the matter, sonny, don't you think you're going to make it?" Aside from the humor, I was very proud of my cousin, one year my junior, but somehow I never related his experience in any way to my own religious life.

In the 50s, the modern Orthodox community was just beginning to make its mark. Orthodoxy had suffered a terrible falloff in the aftermath of the great waves of immigration. There were several prominent rabbis in New York City—Leo Jung, Joseph Lookstein, Emanuel Rackman—who had initiated the process of reestablishing Orthodoxy as a respected Jewish option in modern America, but the process was still incomplete in the 50s. It took the turbulent 60s, with all that decade's variety of experimentation in self-assertion, before the rest of the country could accept ethnicity. And Jews were no different. For many Jews, it took the Six-Day War to invest them with enough self-pride to overcome a stifling self-consciousness.

Meanwhile, in the 50s, Orthodox Jews lived their lives with great fidelity to the Halakhah, even as they tried to "pass" in the larger society. After all, why bring special attention to a particularist way of life? "Be a Jew at home, a man in the streets" was the unspoken social principle. And how did this fine-tuning manifest itself? In one's dress, one's speech, one's name.

The evolution of the *kipah* is a case in point. In the 50s, this headcovering, incumbent upon every observant Jewish male, was still called by its Yiddish name, *yarmulke—kipah* is the Hebrew term—and it certainly wasn't what it is today. In place of those small, neat, attractive, finely crocheted circles you see everywhere nowadays, the 1950s offered only black rayon or silk, measuring a full handspan.

By choice and expectation, my social circle was confined to the yeshiva crowd. Although I don't recall ever discussing with a date how he felt about wearing a *kipah,* I could always observe the different ways of handling the matter in a public situation. One never saw a *kipah* bobbing down Fifth Avenue in the 50s. A hat or a cap was a bit more conspicuous in summer than in winter, but it wasn't all that outlandish. The big test, however, came when the young men entered a public place—a theater, a movie house, a library. Unless it was a restaurant, most of the young Orthodox men of my acquaintance, even the rabbinical students, would go bareheaded for the short duration (something their sons would be horrified at today). In addition, there were all sorts of permutations and combinations—putting on one's *kipah* before saying a blessing over an ice cream soda and then removing it before eating, or waiting until the lights in the theater dimmed before slipping it on. It wasn't that these things were done stealthily or with guilt. It was all a bit of harmless maneuvering to enable a young man and his date to feel at home in a wider range of social, public settings.

How did I relate to all this? With a sense of relief, for I didn't have to cope with the encumbrance of a *kipah* on top of the normal teen load of social self-consciousness. I can recall, in the early courtship with the man who was to become my husband, an occasional sensation of discomfort at the fact that he never removed his *kipah* in public places. Not to my credit, I even remember one evening at the opera, of which I didn't hear a word, while I sat thinking the whole time, "Why can't he be more sensible, less conspicuous?"

This is not meant to be a disquisition on the art of *kipah*-wearing in the 50s. Rather, it is to point out that for a young woman growing up at that time the lines were drawn sharply, and I was glad to be off the hook as far as certain religious responsibilities were concerned. It never occurred to me that these were overt expressions of a religious stamina, a formal statement of what a young man stood for. And although there were no guarantees that this was for life—many a young man broke under the burdens of *kipah* and daily prayer—it was still a more demanding path than that charted for a young woman. The ever-so-subtle side message was that male Jews who passed the tests were a superior breed.

I had a fine Jewish education, the best a girl could have. My father always was more interested in my Hebrew studies than in my secular ones, and he studied with my sisters and me regularly. My mother, the more practical one, also encouraged my Hebrew studies. Having lived through the Depression, she believed that a Hebrew-teacher's license was like money in the bank—the best insurance a girl could buy. Why a Hebrew teacher? That was just about the highest career expectation for a Jewish educated female in the 50s. We were an achievement-oriented family, so along with our secular degrees, my sisters and I and most of our friends added another notch to our dowry belts, a Hebrew-teacher's license.

The fact that teaching Hebrew was a low-paying career didn't matter much. In the 50s, a young Jewish woman really didn't have to worry about earning a living. It was more a matter of waiting for Mr. Right to come along and take over where parental support left off. In her inner soul, perhaps, a young woman's anxieties were greater: She had to wait, somewhat passively, for a man to create a future for her, whereas a young man had a sense of holding the future in his hands. On the surface, however, I think it was easier to be a woman. The loads were neatly packaged, and the one marked "female" was lighter.

After my marriage in the late 1950s, my feelings of contentment and fulfillment were enhanced rather than diminished. The ways of a traditional Jewish woman suited me just fine. All those platitudes about building a faithful Jewish home were not nearly as pleasant as the real thing itself. Moreover, none of those obligations ruled out graduate studies and plans for a career. It was a time of peaceful coexistence between the traditional roles and the initial stirrings of self-actualization for women. I considered myself very lucky to have a husband to care for me and I for him—a man, moreover, who encouraged me to expand my own horizons.

The religious role of a married woman was also perfect in my eyes. I found the clear division of labor, and its nonnegotiable quality, most satisfying. It never crossed my mind that experiencing certain mitzvot vicariously was anything less than the real thing. Quite the reverse. When my husband had to be away on the Sabbath, the act of my reciting the blessings over the wine and the bread for our small children only served to heighten my sense of loneliness for him.

The real thing, then, was for him to perform his mitzvot and for me to attend to mine. I wasn't looking for anything more than I had, certainly not in the way of religious obligations or rights. On those bitter cold Sabbath mornings I was absolutely delighted to linger an hour longer in a nice warm bed and play with the kids rather than to have to brave the elements. I could choose to go to the synagogue when I wanted or pray at home when I wanted; for my husband there was no choice.

The *mehitzah* separating men from women in the synagogue served to symbolize the dividing line. Although there were certain things about sitting behind the *mehitzah* that I didn't exactly appreciate, none seemed an attack on my womanhood. Not only did I not perceive the *mehitzah* to be a denigration of women in the synagogue, but I couldn't understand why some Jews felt that way. At some level, to me the *mehitzah* symbolized the ancient, natural, immutable order of male and female. One didn't question such things.

All of this is not to say that I lived a perfectly docile existence within the boundaries of this natural order. There were certain incidents that made me chafe at the outer limits, but these were isolated, sporadic, and unconnected. I did not see them as part of any meaningful pattern.

During my junior year in college, I studied in Israel for several months at a Hebrew teachers' institute. Nechama Leibowitz was my teacher for Bible. She was the most brilliant, exciting teacher I ever had, and she became an extraordinary model for me. As the time neared to return home, I decided that I wanted to take a year off from Brooklyn College where I had been enrolled and just study intensively with Nechama. She was then teaching at fifteen different places, from army camps to kibbutz seminars to study groups for middle-aged Jerusalem ladies. My intention was to make Jerusalem my home base, follow Nechama to all the places she taught, and learn from her day and night. As an eighteen year old with a singular lack of ambition, it was about the only unusual thing I cared to do. "Come home and finish college," said my parents. "You're crazy," said most of my friends. In the back of my mind, I guess I somehow knew, back in the 50s, that it wasn't the sort of thing a nice Orthodox Jewish girl would do. Not being assertive or terribly independent, I came home to work on Nechama's famous *gilyonot* (Bible questionnaires) and move quickly into the next slot. But even as I did, I quietly knew that had I been a young man wanting to stay on and study intensively with a special Israeli rebbe, every encouragement would have been forthcoming.

Another incident that gave pause for thought was the *oyfruf* of my cousin Allan. (This is the ceremony of calling up a bridegroom to read from the Torah in the synagogue on the Sabbath preceding the wedding.) The *oyfruf* was to be held at a synagogue a mile from where we lived at the time. I was looking forward to the occasion because many of my relatives from Seattle, whom I hadn't seen for a long time, would be there. I had arranged with the baby-sitter to come at 9:30; my husband had left an hour earlier to catch the beginning of the services. The appointed hour passed, then 10:00, 10:30, and still no baby-sitter. At that time there was no eruv (a circumferential boundary that transforms the legal nature of property) in Manhattan that would have permitted me to push a carriage on the Sabbath; there was simply no way I could walk with an infant and a toddler to the synagogue, a mile away. I sat there for an hour, all dressed up, wearing my hat, muttering darkly at the world, while my two young sons played at my feet. Though I couldn't put my frustration into any sort of framework, I had a vague feeling that above my own failure to make any contingency arrangements, there were some situations in which the demarcations brought me up short. If synagogue weren't a man's thing, I mentally pouted, then somehow it would have been I and not my husband at my cousin's *oyfruf.*

These and other incidents nevertheless were quietly put behind me. They didn't total up to anything, and they certainly were not enough to shake my equilibrium.

And then came feminism. In 1963, I read Betty Friedan's *Feminine Mystique,* still the classic text of the women's movement. I was a little intimidated by its force and had trouble with what seemed to me a portent of friction between the sexes, but the essential idea, equality of women, was exciting, mind-boggling, and very just. Still, correct or not, it didn't mean me, nor did it apply to women in Judaism. On that score I was defensive, resistant, and probably just plain frightened. It must have threatened my status quo.

And yet . . . [o]nce I had tasted of the fruit of the tree of knowledge, there was no going back.

The basic idea had found a resting spot somewhere inside me. Little by little, and with a good deal of prodding from my husband, I became sensitized to issues and situations that previously had made no impression on me. Some of my complacency was eroded; my placidity churned up. In place of blind acceptance, I slowly began to ask questions, not really sure if I wanted to hear the answers. Because I was so satisfied, because I had no sense of injustice, some of the new thinking, including my own, came to me as a shock. Things that had run right past me before I now had to grab hold of, for a still moment, to examine under the white light of equality.

I began to think not just about the idea, but about myself as a woman—in relation to people, to a place in the larger society, to a career, and finally to Judaism. I did not look back over my past and say it was bad. In fact, I knew it was very good. What I did begin to say was that perhaps it could have been better. Again, it was not a case of closing my eyes and thinking hard. Instead, it was a series of incidents, encounters, a matter of timing; it was also memories and recollections, a review in which isolated incidents began to emerge as part of a pattern. This pattern now had to be tested against a new value framework.

It was almost ten years before I began systematically to apply the new categories to my Jewishness. As I reviewed my education, one fact emerged—a fact so obvious that I was stunned more by my unresponsiveness to it over the years than by the fact itself. It was this: The study of Talmud, which was a primary goal in my family and community, consistently was closed off to me. Beginning with elementary school, the girls studied Israeli folk dancing while the boys studied Talmud. In the yeshiva high school, the girls' branch had no course of study in Talmud; the boys' branch had three hours a day. In Israel, in the Jewish studies seminar, all of the classes were coeducational except Talmud. The girls studied laws and customs on one day and enjoyed a free period the other four days.

And then there was my father. The great love of his life, beyond his family, was not his business; it was his study of the Talmud. Every day, before he left for work, he would spend an hour studying Talmud with a rabbi friend. In fact, he has not missed a day of study in his life, even during family vacations or times of stress. Yet although he reviewed religious texts regularly with his daughters, it was never Talmud. He even would collar my dates, while I was getting ready, for a few minutes of Talmud discussion. That we didn't participate in those years more directly in our father's passion for Talmud study was not a willful denial on his part; he simply was following the hallowed custom. As a result of all this, when I began to study Rabbinic literature in graduate school in my late twenties, I realized that my male fellow students all had the edge of fifteen or twenty years of Talmud study behind them.

Gradually, too, I became aware of the power of conditioning and how early in life it takes place. On the last Sabbath that my husband served as rabbi of a congregation, the children and I decided to surprise him. Moshe, then ten and a half, prepared the Haftarah reading, David, nine, the *An'im Zemirot* prayer, and J. J., six, the *Adon Olam.* It was a real treat for their father and for the entire congregation; it seemed to the boys as if the whole world was proud of them. On the following Sunday morning, their grandparents visited and gave each of the boys two dollars for doing such a fine job. When the boys told Deborah, then eight, that they each had been given two dollars, she complained that it wasn't fair. At which point Moshe retorted, with the biting honesty of a ten year old: "Well, so what, you can't even do anything in the synagogue!" Click, click, I thought to myself, another woman radicalized.

Oddly enough, until that moment it never had occurred to me that it could or should be otherwise, that perhaps it wasn't "fair" to a little girl. Even more astounding was the fact that with all the weeks of secret practice, all the fuss I had made over the boys beforehand, and all the compliments they received afterward, Deborah never once had complained. It was only the two dollars that finally got to her; to everything else she had already been conditioned . . . to expect nothing.

Other scenes began to pull together. When my Uncle Izzie died, the whole family gathered for his funeral. He had been a cheerful, expansive man, much beloved by everyone. He had had a special spot in his heart for his six grandchildren, especially two girls who grew up in his house. In his eulogy, the rabbi commented on this special relationship. At the end of the service, he asked the grandchildren to accompany the casket out of the synagogue. Three boys and three girls, all in their teens, stepped forward. The president of the congregation hastened over and asked the girls to be seated. The rabbi, he said, meant only male grandchildren.

A few months later, my husband and I went to visit a friend and her daughter who were observing shivah, the seven-day mourning period. We arrived just in time for the evening service. The men rose to pray. The women, including the two mourners, were shunted off to the apartment foyer to stand silently while the men prayed. The men who had arranged the service did not think to provide prayer books for the women, not even for the two female mourners. Nor did it occur to them to move to the foyer themselves at least to allow the women to remain seated in the living room. It was as if once the moment of prayer began, the women no longer existed. None of the men present could be characterized as ill-mannered; each was considerate of women and all were solicitous of the two mourners, the wife and daughter of the deceased. Yet as I stood in my tight corner of the foyer, I recalled a picture I once had seen of Muslim women with their babies, shunted into a similar position, and inwardly I wondered at how smug I had been then.

A turning point for me came in 1973. By sheer accident I was invited to deliver the opening address at the First National Jewish Women's Conference, to be held at the Hotel McAlpin in New York. A month before the conference, two young women, Arlene Agus and Toby Brandriss, came to our house to discuss the conference and to invite my husband to participate in a Sunday morning panel. As we chatted, I chimed in intermittently. Several times I had to leave the room to attend to the children. At one point I went off to put our daughter Goody, then six, to bed. As is the prescribed custom before retiring for the night, Goody got ready to recite the *Shema Yisrael* prayer. A few days earlier we had bought the latest record of the Israeli Hasidic folk festival, which contained a lovely new melody for the *Shema,* quite different from the version we were used to singing at bedtime. When I tucked Goody in, I sang the *Shema* with her to the new tune. Then, just as I was about to leave the room, she said softly, "Now can we say the real *Shema?*" Moments later, I recounted the story to our visitors and added with laughter, "Here you have it, a case in point of why it's going to be so tough to get anywhere with those new ideas of yours." Their response took me by surprise. "Say," said one of the visitors with utter spontaneity, "how would *you* like to speak at the opening session on Friday night with Dr. S. [a well-known woman speaker]?" The next day Toby and Arlene called and with some embarrassment reported that Dr. S. did not want to share the platform, certainly not with a neophyte like me; would I mind giving a workshop instead? "Fine," I said. Two weeks later they called again. The woman had decided to cancel altogether; would I give the opening address? It was definitely a case of being in the right place at the right time.

Until then I had thought through the Jewish issues of feminism only haphazardly—in the shower, watching people, daydreaming in the synagogue or at school, reflecting on the relevant items I came across in the classic Jewish sources, and vaguely relating bits of all this to my own experience. Now I was forced to collect my scattered thought, to research, to focus. When I confronted the sources directly, I found I could no longer accept the apologetic line so popular among those in the traditional Jewish community who were attempting to deal with feminism. Different role assignments? Yes, that part was true. But genuine equality? There was simply too much evidence to the contrary. On the other hand, my background, indeed my love for the tradition, had given me a different perspective on the feminist movement. Untempered, it seemed to me, feminism fell short in some basic human values. Thus, as my talk developed, it ended up being a double-edged critique of Jewish tradition vis-à-vis women and feminism, each from a perspective of the other.

The response was most instructive. I discovered that there were some feminists who relished criticism of the Jewish tradition but would brook no naysaying of feminism. They applauded the first part of my address and hissed at the second part. In my later conversations with them, and in my observations throughout the weekend, I began to realize that it was their counterparts in the broader feminist movement (about whom I had been reading) who had given me pause. I thought of them as "orthodox" feminists, for feminism was to them a religion—sacrosanct, untouch-

able, inviolable. They were the vociferous minority, the radical fringe, whom the self-serving media had projected to the center, passing up the more balanced, less angry elements of the movement. Perhaps the radical fringe is a necessary leaven in any bloodless revolution, but it was also a lesson for me to realize how deeply this fringe could discredit the very movement it held up as ideal. This was an important encounter for me. After that weekend, I found myself less in need of prefacing my comments on the subject with such remarks as "I'm not a women's libber." I found you could still be a mild-mannered yeshiva girl and a card-carrying feminist and not feel out of whack all the time.

More significant was the conference experience itself and the larger group that was present. To my amazement, there were some five hundred women from every point along the continuum, not just the twenty-five hard-core types I had expected to find. Although all were feminists, they were not hostile to Judaism. A good many of them, especially those with no extensive Jewish background had come to Judaism through feminism: In the course of searching for their roots as women, they had begun to search for their roots as Jews. The tone was not as I had feared, a shrill, seventy-two-hour tirade against Jewish tradition. Instead, the whole weekend abounded with a great deal of love for Judaism.

Moreover, as I looked about me, I was astonished to see what the conference organizers—a handful of women in their twenties, inexperienced volunteers for the most part—had achieved: a smooth-running, well-synchronized, rich program with something of value for everyone. I was teaching then at a college that had been founded and successfully run by women, but I had thought that only starched nuns or superefficient Hadassah ladies could pull off something so professional, so successful. It was a striking lesson in women's initiative.

From the conference, I began to understand the value of cohorts, the strength one derives from a like-minded community—the support, the testing of ideas, the cross-fertilization. Until then, except for conversations with my husband, the process for me had been a very private one.

I learned to relax, not to be so rigid when it came to women's experimentation with new responsibilities. I had heard there would be a women's minyon during the course of the conference. Naturally, I wouldn't participate! The first minyon was held on Friday night prior to the formal opening of the conference, when I was to deliver the keynote address. I prayed alone in my room, feeling on the one hand quite self-righteous and, on the other, secure in the knowledge that since I knew only two or three people there, no one would notice my absence. By Saturday morning, however, I was a known quantity, and to stay away from the services would have been conspicuous. So very hesitantly I brought myself down to the women's minyon and sat as far back in the room as I could. I was astounded to hear a woman leading the prayers. Next came another surprise—a woman's melodious voice reading the Torah with the perfect cantillation. Somehow, I had thought that only thirteen-year-old boys were equal to the task. I found it very beautiful.

Finally, there came the real shocker. After the Torah reading, I saw two women, acting in the capacity of gabbaim (synagogue officials), coming down the center aisle toward the back where I was sitting. The last thing in the world I wanted was a synagogue honor. I prayed silently, "Please, don't let it be me." Sure enough, they had come to invite me to step forward for the honor of *hagba'ah* (the raising up of the Torah before it is returned to the ark). Choose someone else, I pleaded. They persisted gently but firmly. It was only good breeding that propelled me down the aisle. Then something happened that was to make me think for a long time about the value of practiced skills. I had seen *hagba'ah* performed at least a thousand times in my life. Yet, as I stood there, I had to ask the woman standing next to me, "What do I do now?" Also, to my surprise, caught as I was with my defenses down, I found it an exhilarating moment. It was the first time I had ever held a Torah scroll.

After the conference, I began to think more seriously and to read some of the Jewish feminist literature that had been around for years but that I, in my private putterings, somehow had missed. I came across an article written two years earlier by Rachel Adler that is still one of the finest and most succinct statements I have read on Jewish feminism, and one by Trude Weiss-Rosmarin written as far back as 1969 that dealt cogently with some of the central problems we are still concerned with today. Little by little, I was able to examine what the other Jewish denominations were doing, without ruling something out just because Conservative or Reform or Reconstructionist Judaism had got there first.

Still, it wasn't a smooth path. Like millions of other women and men, I've pretty much stumbled my way through this revolution. Perhaps because the divisions were so clear and sharp and well defined, I often felt an emotional resistance to things I could accept on a theoretical level. Partly because the lines were so heavily drawn, I found it difficult to know what is form and what is essence in the traditional dichotomy between male and female. It was even more difficult to understand that at certain points in a normative religion, form and essence are one and the same—but who can know these intersecting points?

In 1973, I was still able to say, "Women in the Reform rabbinate, that's one thing. As for Orthodox me, I'll take my rabbis male, thank you." The first time I saw a woman draped in a prayer shawl, my instinctive reaction was, *am ha'aretz,* ignoramus. The first time I spotted a young woman wearing a *kipah* in the library of the Jewish Theological Seminary, I thought she was spoofing; it never occurred to me she might be in earnest. As I drew nearer and saw her studying Mishnah, I began to feel a charge of anxiety. For the rest of the morning I couldn't concentrate on my own work. Instead, I tried to figure out what she was doing under that powder-blue *kipah.* And I tried to figure out why I was so uneasy. Was it because, once again, someone had crossed the lines? I know what my reaction will be on that day when I see some smart-aleck woman marching around with tzitzit—the ritual fringes worn by observant Jewish males—hanging out. Maybe, if she's not some kind of exhibitionist but rather a deeply religious Jew, eventually I'll overcome my palpitations and begin to consider what kind of statement she is making. Maybe I'll even have to consider the possibility that my own great-granddaughters will be obligated to wear some equivalent of tzitzit.

Sometimes I found myself switching gears from one moment to the next. One evening, as I sat in a graduate Rabbinic literature course, the professor departed from his explication of the text at hand to comment on an article that had appeared that morning on the front page of *The New York*

Times about the Conservative movement's decision to count women in a minyon. "This Jew," he said, in a tone not quite free of derision, "gets up in the morning. His five children start to get up, and all at once the house is in an uproar. Now he sets off to the synagogue for the early morning minyon. By the time he gets home, his wife has the children washed, dressed, fed, and off to school. The house is quiet again and he sits down to a peaceful breakfast and an hour of leisurely study. When he comes back in the evening from work, the place is an uproar again. So he takes his prayer book and his Bible and goes off to the synagogue again. Now I ask you, what's he going to do if his good wife has to go to the minyon?" This account was greeted by a sustained roar of knowing laughter.

In the classroom at that moment were fourteen yeshiva men—half of them rabbis, the rest preparing for ordination—and me. I laughed along with everyone else, but after three seconds I said to myself, "Why am I laughing?" Was this not a case of how the primal association of men with synagogue as male refuge and women with home and family was communicated, ever so subtly, from one generation to the next? Not wishing to jeopardize my standing in the group and their gracious acceptance of me, I said nothing. I watched as they laughed along without me. Aware of what had passed at that moment, I began to wonder whether the core issue here had to do with Orthodox versus Conservative, as it seemed, or, on a much deeper level, a matter of male versus female. Or was it both, the two inextricably intertwined? And if so, where did that leave me?

I began to discern that just as I was becoming more open and less anxious about my feminist impulses, there were many in the community who were tightening up and closing off. Some of the issues were political as well as religious. In 1976, for instance, my own synagogue was deciding whether to allow women a membership vote. Several women asked me what the rule was in other synagogues. I had no idea, so I undertook an unscientific survey and called ten Orthodox synagogues in the New York area. About one-third of them allowed women to vote; one even had a woman vice-president. In one case, the associate rabbi told me that women could not vote, but then again, he added, neither could the men; synagogue affairs here were the preserve of a three-man oligarchy. At another synagogue the secretary would not put me through to the rabbi. When she heard what I was calling about, she retorted, "Of course women don't vote here; it's against the Torah. You can't bother the rabbi with such foolish questions." At a third synagogue, the cheery sexton who took my call replied, "When women come to the 7:00 A.M. minyon, I'll give them the vote." I didn't ask him whether he applied that rule to all the voting members of the synagogue; I already knew the answer.

I found certain other issues quite offensive, too, such as the discussion over the Rabbinic precept *kol ishah ervah* ("a woman's voice leads to licentiousness," implying that women may not sing in the presence of men). *Kol ishah* had not been a popular theme in Orthodoxy in the 50s and 60s; if the precept had any religious redeeming value, it clearly escaped me. I half suspected that *kol ishah* was dredged up in the 70s as a counterpoint to women's new freedom of expression, and I openly debated the issue as the need arose. To me, *kol ishah* seemed nothing but an overt slur on the female sex, an arbitrary curb on women in the name of a one-sided modesty meter. Could this be the mild-mannered yeshiva girl speaking?

For me, at least, the process is not over, this interweaving of feminism and Judaism. Because one is continuously exposed to those encounters and incidents that affect one's worldview, I suspect I will have ample occasion to go through several more cycles of thought and feeling before it all stabilizes. I intend to keep my eyes wide open, watching to see what works and what doesn't, what is viable within the framework of Jewish tradition and what isn't. I hope to gain a clearer picture of where the lines should be drawn, which respected authorities should draw them, and where to push further.

Two things I know for sure. My questioning never will lead me to abandon tradition. I am part of a chain that is too strong to break, and though it needs no protection from me, a child of the tradition, I want to protect it with the fierceness of a mother protecting her young. But I also know that I never can yield the new value of women's equality, even though it may conflict with Jewish tradition. To do so would be to affirm the principle of a hierarchy of male and female, and this I no longer believe to be an axiom of Judaism.

I feel instinctively that drawing the lines is important and correct at both fundamental and transcendental levels. Divisions of labor and function are, in fact, humanly expedient; there is a remarkable staying power of sexual identity and distinctiveness, the uniqueness of male and female beyond biology. Yet there are many instances in which the sex-role divisions in Judaism do not work. To deny participation in this or that experience because one is a man or a woman is an act of inhumanity. Somehow, Judaism will have to find a way to bridge the gap.

Meanwhile, there is probably a great deal of tension in store for people like me. But that no longer frightens me, neither personally nor in terms of the system. In fact, I suspect—indeed, I know—that ultimately Judaism will emerge stronger and not weaker from this encounter with feminism. Happiness for a mild-mannered yeshiva girl? Less naiveté perhaps, more unrest, a constant probing, endless queries. Surely that's no blueprint for happiness. But the engagement of Judaism and feminism offers something else: New heights to scale, a deeper sense of maturity, and an enlarged scope of responsibility for oneself, society, and the continuity of tradition—exactly what the religious endeavor is all about.

The Hollywood Image of American Jewish Women

Letty Cotton Pogrebin is a journalist, social commentator, and feminist critic. Here is her account of how Hollywood has treated Jewish women in its films since the 1950s. The essay was published in 1991.

In junior high school, my girlfriends and I used to play a game we called "Choose or Die."

"If you had to give up one of your five senses, which would it be?" we asked each other.

"Suppose there's a nuclear attack and Serkin and Katz, the two worst teachers in school, are the only ones left. Who would you pick for homeroom?"

"Who would you marry if you absolutely *had* to choose between stupid handsome Bobby and smart geeky Ben?"

Such agonizing hypothetical exercises prepared young women for a world of narrow choices, limited social roles . . . and Hollywood movies.

I remembered Choose or Die when I started thinking about how much motion pictures have influenced my life. Until recent years, when I took the trouble to educate myself about Jewish women, I had been exposed to so few religious or historical heroines that movie characters found their way into my psyche with little competition from grander or more mythic personages. Movie women entered, good and bad, with their grating voices and their funny lines, their kind eyes, round bosoms, and oversized gestures; skittish women, brown-haired usually, women with the contours of a cello; screamers and whiners, women who give the anti-Semites plenty to write home about, and women who could have been my grandmothers.

Other than life experience, nothing left a deeper imprint on my formative self than the movies. They took me out of the hothouse of my family, beyond the confines of the Jamaica Jewish Center, and away from the neighborhood where I grew up believing that everyone was either Jewish or Catholic and another word for Catholic was Protestant. Except for a few of my father's conventions, one trip to Miami when I was a baby, and another when I was ten, my parents took me no farther from Jamaica than the Catskills, and until I went away to college I took myself no farther than my cousin's apartment in the Bronx. Hollywood was my bridge to the outside world.

I went to the movies almost every Saturday after shul. My friends and I walked to 165th Street and Jamaica Avenue, to the Loew's Valencia, a three-thousand-seat "atmospheric" movie palace (now the Tabernacle of the Prayer for All People) which in itself was a fantasy world. The interior was a vivid recreation of a Venetian Moorish courtyard at twilight, its vaulted heaven a rival to the Hayden Planetarium. Projected against a cerulean sky were a moon, twinkling stars, and a continuous procession of filmy white clouds. Along the walls was etched the dark silhouette of a medieval skyline with parapets and turrets, crenelated rooftops and Spanish archways, and up front at the center of it all was the movie screen, the bridge to Anywhere.

Woody Allen wasn't the only child of my generation who dived headlong into the world according to Hollywood. I *loved* the movies. I loved anything with Bogart or Gable, Fred Astaire or Cary Grant, and my favorite women—the wholesome blond Bettys—Hutton and Grable—the waterlogged Esther Williams, the terminally cute June Allyson, and also Vera Ellen, Doris Day, Ruth Roman (who was rumored to be Jewish), and the peerless Hepburns, Katharine and then Audrey. These stars taught me what was expected of Americans; but the films I loved best were those that taught me what was expected of Jews. As a child, I used the movies as a litmus test and lesson plan to guide my growing up; and later, as an escape from my impacted religious rebellion into the open field of cultural Judaism where I found something of an alternative identity. I studied the Jewish women: Is that how I'm supposed to behave? Is she what I can hope to become? Am I like that? Is anyone? Above all, the movies helped me define the Jewish women I did *not* want to be.

Recently, to revisit these images, I became the best customer of the local video store, renting two or three cassettes a day to refresh my recollection of films with Jewish characters. Why this sudden desire to saturate myself with movie memories? No doubt the same impulse that has contributed to my writing this book: a need for

answers to the most obscure questions of my identity. A search for how I formulated my ideas of Jewish womanhood; a search for coherence in my past that might even include the movies. As I watched one film after another, I discovered that no matter how good the movie might have been artistically, the female characters left me feeling bad. Not one of them could be considered a complete Jewish heroine, a fully realized, positive, well-balanced, successful, or admirable Jewish woman. Not one aroused in me that uncomplicated "Gee I'd like to be her" fantasy that scores of male film characters activate in the male imagination. Instead, the best I could find were women who made the least intolerable trade-offs, those who did not have to pay too high a price for being themselves.

For instance, Choose or Die: *If you had to live your life as Marjorie Morningstar or Yentl, which would you be?*

If you choose Marjorie, be prepared to give up your identity. You'll be pampered, praised, educated-but-empty—a slate on which men write their dreams and project their inadequacies. But choose Yentl and you'll have to give up love and family; pay for your spirituality by disguising or renouncing your sexuality; pretend to be a man so that you may be a scholar; discover that the only way to be true to yourself is to live a lie. Take your pick: Marjorie's bourgeois subordination or Yentl's lonely rebellion. Some choice!

Again, Choose or Die: *If you had to be the mother in* Marjorie Morningstar *or the mother in* Portnoy's Complaint, *what's your pleasure?*

Here, it's six of one and half a dozen of the other. Both are caricatures, but if you were up against the wall in the forced-choice game, you'd probably opt for Marjorie's mother on the grounds of class. At least she lives on Central Park West, while Mrs. Portnoy hangs her apron strings in a Brooklyn walk-up.

Most films with Jewish characters seemed to have very little human complexity. What I found instead were four debilitating stereotypes, two familiar ones—the Jewish-American Princess and the Jewish Mother—and two that I call the Jewish Man's Burden and the Jewish Big Mouth. By deconstructing these stereotypes and examining how they function in some of the most memorable films of the past thirty years, I began to see where I and my generation got our ideas about

Jewish-American womanhood and why we had so much to unlearn before we could claim a proud Jewish female identity.

To begin with, let me establish some thumbnail definitions of these four stereotypes as the culture sees them:

The Jewish-American Princess is a spoiled, materialistic, vapid, demanding, self-absorbed brat who twists Daddy around her little finger and stalks a husband who will support her in the style to which her father has made her accustomed. She's trendy, sexy-looking, but, alas, frigid. She's tired, she has a headache, sex is inconvenient; she prefers shopping. She's a clotheshorse, an inveterate home decorator, a collector of furs, jewelry, and vacations. She loves to entertain but hates to cook. "What does she make for dinner?" asks the Jewish comedian. "Reservations." What's on her bumper sticker? I BRAKE FOR BARGAINS.

Several movies of the last thirty years have helped mold the JAP image. *Marjorie* started it all in 1958, *Goodbye, Columbus* fleshed it out in 1969, *Private Benjamin* took it into parody in 1980, and in the past decade, *Flamingo Kid* and *Down and Out in Beverly Hills* updated it by inventing a significant sub-genre, the middle-aged Jewish-American Princess.

The second familiar stereotype, the Jewish Mother (J.M.), comes to life on the screen as a loving Yiddishe mama (like Sara in *The Jazz Singer*), hard-working shtetl wife (like Golda in *Fiddler on the Roof*), or repellent shrew (like Aunt Gladys in *Goodbye, Columbus*, the tush-kissing Momma in *Where's Poppa?* and the humiliating Hovercraft mother-in-the-sky in Woody Allen's *Oedipus Wrecks*, from the trilogy *New York Stories*).

At the loving end of the spectrum, the J.M. is a nurturing, self-sacrificing character of warmth and dignity—the 1950s television character Mollie Goldberg, say, or an Old World sage like the grandmother in *Crossing Delancey*—or else a crusty martyr like the mothers in *Brighton Beach Memoirs, Radio Days,* and *Beaches.* Either way, you laugh at her but you love her.

Love is out of the question when it comes to the shrill harpy at the other end of the spectrum. This Jewish Mother is a world-class guilt-tripper. Her every word sets your teeth on edge. She is crass, bullying, asexual, *anti*sexual, and of course a food fetishist. She emasculates her husband, infantilizes her sons, overprotects her daughters,

overfeeds everyone, and obsesses about digestion and elimination.

For instance, take Sophie Portnoy. *Please!* Her turf: the kitchen. Her job: standing with an ear to the bathroom door. Her definition of sin: eating *chazerai.* Her conversational style: "Alex! What is it with those bowels?"

Take your choice: Long-suffering mothers or mothers who made other people suffer. Some choice!

The third stereotype found at the movies is the one I'm calling the Jewish Big Mouth. While the Princess demands her privileges, the Big Mouth demands her rights. Often an Ugly Duckling, she is so bright, funny, accomplished, and confident that people forget her looks. But she has one major problem: She acts like a person. She lets everyone, especially the men in her life, know who she is and what she thinks. If she wants something, she goes for it. A nonconformist, she won't play her assigned role—either as a Jew or as a Woman.

This character is best exemplified in Barbra Streisand's Jewish trilogy, *Funny Girl, The Way We Were,* and *Yentl.* Although these movies were released years apart, watching them more recently in sequence revealed the Achilles' heel, if you will, of the endearing Big Mouth. Although she still appeals to me above all other character types, and holds great promise for self-respecting Jewish women, she comes with a curse: She is not allowed to have it all. She has to pay a price for her independence, and the price is love.

The fourth category, the Jewish Man's Burden, parallels the convention that once described Third World blacks as the White Man's Burden. The Jewish Man's Burden is the Jewish woman whom he views as primitive and underdeveloped. She is an embarrassment to him, like the new immigrant wife in *Hester Street.* She's a drag on his social climbing, like Tina Balzer in *Diary of a Mad Housewife.* She's an albatross, like the bride with egg salad on her face in *Heartbreak Kid,* or the shallow, whiny Bette Midler character in *Ruthless People.* The Jewish Man's Burden stands between him and the American dream. She is an unwanted "too Jewish" reminder of his origins and an unendurable obstacle to his advancement.

These stereotypes operate on different levels depending on whether a film is *implicitly* or *explicitly* Jewish. Implicitly Jewish movies are those in which the character's Judaism is incidental or is implied only by context or cultural reference markers—which is very different from movies in which a character's Jewishness is explicitly stated, intrinsic to the theme, or integral to the story's tension or conflict.

A film is explicit when it is about being Jewish the way *Diary of Anne Frank, Portnoy's Complaint, Hester Street,* and *Yentl* are about being Jewish. Anne Frank's life in hiding during Hitler's Reich is a uniquely, unmistakably *Jewish* story. Portnoy blames his complaint, his impotence, on his Jewish mother and his self-prescribed cure is avoidance of all Jewish women. *Yentl* and *Hester Street* draw on Halachic imperatives and Old World texture to explore the tension between Jewish tradition and women's changing roles and aspirations.

In contrast to these sharply focused Jewish plots, other films have casual, offhand Jewish references. *Hello Dolly!,* for example, is not *about* being Jewish, it is about a woman who happens to be Jewish. It is a story of the time-honored non-sectarian pursuit of a husband, yet it communicates information about Jewish women by implication. The syllogism is subliminal: (a) We know Dolly Levi is meddlesome and manipulative; (b) We know Dolly Levi is Jewish; therefore (c), women who are Jewish are meddlesome and manipulative.

Never mind that Dolly's Judaism has absolutely no bearing on the plot and no relevance to the other characters, all of whom seem to be Gentile. We're not talking logic here, we're talking stereotypes. The minute there is a whiff of Jewishness in the air, the associations are set in motion.

The whiff is weak in *Dolly, Mad Housewife,* and *Flamingo Kid;* somewhat stronger in *Funny Girl, The Way We Were,* and *Dirty Dancing;* and overpowering in *Morningstar, Heartbreak Kid, Private Benjamin,* and *Beaches.* But there's a subliminal syllogism in every one of those films, and because the negative byproduct is so much less conscious than that put out by the explicit *Yentl* or *Portnoy,* its impact may be more pernicious.

Jewish film characters, male or female, no matter how vaguely drawn, seem to be emblematic of Jews in a way that non-Jewish film characters—with the possible exception of Italian Mafia types—are rarely emblematic of a group of Christians. As soon as we know that we are watching Jews, we engage in a circular dynamic. We ascribe weight to these stereotypes because of the power of the film image, and then those weighty character traits become prescriptive. They function as a form of social control, or role modeling by innuendo. For Jewish women, certainly for me, this dynamic has created a choose-or-die game of limited moves.

Looking back at the power of Hollywood's messages, *Marjorie Morningstar* seemed to be my starting point. Ostensibly a love story about a young woman who goes away from home and falls for the wrong man, it is also a Jewish family saga and an ethnic message movie. By including scenes involving a Bar Mitzvah, a family seder, and a Jewish wedding, this movie clearly establishes its ethnic roots. Therefore, the behavior of Rose and her daughter, Marjorie, is seen as unambiguously Jewish feminine behavior. And here is what it says about us.

Rose, the mother, is a climber. "An ordinary Bar Mitzvah wasn't good enough for you," complains her husband. "Ever since we moved from the Bronx, nothing is good enough." Rose buys Marjorie a new outfit for every occasion so her princess can attract the right kind of husband. Rose nags, schemes, is sexually repressive and given to odd monetary references. Faced with Marjorie's rising libido, Rose says, "Save those feelings. Put them in the bank." She sends Uncle Sampson to guard what is "more important than Fort Knox," meaning Marjorie's virtue which is under siege by Noel Airman (formerly Ehrman), the handsome, older theater director at the Catskill resort.

Even though Noel is Jewish, he's not husband material. We deduce that through coded messages. His black outfits, Christianized first name, and Americanized last name establish that he is disconnected from the faith, a luftmensch, an insubstantial, free-floating "air man," a nothing. "A man has to be something," Rose proclaims.

A woman, however, can be nothing. Marjorie Morgenstern takes a job in Noel's summer theater but proves untalented as an actress. Wasp-waisted, whiny, eternally awed, apologetic, and virginal, all she wants is "someone to love." Noel dubs her Marjorie Morningstar, as if changing her name will free her from Jewish moral constraints. But she herself admits she wants excitement without risk. "I'm afraid to break the rules," she says.

For Marjorie—and all of us Marjories of the 1950s—it was a no-win situation: If she rejects Noel's advances, she remains Daddy's little girl, patriarchy's virgin, and Judaism's daughter. But giving in to the apostate in black would mean defying her parents, heritage, and gender imperatives. When she chooses Noel, Marjorie (like the Jews in mid-twentieth-century America) allows herself to be seduced by rebellion and assimilation. With an air man, she is doomed to be as evanescent as a morning star. It's all there in the names.

Hollywood's symbol of second-generation Jewish manhood is not a lawyer, doctor, or businessman, but the precursor of bad boy Philip Roth, the sort of man who describes Jewishness as the antithesis of freedom. Noel ridicules Marjorie for resisting his brand of liberation. He calls her a "Shirley"—his nickname for a Jewish tease who trades sex for matrimony. He predicts Marjorie will end up married to a doctor with a practice in New Rochelle—a prophecy that will be fulfilled thirty years later in another Catskill movie, *Dirty Dancing,* in which the main character has a doctor father and a mother named Marjorie but, significantly, this time the daughter has big plans to be a somebody.

In a line drenched with disdain, Noel says the destiny of a Shirley "was charted by five thousand years of Moses and the Ten Commandments."

Such statements trotted home with me from the movie house on the back of another subliminal syllogism: (a) Marjorie is Jewish; (b) Marjorie is a Shirley; therefore (c), Jewish girls are Shirleys. Shirley, of course, was the first JAP, but not the last.

"Marjorie, you *are* your mother," says Noel, compounding the insult, warning us that JAPs become Jewish Mothers and Jewish mothers raise new JAPs who become again like their mothers. So goes the gospel of Jewish continuity according to Wouk, Roth, Mailer, and other literary princes who created this modern mythology to deal with their own renunciation of their pre-American past.

The concept of the Jewish woman as a reminder of a man's origins is played out more overtly and with varying degrees of offensiveness in movies about The Jewish Man's Burden.

Hester Street opens on the Lower East Side in 1896. Jake has been living here for a few years and feels like a full-fledged American. He speaks English, goes to dance halls, dates the thoroughly modern Mamie. "Here a Jew is a mensch," he says. "In Russia, I was afraid to walk ten feet near a Gentile." When his wife, Gitl, arrives from the Old Country with their son, she threatens to pull Jake back to the old ways. He despises her immigrant habits and superstitions. He wants his son to have a baseball in his pocket, not salt to protect against the Evil Eye. And he wants Gitl to give up her *sheitel,* the wig worn by married Orthodox women to cover their hair from men's view.

Gitl refuses. "I won't be a *goya* even for my husband," she says. Jake demands a divorce so he can marry Mamie. Before Gitl will agree, she makes the happy couple fork up $300, all of Mamie's savings. You want to get rid of your burden? this frankly antiassimilationist film seems to be warning us. Okay, but it'll cost you.

Diary of a Mad Housewife is as vague in its ethnics as *Hester Street* is explicit. But the husband Jonathan Balzer (ballsy?) carries the whiff of Jewishness to anyone who buys the stereotype of the insufferably demanding, upwardly mobile lawyer with an apartment on Central Park West. Along with his maniacal pursuit of brand names and the "right" friends, Jonathan wants his wife, Tina, to be a status object as well. He complains about everything from her hair, to her four-minute eggs, to her shyness.

"Don't hang onto me," he tells her at a party. "Circulate."

He accuses her of holding him back in his career. In the end, when *he* has made a complete mess of their lives, *she* goes into therapy.

Until I saw her again on my VCR, I had forgotten how much the Jewish bride (Jeannie Berlin) in *Heartbreak Kid* had embarrassed me. Rather than deal with my feelings at the time, I laughed at the revolting Lila along with everyone else in the audience. Seeing the film again recalled my sense of passive degradation as I watched the groom, Lenny (Charles Grodin), find fault with Lila immediately after their wedding, ridicule the way she makes love, the way she keeps talking about the next fifty years, the way she sings and eats egg salad and goes to the bathroom and gets hideously sunburned. Oh yes, and she can't swim. For God's sake, every American kid knows how to swim, but not the disgusting Lila. Lenny's view of Lila humiliates *us.*

Three days into his honeymoon, Lenny meets Kelly Corchran (Cybill Shepherd), the golden *shiksa* from Minnesota, blond, rich, spoiled, a JAP in WASP clothing. Kelly *can* swim. Kelly and Lenny swim *together.* You can almost hear *America the Beautiful* playing in the background when he tells her, "I've been waiting for a girl like you all my life." He divorces Lila—his Jewish burden, his Jewish past—and with knavery and pretense, succeeds in marrying Kelly. In the last scene of the movie, surrounded by small talk and Midwestern wedding guests, Lenny sits dazed and lost amid alien corn. He got his wish; now he has to live with it.

Because of that devastating final scene, I can't say whether Jewish men took the movie as pro*shiksa* or anti*shiksa,* but I am sure that no Jewish woman felt good about hailing from the same tribe as the pitiful, loathsome Lila.

The wife in *Ruthless People* (Bette Midler) is a different sort of loathsome and also a transitional figure—a kind of JAP gone gross. She starts out fat, vulgar, and self-indulgent. Her husband married her for her money and now he wants to dump her for his Gentile mistress. He gets rid of *his* Jewish burden by refusing to pay the ransom when she's kidnapped. As for the Jewish wife, captivity brings out the best in her. She makes friends with her kidnappers, loses weight, and discovers she has talent in the *shmatte* game. Which only proves that one man's burden is another man's chief executive officer.

The JAP's capacity for change is developed best in *Private Benjamin,* which is why I ended up liking this movie quite a lot. By the time she was eight, Judy Benjamin knew her heart's desire: "All I want is a big house, nice clothes, a live-in maid, and a professional man." Her wish comes true in the person of her second husband, Yale Goodman. (Again, check out the name: The assimilated Ivy League Jew is a good man to find.) Yale is a sharp, successful lawyer whose sexual artistry ranges from a forced blow job in the back seat of a parked car, to a near-rape on the bathroom floor, both of which Judy tolerates as familiar indignities, that is, until she realizes that he has not just come but gone.

Is his untimely death a warning that a JAP can be fatal to a Yalie? That may be stretching it, but prior to the stunning denouement on the bathroom floor, other unambiguous aspects of the JAP stereotype have already been established. Judy has forcefully reprimanded her upholsterer for using the wrong mushroom-colored fabric on her ottomans, proving herself adept at handling domestic crises. Like Marjorie, Judy has also shown herself to be a skilled Daddy's girl—oriented to the man of the house from whom all bounty flows, but not expecting much more from him than money. On her wedding day, Daddy gives Judy a hefty check, then turns back to his TV. Marjorie's father realized too late, "Maybe I should have spent more time with you; I've been neglectful." Judy's father doesn't know how old his daughter is and doesn't care.

Widowed after six hours of marriage, Judy moans, "I've never not belonged to somebody. If I'm not going to be married, I don't know what to do with myself."

So she joins the army. Too stupid to see through the recruiter's lies about boot camp luxuries, she arrives at basic training asking, "Where are the yachts?" She files her nails, bitches about her fatigues—"Is this the only color these come in?"—and is personally offended by her sleeping quarters. When she realizes this is army life, she wants to revoke her enlistment and go home.

Daddy comes to the rescue, scolding, "How could you do this to your parents? Haven't we given you everything you wanted? Didn't I get you into college? Bail you out of your first marriage? Why are you punishing us? You were never a smart girl. You are obviously incapable of making your own decisions."

This recitation sounds like an indictment of Jewish princesses and their royal families when in fact it could be applied to millions of non-Jews, including the golden Kelly Corchran and her white-bread parents. Yet the movie makes the Benjamins' behavior seem uniquely Jewish—as if only a Jewish daughter is supposed to fulfill certain roles and expectations, as if only Jewish parents take it personally when a child diverges from their teachings, as if only Jewish parents have ever tried to make life easier for their children, or kept a daughter too weak to take care of herself.

When I first saw *Private Benjamin,* I defended against the stereotype from the point of view of its target, the young Jewish woman. This time, I found myself objecting from the perspective of Judy's parents. I had crossed the generational line, but the scene did not get any easier to watch. To me JAPs are no joke.

Private Benjamin didn't find the image funny either. After her father's insulting harangue, she decides to stay in the army despite its hardships, and proceeds to distinguish herself as a soldier of considerable courage and intelligence.

I confess to feeling a tad squeamish about the implied syllogism here: (a) former JAP finds self-respect in the army; (b) the army stands for America; therefore (c), for a young Jewish woman to become self-respecting she must join the American mainstream. This message is not so great either for Jews or women. It takes the position that female emancipation and Jewish culture are incompatible; that to choose personhood, a woman must necessarily renounce peoplehood. Rather than accept such a bifurcation, I wanted to see the army as a kind of Outward Bound program for Judy and not a metaphor for her assimilation. But the movie wouldn't let me off the hook.

To drive home its point, Judy falls in love with a French-Jewish gynecologist. If the army represents assimilation into mainstream America, the new lover represents the next best thing, assimilation into aristocratic Judaism. But gradually, we watch the gynecologist—symbol of both the adored Jewish professional man and all male experts who presume to know more about women than we do ourselves—become unfaithful and belittling, and we watch Judy backslide into domesticated JAPdom. Then, just as they are about to exchange marriage vows, she sees the light. She challenges the doctor (imagine *that!*) when he makes the mistake of calling her stupid. She throws a punch at him, tosses off her wedding veil, and strides into the sunset—presumably to a new life as a strong-willed, self-assured Big Mouth, a breed that, despite its problems, yields Hollywood's most admirable female film characters.

As long as we have to put up with stereotypes, let's admit that some stereotypes are better than others. Just as most Jewish men would rather be denounced as the smart, industrious Jew than the stingy, clannish Jew, I would rather identify with a Jewish Big Mouth than a JAP.

In all the films I reviewed I found only one unlikable Jewish Big Mouth: Naomi, the strident, hypercritical Israeli in, what else, *Portnoy's Complaint.* "I went with a Jewish girl and I can't

get it up in the state of Israel," says Alex, reconvinced that Jewish women are his problem.

Other than Naomi, the Jewish Big Mouth is the closest thing to a winner that we've got in films. From *Anne Frank* to *Funny Girl* to *The Way We Were* to *Dirty Dancing,* the character of the clever, outspoken Jewish girl has become a film convention that empowers everywoman. Most important, films portraying the Ugly Duckling who rises above her appearance have assured girls with big noses and frizzy hair that they too can invent their own kind of terrific and leave Miss America in the dust. Jewish women could take comfort in the triumph of wit and brains over conventional beauty. We may not be able to do much about the WASP ideal and its judgmental view of "ethnic" looks but we could try to get a little smarter every year.

The progenitor of the Jewish Big Mouth character was none other than thirteen-year-old Anne Frank. As powerful as the diary was to read, seeing the film's Anne function despite many confinements—the confinement of her Amsterdam hiding place, of her traditional Jewish family, and of the suffocating Nazi juggernaut—left me with an indelible image of her bravery and spunk. "I'm living a great adventure," Anne says. "I want to write . . . I want to go on living even after my death." "I don't want to be dignified," she tells Peter, the boy whose family shares the attic. "I want some fun."

Anne Frank serves as a shining rebuttal to the insipid antifun *Marjorie Morningstar,* released the previous year. Anne herself, representing the new Jewish woman, directly challenges the other three female archetypes in her story:

She challenges her own Jewish mother— "Mother and I have nothing in common. When I try to explain my views, she asks me if I'm constipated." She challenges her docile sister—"I won't have them walk all over me like Margot. I've got to fight things out for myself. Make something of myself." Though Margot is supposedly the pretty one, Anne outshines her as a bonfire outshines a streetlamp. And she challenges Peter's mother, another middle-aged JAP figure, played by Shelley Winters, who talks of little else but her fur coat and her father, who gave her "the best money could buy."

In contrast to these women, the headstrong, rambunctious Anne sends an electrical charge through the attic, disturbing the peace. "You need an old-fashioned spanking," says Mr. Van Dam, Peter's father, who loses patience with her big mouth. "A man likes a girl who'll listen to him. A domestic girl who likes to cook and sew. Why do you show off all the time? Why not be nice and quiet like your sister Margot?"

"I'll open my veins first," shouts the glorious Anne. "I'm going to be remarkable."

And so she is. By the film's end, when the Nazis barge in, we have seen glimpses of the extraordinary woman she would have become. We see it best in the way she welcomes and comes to terms with her burgeoning sexuality. Thumbing her nose at propriety and defying the realities of confinement, Anne creates a magical romantic separateness, majestically dons a shawl and gloves, and visits Pater alone in his room as if it was an elegant rendezvous rather than a few square feet of space at death's door. Their hours together are filled with palpable sexual energy, good conversation, and mutual respect, a paradigm of friendship and love.

You can't do much better than that. Except of course to survive. But we've never been able to have it all. Something's got to give. In the best of the Jewish Big Mouth films–the Streisand trilogy, *Dirty Dancing*, and *Beaches*–strong Jewish women don't lose their lives, but they lose their loves.

In *Funny Girl*, Fanny Brice loses Nick Arnstein because her success unmans him. The same scenario is played out in *Beaches* when Bette Midler's character, C.C., a singing star very like herself, loses her John. In *The Way We Were*, Katie (Streisand) loses Hubbell (Robert Redford) because her passion and commitment disturb the calm of WASP stability and confidence. Yentl loses Avigdor, her friend, soul mate, and Talmud study partner, because the sources say one cannot be all that, and a woman. And in *Dirty Dancing*, Baby loses Johnny, because a member of the Painters and Plasterers Union is no match for a girl who's planning to change the world.

Compared to other romantic losses in traditional American films, these girl-loses-boy deprivations are oddly, gratefully unhumiliating. That is because all five women are deeply loved in the leaving. It is the *situation* not the woman that is judged to be impossible. It is patriarchy, Orthodoxy, or classism that causes the impasse, each a condition that is not immutable, a condition we

can hope to change. Fanny and Nick, and C.C. and John, would be fine in a society that accepts a wife's public prominence as readily as a husband's. Katie and Hubbell might be together if women activists were viewed as heroes, not troublemakers. Yentl and Avigdor could pursue their passion for Talmud *and* each other, if Judaism did not so vengefully guard its gender ghettos. And Johnny and Baby might have made it if our culture didn't demand that women marry up.

Besides being well-loved, all five female protagonists share another positive quality. When her guy is gone, each woman has something left: Fanny and C.C. have their spectacular careers, Katie her antiwar protests, Yentl has Talmud, and Baby has her whole life ahead of her. The point is, when things don't work out each woman still knows who *she* is.

"I'm a bagel in a place full of onion rolls," proclaims Fanny, who felt destined to be a star, despite her American Beauty nose. "I'm a natural hollerer," she says. She won't let Ziegfeld tell her what to sing, and she refuses to compete with the beautiful Follies showgirls; she comes onstage as a pregnant bride, and wins the spotlight through laughter. Her personal life is not so controllable. Nick wants to be the head of the family and Fanny wants to be a Sadie, a married lady (which I suppose is a grown-up Shirley), but she's not good at faking deference or subordination.

Yentl won't fake it either. After Avigdor learns that his brilliant little study partner is really a woman, he proposes that she be his wife and that he do the thinking for both of them. But Yentl cannot deposit her brilliance in a stewpot. She cannot squelch her passion for Talmudic discourse or overcome her ineptness at the traditional female role. While living with Hadass, a model Jewish wife, she has come to understand the seductive appeal of female solicitousness—the peace in it for a man, the flattery, the comfort. But Yentl can never be a Hadass. "I want to study with you, not darn your socks," she protests. Avigdor insists being his wife should be enough. Echoing Freud's famous question, he asks, "What more do you want?" Yentl answers for millions of us: "More."

In *The Way We Were* and *Dirty Dancing*, the love theme contains an important difference: The object of the woman's affections is a Gentile and the theme is Jewish Big Mouth Wins Gorgeous Goy by Being Her Intense Natural Self. Since we know by now that stereotypes symbolize much more than themselves, we could translate that to read The Jewish People Finally Make Good in America. However, in both movies, girl loses boy, *willingly*. To me, these movies are warning Jews not to sell our souls for a piece of the American dream.

Ultimately, I took *The Way We Were* and *Dirty Dancing* not as antiassimilation stories but as subtle films of Jewish pride in which the ethical standard is upheld by a female. Both are *women's* films. The sex scenes are tuned into female fantasies and in one or two encounters the women are the sexual initiators. Jewish women *kvell* (beam with pride) watching Barbra Streisand and Jennifer Gray, with their frizzy hair and non-pug noses, win the love of Robert Redford and Patrick Swayze. We tell ourselves, "If she can do it, I could do it—if I wanted to."

At the same time, we understand that neither union can last because each woman in her way is too Jewish to compromise; and also because each woman is a cut above her man—and in this culture, that's not allowed; the masculine rules of hegemony hold fast.

Katie Moroski, a working-class woman who fights to save the world from fascism, red-baiting, and nuclear war, is the moral superior of Hubbell Gardner, the Beekman Place Adonis, star athlete, and dashing naval officer, who wrote about himself, "He was like his country; everything came easy to him." *The Way We Were* is about *not* doing it the easy way, not compromising, not selling out your principles, not laughing at Eleanor Roosevelt jokes or ironing your kinky hair, or naming names for the red-baiters.

Dirty Dancing continues what was begun in the Catskills with *Marjorie Morningstar*; in fact, the two stories bracket the thirty-year development of the Jewish female protagonist in American film. *Dirty Dancing* is both a message movie and a showcase for message stereotypes:

There's Baby, the Jewish idealist who's "gonna change the world"; Lisa, her JAP sister, who's "gonna decorate it"; Daddy, the doctor who fixes everything; the Jewish Mother, here a quiet background figure but mischievously and symbolically named Marjorie; the waiters, all Jewish Princes—law students, medical students, and egomaniacs—and Johnny Castle, the new royalty, the working-class idol who attracts Jewish women with his decency and his dirty dancing.

Here, ethnicity's stock characters are flipped on their heads. Gentile Johnny is a kind, sweet, hard-working guy who is exploited by Jewish employers and sex-starved Jewish women. Lest we cry anti-Semitism, Baby redeems the Jews: She wants to send her leftovers to Southeast Asia; she helps people, tells the truth, plans to major in the economics of underdeveloped countries in order to enlist in the Peace Corps. In such a future there's no place for a guy like Johnny Castle.

The movie suggests that for achieving Jewish women, hot sex is as off-limits as working-class Gentiles; there are more important things in life than pleasure. Johnny understands what Noel didn't—that he is a man for one season, a summer fling. He knows Baby is beyond him. At the last big event of the summer, he honors her publicly as "the kind of person I want to be."

You've come a long way, Baby. Thirty years separate Marjorie's Catskill movie from Baby's. In that time, Jennifer Gray, a Jew, has replaced the non-Jewish Natalie Wood in the starring role, and the male love interest is no longer a man in black who calls her a Shirley, but a man in black who calls her his hero. From that summer to this, the Jewish woman has gained a self and a future.

But Baby hasn't come *all* the way. Today, she's going to *be* somebody—but she may not be *with* somebody. The forced choice is still there. Choose or Die. Either/Or. A great love or a full life. In the movies of the next thirty years, I'll be looking for both.

A New York Princess in Nazi-Land

Erica Mann Jong is a New York Jewish novelist and poet, the author of many good books and highly regarded in the Manhattan literary world, as witness to her election as President of the Author's Guild. But to the public at large she is mainly known for one book, *Fear of Flying*, published in 1973. It has gone through innumerable printings and translations and perhaps in the past two decades has been outsold only by the Christian Bible. It is a blatantly autobiographical picaresque novel about the sexual liberation of a New York Jewish princess. Here she encounters the legacy of Nazi anti-Semitism.

There were 117 psychoanalysts on the Pan Am flight to Vienna and I'd been treated by at least six of them. And married a seventh. God knows it was a tribute either to the shrinks' ineptitude or my own glorious unanalyzability that I was now, if anything, more scared of flying than when I began my analytic adventures some thirteen years earlier.

My husband grabbed my hand therapeutically at the moment of takeoff.

"Christ—it's like ice," he said. He ought to know the symptoms by now since he's held my hand on lots of other flights. My fingers (and toes) turn to ice, my stomach leaps upward into my rib cage, the temperature in the tip of my nose drops to the same level as the temperature in my fingers, my nipples stand up and salute the inside of my bra (or in this case, dress—since I'm not wearing a bra), and for one screaming minute my heart and the engines correspond as we attempt to prove again that the laws of aerodynamics are not the flimsy superstitions which, in my heart of hearts, I *know* they are. Never mind the diabolical explanations of air-foil you get in Pan Am's multilingual INFORMATION TO PASSENGERS, I happen to be convinced that only my own concentration (and that of my mother—who always seems to *expect* her children to die in a plane crash) keeps this bird aloft. I congratulate myself on every successful takeoff, but not too enthusiastically because it's also part of my personal religion that the minute you grow overconfident and really *relax* about the

flight, the plane crashes instantly. Constant vigilance, that's my motto. A mood of cautious optimism should prevail. But actually my mood is better described as cautious pessimism. OK, I tell myself, we *seem* to be off the ground and into the clouds but the danger isn't past. This is, in fact, the most perilous patch of air. Right here over Jamaica Bay where the plane banks and turns and the "No Smoking" sign goes off. This may well be where we go screaming down in thousands of flaming pieces. So I keep concentrating very hard, helping the pilot (a reassuringly midwestern voice named Donnelly) fly the 250-passenger motherfucker. Thank God for his crew cut and middle-America diction. New Yorker that I am, I would never trust a pilot with a New York accent.

As soon as the seat-belt sign goes off and people begin moving about the cabin, I glance around nervously to see who's on board. There's a big-breasted mama-analyst named Rose Schwamm-Lipkin with whom I recently had a consultation about whether or not I should leave my current analyst (who isn't, mercifully, in evidence). There's Dr. Thomas Frommer, the harshly Teutonic expert on *Anorexia Nervosa,* who was my husband's first analyst. There's kindly, rotund Dr. Arthur Feet, Jr., who was the third (and last) analyst of my friend Pia. There's compulsive little Dr. Raymond Schrift who is hailing a blond stewardess (named "Nanci") as if she were a taxi. (I saw Dr. Schrift for one memorable year when I was fourteen and starving myself to death in penance for having finger-fucked on my parents' living-room couch. He kept insisting that the horse I was dreaming about was my father and that my periods would return if only I would "ackzept being a vohman.") There's smiling, bald Dr. Harvey Smucker whom I saw in consultation when my first husband decided he was Jesus Christ and began threatening to walk on the water in Central Park Lake. There's foppish, hand-tailored Dr. Ernest Klumpner, the supposedly "brilliant theoretician" whose latest book is a psychoanalytic study of John Knox. There's black-bearded Dr. Stanton Rappoport-Rosen who recently gained notoriety in New York analytic circles when he moved to Denver and branched out into something called "Cross-Country Group Ski-Therapy." There's Dr. Arnold Aaronson pretending to play chess on a magnetic board with his new wife (who was his patient until last year), the singer Judy Rose. Both of them are surreptitiously looking around to see who is looking at them—and for one moment, my eyes and Judy Rose's meet. Judy Rose became famous in the 50s for recording a series of satirical ballads about pseudointellectual life in New York. In a whiny and deliberately unmusical voice, she sang the saga of a Jewish girl who takes courses at the New School, reads the Bible for its prose, discusses Martin Buber in bed, and falls in love with her analyst. She has now become one with the role she created.

Besides the analysts, their wives, the crew, and a few poor out-numbered laymen, there were some children of analysts who'd come along for the ride. Their sons were mostly sullen-faced adolescents in bell bottoms and shoulder-length hair who looked at their parents with a degree of cynicism and scorn which was almost palpable. I remembered myself traveling abroad with my parents as a teen-ager and always trying to pretend they weren't with me. I tried to lose them in the Louvre! To avoid them in the Uffizi! To moon alone over a Coke in a Paris café and pretend that those loud people at the next table were not—though clearly they were—my parents. (I was pretending, you see, to be a Lost Generation exile with my parents sitting three feet away.) And here I was back in my own past, or in a bad dream or a bad movie: *Analyst* and *Son of Analyst*. A planeload of shrinks and my adolescence all around me. Stranded in midair over the Atlantic with 117 analysts many of whom had heard my long, sad story and none of whom remembered it. An ideal beginning for the nightmare the trip was going to become.

We were bound for Vienna and the occasion was historic. Centuries ago, wars ago, in 1938, Freud fled his famous consulting room on the Berggasse when the Nazis threatened his family. During the years of the Third Reich any mention of his name was banned in Germany, and analysts were expelled (if they were lucky) or gassed (if they were not). Now, with great ceremony, Vienna was welcoming the analysts back. They were even opening a museum to Freud in his old consulting room. The mayor of Vienna was going to greet them and a reception was to be held in Vienna's pseudo-Gothic Rathaus. The enticements included free food, free *Schnaps,* cruises on the Danube, excursions to vineyards, singing, dancing, shenanigans, learned papers and speeches and a tax-deductible trip to Europe. Most of all, there was to be lots of good old Austrian *Gemütlichkeit.* The people who invented *schmaltz* (and crematoria) were going to show the analysts how welcome back they were.

Welcome back! Welcome back! At least those of you who survived Auschwitz, Belsen, the London Blitz and the cooptation of America. *Willkommen!* Austrians are nothing if not charming.

Holding the Congress in Vienna had been a hotly debated issue for years, and many of the analysts had come only reluctantly. Anti-Semitism was part of the problem, but there was also the possibility that radical students at the University of Vienna would decide to stage demonstrations. Psychoanalysis was out of favor with New Left members for being "too individualistic." It did nothing, they said, to further "the worldwide struggle toward communism."

I had been asked by a new magazine to observe all the fun and games of the Congress closely and to do a satirical article on it. I began my research by approaching Dr. Smucker near the galley, where he was being served coffee by one of the stewardesses. He looked at me with barely a glimmer of recognition.

"How do you feel about psychoanalysis returning to Vienna?" I asked in my most cheerful lady-interviewer voice. Dr. Smucker seemed taken aback by the shocking intimacy of the question. He looked at me long and searchingly.

"I'm writing an article for a new magazine called *Voyeur*," I said. I figured he'd at least have to crack a smile at the name.

"Well then," Smucker said stolidly, "how do *you* feel about it?" And he waddled off toward his short bleached-blond wife in the blue knit dress with a tiny green alligator above her (blue) right breast.

I should have known. Why do analysts always answer a question with a question? And why should this night be different from any other night—despite the fact that we are flying in a 747 and eating unkosher food?

"The Jewish science," as anti-Semites call it. Turn every question upside down and shove it up the asker's ass. Analysts all seem to be Talmudists who flunked out of seminary in the first year. I was reminded of one of my grandfather's favorite gags:

Q: Why does a Jew always answer a question with a question?

A: And why should a Jew not answer a question with a question?

Ultimately though, it was the unimaginativeness of most analysts which got me down. OK, I'd been helped a lot by my first one—the German who was going to give a paper in Vienna—but he was a rare breed: witty, self-mocking, unpretentious. He had none of the flat-footed literal-mindedness which makes even the most brilliant psychoanalysts sound so pompous. But the others I'd gone to—they were so astonishingly literal-minded. The horse you are dreaming about is your father. The kitchen stove you are dreaming about is your mother. The piles of bullshit you are dreaming about are, in reality, your analyst. This is called the *transference*. No?

You dream about breaking your leg on the ski slope. You have, in fact, just broken your leg on the ski slope and you are lying on the couch wearing a ten-pound plaster cast which has had you housebound for weeks, but has also given you a beautiful new appreciation of your toes and the civil rights of paraplegics. But the broken leg in the dream represents your own "mutilated genital." You always wanted to have a penis and now you feel guilty that you have *deliberately* broken your leg so that you can have the pleasure of the cast, no?

No!. . .

It was after twelve when we finally got to our hotel and we found we had been assigned a tiny room on the top floor. I wanted to object, but Bennett was more interested in getting some rest. So we pulled down the shades against the noon-day sun, undressed, and collapsed on the beds without even unpacking. Despite the strangeness of the place, Bennett went right to sleep. I tossed and fought with the feather comforter until I dozed fitfully amid dreams of Nazis and plane crashes. I kept waking up with my heart pounding and my teeth chattering. It was the usual panic I always have the first day away from home, but it was worse because of our being back in Germany. I was already wishing we hadn't returned.

At about three-thirty we got up and rather languidly made love in one of the single beds. I still felt that I was dreaming and kept pretending Bennett was somebody else. But who? I couldn't get a clear picture of him. I never could. Who was this phantom man who haunted my life? My father? My German analyst? The zipless fuck? Why did his face always refuse to come into focus?

By four o'clock, we were on the *Strassenbahn* bound for the University of Vienna to register for the Congress. The day had turned out to be clear with blue skies and absurdly fluffy white clouds. And I was clumping along the streets in my high-heeled sandals, hating the Germans, and hating Bennett for not being a stranger on a train, for not smiling, for being such a good lay but never kissing me, for getting me shrink appointments and Pap smears and IBM electrics, but never buying me flowers. And not talking to me. And never grabbing my ass anymore. And never going down on me, ever. What do you expect after five years of marriage anyway? Giggling in the dark? Ass-grabbing? Cunt-eating? Well at least an occasional one. What do you women want? Freud puzzled this and never came up with much. How do you ladies like to be laid? A man who'll go down on you when you have your period? A man who'll kiss you before you brush your teeth in the morning and not say *Yiiich?* A man who'll laugh with you when the lights go out?

A stiff prick, Freud said, assuming that women wanted it because men wanted it. A big one, Freud said, assuming that *their* obsession was *our* obsession.

Phallocentric, someone once said of Freud. He thought the sun revolved around the penis. And the daughter, too.

And who could protest? Until women started writing books there was only one side of the story. Throughout all of history, books were written with sperm, not menstrual blood. Until I was twenty-one, I measured my orgasms against Lady Chatterley's and wondered what was *wrong* with me. Did it ever occur to me that Lady Chatterley was really a man? That she was really D. H. Lawrence?

Phallocentric. The trouble with men and also the trouble with women. A friend of mine recently found this in a fortune cookie:

The trouble with men is men,
the trouble with women, men.

Once, just to impress Bennett, I told him about the Hell's Angels initiation ceremony. The part where the initiate has to go down on his woman while she has her period and while all the other guys watch.

Bennett said nothing.

"Well, isn't that interesting?" I nudged. "Isn't that a gas?"

Still nothing.

I kept nagging.

"Why don't you buy yourself a little dog," he finally said, "and train him."

"I ought to report you to the New York Psychoanalytic," I said.

The medical building of the University of Vienna is columned, cold, cavernous. We trudged up a long flight of steps. Upstairs, dozens of shrinks were milling around the registration desk.

An officious Austrian girl in harlequin glasses and a red dirndl was giving everyone trouble about their credentials for registration. She spoke painstakingly schoolbook English. I was positive she must be the wife of one of the Austrian candidates. She couldn't have been more than twenty-five but she smiled with all the smugness of a *Frau Doktor*.

I showed her my letter from *Voyeur* Magazine, but she wouldn't let me register.

"Why?"

"Because we are not authorized to admit Press," she sneered. "I am *so* sorry."

"I'll bet."

I could feel the anger gather inside my head like steam in a pressure cooker. The Nazi bitch, I thought, the goddamned Kraut.

Bennett shot me a look which said: *calm down.* He hates it when I get angry at people in public. But his trying to hold me back only made more furious.

"Look—if you don't let me in I'll write about *that*, too." I knew that once the meetings got started I could probably walk right in without a badge—so it really didn't matter. Besides, I scarcely cared all that much about writing the article. I was a spy from the outside world. A spy in the house of analysis.

"I'm sure you don't want me to write about how the analysts are *scared* of admitting writers to their meetings, do you?"

"I'm *zo* sorry," the Austrian bitch kept repeating. "But I really haff not got za ausority to admit you. . . ."

"Just following orders, I suppose."

"I haff instructions to obey," she said.

"You and Eichmann."

"Pardon?" She hadn't heard me.

Somebody else had. I turned around and saw this blond, shaggy-haired Englishman with a pipe hanging out of his face.

"If you'd stop being paranoid for a minute and use charm instead of main force, I'm sure nobody could resist you," he said. He was smiling at me the way a man smiles when he's lying on top of you after a particularly good lay.

"You've got to be an analyst," I said, "nobody else would throw the word paranoid around so freely."

He grinned.

He was wearing a very thin white cotton Indian kurtah and I could see his reddish-blond chest hair curling underneath it.

"Cheeky cunt," he said. Then he grabbed a fistful of my ass and gave it a long playful squeeze.

"You've a lovely ass," he said. "Come, I'll see to it that you get into the conference."

Of course he turned out to have no authority whatsoever in the matter, but I didn't know that till later. He was bustling around so officiously that you'd have thought he was the head of the whole Congress. He *was* chairman of one of the preconferences—but he had absolutely nothing to say about Press. Who cared about Press, anyway? All I wanted was for him to press my ass again. I would have followed him anywhere. Dachau, Auschwitz, anywhere. I looked across the registration desk and saw Bennett talking seriously with another analyst from New York.

The Englishman had made his way into the crowd and was grilling the registration girl in my behalf. Then he walked back to me.

"Look—she says you have to wait and talk to Rodney Lehmann. He's a friend of mine from London and he ought to be here any minute so why don't we walk across to the café, have a beer, and look for him?"

"Let me just tell my husband," I said. It was going to become something of a refrain in the next few days.

He seemed glad to hear that I had a husband. At least he didn't seem sorry.

I asked Bennett if he'd come across the street to the café and meet us (hoping, of course, that he wouldn't come too soon) and he waved me off. He was busy talking about countertransference.

I followed the smoke from the Englishman's pipe down the steps and across the street. He puffed along like a train, the pipe seeming to propel him. I was happy to be his caboose.

We set ourselves up in the café, with a quarter liter of white wine for me and a beer for him. He was wearing Indian sandals and dirty toenails. He didn't look like a shrink at all.

"Where are you from?"

"New York."

"I mean your ancestors."

"Why do you want to know?"

"Why are you dodging my question?"

"I don't have to answer your question."

"I know." He puffed his pipe and looked off into the distance. The corners of his eyes crinkled into about a hundred tiny lines and his mouth curled up in a sort of smile even when he wasn't smiling. I knew I'd say yes to anything he asked. My only worry was: Maybe he wouldn't ask soon enough.

"Polish Jews on one side, Russian on the other—"

"I thought so. You *look* Jewish."

"And you look like an English anti-Semite."

"Oh come on—I *like* Jews. . . ."

"Some of your best friends . . . "

"It's just that Jewish girls are so bloody good in bed."

I couldn't think of a single witty thing to say. Sweet Jesus, I thought, here he was. The real z.f. The zipless fuck par excellence. What in God's name were we waiting for? Certainly not Rodney Lehmann.

"I also like the Chinese," he said, "and you've got a nice-looking husband."

"Maybe I ought to fix you up with him. After all, you're both analysts. You'd have a lot in common. You could bugger each other under a picture of Freud."

"Cunt," he said. "Actually, it's more Chinese *girls,* I fancy—but Jewish girls from New York who like a good fight also strike me as dead sexy. Any woman who can raise hell the way you did up at registration seems pretty promising."

"Thanks." At least I can recognize a compliment when I get one. My underpants were wet enough to mop the streets of Vienna.

"You're the only person I've ever met who thought I looked Jewish," I said, trying to get the conversation back to more neutral territory. (Enough of sex. Let's get back to bigotry.) His thinking I looked Jewish actually excited me. God only knows why.

"Look—I'm not an anti-Semite, but *you* are. Why do you think you don't look Jewish?"

"Because people always think I'm German—and I've spent half my life listening to anti-Semitic stories told by people who assumed I wasn't—"

"That's what I hate about Jews," he said. "They're the only ones allowed to tell anti-Semitic jokes. It's bloody unfair. Why should *I* be deprived of the pleasure of masochistic Jewish humor just because I'm a *goy?*"

He sounded so goyish saying *goy.*

"You don't pronounce it right."

"What? *Goy?*"

"Oh, that's OK, but *masochistic.*" (He pronounced the first syllable *mace,* just like an Englishman.) "You've got to watch how you pronounce Yiddish words like *masochistic,*" I said. "We Jews are very touchy."

We ordered another round of drinks. He kept making a pretense of looking around for Rodney Lehmann and I came on with a very professional *spiel* about the article I was going to write. I nearly convinced myself all over again. That's one of my biggest problems. When I start out to convince other people, I don't always convince them but I invariably convince myself. I'm a complete bust as a con woman.

"You really have an American accent," he said, smiling his just-got-laid smile.

"I haven't got an accent—*you* have—"

"Ac-sent," he said mocking me.

"Fuck you."

"That's not at all a bad idea."

"What did you say your name was?" (Which, as you may recall, is the climactic line from Strindberg's *Miss Julie.*)

"Adrian Goodlove," he said. And with that he turned suddenly and upset his beer all over me.

"Terribly sorry," he kept saying, wiping at the table with his dirty handkerchief, his hand, and eventually his Indian shirt—which he took off, rolled up and gave me to wipe my dress with. Such chivalry! But I was just sitting there looking at the curly blond hair on his chest and feeling the beer trickle between my legs.

"I really don't mind at all," I said. It wasn't true that I didn't mind. I loved it.

Goodlove, Goodall, Goodbar, Goodbody, Goodchild, Goodeve, Goodfellow, Goodford, Goodfleisch, Goodfriend, Goodgame, Goodhart, Goodhue, Gooding, Goodlet, Goodson, Goodridge, Goodspeed, Goodtree, Goodwine.

You can't be named Isadora White Wing (née Weiss—my father had bleached it to "White" shortly after my birth) without spending a rather large portion of your life thinking about names.

Adrian Goodlove. His mother had named him Hadrian and then his father had forced her to change it to Adrian because that sounded "more English." His father was big on sounding English.

"Typical tight-ass English middle class," Adrian said of his Mum and Dad. "You'd hate them. They spend their whole lives trying to keep their bowels open in the name of the Queen. A losing battle too. Their assholes are permanently plugged."

And he farted loudly to punctuate. He grinned. I looked at him in utter amazement.

"You're a real primitive," I sneered, "a natural man."

But Adrian kept on grinning. Both of us knew I had finally met the real zipless fuck.

PART EIGHT
STRIKING BACK

Jewish economic power: Baron James Rothschild, 1870s.

INTRODUCTION

Victimization, marginalization, adverse discrimination, and martyrdom have constituted a continuous theme in Jewish history. And yet the Jews have survived: Given a modicum of freedom, prosperity, access to the open market, secular learning, and the professions, they have prospered. They have come to play leadership roles in important facets of culture and economics. They have repopulated themselves after devastating genocides. They have exhibited not only intellectual power and business acumen but on occasion—in ancient Judea and modern Israel and even for a moment against insuperable odds in Hitler's Warsaw Ghetto—military skill as well. To the great frustration, indignation and disappointment of their enemies, the Jews have struck back and gained more than a proportionate share of victories, mainly in peace, sometimes in war.

The Jews are a uniquely superior group with an indomitable drive for creativity and accomplishment. Repressed, condemned, and excluded, they come back to haunt their enemies. An example from the field of American literary criticism may be instanced. In 1931 T. S. Eliot, the leading literary critic as well as poet in the English-speaking world, went on a lecture tour of American campuses. His set speech—to enthusiastic applause—was peppered with anti-Semitic portraits of Jews as outside the circle of Western Civilization. At that time Jews were not allowed to teach literature and other humanities in the leading American universities. The gaining of tenure in the Columbia English Department by a Jew, Lionel Trilling, was a unique event in the mid–1930s, bitterly opposed by the faculty and a consequence only of the personal intervention of the University's president, Nicholas Murray Butler. But by 1970, at least a third of the professors of literature in Ivy League Universities were Jewish, including some of the most illustrious critical names—such as Harry Levin at Harvard, M. H. Abrahams at Cornell, and Harold Bloom at Yale.

The Six-Day War of June, 1967, taught the same lesson. At the beginning of that month, the leading British weekly The Economist was trumpeting that the Israelis were "finished" as a political and military power. In their very next issue they had to explain the destruction of Egypt's airforce and tank corps at Israeli hands.

The Jews will strike back; and whatever they say in public, privately they won't forget the bad treatment they had to endure beforehand.

Are the Jews Genetically Superior?

It was discomfiting to liberal American Jews that a 1994 study of the social significance of the results of I.Q. tests shows that among all ethnic groups in the U.S.A., Ashkenazi Jews (those descended from Jews who lived principally in Eastern and Central Europe) had the highest I.Q.s. Chinese people came in second. This is not the kind of data that liberal Jews feel comfortable with—it raises the issue of relationship between intelligence and ethnicity, and conjures up the spectre of Nazi race theory. But the time may be coming when the genetic superiority of Jews can be calmly discussed as it was in 1977 by Raphael Patai.

So far, the environmental factors in the development of Jewish intelligence have been stressed. I emphasized the relatively smaller amount of nutritional and the absence of sociogenic brain damage in the case of the average Jewish child, and the role of the home environment in transmitting and inculcating intellectual interests, a devotion to learning, and preference for academic careers. But such factors are purely environmental ones, which means that they must be present in each generation in order to affect it, and that, if they are eliminated, the very next generation will no longer manifest those intellectual features which resulted from them and which characterized its ancestry for hundreds of years. In fact, something like this has recently begun to appear on the American scene among children who are growing up in thoroughly assimilated Jewish homes from which the traditional Jewish push toward intellectual achievement is absent. . . .

In addition to such environmental influences, however, there is the distinct possibility that genetic factors have also been at work in the development of Jewish intelligence. It has been argued that conditions in the often hostile Gentile environment in which the Jews have lived for two thousand years were such as to favor the survival of the most intelligent among them. . . .

There can be no doubt that the Jews were subject to severe economic restrictions, had to put up with humiliations, were frequently attacked by mobs and victimized by potentates, periodically expelled from cities and whole countries, captured and held to ransom, and exposed to untold other hardships and perils. Other things being equal, those who were mentally better equipped to weather all this had a better chance, not only to survive but to have children, secure *their* survival, and thus perpetuate their genes. In the course of generations, these circumstances brought about a gradual shift in the balance between those of higher and those of lower intelligence; the mean intelligence of the Jewish community tended to increase. If such a process actually did take place—and it seems reasonable to assume that it did—then it was an environmentally induced genetic development, akin to the Darwinian survival of the fittest, and its effects would persist even after the conditions whose pressure had brought it about in the first place had disappeared. . . .

Other students of Jewish intelligence, thinking along similar lines, have suggested that the immense value attributed by the Jews to Talmudic learning contributed indirectly but, in the course of centuries, cumulatively to the development of Jewish intelligence. Their argument, briefly, is as follows. Until the Enlightenment, the Jews considered Talmudic scholarship the greatest of all achievements. The appreciation of this scholarship was inculcated into the children to such an extent that, generally speaking, all the boys who had the mental capacity endeavored to achieve—and many actually did achieve—scholarly status. The most distinguished among the many budding scholars obtained coveted positions as rabbis of Jewish communities or as heads of yeshivot (Talmudic academies). Wealthy Jews sought out the promising young rabbinical scholars to be their sons-in-law. A rich man's daughter, on her part, considered it a great distinction to be chosen as the bride of such a young luminary. Thus excellence in Talmudic study (which this argument considers a mark of high intelligence) enabled a young man to attain a better economic situation, marry earlier, have more children, give them better care, and thereby save more of them from infant and child mortality than other young men. This course, which was followed for many centuries, resulted in an increase in the percentage of the most intelligent element among the Jews, which statistically meant a higher mean intelligence among the Jews than among the Gentiles.

This argument has recently been combined with the contention that among the Gentiles, contrariwise, the most intelligent had the least chance to produce offspring. Throughout the Middle Ages, the greatest, fastest, and, indeed, nearly the only advancement possible for the intelligent sons of the lowly born was offered by an ecclesiastic career. The priesthood attracted the most ambitious and talented sons of the lower estates and the most intellectual ones from the others. Since priestly celibacy was the rule, this meant that the most intelligent portion of the population had no offspring (or had only a few illegitimate children), and this inverse selection, in the course of the centuries, lowered the average intelligence level of the Gentile populations. . . .

The trouble with this hypothesis, as with many others of a similar nature, is that no historical data are available which could substantiate it. All one can say, based on a general knowledge of Jewish history, is that it looks sound, and that it is quite probable that such a historic process of Jewish genetic selection for intelligence (as measured by excellence in Talmudic studies) actually did take place, although of course the people involved remained unaware of it. And if so, then it was an added factor in the modification of the Jewish gene pool in the direction of higher intelligence; added, that is, to the effect of persecution which also favored the survival of those mentally better endowed. So we have these two environmentally induced genetic factors, over and above the effect of the environment on each new generation, which jointly can be considered responsible for the superior Jewish scores on I.Q. tests.

Judaism versus Medieval Christianity and Islam

The greatest Jewish philosopher and Talmudic scholar of the Middle Ages was Maimonides (Rambam, Rabbi Solomon ben Maimon), who lived in the second half of the twelfth century. When he was young he had to flee from Muslim Spain, where fundamentalist groups from North Africa had taken over the Arabic governments and begun harsh treatment of the Jews after three centuries of benign Muslim rule. Eventually Maimonides relocated himself to Egypt where he served as physician to the Sultan's chief minister as well as leader of the Jewish community. The Jews of far-off and isolated Yemen appear to have sought Maimonides' advice on the attitude they should adopt towards Christianity and Islam. Here is Maimonides' reply, a defiant attack

upon both religions and an assertion that the Jews would ultimately prevail, although visible rebellion was unwise. Maimonides' *Letter to the Jews of Yemen* **stands a cry of the heart on the part of the persecuted Jews in medieval and Muslim Christian lands, an affirmation of defiant faith. The translation is by Norman A. Stillman.**

Ours is the authentic religion of truth. It was revealed to us by the master of all the prophets, early and late. Through it, God has distinguished us from all the rest of mankind, as He has said: "Only the Lord had a delight in your fathers to love them, and He chose their seed after them, even you above all peoples" (Deut. 10:15). This was not because of any worthiness on our part, but rather, it was due to divine favor upon us because our forefathers had first come to recog-

Maimonides, aggressive defender of Judaism. Copper and silver locket, Italy, 1700.

nize Him and obey Him, as He has said: "It is not because you are the most numerous of peoples that the Lord set his heart on you" (Deut. 7:7). Because He has singled us out by His laws and precepts, and because our preeminence has been established over all others by His statutes and ordinances, all the nations have risen up against us out of envy for our religion and a desire to suppress it. For this reason, the kings of the earth have devoted themselves to tyrannically and malevolently pursuing us. They seek to oppose God, but He cannot be opposed! From that time (of the Revelation) until now, every obstinate, tyrant king or mighty conqueror has made his first goal and primary concern the destruction of our religious law, and the abolition of our faith by coercion and force of arms, as did Amalek, Sisera, Sennacherib, Nebuchadnezzar, Titus, Hadrian, and others like them. These men represent one of the two classes which strive to overcome the Divine Will.

The second class consists of the cleverest and most educated nations, such as the Syrians, Persians, and the Greeks. They too sought to destroy the religious law and to eradicate it through arguments they concocted and by polemics which they composed. They strove to abolish the religious law by their polemical compositions, just as conquerors have tried to do by their swords. But neither the one nor the other shall succeed!

Later, there arose another faction which combined both approaches, namely physical subjection, as well as argumentation and debate. It seemed that this was more effective for eradicating any trace of our people. This group contrived to lay claim to prophecy and to bring forth a religious law contrary to the law of God, while asserting that it too was from God just like the true Word. This would create doubt and cause confusion since one contradicted the other, while at the same time both were supposed to be derived from a single Deity.

The first to take up this course was Jesus the Nazarene—may his bones be ground to dust. He was of Israel.

Later, there arose a madman [Muhammed] who followed his example since he had paved the way for him. However, he added a further object, namely to seek dominion and complete submission to himself; and what he has established is well known.

All of these men have sought to make religions comparable to the Religion of God—praised be He. But Divine handiwork would resemble human handiwork only for a gullible person who has no knowledge of either. Furthermore, the difference between our religion and the others which resemble it is like the difference between living rational beings and a graven image so expertly fashioned of marble, wood, silver, or gold that it almost resembles a man. Thus when a person who is ignorant of heavenly wisdom or divine work sees a statue which by its outward appearance closely resembles a man in its shape, its features, its proportions, and its coloring, he may think that this workmanship is just like the divine crafting of the human form because of his ignorance of the internal nature of each. As for the wise man who knows what is inside each of them, he perceives that the interior of this graven image possesses no masterly craftsmanship whatsoever, whereas inside the man are true wonders and things which indicate the wisdom of the Creator, such as the extension of the nerves into the muscles and their branching out, the twisting of the sinews, their points of connection, the intertwining of the ligaments, and the way they grow, the articulation of the bones and limbs, the network of pulsating and nonpulsating blood vessels and their divisions, the placement of the organs, some with others, internally and externally, every aspect of these in its proportion, form, and proper place.

Likewise, when a person ignorant of the secrets of the inspired Scripture and the inner meanings of our religious law compares this religious law to the one which was fabricated, he might imagine that there is a similarity between them since he will find in both prohibited and permissible things, acts of worship, negative and positive commandments, promises of reward and admonitions of punishment. If only he understood the inner secrets, then he would realize that all the wisdom of the true divine Law is in its eso-teric meaning, and that there are no mere positive and negative commandments, but rather matters which are beneficial for human perfection, which remove any impediment to the achievement of such perfection, and which produce moral and rational qualities in the masses to the full measure of their potential and in the elite in accordance with their attainments. Through these, the godly community becomes preeminent in two sorts of perfection at once. The first sort of perfection to which I am referring is for a man to achieve an uninterrupted state of existence in this world under the best and most suitable conditions for a human being. The second sort of perfection is the comprehension of the intelligible to the full measure of human capacity.

As for the religious systems which resemble the true one—they have no inner contents, only mere imitations, pale resemblances, and vague similarities. . . .

Therefore, all of you our brethren of Israel scattered in the Diaspora must encourage one another. The elder should guide the younger, and the elite the masses. You should join together in acknowledging the truth which is unchanging and immutable. . . . Keep in mind the theophany at Mount Sinai, which God commanded us to remember always and warned us never to forget. Furthermore, He enjoined us to teach our children about it so that they grow up with a knowledge of it. . . . It behooves you, my brethren, to enhance your children's imagination of that great spectacle and to discuss its significance and its miraculous nature at every gathering. For this is the very pivot of our religion and the proof which leads one to certainty. . . .

You know, my brethren, that an account of our sins God has cast us into the midst of this people, the nation of Ishmael [the Arabs], who persecute us severely, and who devise ways to harm us and to debase us. This is as the Exalted had warned us: "Even our enemies themselves being judges" (Deut. 32:31). No nation has ever done more harm to Israel. None has matched it in debasing and humiliating us. None has been able to reduce us as they have. . . .

We have borne their imposed degradation, their lies, and absurdities, which are beyond human power to bear. We have become as in the words of the psalmist, "But I am as a deaf man, I hear not, and I am as a dumb man that opens not his mouth" (Ps. 38:14). We have done as our sages of blessed memory have instructed us, bearing the lies and absurdities of Ishmael. We listen, but remain silent. . . . In spite of all this, we are not spared from the ferocity of their wickedness and their outbursts at any time. On the contrary, the more we suffer and choose to conciliate them, the more they choose to act belligerently toward us. Thus David has depicted our plight: "I am at peace, but when I speak, they are for war!" (Ps. 120:7). How much worse it would be if we were to stir up a commotion and announce to them with ranting and raving that our dominion is at hand! Then indeed, we would be plunging ourselves into destruction. . . .

May the Creator of the world remember us and you in accordance with His attribute of mercy. May He gather the exiles who are His special portion so that they might "behold the graciousness of the Lord and visit early in His temple" (Ps. 27:4). May He lead us out of the Valley of the Shadows into which He has relegated us. May He dispel the darkness before our eyes and the gloom in our hearts. May He fulfill the prophecy "The people who walked in darkness have seen a great light" (Isa. 9:1).

The Perpetual Superiority of Israel

The Khazars, a Mongolian people who lived north of the Crimea in the tenth century, were heard by Jews in Spain to have adopted Judaism as their religion. If so, they were probably converted by Jewish merchants from Constantinople. By the time the Iberian Jews tried to establish contact with the Jewish Khazars, they were already conquered by the heathen Russians. This is the historical background to Judan Halevi's *The Kuzari*, written in Spain in the later twelfth century, and from which the following paragraphs are taken.

The Kuzari belongs to a familiar medieval genre, the disputation among religious leaders. In this book a rabbi convinces the King of Khazars of the superiority of Judaism over Christianity and Islam.

Judah Halevi was a poet, physician, and philosopher. His book reflects the reconquest of the northern part of Spain by Christian kings (he spent part of his long career in Christian territory) and he therefore takes pains to mention the superiority of Judaism to the religion propagated by Christian monks, who were assiduous in trying to convert Jews. Halevi at this latter point in his life was a kind of Jewish nationalist and believed not only in the superiority of Judaism but in the intrinsic superior quality of Jews over other peoples. Twentieth-century Zionists regarded him as an inspiring forerunner and were fond of citing his proto-Zionist poetry.

In his last year, Halevi made a trip to Zion. We don't know whether he reached the homeland, as legend tells us. We do know from Geniza documents that he was lionized by the wealthy Alexandrian Jews on his way to Zion.

Treatise on the Superiority of Judaism. Page from Hebrew version of Judah Halevi, *The Kuzari*, around 1200.

The root of all knowledge was deposited in the Ark which took the place of the heart, viz. the Ten Commandments, and its branch is the Torah on its side, as it is said: "Put it in the side of the ark of the covenant of the Lord your God" (Deut. xxxi. 26). From there went forth a twofold knowledge, firstly, the scriptural knowledge, whose bearers were the priests; secondly, the prophetic knowledge which was in the hands of the prophets. Both classes were, so to speak, the people's watchful advisers, who compiled the chronicles. They, therefore, represent the head of the people. . . .

The "dead" nations which desire to be held equal to the "living" people can obtain nothing more than an external resemblance. They built houses for God, but no trace of Him was visible therein. They turned hermits and ascetics in order to secure inspiration, but it came not. They, then, deteriorated, became disobedient, and wicked. . . .

Just as the heart is pure in substance and mat-ter, and of even temperament, in order to be accessible to the intellectual soul, so also is Israel in its component parts. In the same way as the heart may be affected by disease of the other organs, viz. the lusts of the liver, stomach and genitals, caused through contact with malignant elements; thus also is Israel exposed to ills originating in its inclinings towards the Gentiles. As it is said: "They were mingled among the heathens and learned their works" (Ps. cvi. 35). Do not consider it strange if it is said in the same sense: "Surely, he has borne our griefs and carried our sorrows" (Is. liii. 4). Now we are burdened by them, whilst the whole world enjoys rest and prosperity. The trials which meet us are meant to prove our faith, to cleanse us completely, and to remove all taint from us. If we are good, the Divine Influence is with us in this world.

The observance of the Sabbath is itself an acknowledgment of His omnipotence, and at the same time an acknowledgment of the creation by the divine word. He who observes the Sabbath because the work of creation was finished on it acknowledges the creation itself. He who believes in the creation believes in the Creator. He, however, who does not believe in it falls a prey to doubts of God's eternity and to doubts of the existence of the world's Creator. The observance of the Sabbath is therefore nearer to God than monastic retirement and asceticism. Behold how the Divine Influence attached itself to Abraham, and then to all those who shared his excellence and the Holy Land. This Influence followed him everywhere, and guarded his posterity, preventing the detachment of any of them, it brought them to the most sheltered and best place, and caused them to multiply in a miraculous manner, and finally raised them to occupy a degree worthy of such excellence. . . .

Now the roots and principles of all sciences were handed down from us first to the Chaldaeans, then to the Persians and Medians, then to Greece, and finally to the Romans. On account of the length of this period, and the many disturbing circumstances, it was forgotten that they had originated with the Hebrews, and so they were ascribed to the Greeks and Romans. To Hebrew, however, belongs the first place, both as regards the nature of the languages, and as to fullness of meanings.

A Jewish Prince in Medieval Baghdad

In the second half of the twelfth century, Benjamin of Tudela, an Iberian Jew, made a trip through the Mediterranean and Middle Eastern Jewish world. Here is his description of the Exilarch, the princely head of the Baghdad Jewish community, who putatively sits in glory next to the Caliph himself.

Here is a theme that is endlessly repeated in Jewish writing through the ages—enthusiastic descriptions of Jews who attain wealth and power and participate in Gentile lordship. Telling such stories made ordinary Jews feel good. They still do—read the New York Jewish press on any given week or the international edition of The Jerusalem Post. Psychologically such success stories were balm for Jewish wounds and poverty.

There are in Baghdad some forty thousand Jews of the People of Israel. They live in peace, tranquillity, and honor under the great Caliph. Among them are great scholars and heads of Yeshivot who are engaged in the study of Torah. There are ten yeshivot in the city.

Over all of them is Daniel B. Hasday, who is called the "Exilarch of All Israel." He has a written pedigree going back to David King of Israel. The Jews address him as Our Lord the Exilarch, and the Muslims as *Sayyidnā Ibn Dā'ūd* (our Master, the son of David). He has been invested with supreme authority over all the congregations of Israel by the *Amīr al-Mu'minīn,* the lord of the Muslims. For thus Muhammad commanded concerning the Exilarch and his descendants, and he issued him a seal of authority over all the sacred congregations living under his rule. Likewise, he ordered that every individual, be he Muslim or Jew, or member of any other people within his kingdom, should rise up before him and salute him, and that whoever does not rise up before him should receive one hundred stripes.

Every Thursday, when he goes to behold the countenance of the great Caliph, he is accompanied by Gentile and Jewish horsemen, and heralds cry out before him: "Make way for our Lord, the scion of David, as is due him!" In their language they say: "*Icmalū tarīq li-Sayyidnā Ibn Dāʾūd*." He rides on horseback wearing garments of embroidered silk with a large turban on his head. Over the turban is a large white shawl upon which is a chain. And on it is the seal of Muhammad. When he comes before the Caliph, he kisses his hand. Then the Caliph rises before him, seats him upon a throne which Muhammad had ordered to be made in his honor. And all of the Muslim princes who have come to behold the countenance of the Caliph rise altogether before him. The Exilarch then sits upon his throne facing the Caliph, for thus did Muhammad command in order to fulfill the scriptural verse:

The scepter shall not pass from Judah,
Nor the ruler's staff from between his feet;
Until he comes to Shiloh,
and the homage of peoples be his. (Gen. 49:10)

The Exilarch grants all communities the right to appoint rabbis and *hazzānīm* [centor] for each and every congregation from Iraq to Persia and Khorasan, and Sheba, which is Yemen, to Diyar Bakr and Mesopotamia; from Armenia to the land of the Alans (Georgia) which is surrounded by mountains and has no outlet other than the Iron Gates that Alexander built, but which were broken; and from Siberia and the land of the Turks to the mountains of Asveh and the land of Gurgan, whose inhabitants, the Gurganites, dwell by the Gihon River (the Oxus)—these are the Girgashites who practice the religion of the Christians; and as far as the Gates of Samarqand, to Tibet and India. These men come to him to be ordained and to receive authority from him. They bring him offerings and gifts from the ends of the earth.

He owns hospices, gardens, and orchards in Baghdad, as well as many plots of land inherited from his forefathers. No man can take anything from him by force. He receives a fixed revenue every week from the Jewish hospices, markets, and local merchants, exclusive of that which is brought to him from distant lands. He is an extremely wealthy man and is learned in both Scripture and Talmud. Many Jews eat at his table each day.

Whenever a new Exilarch is appointed, he must expend a great deal of wealth upon the Caliph, the ministers, and the officials. On the day when the Caliph bestows the writ of authority upon him, he rides in the litter of a viceroy. He is conducted from the Caliph's palace to his home to the accompaniment of tambourines and dancing.

He (the Exilarch) performs the ordination of the Head of the Yeshiva.

The Jews in this city are very learned and wealthy. There are in Baghdad twenty-eight synagogues. These are divided between Baghdad proper and the suburb of al-Karkh which is on the other side of the Tigris—for the river divides the city in two.

The Great American Retailers

Jews in modern times made great reputations as international bankers, such as the Rothschild, Warburg, and Schiff families. But perhaps their greatest contribution to the economy and society in the late-nineteenth and early-twentieth centuries was as founders and managers of great retailing enterprises. This was the case not only in the U.S.A., as witness and role of the Sieff-Marks family in Britain's Marks and Spencer chain of stores. But in the burgeoning economy and expanding immigrant population of America, the Jewish retailing magnates made their most enduring impacts. They were highly innovative managers, gained vast fortunes, and became philanthropists particularly in the fields of medicine, the arts, and education.

Here is a celebratory but reliable account by Leon Harris of two American Jewish retailing giants, Bernard Gimbel and Julius Rosenwald. Gimbel not only developed mighty Gimbel's Department Store in New York (it no longer exists) but took over Saks Fifth Avenue and made it into the elegant and unique store that still flourishes. Julius Rosenwald was the cofounder of the mail order giant Sears, Roebuck that profoundly influenced the lifestyle of small-town and rural America. Rosenwald was also the most generous Jewish philanthropist of his day. He was in the 1930s and 1940s American Jewry's leading anti-Zionist (convincing himself after a visit to Palestine that the Zionist experiment as not fiscally and technologically viable) which clouded his posthumous image, but he deserves to be remembered as a great man.

Bernie [Gimbel] was born in Vincennes in 1885 and had lived as a boy in both Milwaukee and Philadelphia. Therefore it was not surprising that like so many other out-of-towners he should finally become a quintessential New Yorker, boosting it as enthusiastically as any small-town Western merchant would his local community. He became, in fact, "Mr. New York," but first he had had to prove himself in the big city.

To attempt to build a big new store in New York City in 1909 was considerably more unsafe than attending the opera, but that may, in fact, have been its chief appeal to Bernie. For his site he picked the block on Broadway between 32nd and 33rd streets, the terminal of the Pennsylvania and Long Island railroads, thus assuring a flood of commuter traffic. It was also only one block from Macy's, giving him the opportunity to go toe-to-toe with the champion.

On the advice of Sears, Roebuck's Julius Rosenwald, Bernie had the store built by Louis J. Horowitz of the Thompson-Starret Company, who became one of Bernie's intimate friends and invariably referred to him as "Big Casino." The whole undertaking was a big gamble—the "most costly lease in the real estate annals of the city," declared *The New York Times;* the rentals would total $60 million if all renewal options were exercised. Bernie increased even that risk by convincing his reluctant father and uncles not to lease but to buy the Greeley Square land and store outright: More than twenty seven acres of floor area and two acres of window glass, it was a formidably

greater investment than they had in either Philadelphia or Milwaukee.

Also an enormous risk, quite as difficult to sell to his family and finally no less profitable, was Bernie's 1923 purchase of Saks & Company. This included both the store that covered the block between Gimbel's and Macy's and the new $4.25 million Saks store being built way uptown between 49th and 50th streets on the east side of Fifth Avenue. Typically, Bernie worked out the whole deal with Horace Saks sitting on top of a coffin in the baggage car of a train taking them back to the city after a weekend in Elberon. It offered a more informal and private place than the smoking car full of Wall Street bankers.

By 1922, Bernie, a closet smart beneath his dumb-jock pose, had already understood the advantage of buying what he wanted with other people's money, and so had taken Gimbel's "public." He put both common and preferred shares of Gimbel's on the New York Stock Exchange in the pre-1929 boom market, while keeping control firmly in the hands of his family. Rather than parting with always precious cash in order to expand, he was therefore able to pay, with printed-paper stock certificates, some $8 million of which brought him the Saks stores.

When Horace Saks died in 1926, Bernie put in charge of the Fifth Avenue store the other star of the Gimbel third generation, Charles's son Adam Long Gimbel. Not the least of Bernie's talents was the ability, once he had a proven executive, to let him run his own show. For years Adam L. Gimbel and his in-store *couturière* wife, Sophie, made Saks Fifth Avenue the most profitable fashion specialty store in America. Adam lacked Stanley Marcus's genius for personal and institutional publicity, but unlike Neiman-Marcus, Saks Fifth Avenue was a prodigious moneymaker.

For Bernie Gimbel, as for John Wanamaker and every American storekeeper, showmanship was an essential element that must be fostered: the ability month after month and year after year to get for his stores the kind of publicity that Americans equate with success and that therefore makes success. Supplying the stewards' and library's equipment for the great transatlantic liner *Leviathan*; being the first to offer from Paris "colored wigs more brilliant than the rainbow, if not more beautiful;" sponsoring an indoor golf tournament on the store's fourth floor and a $5,000-prize airplane race between the New York and the Philadelphia stores; these and other feats kept Gimbel's in the newspapers and so in the public eye. Then there was always the carefully cultivated, endlessly exploited war with Gimbel's far better known competitor, Macy's, valuable beyond measure in just the same way that years later the debates with the far more famous Richard Nixon would be to the relatively unknown John F. Kennedy.

If Bernie was indifferent to high society for himself, he was delighted when its members could be used to get publicity for the store, as when Miss Ruth Morgan, Mrs. J. Howland Auchincloss, and Mrs. Nicholas Biddle sold in the store for the benefit of Bellevue Hospital. He was even self-assured enough to know, like P. T. Barnum, that "bad publicity" can be good as, for example, when Mrs. O. H. P. Belmont, Mrs. Emmeline Pankhurst, and Mrs. Inez Milholland Boissevain made headlines because the police stopped them—ever so courteously—from distributing a demand for shorter hours for Gimbel's female employees. . . .

But the store's biggest publicity coup (Macy's tried for it and lost) was the sale of millions of dollars worth of William Randolph Hearst's art collection. When the banks and *Los Angeles Times* publisher Harry Chandler (who held the mortgage on Hearst's San Simeon) finally insisted upon repayment from Hearst, his only liquid asset, unless his publishing empire was to go on the block, was some $50 million of art that he had recklessly accumulated for half a century.

Even his three homes in California, his Mexican ranch, his castle in Wales, and his various New York hotel suites (at the Ritz, the Warwick, the Lombardy, and the Devon), couldn't house the collection. Tons of it filled New York and Los Angeles warehouses—much never unpacked since it was purchased—including an entire twelfth-century Cistercian monastery from Segovia, each separate piece carefully numbered and crated.

The deal was brought to Bernie's playboy younger brother, Frederic ("a soft touch for women, especially Cuban or Mexican girls") by his friend Dr. Armand Hammer, who demanded and got ten percent off the top.

The New York police had difficulty controlling the crowds. Half a million dollars' worth had sold the first night, and more than $11 million by the end of the sale, including the monastery. Gimbel's customers got many of the greatest bargains ever bought at the store: a Teniers the Younger sold for $998 that would bring ten times as much today; and a Raffaelino del Garbo sold for $12,998 that would now fetch over half a million.

The value of the publicity to Gimbel's was incalculable. Newspaper and magazine stories appeared around the world, including one about a housewife who as the result of a newspaper photograph showing Bernie and John D. Rockefeller, Jr., examining a bowl, wrote a postcard: "Dear Sirs, Please send me a Benvenuto Cellini bowl as advertised. Kindly choose a good color to go with a blue dining room." The store answered that there was only one bowl—its price, $25,000. . . .

Sears had always had a free hand both as to how much and what kind of advertising was best for his company, and he spent from nine to thirteen percent of sales on promotion. In 1908, he proposed to raise this to seventeen percent. When his own merchandising executives agreed with Julius Rosenwald that this was too much, he resigned.

Rosenwald, now in absolute control, built up a cadre of executives to whom he could leave the day-to-day management while he spent more time at other pursuits. He enjoyed building what he always called "the store" into the greatest retailing operation in the world. But even more, he enjoyed giving away money.

After he had become one of the half-dozen or so best-known philanthropists in America—and before he died he would give away $63 million—reporters frequently asked him, "What is the largest gift you ever made?" Rosenwald invariably replied, "Two thousand five hundred dollars." When he had set up as a clothing manufacturer in Chicago but was still far from rich, he had gone to a meeting where money was being raised for Russian Jews suffering under the czarist pogroms. He was so moved that he pledged $2,500. Given Rosenwald's financial situation at the time, it was an enormous sum, perhaps more than he would earn in that year. He was very worried, therefore, as he walked home from the meeting, as to what his wife would say.

But Augusta assured him, "It will work out," and throughout their life together she enthusiastically encouraged his philanthropy.

As a young man Rosenwald had told a friend that his ambition was someday to have a yearly income of $15,000, so that he could spend $5,000 on his family, put $5,000 away for a rainy day, and have another $5,000 to give away.

Julius and Augusta's commitment to charity was in the Jewish tradition. The Bible is full of injunctions to love, feed, clothe, assist, dower, ransom, and otherwise comfort those in need and not only one's own family and tribe but the outsider as well. "Love ye therefore the stranger: For ye were strangers in the land of Egypt."

As with everything else in the Bible, charity is discussed and defined in endless detail in the Talmud, that accumulation of centuries of rabbinical analyses, although in fact there is no word in Hebrew for charity, and the word most often used, *zedakah,* means righteousness. Helping others was a *mitzvah,* a duty, and far from being a favor to the recipient was something he or she had a right to.

How much charity is enough (in terms of grains of barley or measures of silver) is no more exhaustively discussed in the Talmud than the proper manner of giving, with special emphasis on avoiding any embarrassment or shame for the recipient. The twelfth-century Jewish physician-philosopher Maimonides listed, in order of increasing virtue, the eight ways of giving charity. To give: 1) but sadly; 2) too little, but with good humor; 3) only after being asked; 4) before being

asked; 5) so that the donor does not know who the recipient is; 6) so that the recipient does not know who the donor is; 7) so that neither donor nor recipient knows the other's identity; 8) help to the unfortunate not in the form of a gift but rather a loan or a job or whatever means are necessary for him to help himself and so to maintain his self-respect.

Rosenwald's enormous charitable gifts were influenced both by this Jewish tradition and by the American tradition as well, a tradition he in turn failed to influence. As Daniel J. Boorstin points out, one of the most important and least recognized American contributions is the notion of community. In Europe every person was, after the days of the early adventurers, Aeneas or Beowulf or Siegfried, born into a fixed society with no choice in the matter and lived in the adversary position defined in 1884 by the title of Herbert Spencer's book *The Man versus the State.*

By contrast, in America, from its beginning into the twentieth century, excepting blacks and Indians, almost everyone here (or his father or grandfather) had come by choice and had helped to form a new community before there was formal government or where its writ ran rarely if at all. Unburdened by the obsolete political machinery of Europe, there was first voluntary community collaboration, a kind of do-it-yourself government that slowly became more formal and until relatively recently was viewed by citizens as their servant, not their master.

In Europe everyone paid taxes to the state and its ancient partner, the church. Some part of these funds the two institutions purportedly spent on philanthropic activities. Private charity, if any, was a personal and often secret matter—personal not only in the sense that it was directed to individuals but also that "The almsgiver was less likely to be trying to solve a problem of this world than to be earning his right of entry into the next."

Americans rejected Jesus's promise that "The poor ye always have with you," and changed the focus of philanthropy "from the giver to the receiver, from the salving of souls to the solving of problems, from conscience to community." Like water supply or sewage disposal or educating the young, philanthropy was a prudent social act and Benjamin Franklin's example taught that any useful undertaking, from a police department to a circulating library, should be supported, if not by government then by a group of individuals.

Although it had begun as a traditional Jewish commitment, Julius's own pattern of giving, evolving with his explosively expanding riches, became less and less traditional. Indeed, it offered several new, or at least rare, patterns of charity, some of which were copied, but others unfortunately not.

Initially he had simply given money to whatever Jewish causes were suggested by his Chicago rabbi, Emil Gustav Hirsch. Then in 1905, as increasing thousands of Jews were murdered and driven from their homes in Russia, Rosenwald began, on his own, giving larger sums to help them resettle. At first he supported segregated agricultural communities within Russia; but as it became obvious that there was no hope for Jews in Russia, he helped them to emigrate through the Baron Maurice de Hirsch's organization to resettle abroad in Argentina and Brazil.

Unlike the Baron Edmond de Rothschild, who for more than twenty years had been supporting the resettlement of Jews in Palestine, Rosenwald was an anti-Zionist. Like the Strauses and many other rich American Jews, he feared that a Jewish homeland would increase anti-Semitism and substantiate charges that the first loyalty of Jews was not to America.

In 1914 Julius took Augusta to visit Palestine, where they had contributed money to particular enterprises but had consistently refused to support the Zionist cause. He believed that a Jewish homeland there could never be economically self-sufficient and would exist only so long as massive transfusions of American and European funds supported it—a view yet to be proven incorrect. He also believed that such a homeland would bring into question the patriotism of all Jews living elsewhere in the world.

Similarly, he was strongly opposed to separate relief for Jewish victims of the world war. He believed it would cause non-Jewish victims in the war zones to attack Jews so singled out and would cause existing agencies to ignore Jewish victims or help them last, if at all. Theoretically, of course, he was right. But when the increasingly terrible actual suffering of Jews in Palestine and elsewhere was made clear to him by such distinguished Jewish American leaders as Louis D.

Brandeis and Louis Marshall, his heart overruled his logic. Sending Marshall a check for $10,000 for special Jewish war relief, Rosenwald wrote: "While I have not changed my mind in the least concerning the wisdom of the plan for raising a fund for the relief of distinctly Jewish sufferers . . . I desire, out of respect for the judgement of yourself and your coworkers, to contribute, anonymously, the amount of the enclosed check. Making anonymous contributions is contrary to my policy, since I have always urged that, as a rule, the personality behind the gift is far more valuable than the gift itself, and should be known, but in this case I can see no other means of accomplishing the desired end."

But in his philanthropy as in his business, Rosenwald was able to admit when he was wrong and to change his mind when presented with the facts. Three-quarters of a million Jews in Russia were made refugees by the war, and 300,000 Jews fled from Galicia to Vienna. By 1917 the plight of Europe's Jews was so desperate that American-Jewish leaders such as Jacob H. Schiff and Felix M. Warburg determined to try to raise $10 million—twice as much as ever before. To give their drive the push he believed it had to have, Rosenwald announced that he would donate ten percent of every $1 million raised up to the $10 million. The effect in Jewish communities all across America was electrifying: Rich local Jews were urged to "Be the Julius Rosenwald of Your City," and more than fifty of them, including Governor Simon Bamberger of Utah and Adolph S. Ochs, formerly of Tennessee, each pledged 10 percent of the funds raised in his community.

Jacob Schiff, who two years earlier had been unable to convince Rosenwald to give any support to separate Jewish relief, now declared: "I believe there is no one who has done so much to make the name of Jew respected, to raise it, not only in the eyes of our countrymen, but everywhere, as Julius Rosenwald!"

President Woodrow Wilson said that Rosenwald served both democracy and humanity, and throughout this period Rosenwald made certain that with his time as well as his money he supported his country and the Jews. With others (including Bernard Baruch and Samuel Gompers) Rosenwald served on the Advisory Commission of the Council of National Defense, and in 1918, when he was invited to go to France to tell "our fighting boys" that America was proud of them, he accepted immediately. Offered an army commission by Secretary of War Newton D. Baker, Rosenwald refused it.

In France, when he was presented to American soldiers along with high-ranking generals and field officers, he often introduced himself as "General Merchandise." As he was boarding the S. S. *Aquitania* with crate after heavy crate full of Sears, Roebuck catalogues, the troopship's officers at first refused to load them since they far exceeded the ship's allowance for personal baggage. But Rosenwald insisted, and as he anticipated, nothing presented to the military hospitals in France and England gave the patients more comfort than these reminders of home.

Hollywood Moguls

Jews from a variety of petty bourgeois occupations (from vaudeville to the fur coat business) moved to Los Angeles in the second and third decades of the twentieth century and became the founding heads of the great film studios. It was a risky, undercapitalized business that was attractive only to gambling types outside the ranks of established corporate capitalism.

Most of these film czars were people of vulgar tastes and very little education, but were all the more in tune with the taste and lifestyle of ordinary Americans. They were passionately devoted to projecting puritanical morality and vehement patriotism in their films. That ethos, plus their incessant hard work, and inveterate risk-taking account for their immense success, which profoundly affected world as well as American culture.

The apogee of the film studios came around 1950. At that time a judicial antitrust decision prohibited the major studios from monopolizing film distribution by owning theater chains, and the demoralizing impact of the McCarthyite red scare effected changes in the film industry. But today a leading cable channel does nothing but screen films from the studios' heyday.

Someone who knew the big boys well was Irving "Swifty" Lazar, the leading actors' agent of his day. This description of his pals, the Jewish film magnates, is taken from his 1995 autobiography.

Louis B. Mayer once told me, "A producer will respect you, no matter how tough you are, if he thinks you're representing your clients to the best of your ability. He may not prefer to do business with you, but by God, he'll respect you. If your client is the person he wants, he'll buy him from you, and his agent could be King Farouk."

Well, I wasn't King Farouk. I was someone the moguls had met socially, had grown to like, and then had moved on to do business with without damaging the after-hours friendship.

When I did business one-on-one with Darryl F. Zanuck, Jack Warner, Harry Cohn, Sam Goldwyn, and Louis B. Mayer, I marveled at how much they made decisions on instinct. They weren't as realistic or cautious as their production executives, which is why they didn't usually deal one-on-one with agents. They were lousy businessmen, and they knew it.

Of all these giants, I knew Darryl Zanuck the best. He was short, trim, and iron-hard. He wore a little mustache and had slightly bucked teeth with an aperture in which he could have rested his cigar. He'd stalk his office, frequently holding a riding crop.

For all his toughness, Darryl was a prankster with a flair for slip-on-a-banana-peel humor. I once flew with him from Los Angeles to New York in the days when a cross-country flight took ten hours. Because a late departure meant a night-long flight, there were berths on planes so you could get undressed, put on a pair of pajamas, and go to sleep. But when I flew with Darryl that time, I woke up in the morning to find that my trousers had suddenly become knee pants—Darryl had cut them off at the knees. I looked ridiculous deplaning in New York with my short socks and garters.

I loved to negotiate with Darryl because he was so emotional. If he liked a specific book or play, he had no problem paying more than anyone else. He knew he wasn't a good businessman, so he avoided talking business. In the beginning, I had to siphon my deals through David Brown, head of the Fox story department, or Lew Schreiber, the studio vice president, so Darryl would have time to digest the deal.

But when Darryl was overcome with an insatiable desire to buy a book, nothing could dissuade him—forget Brown or Schreiber, he wanted to close right then and there. Such was the case when he asked me to come to the studio to discuss Romain Gary's *Roots of Heaven,* which he wanted John Huston to direct. I asked for two hundred thousand dollars. He didn't flinch.

"You've got a deal, but you have to sign the contract right now," he said.

"I have to call Gary. I can't sign without telling him about it."

Darryl offered me his phone. I called Gary's office and discovered that as the French Consul General in L.A., he had gone to San Francisco to attend a meeting of colleagues. I tried to locate him at his hotel, then at the convention hall, all to no avail. I didn't want to lose the sale, because it was doubtful that anyone else would pay any real money for the book. Darryl, meanwhile, was eyeing me with a cigar grasped firmly between his two front teeth, looking more like Peter Rabbit than a mogul. He had me exactly where he wanted me.

"If you walk out of here, you can forget the deal," he said. "I don't want you peddling this around."

I knew he meant it. I thought for a moment, then accepted his offer. It wasn't correct for me to do it, and I didn't do it without reflecting on the possible consequences. But I felt in my heart that if push came to shove and Gary was unhappy with the deal, Darryl wouldn't let me swing in the wind.

The next day, I finally got Gary on the phone and asked what he thought would be a fair price for the novel.

"We've been turned down quite a few places, so just do the best you can," he said. "If you could get twenty-five thousand, it would be great."

When I told him to multiply by eight, Gary almost jumped out of the Top of the Mark.

I sold Sloan Wilson's *The Man in the Gray Flannel Suit* to Darryl at Romanoff's, but the next day he didn't remember he had bought it. I had told him the story a few weeks earlier, when we were flying from California to New York. And he absolutely had to have it. I demanded two hundred thousand dollars. He was outraged. But I knew Darryl would come back to me.

When I returned to California, David Brown called. "I wish Darryl would buy that book," he said. "It would make a wonderful movie." I told him of my conversation with Darryl, and David said he would talk to him. That night, I went to Romanoff's for dinner with a client of mine. Darryl was seated at the first table with Michael Romanoff and the director Gregory Ratoff. As I passed by, he motioned for me to come over.

"What will you take now if we close the deal on *Gray Flannel Suit?*" he asked.

"A hundred seventy-five thousand will do it," I said.

"I'm making you a firm offer of one hundred and twenty."

The next day I called the author and told him about the deal. He was very pleased. I immediately called David Brown to accept Darryl's offer.

Very quickly David called me back. "Darryl doesn't remember seeing you last night," he said. Imagine my chagrin. Having closed the deal, I'd informed the author and his publisher. What to do? David suggested that I write Darryl a letter, recounting our conversation in great detail. Darryl then consulted with Ratoff and Romanoff to verify my account. They did, and the deal was honored.

Ethics is not necessarily a word you associate with Hollywood. But during the Golden Era most of these men did deals on a handshake and more often than not lived up to their commitments. Perhaps it was because they were gamblers at heart and understood you paid your debts in full.

In 1946, when I was still handling Moss Hart at MCA, I sat next to Jack Warner at a preview of Moss's play, *Christopher Blake*. For whatever reason, this story of a father who neglects his son had a powerful emotional effect on Jack, and he was soon weeping.

"I want this play," he whispered to me.

I knew I couldn't close a deal because of the Dramatists Guild rule prohibiting the sale of a play that's being performed until three weeks into its run.

"Jack, don't tell anybody," I said at the intermission. "Let's just make a pact. I want a hundred fifty thousand for the play."

He agreed, and we shook hands. I told no one but Moss. Meanwhile, audiences began avoiding the play. It barely made it to the three-week mark. When it did, however, I called Jack to remind him of our agreement. He was more than a gambler, he was a good sport. He knew the play was a flop, but he lived up to his commitment and paid in full.

Of all the moguls, Jack probably had the best sense of humor. He once threatened to bar me from the lot but then relented. "I can't really stick to that," he told me. "I have too much fun with you. Forget it."

"Jack. I never took it seriously."

"Well, if that's the case, you *are* barred. After today, you can't come around any more."

"What about mornings?" I inquired.

"All right. Just mornings."

"You want to give me some time in the afternoon?"

"Okay. You can be on the lot for one hour in the morning and one hour in the afternoon. Otherwise, you're barred."

When I first met Sam Goldwyn, I got the idea that because his accent was so heavy he didn't understand everything I said. So I spoke to him in pidgin-English.

"You like book, Sam?" I would ask. "Book good for you. You have somebody read it, then we talk."

This went on for quite some time until one day he said, "I want to ask you something. How much education have you had?"

I reeled off my educational credentials.

"But you speak strangely," he countered.

That put an end to my talking like an Indian.

Goldwyn admired success in the theater. He always reached out for the best playwrights and was more than happy to pay for them. The fact that he mispronounced the names of the authors or the titles didn't matter—he trusted his instinct. His gut was just as useful when he looked at a film; he knew exactly what wasn't working. He didn't need an audience. His intuition was all he needed to guide him to the making of a successful film.

But Sam was difficult to deal with. During the late 1950s, I had one contretemps with him.

"I cannot tell you what it would mean to me if you found a book that I really cared about," Sam would often say in those years. "I'm anxious to make a picture, but I can't find anything I want to do."

Max Shulman had written a marvelous book called *Rally 'Round the Flag, Boys!*, which was funny, had a great point of view, and was full of Americana. I thought it could bring Sam a success comparable to what he had enjoyed with *The Best Years of Our Lives,* so I sent him the galleys of the book. Two days later, he called: "You've given me a book I'm crazy about, and I want to do it. Let's make a deal right now. I don't want you to show it to anyone else."

"Sam, I haven't given it to anyone. So here's what we want: three hundred thousand for the book, a hundred thousand for Max to write the screenplay, plus a percentage of the profits."

Goldwyn agreed. I went back to my office, called Shulman and his New York agent, Harold Matson, and we all shook hands over the telephone.

Two mornings later, I got a call from Sam's wife, Frances Goldwyn: "We're not buying that book you gave Sam."

"Frances, what do you mean you're not buying it? You already did."

"No, we haven't. It's my money, not Sam's. The book will never make a movie that would sell in Europe. I'm not buying this book, and you can bet on it. Goodbye."

I was startled by this turn of events. Frances had always been very friendly to me. I didn't know what to do next except call Sam.

"Whatever Frances says, goes," he told me.

"I've never dealt with Frances before," I countered. "You didn't tell me the deal was contingent upon her approval."

"Well, that's the way it is."

I wasn't just flabbergasted, I was frantic. That afternoon I gathered up four copies of the Shulman novel and personally visited the head of every other major studio—Mike Frankovich at Columbia, Buddy Adler at Fox, and Jack Warner. I told each of them that I was auctioning the book off to the highest bidder.

Several nights later, I was at Frank Sinatra's for dinner—as were Alder and Frankovich. I asked if they had taken a look at *Rally 'Round the Flag, Boys!* They both said they hadn't gotten to it yet.

"Well, you'd better do it tonight, because I'm selling the book tomorrow," I warned.

When they realized that they were competing with each other, they took early flight from the party. The next morning, Sinatra called and asked me what I had to do with their leaving so early: "It seems to me that after you talked with them, they blew."

"Frank, I merely told them that they hadn't read a book that was going to be sold today."

"You son of a bitch. Try and do business in your own office." Then he added, "Is there a part in it for me?"

Buddy Alder called later that day. "Come on over here. I want to buy the Shulman book." I went over to Fox and got an offer that wasn't as good as the deal I had proposed to Goldwyn; nevertheless, it was an offer.

I called Harold Matson and told him the situation. I had spoken to my lawyer, who felt there was no way we could sue Sam. It would take years before it got to court, and he didn't even think it was a good case. So I suggested that we take the Fox offer because if anyone found out that Goldwyn didn't buy the book, we'd be in trouble selling it elsewhere. Matson wisely agreed.

Weeks later Frances Goldwyn's secretary called to invite me to a dinner party. I told my secretary to tell her I wasn't available. About a week later, another invitation. I declined again. The next time, Sam placed the call himself, but I still wouldn't take it. After that, when I saw the Goldwyns at a dinner party I'd be polite, but I wouldn't let myself get cornered talking to either one of them.

I hadn't told anyone what had happened, but Sam was agitated. He had a great sense of guilt because he fancied himself a man of his word. By his standards, he was. Except that his standards applied only to him. If he made a promise he couldn't keep, he had no difficulty clearing his conscience. My refusal to talk to him made him fear that I would take a stand, perhaps publicly. And that—not his broken promise—was unbearable to him.

One day a distinguished Eastern lawyer called. "I'm in town visiting Sam Goldwyn," he said. "Come over to the studio to see us."

"No, I won't."

"As a favor to me?"

I got into my little Thunderbird, and as I drove along Wilshire Boulevard, I stopped for a light in front of a Rolls-Royce dealership and saw a car in the window that caught my eye. I parked and went into the showroom to look at this beautiful black-and-brown Silver Cloud. It had a custom interior designed for a customer who had put down a five-thousand-dollar deposit and then disappeared. They would sell it to me for sixteen thousand.

At the Goldwyn Studios, I was promptly ushered into Sam's office. Our Mutual Friend was the first to speak.

"Mr. Goldwyn is very, very embarrassed at what happened," he told me. "He doesn't like the idea of your not being friends, and he wants you to reconsider the situation."

"There's nothing to reconsider," I said, not looking at Goldwyn. "I think he behaved very badly. He reneged on a deal and embarrassed me. If I hadn't sold the book to Fox, it would have been disastrous. What Sam did was unconscionable."

"You're right," Sam blurted out. "And I want to make it up to you."

Only now did I turn to Goldwyn. "How?"

"I want to buy you a gift," said Sam.

"What kind of a gift?"

"What do you want?"

"I just saw a Rolls-Royce."

"It's yours."

Goldwyn pressed a buzzer, and in walked Bobby Newman, his general manager. "Bobby, take Mr. Lazar and buy him the Rolls-Royce he wants."

Newman's eyes popped. I shook hands all around, then Newman and I drove to the Rolls-Royce dealership. I'm sorry to report that, after the first couple of years, the car wasn't much good; at that time, there weren't enough qualified Rolls-Royce mechanics in this country. But when it was out of the shop, my Rolls was a great status symbol—particularly in the eyes of friends and clients who had no idea it hadn't cost me a penny.

"There is one man who is not here who is single-handedly ruining the motion picture business as we know it," David Selznick told an assemblage of the most important people in Hollywood at a dinner at Charlie Feldman's house. "The ridiculous prices he demands for books and plays and writers will surely be the end of us all."

It was later reported to me that everyone seemed stunned at this pretentious statement. Then Audrey Wilder, Billy's wife, spoke up. "You're full of shit, David," she said. "You probably wanted to buy something from Lazar, and he didn't want to sell it to you, and you're just mad."

Audrey had it just right. Selznick's outburst was the result of the somewhat legendary sale of Irwin Shaw's novel *Lucy Crown*. When Irwin finished the final draft, he called me from Klosters to say he was sending it only to Random House. "Forget trying to sell it to the movies," he told me. "It's definitely not a film."

Those words only made me more determined.

Irwin's concern was with a crucial scene, in which a child at camp looks through a window and sees his mother having intercourse with his hero, the camp counselor. Irwin thought there was no way that pivotal moment could be depicted on the screen. But Irwin, who was far removed from Hollywood, was wrong. It was possible to shoot such a scene—though not, to be sure, as vividly as he had written it.

The real issue, I felt, was Irwin's pride. He didn't want the book shopped around and possibly turned down. Nor did he want to make a deal that would result in an emasculated version of his story. Because his feelings were strong, I had to agree with him. And, for once, I sat on my hands.

What I didn't know was that Bennett Cerf, at Random House, had slipped David Selznick a copy of the galleys. Selznick had read it and immediately saw a role for his wife, Jennifer Jones. But even if Irwin wanted me to sell the book, I didn't want Selznick to be the buyer. He was a heavy gambler who played for exorbitant stakes—and at

that moment he wasn't in the greatest financial shape.

So here I was in the curious and somewhat contradictory position of trying to dissuade Selznick from making a bid for the book, even as I was working to convince one of my top clients—who was also one of my two best friends in the world—that we could sell the book. True, *Lucy Crown* would have been, in almost any hands, a foolish movie. But if I could get Irwin more money than he'd ever seen before, I felt he could tolerate an embarrassing production.

So when David wrote me a letter stating that I shouldn't interpret his enthusiasm as an opportunity to ask for a lot of money, I told him I'd been offered four hundred thousand dollars. "If you want it, you'll have to pay four-fifty," I continued. "Personally, I don't think you ought to pay it."

"Why can't I buy it for the same amount of money that's been offered?"

"Because you have no preferential status. Nobody does. Whoever buys it has to pay the most money. I'm working for Irwin Shaw."

David asked me not to do anything for a few days. The next day I went over to see Burt Lancaster, Harold Hect, and their partner, James Hill. Under my arm was the manuscript.

"What have you got there?" Burt asked.

"Shaw's new manuscript, *Lucy Crown*."

"Can we read it?" Burt asked.

"David Selznick wants to buy it, so I really can't talk about it," I told them, knowing, of course, that would only pique their interest.

They suggested that I could do them a big favor by letting them read it overnight. As they were big Shaw fans, I let them. And at eight the next morning my houseman awakened me to say that I had visitors downstairs in the living room. Burt, Harold, and James had been up all night reading the manuscript aloud to each other, page by page. They were crazy about it and wanted to buy it on the spot.

"It's a tough way to wake up," I said, "but as long as you're here, let's make a deal."

"Not only do we want to make a deal for the novel, but we were looking at your paintings just now, and our company would like to buy some of them," Harold said, looking lovingly at my two Picassos, a Juan Gris, a Chaim Soutine, and some other large oils.

"The paintings are out. As for the book, I want

four hundred thousand dollars, payable at the rate of forty thousand a year for ten years."

"That's an outrageous price—but we'll pay it."

That afternoon Selznick called inquiring about *Lucy Crown*.

"Sorry, David. I've sold it."

"You couldn't do that without telling me."

"It's done."

"I'm going to Switzerland to see Irwin."

I called Irwin and managed to track him down at the ski lodge at the top of the mountain.

"What's the matter?" he asked, thinking it was some kind of emergency.

"Do you still not want to sell *Lucy Crown?*"

"It's not a movie."

"Say it could be. What would be a fair price for it?"

"I don't think anyone will ever make it, but if you could get fifty thousand, that would be terrific."

"Would you take four hundred thousand?"

"If you can get four hundred, I'm not going to ski down the mountain, I'm going to fly down!"

David, in the meantime, was as good as his threat. He arrived in Switzerland the day after I called, told Irwin he was willing to pay more, and asked why he was willing to take only four hundred thousand.

"I don't know," Irwin said. "But Lazar must have a good reason."

As soon as he could shake free, Irwin called to find out why I wouldn't sell it to Selznick. I explained that David was strapped for cash. I knew he could make the first payment, but by the time the contracts were finalized in two or three months he might not have the rest of the money. If that happened, he was too distinguished for us to badger him for money—we'd have to walk away empty-handed. To me, a real four hundred thousand was better than a vaporous four-fifty. Irwin agreed. And he not only made out all right, he did fine creatively—to this day, *Lucy Crown* has never been filmed.

While I got my commission, I paid a certain price; Selznick shunned me for the next couple of years. Then, as if nothing had happened, he called and asked me to work out a deal on some of his properties. I met him at the St. Regis in New York, where, like an Arab sheik, he had taken over an entire floor. Two secretaries followed him with open notebooks, their pencils flying as they took down the gospel according to Selznick.

L. B. Mayer was a great showman who loved and admired talent. If he thought he spotted a potential star in the making, he was like a kid with a lollipop. And when he met someone who had been recognized as a talent, he was an even more formidable champion. Nothing would stop him from putting all of the muscle, power, and money of Metro-Goldwyn-Mayer behind his judgment, and in some cases, his pure instinct.

By the same token, he was destructive and callous if the talent he endorsed and supported didn't observe his rules, his social standards, and his politics. And that was a problem, for L. B. was one of the fiercest leaders in the search for Communists in Hollywood. He felt completely justified in destroying anyone he identified as un-American—that is, anyone who wasn't a friend of Ward Bond, John Wayne, or John Ford, or who wasn't endorsed by Hedda Hopper.

When Mayer was "eased out" of his position at Metro in 1951, he couldn't comprehend that he was no longer king of the realm and had no power to make or break a star. The way he saw it, he had only to press a buzzer and a minion would produce whomever he wanted. Despite his loss of stature, it was still a given that you showed up when Mayer wanted to see you.

Mayer's secretary called late one morning to inform me that he wanted me in his office at one o'clock that very day, so I changed my schedule around and drove over to his house on St. Cloud Road. As ever, the place was so sanitized that it gleamed. The only paintings Mayer could tolerate here were by Grandma Moses; the only photographs on display—of the Pope and Cardinal Spellman—were both inscribed. Mayer, of course, had not called me to advance his spiritual development.

"I want you to give me your best property," he told me. I knew what that meant: I'd better not offer a potential hit book or screenplay to another producer before giving him first crack. I was a little apprehensive about that because I knew he wasn't accustomed to spending his own money, and he was no longer set up to spend other people's money. Money was even a little bit of a problem—considering that he was once reported to be the highest-paid executive in the United States, he didn't wind up with a fortune.

I had to tell him about something, however, so I recommended *The Shrike,* a play starring José Ferrer that was a big hit in New York. I thought it would work well for Mayer, as it had a strong point of view and could be produced with minimal financial risk. Mayer agreed to pay a hundred and fifty thousand for the property. I then made a deal for Joe Ferrer both to star in and direct the film.

Only after the deal was closed did Mayer want to go to New York to see the show. On the day of our departure, however, various crackpots called him to say that Joe Ferrer was a Communist. As a result, we didn't go to New York.

The next day Hedda Hopper wrote in her column that she thought it was outrageous that Louis B. Mayer was buying a play directed by and starring a Communist, and that the play itself had Communist overtones. Hedda's column was all Mayer needed to renege on the deal. After reading the paper, he called to announce that he was not going to see "that Commie play," nor was he going to pay for it.

As I saw it, Mayer had already committed himself—we were, by this point, waiting for contracts to be prepared. Mayer didn't deny that he had authorized me to buy it. His position was that he would never have done so had he known that José Ferrer was a Communist.

Ferrer didn't behave much better. When I ran into him in London, I extended my hand. "Joe, I'm going to do everything I can to fight this injustice," I said.

"You called me a Communist."

"Don't confuse me with Mayer. He called you a Communist. I'm the one who's fighting for you."

"I don't believe it," he said, and with that, he gave me a shove. I shoved him back a little harder.

My main concern, of course, wasn't clearing Joe Ferrer's name. It was to hold Mayer to the purchase of the play regardless of the outcome. And that I achieved.

My career as a literary agent in Hollywood had just reached its peak when McCarthyism hit the industry. Irwin Shaw, for example, couldn't get a job because Jack Warner had spread it all over town that he was a Communist. At one point, Irwin confronted Warner in a café in the South of France and grabbed him by the lapels. "Come outside and call me a Communist!" he demanded.

When Harry Kurnitz was under contract with Metro, Louis B. Mayer wanted to use his politics as an excuse to break his contract. The idea was that Kurnitz was a member of the Communist party. In fact, Kurnitz had, at one point, been briefly active in party discussion groups but that was the extent of his involvement. Hardly a crime, but in those days, you risked being barred from working in Hollywood just for having a drink with "suspicious" people.

Metro couldn't find the modicum of "proof" that would justify breaking Harry's contract, so the studio arranged to have him assigned to a back lot in the midst of muddy flats quite a distance from the Thalberg Building. This was, in essence, Siberia. If you worked here, you were locked up in a bungalow without any heat. It was a singularly unpleasant experience, and that was the point—after the briefest exposure to Siberia, most writers resigned. Harry, unfortunately, couldn't afford to quit: Quitting would mean not eating caviar and he liked that too much. I eventually had to sell him to studios under the pseudonym of Marco Page.

By 1953, Red-baiting was at its crest. That year, Jerry Wald wanted Peter Viertel to write a script, but before bringing Peter from Paris to Los Angeles and putting him to work, he requested a report on Peter from the Motion Picture Alliance. According to this report, Peter needed to answer some questions about his mother's and his wife's political associations, even though he was now separated from his wife. And, of course, he would have to sign an affidavit stating that he was not now and never had been a Communist, and had never contributed to Communist causes. Peter, too, needed the work and had no choice but to comply.

Chicago Jew Wins Nobel Prize for Literature

American Jews by the third quarter of the twentieth century were taking leadership roles not only in the popular media but also in more upscale literary endeavors. Of the many Jewish fiction writers of his generation, Chicago's Saul Bellow has received the most recognition, being the only American Jew born on this side of the Atlantic to win the Nobel Prize for literature (Isaac Bashevis Singer, the other American Jewish Nobel Literature Laureate was born in Poland). Along with his great success as a novelist, Bellow held a chair in humanities at the University of Chicago for three decades, although he had no academic training.

Here is a succinct and insightful assessment of Bellow's work by Malcolm Bradbury, the English critic and novelist.

In 1976, the Bicentennial year, Saul Bellow—the Jewish-American novelist who was in fact born of Russian-Jewish immigrants in Lachine, Quebec, Canada, and who grew up in the Montreal ghetto until at the age of nine his family moved to his warmly adopted city of Chicago—was awarded the Nobel Prize for Literature. He won it at the age of sixty-one, by which date he had behind him a record of seven major novels, one novella, a good number of short stories, several plays and essays, written over thirty-five years, and the reputation in many quarters of being the leading American novelist of the postwar generation. The award was doubtless intended to recognize the extent to which American fiction had, especially over the postwar period, come to dominate the international development of the novel as a genre. Also, given the spirit of the prize, it meant to recognize that Bellow, in a time when the humanistic development of the novel form had come under a severe questioning, was ready to express and speak for its humanistic purposes. Previous American novelists to win the prize had included Sinclair Lewis, William Faulkner, Ernest Hemingway and John Steinbeck, and in all four the award had been preceded by a movement in their work toward a more humanist intention.

Indeed to glance at the previous winners is to be reminded that the Nobel Prize has never been an easy one to have and to hold, especially if the author is American—part of a cultural system where the prize is tight-bonded to the complex economic operations of the culture-market.

His books show a deep sense of environmental intrusion, of the power of the conditioned, of life as competitive struggle chaotically releasing and suppressing energy. As a novelist he encounters an urban, mechanical, massed world—in which the self may be ironized, displaced or sapped by dominant processes and the laws of social placing, where victimization is real, and the assertion of self and the distillation of an act of will or a humanistic value is a lasting problem. Much of this naturalistic lore Bellow inherited from the 1930s, at the end of which he began to write. But what intersects with all this, and makes his work so convincing, is the deep penetration of his work by the classic stock of European modernism, especially that modernism in its more historically alert, postromantic and humanistically defeated forms.

Bellow is thus a novelist of a very different generation from that of Lewis, Faulkner, Hemingway, Steinbeck or James T. Farrell, all of whom might in different ways be associated with the centralizing of the American novel as a major twentieth century form of expression. He is a novelist writing beyond the end of American pastoral; his works belong to a new order of American and world history.

His social and ethnic origins, as a child of Russian-Jewish immigrants, connected him readily with the neomodernist Jewish writing of the 1920s and 1930s, from Babel to Singer, from Bruno Schultz to Kafka. Politically active in the Depression, he none the less started to write in the mood of abeyance to dialectical politics that came with the Second World War; his first story, "Two Morning Monologues," appeared (in the summer of 1941) in *Partisan Review*—that New York centred, predominantly Jewish, ex-Marxist intellectual journal moving at this date from 30s Trotskyism toward an increased commitment to the spirit of literary modernism, with its bleaker view of man in history. His earliest fictional publication thus immediately precedes the Japanese attack on Pearl Harbor which plunged America into the Second World War, collapsed the 30s political spectrum and allied Americans with the bleakness and bloodiness of modern world history. It was a history that disoriented the liberal progressive expectations of the American left, challenged naturalism as a language of political attention, and raised the question of art's response to a totalitarian and genocidal world. Bellow's response was to write about an America newly exposed to history, affected by the desperations of existentialism and absurdism, war-pained, urban, materialist, *Angst*-ridden, troubled with global responsibility, struggling to distill meaning and morality from the chaos of utopian and progressive thought.

All this was very apparent in *Dangling Man*, Bellow's first full-length novel, which appeared in 1944, as the war moved to an end—an extraordinary book which displays clear debts to a modern European writing of romantic disorientation and historical enclosure that comes from Dostoevsky, Conrad, Sartre and Camus. It is not hard to draw links between his and Dostoevsky's spiritually agonized heroes—caught in the fragmentations of a culture collapsing into urban strangeness, political disorder and waning faith which struggles with existential desire; nor between his world and Conrad's, where civilization is a thin veneer overlying anarchy, calling forth "absurd" existential

affirmations; nor between his imaginings and Kafka's, where the self moves solipsistically through an onerously powerful yet incomprehensible historical world. Yet it is as if this was a tradition which Bellow felt he had the power to qualify and amend, to recall toward humanism; and here his Jewish sources are deeply relevant, constituting another force that "Europeanizes" his fiction.

Perhaps Isaac Bashevis Singer rather than Kafka—Bellow translated Singer's story "Gimpel the Fool"—better suggests this origin, with his classic images of suffering and victimization irradiated with transcendental and mystical hopes; the recovering victim and the "suffering joker" are part of the essential stuff of Bellow's writing, but so is that sense of human bonding which allows him to struggle toward a latter-day humanism and a new civility. Indeed it was that new civility, accommodating the experience of persecution and the path of survival, that made Bellow seem so central a figure in the postwar world, a world postholocaust and postatomic, urban and material, where progressive naturalism and innocent liberalism no longer spoke recognizably to experience.

Bellow thus went on to become a primary voice of a time when the Jewish-American writer, urban, historically alert, concerned to distill a morality and a possible humanism from a bland, material, encroaching reality in which all substantial meanings seemed hidden, moved to the centre of American writing. For now, as Leslie Fiedler noted, the Jewish hero, practised in suffering and survival, persecution and accommodation, became the type of modern man, "the metropolitan at home, though expert in the indignities, rather than the amenities, of urban life." It was an anxious new writing, of mythic inclinations, concerned to measure the large questions of human nature against the material and conformist face of an American life which offered individualist rewards yet base compromises; in Bellow, Bernard Malamud, Delmore Schwartz, Philip Roth and others, the image of disoriented man, the parvenu in the culture, the stranger in the city, the wanderer displaced between origins and the present, offering to substantiate the culture if that culture will show its humane substance, became a central theme for the American fiction of a troubled age.

Bellow, like many of these others, drew his strength from an irritable energy of dissent, and an artistically vigorous view of Jewish metaphysical perception, which attempted to pursue connectedness and moral responsibility in a world that insisted either on bland incorporation into society or else self-privatization, a "hoarding of spiritual valuables," as Bellow would put it. He was to prove most Jewish in his hunger to find a ceremonial of life in a darkened world, to discover some oblique act of human faith. "The world comes after you. . . ," Joseph, the disoriented, hermetic, intellectual protagonist of *Dangling Man,* moving in spirit away from coercive society, reflects. "Whatever you do you cannot dismiss it." But the new humanism was hard to forge, being riddled with doubts and fears—aware of the disjunctive implications of modern experience and modernist writing, conscious of the dark threats of modern totalitarian force, of the justice of apocalyptic imaginings and of the troubled warnings of Freud and others about the imbalance of civilization and desire.

Bellow thus developed as a writer in a period when a distinct stylistic and aesthetic climate, which was also a political climate, was forming. It was a period of revived liberalism, invigorated by the reaction against totalitarianism that arose with the battle against and then the defeat of Nazism, and then with the new cold war struggle of the superpowers. The politics and aesthetics of liberalism were an important version of recovered pluralism and democracy; yet at the same time the postwar social order, with its materialism, its pressure toward conformity, its move toward mass society, threatened the liberal self. The reaction against totalitarian models shaped aesthetic and formal choices; both the lore of modernism and that of naturalism, especially in its thirties form as politico-social realism, came under question. The 1950s seemed hungry for a postpolitical politics, a postideological ideology; in this process literature and cultural concern became the foci of intellectual activity. Modern literature, with its sense of irony, scruple and moral ambiguity, with its bleak report on modern *Angst* and exposure, replaced more ideological texts, especially those of 1930s Marxism, the God that had failed. In the new mood of political abeyance, where there was a strong concern for the rediscovery of a moral humanism that might redeem suffering and destruction, literature became a mode of anxious moral and metaphysical exploration.

It was the Jewish writers, with their sense of traditional alienation and exile, their profoundly relevant witness to the recent holocaust, their awareness of the inadequacies of an older liberalism that could not cope with what Reinhold Niebuhr called "the ultimately religious problem of the evil in man." who concentrated the spirit of the necessary imagination. Lionel Trilling would call this "the liberal imagination," whose natural centre lies in the novel, the testing place where the ideal is perpetually forced to mediate with the contingent and the real, where ideology meets "the hum and buzz of culture," where history and individual are compelled into encounter.

Bellow's fiction, as it developed from the tight form of *Dangling Man* (1944) and *The Victim* (1947) into the looser and more picaresque structures of *The Adventures of Augie March* (1953) and *Henderson the Rain King* (1959), thus seemed to gesture toward a revival of the liberal novel—a form that has had a strained history in our modern and modernist century. The liberal novel is, I take it, the novel of Whiggish history, where there is some community of need between self and society, where individuals may reach out into the world of exterior relationships for reality, civility and maturity, where the possibility of moral enlargement and discovery resides. It is thus attentive to history in both individual and community, finds both equally real, and grants to both a logical chronology of growth. Bellow's novels have certainly moved toward the salvaging of a liberal form. They are hero-centred to a degree unusual in modern fiction; the hero often gives his name to the novel. He is always a man and often a Jew, and often a writer or intellectual; he is anxious about "self," concerned with exploring its inward claim, and about "mind," which may be our salvation or the real source of our suffering. At the same time he is driven by an irritable desire to recognize his relation with others, with society as such, with the felt texture of common existence, with nature and the universe. Around such battles certain prime reminders occur: Man is mortal, and death must be weighed; man is biologically in process, part of nature, and must find his measure in it; man is consciousness, and consciousness is indeed in history; man is real, but so is the world in its historical evolution, and the two substantialities evade understandable relation. So we are drawn toward thoughts of extreme alienation, urgent romantic selfhood, apocalyptic awareness, while at the same time we know ourselves to be in a postromantic universe, Lenin's age of wars and revolutions, where our conditioning is inescapable. Social and historical existence may thus contend with mythical or metaphysical existence, but neither can finally outweigh the other, and the effort must be toward reconciliation—an end displayed in Bellow's own fictional endings, which frequently take the form of some complex contractual renewal between the self and the world, though, despite critical suspicion of them, these endings are less some rhetorical resolution than a suspended anxiety, often returned to in the next novel.

Bellow's books could thus be said to stand at the centre of contemporary enquiry into the possibilities of the novel—an enquiry inherited from those writers of the turn of the century who made naïve realism problematic. For the late Henry James, the novel was driven back symbolistically on to itself, becoming an exploration into the relationship between the perceptions of consciousness and the materiality of the exterior world; in Dreiser's fiction, that materiality becomes a process, a set of systems far larger than the consciousnesses they conditioned, and making them into a facet of things. For the contemporary writer, this space—between what Bellow calls in *Humboldt's Gift* the "it" and the "we"—has been a fundamental area of search. In Bellow's novels, consciousness and history struggle at odds, in a world where, as Joseph notes in *Dangling Man,* the old metaphysical stage of good and evil has been reset, and "under this revision, we have, instead, only history to answer to" (*DM,* p. 73). Yet history may indeed point to excrescence or emptiness, or else to a Byzantine therapeutic self-celebration, a fashionable contemporaneity unaware of its own illusions and decadences. On the one hand there is a lack of cosmic fit between individual and the social mass, the endless proliferation of technologies, systems and abstract social relations; on the other there is the hidden administration of power, truth, "reality" which makes that inner life an aspect of the process from which it seeks to separate itself. Thus there is alienation as a false romantic solipsism, and there is determination as a false acquiescence; the

problem of Bellow's heroes, and of Bellow's novels, is to discover the spaces and the places of that which is both unconditioned and humanly alert and present.

It is indeed because Bellow's novels have in them an intense historical presence that they have survived so vigorously over the four decades of his writing. For many of Bellow's contemporaries, the strain of mastering contemporary American experience has not been easy to face. The Jewish-American novel of the 1940s and 1950s was displaced, in the 1960s, by a novel of historical extremism (*Catch-22, Slaughterhouse Five*) or historical senselessness (*V.*). Indeed, as Morris Dickstein puts it in his *Gates of Eden* (1977), "one of those deep-seated shifts of sensibility that alters the whole moral terrain" occurred, as a new provisionalist radicalism challenged the postwar "new liberal" synthesis. The moral containments of 50s fiction gave way to new aesthetics of black humour, countercultural provisionality, irrationalism and outrage; the new postmodernist text appeared, lexically complex but moving toward indeterminacy of meaning. The nonfiction novel, founded on the conviction that the extremist realities of 1960s America was itself an absurd fiction, linked with the new fictionality. On the writers of the 1940s and 1950s, the impact was clear. J. D. Salinger, whose fragile moral redemptions had seemed an essential metaphysics of possibility, followed his own Glass family into an elected, aesthetic silence. Norman Mailer turned from a formalized naturalism to a fiction of historical self-immersion, offering himself up as a secret agent of the *Zeitgeist,* a risk-taking performer active and participant in the cannibalism of contemporary sensibility. Bernard Malamud's later fiction displayed the strain of applying formal artistic expectations to the unnerving new landscape of modern politicized consciousness; Philip Roth moved from the Jamesian moral management of his early books into the free-form confessional of his later ones.

As for the balance and nature of Bellow's work, that too changed. In the 1950s he had explored the expansive epic, testing out whether man can set himself free in history. By the 1960s that enquiry had tightened again, into the complex structural form of *Herzog* (1964), where historical presence becomes a form of madness, and the bleak irony of *Mr. Sammler's Planet* (1970), which now looks less a bitter assault on the new radicalism than the beginning of a new kind of enquiry into the elements of evil secreted in our modern history, and in modern America, in an age marked by postcultural energy, a new rootless barbarism in which possibility and monstrosity contend for the soul. Bellow's books have grown not easier but harder to read. They have become in some ways more meditative, philosophical, transcendental. So Nathan A. Scott rightly says that we should not see them as some form of latter-day naturalism, but as works where the phenomenology of selfhood is at stake, so that they turn on essential moments when the hero, "transcending the immediate pressures of his environment and the limiting conditions of his social matrix, asks himself some fundamental question about the nature of his own humanity"—a question increasingly answered, Scott suggests, by a falling into peace, a submission to the multilayered mystery of existence. Bellow's lasting concern with questions of the nature of our human contract, our eternality, the worth of our existence on this stony and historically troubled planet, has extended and grown more complex; but so, equally, has his concern with the definition of our late age, the darkening life of our century, the engulfing mechanisms of power and mass, the anxious performance of a consciousness ever more drawn toward excess and extremity.

Bellow is not, in the fashionable sense of the term, a "postmodern" or even an "experimental" novelist. He does not question reflexively his own fictionality, or adopt the nihilist stoicism of black humour. His books still grant the dominant materiality of the outer world, which is process, system and power; and they continue to explore consciousness and mind in struggle with that power, as they hunt to find a significant human meaning, an inward presence and a sense of personal immediacy, and an outward awareness of the nature of the cosmic world. Consciousness and history still struggle at odds, but in an ever-compelled and ever-changing intimacy. His books have, indeed, largely changed by circling their own known subjects, intensifying the elements, deepening the enquiry. Bellow's perception of the nature, the substance and the pressure of the historical world has moved increasingly toward a definition of a new, postcultural America, most clearly manifest in his own home city of Chicago, that "cultureless city pervaded nonetheless by Mind," as its life has changed, accumulated and massed; as its old localities and ways of life fall under the hands of the new developers, as crime and terror haunt its inner city and the *inner* inner city of its inhabitants, as the doors are triple-locked and bourgeois life goes on under siege in some strange modern compact with a new barbarism, it becomes a central image of what the mind and the novel alike must come to terms with. His perception of the world of consciousness has also grown more intense and avid for right feeling, as it finds itself bereft yet busy, having nowhere else but history from which to draw versions of reality in its endless quest for awareness and fulfillment.

Warsaw, April 1943: Germans versus Jews

The struggle in the Warsaw Ghetto of April 1943, between the might of the German army and a handful of Jewish resisters, mostly member of Zionist youth organizations, came to be romanticized after the War into the Revolt of the Warsaw Ghetto. Here is a sobering and heart-rending account of what actually happened in those horrible days by the Israeli historian S. B. Beit Zvi—based on memoirs of participants, German army records, and interviews in Israel with survivors—and privately published in 1991.

That incredible acts of heroism were performed by the Jewish resistors is beyond question. With only the most meager supply of weapons they fought against the German army with its vast numbers and battlefield equipment. But whether this event should be called the Revolt of the Warsaw Ghetto is questionable—a last, desperate, and totally doomed effort to strike back as the Germans proceeded to liquidate the Ghetto would be a more accurate summary description. Nevertheless, these events are destined to be known in Jewish history as the Warsaw Ghetto Revolt.

The uprising in the Warsaw Ghetto began on April 19, 1943, the eve of Passover, on the day the Nazis launched their operation to liquidate the ghetto. The two events, the liquidation and the revolt, intermingled and engendered a further development: the liquidation operation became a massacre, accompanied by the total burning of the ghetto. Their intermixture also created the optical illusion that enabled the obfuscation of the developments. While the liquidation action lasted almost a month, the active revolt ended within a few days. But just as an outside observer who saw the flames rising from inside the ghetto could not know exactly what was happening inside, so it is difficult at first historical glance to discern precisely when and how each event occurred. Under the influence of the combative orientation, the tradition took root at all levels of Israeli research that the revolt paralleled the Nazis' murder and destruction. Thirty years were needed until one of the revolt's participants took the first step toward setting the record straight in a book implying that the active revolt lasted only three days. As we will see, one more day, April 27, should be added to this number.

The abundance of testimonies in the ramified literature on the subject contain solid facts attesting with sufficient certainty to the activity and situation of the insurgents during most of the event. This is particularly true of the "Jewish Fighting Organization" (JFO, *Zydowska Organizacja Bojowa,* or ZOB, in Polish), on which the great majority of the Israeli literature on the revolt is focused.

As the uprising approached, the ZOB was comprised of twenty-two party units, fourteen from Zionist youth movements and parties, and four each from the Bund and the Communists. The units were divided according to the ghetto's three regions: nine (or ten) units in the Central Ghetto under the command of Israel Kanal; five in the Brushmakers' Area commanded by Marek Edelman; and in the Toebbens-Schultz craftsmen's area, eight (or seven) led by Eliezer Geler. The overall commander of the organization, Mordechai Anielewicz, was in the Central Ghetto during the uprising; his deputy, Yitzhak Zuckerman ("Antek"), was on the "Aryan" side of the wall.

Estimates differ regarding the number of ZOB members. Based on a detailed list of the units including the names of their commanders and areas of operation, and assuming that each unit numbered twelve to fourteen persons on the average, Dr. Yosef Kermish estimates that all told, the organization contained some three hundred fighters. Stefan Grajek's estimate that each group was made up of ten to fifteen persons leads to a similar figure. Ber Mark, without explaining his calculations, assesses their number at six hundred, Gideon Hausner increases it to one thousand, while Marek Edelman, a member of the organization's command, insists that there were no more than two hundred members.

The weapons at the ZOB's disposal were meager in the extreme relative to the task they set themselves, and as compared with what the Bialystok group would have four months later. The ZOB's deputy commander, who specialized in acquiring arms, relates: "Our weapons were: pistols, one pistol per person; rifles—no more than ten; a revolver, mines that were laid in five or six places; over a hundred home-made bombs with a very large explosive force; Polish grenades for defense and attack. Marek Edelman's account is similar: "Each fighter received on the average one pistol (ten to fifteen bullets), four to five grenades, four to five petrol bombs. Each area received two to three rifles; in the entire ghetto there was one automatic revolver." Besides that revolver, the ghetto fighters had no automatic weapons, not a single machinegun, no heavy weapons. When the uprising began they discovered that "the pistol is worthless, we hardly used it" (from the letter of Mordechai Anielewicz—see below). The small number of rifles and the absence of long-range automatic weapons meant that from the outset the uprising's possibilities were very limited.

The ZOB's achievements are contained in a document accepted as a letter written by the organization's commander, Mordechai Anielewicz, to his deputy, Yitzhak Zuckerman, on April 23. Several comments have to be made about this document before we can consider it. *The Book of Ghetto Wars,* edited by the letter's recipient, relates that it was originally written in Hebrew, translated into Yiddish "with secret and personal details deleted," and from Yiddish rendered "with changes" into Polish. The Hebrew source went up in flames during the Polish revolt in Warsaw, and the version presented in the book is a retranslation from the Yiddish.

The changes introduced in the letter in the three languages are numerous and diverse, and do not stem only from a desire for secrecy and security. The versions published during and after the Holocaust were marked by some peculiar changes and omissions. To this day opinion is divided as to whether the original letter included a passage praising the aid of the Polish Communists and about the place occupied by the passage in the body of the letter. Some versions try to "correct" statements by Anielewicz that seem unreasonable or cause discomfort. Thus, for example, his twice-repeated comment that as of the writing of the letter only one of the organization's members had been killed, was replaced by Ber Mark with the statement that "our losses in people are very small." The same holds true for the version that appears in the Hashomer Hatza'ir collection, which differs completely from all the other versions, in both wording and tone.

When all is said and done, it is difficult to relate to the letter, as it appears in its different versions, as an exclusive document for gleaning facts. Nevertheless, since it seems probable that the letter was in fact written and sent, and that it was composed on or about April 23, we will use it to illustrate facts that are authenticated by more reliable sources.

The following is Mordechai Anielewicz's assessment of the ZOB's accomplishments up to the fifth day of the liquidation *Aktion* in the Warsaw Ghetto: "The Germans fled twice from the ghetto. One of our units held its ground for forty minutes, and the other for over six hours. The mine planted in the Brushmakers' Area exploded. On our side so far there has been only one casualty. Yehiel. He died heroically manning the machinegun."

The detail about the fighter Yehiel as the organization's only casualty was correct regarding the group of units in which Anielewicz fought personally at the corner of Mila and Zamenhof Streets. It was not correct regarding those who fought elsewhere, including the units whose successes he reports in the letter. The fact that Anielewicz did not know about the death of Michael Klepfisz, a leading ZOB activist and a mainstay in preparing the organization's ammunition, shows how well-founded his complaint was that he had no contact with the units.

The mention of the machinegun also gives rise to doubt, since according to the dual testimony quoted above, the organization did not have a machinegun. Perhaps Anielewicz was referring to the automatic revolver, or perhaps the ZOB did have, after all, some other automatic weapon that became a "machinegun" in the course of the translations and retranslations. The rest of the information about the successes of the ZOB fighters is basically correct and is confirmed by historians and by witnesses who took part in the actual events.

One operation, which forced the Germans to flee, was carried out by a group of four units that seized positions on the upper floors and in attics of the buildings on the four corners of the Mila-Zamenhof intersection. At 6 A.M. on April 19 a German column arrived at the site in order to begin liquidating the ghetto. The Jewish fighters hurled bombs and grenades at the German troops and opened fire with the weapons in their possession. The Germans were taken by surprise and suffered casualties. Fifteen minutes later a tank and two armored vehicles arrived at the site. The tank was twice set ablaze by petrol bombs and the Germans beat a hasty retreat. Soon ambulances arrived to evacuate the wounded and the

Germans then began to shell the fighters with cannons. The Jewish fighters withdrew to a bunker at Mila 29. Anielewicz, who took part in the battle, estimates that the fighters held out for forty minutes, and his testimony is authentic.

Concurrently with the battle at the corner of Mila and Zamenhof, there was a clash on Nalewki Street, near the Gesia-Franciszkanska intersection. Events followed a pattern similar to that described above: A surprise bomb and grenade attack was launched from the upper stories of buildings and fire was opened with all available weapons. The results, too, were identical. The Germans suffered losses and backed off quickly. They did not return for two or three hours. It later emerged that during this respite the commander of the liquidation *Aktion*, von-Sammern, resigned and was replaced by General Stroop. The latter ordered heavy fire directed against the insurgents using a variety of weapons. In the ensuing battle both sides sustained casualties. After the Germans fired incendiary bombs into the buildings, setting them afire, the insurgents were forced to retreat to the bunkers.

It is difficult to determine how long the battle (or battles) at this spot lasted. If we accept Anielewicz's estimate that the fighters held out for six hours, many details are still lacking about what occurred during that time. What is not in doubt is that the operations on Nalewki Street and at the corner of Mila and Zamenhof constituted the peak of the ZOB's success. According to Stroop's reports, the Germans and their collaborators suffered twenty-five casualties (one killed, twenty-four wounded) on April 19—the highest figure on any single day.

The explosion of the mine in the Brushmakers' Area is also confirmed by persons who took part in the fighting. This occurred on the second day of the revolt, April 20. At 3 P.M. an SS company neared the gate of the Brushmakers' Area at the Walowa-Swietojerska intersection. At this spot the insurgents had planted a powerful electric mine beneath the street. When the Germans reached the exact spot, Kazhik hooked up the electricity. The mine went off, causing German losses. In the battle that ensued the Jews defended themselves bravely and stubbornly. The fighting ended when the Germans set the buildings afire from all sides. The fire forced the rebels from the upper floors and attics and they withdrew to bunkers in the burning quarter. At night, when the fire and smoke intensified, they tried to get out of the area. Three units managed to get to the Central Ghetto where they found shelter in the bunker at Franciszkanska 30. The fourth unit returned and were killed when the Germans dynamited their bunker. The Jews had several casualties in the fighting for the Brushmakers' Area, among them, as mentioned, Michael Klepfisz. Stroop's report puts the number of German casualties at thirteen (three killed, ten wounded), far more than on any subsequent day.

These, then, were the three Jewish operations cited by Mordechai Anielewicz. All three took place in the first two days of the liquidation action in the Central Ghetto and the Brushmakers' Area. On the fifth day of the operation, April 23, Anielewicz had nothing to add about additional noteworthy operations in those two quarters.

In the third area, Toebbens-Schultz, the insurgents on April 20 threw two bombs at a company of gendarmes that was marching in formation outside the ghetto, near the wall. They also tried, unsuccessfully, to detonate an electric mine they had planted under the booth of a German patrol. The following morning, April 21, three ZOB units attacked another German squad that was marching outside the ghetto. In this area the Germans delayed setting the buildings afire for a few days in order to complete the transport of several thousand artisans to the Poniatow and Trawnicki camps. As a result, the rebels received a reprieve of three or four days in which they were not forced to seek shelter in the bunkers and enjoyed the advantage of positions high above the Germans who were on the street below. Yet that same factor, the transport, tied the hands of the rebels, as they were reluctant to attack Germans mingling among large numbers of Jews. As the transport operation drew to a close, the Germans began to torch buildings and the rebels were forced to take refuge in the bunkers.

This concluded the military activity initiated by the ZOB. Imprisoned in their places of hiding in the burning ghetto, equipped with only pistols and a few grenades; driven by fire and smoke from one bunker to another; hunger and thirst gnawing at them—in this state of affairs, war is out of the question. The appropriate weapons for the existing conditions were not available. The pistol, as Anielewicz wrote, had "no value" in fighting against rifles and machineguns. The heavy bombs made of steel pipes, if any remained, could only be hurled from above. The few grenades and rifles they still had could inflict no substantial damage.

Anielewicz was aware of the new situation when he wrote his letter. It suggests that he grasped that fighting by day was no longer feasible. But he still hoped to shift to "partisan tactics" during the hours of darkness. He promised that on the following night three units would go into action, their mission being to conduct "an armed patrol and to obtain weapons."

No detailed information exists as to the quantity of arms the night patrols managed to get. Not a great deal, one would assume. The truth is that the pledge of "partisan warfare" was not a realistic proposition at that time, just as today there is no factual basis for the claims of commentators and memoir writers that the goal (or one of the goals) of the patrols was to enter into combat with the Germans, steal their weapons, and kill or harass them. If Anielewicz or any other of the ZOB's leaders entertained thoughts along these lines, reality soon contradicted them. In addition to the gross inferiority in arms, the darkness also worked to the Germans' advantage in the burning ghetto. "The German would lay an ambush for us in the dark. He saw us before we spotted him: The burning buildings lit us up and he would fire at us from afar, while we could not guess when and where the ambush would be. The flames blinded us and we could not see where to aim our bullets." Eventually, when the flames died down, the glare effect was reduced. However, a new and equally dangerous factor now appeared. Beginning on May 1, Stroop dispatched mobile patrols through the streets of the ghetto at night in order to search out Jews who left their places of hiding under cover of dark. These were not bored sentries standing guard along the perimeter of the ghetto or elsewhere; they consisted of special squads—nine soldiers and an officer—whose mission was what a later generation would call "search and destroy." The soldiers were carefully selected and properly equipped, and their effect was devastating.

The patrols of Jewish fighters occasionally encountered Germans, and they even managed to wound a few of them. But of all the concrete descriptions of such encounters contained in the Warsaw Ghetto literature, we recall only one that was deliberately initiated by Jews—in honor of May Day.

This operation is known from the detailed descriptions written by its two participants. The operation was initiated and directed personally by Mordechai Anielewicz. He chose seven fighters, six men and a woman, who were equipped with six pistols and one rifle. Their mission, the commander explained, was to ambush Germans in broad daylight, kill them, and escape. And that is what they did. They went out at midnight, wandered the streets until morning, and picked a convenient site for an ambush. In one account the young man firing the rifle, a superb marksman, hit one German, though another version has him hitting three Germans. The group succeeded in escaping, and after much wandering about for the entire day, made their way back to Mila 18 in the evening. This, then, is the only concrete description we have of an operation planned in advance to attack Germans.

Also working to the Germans' advantage were clashes fought by Jewish patrols that served no truly essential purpose of the latter. The primary mission was to maintain contact between the bunkers in order to convey information, relay orders, and so forth. Subsequently it became more urgent to look for food in buildings and cellars not yet razed by the fire. In certain situations the need arose to search for a different hiding place in order to escape a bunker that was too hot or that was in danger of falling into German hands. And in short order pride of place was taken by the most pressing mission of all—to find a way out of the ghetto.

The initiative to this end did not necessarily come from the organization's command. On April 24, Bozhikovsky relates, "a group of *haverim* from all the units met for a consultation and decided to send four people with 'Aryan' facial features out of the ghetto to get help in extricating the fighters. The four, two men and two women, made their way the following day through the sewage canals toward the Aryan side, but when they tried to get out they were caught and three perished. The fourth, Bozhikovsky, survived miraculously and made his way back to his comrades in the ghetto."

After this, contact with the Aryan side to enlist help and bring out the fighters became a crucial necessity. On April 27 three people were sent to the boundary of the ghetto to talk with Polish firemen. The negotiations ended in a new disaster the next day. On April 29 the ZOB command sent two more people, Simcha Ratheiser and Sigmund Friedrich, out of the ghetto. They succeeded in reaching the organization's deputy commander, Yitzhak Zuckerman, to whom they reported on the situation inside the ghetto. Zuckerman told them about the immense difficulties involved in getting help. "I found that we could not expect any help. We were fated to act alone. Each of us therefore sought to make as many contacts as possible." After a week of toil, initiative and resourcefulness, they succeeded in obtaining concrete results—which for the majority of those slated to leave the ghetto came too late.

The units in the Toebbens-Schultz area got out of the ghetto early and with relative success. The decisions to leave was made in a meeting of activists in the predawn hours of April 28. Prior to the meeting and the decision, the area commander, Eliezer Geler, assembled the organization's personnel in one place. He was not completely successful in this, as several units could not be found. In the morning of April 28 they descended into the sewers for the first time. Following a retreat due to a false alarm (they thought the Germans were pouring gas into the sewer) they reorganized and went down again. Forty people were in the group, including a number of noncombatant civilians. At 2 A.M. they emerged on the Aryan side and hid in the attic of a nearby house. After remaining there for a day, they were given transportation outside the city before dawn on April 30.

It was later learned that on the same day members of units in the Toebbens-Schultz area who had not been able to join the escape two days earlier entered the sewers. After reaching the Aryan side they tried to escape on their own, but were all killed.

In contrast to the decisiveness and energy that characterized the escape operations in the Toebbens-Schultz area, the organization's leadership in the Central Ghetto was wracked by uncertainty and indecision. This situation developed due to personal and circumstantial factors, one of which strikes us as particularly important. This was a convenient circumstance that was transformed, it seems, from a blessing into a curse.

As they wandered from place to place to escape the fire and smoke, the organization's command happened on the bunker of the Warsaw Ghetto underworld. Their huge bunker consisted of a series of cellars, burrows and caves, well camouflaged and outfitted with all possible conveniences. The occupants received the commanders and other fighters warmly. Within a short time more fighters arrived, until nearly a hundred people were in the bunker—nearly all the remaining ghetto fighters.

Conditions in the bunker were difficult, particularly in some of the sections to which the fighters were assigned. The air and heat in the "Treblinka" and "Piaszci" sections, as the fighters called them, were intolerable; the electricity, which had functioned in the first days, went off; the water tap produced only drops; contamination spread, hunger grew sharper.

Yet these conditions were passable as compared with hundreds of other bunkers. In the "Trawnicki" and "Poniatow" sections the heat was average, and people could occasionally switch from one section to another. The night patrols to search for food were conducted with the participation and active advice of the bunker's occupants, whose profession made them past masters at this kind of work. Rarely did patrols return empty-handed. The leader of the bunker saw to it that the food was properly and fairly distributed and that people moved about from one section to another.

The agility of the bunker's occupants, their self-confidence and their ability to adapt to the extraordinary conditions of life in hiding made a great impression on the young fighters. The knowledge that the fire and smoke did not threaten them here (the bunker was established under the ruins of a building that had already been razed to the ground) was also a contributing factor. Overall, it seems probable that together with the relief ensuing from the cessation of the unbearable wandering through a sea of fire and death, the fighters began to feel a sense of something approaching security—that in this wonderful bunker and under the protection of its omnipotent masters, no harm would befall them, at least not this day.

This conjectured blunting of the sense of urgency and danger may help account for the passivity that marks the period which the fighters spent at Mila 18. As the days passed, fewer attempts were made to communicate with the "Aryan" side at all costs or to find ways out of the ghetto. After the two boys were sent on April 29, as described above, nothing more was done until the fateful night between May 7 and May 8.

Not only was action paralyzed, so too were thought and initiative. The rank-and-file fighters, under the influence of the dual psychology—of their commanders and their hosts—spent their time singing, exchanging stories about their experiences, listening to the tales told by the ringleaders among the thieves, and arguing about Yiddish vs. Hebrew, Zionism vs. Communism. The commanders, for their part, sat about in the bunker's corridor holding endless consultations. Various opinions were voiced and diverse proposals were adduced. But no decision was made that necessitated action. The commander, Mordechai Anielewicz, "considers every suggestion, but the truth is that he does not know which way to turn."

This was the situation as the events of May 7 began—the day on which the Germans discovered the location of the bunker at Mila 18. At 3 P.M. the bunker's inhabitants heard heavy movement above them, the stamping of feet and the noise of various tools. Plaster and sand fell on them from the ceiling. The ruckus lasted about three hours. At 6 P.M. the Germans left.

A burst of activity followed. Three missions set out from the bunker that night. Two were dispatched to the Aryan side to look for ways out and enlist help; both groups were too big for a task requiring maximum mobility and evasive capability. Tuvia Bozhikovsky, who was in one of the groups, and Tzivia Lubetkin, who also went out, explain that only a few, with "non-Jewish" features, were supposed to cross to the Aryan side, while the others were to wait in the sewers until the appropriate message arrived from those who had crossed over. This testimony suggests that quite a few of the fighters (among them one of the commanders, Israel Kanal, who had unmistakably Jewish features) preferred the agony of expectation and uncertainty in the inferno of the sewers over the continuing wait at Mila 18.

Both missions ended in failure. One group, with eleven members, headed by Aharon Bruskin, was caught as they emerged from the sewers; most of them perished. The second group, containing ten people, encountered a German night patrol while still inside the ghetto. Four of them were seriously wounded but with the help of three others managed to return to Mila 18. The remaining three were pursued without letup from 2 A.M. until 6 A.M., when the Germans changed their guard. During the day they found shelter in a disused bunker and the following night they arrived back at the bunker they had left 24 hours earlier—only to find it in ruins.

The third group completed its mission in full. It consisted of two people, Tzivia Lubetkin and Haim Frimmer as escort. They were sent to the bunker at 22 Franciszkansa Street, where Tzivia Lubetkin was to do three things: meet with the fighters in the bunker; ascertain that the sewers were accessible from the bunker; make contact with a certain youth and send him to guide Bruskin's group; and finally, to convince the bunker's inhabitants (noncombatants) to admit the fighters from Mila 18 so that they could get to the sewers.

This was a saliently solo operation and the available information about it sheds little light on the circumstances of its conception and realization. Incomplete testimonies indicate that the negotiations with the bunker's occupants was the primary mission, and that for this reason a very influential member of the organization's hierarchy was sent.

At first glance it appears that this mission could have constituted a fateful turning point had it been more fortunate. It was totally successful, as already mentioned, and the assent of the bunker's occupants was secured. True, it later emerged that the exit of Bruskin's group ended in disaster, and the guide was found not to be sufficiently expert in the underground canals. However, confirmation was received that the way from the bunker to the sewers was open and that all could assemble in the bunker prior to leaving.

If Tzivia Lubetkin had *hurried* back to her bunker and reported to her friends about what she had learned, would a miracle have occurred? Perhaps her news would have encouraged more and more of the fighters to leave urgently in the wake of the twenty-one who had left with the two unsuccessful missions? And maybe the command would have found the mental resilience to shake off its hesitations and decide to leave with all the fighters at the last minute under cover of dark?

Perhaps . . . But it's doubtful whether the organization's leadership, bewildered and mentally exhausted, could have been pushed to take action beyond endlessly discussing all kinds of proposals. The behavior of Tzivia Lubetkin herself that night was not characterized by a sense of urgency—in terms of hours—such as might have infected her comrades and roused them to immediate action. Testimony does exist suggesting that on the way there she intended to return "shortly after midnight," but the emotional reunions with friends brought a slackening of alertness. The conclusion of the mission is related by the two participants simply and convincingly:

Haim Frimmer:

Tzivia met with the command people and they sat down to discuss their business . . . I washed and drank some good water. I was very tired and I lay down in some corner and fell asleep. The meeting went on for a long time, and when I was awakened after it ended, dawn was already beginning to break. To return to Mila 18 now would mean to move in broad daylight. The danger was great. Tzivia insisted that we return. Her argument was that it would not be fitting for people to think we were cowards. But I considered myself responsible for escorting her, and I was adamant: To return in broad daylight meant certain death. We therefore stayed there the whole day.

Tzivia Lubetkin:

The night passes. We want to leave in order to return and report on the situation as regards getting out. But they plead with us not to go. Soon it will be daylight, and we must not walk about the streets! I refused to remain here for a whole day, but I was so tired, the body yearns for a little rest, and even Marek Edelman, the commander of the unit in this bunker, implores us to stay. He too is going out tonight and will accompany us. And the dawn is already visible outside.

The decision to stay saved the lives of the three fighters. The fate of the fighters at Mila 18 was then already sealed, since they no longer had a way out during the daylight hours.

On May 8 the Germans returned to the bunker at Mila 18 which they had discovered the previous day. They took up positions at all five exit points and called on the occupants to come out and surrender. All (or most) of the noncombatants complied. Not one of the fighters came out. The Germans injected gas into the bunker, initially in small quantities, in order to force everyone out; then they poured in gas in large doses to suffocate whoever remained inside. One of the fighters urged everyone to commit suicide, and many did so. The commander, Mordechai Anielewicz, suggested that they try to overcome the effect of the gas by immersing their heads in water. He himself put his head in a pail of water that was standing under the tap, and thus died. The others died of suffocation.

Miraculously, a few people survived. They had been next to one of the openings and the air they inhaled was partly pure. They were found in a semiconscious state and extricated by Tzivia Lubetkin and her companions who returned from 22 Franciszkanska, and by Bozhikovsky and his friends who returned just then from their unsuccessful mission.

The gassed fighters and their rescuers moved to 22 Franciszkanska. But the events that had occurred at Mila 18 the previous day were now replayed at this bunker: The occupants heard footsteps outside and concluded that the Germans had discovered their location. Immediately Tuvia Bozhikovsky led another group on a third mission to the Aryan side. This time he was surprisingly successful. In the subterranean maze of canals they encountered Ratheiser-Kazhik who said he had gone to the ghetto with two guides in order to rescue the fighters, but after failing to find anyone in the places he looked was about to return to the Aryan side in great disappointment and despair.

On the morning of May 9 all the fighters from 22 Franciszkanska and a number of noncombatants, about sixty people altogether, entered the sewers. A stormy argument preceded the decision to leave when some of the group refused to go without taking the remnants of three units of fighters located at Nalewki 37—which was impossible until after dark. At 11 A.M. the group reached the opening of the sewer on the Aryan side, where they were told they would have to wait until nightfall before they could come out. When night came a note was handed down saying that the streets in the area were crawling with gendarmes and the exit would have to be postponed until the following night.

Mentally and physically, the fighters were almost at the end of their tether. The rescuers finally yielded to their insistent appeals and agreed to take them out during the day. They left the sewer on May 10. The operation was both successful and disastrous: Thirty-two (or thirty-four) people were pulled on to a truck and got out of the city. When the others tried to follow they were spotted by Germans and all perished. Nothing is known about the fate of the fighters who remained at Nalewki 37.

The description thus far indicates that the active uprising in the Warsaw Ghetto lasted two or three days. As for the subsequent events, they can be subsumed under the term commonly used by the spokesmen for the Holocaust history establishment: "defense of bunkers." But as we explained, the bunkers were no more than hiding places and they were not fortified. To reach them, the enemy had no need to overcome obstacles, only to discover their location. And once discovered, the bunkers were doomed.

As we pointed out, the great publicity surrounding the revolt was in large measure the result of the optical illusion that *enabled* the blurring of the boundaries between the Germans' liquidation operation in the ghetto, and the Jews' uprising. This blurring was not a spontaneous act and was not effected at the time of the events by the insurgents and their colleagues, who in any case did not think in terms of a "revolt" but took a more modest view of their actions. All the versions of Anielewicz's letter speak of "Jewish defense," not a revolt. Nor was a revolt mentioned in Zuckerman's 1944 survey, later published verbatim in Neustadt's book. Batya Temkin-Berman, who wrote her diary on the "Aryan" side of Warsaw, calls the events of April-May "the third extermination operation," or "the third *Aktion*;" she reserves the word "revolt" for the Polish uprising in Warsaw in August 1944.

Most convincing of all is the testimony of Emanuel Ringelblum in his essay, *The Relations Between Poles and Jews in World War II*. Ringelblum devotes considerable space to the Jewish resistance during the liquidation of the ghetto, and does not even think of calling it a revolt. Dozens of times he speaks about the "April *Aktion*" and once about a "struggle"—never about a revolt.

Ringelblum is the first to point out that there was one party with a vested interest in presenting an exaggerated description of the resistance and describing it as a revolt—namely, the Germans. According to Ringelblum: "With German methodicalness they laid a suitable foundation for their acts of cruelty. It was to this end in particular that both the German administration and the press maintained that a Jewish revolt was being suppressed. The Jews [the Nazis claimed] had established partisan units to kill German soldiers."

What Ringelblum could not have known was that in addition to the propaganda angle, the ghetto's liquidator, Stroop, had a strong personal motivation for inflating the dimensions of the events and their military significance. As is clear from the collection of reports and photographs the Nazi general presented as a gift to his superior, he was determined to exploit the situation to the full in order to advance his military and party career. With this in mind he tried to depict the events as a broad-based military episode. It is doubtful whether he could afford to take the chance of distorting facts and figures—the manner in which the reports were drawn up and sent dictated limitations which he could not ignore. However, he had wide latitude in the area of description and interpretation. Here he could exercise a free hand and his appetite grew. The operation itself, called the "operation in the ghetto" during the first ten days, on April 30 became the "large-scale operation in the ghetto." As the days went by with the ghetto in its death throes, the reports were increasingly full of descriptions of the Jews' fierce resistance, the intensity of the operation to suppress them, and the excellent merits of the suppressors. Stroop's persistence paid off: For his work in liquidating the ghetto he was awarded a high Nazi decoration, the Iron Cross Class A. He was promoted and given important assignments.

In December 1945 Stroop's reports were submitted as evidence in the Nuremberg trial. During a break in the trial the professional Nazi General Jodl exclaimed: "The dirty arrogant SS swine! Imagine writing a seventy-five-page boastful report on a little murder expedition!" But the report's publication had its effect. Alongside the invaluable statistical and factual material, his tendentious tales were absorbed and helped blur the boundaries of time between the liquidation action and the revolt.

But as it turned out, all the ploys were totally unnecessary. The blurring of boundaries and the confusion of concepts, the stylistic and terminological deceptions, all the glorifications resorted to by the chroniclers of the uprising of the young Jews in the Warsaw Ghetto, were not needed. The aura of the revolt would not have been tarnished, and historical credibility would have gained immeasurably, if instead of all these ploys the historians and memoir writers had told the simple truth they knew, without concealing a thing.

Yet astonishingly, for years the flags were not mentioned by so much as a word in Israeli literature on the Holocaust. The memoir writers forgot them and the researchers did not discover them. For years great efforts were invested in uncovering and commemorating every detail about the revolt. Every fact, every rumor, every scrap of a story was collected and set down in writing, for the sake of history. No detail was found to be unimportant, unreliable or insufficiently verified. Everything was considered fit for publication and perpetuation. Only one "detail," a solid, well-known fact of far-reaching importance—the hoisting of the flags—was barred from mention in amazing agreement between the community of memoir writers, researchers and commemorators.

The reason, it turns out, is that the flags were flown by the "wrong" people. They were from Betar, the youth movement of the Revisionists, who were passionately despised by their opponents in the Zionist movement. Embarrassingly, besides hoisting the flags, they did other things which, if made public, were liable to wreak havoc in the party alignment which was supposed to represent the revolt in the eyes of the public. Since nearly all the Revisionist fighters, with only a few exceptions, were killed during or shortly after the revolt, they and their deeds could be ignored for years.

The flags that Ringelblum saw from the fourth floor of Nalewki thirty-two were hoisted in Muranowska Square, a central assembly place of the Betar organization. Its name was the "National Military Organization," or ZZW according to its Polish initials.

The ZZW fighters were for the most part members of Betar, although the organization also had unaffiliated persons and members of youth movements ranging across the entire political spectrum, including Communists, as individuals and as autonomous groups. The ZZW had three leaders: David-Mordechai Appelbaum, a former Polish Army officer; Pawel Frankel, a student who was one of the organization's founders; and Leib-Leo Rudell, a journalist who headed the information department. As with the ZOB, the number of ZZW members is in dispute. The historian of the ZZW, Haim Lazar Litai, speaks of an estimated five hundred members at the end of 1942, and twelve hundred on the eve of the revolt. Ber Mark estimates that there were four hundred ZZW members at the beginning of 1943, and concurs with Litai regarding the number when the revolt broke out. Yosef Kermish is skeptical about Mark's estimate, hinting that it is exaggerated.

No one, however, disputes that the Revisionist group was well armed. Unlike the ZOB, it possessed a relatively large quantity of weapons and ammunition of various kinds, including automatic weapons, among which was the only heavy machinegun in the ghetto. The arms were acquired from various sources, thanks, among other connections, to the ZZW's excellent relations with groups in the Polish underground—one of the significant differences between the two organizations. The ZOB leaders (with the exception of Mordechai Tenenbaum) had a strong pro-Soviet orientation ("anti-Fascism" in the accepted terminology). This generated suspicion and mistrust among the Poles, who had hardly forgotten the division of Poland by Hitler and Stalin. The ZZW, by contrast, being composed of diverse political elements, espoused demonstrative Polish patriotism, and indeed started out as a Jewish branch of the Polish underground. Besides a direct supply of arms, the friendship with the Poles opened up other routes of procurement for the ZZW from sources where the ZOB faced insurmountable obstacles.

An important ZZW asset consisted of two tunnels its members had prepared some time earlier, linking the ghetto with the Aryan side. A sophisticated tunnel, the result of a considerable engineering feat, connected the two sides of the wall at Muranowska Square and played an important part in the course of the fighting there. A second tunnel, integrated with sewage canals, joined the two sides of Karmelicka Street in the Toebbens-Schultz area.

Their advantages in ammunition, organization and military planning enabled the Betar group to make impressive visual achievements. At their main place of assembly—Muranowska 7–9 and the corner of Muranowska and Nalewki—they demonstrated the ability to stand up to the Germans in face-to-face combat for hours on end in a battle that lasted for two days. They defended the flags they had hoisted by opening fire with the machinegun in their possession. They repulsed a German assault on the afternoon of April 19 and held their ground until nightfall. The following morning the flags, riddled with bullet holes, were still flying and had not fallen to the enemy. Only after a stubborn battle involving tanks, cannons and other heavy weapons were the Germans able to take the buildings, seize the flags, and wreak revenge on the defenders.

The Romantic Image of the Warsaw Ghetto Revolt

How the events of April 1943 in the Warsaw Ghetto have become enshrined in Jewish memory was already set down in 1946 in this encomium by the American Yiddish popular novelist, Sholem Asch. Variants of it are heard every April from politicians and publicists in America and Israel. Asch later had a big falling out with the American Jewish community for writing a sympathetic novel about Jesus of Nazareth.

So, united, Zionist, Bundist, [Socialist] Communist around the Jewish flag of the Battle of the Warsaw Ghetto they now come marching down the pages of Jewish history, after their death. A warning for the present, consolation for the future.

The martyr-heroes march together in closed ranks, united as they were when they fought together, in the streets, in the bunkers, in the cellars, on the roofs, Zionist, Bundist, Communist, religious Jew, Chassid and assimilationist, all together, each marked with the seal of Kidush Hashem by God's angels. Each wears the distinction of German knife and bullet wounds, all dripping blood as they go. It is the same blood from them all, Bundist, Zionist, Communist, religious Jew—all Jewish blood. The same devil shed it all. The same enemy, the same vengeance, the same triumph, the same liberation and redemption. The past is one, and the future is one. Am Yisroel Chai!

Then by herself, alone, comes a Jewish mother, tall, wrapped in the folds of a black mantle, carrying a dead child in her arms; she weeps quietly to herself, like a dove. Like Mother Rachel she complains to God. She has only one complaint: "Abraham was only tried. From me you took the full sacrifice." That is all she has to say.

This was the end of the march of the dead. Then came the march of the living.

Suddenly everything vanished. Like a dream. Gone were the crowds, the sea of faces had disappeared as though they had never been there. The whole Jewish population of Warsaw had flown up into the air, and left the earth free. The air was silent. Only the bells went on ringing to the tune of Chopin's Funeral March, echoing the tramp of the entering liberation armies.

Out of a side street came a small group of people with torn clothes, barefoot, with disheveled hair. Mothers looking like madwomen, with flaming eyes and sick children in their arms, or leading them by the hand. Fathers, wild-eyed, with flying hair and beards, rifles slung over their shoulders, the wounded flesh showing through their rags, their naked feet torn and bleeding. The eyes of the children wide with terror, looking round all the time, terrified, as if pursued.

This group of people came rushing toward the advancing liberation armies. Suddenly everything was silent. The music stopped, the church bells no longer rang. The general leading the liberation armies shouted an order, and his armies withdrew, making room for the oncoming group with their tattered clothes and bleeding bodies, and each whispered to the other: "These are all that are left of the Jews of Warsaw."

The general dismounted from his white horse. "I bend my head," he said, "to the Jewish martyrs of Poland. You are Hitler's greatest victims, yet you are also the greatest heroes of the Hitler war. You, with your endurance, won the war against Hitler."

The generals of the other liberation armies and of the armies all came forward, bowed to the handful of surviving Jews, said: "Warsaw will live. Warsaw will live, with you. There will be no Warsaw without Jews."

Suddenly a voice rose, the voice of the half-million Jews of Warsaw, the voice of the three million Jews of Poland. The voice came from invisible heights, falling down to earth, the voice of the whole Jewish population that had lived in Poland, all the rabbis, all the writers, the social workers, the thieves, the fighters, the vulgar common folk, the Chassidim, the Communists, the Bundists, the Zionists, all the women and children who perished for Kidush Hashem, by all Hitler's terrible ways of slaughter. The voice cried: "Jews of Poland, your blood is Jewish history for a thousand years. In your heart beats the pulse of generations, of scholars, rabbis, writers, leaders. Jewish destiny depends on you. You are the remnant of us all. You must live! You will live. In you we all shall live!"

Then came an echo, the voice of hundreds of thousands, of millions of Polish people whom Hitler tortured to death, and they cried to the Jews: "Jews of Poland! We died for a free Poland. Without you, without the Polish Jews, there is no Poland. Live, live on!"

Victory

Yael Dayan is a prominent Israeli writer, feminist, and left-wing member of the Israeli parliament. She is also the daughter of Moshe Dayan, who more than any other Israeli general came to symbolize the great victory in the Six-Day War of June 1967 over Egypt and Jordan. The victory resulted in the taking of East Jerusalem—which the Israelis had failed to do in the War of Independence of 1948, in which Moshe Dayan lost an eye during the fighting—and the West Bank and Gaza, which have given the Israelis so much trouble since 1988.

In 1985, Yael Dayan published *My Father, His Daughter*, a work that combines memoirs with a biography of her father, about whom she has ambivalent feelings—mostly but not entirely admiring. Moshe Dayan was a great womanizer and had divorced Yael Dayan's mother. Moshe was also a brilliant if controversial amateur archaeologist and a tough-minded politician. As defense minister in 1973, he did a bad job in preparing the Israeli Defense

Forces for the Egyptian counterattack in the Yom Kippur War, and was soon forced to resign and withdraw from public life.

In this remarkable chapter Yael Dayan give her highly personal recollection of the great victory of 1967. It is an interesting perspective because she knew personally most of the leaders involved in the event, or had at least observed them in relation to her father. There is an air of family business about her version of what happened.

Yael Dayan's work is the single best book ever written about modern Israel. It is, of course, not touted at Israeli Bond Dinners or on the rightist pages of Commentary magazine.

On May 20, 1967, my father celebrated his fifty-second birthday. For a few days prior to what for him personally was just another insignificant birthday, a huge Egyptian force, comprising about eighty thousand soldiers and eight hundred tanks, was moving in the Sinai Peninsula toward the Israeli border.

On May 22, Nasser declared a blockade of the Straits of Tiran to all ships bound to or from Israel.

On May 23, I received a cable in Athens, summoning me home. My father was sure we were facing another war, and very soon, and he knew I would rather be home when that happened.

On May 25, my BEA flight landed in Lydda airport, where my mother met me and drove me to my reserve-unit HQ in Tel Aviv, where I reported. I was listed as a lieutenant in the Military Spokesman's unit, and I made it clear that I didn't intend to stay in the Tel Aviv area and brief foreign journalists. It was Friday, and I was told to report the next day. They'd see what they could do, the officers promised. "As long as it is in the south," I pressed. "And where do you think everyone requests to be sent?" On the way home, we listened to Nasser's bragging speech. "Egypt will destroy Israel," he declared. He announced that the armies of Egypt and Syria were now one, and invited Jordan to join. He praised the Soviets, scorned the U.N., and his voice held a new self-confidence rather than the familiar Middle East hysteria.

After my rather long absence, the house in Zahala seemed like a safe shore that no war could shatter. Both my brothers were mobilized, and my father was truly glad to see me. "Just in time," he said. "The war may begin tomorrow with dawn, unless it is postponed again, which would not surprise me." He must have been certain enough, though, for he took me out to a "festive" dinner and was quite relaxed during the four-course meal. I couldn't take my eyes off him, and was fascinated by the changing expressions on his face rather than by what he told me. He had been in uniform for a week now, "getting the feel of it" again. Many reservists were mobilized, and the long, nervous wait was demoralizing. His face lit up, as if transformed chemically from inside, when he spoke of the troops, of the commanders he knew; his heartbeat was with them, and all the parental love, all the camaraderie this man could summon glittered in his one eye. When he spoke

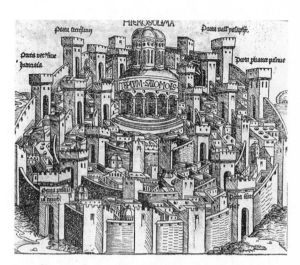

Jerusalem as a fortress city, 1493.

of the diplomatic efforts to attain American consent and guarantee for free passage in the Gulf of Suez, or the negotiations with the U.N. and with European heads of state, his face showed dismay, if not contempt. He mentioned Udi and Assi and Zorik's son Uzi and Aviva's son Jonathan with anxiety and pride. They were all good fighters, responsible, reliable, and he said: "I am happy about the fact that they are motivated by love of their country rather than by hate for the enemy."

He was confident of our strength, of our morale, and in all his eagerness for the operation to begin, he did not sound trigger-happy, bent on destruction, or in search of some personal satisfaction. Some of the plans were not perfect, he suggested, but all war rooms and command "pits" were open to him, and his advice at least was heard. It didn't bother him to have no official authority, as long as they let him—"they," meaning Eshkol, who was prime minister as well as minister of defense—be in on it. And where he asked to be, which was naturally the Southern Command, with an armored brigade. "Make sure you're sent south," he advised me, as if I were a tourist talking to a travel agent. "The best, of course, is Sharon's division, if you can get there!"

The end of May is blessed with warm days and cooler nights, and a reminder of orange blossom is still in the air. We parted, not knowing when and how we would meet again, but sensing a deep harmony. For both of us, for my father in a deep and vast national sense, and for me in a purely personal way, it was a comeback. I came home, and soon I knew it was for good. He was at his best, freed of the frustrations, melancholy, and bitterness of the past few years. His car was waiting, and he drove—it was almost midnight—to the Southern Command in Beersheba, and I drove home to Zahala, to spend one last night, for many days to come, in a comfortable bed.

Twenty-four hours later, there was no orange-blossom scent in the air. The evening breeze scattered the loess dust, powdering my face, my sandaled feet, my writing pad, and the ration biscuits I was eating. I was attached to Arik Sharon's division HQ, "the best post," as my father suggested, for however long the general mobilization lasted. I was to send daily reports to the correspondents' pool, which were to be distributed for publication in Israel and abroad. The definition of my objectives didn't matter. I was in the one and only

place I cared to be. The Egyptian threat, less than a mile to the west of where our tents were pitched, was my only reality, and my pulse beat in an impatient unison with the men around me, officers, soldiers, reservists, and innocent, eager conscripts.

The steam that had been bottled up for the last few years had to surface, and an all-out war seemed inevitable. A series of incidents between Syria and Israel and between Jordan and Israel led to the flawed judgments of President Nasser, who believed this was the perfect time to strike and retrieve his supremacy in the Arab world. The Six-Day War, as it was later called, was the third major armed conflict Israel had had to engage in since its birth, and on the last days of May we did not need to analyze or look for a historical perspective. We almost took for granted the fact that we were not accepted as an equal nation by our neighbors, that we were doomed to fight wars for our survival at what seemed to be ten-year intervals. The cycle of hatred, rejection, accumulation of arms, buildup of confidence in their own strength, and internal needs of a military dictatorship offered a seemingly endlessly repeatable pattern, leaving us no options other than tactical ones. Defense, a preemptive attack, the capture of the populated northern Sinai and the Gaza Strip, or a sweeping move toward the canal, one front at a time or all-out war on three fronts, the bombing of civilian targets or the use of the Air Force as an auxiliary to armor and infantry. The preoccupation with these options and others was not limited to government and General Staff meetings. Women in the supermarket as well as farmers in border settlements, schoolchildren, and newspaper editorials, with a varying degree of expertise and anxiety, were hectically assembling the pieces of this political-military jigsaw puzzle. The questions were not "why," as there the answer seemed to be "survival," but were mostly "when" and "how."

Near the Nabatean ruins of ancient Shivta, where Sharon's HQ was camouflaged sloppily, we had all the answers. The "when" was yesterday—at the latest, today—and the "how" was mapped out in the war-room tent in large red-and-blue arrows crossing the green border line into the Sinai all the way west. The "how" was also mapped in the experienced, wrinkled faces of reservists, in the shining eyes of tank crews, and in Arik Sharon's diabolically brilliant military brain. Where the question marks were left open and gaping was the corridors of the Foreign Ministry and the Prime Minister's office. It was evident that the political leadership was unable to commit itself to an irreversible course of action and was hesitant to derive the courage and determination to do so from the people and the Army, rather than, as normally expected of leadership, inspire them.

Ceaseless interparty contacts attempted to broaden the framework of Eshkol's government to form a national unity government. Some of the parties, including Begin's Herut, asked Eshkol to hand over the premiership to Ben-Gurion, but the real need was expressed in popular demonstrations, petitions, and tireless exhortations by a stream of individuals. "Dayan for Minister of Defense" was almost a unanimous request. As Shimon Peres was effectively negotiating the proposition, fully backed by Ben-Gurion, his task was made easier by an enormous surge of popular demand. A myth? A craving for what represented military glory and personal courage? Idealists, pragmatists, followers, and political adversaries who joined in a request to have my father named Defense Minister were mostly motivated by a crying need for decision-taking leadership. The emotional horses were pulling the hesitant political cart, and either to steer, speed, or stop it, it needed a superb coachman. The candidate himself, my father, did not cooperate. He would do, he declared, anything he was asked to do, provided it did not keep him from the active front. He was not going to be an "adviser" in a Jerusalem office; he'd rather command a tank battalion. He was not going to interfere with the existing IDF hierarchy or replace someone, thus discrediting him. He rather fancied a position as commander of the southern front, with the current GDC Southern Command as his deputy.

Meanwhile, Peres, Begin, the Religious Front leaders, and others calling on the government to entrust the defense portfolio to Dayan's hands were against compromising. When Golda Meir suggested Allon for Defense, and it was clear that the Defense portfolio was to be separated from the premiership, the pressure mounted, and Allon himself withdrew his candidacy.

On May 30, King Hussein signed an Egyptian-Jordanian defense pact in Cairo, and on June 1 my father inspected the Jerusalem area. His trip was interrupted. At 7 P.M., Eshkol telephoned Father to report that the cabinet had approved the decision to give him the Defense portfolio. As my father said, the following morning: "It took the entry of eighty thousand Egyptian troops into the Sinai to get me back into the government."

The precise series of events, the pressures, the intricate political scheming, are of little consequence now, or even then—once the decision was taken. What was evident then, and later, as before, was the fact that my father's career would never benefit from his own ambition. He would never push or pull to get a position, or even cooperate with those who wished it with his consent and on his behalf. He was content to announce his availability, and his neutrality, meanwhile wasting no time, doing his homework, planning, and applying his mind and talent to what should be done rather than to who would do it. As a result, he did not feel in debt or make an emotional or ideological commitment to the people and movements which placed him where they did. He felt he derived his power, authority, and sense of mission directly from the people, and to them it was owed. Eighty thousand Egyptians motivated three million Israelis to want him there, and the three million's gain was the eighty thousand's loss. There was no time to waste.

That same Thursday, June 1, I was busy brigade-hopping. The frustration was reaching a peak, and an afternoon sandstorm didn't help. Cooks, drivers, privates, and colonels fought apathy and desperately tried to boost morale. Mordechai Zipori, an armored brigade commander, recited Jabotinsky's patriotic verse. Arik Sharon restlessly went over the attack plans for the thousandth time—they were flawless, to begin with—and Kuti, the infantry commander, walked the desert plateau, where I joined him, looking for flintstone arrowheads. He piled them on the sand and sorted them out. The small or broken he said were common; he gave them to children. A few perfect ones he kept; but the best, the largest, and one extraordinarily shiny white one he asked me to bring to my father. "And one for you, to keep you safe," he said, and I put it in my shirt pocket. The night before, Arik issued orders to move our half-tracks to the border. "I want them on the frontier, even if exposed. From border stone to border stone, on the last inch which is Israel." I was watching with Kuti the dusty trails of the approaching vehicles. "An exercise in wishful thinking," Kuti commented. "Lining up for a race does not mean the race will take place." Colonel Kuti Adam looked like a fierce warrior. He was dressed in battle fatigues and a black beret, a pistol and a knife dangling from his belt; a canteen, binoculars, a large map on the hood of his jeep—all contrasting with the extraordinary softness of his voice, and the warm, nostalgic look in his black eyes. He talked of my father, whom he loved and admired, saying simply: "If he leads us, it isn't that we'll go to war, as we should; it is the way we are going to win it which is going to be different." He talked at length, gazing west, as the half-tracks were pulling into a set formation. "Moshe," he said, "is not a mystic mascot. It isn't his military genius either, as he approved of the battle plans and made only a few changes. It is a quality which can't be defined, which represents, and demands, the best in all of us. For me, he is a link between those arrowheads and the half-tracks, and forward in time to, alas, nuclear warheads. At the same time, if we ever have peace, it will be under his leadership, or in his spirit." Kuti felt he talked too much, as he was a gentle, shy person, and to his relief, Colonel Dov Sion arrived to take me to the field hospital and back to Shivta. We had dinner with Arik, in his trailer, and I was too tired to wait for the midnight news, on which my father's appointment was announced.

On Friday morning, the change was noticeable in every face, word, and action. As if we all got a second wind, as if a large brush had painted off the past two weeks and splashed new vivid colors and feeling into the dormant desert, the steel war machines, the spirit of the commanders, all of us. Even the long wait suddenly made sense, and for once I wasn't embarrassed by expressions of affection and pride which were bestowed on me but directed at my father.

At the first cabinet meeting in which my father participated, the die was cast. Eshkol, willingly and with a tremendous sense of relief, asked my father what his proposals were, and without hesitation Father declared: "We should launch a military attack without delay. If the cabinet takes such a decision at its next scheduled meeting, Sunday, June 4, we should strike the next morning. The campaign would last from three to five days." He added his objections to advancing too close to the Suez Canal, and to a suggested transfer of refugees from the Gaza Strip to Egypt. This war should not lay the grounds for a next, harder war. It should eliminate a direct threat and rule out a major armed confrontation.

The long days of avoiding a decision were over. The mood of the entire cabinet was changed, and the Army's self-confidence was restored as if by a magic touch. Those who were in favor of waiting another week, to protect the political flanks, listened to him describe the merits of a preemptive strike. "The first shot would determine which side would suffer the heavier casualties, and if we took the enemy by surprise, their damages would be the equivalent of all additional arms supplies we might receive for the next six months. The course of the campaign should be dictated by us, and the enemy should be forced to fight according to our moves." The next cabinet meeting ended with a vote on my father's proposal that "orders be given to the Army to choose the time, place and appropriate method." All but two ministers voted for the resolution.

Dov, who was Sharon's liaison officer with GHQ and the Southern Command, agreed to drive with me to Zahala and back that Friday evening, on the scant hope that I might get a minute with my father.

The house was full of flowers, boxes of chocolate, baskets of fruit, as if for a wedding. Gifts from people, mostly unknown to us. The comforting aroma of chicken soup filled the kitchen, and my brother Assi, on a three-hour leave from his antiaircraft gunners unit, was the recipient of my first hug and kiss. Father was taking a bath—between meetings. My mother's eyes, though glittering with pride, still had a tear in them when she saw us, both in uniform, aware as she was of what would happen shortly. We were, in fact, prematurely celebrating a victory, but she could not ignore the inevitability of casualties that even the greatest of triumphs incurs.

Father walked out of the bathroom in his underpants and slippers, and without his eye patch. He hardly fit the confidence-inspiring image he represented since the previous day. Yet it was all there. The brightness in his direct look, the youthful stride as if a burden had been shed, the seriousness of a tremendous responsibility, and the bemused half-smile of self-assurance. Most of what we had to say to each other we expressed in a long embrace, and he was as delighted as an infant when he examined Kuti's arrowheads. He spoke admiringly of Arik and his brigade commanders, and promised me I was "in the best of hands." He talked about being for the first time endowed with the highest authority, as Eshkol left all military decisions to him.

In 1956, as Chief of Staff under Ben-Gurion, he carried out orders even when he considered them mistaken. Now the responsibility was his. "For good or for ill, I will be on my own." We all had to leave soon, and wished each other luck. None of us knew when, or how happy, our next encounter would be. Mother packed fruit and nuts and chocolates for me to take to Shivta, and with them her anxiety and love.

Dov called for me, giving me time to get into and out of a hot bath and change, and I hastily introduced him to my mother. I couldn't at that moment share with her the vague but mounting feeling I had for him. I myself referred to it as "nothing personal," just an emotional affinity of two people facing a surge of events.

We did not talk much on the long drive back. Beersheba's main street was dark and dead, and Arik's trailer and the HQ tents in Shivta felt like home. I could not mark it on a calendar, but D-Day tension was in the air, and the precise date didn't matter. We were on our way.

On Sunday afternoon, Dov said to me: "You had better get some equipment." We went to the supply tent, where I exchanged my boots for a better pair, got a new canteen, spare woolen socks, and some ammunition. I handed in my identity discs and received in their place a "prisoner's card" on which were the details I was allowed to give if I was captured. Name, rank, number, blood type. I placed the card in my pocket, next to Kuti's arrowhead, and tried on the helmet, which felt heavy and uncomfortable. Trucks were being loaded, engines warmed, communications systems tested, field kitchens packed, but nobody said D-Day is tomorrow. The most I could get from Dov to my "So that's it" was an enigmatic shrug and a suggestion which seemed wild: "Try to get a few hours' sleep." My father reviewed the final plans that Sunday evening, flew to the Northern Command to get a situation report, and arranged for a field bed to be available to him in the emergency HQ. It was a cool, pleasant night, almost romantic, had it not been for hordes of mosquitoes, and to my amaze-

ment, I managed three hours' sleep. I woke up in a dark A.M., with a dramatic feeling. For a brief moment, the last in many days to come, I was an observer. A few soldiers were in prayer next to the war room; two reservists were writing letters; Arik was shaving in his trailer and very carefully applying aftershave lotion, like a youth before his first date; and Dov was packing. A small bag to take along, and the rest of the things to be left behind. I was taking the same stock, mentally and emotionally. Nahalal, my brothers and cousins, my parents, high-school history and geography lessons, oil lamps and arrowheads, were placed close to my skin and would come along, with the reliable boots, the writing pad, and "Don't forget the toilet paper," Dov had said. Athens; Michael, regretfully and affectionately; Rome's cakes and Paris restaurants; London publishers' talk and New York sophisticated dinner parties; Vietnam jungles and Singapore markets—all were neatly compressed and packed, to be left behind. I left on my wrist a gold bracelet given me by that gentlest and most understanding friend, Alain de Rothschild, as a token link between the worlds. He was in Paris, and I knew his heart was with me and the men around me.

When the sun mounted, blessing us with its golden touch, we had already advanced in a compact, mobile HQ formation. Arik's two half-tracks were to move with the force, together with a couple of jeeps equipped with machine guns, and the supply car would trail behind. The brigades were spread out on our flanks, and for the time being the communications system was not activated.

I helped Rachamin, the cook, with breakfast and, when the tea was ready, woke up Arik. On a blanket spread on the hard sand, I got our last "civilized" breakfast of fried eggs, fresh salad, and bread. Next would be C-rations, and who could tell for how long.

My mother prepared an early breakfast in Zahala on June 5. My parents sat at the table at 6:30, had coffee and toast, and Mother mentioned that she was going to Jerusalem for a meeting later. From Zahala my father left for HQ, made sure the timetable was planned, and took off for a small café around the corner, where he met with Rahel for another coffee and a croissant. He didn't mention to either woman, or as much as indicate, what was to happen within the hour.

At 7:30, my father was in the Air Force "pit," and Arik told us to put on helmets and get packed and ready to move. Very few words were spoken. The buildup to this moment was so long, it left no room for last-minute, dramatic excitement. The spring was stretched to capacity and ready to be released, and there was a severe sense of professional awareness in the air.

Between 7:14 and 8:55 A.M., Israeli planes carried out an attack in two waves. In the first wave, 183 aircraft were engaged, rendering six Egyptian airfields inoperable and destroying 205 enemy aircraft, putting sixteen radar stations out of order. The second wave, comprising 164 planes, attacked fourteen bases and destroyed 107 enemy aircraft. The Egyptians lost three-quarters of their air strength. Our casualties were eleven pilots—six killed, two taken prisoner, and three wounded. The air operation was carried out in complete radio silence and at a low altitude, below the radar; and the ground forces did not switch radios on until their own H-Hour, which followed the positive reports of the returning pilots.

Our own generator was activated at 0800, and at 0815, in a strong, confident voice, Arik gave the order: Nua! Nua! (Move! Move!). The vehicles, already in gear, with engines running, headed west, and I could soon see our tanks descending toward the frontier. Arik was standing up, looking through his binoculars, and a few moments later, to the first sound of our own shells, he announced: "Here we go, we are firing!"

On my small transistor radio I heard my father's voice, through the shots and the shells, broadcasting to the advancing troops, to the mothers and wives at home, and, as I felt, speaking to me personally. "Soldiers of Israel," he said, "we have no aims of conquest. Our purpose is to bring to naught the attempts of the Arab armies to conquer our land, and to break the ring of blockade and aggression which threatens us. . . . They are more numerous than we are, but we shall overcome them. We are a small nation, but strong. Peace-loving, yet ready to fight for our lives and our country. . . . The supreme efforts will be demanded of you, the troops, fighting in the air, on land, and on the sea. Soldiers of the Israel Defense Forces, on this day our hopes and our security rest with you." Dov's eyes met mine, and he understood how I felt. There are peaks in life, national and personal, which one is aware of

at the moment they take place. Not in perspective, not as an afterthought or in a final accounting or a historical assessment. We simply knew that what was happening on June 5, between 7:45 and midday, was one of those unique peaks. Everything that was in us, all the accumulated energies and convictions, past tragedies and future hopes, were compressed into the effort of these few hours.

My father was hundreds of miles away from me, finalizing orders to attack Jordanian airfields and prepare the offensive against the outposts around Jerusalem. Jordan and Syria joined the war, Jordan with artillery on the Jewish quarters in Jerusalem, and Syria with its Air Force bombing Tiberias and Megiddo. I was entering the first enemy post that was destroyed. I never felt as close to my father as I did during those hours; in spite of the distance, I could feel his physical presence. His face was with me, his strong, stable gaze, his calm, composed confidence, brain ticking away like a radar searching for options in a circular movement. With the deepest of emotions, I felt privileged. There was my complex, beloved father, living through his greatest hours perhaps, towering above us all in a multidimensional way.

My mother was caught in the first shelling of Jerusalem, in a petrol station near the King David Hotel. She managed to abandon her car, get to a telephone, and reach the Knesset shelter in time for the swearing-in ceremony of the new cabinet. Father showed up, but couldn't wait for Eshkol, who was delayed. They drove back to Tel Aviv, missing the actual ceremony, Mother again witnessing with pride and love the unfolding of events, as Father issued orders and received reports in the car. In the opposite direction, a long line of heavy, dark tanks was silhouetted in the dark night, advancing along the curving road to Jerusalem.

My father returned to the pit as we were preparing for the major breakthrough battle in mid-Sinai. The objective was the Um Katef stronghold, difficult to approach, flanked by mine fields and impassable dunes, and manned by dug-in infantry brigade and heavy artillery. But once the defense line was broken, the central axis to the Suez Canal would be open to race through, since the same operations were in progress in the northern Sinai sector (Tal's force) and the southern sector—all the way to Sharm el-Sheikh and the blockaded Straits of Tiran. Mother refused to join the neighbors in their shelter and felt safe enough in her own bed, listening to the all-night radio reports.

Dov explained the battle plan to me, drawing lines on my writing pad. If we knew we were in love then, there was no room to express it. War does strip one of all fringes, and the bare essentials are so evident that emotional communication is almost telepathic. He was talking of the Russian defense system, of our mobility and their loss of air support. We heard reports of one of our battalions suffering casualties, trapped in a mine field. We listened to reports on the radio, and Dov carried out his own liaison job, consulting occasionally with Arik, and with a matter-of-fact, almost casual, efficiency. I knew very little about him, and had a feeling I would have a lifetime to find out. The bond was there, and there was no call to analyze, examine, or even take joy in it. Just after 2230, the artillery commander, in whose half-track I placed myself that night, was given the order to open fire. The paratroopers landed in helicopters at an assembly point; Kuti's infantry was positioned in the sand dunes near the Um Katef northern trenches, waiting for the artillery softening, and the long, swift fist of Motke's tanks was charging straight for the center of the fifteen-kilometer-wide defense line. Our major battle had begun. Arik's orders were colorful. He used first names for the commanders, announcing: "Let the earth shake." And next to me I could hear the artillery commander answering softly: "Shake it shall," when he ordered a barrage of six thousand shells on Um Katef in the next twenty minutes.

My heart was with the infantry. I carefully isolated Kuti's voice whenever it was heard. They were advancing under heavy fire in the trenches. Casualty reports came in, and I clutched my arrowhead with a primitive faith. The Egyptians in their strongholds were well prepared for the battle, and flanked, they had no escape route. Our timing, coordination, and superior fighting capacity gave us victory, but it took all our flexibility in combat deployment to achieve this.

While we were still in the midst of the battle of Sinai, Mota Gur's parachutes had gone into action in Jerusalem in frontal assaults on the police school compounds and on Ammunition Hill. The parachutists suffered heavy casualties, cutting their way under withering fire to take these two major bastions by dawn of June 6. When I drove in Dov's jeep to the smoke-covered Um Katef battlefield, my father, with Ezer Weizman and Uzi Narkiss, exposed in an open jeep, entered the gates of Mount Scopus. The Old City of Jerusalem was spread out below, and he was under strong government pressure to capture it immediately. The difference between his reactions as Chief of Staff and as Defense Minister was nowhere more evident than in his attitude toward the battle of Jerusalem, and in the south, at the capture of the east bank of the Suez Canal. His restraining attitude called for the Old City to be surrounded first. Entry should be without air or artillery support, causing as little damage as possible to the city and its holy places. When the encirclement was complete, and Jerusalem was cut off from Jordanian reinforcements from the east, we were already on our way on a chase-and-destroy mission into the central Sinai. Our division was lighter and smaller, as Kuti's infantry left for El Arish in the north. "Don't you want to join us for a swim?" he suggested, but Arik promised me a swim in the canal soon, and nothing at that point could tempt me away from Dov's jeep. We were advancing fast, often under an occasional barrage, and I soon became experienced in judging where the rocket would hit and how to avoid it. Holding to a heavy machine gun in the front seat, hearing Arik's voice on the wireless, and finding comfort in Dov's short, well-spaced utterings, I never felt safer. All the years with or alongside my father had obviously contributed to this lack of fear, and I didn't think of it as anything but natural, taken for granted, that there I was, on a dirt road in the Sinai, face covered with a mask of baked mud, and surrounded by tough warriors, fighting my way to the Suez Canal.

On Wednesday, June 7, a helicopter landed with the first newspapers and mail. The headlines declared in big type: "Gaza Strip in Our Hands," "Ramallah Is Ours," "West Bank Cities Are Captured." The small print had greetings from plants and factories, kibbutzim and schools, to "Our workers, sons, or members: We are with you wherever you are." There was an announcement from the American embassy, "advising all American citizens to leave Israel," and in the inside pages, the first terrible sight of names in black borders—the price we were paying. "Captain Yoram Harpaz, killed in action, in the performance of his duty . . . ," "Lt. Amiram Manor, killed in action . . . ," "Our blessed Chaim . . . ." With gray faces, the older reservists among us searched through the lists—their sons were serving on another front—and I couldn't hold back my tears. We were winning on three fronts. We were between Um Katef and Nakhl, and were immersed in our own reality, and suddenly, in the black rules in the paper, war acquired its real horrible meaning of destruction and the loss of lives. A young soldier was looking at the paper over my shoulder, and when I turned to look at him, his eyes were wet. Had he found a familiar name? Or did he imagine his own name edged in black?

We had to move on, and with nightfall, we were advancing very slowly. The wind was blowing. The route climbing up the higher plateau was not fit for a convoy like ours, and soon the reconnaissance patrol ordered us to stop. We hit a mine field and we had to wait until the engineers cleared a path through it. We didn't budge and simply registered the proximity of danger. Arik was listening in on the next frequency when he repeated what he heard. His voice had a dreamlike quality as he said: "The Old City of Jerusalem is in our hands." The news was passed from jeep to tank, from the engineers' bulldozers to the supply trucks, from the mobile hospital unit to the artillery, and clusters of huddled men, tired and hungry and weary, started singing softly "Jerusalem of Gold," in hoarse but wistful voices. As if this song was a prayer, answering the prayers of thousands of years. We couldn't move, but we had wings. The night was cold and the wind brushed us with cutting grains of sand, but there was a warmth of surging feelings and an unseen rainbow in the desert sky.

A few hours earlier, my father had walked with Rabin, then Chief of Staff, and Uzi Narkiss, then head of Central Command, through the gates of the Old City, in the footsteps of the paratroopers. They entered the Lions' Gate, turned left, and reached the Temple Mount. The Israeli flag was hoisted on the spire of the Dome of the Rock (and it was typical of my father that he ordered it down, refraining from any national demonstrative acts regarding the holy sites). They turned right through the Mograbi Gate and into the narrow plaza in front of the Wailing Wall. Father, dramatically aware of the historic moment, scribbled on a note: "May peace descend upon the whole house of Israel," and inserted the folded paper into an opening between the ashlars. The place was crowded with soldiers who had been in the battle, some wounded and many weeping, touching the huge stones and praying softly. For most of them, it was the first prayer ever.

On leaving the Western Wall, he was asked to say a few words, and later in the Sinai I heard his voice, as did my brothers in their units, my mother and grandparents, as did every Israeli wherever he was, words spoken with wisdom and thought but expressing a great emotion. He didn't really speak to us, but for us. He said: "We have returned to the holiest of our sites, and will never again be separated from it. . . ."

Elation

Saul Friedlander, born in Prague, survived the Holocaust by being adopted by a French family and raised as a Catholic (the current Cardinal Archbishop of Paris became a Catholic in the same way). After the War, Friedlander gradually gained knowledge of his true lineage and reverted to Judaism. He immigrated to Israel just as the Six-Day War occurred and this passage in his 1979 memoirs relates his feeling of elation at the time, an elation shared by nearly all Jewish Israelis and by millions of Jews all over the world. Friedlander subsequently became a distinguished historian at Tel Aviv and Stanford universities.

How can I describe my enthusiasm when I first arrived in Israel during the War of Independence? Everything seemed a miracle to me: the local chocolate quite as much as the Jewish state itself.

I began by talking about the people in Nira, but I should also describe the village. The bus from Natanya deposited you in front of a little textile factory with ocher walls, which, before my arrival, produced cotton goods, and afterward was converted for the production of camouflage nets for our nascent army.

The houses of Nira were all alike, and had been built, I believe, shortly before the Second World War: little square houses with white walls, topped by red tile roofs, which stood out against the dark green background of the orange groves. Climbing plants on the walls added brighter, ever-changing colors according to the season: wisteria, honeysuckle, and sometimes, at the entrance to a garden, beds of rhododendrons.

I almost forgot the hen yards. They constituted an essential feature of the *meshek,* a word that could be translated as *farm,* but meaning a modern model farm. When I say hen yard, you probably think of a poultry yard where the hens move about freely, pecking leisurely at grain. This was not at all the case in Nira. The hens were housed in cages alongside each other, forming geometric shapes, illuminated around the clock by electric lights to encourage egg laying. It was this that was responsible for the monotonous, incessant cackling which went on around us night and day.

Pleasures in Nira, in Beit Itzhak and the villages of the plain were simple ones. Apart from the evenings playing bridge, the most enjoyable thing at the end of a long day in the sun was to meet in the café that overlooked all the surrounding countryside, beneath the water tower of Beit Itzhak, summon "Herr Ober," order a beer, and watch the slow approach of darkness, as the lights of Natanya went on one by one along the line of dunes.

On Friday evenings we went to the movies at Shaar Hefer, a neighborhood village. The benches were set out in rows beneath two eucalyptus trees in front of the door of the grocery store. The screen was put in place, Herr Cohen set up the projector, and the show would begin, punctuated by breakdowns and interruptions that bothered no one; in the heat of those nights, there was at least as much hugging and kissing on the benches

Our world: *The Gates of the Cemetery,* by Marc Chagall.

in front of Shaar Hefer's grocery store, as in the heart-throbbing melodramas that reached us at the end of their run.

After several months in Nira, I became a boarder at an agricultural center for the education of newcomers which hugged the sea near Natanya. There I learned Hebrew and discovered the rudiments of a Jewish culture entirely new to me.

That year, most of the boarders at Ben Shemen came from Bulgaria, bringing with them all the charm of a prosperous Sephardic community that on the whole had been spared the lot of the Jewish communities in North Africa and the Middle East. Our daily life unfolded amid general gaiety, which reached its climax in the interminable *horas* we danced every night, and in the Bulgarian songs celebrating the valley of Maritza— all this a few hundred meters from a very gentle sea, beneath a sky sparkling with stars.

Learning Hebrew meant, above all, discovering the Bible. The Bible soon fascinated me, and the simplest passages we read were perhaps those that bore the most powerful message, that were infused with the most intense poetry. For me, for example, who had changed my name from Paul to

Shaul (Saul) upon arriving in the country, the story of this first king of Israel, told in the Book of Samuel with so much controlled force, became the very image of the tragic: Called against his will, and then abandoned by all, even by God, who refuses to answer, Shaul on the eve of his greatest trial is reduced to resorting to necromancy, learning his destiny from the witch of Endor.

Along with the Bible, we also discovered Jewish life at the beginning of the century, the life that had flowered in Eastern Europe. The typical tiny Jewish village in Russia came alive for us through the stories of I. L. Peretz and Sholem Aleichem. They may not be great literature, but they have all the warmth and flavor of an authentic tradition.

Should I confess that since the beginning I had nonetheless had vague, confused, intermittent feelings that something was missing? From time to time I would go sit on the beach behind a sandy rock, and open a book that was merely a symbol—Fromentin's *Dominique,* in one instance that occurs to me. I thought that I was thus affirming,

for myself alone, the permanence of a culture that remained the only one that mattered in my eyes. This was a slight premonition of future dilemmas, though entirely eclipsed by another habit of mine, equally harmless but much more indicative of my state of mind at this time. At midday we students had a two- or three-hour recess on account of the heat. Every day, after the noon meal, I would start out for Natanya along the beach (the shortest route, but also the one least sheltered from the sun), all alone and almost running, to buy the daily paper—which I could barely understand—and take pleasure in the announcement in it of some feat of valor, some new victory, or simply in its accounts of the everyday life of the country. Yes, I was insatiable, and the most trivial news story filled me with joy: A stretch of road had just been inaugurated here or there; this or that many kilometers of irrigation pipe had been laid; in short, Israel lived (as a Hasidic song has it), and I could see the miracle taking place before my very eyes, on pages I had deciphered slowly, but with that much more pleasure for so doing.

Jerusalem the Golden

In his 1989 book, leading Israeli journalist Amos Elon communicates what Jerusalem means in the Israeli consciousness. The discussion is notable for its historical insight and its restraint.

On a winter day on the wall, the fog sweeping over the rooftops blots out the New City, the television antennas, and the parked cars, leaving the historic core shorn of all modern accouterments. Very briefly, the view is what it must have been in Isaiah's or Josephus's days, timeless—"your heaven as iron and your earth as brass." We know these flat roofs of stone from Isaiah's "What aileth thee now, that thou art wholly gone up to the housetops?" The compact little houses, which crowd in close on somber, narrow lanes, climb steeply. In a moment, the narrow lanes that Josephus often wrote about in the first century sparkle again with

a glassy beauty as the sun breaks out through the clouds and hits the wet stones.

In the soft light, there is a good view now from the ramparts into the Upper City, on Mount Zion, where the last of the Jewish zealots held out for another month after the rest of the city had fallen to the Romans. The rich and the priestly families lived in the Upper City, where they looked down, as high priests often do, on the Mountain of God, which gave them their livelihood. The Upper City was separated from the burning temple by a great bridge, across which, Josephus says, the Romans harangued and harassed them. The past nineteen

356　THE JEWISH EXPERIENCE

The old-new land: Jewish agricultural workers in Palestine, around 1910.

hundred years have wrought additional havoc on this hill. Of the temple below it and its courts, only the vast platform has remained. Yet it is still possible to identify many prominent points mentioned in Josephus, including the bridge. They conjure up in the mind's eye the vanished splendor of the city and the last bloody scenes of her overthrow. It is clear why the Upper City held out to the very end. The Romans were unable to take it by storm after they had taken the temple platform below. They were forced to raise additional banks against it. Wood had to be hewn and brought in from afar; there were no trees left in the environs to a distance of a hundred furlongs (twelve and a half miles). Fierce house-to-house fighting was followed by close man-to-man combat in underground passages, and by another great fire. The slaughter, claimed Josephus—and perhaps he was not exaggerating by much—"made the whole city run down with blood to such a degree indeed that the fire of many of the houses was quenched with these men's blood."

Of the destruction of A.D. 70, several dramatic sights have been unearthed in recent years by two leading archaeologists, the Britisher Kathleen Kenyon and the Israeli Nahman Avigad. In some

ruins, churned up by the winter rains outside the present walls, Kenyon found human bones, including three smashed skulls, "a reminder of the slaughter described by Josephus which filled the streets with blood." The dating of these skulls was facilitated by a purse, found among the bones, filled with coins minted a few months before the destruction of the city. The site excavated by Kenyon was never inhabited again. The remains she found lay immediately under the topsoil, with nothing Byzantine, Arab, or Crusader in between.

Inside the Upper City, Avigad has uncovered the remains of several priestly palaces. Each is covered in soot. Here again, the date of the fire was suggested by coins minted in A.D. 69, as well as by household utensils and other identifiable objects found in the ashes. But it was a family seal found in the debris that gave the excavator that rare and exhilarating feeling that he was in touch with specific human beings. The inscription on the seal suggested that one of the burned mansions belonged to the rich Kathros, a high priest much hated for his rapacity and corruption, and remembered in a well-known Talmudic skit on the priestly oligarchy:

*Woe is me from the House of Baytos, woe is me
from their sticks,*
*Woe is me from the House of Hannin, woe is me
from their whispers.*
*Woe is me from the House of Ismael, woe is me
from their fists,*
*Woe is me from the House of Kathros, woe is me
from their poisoned pens.*
*All are high priests and their sons are tax collec-
tors, their sons-in-law are cashiers and their
servants beat the people with whips.*

The ruins were still smoking when the survivors began to spin the theology of the disaster.
They refused to believe that God had given them
up. He could be weary or old, or simply in exile,
as they were. But he would come back one day.
There would be a Return. Until that day, they
would be a people of sorrows. On the anniversary
of the destruction, they would fast. They would
sit on low stools and cover their heads in ashes.
For centuries, they would speculate on the meaning of the event.

Some of these speculations—transmitted orally
at first—were collected in the fifth century and
codified in the Midrash (the rabbinical commentary) on the Book of Lamentations. The end of the
physical city made the survivors redouble their
speculations on the spiritual. In the process, the
tradition of exegesis acquired a sacredness of its
own.

Lamentations was the great elegy on the first
destruction of Jerusalem in 586 B.C. In the Midrash
on Lamentations, every word, every phrase in the
original text was applied to the later tragedy, thus
presaging similar preoccupations and perplexities
that would manifest themselves down through
the centuries. The first sentence in Lamentations
reads: "How lone she sits, the city big with people, is widowed." The key word here, according
to the exegetes, was the first: *How (Eykha)*.

In Hebrew, as in many other languages, *eykha*
(pronounced "ay-haa") has a distinctly woeful,
onomatopoeic sound. *Eykha* sounds like a howl.
"How *could* you!" *Eykha*, not Lamentations, is the
Hebrew name of this book. But the Midrash on
Lamentations is not just obsessive anguish, self-
pity, or lament. There is wit in it, and the free-
wheeling philosophy of a fascinating and complex
society of scholars—rabbinical Sherlock Holmses
in search of a new religious philosophy. They
inhabit a unique republic of letters where the religious drama is no longer enacted in a physical setting, as in the destroyed temple, but in the mind.
God is everywhere. Men are called upon to con-
template his glory by concentrating on the study
of the sacred books. For this purpose, any study
room, any little synagogue in the world will do.
Jerusalem is still the code word that releases glorious visions of a messianic age. The exegetes do
not, at this stage, take such daydreams too literally. The memory of the lost city is still alive; the
messiah, however, is no longer necessarily *The
Historical Geography of the Holy Land*. He was
able in the end to take the city without firing
a single shot. "It has never fallen so tamely
before," T. E. Lawrence ("Lawrence of Arabia"),
who marched into Jerusalem with Allenby, wrote
his mother, adding rashly: "These modern wars of
large armies and long-range weapons are quite
unfitted for the historic battlefield." Before fifty
years passed, he would be proved twice wrong.

Climbing onto the wall again after the breach
and walking farther north, you discover small gardens inside the Old City and good views over the
stone roofs and towers, despite a forest of television antennas. A plaque on the rampart bears the
words "Jordanian Post." It denotes its function
between 1948 and 1967, when this part of the
wall was a military zone, on the edge of a narrow
strip of no-man's land between Israeli and
Jordanian-held Jerusalem. Jordanian snipers sometimes used this spot to shoot at Israelis passing
through the deserted border area. There were also
lighter moments during those years of intermittent warfare, as when a nun, on the Israeli side of
the line, coughed her dentures out a window into
no-man's land and a temporary cease-fire was
negotiated under United Nations auspices. A
brace of blue-helmeted U.N. truce supervisors,
brandishing white flags, combed the debris-cov-
ered terrain where few persons had ventured for
years and fewer still had come back alive. The
false teeth were successfully retrieved. Nowadays,
this section of the ramparts is a popular tourist
attraction. The former no-man's land has become
a busy traffic artery. The Franciscan fathers sometimes complain that tourists wandering on the
wall peer into their bedroom windows—which
brings to mind the chorus in *Oedipus Rex*: "Walls
are nothing when no life moves in the empty pas-
sageways."

Below the walls, underfoot almost everywhere, are the tombs. The city is ringed by a great necropolis. South, east, and west of the city walls, old and new cemeteries present themselves as in a single tableau: tombstones of all kinds, caves, crypts, vaults, catacombs, mastabas, rock monuments, churchyards, and burial grounds of all races and faiths. In Jerusalem, tradition long ago gave the vote to remote ancestors, establishing a kind of democracy of the dead. As Rimbaud said of baroque Rome, death seems to have been born here. The most enduring monuments in Jerusalem are tombs and cenotaphs. They seem to be among the oldest in the Near East. In summer, when the heat hangs heavily over the twisted spurs of hardened dust, children climb over the scattered tombstones and sense the slow fire inside. It is amazing how much trouble people who treated life so casually took with death and with their tombs—kings as well as paupers.

The author of the Book of Nehemiah called Jerusalem "the city of my fathers' sepulchres." The oldest Jewish sepulchres are cut into the rock, in deep, sunken courts. As usual in the East, the fear of grave robbers gave birth to elaborate devices to keep them out. Some tombs still have a heavy round stone rolled back from their mouths, revealing dark, cavernous chambers with finely chiseled walls inside, and holes (*kokhim*) for the disposal of bones. A fifth- or sixth-century Jewish epitaph, perhaps that of Shebna, the king's steward whose hewn-rock sepulchre is mentioned in Isa. 22:15, reads: "No silver and gold here . . . cursed be the man who . . . opens this." A first-century anklebone with a nail driven through it and thus suggestive of a crucifixion by the Romans has also been found—the only one anywhere found so far. The city's museums are filled with coffins and elaborately decorated bone-pots and urns. The connection between religion and death, or the fear of death, is well known. There was a widespread Jewish cult of tombs. The rabbis were opposed to it and yet their own tombs eventually became objects of veneration. Later on, a belief grew that dying and being buried in Jerusalem was a shortcut to paradise. "Men from all parts of the world" come to Jerusalem to die, the Persian traveler Nasir-i-Khusrau reported in 1047. Jews and Moslems believed that if they died in Jerusalem their flesh would not rot. At the End of Days, when they are finally summoned by their maker to free them of all memory, they would be spared the ordeal and discomfort of rolling to Jerusalem under the ground.

There are tombs of all ages, beginning in the eighth century B.C., and a few noteworthy gaps: no tombs from the time of the Persian conquest, even though hundreds of thousands were massacred then (Zoroastrian religion forbade defiling the pure earth with unclean corpses), and only one grave of a Crusader. There must have been thousands of Crusader tombs, including many monumental sepulchres. But tombs have habitually played a part in the struggles over Jerusalem. Their destruction has often marked the transition from one faith or sect to another. The Greeks waited till 1810 to dismantle two royal Crusader tombs, which Chateaubriand had seen still extant four years earlier. Tombs describe conflicting domains of memory in the city. Of approximately seventy thousand Jewish graves on the Mount of Olives and its slopes, some fifty thousand were destroyed or defaced during the nineteen years of Jordanian rule between 1948 and 1967.

Moslem sepulchres of some importance were built conspicuously on the surrounding hilltops. Henry Maundrell, a seventeenth-century English traveler, observed (perhaps sardonically) that "you will find among the Turks far more dead saints than living ones." In the more recent cemeteries, Moslem tombstones are twin-posted like "husband and wife facing each other across the breakfast table." A memorial to the Arab dead in the Six-Day War, erected in 1967 with the encouragement of the liberal Israeli mayor Teddy Kollek, nearly proved to be Kollek's political undoing. Where in London is there a memorial to the German dead? the critics cried. Kollek's answer was that London was not a German city as well, as Jerusalem is partly Arab.

In a Protestant cemetery that occupies the side of Mount Zion, several Hebrew tombstones commemorate the extremely meager results of great efforts by English missionaries last century to convert the Jews. Opposite the northeast corner of the Old City, on top of Mount Scopus, there is a British military cemetery for the casualties of World War I. Its boisterous tone is quite inappropriate to the horrors of that war fought in the crusading and salvationist style of the imperialist heyday.

Further in the west, an entire mountain is covered by new Jewish cemeteries. It is known as Mount Herzl. In 1949, forty-five years after his death, the remains of Theodor Herzl, founder of modern Zionism, were flown to Israel from Vienna and buried here under a square block of black marble. The national movement Herzl helped found and that he hoped would lead to the reestablishment of a Jewish state in peace with its Arab neighbors has not yet reached its goal. The north slope of Mount Herzl is a military cemetery, a reminder of the heavy toll exacted by five Arab-Israeli wars since 1948 and of the many skirmishes in between.

The south slope is occupied by a monumental tomb of another sort, entirely symbolic, awesome, called Yad Vashem (literally, "Memory and Name"). It honors the memory of the six million exterminated Jews of Europe, who Herzl, sensing the approaching catastrophe, vainly tried to rescue.

As a ritual site in the civil or political religion of Israel, Yad Vashem is second only to the Western Wall. It bears witness to the fact that Israel is founded on new ashes as much as on its biblical past. Yad Vashem does not face the city but instead looks toward the sea, the direction from which those who were slaughtered by the Nazis might have come. Its architecture of pain is the most powerful where it is understated. In the austere Memorial Hall, the names of the main annihilation camps are inscribed in the floor. Stunned visitors of all nationalities stare at them at all hours of the day: Majdanek, Sobibor, Buchenwald, Theresienstadt, Bergen-Belsen, Mauthausen, Dachau, Treblinka, Auschwitz. An eternal flame rises from a kind of vault in the ground where ashes found in one of the death camps have been buried. Cantors intone the ancient Hebrew prayer for the dead, a rapt, intense lament, which by its primitive strength might have been composed only yesterday.

As a "sacred space," Yad Vashem fulfills a political and religious function in Israeli public life similar to that of the Tomb of the Unknown Soldier in other countries. As a monument, it triggers awe. Foreign heads of state and ambassadors come here to lay wreaths. In the austere Memorial Hall, they solemnize their recognition of the new state and legitimize its raison d'être. President Sadat of Egypt visited Yad Vashem in 1977 and wrote in the visitor book: "May God guide our steps toward peace. Let us end all suffering for mankind."

In the Jewish tradition, catastrophe is theologically linked with redemption. Death and rebirth are juxtaposed. This gives Yad Vashem its peculiar political twist. The historian Saul Friedlander has written about Yad Vashem: "Redemption here loses its explicit religious connotation and becomes rebirth, in secular but no less mythic and metahistorical terms." Yad Vashem symbolizes the negative pole of the positive energy that went into the building of the Jewish state during the past hundred years. This was made clear during the 1953 Knesset debate over establishing an annual day to commemorate the annihilation of European Jewry. Mordechai Nurok, who headed the subcommittee in charge, said: "We have seen a graveyard in front of us, a graveyard for six million of our brothers and sisters. Maybe because of their blood, shed like water, have we been privileged to have our state."

The Clan

In the twenty years after the Second World War, the two developments in world Jewry that had the greatest consequences were the advancement of Jewish corporate magnates, and the rise of Israel. These two developments became intertwined. The military and economic strength that Israel exhibited by the time of the Six Day War in 1967 would have not occurred without all sorts of help and support from Jewish billionaires in Europe and America.

Of course not all very wealthy Jews were committed to Israel, but a substantial number were, and this involvement heightened their consciousness as Jews and helped to retain them in the Jewish faith. Through how many succeeding generations of billionaire Jewish families this Jewish consciousness fostered by Zionist enthusiasm will continue is problematic. Israelis always assume that it will last indefinitely but by the last decade of the twentieth century there were ample signs that it was a phenomenon of the wartime and postwar generation and then an erosion of Zionist enthusiasm and Jewish consciousness could easily set in among the scions of many of these exalted families.

While corporate capitalism would seem to be as far as possible from Ben-Gurion, the Israeli Labor party, and its doctrinaire socialist principles, the Israeli socialist leadership never experienced discomfort in soliciting funds from and working effectively with these Jewish billionaires from abroad. Is that a demonstration of Israeli pragmatism, desperation, or greed? A bit of all three.

The most successful Jewish business family in Britain were the great retailers Simon Marks and Israel Sieff who owned and greatly expanded the Marks and Spencer department stores. They were also vehement and generous supporters of Israel. George Weidenfeld, the British publisher (he came to England from Vienna in 1938) was for a time married to Jane Sieff. Here is his knowledgeable assessment of the clan's triumphant operations and its distinctive culture, which some will greet with adulation and others with misgiving.

The Marks & Spencer clan, known in the Jewish world simply as "the Family," also belonged to Flora's intimate circle. Simon Marks and Israel Sieff, two childhood friends from Manchester, had married each other's sisters. The husbands of the other two Marks sisters were also in the business, and so were some of their children. The clan centered on three men and their wives, Simon Marks, Israel Sieff and Harry Sacher. Harry Sacher, a barrister who had been leader writer on *The Manchester Guardian* in the days of C. P. Scott, that great prewar editor known as "the Thunderer of the North," had married Simon's sister Miriam. A close collaborator of Chaim Weizmann, Sacher had been instrumental in committing the *Manchester Guardian* to a pro-Zionist line. He was the intellectual of the Family. Caustic, sharp-witted and ultracautious, he sat in his book-lined office in Baker Street and acted as a dam to the revolutionary business ideas of the two brothers-in-law, Simon and Israel. He was an active member of the Jewish Agency for Palestine.

The youngest of the four Marks sisters, Elaine, first married Norman Laski, one of the distinguished family of Manchester Jews which produced a top lawyer, Neville, the Labour Party's theoretician, Harold (who was Norman's uncle), and the writer Marganita. Norman also worked in the firm, but Elaine's second husband, Neville Blond, did not. He was a textile magnate with a bulldog face who supplied Marks & Spencer and was one of the founders of the Royal Court Theatre. His son is Anthony Blond, a gifted rebel who turned his hand to publishing and wrote a *roman à clef* about the Family which caused much discomfort.

Simon Marks was a business genius. Sensitive to a fault, he was incapable of articulating himself explicitly and functioned intuitively. He was a master of the worm's-eye view. He would enter a suburban store, see a speck of dust on the counter and launch a hygiene campaign. He would detect a momentary hesitation on the part of a salesgirl in Leeds and decide that the whole system needed a time and motion study.

Israel Sieff was just the opposite. He had a degree from Manchester University and thought in categories and concepts. Like the Markses he came from a family of Russian-Jewish merchants, but the Sieffs were higher up in the social structure of the ghetto. Israel was cultivated and benign. He had cofounded PEP, Political and Economic Planning, an early think-tank of mildly left-of-centre bearing, and represented all that was *bien-pensant* in the world of business and philanthropy.

When his father, the original founder of the Penny Bazaar, died, Simon won a High Court case against the Spencer interest and persuaded Israel, who was already a successful businessman in his own right, to become his main partner. The Marks and Sieff partnership was not only crucial to the making of Marks & Spencer, it also made a major contribution to the creation of the State of Israel. They had a deep faith in Zionism which was inspired by their friendship with Chaim Weizmann, whom they had known from the days when he had taught at Manchester University. They were his disciples and his benefactors. His thoughts on scientific method in industry and the importance of science to any future colonization of Palestine made a deep impression, and they were tireless in their commitment to Zionism. During the First World War, Simon Marks organized a London Zionist office for Weizmann and went with him to the Versailles Peace Conference, while Israel Sieff was appointed to the Palestine Commission which Weizmann set up after the Balfour Declaration to advise the British authorities on the establishment of the Jewish National Home.

Very much in keeping with Tawney's *Rise of Capitalism*, Simon Marks and Israel Sieff became enlightened businessmen rather than narrow-minded traders. Weizmann's scientific input, for which they felt indebted, and their passionate desire to combine merchandising with science were the real secrets of the firm's success. Simon Marks often said that, but for Weizmann's belief in combining politics and science, or, as he put it, "his philosophy combined with our commercial flair," he and Israel Sieff would never have gone beyond being conventional businessmen in Manchester.

The Family was a highly structured clan with its own social ceremonial governed by unwritten laws. There were four solar systems: the Markses, the Sieffs, the Sachers and the Blonds. The various strands formed a powerful framework within which the professional and social lives of its members prospered and proliferated. They all lived in or around Grosvenor Square, having moved collectively from the Addison Road area in the 1930s and from Hampstead before that. Their houses were done up in the same conventional way, with eighteenth-century English furniture and Impressionist paintings. Their style of entertaining was similar and they all had country houses with adjacent farms which they kept partly for tax reasons. They had a collective identity and a common body of friends whom they invited to luncheons, dinners and weekend parties. These included rich Anglo-Jews, but also the big suppliers, the nouveaux riches and some recent immigrants. Besides them there were certain *hausfreunde*, like Robin and Angela Fox, the parents of the actors Edward and James Fox, and the plastic surgeon Sir Archibald McIndoe and his daughters, who enjoyed near-Family status. Years later I overheard a conversation in the house of Nigel Lawson, then married to his Lyons heiress wife Vanessa, at one of their parties in Hyde Park Gate. In the queue for the buffet I found myself standing behind Alun Chalfont, who was talking to one of the McIndoe daughters. She was married to Dennis Walters, a pro-Arab Tory, and Alun asked her: "Tell me, Vanora, why are you so passionately anti-Israel?" She replied, "If you had spent every weekend as a child at the Markses in Sunningdale hearing about the kibbutzim, you would feel the same."

There was also a group of courtiers, self-seeking adventurers and hangers-on. Some found only temporary favour and, once banished from one of the major courts, would automatically be dropped by the whole clan. Others were regularly in attendance. They were a mixed bunch, encompassing lawyers, accountants, a former tennis champion, a Scottish laird who had run into debt and lived on favours, aristocrats who traded on their wits, interior decorators and a florist. In his sardonic way, Chaim Weizmann referred to them as the "Ps and Ws," short for Pimps and Whores.

Lajos Lederer, a dashing Hungarian who worked on the *Observer,* was part of the family entourage. He had come to England in the 1920s with a delegation of Hungarian monarchists who wanted to offer Lord Rothermere's son, Esmond

Harmsworth, the Hungarian crown because of the former's passionate advocacy of their cause in his *Daily Mail*. Rothermere had turned it down after some reflection. Lederer never went back to Hungary and finally persuaded David Astor to give him a job on the *Observer*. Jan Gehrke was also taken into the fold. He had been number two at the Czechoslovak Embassy when Jan Masaryk was ambassador. Munich left him a penniless refugee and the Family appointed him transport officer of Marks & Spencer. He was said to be the lover of Daphne Sieff, the wife of Israel's elder son, Michael.

All the senior members of the clan had their favourite segment in British society, and the various families formed subclans. Simon and Miriam Marks sought the company of politicians, fashionable journalists and big business celebrities, but they also entertained titled decorators, brokers and favourites from the worlds of sport, film and theatre. Miriam had a lively, seemingly dotty manner, but was shrewd and very generous. Israel and Rebecca (Becky) Sieff preferred intellectuals to the social crowd. Most of the "court intellectuals" had a limited life span with the Family. Some of them were given a temporary office in Baker Street and were commissioned to write papers, or indeed the history of Marks & Spencer. Simon Marks was never happy with the result. He did not realize that if a flourishing business made for spectacular balance sheets, it was not necessarily the stuff of a breathtaking narrative. So the hapless authors would be dismissed with Simon's chilling epitaph: "Alas, he did not grasp the essential philosophy of our business."

Newcomers were treated with benign curiosity. Once they had been suitably vetted they would make the circuit. As a friend and protégé of Flora, I was taken up by the Family and spent many weekends in a Marks, Sieff, Sacher, Blond or Laski house in the years before I married Jane, the daughter of Israel's younger brother Edward (Teddy). It was quite an adventure for me to move in this world with its own hierarchy and codes, conversational patterns, interests and prejudices. I saw a great deal of Marcus Sieff, Israel's son, who became my closest friend in the Family. A rugger blue at Cambridge, he was very good-looking and something of a ladies' man. Marcus had a distinguished war record. He inherited his father's dedication to Zionism and contributed more than any-

one else in this country towards smoothing the transition from turmoil in Palestine to a functioning State of Israel, engaging a circle of able people to develop a new infrastructure.

For the Jewish community in Britain it was a time fraught with tension and problems. The Attlee-Bevin Government was adopting an increasingly pro-Arab, anti-Zionist course, and prominent Jews were torn in their loyalties between Britain and Zionism. Men like Simon Marks, Israel Sieff, his son Marcus and Sigmund Gestetner, a blunt but warm-hearted businessman who was one of Flora's admirers, took considerable personal risks in financing the purchase and transport of arms to support the Zionist cause. They also helped finance the illegal immigration of Jews from displaced-persons camps all over Europe.

A whole floor of Marks & Spencer was given over to the cause. The headquarters in Baker Street became the brain centre of a Jewish State-to-be, a sort of government-in-exile. Drawing on their retailing and management experience, the directors and senior executives were detailed to help set up systems for procuring supplies, training future civil servants and coordinating a forceful political lobby in Westminster. Marcus was responsible for influencing public opinion. He met with leading members of all parties to lobby for the cause and I used whatever contacts I had to help.

It would be difficult to exaggerate the enthusiasm that swept the Jewish community in Britain and elsewhere during that period from November 1947, when the United Nations decided to partition Palestine into a Jewish and Arab State, through the War of Independence up to the early stages of statehood. Even hitherto uncommitted people wanted to contribute to the cause. Flora undertook an important and consuming mission at the behest of Golda Meir, then Minister of Labour and in charge of absorbing the survivors from Hitler's death camps who were streaming into Israel from Europe. Most of the immigrants arrived without any possessions and had to be put up in makeshift camps. Conditions were appalling, and the local population could not cope with the influx. Flora was famed for her organizational skills—during the Second World War she had applied her Marks & Spencer reforms on a far larger scale, organizing soup kitchens and medical services for those who had lost their homes in the Blitz. She applied the same Marks & Spencer techniques in helping suppliers develop standards and efficiency in Israel. She also introduced cottage industries in the camps. The immigrants wove rugs and made pottery which they sold to buyers whom Flora

brought in from all over the world. Her efforts did much to raise morale.

It was around this time that Flora turned to me one day and said, "Georgek, it's time you did your bit."

Stalin's Jews

Not only in American business and cultural life and in Israel's military triumphs have the Jews in this century struck back against their age-old enemies. The Bolshevik Revolution and some of its aftermath represented, from one perspective, Jewish revenge.

As the Tsarist government in the late-nineteenth century found itself increasingly in confrontation with the Empire's Jewish population, there was a strong leftist and revolutionary drift among the younger Jewish generations. Most became members of the Bund, a democratic, peaceful, labor union organization. But some became bomb-throwing anarchists and revolutionary Communists. In the Bolshevik government that was in control of most of Russia by 1920, three out of the six members of the Politburo executive were Jews, not counting Lenin himself whose father had a Jewish grandparent.

The founders of the Soviet secret police (later KGB), headquartered in Lubyanka prison in Moscow, were mostly Jews. Jews also took leadership roles, down into the early 1950s, in the Communist parties of Germany, Hungary, Poland, Czechoslovakia, and Rumania. In the struggle for succession to Lenin in the 1920s, leading to the defeat and exile of the Jewish Trotsky (Bronstein), most of the high-level Soviet Jews made the mistake of supporting Stalin, an Asiatic anti-Semite who in the purge trials in the mid-1930s eventually eliminated these Jewish "Old Bolsheviks." But even to some degree after the Great Purge, Jews were still prevalent in powerful Soviet government positions and many of Stalin's cohorts in the 1940s had Jewish wives. Here is a cool appraisal of Stalin's Jews, published in 1994 by the Russian writer Arkady Vaksberg.

During the heyday of the Cold War, American Jewish publicists spent a lot of time denying that—as 1930s anti-Semites claimed—Jews played a disproportionately important role in Soviet and world Communism. The truth is until the early 1950s, Jews did play such a role, and there is nothing to be ashamed of. In time, Jews will learn to take pride in the record of the Jewish Communists in the Soviet Union and elsewhere. It was a species of striking back.

Stalin's anti-Semitism juxtaposed to the unquestionable fact that a large part of his milieu—both professional and personal—was made up for almost a quarter-century by Jews, may seem to pose an inexplicable contradiction. Yet this paradox is quite natural. In fact, the two phenomena are interdependent. The more people of "undesirable background" there were around him and part of his everyday life, the deeper and fiercer grew his truly biological hatred of them, gradually turning into a mania. . . .

The people who surrounded Stalin and who had rendered him services in the 20s and 30s were mostly Jews. Among the first leaders of the repressive apparat created almost immediately after the revolution to terrorize the whole country, first in the form of the VChK, or Cheka (the All-Russian Extreme Commission), then turning into the GPU (the Main Political Directorate), the NKVD (People's Commissariat of Internal Affairs), and finally the KGB (Committee on State Security), the man who was closest to Stalin and worked totally on his behalf was Genrikh Yagoda. Two other leaders, both Poles—Felix Dzerzhinsky and Vyacheslav Menzhinsky—were more distant from Stalin and, paradoxically, from the institution they headed. While formally head of that typical Soviet police monster until his death, Dzerzhinsky focused most of his attention on agriculture, simultaneously as head of the Higher Council on Agriculture, and seemed to be more a member of the GPU than its director. His first deputy, Menzhinsky, was a sickly and totally indifferent man, a cynic and aesthete, who spent his time lying on a couch and reading books in the many languages he knew. That alone would keep him from learning (nor, probably, did he wish to learn) one more language, the most important for his career—that of direct contact with Stalin.

But Yagoda, another of Dzerzhinsky's deputies, knew that language—and no other. He was the real chief of the Lubyanka [Secret Police] even when he was second deputy director.

Born in Nizhni Novgorod, Yagoda was trained as a pharmacist (which came in handy later when the NKVD under his direction began a secret laboratory for the preparation of poisons), but worked as an apprentice in the jewelry studio of Moisey Sverdlov, whose son Yakov (Yanekl) would be "president" of Soviet Russia for a brief time—November 1917 to March 1919—and whose granddaughter (Yakov's niece) Ida would marry Yagoda. These court marriages were much more popular among the Soviet elite than even among European royalty. Almost all of them married people of their own circle, and this tradition was continued with even greater intensity by their children and grandchildren. Yakov Sverdlov's nephew and Yagoda's brother-in-law was Leopold Averbakh, the chief supervisor of Party purity in Soviet literature. It was not easy for outsiders to break into the family network.

And Yagoda was the man Stalin trusted most within the repressive apparat without which no totalitarian regime can exist. The Soviet version of dictatorship and Stalin personally would not have survived without the "faithful watchdogs of the revolution" and their "punishing swords."

The Soviet political police had "aliens" in its makeup from the start, particularly Latvians, Poles, and Jews. It is important to note that "aliens" (including Armenians and Georgians) formed a very large percentage of all Soviet departments and ministries—for obvious reasons. Oppressed, or at least discriminated against, second- and even third-class citizens in the old Russia, they felt a new energy in the new regime and with fanatical dedication launched themselves on revolutionary careers. But their presence was most visible (again for obvious reasons) in the activities of the vicious Cheka-GPU, noticed by both the public at large and the leaders who paid attention to the national question. The very fact that the life and death of hundreds of thousands, of millions of people depended on these men caused them to be scrutinized closely. Certain characteristics were noted even by internationalists who were not in the least interested in ethnic background.

The revolution brought to the top not the intellectual Jews, who had suffered discrimination under the tsars and had had to struggle to get an education and a university degree, to be able to master a profession and practice it wherever they wanted. The majority of Jewish intellectuals emigrated or became "fellow travelers," the "specials," scornfully tolerated by the Soviet regime. And a huge number of them ended up in the GULAG, or exile, or mass graves. But the illiterate petty craftsmen, who had ambitious dreams of careers and power over their kind—power of any sort—rushed to the capitals, and because of their flawless social background they received Party posts. The rest depended on their zeal and capacity for intrigue to make connections and to advance themselves.

The percentage of Jews in key posts in the Lubyanka did not differ markedly from the percentage in other departments, but the other departments interested only the people dealing with them, while the Lubyanka interested everyone. And therefore if someone named Rabinovich was in charge of a mass execution, he was perceived not simply as a Cheka boss but as a Jew, while if someone named Abramovich was in charge of a mass epidemic countermeasure, he was perceived not as a Jew but as a good doctor. This was natural and not surprising.

It was the same reasoning that led to portraying the vicious murder of the tsar's family in Ekaterinburg in 1918 as the work of Jews, even though the vast majority of the executioners were Russian. Inflamed anti-Semites proclaimed one of the main organizers—chairman of the executive committee of the Urals Soviet, twenty-seven-year-old Alexander Beloborodov—to be the Jew Weisbrot, even though Oleg Platonov, a leading contemporary exposer of "Jewish crimes," has been forced to admit that "research in archives does not support this version." In their desire to find Jewish roots for Beloborodov, some people gave his father's name as Grigori (which is common in Jewish families) when it was actually Georgy.

But there is no getting around the fact that the first violins in the orchestra of death of the tsar and his family were four Jews—Yanker Yurovsky, Shaia Goloshchekin, Lev Sosnovsky, and Pinkus Vainer (Pert Voikov). The concert master and conductor was Yakov Sverdlov. It is quite possible, taking into account the extreme character of this murder against the background of the others that had become mundane, Lenin consciously left the organization of this Bolshevik act to Jews, so as to channel the wrath of the Whites and the Russian diaspora against them and then be able to accuse the indignant Russians of being anti-Semitic.

Could Stalin, as a member of the Central Committee and part of the innermost circle of the Party elite, been unaware of all the undercurrents in this scheme? Apparently he did not play a direct part in the murder of the tsar's family, but he learned a good lesson from the method of organizing bloody intrigues and manipulating public opinion. It goes without saying that the organizers and participants in the murder of the tsar's family came to the same end. Sosnovsky was shot in 1937, Beloborodov in 1938, Goloshchekin in 1941. Yurovsky died of cancer on the eve of his arrest in 1938 (the warrant had been signed), and Voikov was assassinated by an émigré student in 1927 in Warsaw, where he had been sent as ambassador, and became a Soviet martyr saint. His name (his Party pseudonym, that is) remains on a Moscow street and metro station, despite the trend of restoring old names to cities and streets.

Working side by side with Yagoda was another professional Chekist (a euphemism for professional executioner), Meer Trilisser. He joined the Party in 1901 (at the age of eighteen) and remained a little-known figure among Bolsheviks until he started working in the "organs" and came to Stalin's attention. With Stalin's intervention, this unknown Jew became a top-ranking Chekist by 1921, heading the foreign section of the Cheka (and later the GPU and OGPU—United Main Political Directorate). His work included keeping an eye on foreign Communists and reporting on their sympathies and antipathies and their contacts with various Bolshevik leaders. Stalin was impressed that Trilisser had an obviously negative attitude toward Zinoviev. Of course, Trilisser could tell which way the wind was blowing and whom his benefactor liked and did not like.

This successful Chekist quickly received a promotion to the same level as Yagoda—deputy chairman of OGPU—becoming the second Stalinist at the helm of Lubyanka. The many actions undertaken by Trilisser's agents included blowing up the cathedral in Sofia with the Bulgarian tsar and his government inside and a much, much more important action—an attempt in Paris on the life of Boris Bazhanov, Stalin's secretary who fled the country. The attempt was a failure, but even that did not cause Trilisser to lose Stalin's favor.

In 1927, on the tenth anniversary of "the revolution's punishing sword" (the traditional high-flown Bolshevik epithet for the Soviet secret police, which became part of the political jargon), Trilisser was given the Order of the Red Banner. The anniversary "luckily" coincided with the total defeat of Trotsky, as well as of Zinoviev and Kamenev, who three years earlier had joined in a conspiracy with Stalin against Trotsky. Now all three were expelled from the Party.

Stalin "gratefully" acknowledged Trilisser's role, his help in supplying the General Secretary with valuable secret information about his sworn "friends," and furnished a solemn motivation for bestowing the order on his informer that is meaningless to the uninitiated but transparent to those who are familiar with the language of the apparat: ". . . for especially promoting the strengthening of the dictatorship of the proletariat with his courage, loyalty to the revolution, and tireless persecution of its enemies and for especially valuable achievements in the struggle against counterrevolution, espionage, banditry, and other organizations hostile to Soviet power." Along with Trilisser, and with similar formulations, this glorious battle order was awarded to many other famous Chekists who were part of Stalin's entourage and who had already distinguished themselves with a talent for execution—Yakov Agranov, Matvei Berman, Karl Pauker, and other representatives of the Jewish proletariat.

There is evidence that Trilisser used his close relations with Stalin to dig up some "dark spots" in Yagoda's biography (hinting at former ties with the tsar's secret police) and reported them directly to the dictator in the hope of further improving his position. The fierce war for the throne of the ailing Menzhinsky as chief of OGPU was being waged behind closed doors, and all the deputies dreamed of replacing him. Stalin did not act on the valuable information, but remembered it. At that time Yagoda was, on Stalin's orders, preparing the murder of Kirov, and his own hour had not come. But Trilisser was not fired for his inappropriate initiative; rather, he was promoted.

Soon afterward Stalin made the professional punisher the chief figure of the Comintern, the Communist International, as a member of its executive committee, presidium, and political secretariat. He used the banal pseudonym Moskvin. Amazingly, that name, demonstrating with dreary literalness the bearer's loyalty to Moscow, was used by several other Comintern members, including foreign Communists, and I have no idea how they kept the "Moskvins" separated.

As secretary of the executive committee of the Comintern, Trilisser-Moskvin was in charge of personnel, a key position. The job was always held by someone from the organs, but in this case, it was of an order higher, since Trilisser had direct access to Stalin and got his orders from Stalin. On all personnel issues (which included leading comrades of all the fraternal parties), his word was law. His word was not only the word of the NKVD but also the word of Stalin. The Comintern archives are filled with respectful letters from friends abroad to Comrade Moskvin with requests to confirm someone, replace someone, appoint someone, report on someone. Remarkably, even in the latest edition of the *Great Soviet Encyclopedic Dictionary* (1991)—not to mention the earlier ones—there is no mention in Trilisser's biography of the almost four years he spent as personnel head of the Comintern at the peak of the nightmare, 1935–1938.

Meer Trilisser (Mikhail Moskvin) met the fate that was inevitable for them all. His case was run by Jewish investigators, some of whom he had hired and who later followed him into that cellar to be shot. Trilisser was accused of "placing Trotskyites, spies and provocateurs in the fraternal communist parties of Greece, Poland, England, Estonia, France, Hungary, Latvia and other countries." Not a single Trotskyite, spy, or provocateur was named; nor was it necessary in those days. His students and colleagues at his beloved Lubyanka also claimed that he became a spy for Japan in 1920 and for England in 1925. They could have added many other countries, but they were too lazy. Besides, Stalin did not like reading very long documents, and this transcript was sent to him.

Trilisser was executed on February 2, 1940, on the same day as the great theater director Vsevolod Meyerhold; as Mikhail Koltsov (Fridland), a worker of the NKVD and the Comintern and the country's premier journalist, close to Stalin, yet hated by him for his "pushiness;" and as Stalin's comrade-in-arms Robert Eikhe, among many others. They were very different men, but there was one factor that put them all on the same level—a bullet from the same executioner and burial in a mass grave.

Even closer to Stalin than Trilisser were two high-ranking figures at Lubyanka—Yakov Agranov, Yagoda's first deputy, and Karl Pauker, head of the operative department.

Pauker—one of the Hungarian Jews who took an active part in the Russian revolution (another, Bela Kun, spread bloody terror in the Crimea with Rozalia Zemlyachka-Zalkind and was executed by

Stalin in 1938; yet another, Matyas Rakoszy, became dictator after the Red Army occupied Hungary)—pleased Stalin and became chief of his bodyguards. An illiterate barber, he compensated for his pathological ignorance with pathological cruelty and unbounded toadying. Stalin's trust in Pauker was so great that he allowed him—and only him—to shave him with a dangerous razor.

This satrap participated in many operations personally developed and approved by Stalin, and showed especial zeal and readiness to serve. For instance, he was a member of the group who arrested Kamenev. But this was not his primary role for Stalin. The toady knew that Stalin adored Jewish anecdotes, and he was an incomparable storyteller, amusing his boss with an ever-new store of jokes.

Jewish jokes come in two models. The first is imbued with irrepressible Jewish humor, a mixture of sadness with a strictly measured dose of self-irony, always evidence of spiritual health and faith in the solidity of the national spirit.

Pauker was a masterful teller of such anecdotes, and he needed clever writers to keep his repertoire fully stocked. Pauker himself was incapable of creating anything. According to reliable though unchecked sources, his main creative partner was none other than Karl Radek, the notable Bolshevik columnist and political figure, whose real influence was much greater than his official posts would indicate. This very talented and absolutely unprincipled politician, of Jewish extraction, would have been happy to amuse Stalin himself with his anti-Semitic jokes, but he did not enjoy the leader's trust to that degree, and so had to settle for anonymous ghostwriting that improved Pauker's standing in the boss's eyes. Pauker had a wonderful way of rolling his R's, and did a small-town Jewish accent that made the usually affectless Stalin roar with laughter. He did not even get too upset if Pauker ran short of new material, but enjoyed hearing the old stories over again.

There is a fairly well substantiated story that Pauker was personally present at the execution of Zinoviev and Kamenev, and that he is the source of information about the final minutes of Lenin's closest comrades, who with him had formed the leading circle of the revolution. After a late party, Pauker did an imitation of Zinoviev being dragged away to his execution by two guards, and with a Jewish accent (which Zinoviev did not have), moan-

ing as he grabbed hold of the guards' legs, "For God's sake, comrades, call Josif Vissarionovich. Josif Vissarionovich promised to save our lives!" Delighted, Stalin choked with laughter and demanded a reprise.

The defector Alexander Orlov (Lev Feldbin), who knew the backstage life of the Kremlin and Lubyanka well, recounts in his memoirs, *The Secret History of Stalin's Crimes,* that the performance did not end there. "Pauker," Orlov writes, "added a new element to his performance. Instead of falling on his knees now when he depicted Zinoviev, he straightened up, reached to the heavens, and shouted, 'Hear O Israel, the Lord is our God, the Lord is One!' Stalin couldn't stand it and, laughing and sobbing, he waved at Pauker to stop the show."

Actually, the truth of this episode (I do not mean "Pauker-Stalin" but "Zinoviev-executioners") is seriously open to question. Zinoviev, as he (literally) licked the boots of his killers minutes before his death, certainly must have shouted out some words. But *those* words are least likely to have been the ones. Pauker, however, knew what would make his boss laugh. He knew his hobbyhorse. And he played on the string that would please.

Either his incredible stupidity or the blindness that afflicted almost everyone kept Pauker from seeing his inevitable end. The recipient of every possible medal and order, he was arrested on April 21, 1937, and shot less than four months later, on August 14. The comic element (if that word can be used at all in the context of the great tragedy) was that the Jewish Pauker was seriously accused of being a Gestapo agent.

A year later the same fate befell another Chekist who was even closer to Stalin than Pauker. Yakov Agranov, deputy chief of the OGPU and then Deputy Commissar of Internal Affairs, was no illiterate Pauker. Stalin probably did not consider the sensible and well-educated man a friend (he never had a friend in his entire life) but certainly a "close comrade." In any case, he moved him into the Kremlin and gave him a dacha next to his own in the village of Zubalovo near Moscow.

Agranov began his "Soviet work" in Lenin's apparat as secretary of the Small Council of Commissars, and then moved to the Lubyanka, where he remained until his dying hour. A list of the cases that Agranov was in charge of would be enough for the Russian reader to learn everything he needs to know about the man. The most controversial cases of "counterrevolutionary conspiracies" fabricated by the Bolsheviks in the early twenties were investigated by Agranov, and it is likely that he himself wrote the scenarios that he later produced. We can find his name in Solzhenitsyn's *Gulag Archipelago*, where one passage is particularly illuminating about him.

The case involved one of the first large-scale fabrications created by Iron Felix [Dzerzhinsky], the case of the Petrograd military organization—an invented anti-Bolshevik conspiracy (1921), headed allegedly by Professor Vladimir Tagantsev, of Petrograd University and the Mining Institute. Here is what Solzhenitsyn writes:

Professor Tagantsev kept heroically silent through forty-five days of investigation. But then Agranov persuaded him to sign an agreement with him:

"I, Tagantsev, consciously begin giving evidence about our organization, hiding nothing. . . . I am doing all this to ease the lot of the defendants in our case."

"I, Yakov Saulovich Agranov, with the aid of Citizen Tagantsev, undertake to end the investigation quickly and afterward turn the case over to an open trial. . . . I promise that none of the accused will be given the highest measure of punishment."

"None of the accused"—Stalin similarly gave his personal word to Zinoviev and Kamenev that they would not be executed if they "honestly performed the will of the Party." They were executed, and all that was left of Comrade Stalin's word of honor was Pauker's drunken story that gave Stalin so much merriment.

And in the case of Tagantsev, sixty people (including fifteen women) were shot on the night of August 14, 1921. One of the people executed was the Russian poet, and Anna Akhmatova's first husband, Nikolai Gumilev. A man of immense talent and great personal courage, he had looked death in the eyes several times and met it with amazing and proud dignity. Six years before his execution, in one of his most famous poems, he foretold his death at the hands of an executioner.

Another of Yakov Agranov's achievements is the case of his colleague, a zealous Chekist and former left Social Revolutionary, Yakov Blumkin—the killer of the German ambassador Count Meerbach. (He was forgiven for the murder—he was executed for his closeness to Trotsky, which was the case Agranov investigated.) Another case invented by the Lubyanka was that of the Labor Peasant Party, which never existed, and on whose account Professor Alexander Chayanov, a leading agrarian economist and writer (of sociophilosophical novels) was executed. But the most important case is that of the murder of Sergei Kirov, the Party boss of Leningrad and Stalin's great rival. Stalin took Agranov, along with the prosecutor Andrei Vyshinsky and the investigator Lev Sheinin (more of him later), with him in the government train that rushed to Leningrad upon news of the fatal shot. Therefore, Stalin knew whom to take and why.

Agranov justified the trust of his leader and teacher. He ran an investigation that removed any possible suspicions against Stalin. He beat the statements he needed for his boss out of the wounded Nikolayev and the other arrested suspects. And he became, in the course of just a few days, the head of the Leningrad NKVD, and soon after that, First Deputy to Commissar of Interior Affairs Yagoda. The show trial of Zinoviev and Kamenev in 1935, which ended with prison sentences for them for conspiracy and murder, had been prepared entirely by Agranov. He headed the investigation team and personally interrogated the former leaders of the revolution. And it was then, in addition to his high post, that Agranov received from his "close comrade" and mentor an apartment in the Kremlin (to always be nearby) and the dacha in Zubalovo, the village that Svetlana Allilueva describes with such nostalgic warmth in *Twenty Letters to a Friend*.

Agranov, one of Stalin's "main Jews," until recently was known in the Soviet Union only as a friend of the poet Vladimir Mayakovsky and his mistress Lili Brik (née Kagan), the sister of the French writer Elsa Triolet. Without divorcing her husband, the writer Osip Brik, she was considered (and according to the literature of recent years, is still considered) the wife simultaneously of several other men, including Mayakovsky and an outstanding Soviet military leader, Vitaly Primakov, who was executed with Marshal Tukhachevsky in 1937. Like Osip Brik, Lili collaborated with the NKVD, performing delicate assignments, not yet fully documented (but apparently on the friendly recommendation of Agranov), at home and abroad—in Latvia, Germany, France, and England. Lili Brik's "salon," which Anna Akhmatova described with undisguised scorn, gathered major literary and artistic figures of the period as well as major Chekists. These were not secret agents, but official staff personnel of the Lubyanka, who not only did not hide their work but were proud of it.

It is important to understand that in those years the attitude toward the OGPU-NKVD was not like that of any decent person today—if for no other reason than the fact that no matter how grievous the crimes of the Cheka in the 20s, this was still before the era of the Great Terror, and the country had not yet lived through the NKVD under Yezhov and Beria, had not yet been inundated by the blood of occupied Eastern Europe, had not yet started persecuting dissidents. There was still a revolutionary, romantic aura that permeated society, especially that milieu, and it particularly related to the activities of the "glorious Chekists." If a host introduced an acquaintance to a new guest as someone who worked for the OGPU, he could be sure that the guest would break into a polite smile and make a respectful bow.

I doubt that there was another poet (or novelist or playwright or artist) who was as surrounded by Chekists as Mayakovsky. And sadly, they were almost all Jewish. But not because it was a Jewish plot to harass a Russian poet, but because they were placed, according to Stalin's plan (more below), in every level of Lubyanka. The only other salon that could compete with Lili Brik's in terms of permeation by OGPU officials was that of the actress Zinaida Raikh, whose husband, the director Vsevolod Meyerhold, also a friend of Mayakovsky's, was surrounded by them. Of the twenty-seven people who signed the poet's obituary notice published in *Pravda*, in which they called him their "close friend" (eleven of them would soon be executed), at least three were generals in the Cheka—Yakov Agranov, lovingly called "Yanya" by the literary-theatrical world of Moscow, Moisey Gorb, and Lev Elbert. A fourth, Zakhar Volovich, could have signed (with as much right as the other three), but did not only because he was on "diplomatic" assignment in Paris under an assumed name.

Zakhar Ilyich Volovich was involved in many of the dirty crimes of the NKVD, crimes enveloped even today in deep secrecy. In 1928 he worked undercover as Vladimir Borisovich Yanovich, an attaché of the Soviet embassy in Paris. That is where he became close to Mayakovsky. The true role of the "diplomat" was no secret in Paris. The French newspapers openly called him "chief of the Paris GPU." Volovich-Yanovich (aka Vilyansky) took part in the kidnapping and murder of the tsarist General Kutepov, who headed the Russian Military Union. This piece of banditry caused a lot of noise in its time. When he returned to Moscow, he became deputy to the chief of the Operative Section of the NKVD, Pauker. He personally participated in the arrest of Grigori Zinoviev. With Pauker, he guarded Stalin, not leaving him for a minute. On March 27, 1937, he was arrested and charged with planning a terrorist act against Stalin (why he didn't execute it, seeing him daily, was never explained) and with espionage on behalf of Nazi Germany. His chief, Karl Pauker, was also arrested on this latter charge. Both these Jewish "Nazi spies" were killed by the bullets of an unknown colleague on the same day, August 14, 1937.

If Mayakovsky had only known how high his friend Yanya, Yakov Agranov, would soar! Whose cases he would investigate! Life creates the most unbelievable scenarios. Agranov supervised the investigation of one of the de facto husbands of his close friend and associate Lili Brik. The husband was Vitaly Primakov, whom Agranov had met at Lili's salon many times. From his prison cell Primakov wrote the first deputy commissar (his acquaintance and his wife's friend), "Please interrogate me personally. . . . They are confusing me more and more, something I do not understand at all. I am completely innocent. I have heart spasms every day." Agranov heard his pleas and called the prisoner in, after which he "confessed" to everything. And at the so-called trial with other "confessed" defendants he was the chief exposer of himself and others. And got a bullet in the back of the head.

The fall of Stalin's man Genrikh Yagoda meant the fall of the leader's friend Agranov. Yagoda's arrest was preceded by a brief appointment as Commissar of Communications. And Stalin decided to follow the same approach, but in a farcical variation, with Agranov. Yagoda was arrested on March 27, 1937, and on June 1 his former first deputy was sent by the "marvelous

Georgian" to Saratov as head of the local ministry of internal affairs and instructed to expose "the nests of German intelligence in the autonomous republic of the Volga Germans." Agranov was a smart man, but he did not understand the meaning of this "responsible assignment." Or did he just not want to believe it?

He took on his new job with such zeal that his provincial colleagues were stunned. In just a few days his unbridled imagination created dozens of "spying, conspiratorial, terrorist, and diversionary groups" on his new territory. People were arrested by the hundreds and thousands, the local prison could not hold them, and they all confessed, all of them.

There was a small hitch. Many of the people charged with creating "German nationalist, anti-Soviet organization" were Jewish—and the local Chekists, who knew their "clients" better, pointed this out to the new boss. Perhaps he had been thrown off by the similarity of German and Jewish names. But Agranov simply changed the organizations he had uncovered to "German-Jewish nationalist anti-Soviet" ones. The patent for this fantastic hybrid is his.

Agranov was trying to save his life—he had to show that in far-off Saratov he had discovered enemies living in Moscow. Among the German spies he found were Lenin's widow, Nadezhda Krupskaya, and Georgi Malenkov, just starting out on his Party and state career. Stalin hated Krupskaya, which Agranov knew, but he could not allow Agranov to take such liberties with an icon's widow, and he had plans for Malenkov to replace the government "enemies of the people" who had been destroyed. Agranov had overreached. Agonizing, he lost all his abilities as an experienced and clever intriguer. His crazy letter to Yezhov (which was immediately forwarded to Stalin), with a proposal to arrest Krupskaya and Malenkov as "protectors of the counterrevolutionary, nationalist German-Jewish underground," speaks for itself.

By July 16, Agranov had been recalled to Moscow. He expected to be rewarded for his zeal. But Yezhov, who had orders from his leader, gave him a crude and ruthless chewing-out. The inexorable end was approaching. Other tenants had been moved into his Kremlin apartment. But Agranov had a spare flat in the grim ten-story building for the Cheka, at 9 Markhlevsky Street (that prison-like edifice is still standing), where Yagoda had recently been arrested. And Agranov was taken there too. He knew perfectly well what awaited him. He did not resist. He signed without a murmur everything that his more fortunate colleagues (for the time being) had prepared. A year later, on August 1, 1938, an executioner's bullet ended his life. On August 26, his wife, Valentina Agranova, who had also been a friend of Mayakovsky, was shot. She was rehabilitated posthumously in 1957. Despite the efforts of their daughter (who in the 50s wrote to Voroshilov, Kaganovich, and other former colleagues of her father), Agranov was refused rehabilitation. He is still considered an agent of Germany and Poland, on whose orders he planned to kill Stalin (but for some reason did not, despite seeing him on a daily basis at work and socially, with their families). God is his judge and the judge of his judges.

There is a widespread belief that whenever Jews find a niche, they start protecting one another and helping other Jews get on board too. Soviet reality, created by the genius of Stalin, refutes this point of view. A much more general and obvious rule was mutual destruction, and the desire not to be suspected of protectionism and nepotism prompted many well-situated Jews, especially those in positions of power, to bend over backward to show their "objectivity" and unlimited loyalty to the Party and its beloved leader. This was supposed to confirm in a monstrously deformed way Lenin's concept of solidarity based on class rather than nationality and Stalin's idea that there was no Jewish nation.

But that nation existed for the author of the idea that the nation did not exist. In examining the factors that shaped Stalin's anti-Semitism, which grew fiercer with every year, we cannot limit ourselves to the political sphere and the power struggle. A great influence on Stalin was his personal entourage and the daily life of the Kremlin—especially in the 20s, when the Party leaders saw one another socially, including families, with the spontaneity of the recent prerevolutionary past and of the Civil War, before the socializing became formalized into a Party ritual.

There were not that many Jewish leaders, but there was a plethora of Jewish wives. Their presence created an atmosphere in the Kremlin that would go unnoticed only by a normal person without prejudices. But the Kremlin's chief specialist on ethnic issues was by no means a normal person.

The wives of Zinoviev (Zlata Lilina) and Kamenev (Olga Bronstein, Trotsky's sister) were not only their husbands' helpmeets but political activists in their own right. Lilina held important posts in the Party and Soviet apparat (she was fortunate to have died a natural death in 1929), and Kameneva was in charge of culture (she was shot in September 1941 in a forest near Orel). Some authors use the fact that the leaders of the "right opposition" (the last opposition to Stalin in the late 20s) were almost all "pure-blooded" Russians to show that Stalin was not anti-Semitic in his struggle with his political foes. Konstantin Simonov stressed, "At the head of the right opposition, with which Stalin . . . dealt ruthlessly, were people with Russian names and Russian background, as if they had been specially selected."

But both Bukharin and Rykov, leaders of the right, who lived in the Kremlin, were close neighbors of Stalin, and shared the family table with him, were married to Jewish women. Nina Rykova (Marshak) was active in Party and administrative work in various districts of Moscow and was in leading elective Party organs (she died in the GULAG). Bukharin's second wife (although they never made the marriage legal, which was not an issue in those days) at the period of his greatest closeness to Stalin, who called him "Bukharchik," was Esther Gurevich, Party member and famous economist. Soon after, he married the young and lovely Anna Larina (Lurie), who was the daughter of Mikhail Lurie, a prominent Bolshevik and friend of Lenin, economist, member of the parliament of the Union and of Russia, and a writer under the pen name Yu Larin. This marriage elicited envy and jealousy in Stalin and left a deep wound in the rancorous leader.

Sergei Kirov, "beloved friend and brother" of the great leader, was also married to a Jew. Of Stalin's closet entourage, Molotov, Voroshilov, and Andreyev all married Jewish women. There was nothing remarkable about this. Jewish girls from poor families (primarily the families of village craftsmen) joined the revolution in great numbers and gave it their passion and fire. And it was among them that the future leaders found their love. Voroshilov, for instance, married Ekaterina Gorbman in 1907 or 1908. Molotov found his love, Perl Karpovskaya, in 1921 in Moscow, where the twenty-four-year-old Communist had come for a conference from the Ukrainian city of Zaporozhie. She would later take the name Polina Zhemchuzhina and become famous in the Party and the country.

But surely it was no accident that these two comrades-in-arms, Molotov and Voroshilov, who passed unharmed through the maws of the Great Terror and escaped its revival in the late-40s and early-50s, were suspected by Stalin toward the end of his life when he was completely paranoid. In Voroshilov, Stalin saw a British spy and in Molotov, an American one. It would be a grave mistake to consider these family particulars as being incidental or insignificant and unworthy of historical analysis. By virtue of circumstance, every detail of Kremlin life, the life of that building which was basically a communal flat, willy-nilly became a factor in politics. For a man of a different mentality, a different upbringing, roots, and character—in other words, a man from the intelligentsia influenced by culture—the ethnic background of his colleagues' wives would not have mattered. But Stalin was made of other stuff; and as the years passed, the constant presence of the wives became harder and harder to deal with for the Georgian leader of the Russian people.

Let us also add the wife of a man extremely close to him for almost two decades, his personal secretary and a Lubyanka general, Alexander Poskrebyshev. Bronislava Solomonovna Poskrebysheva was the sister of the wife of Lev Sedov, Trotsky's son. That alone doomed her. Poskrebyshev dared to defend his wife, but Stalin's sole response was: "We will find you another wife." And one evening, when Poskrebyshev came home, he found a woman selected by Stalin going about the housework. I need not say that she was not an "alien." But still, in 1952, when the fear of a Zionist conspiracy drove Stalin to his final madness, he not only planned the liquidation of Molotov and Voroshilov (the only two survivors out of the entire ruling elite) but also fired Poskrebyshev, the most loyal of the loyal. His logic (if it could be called that) is clear. If not for the grace of God, all three would have followed the millions of other victims, many of whom had died thanks to them.

The figure of Lazar Kaganovich stands out, and deserves separate discussion. The last of Stalin's entourage, Kaganovich, who died recently at age ninety-eight, spent almost three decades as the leader's favorite and closest comrade. For some time (in the first half of the 30s) he was the second most important man in the country. Many letters from the provinces on current questions of party or economic life were addressed to "Comrades J. V. Stalin and L. M. Kaganovich." It was he who was designated by Stalin to announce to the Politburo that Stalin's wife, Nadezhda Alliluyeva, had shot herself. Until then, Stalin had told his party comrades that Nadezhda had "died suddenly."

When Stalin took a vacation, Kaganovich, as acting General Secretary, replaced him. He chaired the meetings of the secretariat of the Central Committee and the Politburo. It was probably that exceptional position that gave him the "moral" right to be rude to Krupskaya, which Stalin liked (and which Kaganovich knew he liked). In particular, in 1930 Kaganovich announced at a regional Party conference in Moscow, "Krupskaya shouldn't think that just because she was Lenin's wife that she has a monopoly on Leninism." Not many people would have dared to say something like that publicly, even in 1930.

A cobbler by profession, from a poor Jewish family, uneducated, writing with an enormous number of grammatical and spelling mistakes, Lazar Kaganovich was brought into the Bolshevik underground before the revolution by his older brother, Mikhail, but he did not earn any fame in the Party. In July 1936 an unnamed versifier sent "A Message from the Belorussian People to Comrade Stalin," which said, "Kaganovich's word resounded, He grew our Party in Gomel." But in fact no one heard Kaganovich's word and no one had any idea that he was "growing the Party," if only in Gomel. In the thousands of letters, notes, notations, and resolutions by Lenin, lovingly preserved in the Party archives, innumerable names appear, most of which are forgotten even by specialists in Party history and require footnoting, but Kaganovich's name does not show up even once.

But Stalin, with his unerring nose, found Kaganovich in the mass of middle-level Party apparatchiks and elevated him as soon as he himself became General Secretary of the Party (1922), bringing him into his innermost entourage. Just two years later, on Stalin's direct "recommenda-tion," the previously unknown Kaganovich became secretary of the Central Committee, and a short while later a member of the Politburo.

This dizzying career, created by Stalin himself, might seem to disprove the idea of Stalin's anti-Semitism. But in fact, no matter how paradoxical it may seem, it confirms it. First of all, with the very large number of Jewish Party apparatchiks and officials at all levels, the question of ethnic background was not an issue in the twenties—and personal loyalty was much more important for Stalin than data in a curriculum vitae. Kaganovich suited him because he had never been part of Lenin's group (even at a great remove), or of a leading nucleus, had no ties to the old cadres who were fighting for the inheritance of their respected founder, and owed his job solely to Stalin. Secondly, the presence of at least one Jew in the leading elite (Trotsky, Kamenev, and Zinoviev were gone by then) automatically obviated any possible accusations of discrimination. In those days a hint of even hidden anti-Semitism was a grievous sin that in some cases meant expulsion from the Party. Stalin, almost to the very end, maintained his image as a militant internationalist.

When in the late-20s Kaganovich was sent by Stalin "to bring order" to Ukraine, he showed his boundless energy and organizational abilities through merciless beatings of the cadres on any demagogic excuse. Two other Ukrainian leaders—Grigory Petrovsky and Vlas Chubar—came to Stalin to beg him to recall Kaganovich from Ukraine before he beat up all the most talented workers. Defending his man, Stalin accused them of anti-Semitism. That was a favorite tactic of his, allowing him to kill several birds at once. He not only rejected accusations against Kaganovich, who was merely doing what Stalin told him to do, but he made it impossible to accuse Comrade Stalin of a sin unbefitting a Communist. Of course, Stalin did recall Kaganovich from Ukraine a year later and made him secretary of the Central Committee again, which brought them even closer because of the zeal with which Kaganovich did Stalin's bidding (the zeal that so upset Petrovsky and Chubar). Eventually Chubar was shot, Petrovsky was removed from all his posts and left to anticipate arrest, Petrovsky's son was arrested and executed, while Kaganovich remained on the Party Olympus as the only Jewish representative, demonstrating the absence of state anti-Semitism in the most international and most democratic country in the world.

Kaganovich actively participated in the forced collectivization of agriculture, in the cruel campaign against Cossacks in the Northern Caucasus (that is, in the deportation and killing of Cossacks only because they or their fathers had belonged to the Don Cossack Army in tsarist times). He ruthlessly purged the transport sector and for a time was the Commissar of Transportation. The list of his villainous deeds is enormous.

PART NINE
ICONS

INTRODUCTION

Every culture and society needs and has individual people etched into its collective historical imagination and memory that may be called icons, totems, or talismans. These are people who made a tremendous impact on culture and society in their lifetimes, who rose transcendentally above almost everyone else in the ambiance, and who came to symbolize important and, for nearly everyone, vehemently applauded activity. Examples in American history are George Washington, Abraham Lincoln, Franklin Delano Roosevelt, Thomas Edison, and Babe Ruth.

When professional historians look closely, empirically, and critically at these icons, they may see a downside to their characters and behaviors. But even if lengthy and learned books pointing out these downsides are published, and even if these books gain a substantial audience, the iconic figures remain transcendent and symbolic in their greatness for nearly everyone.

So it has been also with the Jews. Because critical, empirical Jewish historical writing has been so meager in amount, and because the Judaic Studies Departments are captives of their conservative, under-educated rich benefactors, there has been in recent years more caution than might otherwise be expected in pointing out the chinks in the armor of the Jewish icons. But even when these downsides are revealed in good books—for example, Moses probably had no historical existence; Maimonides at one point in his earlier lifetime for safety reasons quite possibly pretended to be a Muslim; Herzl died

Reconstruction of the Temple of Solomon.

376

young of venereal disease; Ben-Gurion engaged in petty corruption, using labor union funds to finance trysts with his mistress in European spas—these revelations have had virtually no public impact. The great names continue to be tendered forth from Jewish pulpit and lecture platform and in the Jewish press.

Such is the nature of Jewish public culture. But the Jews are not singular in protecting and forever gilding their icons. They are perhaps only a little more aggressive than most others in doing so, because they have suffered so much. They have such nightmarish memories of powerlessness, exile, and extermination, that their icons are all the more precious, all the more to be vehemently held onto and elevated with epiphanic hymns.

Functionally, sociologically, and psychoanalytically, this persistent icon worship and totemic and talismanic adulation makes sense, serves therapeutic needs, and brings personal comfort and strengthens community.

In the 1940s every Jewish Bar-Mitzvah boy in the U.S.A. and Canada received as a gift, along with the fountain pens, a copy of a volume called *They All Are Jews*—a collection of romanticized pages of penciled visages and of sticky prose about how good each was, how wonderful the particular Jewish man's and woman's accomplishments were. And it wasn't a set of lies. By and large, this inspirational volume was grounded in truth.

Moses

Along with the Bible and Halachic (legalistic) commentaries on the Bible, which became solidified in the Talmud, there were stemming from about 200 B.C. to A.D. 500 vast collections of material in a legendary genre, the Haggadah, and Midrash, which along with the Halachic works, similarly constituted an amplification and explanation of the Biblical text.

Here is the view of Moses presented in the Haggadic literature, translated by Louis Ginzberg. This passage features a characteristic of the Haggadic literature, namely a conflation of time, so that Moses is connected to other great religious leaders who came much later, such as Rabbi Akiba in the second century A.D., and the Talmudic sage Rabbi Eliezer.

This obliviousness to time sequences remains today a character of rabbinical sermons, even of Reform rabbis. Of course, more than a century of archeological work in the Nile delta has turned up not a shred of evidence that Moses ever existed. Orthodox Jews totally block out this historical fact. More secular, liberal, believing Jews take one of two lines: First, there is no certainty of evidence that Moses did not exist (so much for archeological science); and second, historical quibbling is of no relevance to faith.

In general—and this passage about Moses clearly illustrates this point—the Haggadah, a body of literature as vast as the Talmud, constitutes the exercise of romantic imagination on the Biblical stories—their amplification and

elaboration. Until modern times and full Jewish access to secular literature, the Haggadah was an important and necessary outlet for imaginative fantasizing, which because it was focused on the Biblical tradition, was legitimated by the Orthodox rabbis.

Moses now stayed forty days in heaven to learn the Torah from God. But when he started to descend and beheld the hosts of the angels of terror, angels of trembling, angels of quaking, and angels of horror, then through his fear he forgot all he had learned. For this reason God called the angel Yefefiyah, the prince of the Torah, who handed over to Moses the Torah, "ordered in all things and sure." All the other angels, too, became his friends, and each bestowed upon him a remedy as well as the secret of the Holy Names, as they are contained in the Torah, and as they are applied. Even the Angel of Death gave him a remedy against death. The applications of the Holy Names, which the angels through Yefefiyah, the prince of the Torah, and Metatron, the prince of the Face, taught him, Moses passed on to the high-priest Eleazar, who passed them to his son Phinehas, also known as Elijah.

When Moses reached heaven, he found God occupied ornamenting the letters in which the Torah was written, with little crown-like decorations, and he looked on without saying a word. God then said to him: "In thy home, do not people know the greeting of peace?" Moses: "Does it behoove a servant to address his Master?" God: "Thou mightest at least have wished Me success in My labors." Moses hereupon said: "Let the power of my Lord be great according as Thou hast spoken." Then Moses inquired as to the significance of the crowns upon the letters, and was answered: "Hereafter there shall live a man called Akiba, son of Joseph, who will base in interpretation a gigantic mountain of Halakot upon every dot of these letters." Moses said to God: "Show me this man." God: "Go back eighteen ranks." Moses went where he was bidden, and could hear the discussions of the teacher sitting with his disciples in the eighteenth rank, but was not able to follow these discussions, which greatly grieved him. But just then he heard the disciples questioning their master in regard to a certain subject: "Whence dost thou know this?" And he answered, "This is a Halakah given to Moses on Mount Sinai," and now Moses was content. Moses returned to God and said to Him: "Thou hast a man like Akiba, and yet dost Thou give the Torah to Israel through me!" But God answered: "Be silent, so has it been decreed by Me." Moses then said: "O Lord of the world! Thou hast permitted me to behold this man's learning, let me see also the reward which will be meted out to him." God said: "Go, return and see." Moses saw them sell the flesh of the martyr Akiba at the meat market. He said to God: "Is this the reward for such erudition?" But God replied: "Be silent, thus have I decreed."

Moses then saw how God wrote the word "long-suffering" in the Torah, and asked: "Does this mean that Thou hast patience with the pious?" But God answered: "Nay, with sinners also am I long-suffering." "What!" exclaimed Moses, "Let the sinners perish!" God said no more, but when Moses implored God's mercy, begging Him to forgive the sin of the people of Israel, God answered him: "Thou thyself didst advise Me to have no patience with sinners and to destroy them." "Yea," said Moses, "but Thou didst declare that Thou art long-suffering with sinners also, let now the patience of the Lord be great according as Thou hast spoken."

The forty days that Moses spent in heaven were entirely devoted to the study of the Torah, he learned the written as well as the oral teaching, yea, even the doctrines that an able scholar would some day propound were revealed to him. He took an especial delight in hearing the teachings of the Tanna Rabbi Eliezer, and received the joyful message that this great scholar would be one of his descendants.

Solomon

Through centuries of misery and poverty in ghetto and shtetl, Jews could feel good about King Solomon and the Temple he built in Jerusalem. In this selection from the Haggadic literature, the authors are sensitive to Solomon's position as the offspring of King David's tempestuous and not-very-ethical union with Bath-sheba, and try to portray it in a way that satisfies religious and moral tradition. Or maybe they just wanted to jazz up the account of the building of the First Temple with reminiscence of a suggestive sexual story imbedded in the Bible. Haggadic writers were very market-conscious: They knew what their readers wanted.

Among the great achievements of Solomon first place must be assigned to the superb Temple built by him. He was long in doubt as to where he was to build it. A heavenly voice directed him to go to Mount Zion at night, to a field owned by two brothers jointly. One of the brothers was a bachelor and poor, the other was blessed both with wealth and a large family of children. It was harvesting time. Under cover of night, the poor brother kept adding to the other's heap of grain, for, although he was poor, he thought his brother needed more on account of his large family. The rich brother, in the same clandestine way, added to the poor brother's store, thinking that though he had a family to support, the other was without means. This field, Solomon concluded, which had called forth so remarkable a manifestation of brotherly love, was the best site for the Temple, and he bought it.

Every detail of the equipment and ornamentation of the Temple testifies to Solomon's rare wisdom. Next to the required furniture, he planted golden trees, which bore fruit all the time the building stood. When the enemy entered the Temple, the fruit dropped from the trees, but they will put forth blossoms again when it is rebuilt in the days of the Messiah.

Solomon was so assiduous that the erection of the Temple took but seven years, about half the time for the erection of the king's palace, in spite of the greater magnificence of the sanctuary. In this respect, he was the superior of his father David, who first built a house for himself, and then gave thought to a house for God to dwell in. Indeed, it was Solomon's meritorious work in connection with the Temple that saved him from being reckoned by the sages as one of the impious kings, among whom his later actions might properly have put him.

According to the measure of the zeal displayed by Solomon were the help and favor shown him by God. During the seven years it took to build the Temple, not a single workman died who was employed about it, nor even did a single one fall sick. And as the workmen were sound and robust from first to last, so the perfection of their tools remained unimpaired until the building stood complete. Thus the work suffered no sort of interruption. After the dedication of the Temple, however, the workmen died off, lest they build similar structures for the heathen and their gods. Their wages they were to receive from God in the world to come, and the master workman, Hiram, was rewarded by being permitted to reach Paradise alive.

The Temple was finished in the month of Bul, now called Marheshwan, but the edifice stood closed for nearly a whole year, because it was the will of God that the dedication take place in the month of Abraham's birth. Meantime the enemies of Solomon rejoiced maliciously. "Was it not the son of Bath-sheba," they said, "who built the

Temple? How, then, could God permit His Shekinah [Divine Presence] to rest upon it?" When the consecration of the house took place, and "the fire came down from heaven," they recognized their mistake.

The importance of the Temple appeared at once, for the torrential rains which annually since the deluge had fallen for forty days beginning with the month of Marheshwan, for the first time failed to come, and thenceforward appeared no more.

The joy of the people over the sanctuary was so great that they held the consecration ceremonies on the Day of Atonement. It contributed not a little to their ease of mind that a heavenly voice was heard to proclaim: "You all shall have a share in the world to come."

The great house of prayer reflected honor not only on Solomon and the people, but also on King David. The following incident proves it: When the Ark was about to be brought into the Holy of Holies, the door of the sacred chamber locked itself, and it was impossible to open it. Solomon prayed fervently to God, but his entreaties had no effect until he pronounced the words: "Remember the good deeds of David thy servant." The Holy of Holies then opened of itself, and the enemies of David had to admit that God had wholly forgiven his sin.

In the execution of the Temple work a wish cherished by David was fulfilled. He was averse to having the gold which he had taken as booty from the heathen places of worship during his campaigns used for the sanctuary at Jerusalem, because he feared that the heathen would boast, at the destruction of the Temple, that their gods were courageous, and were taking revenge by wrecking the house of the Israelitish God. Fortunately Solomon was so rich that there was no need to resort to the gold inherited from his father, and so David's wish was fulfilled.

Akiba

The historical Rabbi Akiba was a venerable and influential sage who supported the second Judean rebellion against Rome, led by Bar Kochba ("son of a star," originally Bar Koseba) 132–135 B.C. which was doomed to failure and put down savagely by the Romans. The Romans vengefully expelled all Jews from the southern half of the country and turned Jerusalem into a pagan city. Akiba was killed by Romans. There is a passage in the Talmud that indicates that some other rabbis severely criticized old Akiba for supporting Bar Kochba's rebellion.

Yet Akiba became an icon of Jewish tradition as a great and wise sage. In the Haggadah he is indeed hailed as the last of the ancient sages, which is not true. Note how in the legendary account Akiba still dies a martyr's death at Roman hands.

The Haggadah's account of Akiba's life is embellished with soap-opera-like popular romanticism—he is very wealthy; he marries the converted wife of the Roman governor; he is accompanied on a trip by beautiful young women; etc.

When Moses ascended to heaven he saw God busy adorning some letters of the Torah with decorative crowns. Moses asked God, "Why are You doing this?" God answered "Some time in the future a great teacher will arise by name of Akiba ben Joseph and he will teach many new laws from each of these crowns." Moses asked, "Can I see him?" God did this for Moses who was then carried off into the future and placed in the school room of Akiba where he sat at the back of eight rows of students. As he listened to the lesson, Moses felt distressed because he did not understand what Akiba was teaching. Then one of the disciples asked Akiba what was the authority for the new law which the master was expounding. Akiba answered, "It is a tradition which we have received going back as far as Moses on Mount Sinai." At that, Moses felt at ease again. He came to God and said, "Master of the World! with such a man why did you give the Torah through my hand?" God answered him, "Moses be still; this is My decision." Moses thought for a while and said, "Dear God, You have shown me the man and his great teaching of Torah. Now show me his reward." God then said, look into the future at this picture. When Moses looked, he saw how Akiba was being tortured to death by the Romans. "Is this his reward for teaching Torah?" asked Moses in pained astonishment. Again God replied, "Moses, be still: This is My decision."

Rabbi Akiba was a shepherd for forty years, studied for the next forty years and taught for the next forty years.

Who are the fathers of Israel? Rabbi Ishmael and Rabbi Akiba.

Had it not been for Shafan (the scribe to King Josiah, IIKg. 22) and Ezra and Akiba in their respective periods, the Torah would have been forgotten in Israel.

With the death of Jose ben Yoezer of Zereda and Jose ben Johanan of Jerusalem, there were no more "clusters" i.e., encyclopedic scholars, as it is written, *There is no cluster to eat; nor first ripe fig which my soul desireth* (Mic. 7, 1). Then came Akiba.

Akiba worked as a shepherd for Kalba Savua. This man had a daughter, Rachel, who was impressed with Akiba's superior character. One day she said to him, "If I agree to marry you will you go to the school to study?" Akiba agreed to this arrangement, and they became secretly betrothed. But the father learned what had happened and he expelled them both from his house, vowing to cut off his daughter from benefit of his wealth. The couple married and went off. It was winter, and they were so impoverished that they slept on a pile of straw. Each day Akiba would remove some straw from Rachel's hair. "If I were rich" he said, "I would get you a golden diadem for your hair." The prophet Elijah appeared to them in the guise of a poor beggar and asked, "Give me some of your straw. My wife is in labor and has nowhere to lie down." They gave him the straw. "See!" said Akiba, "there are some poor people who don't even have straw." Rachel then reminded him of the arrangement. "Go and study" she said. And Akiba went away for twelve years to study in the schools of Rabbis Eliezer and Joshua.

At the end of twelve years, Akiba made his way back to Rachel, accompanied by twelve thousand students and the whole town went out to greet him. When Rachel learned what was happening she too went out. Her neighbors said to her, "Borrow some clothes and cover your rags." But she replied, "Don't worry, *A righteous man regardeth the life of his beast* (Prov. 12,10)." When she saw Akiba, she ran forward, fell on the ground and began to kiss his feet. The astonished disciples rushed to push her away, but Akiba said to them, "Leave her alone. For everything I am and everything you have learned is due only to her."

When Kalba Savua heard that a great man had arrived in the town he said, "I will go to see him to have my vows annulled." On appearing before Akiba, whom he did not recognise, the scholar asked him, "Would you have made your vow had you known that the shepherd would become a scholar?" Kalba Savua replied immediately, "If he had only learned one chapter or a single law, I would not have cut off my daughter from benefiting from my will." Then Akiba turned to his wealthy visitor and said, "I am your former shepherd!" Kalba Savua fell on his face and kissed Akiba's feet. He gave the scholar and his daughter half of all his wealth.

How did Akiba get started on his studies? He was forty years old and quite ignorant. One day, as he was sitting by a water stream near Lydda he saw an indented stone. "Who made this hollow in the stone?" he asked. His companions answered him, "Akiba, this has been done by the constant dripping of the water on the stone. Even the Bible says, *The waters wear away the stones* (Job 14,19)." Akiba then said, "Surely my heart is more impressionable than the stone, and the Torah is stronger than water. I will go and study." So with his son he went to the school house and he began to read from the slate. They learned the aleph bet. After that he studied the book of Leviticus, then book after book until he had studied the whole Torah.

The scholars Rabbis Eliezer and Joshua became his teachers. They began by teaching him Mishnah, and everything he learned he examined thoroughly and critically. He was full of questions on everything which they taught him, and sometimes his teachers were unable to answer his curiosity.

During the time he was a poor student, Akiba gathered a stack of wood every day. He would sell it and use half of the proceeds to buy food and the other half for additional expenses to live on. One day, his neighbors complained of the smoke from the wood fire by which Akiba studied. "Why don't you sell all the wood and buy some oil to give you light for study?" they asked. Akiba told them, "I use some of the logs for a variety of purposes—for study by its light, for warmth from its fire and to sleep on."

By the time he died, Akiba was so wealthy that he had tables of gold and silver as well as a stool of gold leading to his bed. His wife was provided with such costly jewels that Akiba's disciples said to him one day, "Rabbi, you put us to shame because we cannot give our wives such costly jewels." Akiba told them, "I do it because for many years she sacrificed everything to make it possible for me to study Torah."

When Rabban Gamaliel's wife saw the expensive jewelry which Akiba's wife was wearing, she became very jealous and complained to her husband. Gamaliel said to her, "If I could afford it, I might have done the same for you had you done what Akiba's wife did. While he was a poor student she even sold her hair and sent him the money!"

Akiba was in a reminiscent mood one day and he told his students that when he was an ignorant peasant he was so antagonistic to the scholars that he once vowed to "bite them like a donkey." The students said, "You mean 'like a dog'" and the teacher said, "No; a dog bites and doesn't break bones but an ass breaks bones."

Johanan ben Nuri said: I swear that on many occasions Akiba suffered on my account because I frequently complained about him to Rabban Gamaliel in Jabneh. Still, the more I criticized him, the more love he showed me, and so he fulfilled the teaching of the Bible, *Reprove a wise man and he will love thee* (Prov. 9, 8).

Once when Akiba was late in arriving at the study house, he sat outside. Then a problem arose and the disciples said, "The answer can be found outside." The second time it happened they said more explicitly, "Akiba is outside." So they made room for him and had him sit before Rabbi Eliezer.

Rabbi Akiba was likened to a cornucopia filled with many kinds of knowledge, and to a workman who carries his sack into the fields. There he finds wheat, barley, spelt, beans and lentils, all of which he puts into his sack. Then when he gets home he separates all the produce into different heaps. So Akiba dealt with all the laws of the Torah, classifying them and separating them into different categories.

Rabbi Jonah said: Scripture declares, *I will grant whole hordes for his tribute, he shall divide the spoil with the mighty* (Isa. 53,12). This applies to Rabbi Akiba who systematized the exposition of all the law and folklore. Another opinion has it that this classification and systemization was done by the Men of the Great Synagogue.

Akiba's contribution was in laying down all the guiding principles, large and small.

One day while Akiba was lecturing to his students the memory of what he did in his early years crossed his mind. He interrupted the lesson to express his gratitude and said, "I give thanks to Thee O Lord, my God, that you have placed my lot among the students of the Torah and not among the idle good for nothing."

Rabbi Tarfon once said to Akiba, "Akiba, whoever goes away from you separates himself from life itself." On another occasion he said, "The verse, *He brings to light secret things that were hidden* (Job 28,11) can be applied to you because you illumine things otherwise hidden from our understanding."

Ben Azzai said, "All the sages in Israel are as thin as vegetable peel compared to me; all with the exception of that bald head Akiba!"

A question concerning the red heifer was being discussed by the sages in Jabneh. They made a ruling permitting the eating of the flesh of such an animal. This was the time when Rabbi Jose Hagelili ruled in the presence of his teacher Akiba and was therefore expelled from the academy for a breach of discipline and ethics. Subsequently, Jose found a reason which supported his view against that of Akiba and he sought to return to the academy. Whereupon Akiba said, "I wouldn't do this for anyone else but you." and Akiba was able to refute the disciple's criticism.

It was said that Akiba never said to his students, "It is time to finish the lesson" except on the eve of Passover and on the eve of Yom Kippur. On the Passover eve because of the children who might fall asleep if the Seder began too late, and on Yom Kippur eve so that the students could get home in time to eat with their family.

During the illness of Simeon, his son, Akiba did not miss teaching, but sent messengers to his house to enquire about his son's condition. When the first messenger came and reported that it was serious he said to his disciples, "Pray for him." A second report came later with the news that the situation was getting worse and Akiba went on with his teaching. When a third messenger came to inform the rabbi that his son was near to death, Akiba again asked his students to pray for him. Then a fourth report came with the news that his son had died. Akiba then stood up, removed his tephillin, rent his garment and said, "Up till this moment we were obligated to study Torah, but now we are bound to honor the dead."

A huge gathering came to the funeral and eulogy for Akiba's son. Before they left, Akiba stood on a bench and cried out, "My fellow Jews! Because of your expression of friendship I would have been comforted even if my son had been a bridegroom when he died. You are not here because I am a wise man; there are wiser men than me here. Nor because I am rich; there are richer men than me here. People of the south know Akiba, but how should the northerners know him? The men might know Akiba, but how should the women and children know him? And you haven't come here because of the name 'Akiba' for there are many people with that name. I know therefore that you have come here to mourn with me only because of your piety and in honor of the Torah. I want you to know that I am comforted by all this. Return to your homes in peace!"

Rabbi Akiba was crying on the Sabbath. "Master" said his students, "you always taught us the importance of the verse, *You shall call the Sabbath a delight* (Isa. 58, 13)." Akiba said to them, "Just now this is my delight."

Once the leader of the synagogue asked Akiba to go forward and read from the Scroll but he refused. After the service he explained himself to his disciples, "I swear to you that it was not on account of any pride or haughtiness on my part I refused to read the Scrolls; it was simply because I had not prepared myself."

Rabbi Judah told that whenever Akiba read the prayers before the congregation he read the service quickly in order not be a burden on the congregation. But when he prayed privately then you could leave him in one corner of the room and find him in another corner some time later. That was because of the enthusiasm of his devotions with many bowings and prostrations.

Our rabbis taught that there were four men who entered Paradise. That is, they engaged in experimentation with the esoteric mysteries. The four were Ben Azzai, Ben Zoma, Elisha ben Avuyah and Akiba. It was Akiba who warned the others, "When you approach the pillars of marble do not cry out 'Water, Water!' and don't be misled by the outer appearances of what you see." Ben Azzai looked at the mysteries too long and he died; Ben Zoma lost his mind; Elisha became a heretic. Rabbi Akiba was the only one of the four who entered in peace and came out of the experience in peace. Even Akiba nearly came to a bad end because the ministering angels wanted to push him away. But God defended him from them and said, "Let him be. This old man is destined to minister to Me in my heavenly court."

History records that Akiba had twenty four thousand students throughout the land. They all died in their teacher's lifetime and during one period, between Passover and Shavuot, because they showed no respect for each other. The Jewish world was desolated by this disaster, until Akiba traveled south and taught the Torah to Rabbis Meir, Judah, Jose, Simeon and Eleazar ben Shammua. Akiba warned them, "Your predecessors died only because they were jealous of each other even in matters of Torah study. Now beware that you don't repeat their failings." The new generation of students took heed of their master's warning and filled the land with sincere Torah study.

Rabban Gamaliel told of the time when he was on a ship and he saw another vessel wrecked in the water. "I knew that Rabbi Akiba was on that shipwreck and I grieved for his fate. To my surprise, after I came ashore Rabbi Akiba arrived and even taught Torah in my company. I asked him, 'How did you survive?' and he told me, 'A wooden plank from the ship floated my way. I got on it and managed to ride the waves with it.'"

On one of his journeys Rabbi Akiba wanted to stay at an inn which was full and he was refused entry. Like an earlier teacher, he also comforted himself with the thought that whatever happens happens for the best and he went to sleep in an open field. He had with him an ass, a cockerel and a lamp. During that night, a wild animal came and killed his ass, a cat devoured the cockerel and the wind blew out the lamp. Still, after each accident Akiba said, "Whatever happens happens for the best." Before dawn a gang of murderous robbers attacked that inn and killed and robbed.

Learning of the attack, Akiba confirmed his philosophy and understood that his own losses saved his life. First, that he had no accommodation in the inn. Then had his ass brayed or the cock crowed or the lamp been alight, he would have been discovered by the murderous gang and suffered at their hands.

Rabbi Akiba gave his son Joshua seven pieces of advice. He said, "My son, do not study at the cross-roads of the town because of interruptions. Do not live in a town where everyone is a scholar because then the civic affairs are badly neglected. Do not enter your own house without warning, how much less so the house of a stranger. Do not skimp yourself in sandals since it is not fitting for a scholar. Eat breakfast early, in the summer because of the heat and in the winter because of the cold. Make your provisions for the Sabbath like for a weekday, rather then depend on the generosity of other people. And be friendly to those who are in a position of influence."

■ ■ ■

One of Akiba's students fell ill and the others did not go to visit him. Akiba did go, and when he arrived he swept the room and made the patient comfortable. The patient recovered and he said to Akiba, "Master, you brought me back to life." On account of this, Akiba taught his pupils, "Whoever refuses to visit the sick is like one who is guilty of murder."

Rabbi Akiba said, "Let me tell you what made me meticulous in following the teaching of my masters. One day as I was walking in the country, I came across a corpse which had been left without burial. I carried the body four miles to the nearest cemetery where I buried it. Then when I came to Rabbis Eliezer and Joshua and told them what I had done they said to me, 'For every step you took with the body you are guilty as if you had shed blood. You should have buried him in the place where you found him.' So I thought that if I am guilty at a time when my intentions are good, how much more so at a time when I am not so motivated. Since then I have never ceased to remain close to the sages."

Rabbi Akiba's wealth came from six sources. The first was from Kalba Savua his father-in-law, as we have told. The second was from a ram's head mascot made for a ship which was abandoned on the sea shore. Akiba found it and discovered that it was filled with gold coins. The third source was an old chest. Once Akiba gave some sailors four zuzim to bring him back something from their voyage. They couldn't find anything except an old box which they picked up on the sea shore and which they gave to Akiba. When he opened it he found it full of coins. Subsequently he discovered that it was from a pirate's shipwreck.

The fourth source of Akiba's wealth came from a certain wealthy lady. It happened this way. Once the school was in urgent need of funds and the rabbis decided to approach a wealthy lady for her assistance. They appointed Akiba as their representative to obtain the loan, and in due course he arrived at her home and requested the large loan. "Who will be my sureties?" she asked. "Whoever you wish." answered the rabbi. "In that case." she said, "I want God and the seashore to be my sureties against non-repayment by a certain date." Akiba agreed with the condition and received the loan for the school. On the day that the loan had to be repaid Akiba was ill and could not travel to repay the money. Whereupon the lady went out to the seashore which was near her house and addressed God, "Dear God, You know that your servant Akiba is ill and unable to come with the repayment of the loan. But as You and the seashore were appointed sureties for the loan I now turn to You for repayment." Then God sent a mood of madness into the emperor's daughter who went into the royal treasure house, filled a chest with jewels and gold and threw the chest into the sea. The box floated on the waves and reached the seashore close to that matron's house. She forthwith took it. In due course, Akiba recovered and traveled to the lady with the money to repay the loan. "Keep it." she said to the rabbi "the sureties we appointed have already repaid the debt and much more." With that she gave Akiba the surplus and many precious gifts, and she sent him away in peace.

The fifth source of wealth was the wife of the Roman governor Tinneius Rufus. He used to have many debates with Akiba which the latter would win. One day the governor looked particularly dejected and his wife asked him the reason. "It's Akiba" he said. "He defeats me in arguments every time." She said to the governor, "You leave him to me." So next day, dressed up in her finest, she came to Akiba. When he saw her he spat, wept and laughed. When she asked him the meaning of his strange behavior he said, "I cannot tell you the reason for the third thing I did but I will explain the first two. I spat out thinking of your origin from a putrefying drop. I wept because of your great beauty which is destined to rot in the grave." Thinking on these things, the Roman matron asked, "Is there any remedy for this?" He told her that there was a remedy in converting to Judaism and coming to the belief in the only true God. So she did that. Some time later Akiba's wife died and he married the former Roman convert who brought him great wealth. It was this which Akiba had seen in a prophetic vision and which brought him to laugh. But of course, this he did not tell her.

The last source of Akiba's fortune was Katia bar Shalom who was also a convert. He was sentenced to death by the Romans and willed all his wealth to Akiba and his colleagues.

Tinneius Rufus asked Akiba, "It says in your Bible, *But Esau* (that is Edom or Rome) *I hated* (Mal. 1, 3). Now why does your God hate us?" Akiba said, "Give me till tomorrow and I will answer you." Next day the Roman taunted Akiba, "What answers did you dream up last night?" Akiba replied, "I dreamed of two dogs, one called Rufus and the other Rufina." Tinneius Rufus was outraged. "Could you think of no other names for the dogs but mine and my wife's?" he yelled at the rabbi. "You deserve to be executed." Akiba answered him, "But really what is the difference between you and them? You eat and drink and they eat and drink. You propagate and they propagate. You are mortal and they are mortal. And as for you, getting angry just because I gave them names similar to yours, look what you yourselves do. You take an idol of wood or stone and give it a name similar to the Creator of the universe. Don't you think that He has more cause to hate you? Now that is why the Bible says in His name, *But I hate Esau.*"

When Akiba had to travel on a mission abroad, the Roman governor provided him with two beautiful young girls to accompany him. The first night they bathed, anointed themselves and dressed up like brides. All night long they pestered Akiba pleading with him. Each one wanted him. But Akiba sat between them and would not be moved. He even refused to look at them. Next morning they went to the governor and complained saying, "We would rather die then be subjected to such insulting rejection from this man!" The Roman governor summoned Akiba and demanded, "Why don't you behave towards these women like a normal man? Aren't they good enough for you?" Akiba defended his behavior and said, "What can I do? When they are near me I am reminded of my death."

Rabbi Akiba criticized those who were too weak to overcome their passions. So one day Satan put him to the test. He disguised himself as a beautiful woman and sat on a tree top. Akiba started to climb the tree but about half way up his passion left him. At this Satan said, "Had they not announced in heaven 'Be careful with Rabbi Akiba and his Torah' I would have dealt with you, and your life would not have been worth a penny!"

When the Romans issued an edict prohibiting the study of Torah upon penalty of death, Rabbi Akiba ignored the edict and continued to teach before large assemblies of students. One day, Pappus ben Judah said to him, "Aren't you afraid of the Romans?" Akiba replied, "I am surprised at you, Pappus. You have a reputation of being a clever man." And Akiba went on to illustrate his point with the following parable.

A fox was walking by the river bank when he saw some fish swimming frantically about.

"What's the trouble?" asked the fox.

"We are afraid of the fisherman's nets." they replied.

"In that case" suggested the fox "why don't you come over with me to my cave where there are no fishermen?"

"Foolish fox!" said the fish. "We cannot understand why people call you clever. If we are not safe in the water which is our natural home, how much less safe we would be if we were to leave our life-sustaining habitat!"

"So it is with us" concluded Akiba. "If we are in danger while we are engaged in Torah which is described as "Your life and the length of your days' how much worse would it be for us if we forsook our life-giving Torah!"

It wasn't long before Akiba was arrested and put in jail. Who should he see there but Pappus ben Judah. "Why are you imprisoned?" Akiba asked him. Pappus replied, "Blessed are you Akiba. You were arrested for the sake of Torah. Me they arrested on some trumped up nonsense charge!"

When Rabbi Akiba was jailed by the Romans, Rabbi Joshua Hagarsi was appointed to attend to him. Every day he was given a measure of water to bring to Akiba. One day the jailer stopped him and demanded, "Why have you got so much water with you today? I bet you are planning an escape!" With this accusation, he poured out half the water from the pitcher, leaving Rabbi Joshua with a very small amount. When he came to Akiba's cell, Akiba said to him, "Joshua, what kept you so long? You know my life depends on you." Joshua told him what had happened. Then Akiba said, "Fetch me the water that I can wash my hands." But Joshua argued, "There isn't even enough to drink, so why should you worry about

washing?" Akiba replied, "There is nothing that I can do. It is better that I die from thirst rather than I should transgress the law instituted by my colleagues." And he refused to eat a thing until Joshua had brought him the water with which to wash his hands. When the sages heard what had happened they said, "If he is so particular when he is a feeble old man, imagine how careful he must have been when he was younger and stronger. And if in jail he is so meticulous, imagine how strict in every detail he must have been in his own home!"

Rabbi Johanan the shoemaker disguised himself as a peddlar and went and stood outside the window of Akiba's prison and called out, "Who wants pins? Who wants needles? Is a *halitzah* (levirate divorce) without witnesses valid?" In this way he slipped in his legal question between his advertisement for goods. Akiba heard the question from his cell, went to the window and called out, "Do you sell weaver's pins, called kushin? kasher . . . it is valid!" In that way he hid his answer by masking it in market language so that the guards would not suspect what was going on.

As Rabbi Akiba was awaiting sentence from the Romans, Rabbi Joshua Hagarsi was with him and they prayed together. During their prayer, a cloud descended and enveloped them. Rabbi Joshua said, "It seems to me that the cloud came down so that my master's prayer should not be heard, in accordance with the verse, *Thou hast covered Thyself with a cloud, so that no prayer can pass through* (Lam. 3, 44)."

After the Romans brought out Akiba for execution, they tied him up and combed his flesh with iron combs. During his agony, the sage concentrated on declaring God's unity out of love. His disciples who witnessed this were astounded at their master's courage and cried, "Master! How much more of this can you stand?" Akiba said to them, "My children, all my life I thought about the meaning of loving God *with all your soul* (Deut. 6, 5), which means even if God takes away your life. And I wondered when I would be able to carry out such a commandment. Now that the moment has arrived, shall I not embrace it?" Akiba cried out the final proclamation "*Shema Yisrael Adonai Eloheinu Adonai Ehad!* Hear O Israel, the Lord our God, the Lord is one!" and he died as he fervently articulated the sounds of the last word, *Ehad*. A heavenly voice was heard to say, "Blessed are you Akiba that you died with the word *Ehad* on your lips." The heavenly angels came up to God's throne and asked, "Is this martyrdom the just reward for one who has taught so much Torah?" God said to them, "The portion of such people is in eternal life in the World to Come." Again a heavenly voice was heard to confirm, "Blessed are you Akiba for you are assured of your place and eternal life in the World to Come."

That happened as it was approaching Yom Kippur eve when Akiba's attendant, Joshua Hagarsi, had already left and returned to his house. Elijah the prophet appeared at Joshua's door.

"Peace to you, master." said the rabbi.

"Peace to you master and teacher" returned the prophet.

"Is there anything you require?" asked Joshua. "Who might you be?"

"I am a priest and I have come to inform you that Rabbi Akiba has died as a martyr in prison."

Both of them then left for the jail where they found the door open, and the guard and all the prisoners fast asleep. They lifted Akiba on to a bed

and were about to leave, when Elijah turned round, went back and took Akiba on to his shoulders.

"Master!" cried Joshua. "You told me that you are a priest, and a priest is not allowed to be defiled by a dead body!"

Elijah said to him, "Do not be concerned over that point. I want to tell you, Joshua my son, that there is no source of defilement in scholars or their disciples." They carried Akiba all the way to Antipatras near Caesarea. There they came to a place where they ascended three steps and went down three more steps when a cave mysteriously opened for them. Inside they saw a chair, a bed, a table and a lamp. They laid Akiba on the bed and left. As soon as they left, the cave closed and the lamp lit by itself. Before departing from that place Elijah proclaimed, "Blessed are the righteous; blessed are those who labor in the Torah; blessed are those who fear God, because a place in Paradise is allotted to them. And blessed are you Akiba for whom a place of honor was appointed at your death."

After Akiba's death the glory of the Torah departed; giants of the Torah and sources of wisdom were no more found.

Maimonides

"From Moses unto Moses there was none like Moses," said the medieval sages. They were referring to Moses Maimonides, Rambam—physician, rabbi, communal leader, the greatest Talmudic scholar of his day, a man of exemplary courage and wisdom. Maimonides lived in the second half of the twelfth century, first in Spain, then briefly in Morocco, then in his last three decades in Cairo. He had all the iconic qualities that many observant Jews admired then and now.

His name still adorns Jewish schools and hospitals. The more moderate, mainstream kind of Orthodox Judaism today follows in his wake. Yeshiva University, founded in the 1920s with an intention of cultivating both Talmudic and secular learning, while seeing no fundamental contradiction therein, reveres Maimonides as a totemic exemplar. The writings of the current, long-serving President of Yeshiva University, Rabbi Norman Lamm, are closely within the Maimonidean tradition.

Yet Maimonides got himself into trouble with some of the rabbis of his day in the century following his death because of one book, The Guide of the Perplexed. Maimonides was a keen student of Greek and Arabic philosophy and he sought to walk a fine intellectual line in The Guide of the Perplexed, indicating how far the learned, Halachic Jew might go in finding compatibility between traditional Judaism and vanguard Aristotelian philosophy, the dominant rationalist intellectual system of his day in the Mediterranean and Western Europe.

In the early-thirteenth century, the rabbis in Provence, France, turned sharply against Maimonides' quasi rationalism and scientism and condemned The Guide of the Perplexed as heretical. There is a story that they asked the Papal Inquisition to burn it. In response to Maimonides rationalist scientism, the Provençal rabbis dredged up and expanded upon the antirationalist Haggadic, astrological, mystical, and demonological tradition in Judaism, which became known as Kabbalah. In the late-thirteenth century the most respected rabbinical thinker in Spain, Nachmanides, came out on the Kabbalistic side, resulting in the suppression of Maimonides' philosophical tradition in Orthodox Judaism until the nineteenth century.

These selections from the excellent translation of The Guide of the Perplexed by Shlomo Pines indicate what the French rabbis found so troubling in it. It was not so much that philosophical inquiry was to be preserved for a small and learned elite—Kabbalistic speculation was also at the time so restrained. It was rather that Maimonides was walking a fine line with Aristotelian science—trying to explain away Aristotle's doctrine of the eternity of the world; seeing God as a scientific First Cause; struggling to maintain the validity of prophecy within a rationalistic continuum; interpreting human nature in accordance with Aristotle's difficult doctrine of form and matter.

Nothing that Maimonides says is actually heretical: Nowhere does he abandon Jewish theology for Greek philosophy. He is careful to stress limitations of human intellect. It is his general tone of great respect for Aristotelian science; his strenuous efforts to express Biblical view of God and man in philosophical language; his stubborn insistence that this difficult inquiry is worth pursuing that was so provocative.

Put another way, if The Guide of the Perplexed was legitimated in Jewish culture, then all the rabbis would have to learn to speak in this Greek/Arabic philosophical discourse. That is something they did not want to do. They would rather quarry out the Haggadic tradition, the irrationalist romantic pastiche known as Kabbalah. Was this an unfortunate turning-point in Jewish history? Probably it was. Maimonides was willing to face the scientific future; They were not.

In the late-twentieth century the issue was joined again. But this time the Orthodox mainstream like Joseph Soloveitchik and Norman Lamm stood with Maimonides and thereby strengthened his position as an iconic figure.

Do not think that only the divine science should be withheld from the multitude. This holds good also for the greater part of natural science. . . .

How much all the more is it incumbent upon us, the community of those adhering to Law, not to state explicitly a matter that is either remote from the understanding of the multitude or the truth of which as it appears to the imagination of these people is different from what is intended by us. Know this also. . . .

It may thus happen that whereas one individual discovers a certain notion by himself through his speculation, another individual is not able ever to understand that notion. Even if it were explained to him for a very long time by means of every sort of expression and parable, his mind would not penetrate to it in any way, but would turn back without understanding it. This difference in capacity is likewise not infinite, for man's intellect indubitably has a limit at which it stops. There are therefore things regarding which it has become clear to man that it is impossible to apprehend them. And he will not find that his soul longs for knowledge of them, inasmuch as he is aware of the impossibility of such knowledge and of there being no gate through which one might enter in order to attain it. Of this nature is our ignorance of the number of the stars of heaven and whether that number is even or odd, as well as our ignorance of the number of the species of living beings, minerals, plants, and other similar things.

On the other hand, there are things for the apprehension of which man will find that he has a great longing. The sway of the intellect endeavoring to seek for, and to investigate, their true reality exists at every time and in every group of men engaged in speculation. With regard to such things there is a multiplicity of opinions, disagreement arises between the men engaged in speculation, and doubts crop up; all this because the intellect is attached to an apprehension of these things, I mean to say because of its longing for them; and also because everyone thinks that he has found a way by means of which he will know the true reality of the matter. Now it is not within the power of the human intellect to give a demonstration of these matters. For in all things whose true reality is known through demonstration there is no tug of war and no refusal to accept a thing proven—unless indeed such refusal comes from an ignoramus who offers a resistance that is called resistance to demonstration. Thus you can find groups of people who dispute the doctrine that the earth is spherical and that the sphere has a circular motion and with regard to other matters of this kind. These folk do not enter into our purpose. The things about which there is this perplexity are very numerous in divine matters, few in matters pertaining to natural science, and nonexistent in matters pertaining to mathematics. . . .

Do not think that what we have said with regard to the insufficiency of the human intellect and its having a limit at which it stops is a statement made in order to conform to Law. For it is something that has already been said and truly grasped by the philosophers without their having concern for a particular doctrine or opinion. And it is a true thing that cannot be doubted except by an individual ignorant of what has already been demonstrated. . . .

In natural science, it has been made clear that there are causes for everything that has a cause; that they are four: namely, matter, form, the efficient cause, and the end; and that some of them are proximate causes and others remote ones. Every cause belonging to one of these four is designated as cause and ground. Now one of the opinions of the philosophers, an opinion with which I do not disagree, is that God, may He be held precious and magnified, is the efficient cause, that He is the form, and that He is the end. Thus it is for this reason that they say that He, may He be exalted, is a cause and a ground, in order to comprise these three causes—that is, the fact that God is the efficient cause of the world, its form, and its end.

What led me to speak of this is the fact that the latter-day followers of Aristotle believe that Aristotle has demonstrated the eternity of the world. Most of the people who believe themselves to philosophize follow Aristotle as an authority in this question and think that everything that he has mentioned constitutes a cogent demonstration as to which there can be no doubt. They regard it as disgraceful to disagree with him or to suppose that some concealed point or some false imagining in one of the issues has remained hidden from him. For this reason I thought that it was indicated to challenge them with regard to their opinion and to explain to them that Aristotle himself did not claim to have a demonstration in this question.

[The Lord] may He be exalted, is a cause and this world an effect and it was necessary that this should be so. Just as one does not ask with regard to Him, may He be exalted, why He exists or how He exists thus—I mean to say as One and incorporeal—so it may not be asked with regard to the world as a whole why it exists or how it exists thus. For all this, both the cause and the effect, exist thus necessarily, and nonexistence is not possible with regard to them in any respect nor their changing from the way they exist. Hence it follows necessarily from this opinion that of necessity everything must remain permanently as it is according to its nature and that nothing can change as far as its nature is concerned. For according to this opinion, it is impossible that a thing from among the existents should change as far as its nature is concerned. Accordingly no thing has come into being in virtue of the purpose of One possessing purpose who chose freely and willed that all things should be as they are. For if they had come into being in virtue of the purpose of One possessing purpose, they would not have existed thus before they were purposed.

Now as for us, the matter is clear in our opinion: Namely, that all things exist in virtue of a purpose and not of necessity, and that He who purposed them may change them and conceive another purpose, though not absolutely any purpose whatever. . . .

Now we desire to make a sufficient inquiry. For it is obligatory for us to inquire into them and to speak concerning them according to the capacity of our intellects, our knowledge, and our opinion. However, no one ought to attribute this undertaking to overboldness and temerity on our part, but rather should our desire and ardor for philosophy be admired. When, therefore, we seek out noble and important questions and are able to propound for them—though it be only to some small extent—a well-founded solution, it behooves the hearer to feel great joy and jubilation.

Know that our shunning the affirmation of the eternity of the world is not due to a text figuring in the *Torah* according to which the world has been produced in time. For the texts indicating that the world has been produced in time are not more numerous than those indicating that the deity is a body. Nor are the gates of figurative interpretation shut in our faces or impossible of access to us regarding the subject of the creation of the world in time. For we could interpret them as figurative, as we have done when denying His corporeality. Perhaps this would even be much easier to do: We should be very well able to give a figurative interpretation of those texts and to affirm as true the eternity of the world, just as we have given a figurative interpretation of those other texts and have denied that He, may He be exalted, is a body.

Two causes are responsible for our not doing this or believing it. One of them is as follows. That the deity is not a body has been demonstrated; from this it follows necessarily that everything that in its external meaning disagrees with this demonstration must be interpreted figuratively, for it is known that such texts are of necessity fit for figurative interpretation. However, the eternity of the world has not been demonstrated. Consequently in this case the texts ought not to be rejected and figuratively interpreted in order to make prevail an opinion whose contrary can be made to prevail by means of various sorts of arguments. This is one cause.

The second cause is as follows. Our belief that the deity is not a body destroys for us none of the foundations of the Law and does not give the lie to the claims of any prophet. The only objection to it is constituted by the fact that the ignorant think that this belief is contrary to the text; yet it is not contrary to it, as we have explained, but is intended by the text. On the other hand, the belief in eternity the way Aristotle sees it—that is, the belief according to which the world exists in virtue of necessity, that no nature changes at all, and that the customary course of events cannot be modified with regard to anything—destroys the Law in its principle, necessarily gives the lie to every miracle, and reduces to inanity all the hopes and threats that the Law has held out, unless—by God!—one interprets the miracles figuratively also, as was done by the Islamic internalists; this, however, would result in some sort of crazy imaginings. . . .

Know that the true reality and quiddity of prophecy consist in its being an overflow overflowing from God, may He be cherished and honored, through the intermediation of the Active Intellect, toward the rational faculty in the first place and thereafter toward the imaginative faculty. This is the highest degree of man and the ultimate term of perfection that can exist for his species; and this state is the ultimate term of perfection for the imaginative faculty. This is something that cannot by any means exist in every man. And it is not something that may be attained solely through perfection in the speculative sciences and through improvement of moral habits, even if all of them have become as fine and good as can be. . . .

All bodies subject to generation and corruption are attained by corruption only because of their matter; with regard to form and with respect to the latter's essence, they are not attained by corruption, but are permanent. Do you not see that all the specific forms are perpetual and perma-

nent? Corruption attains the form only by accident, I mean because of its being joined to matter.

All man's acts of disobedience and sins are consequent upon his matter and not upon his form, whereas all his virtues are consequent upon his form. For example, man's apprehension of his Creator, his mental representation of every intelligible being, his control of his desire and his anger, his thought on what ought to be preferred and what avoided, are all of them consequent upon his form. On the other hand, his eating and drinking and copulation and his passionate desire for these things, as well as his anger and all bad habits found in him, are all of them consequent upon his matter. Inasmuch as it is clear that this is so, and as according to what has been laid down by divine wisdom it is impossible for matter to exist without form and for any of the forms in question to exist without matter, and as consequently it was necessary that man's very noble form, which, is the *image of God and His likeness,* should be bound to earthy, turbid, and dark matter. . . .

Dreyfus

Captain Alfred Dreyfus, who died in 1935, occupies a peculiar place in the Jewish iconic firmament. He has come to be a totemic symbol of injustice and persecution, but one later triumphant over anti-Semitic prejudice and scheming enemies. Through the course of Jews making their way, at times with difficulty, up the ladder of business and professional success, Dreyfus's story has been transformed into a paradigm of beating the anti-Semitic odds in modern western society.

Dreyfus came from an old Alsatian Jewish family. He was a professional soldier in French intelligence at a time of increasingly intense rivalry with the power of Germany. Dreyfus had no particular interest in Jewish things. In 1895 he was charged on the basis of slim evidence, which later turned out to be perjured testimony, of passing military secrets to the Germans. After a sensational trial he was cashiered as a soldier and sentenced to the French penal colony on Devil's Island, off the coast of French Guiana.

Dreyfus' family stood by him. The novelist Marcel Proust, who came from a prominent Jewish family on his mother's side, was among those who raised funds to reopen the case. The prominent liberal politician Georges Clemenceau (later prime minister) and the outspoken novelist and radical journalist Emile Zola demanded another trial. The second trial was inconclusive but Dreyfus was cleared by presidential pardon and restored to his military career (which was uneventful). Two other officers were exposed as manufacturing evidence against Dreyfus and one may have been the real spy; one fled to England, one committed suicide.

The story is thus a very dramatic one and from a Jewish point of view, appears to have a highly satisfying outcome. But in truth the Dreyfus affair had disastrous consequences for the Jews in France and elsewhere in Western Europe. In the late-nineteenth century, Jewish academics and community leaders had supported the efforts of liberal left politicians to divest the Catholic Church of its centuries-old hold over French education. This secularization was largely successful. This came at a time of an intense neo-medieval intellectual revival among a younger generation of French Catholics. The Dreyfus case became for them a flashpoint for developing a frenetic journalistic and literary campaign against Jews as secular allies of conspiratorial Freemasons and as a formentors of a liberal and capitalist conspiracy to take control of modern societies.

The reversal of Dreyfus' conviction did little to moderate this "anti-Dreyfus," anti-liberal, anti-Semitic furor. It led directly to the anti-Semitic activities of militant rightist French groups in the 1930s; to the Vichy Government's collaboration with the German occupation in sucking Jews into the Holocaust; to the intense anti-Semitism among Polish and Quebec Catholics, who took their intellectual cues from Paris; to the Russian-Ukrainian–authored *Protocols of the Elders of Zion*, the most widely disseminated anti-Semitic tract of the century. French anti-Dreyfardism was also one of the sources of Nazism, which had its pre-1933 strength in Catholic Bavaria, not in Protestant northern Germany.

Dreyfus remains an icon of persecution and then vindication, but the Dreyfus case left a terrible legacy. The following are extracts from Dreyfus' diary on Devils' Island and one of Zola's provocative appeals in the press on his behalf.

September 29, 1895

I had violent palpitations of the heart this morning. I was suffocating. The machine struggles; how long has it still to run?

Last night also I had a fearful nightmare, in which I called out to you for help, my poor, dear Lucie.

Ah! if there were only myself, my disgust for men and things is so deep that I should look forward only to the great rest, to eternal repose.

October 1, 1895

I no longer know how to write down my feelings; the hours seem centuries to me.

October 5, 1895

I have received letters from home. Still nothing done! From all these letters there rises such a cry of suffering that my whole being is shaken to its depths.

I have just written the following letter to the President of the Republic:

"Accused and then found guilty on the sole evidence of handwriting, of the most infamous crime which a soldier can commit, I have declared, and I declare once again, that I did not write the letter which was imputed to me, and that I have never forfeited my honour.

"For a year I have been struggling alone, with a clear conscience, against the most terrible calamity which can befall a man.

"I do not speak of physical sufferings; they are nothing; the sorrows of the heart are everything.

"To suffer thus is dreadful in itself, but to feel those who are dear to me suffering with me is horrible. It is the agony of a whole family, expiating an abominable crime which I never committed.

"I do not beg for pardon, or favours, or compassion; I only ask, I beg, that light full and complete may be shed upon this machination of which my family and I are the unhappy and miserable victims.

"If I have lived on, M. le President, and if I still continue to live, it is because the sacred duty which I have to fulfill towards my family fills my soul and governs it; otherwise I should long since have succumbed under a burden too heavy for human strength to bear.

"In the name of my honour, torn from me by an appalling error, in the name of my wife, in the name of my children—oh! M. le President, at this last thought alone my father's heart, as a Frenchman and an honest man, cries out in its anguish!—I ask justice from you; and this justice, which I beg of you with all my soul, with all the strength of my heart, with hands joined in supreme prayer, is to probe the mystery of this tragic history, and thus to put an end to the martyrdom of a soldier and of a family to whom their honour is their all."

I am writing also to Lucie to act with energy and resolution, for this cruelty will end by prostrating us all.

They tell me that I think more of the sufferings of others than of my own. Ah, yes, assuredly; for if I were alone in the world, if I allowed myself to think only of myself, long since the tomb would have closed over me.

It is the one thought of Lucie and my children that gives me strength.

Ah, my darling children, to die is of little matter to me. But before I die, I wish to know that our name has been cleared from this stain.

On Monday, June 8, 1899, half an hour after noon, the chief warder entered my hut precipitately and handed me the following note:

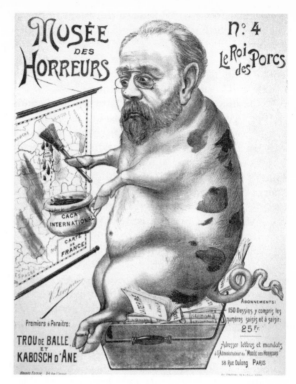

Anti-Semitic caricature of Captain Alfred Dreyfus, 1895.

"Be good enough to let Captain Dreyfus know immediately of the order of the Court of Cessation. The Court quashes and annuls the sentence pronounced on December 22, 1894, against Alfred Dreyfus by the first court-martial of the Military Government of Paris, and orders that the accused shall be tried before a court-martial at Rennes, &c.&c.

"The present decision is to be printed and transcribed in the Book of Records of the first court-martial of the Military Government of Paris, on the margin of the annulled sentence. In virtue of this decision, Captain Dreyfus ceases to be subjected to the convict regimen; he becomes a simple prisoner under arrest, and is restored to his rank and allowed to again wear his uniform.

"See that the prison authorities cancel the commitment and withdraw the military guard from the Ile du Diable. At the same time, have the prisoner taken into custody by the commandant of the troops and replace the warders by a squad of gendarmes, who will do guard duty on the Ile du Diable, according to the regulations of military prisons.

"The cruiser *Sfax* leaves Port-de-France to-day, with orders to take the prisoner from the Ile du Diable and bring him back to France.

"Communicate to Captain Dreyfus the details of the decision and the departure of the *Sfax*."

My joy was boundless, unutterable. At last, I was escaping from the rack to which I had been bound for five years, suffering martyrdom for the sake of my dear ones, for my children. Happiness succeeded the horror of that inexpressible anguish. The day of justice was at last dawning for me. After the Court's decision, I thought that everything was going to be terminated speedily; that there was no further question of anything but mere formality.

Of my own story I knew nothing. As I said, I was still back in 1894, with the Bordereau as the only document in my case, with the sentence of the court-martial, the terrible parade of degradation, and its attendant cries of death from a deluded people. I believed in the loyalty of General de Boisdeffre; I believed in the head of the State, Félix Faure; I thought both eager for justice and truth. After that, a veil had been interposed before my eyes, and had become more impenetrable every day. The few facts I had gleaned during the last month remained incomprehensible to me. I had learnt the name of Esterhazy, the forgery of Lieutenant-Colonel Henry, and his suicide. I had only had official relations with the heroic Lieutenant-Colonel Picquart. The grand struggle undertaken by a few great minds, full of the with my friends and my defenders took place here. Strong as I was, violent trembling seized me, my tears flowed—tears which I had not known for so long a time; but I was soon able to control myself again.

It is impossible for words to describe the deep emotion which my wife and I both felt at seeing each other once more. In our meeting were mingled feelings of joy and grief; we sought to read in each other's faces the traces of our sufferings; we longed to tell each other all that throbbed in our hearts, all the emotions suppressed and stifled during these long years; and the words died away upon our lips. We remained content to look at each other, concentrating in this interchange of looks all the strength of our affection and of our determination. The presence of a lieutenant of infantry, who was ordered to be present at the interview, prevented us, however, from giving way to our feelings. On the other hand, I knew nothing of the events which had occurred during the previous five years, and had returned to France full of confidence in the speedy reparation of my wrongs. But, though this confidence had been rudely shaken by the varied events of the night I had just passed, I did not dare to question my dear wife, for fear of giving her fresh grief, and she too preferred leaving to my lawyers the task of informing me of all that had happened.

My wife was authorised to see me every day for an hour. I also saw in succession all the members of our family; and nothing could equal the joy of our meeting after so many painful years.

I know well that today, once more, the pretext is that the country is in danger, that France has been given away to the victorious enemy by a band of traitors. Only, I ask where shall we find a clear intuition of things, an instinctive perception of what is true, of what is just, if we do not find it in those fresh young souls now entering upon public life with honest and upright minds which nothing yet has come to sully? That politicians, perverted by years of intrigue, that journalists who have lost their mental balance through the perpetual chicaneries of their profession, are found to accept the most impudent lies and to shut their eyes to the most blinding light, can be explained, can be understood. But the youth of the country must be already badly gangrened if its natural candor and purity do not of a sudden pull themselves together in the midst of such untenable errors, and go straight for that which is self-evident, limpid, and full of the honest light of day!

The story is one of the simplest. An officer has been condemned, and no one impugns the good faith of his judges. They dealt with him according to their conscience, on what they considered to be certain proofs. Then one day it came about that first one man and then several men began to entertain doubts of these proofs, and ended by convincing themselves that one, the most important proof, the only one at least on which the judges had publicly relied, had been attributed falsely to the condemned man, and was most assuredly the work of another person. On expressing their conviction, this other person was denounced by the brother of the prisoner, who was thus doing his strict duty; and, in consequence, a new trial is held, which should it end in a verdict of guilty, must bring about the revision of the first trial. All this is perfectly clear, just, and reasonable, is it not? Where does one find in it a machination, a black plot to save a traitor? No one denies that there has been a traitor, all one asks is that it should be the guilty man and not the innocent one to expiate the crime. You will always have them, your traitors; the thing is to put your finger on the right ones.

A little common sense should be sufficient to do this. What is the motive actuating those who desire the revision of the Dreyfus case? Put aside the imbecile anti-Semitism, with its ferocious monomania which sees a Jewish plot sustained by Jewish gold seeking to thrust a Christian in the place of the Jew into an infamous gaol. This will not hold water. The improbabilities, the impossibilities stumble over one another. There are certain consciences which all the gold in the world could never buy. We come perforce to the real motive, which is the natural, slow, and invincible expansion of every judicial error. There you have the whole story. A judicial error is a power which spreads, which conquers the conscience, which haunts it, which drives men to risk their fortune and their life, while they devote themselves more and more obstinately to the consummation of Justice. There is no other possible explanation of what is taking place amongst us today; the rest is nothing but the most abominable political and religious animosities, nothing but an overflowing torrent of calumnies and abuse.

Yet what excuses shall avail our young men if they allow their ideas of Justice and of Humanity to be tarnished, were it only for an instant! When the French Chamber met on December 4th, it covered itself with shame by voting an order of the day "to brand with infamy the ringleaders of the odious campaign which is troubling the public mind." For the benefit of those who, I hope, will read me in the future, I say boldly, that such a vote is unworthy of our generous country, and constitutes an ineffaceable stain. "The ringleaders" are those brave and conscientious men, who, certain that a judicial error had been committed, denounced it in order that reparation might be made in the patriotic conviction that a great nation, among which one innocent man agonized

in torture, must be a doomed nation. "The odious campaign" is the voice of truth and justice on the lips of these same men; it is their pertinacity in wishing France to continue to be in the eyes of all who watch her, the humane France, the France who having accomplished freedom, will yet do justice. And as you see, the Chamber has fallen into crime, since it has corrupted the youth of the Schools, which deceived, led astray, let loose upon our streets demonstrates—a thing which has never been known before—against all that is noblest, all that is bravest, all that is most divine in the human soul!. . .

Oh young men, young men! Remember all your fathers suffered, the terrible battles which they fought and gained in order to win for you the freedom which you enjoy today. That you find yourselves independent, that you may come and go as you please, that you may say what you think in the press, is due to your fathers, who purchased liberty for you with their genius and with their blood. You have not been born beneath a tyranny; you do not know what it is to awake every morning with the heel of the master upon your neck; you have not fought to escape from the sword of the dictator, from the false scales of the unjust judge. Thank your fathers for this, and do not commit the crime of applauding lies, of joining the ranks of brute force, of fanatical intolerance, of ambitious greed. The dictatorship is at an end.

Young men, young men! side always with justice. Should the idea of justice grow dim within you, you expose yourselves to every peril. I am not speaking of legal justice, which is but the safeguard of social ties. Such justice, certainly, one must respect; but there is a higher justice than this, which accepts as fundamental principle the fallibility of all human judgment, and which admits the possible innocence of a condemned man without thereby in any way insulting the integrity of his judges. Have we not, then, here an enterprise which should uplift your burning love of righteousness? Who will get up and insist that justice be done if it is not you, who have no part in the conflict of personalities and interests, who are not yet engaged in or compromised by any crooked schemes, who dare to speak aloud in all sincerity and good faith?

Young men, young men! Be humane, be generous! Even if we are mistaken, stand by us when we say that an innocent man is enduring a most horrible penalty, of which it breaks our hearts to think. If you admit for one instant the possibility of a mistake, the tears rush to your eyes, and you feel yourself suffocating as you remember the enormity of his punishment. Let the convict-warders remain unmoved; but you, how can you so remain? You, who still can weep, who should be filled with pity for suffering of every kind. How is it that while one single martyr exists, no matter where, sinking beneath the burden of unmerited hate, the spirit of chivalry does not prompt you to espouse his cause and achieve his deliverance? Who, then, if it is not you, shall attempt the glori-ous deed, shall dare to fling himself into a danger-ous and noble cause, and in the name of ideal jus-tice, bid defiance to the mob? Ah! does it not cover you with shame that it is not you, but the old men, the men of a past generation, who, full of the enthusiasm which should be yours, are per-forming your work today?

Whither are you going, young men? And you, students, who parade the streets, flinging down, in the middle of our discords, the reckless courage and the high hopes of your twentieth year?

"We go to combat for Humanity, for Justice, and for Truth!"

Einstein

There has been no icon more revered among twentieth-century Jews than the physicist Albert Einstein. He was made a professor at the University of Berlin after World War I in spite of the strict quota against Jewish full professors and a somewhat skimpy academic resume. But in the early years of the century, while working in the Zurich Patent Office, Einstein published two papers that made him the leading theoretical physicist since Newton in the early-eighteenth century. Furthermore his theory of relativity was a least partly con-firmed by empirical observations in 1919.

Einstein, who had a difficult upbringing, was a political radical and vehe-ment Zionist. He left Germany in 1933 with Hitler's advent to become the first professor at the research Institute for Advanced Study in Princeton, New Jersey, which had been especially created for him and such other German Jewish émigrés he might designate, with funds provided by a New Jersey retailing family. Privately, Einstein held the town of Princeton and its upscale suburbanites in contempt.

He never repeated his early sensational breakthroughs, but he was the revered master scientist of his generation. He helped to persuade President Franklin Roosevelt to start up the Manhattan Project, the American atom bomb effort in competition with that of the Germans. He turned down, on the grounds of old age, Ben-Gurion's offer to be the first president of Israel in 1948.

Here are two coinciding views of Einstein. The first is a general evaluation of his importance by Isaiah Berlin, an Anglo-Jewish academic and something of an icon himself. The second is an account of Einstein's visit to Jerusalem in the 1920s by his best biographer, Ronald Clark.

Ben Shahn, *Einstein and Other Immigrants*.

Certainly Einstein presented a heroic image of a man of pure heart, noble mind, unusual moral and political courage, engaged in unswerving pursuit of the truth, who believed in individual liberty and social equality, a man sympathetic to socialism, who hated nationalism, militarism, oppression, violence, the materialistic view of life. But apart from embodying a combination of human goodness with a passion for social justice and unique intellectual power, in a society in which many seemed to live by the opposite values—apart, that is, from his exemplary life, from being, and being seen to be, one of the most civilised, honourable and humane men of his time—what impact did Einstein have?

It is true that the word "relativity" has been, to this day, widely misinterpreted as relativism, the denial of, or doubt about, the objectivity of truth or of moral and other values. But this is a very old and familiar heresy. Relativism in the sense in which Greek sophists, Roman sceptics, French and British subjectivists, German roman-

tics and nationalists professed it, and in which theologians and historians and ordinary men have, in modern times, been tormented by it— this was the opposite of what Einstein believed. He was a man of simple and absolute moral convictions, which were expressed in all he was and did. His conception of external nature was that of a scientifically analysable, rational order or system; the goal of the sciences was objective knowledge of an independently existent reality, even though the concepts in which it was to be analysed and described were free, arbitrary human creations.

What general impact did his doctrines have? Modern theoretical physics cannot, has not, even in its most general outlines, thus far been successfully rendered in popular language as Newton's central doctrines were, for example, by Voltaire. High-minded public men in England like Haldane and Herbert Samuel tried to derive general metaphysical or theological truths, usually somewhat trite ones, from the general theory of relativity, but this only showed that their gifts lay in other spheres.

But if the impact of Einstein's scientific thought on the general ideas of his time is in some doubt, there can be none about the relevance of his non-scientific views to one of the most positive political phenomena of our time. Einstein lent the *prestige mondial* of his great name, and in fact gave his heart, to the movement which created the state of Israel. Men and nations owe a debt to those who help to transform their realistic self-image for the better. No Zionist with the least degree of self-esteem can refuse to pay him homage if the opportunity of doing so is offered to him. Einstein's support of the Zionist movement and his interest in the Hebrew University were lifelong. He quarreled with Weizmann more than once; he was highly critical of the Hebrew University and, in particular, of its first President; he deplored the shortcomings of Zionist policy towards the Arabs; but he never abandoned his belief in the central principles of Zionism. If young people (or others) today, whether Jews or Gentiles, who, like the young Einstein, abhor nationalism and sectarianism and seek social justice and believe in universal human values—if such people wish to know why he, a child of assimilated Bavarian Jews, supported the return of the Jews to Palestine, Zionism, and the Jewish state, not uncritically nor without the anguish which any decent and sensitive man cannot but feel about acts done in the name of his people which seem to him wrong or unwise, but nevertheless steadily, to the end of his life—if they wish to understand this, then they should read his writings on the subject. With his customary lucidity and gift for penetrating to the central core of any issue, whether in science or in life, Einstein said what had to be said with simplicity and truth. Let me recall some of the things he said and did, and in particular the path which led toward them.

He was born in Ulm, the child of irreligious parents. He was educated in Munich, where he seems to have encountered no discrimination; if he reacted strongly against his school and suffered something approaching a nervous breakdown, this does not seem to have been due to anti-Jewish feeling. What he reacted against was, perhaps, the quasi-military discipline and nationalist fervour of German education in the 1890s. He studied intermittently in Milan and Zurich, taught in Zurich, obtained a post in the Patent Office in Bern, then held university chairs in Prague and Zurich, and in 1913 was persuaded by Nernst and Haber, as well as Planck, whose reputations were then at their peak, to accept a research post in Berlin.

I do not need to describe the atmosphere of Prussia on the eve of the First World War. In a letter written in 1929 to a German Minister of State, Einstein said, "When I came to Germany fifteen years ago [that is, in 1914] I discovered for the first time that I was a Jew. I owed this discovery more to Gentiles than Jews." Nevertheless, the influence of some early German Zionists, in particular Kurt Blumenfeld, the apostle to the German Jews, played a significant part in this—and Einstein remained on terms of warm friendship with him for the rest of his life. But, as in the case of Herzl, the decisive factor in his awakening as a Jew was not so much encounter with an unfamiliar doctrine (he had met adherents of it in Prague but apparently took no interest in it then) as the chauvinism and xenophobia of leading circles, in this case in Berlin, which led him to a realisation of the precarious predicament of the Jewish community even in the civilised west. "Man can flourish," he declared, "only when he loses himself in a community. Hence the moral danger of the Jew who has lost touch with his own people and is regarded as a foreigner by the people of his adoption." "The tragedy of the Jews is . . . that they lack the support of a community to keep them together. The result is a want of solid foundations in the individual which in its extreme form amounts to moral instability."

The only remedy, he argued, is to develop a close connection with a living society which would enable individual Jews to bear the hatred and humiliation to which they are often exposed by the rest of mankind. Herzl is to be admired, Einstein tells us, for saying "at the top of his voice" that only the establishment of a national home in Palestine can cure this evil. It cannot be removed by assimilation. The Jews of the old German ghettos were poor, deprived of civic and political rights, insulated from European progress. Yet

these obscure, humble people had one great advantage over us—each of them belonged in every fibre of his being to a community in which he was wholly absorbed, in which he felt himself a fully privileged member, which asked nothing of him that was contrary to his natural habits of thought. Our forefathers of those days were pretty poor specimens intellectually and physically, but socially they enjoyed an enviable spiritual equilibrium.

Then came emancipation: rapid adaptation to the new open world: eager efforts to don clothes made to fit others, involving loss of identity, the prospect of disappearance as a group. But this was not to be:

However much the Jews adapted themselves, in language, manners, to a large extent even in the forms of religion, to the European peoples among whom they lived, the feeling of strangeness between them and their hosts never vanished. This is the ultimate cause of anti-Semitism, which cannot be got rid of by well-meaning propaganda. Nationalities want to pursue their own goals, not to blend.

To ignore, or argue against, emotional prejudice or open hostility, Einstein declared, is wholly futile; the baptised Jewish *Geheimrat* [Gentry] was to him merely pathetic. National frontiers, armies, he regarded as evil, but not national existence as such: The life of peaceful nations, with reciprocal respect for one another and toleration of each other's differences, was civilised and just. There follows a statement of Zionism not unlike the reaction to a similar predicament of another internationalist and socialist, Moses Hess, in the 1860s. Let me quote Einstein's words in 1933: "It is not enough for us to play a part as individuals in the cultural development of the human race, we must also attempt tasks which only nations as a whole can perform. Only so can the Jews regain social health." Consequently: "Palestine is not primarily a place of refuge for the Jews of Eastern Europe, but the embodiment of the re-awakening of the corporate spirit of the entire Jewish nation."

This seems to me a classical formulation of the Zionist creed, with an affinity to the unpolitical cultural nationalism of Ahad Ha'am: What Einstein was advocating was, in essence, the creation of a social and spiritual centre. But when British policy and Arab resistance, in his judgement, made the state inevitable, he accepted it, and the use of force to avoid annihilation, as being, perhaps, something of a necessary evil, but nevertheless as a burden and a duty to be borne with dignity and tact, without arrogance. Like all decent Zionists he was increasingly worried about the relationship with the Arabs of Palestine. He wished for a state in which Jews and Arabs could fully cooperate. But he realised, sadly, that events made this unlikely for the time being. He remained a consistent supporter of the Jewish state of Israel: Here Jewish ideals must be pursued, especially three among them: "knowledge for its own sake; an almost fanatical love of justice; desire for personal independence."

I need hardly say how sharply this differed from the general attitude of the educated German Jews of his milieu, not to speak of men of similar origin and social and intellectual formation elsewhere in western Europe. When one remembers Einstein's earlier life, remote from Jewish affairs, his lifelong idealistic internationalism, his hatred of all that divided men, it seems to me to argue a remarkable degree of insight, realism and moral courage, of which his fellow Jews today have good reason to feel proud. After all, other eminent German-Jewish scientists, honourable men of unimpeachable personal integrity, Fritz Haber, Max Born, James Franck, reacted very differently. So did writers and artists like Schnitzler, Stefan Zweig, Mahler, Karl Kraus or Werfel, who were all too familiar with anti-Semitism in Vienna.

I do not wish to imply that Einstein necessarily condemned assimilation to the culture of the majority as always ignoble or doomed to failure. It was plainly possible for children of Jewish parents to find themselves so remote from their community and its traditions that, even if they considered it, they were unable psychologically to reestablish genuine links with it. He was clear that in a civilised society every man must be free to pursue his own path in the manner that seemed to him best, provided that this did not do positive harm to others. He did not accuse these scientists and writers and artists of dishonourable or craven motives; their human dignity was not, for him, in question, only their degree of self-understanding.

It was his incapacity for self-deception or eva-sion, his readiness to face the truth, and—if the facts demanded it—to go against the current of received ideas, that marked Einstein's bold rejection of the central elements in the Newtonian system, and it was this independence that characterised his behaviour in other spheres. He rejected conventional wisdom: "Common sense," he once said, "is the deposit of prejudice laid down in the mind before the age of eighteen." If something did not seem to him to fit, morally or politically, no less than mathematically, he would not ignore, escape, forget it; adjust, arrange, add a patch or two in the hope that it would last his time; he would not wait for the Messiah—the world revolution—the universal reign of reason and justice—to dissolve the difficulty. If the shoe does not fit, it is no use saying that time and wear will make it less uncomfortable, or that the shape of the foot should be altered, or that the pain is an illusion—that reality is harmonious, and that therefore conflict, injustice, barbarism belong to the order of appearances, which superior spirits should rise above. If his philosophical mentors, Hume and Mach, were right, there was only one world, the world of human experience; it alone was real: Beyond it there might be mystery; indeed, he regarded the fact, of which he was totally convinced, that the universe was comprehensible as the greatest of mysteries; yet no theory was valid which ignored any part of direct human experience, in which he included imaginative insight, arrived at by paths often far from conscious.

It was this sense of reality that saved him, despite his deep convictions, from being doctrinaire. When what he knew understood directly, was in conflict with doctrinal Orthodoxy, he did not ignore the immediate evidence of his moral, social or political sense. He was a convinced pacifist; during the First World War he made himself unpopular in Germany by denouncing it. But in 1933 he accepted the necessity of resisting Hitler and the Nazis, if need be by force, which horrified his pacifist allies. He was an egalitarian, a democrat, with an inclination towards socialism. Yet his sense of the need to protect individuals from the state was so strong that he believed that Bills of Rights would be trampled on unless an élite of educated and experienced persons in authority at times effectively resisted the wishes of majorities. He praised the American Constitution, and in par-

ticular the balance of power between the President, Congress, and public opinion (his early political mentor, the Austrian socialist Fritz Adler, would scarcely have approved). He hated walls between human beings, exclusiveness. But when Jewish students were being hounded by nationalist students in German or Polish universities, he declared that Weizmann was right; liberal and socialist resolutions were useless; the Jews must act, and create their own university in Jerusalem.

He hated nationalism all his life. But he recognised the acute need of the Jews for some form of national existence; above all, he did not regard a sense of national identity and nationalism as being one and the same thing. It is clear that he took political allegiance seriously. He renounced his German nationality twice. He would not, as a young man, have chosen to adopt Swiss, or, after Hitler, American citizenship, had he not felt that he could give his full allegiance to these democratic countries when, for obvious reasons, he found it unbearable to retain his German passport. It was this combination of social sensitiveness and concrete insight into what it is that men live by that saved him from doctrinaire fanaticism; it was this that made him morally convincing.

He was an innocent man, and sometimes, I should think, taken in by fools and knaves. But innocence has its own modes of perception: It sometimes sees through its own eyes, not those of the spectacles provided by conventional wisdom or some uncriticised dogma. The very same independence which caused him to reject the accepted notions of physical space-time, and boldly offer the hypothesis of gravitational waves and light quanta against the resistance of physicists and philosophers, also liberated him morally and politically.

Consequently this man who sought privacy, who remained wholly uncorrupted by adulation and unparalleled fame in five continents, who believed in salvation by work and more work to unravel the secrets of nature—secrets miraculously amenable to analysis and solution by human reason—this gentle, shy and modest man displeased many establishments: German nationalists, Germanophobe Frenchmen, absolute pacifists, Jewish assimilationists, Orthodox rabbis, Soviet Marxists, as well as defenders of absolute moral values in which, in fact, he firmly believed.

He was neither a subjectivist nor a sceptic. He

believed that the concepts and theories of science are free creations of the human imagination, not, as Bacon or Mill or Mach thought, themselves abstracted from the data of experience; but what the scientist seeks to analyse or describe by means of these theories and concepts is itself an objective structure of which men, viewed scientifically, are themselves a part. Moral and aesthetic values, rules, standards, principles, cannot be derived from the sciences, which deal with what is, not with what should be; but neither are they, for Einstein, generated or conditioned by differences of class or culture or race. No less than the laws of nature, from which they cannot be derived, they are universal, true for all men at all times, discovered by moral or aesthetic insight common to all men, and embodied in the basic principles (not the mythology) of the great world religions.

Like Spinoza, he thought that those who deny this are merely blinded by the passions; indeed, he felt Spinoza to be a kindred spirit. Like Spinoza, he conceived God as reason embodied in nature, as being, in a literal sense, a divine harmony, *Deus sive Natura*; and, again like Spinoza, he showed no bitterness toward his detractors, nor did he compromise with them–he remained serene and reasonable, humane, tolerant, undogmatic. He did not wish to dominate, and did not demand blind fidelity from his followers. He supported any movement–say, the League of Nations or left-wing groups in America–if he thought that on the whole it did good, or at least more good than harm.

So with Jewish Palestine. He hated the chauvinists; he was critical, at times to an unrealistic degree, of the attitude of the Zionist leadership towards the Arabs, but this did not make him lean over backward occasionally as it did others; he denounced the Eisenhower Administration for seeking to please the Arab states at the expense of Israel, a policy which he attributed to American imperialism. He was critical of some of the Hebrew University's policies: For instance, he thought that, among the academic refugees from Fascist Europe, young scholars, not the old and famous, should be offered appointments. But his loyalties remained unimpaired. He was not prepared to abandon the Zionist movement because of the deficiencies of some of its leaders. His Zionism was grounded in the belief that basic human needs create a right to their satisfaction:

Men have an inalienable right to freedom from hunger, nakedness, insecurity, injustice, and from homelessness too.

He was somewhat homeless himself. In a letter to his friend Max Born he wrote that he had no roots; that he was a stranger everywhere. He was, on his own admission, a lonely man who instinctively avoided intimacy. He was a solitary thinker, not easy to know as a human being. His deep humanity and sympathy with the victims of political oppression, social discrimination, economic exploitation, were central to his outlook and need no special explanation; they were in part, perhaps, a compensation for his difficulty in forming close personal relationships.

Like many physicists connected in some way with the production of the atom bomb, he was, in his later years, oppressed by a sense of the responsibility of scientists for introducing a terrible new means of destruction into the world; and he condemned the use of it made by his adopted country, which seemed to him bent on a dangerously imperialist course. His hatred of the cruelty and barbarity of reactionaries and Fascists at times led him to believe that there were no enemies on the left–an illusion of many decent and generous people, some of whom have paid for it with their lives.

Perhaps his very gifts as a scientist led him to schematise, to oversimplify practical problems, including complex political and cultural ones, which allow of no clear-cut solutions, to be too sweeping and to ignore the wrinkles and unevennesses of daily life, insusceptible as they are to exact quantitative analysis. For it seems to me that there may exist a certain difference between the gifts of scientists and humanists. It has often been pointed out that major discoveries and inventions–as opposed to demonstrations of their validity–require great imaginative power and an intuitive sense–not rationally analysable–of where the right solution must lie, and that this is not dissimilar from the vision of artists or the sympathetic insight into the past of gifted historians or scholars. This may well be true. Yet those who deal with human beings and their affairs need some awareness of the essential nature of all human experience and activity, a sense of the limits of what it is possible for men and women to be or to do; without some such awareness of the limits imposed by nature there is no criterion for dismissing an infinity of logically possible but wildly improbable or absurd historical or psychological hypotheses.

About what makes men rational Aristotle and Kant and Voltaire and Hume may well be right: On this sense of what can, and what clearly cannot, be the case in human affairs, on the normal association of ideas, on such basic concepts as those of past, future, things, persons, causal sequence, logical relations—a closely woven network of categories and concepts—human rationality, perhaps even sanity, in practice, depends. Departure from these, as attempted, for example, by surrealist painters or poets, or aleatory composers, may be interesting, but it is deliberately counter-rational.

But in mathematics or theoretical physics this sense of reality does not necessarily seem to be required. Indeed, something close to the opposite may, at times, be needed. In the case of seminal discoveries—say, of imaginary numbers, or non-Euclidean geometry, or the quantum theory—it is precisely dissociation of commonly associated ideas, that is, departure from some categories indispensable to normal human experience, that seems to be required, namely a gift for conceiving what cannot in principle be imagined, nor expressed in ordinary language which is concerned with day-to-day communication, with the facts and needs of human life. It is this detachment from, even flouting of, everyday reality that leads to the popular image of the abstract thinker—Thales who falls into a well, the absent-minded professor who boils his watch in place of an egg.

This kind of escape into abstractions—an ideal world of pure forms expressed in a specially invented symbolism free from the irregularities and untidiness, or even the basic assumptions, of ordinary experience—may possibly, at times, be connected with a psychic disturbance, some kind of displacement in early life. Einstein's breakdown as a schoolboy in Munich is paralleled by similar childhood experiences of Newton and Darwin, who also remained somewhat inaccessible emotionally. These thinkers, too, spoke of a type of experience which Einstein described as a deeply religious feeling before a vision of the divinity revealed in the all-embracing unity and rational harmony of the rigorously causal structure of nature. This was a vision of reality which nothing could shake: Consequently, Einstein remained an unyielding determinist, and never accepted the uncertainty principle as an ultimate category of natural knowledge, or as an attribute of objective nature—only as part of our provisional and incomplete analysis of it.

Such addiction to pure abstraction and generalisation may, at times, be connected with an incapacity for close personal relationships with others, a full social life; this appears to me to be a plausible hypothesis. It may well have been so with Albert Einstein. What he withheld from private life he gave to the world. Not only the fame of his achievement, but his figure, his face, are known to millions of men and women. His appearance became a visible symbol, a stereotype, of what people supposed a scientist of genius should look like, much as an idealised Beethoven became a commercialised image of the inspired artist.

Back in Berlin, Einstein reflected on his experiences. There is no doubt that the Jews of America had given him a concept of Jewry quite different from the one he had grown up with in Europe. "It was in America," he wrote, "that I first discovered the Jewish people. I have seen any number of Jews, but the Jewish people I have never met either in Berlin or elsewhere in Germany. This Jewish people which I found in America came from Russia, Poland, and Eastern Europe generally. These men and women still retain a healthy national feeling; it has not yet been destroyed by the process of atomization and dispersion. I found these people extraordinarily ready for self-sacrifice and practically creative."

Einstein's optimism was further expressed when he spoke in Berlin's Bluthner Hall on work in Palestine a few days after his return, and in a letter to Ehrenfest on June 18 he noted that "our activities on behalf of the Hebrew University were very successful. . . . The university seems financially assured to the extent that the building of the particularly important medical facilities can soon be started. The middle classes, rather than the rich Jews, have made this possible and, in particular, the six thousand Jewish doctors in America." This mood soon passed and the Zionist leader Selig Brodetsky, reporting on his visit to Einstein in Berlin shortly afterwards, relates that he was told "of the failure of his mission to the

United States." Three months later Weizmann was writing almost plaintively asking Einstein to sign a letter to the Boston New Century Club where they had drummed up considerable support—"the Club has made difficulties regarding the handing over of the money collected; of the $20,000 promised, we have actually so far collected $4,000," he noted. The different views are not contradictory. Like the mythical bottle of whiskey, half-full or half-empty, Weizmann's tour could be considered either failure or success according to expectations. But as the enthusiasm engendered by the visit began to slip away, the facts began to look less rosy. It was some years before the Hebrew University pulled in the really large contributions hoped for in 1921.

Einstein's already slightly jaundiced view of the tour was increased when he realized the price to be paid for the support gained. Forever the idealist, he could not stomach the shifts, the horse trading, and the accommodations necessary in an imperfect world. Above all, he could never reconcile himself to the fact that whoever pays the piper calls the tune; that the American Jews who provided most of the finance for the Hebrew University would in practice have a hand in the way it was run almost as powerful as the Board of Governors.

In 1921 this was still a small cloud on the horizon. Einstein remained the great Zionist capture; it followed therefore that he should be asked to visit Palestine on his return from the Far East early in 1923 and to give the inaugural address at the university. For Einstein himself the visit was a deeply emotional experience, doubly important to a man who had excluded emotion from his life whenever possible.

The Palestine Mandate, under which the former Turkish territory was administered by the British with the ultimate aim of creating a Jewish National Home, had been approved by the Council of the League of Nations only six months previously, and was not to become operative until the end of September, 1923. But the British High Commissioner had already been appointed, and Jewish immigration and reconstruction were being pushed ahead. The High Commissioner, with whom the Einsteins were to stay, was Sir Herbert, later Lord Samuel. Like Lord Haldane, he was both philosopher and statesman, a man who had been deeply moved by the implications of rel-

ativity, and one of the few outside the field of science to become a comparatively close friend. Samuel was not only a first-class administrator, he was also a Jew; and while his appointment had been intended to show the British government's favorable attitude towards Jewish aspirations, there were repercussions which only the most Machiavellian foresight could have predicted. For Sir Herbert was also a British official whose neutrality must be above suspicion. It was therefore almost inevitable that in the Jewish-Arab disputes that spattered the unhappy history of the country during the years of his appointment the High Commissioner should stress his impartiality by giving utmost consideration to the Arabs. In this he was no more than just; but among Jews it was often felt that he was so busy returning good for evil that he had little time to return good for good. Therefore his long friendship with Einstein, begun in the first months of 1923, was to be marked more than once by differences as to what should be done for Palestine.

Einstein arrived with his wife at Tel Aviv on February 2, 1923, and was greeted by Colonel Frederick Kisch, who had retired from the British army with a fine war record to join the Zionist Executive. "Found him rather tired as he had sat up all night," Kisch recorded in his diary, "but I later learned that this was his own fault, as he had insisted on traveling second class in spite of every effort to persuade him to go into a *wagon-lit* which had been reserved for him." Three days later he was formally received by the Palestine Zionist Executive. "He made," Kisch recorded, "a little speech explaining the nature of his brain which he said was such that he was afraid it would be unproductive work for him to attempt to learn Hebrew."

But there was no doubt about Einstein's almost embarrassing enthusiasm for Palestine—or of Palestine for him. This was shown the following day. That the most famous scientist in the world—if the most controversial one—should give such unqualified support to their efforts genuinely roused the inhabitants and emboldened them to think that the reward would be equally unqualified. Einstein responded with an answering enthusiasm. The interaction was shown when on February 6 he drove through streets lined with crowds of waving schoolchildren to a reception at the Lemel School organized by the Palestine

Zionist Executive and the Jewish National Council. After he entered, there was, the *Palestine Weekly* reported, "no holding back the crowd who had assembled outside. The outer gates were stormed, and the crowd burst into the courtyard, and tried to force the inner gates which were stoutly held by three or four stalwarts."

Inside, Einstein was baring his soul. "I consider this the greatest day of my life," he said. "Hitherto I have always found something to regret in the Jewish soul, and that is the forgetfulness of its own people—forgetfulness of its being almost. Today I have been made happy by the sight of the Jewish people learning to recognize themselves and to make themselves recognized as a force in the world. This is a great age, the age of the liberation of the Jewish soul; and it has been accomplished through the Zionist movement, so that no one in the world will be able to destroy it."

The following day he was to perform his main task in Palestine: delivery of the inaugural address at the Hebrew University, which had been founded five years earlier as the British and Turkish guns still faintly boomed away fifteen miles to the north. Before the ceremony he had a long talk with Kisch, which reveals the state of his mind.

"Interview with Deedes," Kisch recorded, "then a walk back from Mount Scopus to the city with Einstein to whom I explained the political situation and some of the intricacies of the Arab question. Einstein spoke of Ussishkin's attempt to persuade him to settle in Jerusalem. He has no intention of doing so, not because he would sever himself from his work and friends, but because in Europe he is free and here he would always be a prisoner. He is not prepared to be merely an ornament in Jerusalem."

At 4:30 the same afternoon some hundreds of men and women, including members of the consular corps and the newly created Palestine government and their wives, packed into the temporary building of the Hebrew University on Mount Scopus. "Many . . . like myself . . . could have no claim to understand his theory," wrote Helen Bentwich, wife of Norman Bentwich, then attorney general to the government. "But we all wanted to hear and meet this great man, probably to be able to say in the years to come that not only had we heard Einstein lecture about his the-ory, but that we had attended the first lecture given at the Hebrew University of Jerusalem."

The hall was hung with Zionist flags and the insignia of the twelve tribes. Above the platform hung the Union Jack with a portrait of the High Commissioner and a Zionist flag with a portrait of Dr. Herzl, while from the ceiling descended a banner bearing the words "*Orah ve Torah*" ("Light and Learning").

Ussishkin introduced Einstein with the announcement that two thousand years ago Titus and his avenging armies had stood where they now stood. But today they were inaugurating a temple of science. "Mount the platform which has been waiting for you for two thousand years," he concluded grandly.

Einstein did so, delighting those present by giving what Samuel called "an opening sentence pro forma in a Hebrew that was evidently unfamiliar." Then he continued in French; and, at the end of the comparatively short address, repeated it in German. Nevertheless the first official words spoken from the university had been in Hebrew.

During the next few days Einstein toured the country, planting a tree in the garden on Mount Carmel outside Haifa and visiting the city's high school and technical college. "Suitably impressed by the work so far done," he wrote to Weizmann on a leaf torn from his notebook. "It would be of great benefit if teaching could start at the Tech. Coll. as everything is ready and the need is great. Here the difficulties are great, but the mood is confident and the work to be marveled at." In Tel Aviv he was created a free citizen and at a banquet held in his honor he spoke with an honesty that tact might have blue-penciled: "I have already had the privilege of receiving the honorary citizenship of the City of New York, but I am tenfold happier to be a citizen of this beautiful Jewish town." At Rishon Le Zion, which he visited from Jaffa, he promised to "rouse the Jewish world and tell them of the strength that has been invested here," adding that until his last hour he would "work for our settlement and for our country."

His enthusiasm for the opportunities which Palestine would now be able to offer was stressed as he walked on the Mount of Olives with the attorney general. "The Jews had produced no genius of rank in the nineteenth century save a mathematician—Jacoby—and Heine," he said, according to Bentwich. "The National Home in

Palestine could release and foster their genius. For two thousand years their common bond had been the past, the carefully guarded tradition. Now they had a new bond, the active cooperation in building up a country. Then he went on to talk of other things. He delighted in the beauty of the Arab peasant dress and the Arab village growing out of the rock, and equally in the beauty of life in Japan and in their sense of corporate union. The Japanese dinner made you understand the meaning of eternity. . . . On the journey from Japan, he had been thinking out a new theory of the relation of light to gravity. The ship gave the best conditions for thought; a regular life and no disturbing influence." And then, a decade before the same thought was to be awakened by solitude in England, Einstein commented: "For similar reasons he found light-houses attractive; a man could be alone there."

Palestine strengthened his Zionist sinews, and the memory of it helped him during the difficult decade that lay ahead. When he dined with the attorney general and his wife, borrowing a violin and making up a quartet with Bentwich and his two sisters, he not only played remarkably well, but "looked so happy while he was playing that I enjoyed watching as much as listening," Mrs. Bentwich remembered. "We talked of books, and of one he said, with a happy twinkle in his eye: 'It's not worth reading. The author writes just like a professor.'"

This was but one side of the coin. The other was represented by the formality of Government House, by the mounted troops that accompanied the High Commissioner as he traveled with his guests, and by the boom of the cannon which echoed every time he left the official residence. All this worried him. He had already perfected a technique of behaving as if formality did not exist—a technique which was perfectly sincere but which at times gave a misleading impression of playing to the gallery or of being eccentric for eccentricity's sake. Elsa was also uncomfortable, but for her own reason. "I am a simple German housewife," she told Philip Frank. "I like things to be cozy and comfortable and I feel unhappy in such a formal atmosphere. For my husband it is a different matter; he is a famous man. When he commits a breach of etiquette, it is said that he does so because he is a man of genius. In my case, however, it is attributed to a lack of culture."

Despite the contrasts between Samuel, the shrewd able statesman, and the less worldly Einstein, the two men were attracted to one another, and talking in the grounds of Government House their conversation ranged across the future not only of Israel but of relativity. Here Samuel quoted T. H. Huxley's famous remark: "Herbert Spencer's idea of a tragedy is a deduction killed by a fact." Einstein's reply was recorded by Samuel: "Every theory is killed sooner or later in that way. But if the theory has good in it, that good is embodied and continued in the next theory."

Einstein and his wife left Palestine for Europe in mid-February. His final impression, as he put it to Solovine in a letter that Easter, was that it would "become a spiritual center but will not be able to receive a big proportion of the Jewish people. I am, nevertheless, convinced that the colonization will succeed." His advice was severely practical. Kisch records that as he said good-bye to his visitor in Jerusalem, he asked Einstein "to let us know if during his tour he had observed that we were doing anything which in his opinion we should not do, or if we were leaving undone things which should be done. He answered: 'Ramassez plus d'argent'" ("Collect more money").

Albert Einstein.

Brandeis

The name of Louis D. Brandeis is as revered among American Jews as that of Einstein. One of the United States' two Jewish-sponsored universities is named after him, along with sundry schools. Brandeis came to Harvard Law School from the comfortable German Jewish community in Louisville, Kentucky, and stood first in his class. He did not take a teaching position at Harvard Law, although he occasionally lectured there because he needed money. Instead, he went into a lucrative partnership with a classmate from a Boston Brahmin family. Along with serving rich and corporate clients, Brandeis was also active as counsel to labor unions and he pioneered in getting the courts to take social data into account in rendering decisions.

Brandeis was a close associate of the former Princeton professor and historian, President Woodrow Wilson. In 1916 there was a huge public outcry, headed by the American Bar Association no less, against Wilson's nomination of Brandeis to the U.S. Supreme Court, partly on anti-Semitic grounds (Brandeis would be the first Jewish justice on the court) and partly because of Brandeis' sympathy with labor unions and the principles of the regulatory and welfare state. Nevertheless, Brandeis was confirmed by the Senate and served for close to two decades in a not particularly prominent and influential manner. By 1920 Brandeis' chief interest was in Zionism, and he wanted to be head of the World Zionist Organization but Chaim Weitzmann stood in his way.

In the following selection from a speech given in 1915 Brandeis argues for the need of Zionism in Palestine and deals with the issue of allegations of dual loyalty made against American Zionists, an argument that would be made by a Zionist leader today.

There is a striking similarity between Einstein and Brandeis. Brilliantly successful in their own fields, they used their success not to maximize their ascent into the establishment but rather to express radical ideas that offended conservative groups and classes. Both were therefore highly autonomous and courageous men. Both were also strong supporters of Zionism at a time when this was a minority position even among Jews.

Zionism seeks to establish in Palestine, for such Jews as choose to go and remain there, and for their descendants, a legally secured home, where they may live together and lead a Jewish life, where they may expect ultimately to constitute a majority of the population, and may look forward to what we should call home rule. The Zionists seek to establish this home in Palestine because

they are convinced that the undying longing of Jews for Palestine is a fact of deepest significance; that it is a manifestation in the struggle for existence by an ancient people which has established its right to live, a people whose three thousand years of civilization has produced a faith, culture and individuality which enable it to contribute largely in the future, as it has in the past, to the advance of civilization; and that it is not a right merely but a duty of the Jewish nationality to survive and develop. They believe that only in Palestine can Jewish life be fully protected from the forces of disintegration; that there alone can the Jewish spirit reach its full and natural development; and that by securing for those Jews who wish to settle there the opportunity to do so, not only those Jews, but all other Jews will be benefited, and that the long perplexing Jewish Problem will, at last, find solution.

They believe that to accomplish this, it is not necessary that the Jewish population of Palestine be large as compared with the whole number of Jews in the world; for throughout centuries when the Jewish influence was greatest, during the Persian, the Greek, and the Roman Empires, only a relatively small part of the Jews lived in Palestine; and only a small part of the Jews returned from Babylon when the Temple was rebuilt.

Since the destruction of the Temple, nearly two thousand years ago, the longing for Palestine has been ever present with the Jew. It was the hope of a return to the land of his fathers that buoyed up the Jew amidst persecution, and for the realization of which the devout ever prayed. Until a generation ago this was a hope merely, a wish piously prayed for, but not worked for. The Zionist movement is idealistic, but it is also essentially practical. It seeks to realize that hope; to make the dream of a Jewish life in a Jewish land come true as other great dreams of the world have been realized, by men working with devotion, intelligence, and self-sacrifice. It was thus that the dream of Italian independence and unity, after centuries of vain hope, came true through the efforts of Mazzini, Garibaldi and Cavour; that the dream of Greek, of Bulgarian and of Serbian independence became facts.

The rebirth of the Jewish nation is no longer a mere dream. It is in the process of accomplishment in a most practical way, and the story is a wonderful one. A generation ago a few Jewish emigrants from Russia and from Roumania, instead of proceeding westward to this hospitable country where they might easily have secured material prosperity, turned eastward for the purpose of settling in the land of their fathers.

To the wordly-wise these efforts at colonization appeared very foolish. Nature and man presented obstacles in Palestine which appeared almost insuperable; and the colonists were in fact ill-equipped for their task, save in their spirit of devotion and self-sacrifice. The land, harassed by centuries of misrule, was treeless and apparently sterile; and it was infested with malaria. The Government offered them no security, either as to life or property. The colonists themselves were not only unfamiliar with the character of the country, but were ignorant of the farmer's life which they proposed to lead; for the Jews of Russia and Roumania had been generally denied the opportunity of owning or working land. Furthermore, these colonists were not inured to the physical hardships to which the life of a pioneer is necessarily subjected. To these hardships and to malaria many succumbed. Those who survived were long confronted with failure. But at last success came. Within a generation these Jewish Pilgrim Fathers, and those who followed them, have succeeded in establishing these two fundamental propositions:

First: That Palestine is fit for the modern Jew.

Second: That the modern Jew is fit for Palestine.

Over forty self-governing Jewish colonies attest to this remarkable achievement.

This land, treeless a generation ago, supposed to be sterile and hopelessly arid, has been shown to have been treeless and sterile because of man's misrule. It has been shown to be capable of becoming again a land "flowing with milk and honey." Oranges and grapes, olives and almonds, wheat and other cereals are now growing there in profusion.

This material development has been attended by a spiritual and social development no less extraordinary; a development in education, in health and in social order; and in the character and habits of the population. Perhaps the most extraordinary achievement of Jewish nationalism is the revival of the Hebrew Language, which has again become a language of the common intercourse of men. The Hebrew tongue, called a dead language for nearly two thousand years, has, in the Jewish colonies and in Jerusalem, become again the living mother tongue. The effect of this common language in unifying the Jew is, of course, great; for the Jews of Palestine came literally from all the lands of the earth, each speaking, excepting those who used Yiddish, the language of the country from which he came, and remaining, in the main, almost a stranger to the others. But the effect of the renaissance of the Hebrew tongue is far greater than that of unifying the Jews. It is a potent factor in reviving the essentially Jewish spirit.

Our Jewish Pilgrim Fathers have laid the foundation. It remains for us to build the superstructure.

Let no American imagine that Zionism is inconsistent with Patriotism. Multiple loyalties are objectionable only if they are inconsistent. A man is a better citizen of the United States for being also a loyal citizen of his state, and of his city; for being loyal to his family, and to his profession or trade; for being loyal to his college or his lodge. Every Irish American who contributed towards advancing home rule was a better man and a better American for the sacrifice he made. Every American Jew who aids in advancing the Jewish settlement in Palestine, though he feels that neither he nor his descendants will ever live there, will likewise be a better man and a better American for doing so. . . .

There is no inconsistency between loyalty to America and loyalty to Jewry. The Jewish spirit, the product of our religion and experiences, is essentially modern and essentially American. Not since the destruction of the Temple have the Jews in spirit and in ideals been so fully in harmony with the noblest aspirations of the country in which they lived.

America's fundamental law seeks to make real the brotherhood of man. That brotherhood became the Jewish fundamental law more than twenty-five hundred years ago. America's insistent demand in the twentieth century is for social justice. That also has been the Jews' striving for ages. Their affliction as well as their religion has prepared the Jews for effective democracy. Persecution broadened their sympathies. It trained them in patient endurance, in self-control, and in sacrifice. It made them think as well as suffer. It deepened the passion for righteousness.

Indeed, loyalty to America demands rather that each American Jew become a Zionist. For only through the ennobling effect of its strivings can we develop the best that is in us and give to this country the full benefit of our great inheritance. The Jewish spirit, so long preserved, the character developed by so many centuries of sacrifice,

should be preserved and developed further, so that in America as elsewhere the sons of the race may in future live lives and do deeds worthy of their ancestors.

But we have also an immediate and more pressing duty in the performance of which Zionism alone seems capable of affording effective aid. We must protect America and ourselves from demoralization, which has to some extent already set in among American Jews. The cause of this demoralization is clear. It results in large part from the fact that in our land of liberty all the restraints by which the Jews were protected in their Ghettos were removed and a new generation left without necessary moral and spiritual support. And is it not equally clear what the only possible remedy is? It is the laborious task of inculcating self-respect, a task which can be accomplished only by restoring the ties of the Jew to the noble past of his race, and by making him realize the possibilities of a no less glorious future. The sole bulwark against demoralization is to develop in each new generation of Jews in America the sense of *noblesse oblige*. That spirit can be developed in those who regard their people as destined to live and to live with a bright future. That spirit can best be developed by actively participating in some way in furthering the ideals of the Jewish renaissance; and this can be done effectively only through furthering the Zionist movement.

Since the Jewish Problem is single and universal, the Jews of every country should strive for its solution. But the duty resting upon us of America is especially insistent. We number about three million, which is more than one-fifth of all the Jews in the world, a number larger than comprised within any other country except the Russian Empire. We are representative of all the Jews in the world; for we are composed of immigrants, or descendants of immigrants coming from every other country, or district. We include persons from every section of society, and of every shade of religious belief. We are ourselves free from civil or political disabilities; and are relatively prosperous. Our fellow-Americans are infused with a high and generous spirit, which insures approval of our struggle to ennoble, liberate, and otherwise improve the condition of an important part of the human race; and their innate manliness makes them sympathize particularly with our efforts at self-help. America's detachment from the old world problem relieves us from suspicions and embarrassments frequently attending the activities of Jews of rival European countries. And a conflict between American interests or ambitions and Jewish aims is not conceivable. Our loyalty to America can never be questioned.

Let us therefore lead, earnestly, courageously and joyously, in the struggle for liberation. Let us all recognize that we Jews are a distinctive nationality of which every Jew, whatever his country, his station or shade of belief, is necessarily a member. Let us insist that the struggle for liberty shall not cease until equality of opportunity is accorded to nationalities as to individuals. Let us insist also that full equality of opportunity cannot be obtained by Jews until we, like members of other nationalities, shall have the option of living elsewhere or of returning to the land of our forefathers.

The fulfillment of these aspirations is clearly demanded in the interest of mankind, as well as in justice to the Jews. They cannot fail of attainment if we are united and true to ourselves. But we must be united not only in spirit but in action. To this end we must organize. Organize, in the first place, so that the world may have proof of the extent and the intensity of our desire for liberty. Organize, in the second place, so that our resources may become known and be made available. But in mobilizing our force it will not be for war. The whole world longs for the solution of the Jewish Problem. We have but to lead the way, and we may be sure of ample cooperation from non-Jews. In order to lead the way, we need not arms, but men; men with those qualities for which Jews should be peculiarly fitted by reason of their religion and life; men of courage, of high intelligence, of faith and public spirit, of indomitable will and ready self-sacrifice; men who will both think and do, who will devote high abilities to shaping our course, and to overcoming the many obstacles which must from time to time arise. And we need other, many, many other men, officers commissioned and noncommissioned, and common soldiers in the cause of liberty, who will give of their efforts and resources, as occasion may demand, in unfailing and ever-strengthening support of the measures which may be adopted. Organization, thorough and complete, can alone develop such leaders and the necessary support.

Organize, Organize, Organize, until every Jew in America must stand up and be counted, counted with us, or prove himself, wittingly or unwittingly, of the few who are against their own people.

Frankfurter

A juristic icon equal in stature to Brandeis among American Jews was another Harvard Law graduate (and professor) and U.S. Supreme Court justice, Felix Frankfurter. The iconic stature Frankfurter gained among American Jews in the 1940s and 1950s, he has largely retained. He came from a German Jewish family of moderate means in New York City and before he went on to star at Harvard Law School, Frankfurter graduated from City College—then the favorite route of upward mobility for middle-class New York Jews.

Brandeis made Frankfurter his chosen disciple and virtually adopted him, secretly giving Felix generous monetary gifts for many years. Frankfurter had as close a relationship with FDR as Brandeis did with Woodrow Wilson.

It is not easy to categorize Frankfurter's position on the Supreme Court. He began as a New Deal liberal, and played a major role in securing *Brown* v. *Board of Education*, the landmark 1954 decision that desegregated public

The two men were alike in many ways. Both held the same public office, of course; their terms even briefly overlapped: Frankfurter joined the Court on January 30 and Brandeis resigned on February 13, 1939. Both were Jews who had been educated at the Harvard Law School. And they were close friends for some twenty-five years. Indeed, though Frankfurter had a wide circle (his wife once observed that "Felix has two hundred best friends"), for Brandeis their friendship was apparently the most intimate male relationship in his adult life. Most uncharacteristically, Brandeis referred to Frankfurter, in a letter to him in 1925, as "half brother–half son."

Their differences were, however, substantial and are more significant in understanding the two men. There was first of all a difference in personal style. Compare Brandeis's guarded reserve, his apparent aloofness, with this description of Frankfurter:

He talked copiously, with an overflowing gaiety and spontaneity which conveyed the impression of great natural sweetness. . . . Whenever I met him . . . the same phenomenon was always to be observed: He was the centre, the life and soul of a circle of eager and delighted human beings, exuberant, endlessly appreciative, delighting in every manifestation of intelligence, imagination or life.

This was Isaiah Berlin's testimony of Frankfurter's visiting year at Oxford in 1934. Or compare the account by Brandeis's biographer of his clients' efforts to remain in his company "by clinging to some substantial object" with Marion Frankfurter's description of her husband as a "door-hanger" who could not let a guest leave their home without "adding another paragraph." Or compare the physical distance Brandeis kept between himself and his law clerks with Frankfurter's "habit" of taking other men's arms and "squeezing," as reported by one of his law clerks, among others. (As one of Frankfurter's eulogizers put it after his death, "Who of us will not continue to feel that iron grip on the arm?") Indeed, the best explanation of Brandeis's intimacy with Frankfurter is suggested by Isaiah Berlin's general observation that Frankfurter "had an uncommon capacity for melting reserve, breaking through inhibitions, and generally emancipating those with whom he came into contact."

There were also substantial differences in their experience as Jews. By the time Frankfurter reached the Harvard Law School as a student in 1903 (and even more when he joined its faculty in 1914), Jewishness had assumed an openly stigmatized meaning in American life. The two men's Jewishness also had very different meanings in personal terms. Unlike Brandeis, Frankfurter was raised as a practicing Jew. "As a boy," he recounted, "I was religiously observant. I wouldn't eat breakfast until I had done the religious devotions in the morning." Jewish ritual, he said, later "ceased to have inner meaning" for him; he first fully recognized this at a Yom Kippur service during his junior year at the City College of New York and thereupon "left the service in the middle of it, never to return."

Frankfurter never denied that he was a Jew; he was quite pointed throughout his life in identifying himself as such. But there was no spiritual or "inner meaning" to this affiliation for him, whereas Brandeis, who never had any childhood involvement to abandon, did imbue his latter-day Zionism with a spiritual fervor. (Frankfurter also became active in Zionist affairs around World War I, but only as an aide-de-camp to Brandeis; after Brandeis's death in 1941, Frankfurter showed no special interest in the movement.)

Jewishness also had different cultural meaning for the two men. Brandeis believed that his religious affiliation (which he equated with his Zionism) was wholly consistent with his Americanism. Frankfurter did not fully believe this; his early experience, in particular, taught him otherwise. For Frankfurter, Jewishness was inextricably linked to the immigrant world in which he had been raised. Brandeis was born here; Frankfurter arrived, when he was twelve, with his parents from Vienna. The family lived on the East Side of New York in the midst of a German-Jewish immigrant settlement. Frankfurter recounted that when he arrived in New York, he "never had heard a word of English spoken;" he counted among the "greatest benefactors" in his life his first public school teacher, a "middle-aged Irish woman":

She believed in corporal punishment—I was going to say capital punishment. She evidently saw this ardent kid who by that time had picked up some English—I'm not a linguist and haven't got a good ear for languages—but she told the boys that if anybody was caught speaking German with me, she would punish him. She would give gentle uppercuts to the boys. It was wonderful for me that speaking English was enforced upon my environment in school, all thanks to Miss Hogan.

To become a full-fledged American, then, Frankfurter had to separate himself from his immigrant past—as it were, by force majeure, by corporal, if not capital, punishment. Frankfurter's boyhood Jewishness, like that of many other Jewish immigrants, was bound up in this struggle.

All of these differences found expression in the underlying attitudes of the two men to American society. Brandeis, as I have suggested, always stood apart; he was content, even eager, to remain at the margin—in effect, homeless. This was not Felix Frankfurter's way. Early in his career, Frankfurter alluded to this issue in a letter to his mentor, Henry Stimson, explaining his regret that he could not affiliate with any political party: "I have to be one of those who, by being outside of both camps, is going to pick and choose from election to election. . . . I don't like the situation. It is not comfortable to be politically homeless, but I don't see my way clear to being other than a tenant at will until better days."

Happier days did come later for Frankfurter when he embraced a political affiliation with a passion that many reserve for other pursuits. Two days before his death, Frankfurter told his chosen biographer, "Tell the whole story. Let people see how much I loved Roosevelt, how much I loved my country, and let them see how great a man Roosevelt really was." Franklin Roosevelt was not the sole object of Frankfurter's adulation. At different times he spoke in similar terms of other national institutions—of the Supreme Court, on which he served ("Of all earthly institutions this Court comes nearest to having, for me, sacred aspects"); of Harvard, where he studied and taught ("I have a quasi-religious feeling about the Harvard Law School"); and about America itself.

In 1942 Frankfurter said this at a case conference with his brethren (as he later recorded in his diary):

I am saying what I am going to say because perhaps this case arouses in me feelings that could not be entertained by anyone else around this table. It is well known that a convert is more zealous than one born to the faith. None of you has had the experience that I have had with reference to American citizenship. . . . As one who has no ties with any formal religion, perhaps the feelings that underlie religious forms for me run into intensification of my feelings about American citizenship. I have known, as you hardly could have known, literally hundreds of men and women of the finest spirit who had to shed old loyalties and take on the loyalty of American citizenship. Perhaps I can best convey what is in my mind if I read to you from a letter written by as distinguished an historian as is now alive when he went through this experience of becoming an American citizen.

Frankfurter then recited to his brethren, and transcribed in his diary, a letter from Professor Gaetano Salvemini of Harvard:

There is in this country a wider area of generosity than in any other country, at least in Europe. It is this feeling that one is at home here that conquers you little by little. And one fine day you feel that you are no longer an exile but a citizen in your own country. When I took my oath I felt that really I was performing a grand function. I was throwing away not my intellectual and moral but my juristic past. I threw it away without any regret.

Frankfurter thus, according to his testimony, embraced American citizenship with an almost religious fervor, so that, like his correspondent, he was "no longer an exile" but "at home." The context in which Frankfurter gave this testimony suggests how this embrace found expression in his conception of the judicial role. The context was the Court's consideration of *Schneiderman* v. *United States*, a case in which the government sought to revoke the petitioner's naturalized citizenship on the grounds that he was an active Communist party member when naturalized and that such membership in itself was necessarily inconsistent with his required oath of attachment "to the principles" of the Constitution. (The naturalization statute in effect at the time did not specify Communist party membership as a disqualification, and Schneiderman had neither revealed nor denied his membership then.)

Frankfurter voted for revocation in the case, though he wrote no opinion. From his diary entry, I would paraphrase his underlying attitude as follows: I, like Schneiderman, was once an alien; unlike him I "shed old loyalties," and he must do the same; I say this not as a private individual but as a judge charged with defining what it means to be an American, to be truly welcome and "at home" here. Frankfurter, in my paraphrase, portrays himself as a quintessential insider—even as a "convert . . . more zealous than one born to the faith."

This self-portrayal found more open, and even more dramatic, expression in a case that had come to the Court two years earlier, *Minersville School District* v. *Gobitis*. The school board required all children to salute and recite allegiance to the American flag at the beginning of each school day. Jehovah's Witness children refused on the grounds that this was idolatry forbidden by their religion; they were accordingly expelled, and their parents were convicted of truancy law violations for effectively withholding them from school attendance. Frankfurter wrote the Court's opinion affirming the school board's authority to compel the flag salute.

Chief Justice Charles Evans Hughes recounted that he had assigned the opinion to Frankfurter because of the emotion with which Frankfurter had invoked, in the conference deliberation, the "role of the public school in instilling love of country," based on his own experience as an immigrant child. As Richard Danzig has observed, Frankfurter's *Gobitis* opinion echoes his reminiscences of one of his "greatest benefactors," Miss Hogan, who forced Frankfurter to speak only English by threatening "gentle uppercuts," if not "capital punishment," to anyone conversing in an alien tongue with him.

This resonance is only indirect. In his opinion Frankfurter carefully confined himself to the proposition only that a reasonable legislature might favor compulsory observances to "best promote in the minds of children . . . an attachment to the institutions of their country," to "evoke in them appreciation of the nation's hopes and dreams, its sufferings and sacrifices," and that a court must defer to such reasonable legislative judgment. It may be that the local school board were thus benignly motivated in expelling the Jehovah's Witness children and prosecuting their parents. It may also be that the board were more intent on expressing disdain for these stiffnecked aliens in their midst who refused to acknowledge the supremacy of their secular authority. Even this less appealing state policy found some implicit deference in Frankfurter's opinion. The Jehovah's Witnesses, he suggested, were "dissidents" asking for "exceptional immunity;" the question at issue was the "respect" required for their "individual idiosyncracies." In a gentle uppercut of his own devising, he wrote: "For ourselves, we might be tempted to say that the deepest patriotism is best engendered by giving unfettered scope to the most crochety beliefs. . . . But the courtroom is not the arena for debating issues of educational policy."

Thus Frankfurter was prepared to assume the most benign legislative motive, but even to accept a more disdainful hostility to alien beliefs and practices, in order to vindicate "authority to safeguard the nation's fellowship" by imposing "the binding tie of cohesive sentiment" toward the symbols of the nation. His is the voice of the insider—unsympathetic, uncomprehending, dismissive of the outsider's "idiosyncrasies," his "crochety beliefs." This is a far remove from Brandeis's habitual stance of trying "to appreciate [the other man's] point of view" and his persistent effort in judicial opinions to set out the most sympathetic case for others' perspectives in order "to enrich our knowledge and enlarge our understanding" of them.

Frankfurter carried all but one of his brethren with him in *Gobitis*; only Harlan Fiske Stone dissented. Just three years later, however, in one of the most abrupt reversals in its history, the Court overturned *Gobitis*. Frankfurter dissented, while three justices—Hugo Black, William O. Douglas, and Frank Murphy—who had previously voted with him in *Gobitis* now reversed themselves to form the new Court majority (with Stone and two new arrivals, Robert Jackson and Wiley Rutledge). These were the opening words of Frankfurter's dissent:

> One who belongs to the most vilified and persecuted minority in history is not likely to be insensible to the freedoms guaranteed by our Constitution. Were my purely personal attitude relevant I should wholeheartedly associate myself with the general libertarian views in the Court's opinion, representing as they do the thought and actions of a lifetime. But as judges we are neither Jew nor Gentile, neither Catholic nor agnostic. We owe equal attachment to the Constitution and are equally bound by our judicial obligations whether we derive our citizenship from the earliest or the latest immigrants to these shores.

This is an extraordinary statement for the pages of the United States Reports; nothing else in all of those volumes, so far as I have read in them, approaches this intense confessional tone. But Frankfurter denied that there was anything "personal" about this statement. In his diary he recorded his response to Justice Murphy's plea "as a friend" and "for your benefit" to delete these opening sentences:

> I said I could understand that a reference to the fact that I am a Jew would be deemed to be personal if I drew on that fact as a reason for enforcing some minority rights. . . . But I do not see what is "personal" about referring to the fact that although a Jew, and therefore naturally eager for the protection of minorities, on the Court it is not my business to yield to such considerations, etc.

There is a sharp line, a disjunction as he sees it, between Frankfurter the person and Frankfurter the judge. For one to become the other, indeed, this line must be drawn. In this formula there is no room for an empathic understanding between judge and litigant based on the judge's personal identifications. Thus the judge guards himself against favoritism, against prejudicial bias in favor of "people like himself." But if this judge's personal experiences and sympathies lean toward those who are "vilified and persecuted," as Frankfurter put it, there is considerable risk that rigorous exclusion of this empathic identification will push this judge into an alliance with the vilifiers and persecutors. Brandeis protected himself from this trap by building from this identification with oppressed outsiders towards a judicial role as their advocate, an instrument of their acknowledged social inclusion. Frankfurter—perhaps because identification with alien outsiders was rawer and more exposed for him than for Brandeis—excluded any such special understanding from his self-definition as a judge.

The most Frankfurter would extend to outsiders was an invitation to join the inner circle on the same terms and at the same costs that he had accepted. This, as Danzig has suggested, was the alternative Frankfurter was content to offer the Jehovah's Witness children—that they would find ready acceptance if they became full-fledged Americans (as he had done) by turning away from their alien language and idiosyncratic beliefs. This was also the role Frankfurter saw for himself as a judge in the race segregation cases. There was an almost precise parallel between Frankfurter's passage from alien to citizen and the claims then articulated by Negro spokesmen for assimilation into the American mainstream. Because segregation laws visibly blocked such assimilation, they violated the "fundamental values" that Frankfurter saw as the essence of American society for himself.

Frankfurter would not have said that his personal experience as an immigrant and a Jew was irrelevant to his conception of himself as a judge. I surmise that he believed his successful passage from alien to fully assimilated citizen gave him special insight as a judge into fundamental American values because he embodied those values in his own experience. He drew no protective mandate or special sympathy for outsiders, however, from this experience. He instead derived a mandate zealously to protect the values and status of insiders, such as he had become.

The irony of this special zeal occasionally struck even Frankfurter himself; in his reminiscences, he told of a question he posed at social encounter in 1940 to an isolationist senator who fervently opposed lend-lease aid to Great Britain:

How is it that I who, as far as I know, haven't remotely a drop of English blood in me, who never heard the English language spoken, certainly never spoke a word of it until I was twelve, who never saw England until I was past thirty, have such a deep feeling about the essential importance of the maintenance of England, have such a sense of kinship professionally speaking with English institutions and feel that ours are so deeply related to their history and therefore am profoundly engaged in this cause with Englishmen, whereas you who I believe have nothing but English ancestry would on the whole view with equanimity the destruction of England?

The senator, who was a direct descendant of one of the signers of the Declaration of Independence, responded that he, unlike Frankfurter, had "a memory of the red coats." But for present purposes, Frankfurter's question is more interesting than the answer he received. Perhaps a better answer to that question is found in the special zeal of the convert. Whatever the answer, in his role as justice, Frankfurter saw himself specially obliged and specially qualified to discern the fundamental values of American society— as he put it in one case, "canons . . . which

express the notions of justice of English-speaking peoples" (such as he had become). . . .

But, by my estimation, when Frankfurter joined the Supreme Court in 1939, he lost his balance. His judicial office meant for Frankfurter that he now stood at the very center of American society as an embodiment of its values and traditions. Because he claimed that there was such a center, and that he could not only perceive it but had attained it, he was also prepared to force it on others who appeared as litigants in his Court. To be a Supreme Court justice was for Frankfurter a culminating expression of his passion for America, and the status itself seemed conclusive proof that the passion was reciprocated. His wish to achieve insider status, to find a home and an end to his personal exile, seemed finally to be within reach; and so he grasped it. But in this grasp he lost an essential aspect of his judgmental capacity; he became too single-minded, an overeager apologist for the existing order. He embraced an attitude to America that provided no critical distance for him in reaching judgment on his contemporary society or on himself.

Yet even at this personally culminating accession for Frankfurter, the long-sought prize of homecoming still eluded him. One episode at the very beginning of his tenure symbolizes the matter. James Landis, then dean of the Harvard Law School, recounted it (according to Joseph Lash in his biographical essay preceding Frankfurter's diaries):

A gaffe in dress marked [Frankfurter's] first conference with his Brethren. He had the habit of wearing, unless in the classroom, "one of those little alpaca coats," when he was working, recalled Landis. So he came to the conference in an alpaca coat, only to discover the other justices fully dressed up. He was quite embarrassed, he later confided to Landis, and after the lunch break came back properly attired, only to see that Chief Justice Hughes had put on an alpaca coat.

Frankfurter may have told the story to demonstrate Hughes's exquisite consideration and breeding in putting this new boy at ease; and it does indeed show this. But I would read more into it. Here was Frankfurter, at last eligible to dress up and march with his judicial brethren "in lock step in top hat to the Union Club for lunch," and he wore the wrong outfit. The chief justice then conformed his dress to that of this "latest immigrant to these shores" and thereby elegantly demonstrated his own social ease, his own unquestioned sense of belonging. And still, it turned out, Frankfurter dressed wrong.

Somewhere in this intricate minuet, Frankfurter had lost his bearings. Where was the "thesis of independence" that he had fixed as a marker on his doorpost in Oxford when he had previously been swept into a costume party? Where was his sense of self?

Herzl

Among twentieth-century Jewish icons, a handful of Zionist leaders occupy a special place. By their indomitable wills they created a Jewish homeland in Turkish (after 1917 British) Palestine, militarily secured the independence of the State of Israel in 1948, made it stronger and bigger in 1967, and were able to absorb millions of refugees from Hitlerian and Arab persecution, as well as convince a small number of dedicated Zionists from elsewhere to return voluntarily to the homeland.

In 1896 when the first Zionist Congress met in Basel, Switzerland, these achievements would have seemed impossible. Therefore it is the mind and will and image of the Congress' Chairman—the tall, handsome man, with the big black beard, impeccably dressed in a high bourgeois Viennese morning coat, and addressing the Congress delegates in eloquent German—that looms powerfully and perpetually in Jewish memory. This was Theodore Herzl, to die only eight years later at the age of forty-four.

In Israel, Herzl's physical image is everywhere and justifiably so—in government offices and on currency, the tall man with the big black beard still presides iconically over each Israeli consulate around the world, at Zionist world congresses, at Israeli Bond Dinners.

Like Moses, Herzl began as an outsider among Jews. He knew very little Jewish history or Hebrew; he could only make himself understood to Yiddish-speaking crowds because Yiddish is a German dialect. He was the indulged son of affluent, assimilated Jewish parents in Vienna. He graduated in law but never practiced it. Instead he became a successful author of light comedies for the stage and a much-read journalist for what today would be called a tabloid newspaper started up by two enterprising Austrian Jews.

Herzl as a correspondent witnessed the Dreyfus trial, which moved and alarmed him deeply, but he was already conscious of the spreading race hatred in Western Europe—Vienna competed with Paris for being the center of anti-Semitic fervor—and he transformed a romantic vision of Jews returning their "old-new land" into the rudiments of a world organization to raise funds to lobby governments, and organize the true return to Zion.

For two decades Lovers of Zion already had a similar program in Odessa and other Eastern European centers, but they had accomplished little in a practical sense. Herzl overtook them, got the Zionist momentum going, and furthermore greatly increased support for Palestine immigration in Western Europe. As a prominent journalist, he was used to getting easy access to dignitaries, and therefore sought and gained interviews with both the German Kaiser and—more importantly, since Palestine was ruled by the Turks—the Sultan in Istanbul. Neither interview achieved anything tangible, but it greatly impressed the Jewish masses in Eastern Europe.

Here is the account in Herzl's diary of his encounter with the Sultan and his corrupt, incompetent officials in 1901. It shows that Herzl lacked no illusions about the difficult task ahead, but nothing could quench his ardor. The sharp eye for detail of the tabloid journalist and the skillful composition of a scene by a successful popular dramatist are evident.

Herzl v. Sultan is followed by an assessment of Herzl as a leader written in the 1930's by Vladimir Jabotinsky, the founder of the right-wing, militant branch of Zionism, then called Revisionists and now called Likud. Jabotinsky was impressed by Mussolini and the authoritarian leaders of the inter-war period and his assessment of Herzl should be read in this context.

May 21, [1901].

On board the "Principessa Maria."

We have just sailed out of the Bosphorus, the beauty of which shortened the morning hours, and at last I can feel that a good part of our adventure is happily over with—an adventure not without its dangers.

I was placed in the grasp of a despot whom I had every reason to consider half-insane, and whose Government, as the debate in the Italian parliament showed, had twice during the past year demanded the intervention of the Great Powers against Jewish immigration.

My situation was rendered hazardous from another side by reason of the fact that I was obliged to introduce myself, at first, not in my real and universally known capacity as head of the Zionist movement, but as an editor of the "Neue Freie Presse"—which they promptly turned into *directeur* and which again I had to modify by the adjective *littéraire*.

As a matter of plain fact I stood in constant fear of running into some hidden snag, and not only foundering but making myself impossible for ever after. In addition, all the money would have been thrown away, and I would have rightly been held responsible.

Well, it turned out not so bad, but it has brought me tremendous new cares and troubles. Not the least of them is over making a living for myself and my family, for I shall probably have to forfeit my position on the "Neue Freie Presse" and run the risk of becoming a financial free-lance. *Mais c'est un engrenage. Quand on y a mis le doigt, il faut y passer tout entier.* [It's the wringer: Put in a cuff and the whole shirt's got to go through.]

I have seen Yildiz Kiosk as it really is—and in doing so have caught a picture which may not be without value for history.

Many times in this diary, I have been compelled to gloss over my original impressions, for I was recording them on the spot, where bad luck or a trick of espionage could have twisted the book into damning evidence. But here and now, aboard a Rumanian ship in the Black Sea, I feel altogether free, safe, and out of it—as that time on the "Dundee" after leaving Jaffa.

Hence anything I may presently write that is favorable to Sultan Abdul Hamid has, for posterity, the full merit of truthfulness. Needless to say, neither his red cordon nor his yellow diamond has influenced me in the least. Such things leave me, as they would any sensible person, entirely cold. They have for me merely political value, which my judgment weighs in impartial scales. I believe that some capital can be made out of these things, which will benefit the movement, strengthen it, increase its influence, and thus hasten its advance.

The Sultan impressed me as a weak, craven, but thoroughly good-natured man. I believe him to be neither clever nor cruel, but a profoundly unhappy prisoner in whose name a thieving, infamous, scoundrelly camarilla perpetrate the vilest abominations. If I didn't have the Zionist movement to look after, I would go and write an article that might help the poor prisoner gain his freedom. I never before had the opportunity of even suspecting the existence of such a troupe of *malfaiteurs*. The indecent clutching for hand-outs, which begins at the palace gate and ends only at the foot of the throne, is probably far from the worst of it. Everything is done for what there is in it, and every official or functionary is a swindler. At least, this is what I heard on all sides, and what I came to learn about the business leads me to believe it is no calumny.

I can only compare that horde of wastrels to a tangle of venomous snakes. The weakest, poorest, and most harmless snake wears a tiny crown. But this particular den of snakes is fixed to appear as though its crowned king-snake were the one that bit and poisoned everything in sight.

The Yildiz gang is your true *bande de malfaiteurs*. Having committed some atrocity, they disperse; and since any number of them were involved, no one is held responsible except the "master" in whose name the deed was done. His name spreads a terror such as could be earned only by the expert cruelty of a criminal seated on a throne, whereas in reality the criminals *surround* the throne. In my idea for a play, "The Master," I had envisioned just such an unprincipled, cowardly set of underlings, enfeebled and demoralized by the slavish fears born of their dependent state in a capitalistic enterprise. But the "master" himself, played by a comedian, was to be a stupid, weak, and ludicrous figure, so that the tragedy of dependence would be brought into greater relief by the very absurdity of the great lord. Our ridiculous Sultan in Constantinople is virtually the embodiment of my conception—but again he is not, for I cannot help pitying him. Perhaps it would deepen the idea of my play if I made the manufacturer, that is, the "master," secretly a bankrupt.

I can see him before me now, the Sultan of this

The visionary: Theodore Herzl.

declining robber empire. Small, shabby, with his badly dyed beard touched up apparently once a week for the *selamlik*, the hooked nose of a Punchinello, the long yellow teeth with a big gap to the right in the upper set, the fez pulled low over his doubtlessly bald head, his stuck-out ears serving, as I say to my friends, as a pants protector—to keep the fez from slipping down below his waist, the feeble hands in their white over-size gloves and the loud-colored cuffs that don't match his suit, the bleating voice, restraint in every word and fear in every glance. And *this* rules!

Only in show, of course, and nominally. But who is the real blackguard behind the grotesque mask of the poor Sultan? Is it the First Secretary Tahsin Bey? Is it the Second Secretary Izzet Bey? Or is it others, whom I didn't know, lurking somewhere among the slime-pits and bracken of that glorious Yildiz Kiosk?

Tahsin is a man of cold impassiveness, Izzet ready for the pounce—like a tiger.

Likely my best piece of work on the present expedition was the way I tamed the tiger Izzet. He is assuredly ready to tear me to pieces at the first opportunity, but for the moment he had to slink away, snarling and craven, his tail between his legs.

And now for those events of yesterday.

May 20, [1901].

Trudel's birthday.

We packed all our trunks and bags the first thing in the morning, preparatory to leaving at noon. Oscar Marmorek had the assignment to get everything ready for our drive to the station, so that even if we turned up at the last moment we could catch the Orient Express.

I wouldn't let Wellisch accompany me this time, for Wolffsohn told me that, on the previous day, he had fingered and sniffed the letter to Tahsin in a rather tell-tale manner. I took Wolffsohn with me to the palace, and he had the letter with the ten thousand francs to hand over to Tahsin in case a *circonstance favorable* could be contrived. I wanted to make a friend of Tahsin, and yet not risk a scandal, a refusal of the money. The turn of events had to be put to account.

Ibrahim was waiting for me when I entered the palace at 9 o'clock. I left Wolffsohn in the ante-room and went with Ibrahim into his office.

First he imparted to me a message from the Sultan. His Imperial Majesty—an awestruck bow at each mention of that hallowed pseudonym—was too occupied to receive me at present, but had requested him, Ibrahim, to communicate to him whatever I had to say. His Imperial Majesty had immediately read my yesterday's letter, or rather, had it translated by the honest Ibrahim. His All-Highest Self had even been pleased to take note of my missive during his postprandial walk. The noble lord was very curious to learn my proposals, the more so as the finances just now were in a sadder state than at any time since the inauguration of his glorious reign. The Sultan had also repeated a number of times my saying about the lion's thorn. Hence I might have the goodness to express my views to Ibrahim; it would come almost to the same thing as submitting them direct to the All-Highest, inasmuch as he would immediately write everything down and transmit it forthwith to the Sultan.

So I set to work, and Ibrahim made notes.

I outlined a sort of systematic presentation, calculated for the feeble brain of His Imperial Majesty the Caliph. My oral *exposé* fell into three parts, which I clarified for poor Ibrahim, and directed him to write down in the following manner:

I. CRITICAL PART

A. Izzet's unification plan is impracticable; and to attempt it, injurious.

B. All loans are inadvisable at present, chiefly because in her present situation Turkey could only obtain money on the most usurious terms—*et encore*!

C. Buying up the bonds of the Public Debt on the stock exchanges should be carried out in complete secrecy by a trustworthy syndicate: An operation which under favorable circumstances might be concluded within three years.

D. Meanwhile, immediate requirements must be provided for, and, in particular, steps taken to meet the £1½ million deficit by October 1st.

E. During that time, however, tapping new sources of revenue should be studied and put into effect. . . .

III. GENERAL CONSIDERATION

We Jews need a protector in the world, and we want this protector (the well-known Lion) to regain his full strength.

Ibrahim wrote and wrote, and made a fair copy of his notes: doing it all on the palm of his hand, which was propped on his knee, Turkish fashion. Meanwhile I asked him to have me announced to Tahsin, to whom I wanted to pay a farewell visit. But Tahsin again sent word that he was engaged; and afterwards he was summoned to His Majesty.

At 11 o'clock Ibrahim had finished, sealed the report reverentially, and sent it to His Imperial Majesty.

A few minutes later, he was called in to the Sultan, as I could see when he slipped on his Turkish court-jacket. When he returned after a brief absence, Tahsin Bey was with him, positively cordial this time—something I couldn't at the moment account for. He pressed my hand, smiled, regretted he hadn't more time for me, and counted with delightful certainty upon seeing me soon again in Constantinople.

Then I had to wait some more. Time was passing; it was already unlikely that I could catch my train. Suddenly the door opened and in pounced the lean and malignant panther Izzet. He held in his hand a paper which I immediately recognized: the strictly confidential *exposé* intended only for His Imperial Majesty, which I had dictated to Ibrahim. The former American Ambassador, Straus, had told me long ago in Vienna that His Imperial Majesty was a "scoundrel." Was this the *secret, secret* he had promised me, with eyes solemnly raised to heaven?

Izzet brandished the paper grimly and triumphantly, as if to say: "What? you never guessed, you Jewish dog, you, that I would get hold of your little proposals and tear your intrigue to pieces!"

He stripped for action. So did I.

"En quoi, Monsieur, le projet de l'unification de la dette est-il nuisible?" he demanded crudely, and I recognized that his thievish scheme had been balked.

At first I gave ground before the onslaught. I endeavored to be polite.

"Je ne dis pas que l'idée n'est pas bonne," I said.

"Ah, elle est donc bonne?" he sneered, and then he turned upon Ibrahim: "Ecrivez!"

So Ibrahim was to draw up a statement, which would evidently be submitted to the Sultan, garnished with lies.

But that *"Ecrivez!"* and Izzet's glance of fury brought home the full danger. He purposed to destroy me and make me impossible in the eyes of the Sultan. I at once recovered my fighting spirit, and said serenely to Ibrahim:

"Oui, Excellence, écrivez—L'idée est bonne et belle, comme il serait beau aussi de voler. . . ."

Izzet's eyes suddenly turned furtive. Did I mean stealing or flying?

I politely added: ". . . de voler dans l'air. But that, under the circumstances, is impossible. And since in attempting an aerial flight you might fall and break something or other, the idea is *nuisible.* The attempt would have no other results than to kite the price of Turkish bonds on the stock market. Besides, the operation itself is unfeasible. You will never find the thirty million pounds needed to begin the funding. And even if you found them, the price, as the result of your purchases, would rise, and the thirty millions would fall far short of enough."

"Ce n'est pas ce que j'ai voulu dire [that's not what I meant]," the rogue said, trying to veer around, for it was precisely what he did say yesterday.

I made it easy enough for him to come round. For of course I wanted to win him over to my side. After I had shown him my fist, I tried to render him pliant by my expression. As Ibrahim was present, I couldn't speak out; I could merely look deep into his eyes and say, "In our hands every financial operation will turn out well for His Majesty's interests. In our hands you will prosper," etc. And many other attractive and inciting *sous-entendus,* while accompanying my words with a wink.

I looked at my watch. We had missed the train.

Then I committed what was perhaps a great mistake, perhaps no mistake at all. I went outside to Wolffsohn and handed him a letter for Tahsin which had been drawn up at the hotel, and asked him to deliver it at once. In it I had written him that I would send him, through Vámbéry, the communication which he had not been willing to receive from Wolffsohn yesterday.

When I re-entered the office, Ibrahim and Izzet, in Turkish manner, arose and did not sit down until I had done so. The conversation proceeded. Izzet was more amenable. We talked about the *resources à créer* [revenues to be created]. His Imperial Majesty proposed to offer me the exploitation of five monopolies: mines, oilfields, etc. Presumably it meant that we were to raise the money for the purpose. They'd like to bleed us. I looked agreeable and dense: That would all be possible.

Then Izzet blurted out:

"We need about four million pounds in the near future. We've ordered warships, etc. In short, roughly four million is what we need. Could you get them for us?"

"I think it possible. I should have to consult my friends. Everything depends on what attitude His Majesty would adopt toward us Jews."

"What is your idea," Izzet asked, "for raising and covering such a loan?"

I still didn't wish to speak about the charter, but angled for their continued interest, and I said I should let them know in three or four weeks, after consultation with my friends.

It was, I believe, at this point that Ismail Hakki Bey, Tahsin's confidential dragoman, came in, and with a distinctly frigid air—obviously on purpose, because of the presence of Ibrahim and the mortal enemy Izzet—asked me the nature of the communication mentioned in my letter. Tahsin requested me to send him the communication through Ismail.

Izzet pricked up his ears, and I saw him give Ibrahim a knowing look. They guessed that it had to do with money. I found the whole thing beyond me. Did Tahsin want to nail my attempt at bribery to the counter, or was he simply demanding the cash? Since I wasn't clear on how they work things here, but knew well enough that I was in the presence of the enemy, I told Ismail in an off-hand way that it was something Prof. Vámbéry had asked me to communicate to Tahsin and which I would write him before I left.

Ismail Hakki went out, angrily.

We pursued our talk, which now reached an unexpected climax. His Imperial Majesty asked—through Izzet and Ibrahim—how I envisaged the future citizenship of those Jews who in one form or another would do business with Turkey or inside Turkish territory.

"The Israelites can come in," said Izzet in his barbarous French, "but they must become Ottoman subjects. For example, if you buy in the bonds of the Public Debt, the members [of the syndicate?] will have to become subjects of His Imperial Majesty. Also, the same for those who enter as colonists. They must not only become Turkish subjects, but they must renounce their previous allegiance and show proof of this renunciation, attested to by the government in question."

"And perform military service," said Ibrahim, "if His Majesty calls them to the colors."

"Under these conditions we could take in here the Israelites of every land," remarked Izzet, pleasantly, like a hyena.

I thought to myself: "The devil you will!" It would just suit Messrs. Izzet & Co. that we should bring them in, rich and poor, to be plundered. But it was not the moment to raise objections in dealing with blackguards from whom, in any case, every paragraph of a charter will have to be bought.

Accordingly, I affected delight at the prospect of coming under the old reliable and glorious sceptre of Abdul Hamid, and declared that I was ready to enter into details.

"Also," continued Izzet, "colonization must not have a mass character. Instead, let us say, five families here and five there—scattered, without connections."

"The easier to plunder and slay them," I told myself, as I assumed a contented and convinced expression.

"Although I should not have the slightest objection to such a dispersion," I said, "there are nevertheless technical and economic difficulties which militate against this method. Last year, as we know, His Majesty was graciously pleased to place some land in Anatolia at the disposal of Rumanian Jewish refugees. Notwithstanding all my gratitude for this great magnanimity I was opposed to these scattered settlements, because they lack an economic basis. Such haphazard forms of immigration are not to be encouraged. They serve no purpose.

"What could be done, however, is to organize a great land company, to which uncultivated territory could be assigned, and which would then proceed to establish settlers on it. In Palestine, of course, there is plenty of land for such a purpose. If this land company, which would no doubt have to be an Ottoman corporation, received a suitable concession, it could make the land arable, settle people, and pay taxes. On the prospective income of such a company, money might perhaps be borrowed in advance. There you would have at once a new *resource*."

In that inoffensive form I propounded the charter to the Sultan's representatives for the first time, and was content to let the suggestions sink in.

It will be time enough to elaborate the matter at subsequent negotiations, and money will dissipate all the misgivings of honest Izzet and his likes.

Izzet disappeared, it was transparent, in order to repeat to His Majesty all that I had said. Presently he returned with a farewell message from His Majesty, who expects my definite proposals within a month.

Thus we have actually entered upon negotiations for the charter. It needs now only luck, skill, and money, to put through everything I have planned.

At the present stage, I am giving the grant of a

charter more or less the character of a favor rendered us in order to awaken our sympathies for the Turkish Empire.

Et nous verrons après.

These were the noteworthy incidents of May 20, 1901, the ninth birthday of my daughter Trudel.

So far there is nothing very tangible in the results, and yet I already see in them the embryo of the perfected whole.

Is it a law of nature that the more intently you look at the vision the more it fades, the less comprehensible it becomes? The more I think of Herzl the more inexplicable he is. Why a Hungarian Jew, brought up in Vienna, who became a Zionist in Paris? In Hungary he could only have seen Jews assimilating with romantic ardor. Vienna, in the days of Herzl's youth, was the scene of internal Jewish decomposition—decomposition without tragedy, without regret. It was a gay, waltzing decomposition. And life in Paris in the 90s, for a young correspondent of a rich and famous paper, a handsome young fellow like Theodor Herzl at that, must have been the most ideal imaginable for forgetting all the troubles of the world, let alone the troubles of being a Jew.

True enough that in all three countries he would have observed various forms of anti-Semitism, especially in the Vienna of Lord Mayor Lueger. And in Paris there was the Dreyfus Affair. Yet we know that blows alone are not enough to make a man a Zionist. There must be some positive Jewish seed, and where in Herzl did that come from?

There is another, a still greater mystery. Where did the magic force come from that in the space of seven short years transformed the face and the soul of a people such as we are? All our leading men today have had to toil twice and thrice seven years before they could attain the position of being leaders. And here comes a stranger, writes a book, and he is immediately the leader.

You will say it was because of the pleasant surprise of a man like Herzl coming from "outside." Or because Jews were flattered that Herzl was an important journalist in the Christian world. I think this may explain some of the mystery. It may be enough for the beginning, for the first sensation. But congresses and world organizations are not built on pleasant surprises and flattering personal positions. And after you have held a congress and founded a world organization it must take more than seven years for it to materialize, to be noticed and recognized, even as a hostile force. Let alone as a leading body. Yet here comes a stranger, speaks a word, and seven years later he dies and leaves behind him—where there was previously a man—a nation.

Of course the secret is that Herzl was a born leader. But what is a leader? I can't remember the word leader in any common use among Jews in Herzl's time. I don't think it was. Nor was it general among the nations in whose midst we lived. England was the only country where the word leader was known, but there it meant something quite different. The leader was the chairman of a committee, a kind of manager who could be dismissed at a moment's notice. He was certainly not the superman who is followed blindly. In Russia people would have laughed at anyone who talked of a leader. A movement was directed by a committee, which might or might not have a chairman. In the Latin countries no one had yet heard of such a thing as a political leader. The French language even now has no equivalent for this term. Even the Italian word *duce* is not Italian. It did not exist in the ordinary language till 1922. It is an adaptation of the Latin word *dux*, specially introduced for Mussolini.

It is different today, when it has become the fashion almost everywhere to have a "leader," so that if there is no one fit for the position it goes to someone who is not fit for it. So long as there is somebody to bear the title. And we Jews, who even in our Zionism are firm believers in the virtues of assimilation, follow the general trend, with the same result.

And since there is, alas, no superman, we get hold of an ordinary man, and we thrust the title on him. If he is a fool he accepts it, struts around, and tries to play the part. And we have no lack of fools. I think I know all the Jewish parties, and I can honestly say that there isn't a single born leader among the lot of them. Yet some bear the title, and a few, I am sorry to say, are inclined to take it seriously. And I know of at least another dozen who are candidates for the title, overtly or covertly.

The present-day conception has indeed wandered far from its philological source. The English term leader meant in actual fact the man who did what his party told him. A leader in the modern sense is a man who has been given authority to do all the thinking for the entire party. A program agreed upon at a conference means nothing now. The only thing that counts is what the leader of the moment thinks is necessary. It is useless for anyone to show logically, with facts and arguments, that this or the other is unwise. The answer is always that the leader knows best, and that if it were unwise he wouldn't do it.

One must indeed be a superman to wear such a crown of omniscience. In actual practice, however, the official "leaders" always act under the influence of a general vote, it is the influence of chance favorites. Our children will gasp in amazement when the naked truth will be revealed one day about these "leaders," who swarm in so many countries now, and they see that most of them were really only tools in the hands of those who happened to be close to them.

It is hard to understand the mentality of those who pray for "leaders" and are happy when they have found a "leader." Things were different when I was young, and I am of the opinion that they were much better than they are now. It was our belief that every movement consists of people who are equal. Each is a prince or a king. When elections come it is not individuals who are chosen, but programs. Those who are elected are the instruments to carry out the program. We, the mass of the people, listen to them and obey them not because they are leaders, but because we have

elected them to do what we want done. When you have voluntarily appointed a number of people and told them to work for you, it is your duty to assist them, or depose them. You do not obey their will, but your own will, expressed in the election.

There were a good many contradictions of course in this doctrine, which was held by all who belonged to the generation of my youth. It was often too a fiction, as all human doctrines are; but I prefer it to what we have now. There is more pride and glory in it, though it bears the discredited name "democracy."

Herzl was an entirely different kind of "leader." To him it was no title, nor a predestined function. People simply obeyed him, and therefore he was their leader.

There is a term in Russian that is more appropriate than the word "leader." In past generations a beloved and venerated thinker was called "ruler of thought." Michailovsky, a publicist of the 80s, who didn't belong to any party, was described in this way. That is what Herzl was. He ruled our thoughts. It was a fact, not an office.

In other words, it was real. Real leaders are born rarely, and often they are recognized by the fact that they have no desire, no claim to lead. Following them is not a matter of discipline. You follow them as you follow raptly a wonderful voice. Because the melody expresses our own yearning, our own desire. There is one other point. A Herzl, when he dies, remains our leader, even thirty years after and longer.

Weizmann

Chaim Weizmann, the leader of world Zionism from around 1915 to the late-1930s, the man most responsible for the Balfour Declaration of 1917 that committed Britain to a "Jewish National Home" in Palestine, a cofounder of the Hebrew University and founder of Weizmann Institute of Science in Rehoveth, Israel, and the first President of Israel, left behind a voluminous archive of biographical material. Two historians, Jehudah Reinharz, the current President of Brandeis University, and Norman Rose of the Hebrew University, have now gone through this material and published authoritative biographies.

There are only two things in Weizmann's life that are open to criticism: He had a penchant for expensive underwear and, depressed by being evicted from leadership of the World Zionist Organization in the late 1930s, he perhaps was not as voluble he might have been in demanding that Winston Churchill do something to stop the Holocaust. Otherwise, Weizmann looms as not only a great leader and visionary but also as an extremely capable politician and administrator, and a scientist and educator of the first rank. It appears that following an old Talmudic and ghetto tradition, about remuneration of a Jewish community leader, he did not even draw a salary from a Zionist organization after the early 1920s when litigation established his control of remunerative patents to chemical munitions formulae that he developed for the British military in the First World War. His handsome house on the grounds of the Weizmann Institute, which is now a museum, was built with his own money.

Weizmann came from an affluent Polish family and was sent to be educated in Germany, where he received a Ph.D. in chemistry. He then got a job teaching at the University of Manchester, which was fortunate for him and his vivacious wife Vera because Manchester had a small but very wealthy Jewish community. Through the Manchester Jewish business magnates, he established good personal relations with aristocrats and prominent politicians in both the Liberal and Conservative parties, making possible the maneuvers that brought about the Balfour Declaration.

Weizmann was a man of the highest integrity and probity in any area of life. For example, he founded the Weizmann Institute of Science because he felt that the academic standards of the Hebrew University were not high enough. Politically he was slightly right of center. While not opposed to a welfare state in Zion, he thought that the Jewish state required heavy capitalist investment and should not go to extremes in a socialist direction. Time and experience has fully sustained this judgment.

These selections from Weizmann's letters and other writings, skillfully edited by Barnet Litvinoff to demonstrate the mind and temperament of a very great man.

Palestine is not an empty country. It contains today about six hundred thousand non-Jews, the overwhelming majority Moslems, a small minority of Christians and another small minority of Jews. Roughly, there are five hundred thousand Moslems, one hundred thousand Christians and one hundred thousand Jews. We recognize that since the war, and even earlier, there has been a striving on the part of the Arab people for a revival; and being anxious for the revival of the scattered Jewish people, we treat with respect and reverence any attempt of revival amongst other people. We are the last, and should be the last, to look down on other people and say: "You cannot do it." We shall assume that Arab culture will blossom again as it had in Spain, as it had when Europe was completely in darkness, for it was the Arab people together with the Jews who were the bearers of the torch and the preservers of civilization, who prepared and paved the way for the great renaissance which followed. We recognize today that between us and the Arabs in the Near East, and particularly in Palestine, stand many forces—perhaps destructive forces—which

The statesman: Chaim Weizmann.

try to emphasize this estrangement which has taken place between two races which are akin to each other. But we also see at present in Palestine that the tendency which was so marked three or four years ago, the tendency of two entrenched camps watching each other with suspicion, is gradually declining. We are trying to cooperate with them. We work with them. We are looked upon with a certain amount of suspicion. We are looked upon with suspicion particularly because to the Eastern races we represent the West, and the West is looked upon with suspicion at present in the Near East. The various tribulations through which Europe and the East is passing today, Bolshevism, Kemalism, the unsettlement of European affairs, the fact that no conference of European Powers comes to any definite issue, all this reflects on the fancy of an Oriental people. Every rumour in the Press is exaggerated. Every vibration in the political world is reflected and exaggerated in Palestine.

Palestine is a peculiar country. There is no other country in the world where the distance between the sublime and the ridiculous is so small. One stands constantly with one foot in the sublime, for eighteen generations gaze down. Palestine is like a sounding-board. Every noise is blazoned forth over the world. If a Jew is killed in Piccadilly, in the Ukraine, or run over by a motor-car on Broadway, it is an ordinary affair. If something of this kind happens in the Holy Land, it becomes an act of state, an act of violence, two races clashing with each other. All these factors, the unsettlement in Europe, the tribulations of Europe, mental and moral strife, contribute to make life in Palestine much more difficult than elsewhere.

From a speech to Jewish journalists. New York, 13 March 1923.

PALESTINE IS NOT RHODESIA

I admit that by a political impression, by an effective speech or demonstration, some minister or official may be influenced, but that is only for the moment. Once the moment has passed there comes the reaction for which one has permanently to pay. I will not conceal from Jabotinsky, and certainly I am making no personal attack (it is hardly necessary to say that our personal relations remain those that are customary among gentlemen): I helped you against the will of my friends according to the measure of my powers at the time of the raising of the Legion, because at that time I could go along with you. I would, however, regard such a demand today not only as useless but even as harmful. The key to the situation lies in another direction. Not in the 900,000 dunams which the government can or cannot give us. Not in the *Machlul* lands, not on the hills of Judea, the cultivation of which costs perhaps twenty times as much as the government has to be paid for rent. The key lies in opening up the Near East to Jewish initiative in real friendship and cooperation with the Arabs. Palestine must be built up without disturbing a hair of the legitimate interests of the Arabs. The Zionist Congress must not confine itself to platonic formulae. It must recognize the fact that Palestine is not Rhodesia, but that six hundred thousand Arabs are there who, from the point of view of international justice, have just as much right to their life in Palestine as we have to our National Home.

Don't call me a fanatic, or a narrow-minded man. Zionism exercises its Maccabean force of attraction and its greatness as a freedom movement so long as it solves the Jewish question radically, or strives to do so. The moment it chases after transient successes at the expense of Jewish distress the gates are opened wide for the politics of the ghetto.

From a letter to Judah L. Magnes. Manchester, 13 February 1906.

ABNORMAL SITUATION

Zionism is often briefly defined as a solution, or rather *the* solution, of the Jewish question. The Jewish question consists in the endeavour to bring about an adjustment of the Jews to their environment, and Zionism maintains that the only effective adjustment can be achieved by a restoration of the Jewish people to their ancestral country. Whatever country we examine in which Jews are settled in large numbers, we find the position abnormal. In Russia and Galicia there are compact masses of Jewry who live a life of their own, preserving the culture of ancient times, and producing a literature of their own at the present day. But the confinement of the Jews to the Russian Pale and their voluntary seclusion from the national life in Galicia are both abnormal phenomena.

Russia is frank in its hatred of the Jews, and tries its best to crush them out of existence. As for the Jews of Galicia, the mere fact that they pursue their own national life in an alien environment and upon alien soil inevitably produces something unnatural in their character. In Western Europe, Jews participate very freely and largely in the life of their respective countries, socially and politically. Nevertheless they find it necessary constantly to emphasize that they are Frenchmen, or Germans, and so forth. In France, the great majority of Jews are differentiated in very few respects from ordinary Frenchmen; in appearance, habits, views and prejudices, they are very much alike. And yet the Jews in France feel compelled every now and again to assert their French citizenship, as though fearing they might be suspected of disloyalty. This tendency of Jews towards chauvinism can be observed in every country in Western Europe, and to a certain extent it is evident even in Eastern Europe.

From this it may be gathered the Jews never feel rooted in the country of their residence. However comfortably they might be established, they can hardly be animated by the same sentiments and traditions that fill the hearts and minds of their fellow-citizens. The reason has nothing to do with patriotism. It is simply a question of history. The Jew, with his long, glorious and chequered history, and thousands of years, cannot help feeling somewhat apart in relation to the modern country in which he lives—a country which, even upon the most liberal reckoning, began to have a continuous history only some hundreds of years after the downfall of the Jewish State. As for the culture of his native country, the Jew feels he is above it; in other words, his own life has grown up from a different moist soil. The Jew might even contribute to the culture of his country, to its science, its learning, its general advancement; but the Jewish people obtain no profit from this. The persecution in an Eastern country would not be less because Jews had contributed to the improvement of Western countries. Surely such a position must seem unfair and unjust to all who consider the Jewish people as a whole. So much energy is put forth in producing for others, so much energy expended in the mere effort of self-preservation, and yet if only the same amount of energy were applied in a positive direction in a Jewish land it would be productive of such great national benefits.

It should also be noted that the Jew is very adaptable, no matter in what country he settles; but the culture he picks up in each successive place is superficial. He remains a Jew after all. Zionism contends that the abnormal position involved by the dispersion of the Jews should be brought to an end, and that this can be accomplished only by a national rehabilitation on a territory of our own. There are some who say that any territory will do. But as a Zionist I maintain that only one territory can answer the desired purpose—the land of Palestine. I shall not enter into questions of climate, soil and politics. I would simply remind you of the long history and the innumerable traditions that bind the soul of the Jew to Palestine. To cut the future of the Jewish people off from that country would damage its moral development; it would produce a new type, which would not be a natural and normal development from the past. We have only to remember how, throughout our dispersion, we planted a moral Palestine in our communities. That will bring home to you how intimately the Jewish soul is knit with the idea of a return to that country. To be a Zionist it is only necessary to be convinced of the necessity of rebuilding the Jewish nation in the Holy Land. It is not necessary, in the first place, to be convinced that the idea can be carried out. But those who are convinced of the ideal will surely be animated by sufficient enthusiasm to do everything in their power, to the extent of personal sacrifice, to translate the ideal into reality.

From a lecture to London University Zionist Society. 21 March 1909.

SWINGING BETWEEN EXTREMES

The Jews are strong enough not to disappear completely and too weak to be able to lead an independent existence. So in every relationship, and dearest might have been saved. When millions died, a few thousand escaped, but even the thought of their rescue is marred: It is associated with the images of the *Patria* and the *Struma*, with the deportations from Athlit Camp, and exile to Mauritius. The mental torture which Palestine Jewry has suffered explains the madness of some, and the direction it takes.

This emotional background does not imply sympathy with the violent methods of the groups, which every responsible Jew, in Palestine and elsewhere, condemns. But it should be remembered in handling the situation. The Palestine authorities can arrest and shoot a hundred Jews, and after that five hundred, etc., but if they do so while continuing their present policy and methods in Palestine, they will implant a Sinn Fein mentality in a hundred thousand.

From a memorandum to Jan C. Smuts. London, 4 May 1944.

MOST TERRIBLE CALAMITY

The terrorist acts in Palestine are the most terrible calamity that could befall us; they are already doing us incalculable harm, and will do worse if they continue. I have been trying my level best, directly and indirectly, to impress upon the *Yishuv* that they have to do everything in their power to stop it.

From a letter to Abba Hillel Silver. London, 18 October 1944.

RELIGION SHALL NOT CONTROL THE STATE

Many questions will emerge in the formative stages of the State with regard to religion. There are powerful religious communities in Palestine which now, under a democratic regime, will rightly demand to assert themselves. I think it is our duty to make it clear to them from the very beginning that whereas the State will treat with the highest respect the true religious feelings of the community, it cannot put the clock back by making religion the cardinal principle in the conduct of the State. Religion should be relegated to the synagogue and the homes of those families that want it; it should occupy a special position in the schools; but it shall not control the ministries of State.

I have never feared really religious people. The genuine type has never been politically aggressive; on the contrary, he seeks no power, he is modest and retiring—and modesty was the great feature in the lives of our saintly rabbis and sages in olden times. It is the new, secularized type of rabbi, resembling somewhat a member of a clerical party in Germany, France or Belgium, who is the menace, and who will make a heavy bid for power by parading his religious convictions. It is useless to point out to such people that they transgress a fundamental principle which has been laid down by our sages: "Thou shalt not make of the Torah a crown to glory in, or a spade to dig with." There will be a great struggle. I foresee something which will perhaps be reminiscent of the *Kulturkampf* in Germany, but we must be firm if we are to survive; we must have a clear line of demarcation between legitimate religious aspirations and the duty of the State towards preserving such aspirations, on the one hand, and on the other hand the lust for power which is sometimes exhibited by pseudo-religious groups.

From Trial and Error.

Ben-Gurion

David Ben-Gurion, the first prime minister and the main founder of the State of Israel in 1948, was, like Weizmann, from an affluent Polish family. Also like Weizmann, he was fiercely dedicated to Zionism from an early age and was a man of great courage and charismatic qualities. But otherwise, Ben-Gurion, who pushed Weizmann out of the leadership of world Zionism in the late-1930s and condescended to invite Weizmann to be the first President of Israel (a powerless position) only after Einstein declined, was very different than Weizmann both in ideas and character.

Ben-Gurion came to Palestine as a young man in the Second Aliyah (immigration wave) before the First World War. He was already a vehement socialist but in spite of his life-long affiliation with the commitment to the kibbutz movement, the first source of his political power, he actually spent only a few months as a kibbutz worker. Ben-Gurion was in fact from the start a professional politician—it was his sole interest and career. By the 1930s he was the head of both the kibbutz movement and the Histadrut, the national labor union that was also a corporate giant, and by far the most powerful leader within the yishuv, the Jewish community in Palestine. He formed a coalition of socialist parties into the Mapai which ruled Israel until 1977. His taste for power was insatiable.

When in late-1947 the British suddenly announced their early withdrawal from the country and most of it appeared ready to fall into Arab hands, Ben-Gurion showed the greatest courage in declaring the existence of the State of Israel and willingness to fight to the death against well-armed Palestinians and the powerful Jordanese army to back up this declaration of independence.

Until 1945 Ben-Gurion was fortunate in having the quiet collaboration of Beryl Katznelson in administrating the affairs of the yishuv. Ben-Gurion himself was not a good administrator, and his record as prime minister in the late 1950s is a checkered one. Neither he nor his ministers were free of petty corruption. Yet under his aegis, Israel incorporated a million refugees from Europe and a like amount from Arab lands, and established the economic and political foundations of a modern state as well as building up a great military machine. He did nothing to solve the Arab problem and the state he created was unwisely overcommitted to socialist control of the economy.

In his early years, Ben-Gurion was not an impressive speaker. When he visited America in 1916, the head of the Zionist organization in Milwaukee—a school teacher who under the name of Golda Meyer was later a successor to Ben-Gurion as prime minister of Israel—told him not to come to her city because she heard he was a bad speaker in any language. Over time Ben-Gurion became a powerful, if forever long-winded, public speaker in the Eastern European manner and in his later years, with his broad face, husky body, and shock of white hair, an instantly recognizable iconic figure matching Herzl and Weismann in the Zionist pantheon.

Ben-Gurion had almost no formal postsecondary education. He was, however, an autodidact, read widely in history and philosophy, and was an avid collector of books and thought of himself as an intellectual. This speech, delivered after the Six Day War in 1967 had thoroughly vindicated his policies and towards the end of his life is characteristic of his ideas, his learning, and the texture of his rhetoric.

Every man has a conscience and the faculty within himself to discern between right and wrong. That is the meaning, at least to me, of Elijah's still, small voice and of Jeremiah's counsel.

I am not religious, nor were the majority of the early builders of modern Israel believers. Yet their passion for this land stemmed from the Book of Books. That is why the socialists of the Bilu movement named themselves with reference to Ezra. And it is why, though I reject theology, the single most important book in my life is the Bible.

Like many Jews, no doubt because of early traditional training, I have a fondness for study. I have read in various cultures, all of which have made me richer as an individual. I learned Greek so that I could enjoy Plato, for whom I have deep respect and who has given me many happy and speculative hours. I have also studied Hindu and Buddhist thought. From Plato, one learns elegance in reasoning; from Hinduism humility; from Buddhism the peace that comes of meditation. But from Torah one principally learns a moral activism that characterizes the Jews and that, I believe, has made them so admired and so detested whenever they have lived among others.

Jewish history in dispersion is a stormy one, ranging to extreme high points and to the lowest depths. In accordance with the dictum that evil outlasts good in human memory, we are particularly sensitive to the continual sufferings inflicted upon us during our two-thousand-year journey round the civilized world and back to Israel again. But the Jews were also respected of their fellow men. They flourished in Islam for many centuries, helping to guide the destiny of this daughter culture. And they are the architects of Christianity.

Who could have been more of a purist in Judaism than Jesus?

Jews are activists, that is they have a Messianic spirit. They are not missionaries since they don't seek to convert others to their ways. But they are merciless with themselves. The Bible has imparted to them that divine discontent leading at its best to initiatives such as the pioneering life, at its worst to persecution by their fellow men. It has never allowed them as a people to enjoy for long comfortable mediocrity.

Certainly in Israel today we are Messianic. The Jews feel themselves to have a mission here; they have a sense of mission. Restoration of sovereignty is tied to a concept of redemption. This had determined Jewish survival and it is the core of Jewish religious, moral and national consciousness. It explains the immigration to Israel of hundreds of thousands of Jews who never heard of Zionist doctrine but who, nevertheless, were moved to leave the lands wherein they dwelt to contribute with their own effort to the revival of the Hebrew nation in its historic home.

A secular vision of the Bible must examine the postulate of the Jews as a Chosen People. I believe firmly that the true situation in history was the reverse of what the phrase implies. I think the Jews chose their God and not, as Torah puts it, that He chose us. . . .

When I came to Israel, language was a big issue. At that time, the overwhelming majority of immigrants were coming from Russia and Eastern Europe. They all spoke Yiddish. So there was a sizable move to adopt this "Jewish" language as the official tongue here. Yet, despite the fact that Yiddish really was a *lingua franca* among the Jews of the day, we didn't declare it the speech of

The political leader: Ben-Gurion proclaiming the State of Israel, May 15, 1948.

Eretz Israel. Why? Because its association was basically one of sadness, of exile, of loss and of persecution.

So others said: "Let's speak German. It's close to Yiddish and easy, therefore, to learn. And it is universal, one of the great languages of the world." Had we decided to speak German, we would today be communicating in the tongue of those who destroyed European Jewry. Not only that; while trying to destroy us they successfully destroyed themselves in large measure. Today, German is just one among many European languages and the Germans themselves are all busy learning either English or Russian depending on which side of an artificial boundary they live on. These are the two great tongues of the moment, with English leading the field.

At Independence, it was obvious that English would be the most useful vehicle of world communication. And we were coming to nationhood under British tutelage. We could have decided to make this our national tongue. Of course, by that time the argument was academic since we were all speaking Hebrew and enjoying it.

However, suppose we had become English-speakers. Again, as with German, we should be adopting someone else's culture. We, the oldest civilized people in the West! That would have been ridiculous. And how do we know that in fifty years English won't be a secondary language with Chinese replacing it at the top of the Tower of Babel?

Had we decided to adopt the language of current fashion, we might have found ourselves having to change official tongues every twenty-five years or so. History is a far better guide. So we opted for our natural speech, the language of our inheritance, our sovereignty and our association with this part of the world.

At once, everything became simple. We brought it up to date so that we could discuss problems of microbiology and nuclear physics in Hebrew, and yet at the same time every inhabitant here possessed the tool to unlock the treasure of his culture to its earliest known record. We had in depth what we lacked in breadth.

For this reason I must say to my friends in the Galuth, in dispersion, that it is not we who have lost contact with you by resuscitating our cultural vehicle and making it live again. Rather, it is you who have cut yourselves off from your roots by denying yourselves knowledge of your own language. If there is a communication gap between the Jewish world and Israel, it is up to the former to close it. We are making history, living history. The Jew in Argentina, France, the United States, India, Russia, New Zealand, South Africa and elsewhere is a watcher on the sidelines. Sometimes, as in the Soviet Union or Iraq, he is a prisoner and forced to stay behind as his people advance. That is a personal tragedy, and a tragedy we share since his absence, his inability to contribute to our Jewish life, is a gap that can never be filled— just as the death of six million potential Israelis in Europe is an overwhelming tragedy for us here today.

But life must continue in the face of sorrow and disaster. The Jewish redemption is here and it is now. We are very privileged to live at a time when we are not forced to survive culturally on mysticism and dreams. It is not next year in Jerusalem but today!

The Jews of the world are coming to realize this, and they are making a choice. Many will cease to be Jews, will assimilate into other cultural traditions. We wish them well. But many more will see their link with us and reach over to grasp our hand of friendship. They will learn Hebrew, will come and will cherish their reinsertion into history.

And I am sure that now we are home again, we shall once more be creative as a people. We have already begun to be so. Today, we are in the process of writing a new Torah not only with scribes but with pioneers and farmers, artists and scientists, architects, teachers, engineers, legislators, collectivists, citizens in every walk of life. All speak the language of Moses and even the freethinkers among them study deeply in the Book, the source of inspiration, provider of a past and of a vision for the future. Our new Torah is being written now but its best chapters are still to come. It is my conviction that they will tell the story of our taming of the desert.

Ahad Ha'Am

Among the three Eastern European Jews who dominated the Zionist movement after Herzl's premature death, Asher Ginzberg, who wrote as Ahad Ha'Am ("One of the People"), is today much less known to the public than Weizmann and Ben-Gurion. There is, however, an excellent 1993 biography of Ahad Ha'Am by Steven J. Zipperstein that has restored some of the iconic luster he enjoyed in the second and third decades of the century.

Ahad Ha'Am, from an aristocratic Hasidic family, was a product of the Odessa cultural renaissance at the beginning of the century. Nevertheless, his firm commitment to making Hebrew rather than Yiddish the international language of Zionism and the Zionist homeland contributed importantly to the decline of the Yiddish-speaking Odessa-based renaissance.

Unlike Weizmann and Ben-Gurion, Ahad Ha'Am (who immigrated to Palestine only shortly before his death in 1927) saw the new Israel not as a political homeland drawing in the dispersed people, but a moral and cultural center for World Jewry. For a long time this view of Israel was marginalized,

This idea of Israel as the Supernation might be expanded and amplified into a complete system. For the profound tragedy of our spiritual life in the present day is perhaps only a result of our failure to justify in practice the potentialities of our election. On the one hand, there still lives within us, though it be only in the form of an instinctive feeling, a belief in that moral fitness for which we were chosen from all the nations, and in that national mission which consists in living the highest type of moral life, in being the moral Supernation. But, on the other hand, since the day when we left the Ghetto, and started to partake of the world's life and its civilization, we cannot help seeing that our superiority is potential merely. Actually we are not superior to other nations even in the sphere of morality. We have been unable to fulfill our mission in exile, because we could not make our lives a true expression of our own character, independent of the opinion or the will of others. And so it may even be that many of our latter-day Zionists, who base their Zionism on economic and political grounds, and scoff at the national "election" and the moral "mission"—it may even be that many of these have been driven to Zionism simply by force of this contrast between the possibilities and the actualities of Jewish history: being forced thereby, all unconsciously, to seek some firm resting-place for their people, in order that it may have the opportunity once more of developing its genius for morality, and fulfilling its "mission" as the Supernation.

But enough. I mean no more than to show that the doctrine of the "transvaluation of values" is really capable of being assimilated by Judaism, and of enriching Judaism without doing violence to its spirit, by introducing "ideas which are new, but not foreign," or, rather, by introducing ideas which are not even essentially new. For, more than eight hundred years ago there lived a Jewish philosopher-poet, Rabbi Jehudah Halevi, who recognized the inner meaning and value of the election of Israel, and made it the foundation of his system, very much on the lines of what I have said above, though in a different style.

And now what have our young writers done with this doctrine?

They have neglected what is essentially original in it, and have seized only on the new phrase and the Aryan element which its author introduced: and with these they come to their own people, as with a medicine to cure the diseases of its old age. For them the essential thing is not the emancipation of the superior type from its subservience to the multitude; it is the emancipation of physical life from its subservience to the limiting power of the spirit. Such a point of view as this can never ally itself with Judaism. No wonder, then, that they feel a "cleft in their souls," and begin to cry, "Transvaluation! New values! Let the Book give place to the sword, and the Prophets to the fair beast!" This cry has become especially prominent during the last year; and we are told every day that our whole world must be destroyed root and branch, and rebuilt all over again. But we are never told how you can destroy with one breath the national foundation of an ancient people, or how you can build up a new life for a nation after destroying the very essence of its being, and stifling its historic soul.

One can understand—and one can tolerate—the individual Jew who is captivated by the Superman in Nietzsche's sense; who bends the knee to Zarathustra, throws off his allegiance to the Prophets, and goes about to regulate his own private life in accordance with these new values. But it is difficult to understand, and still more difficult to tolerate, the extraordinary proceeding of these men, who offer such a new law of life as this to the whole nation, and are simple enough to think that it can be accepted by a people which, almost from the moment of its first appearance in the world's history, has existed only to protest vehemently and unceasingly on behalf of the rights of the spirit against those of the strong arm and the sword; which, from time immemorial to the present day, has derived all its spiritual strength simply from its steadfast faith in its moral mission, in its obligation and its capacity to approach nearer than other nations to the ideal of moral perfection. This people, they fondly imagine, could suddenly, after thousands of years, change its values, forgo its national preeminence in the moral sphere, in order to become "the tail of the lion" in the sphere of the sword; could overthrow the mighty temple which it has built to the God of righteousness, in order to set up in its place a mean and lowly altar (it has no strength for more) to the idol of physical force. . . . was not for the existence of the Book in itself, but for its petrifaction. I lamented the fact that its development has been arrested, that it no longer corresponds to the inner moral feeling, as it used to do, in the earlier days of Jewish history, when "the voice of God in the heart of man" used to draw its inspiration direct from the phenomena of life and nature, and the Book itself was compelled to change its contents little by little, imperceptibly, in order to conform to the moral consciousness of the people. And so I was not advocating the dominance of the sword over the Book; I was pleading for the dominance of that moral force which was implanted in our people centuries ago, which itself produced the Book, and renewed the spirit of the Book in each successive period, according to its own needs.

PART TEN

ALTERNATIVE INTIMATIONS

INTRODUCTION

What is recognized as mainstream Jewish culture by the Jewish press, Judaic Studies departments, the Israeli political elite, American Jewish billionaires and the organizations they control directly or inferentially, and the overwhelming majority—to the point of near unanimity—of Conservative, Reform, and conventional Orthodox rabbis, is a relatively benign, politically correct, and moderately and humanistically liberal set of assumptions and attitudes. But it is a narrow, dry, quite placid and homogeneous texture of ideas and assumptions.

A world governed by these principles would be rough for the Palestinians and underprivileged for other Arabs, but would be otherwise progressive and decent in the conventional liberal sense. It is also a stagnant cultural world that excludes some of the best Jewish minds, that marginalizes pejoratively less mainstream religious behavior, and that drives out of connection with collective Jewry thousands of intellectuals, artists, scientists, behavioral scientists, journalists, academics, and professionals, especially in the U.S.A. but also in Canada, Britain, France, and in a kind of internal exilic way even in Israel itself.

A recent book about American Jews by Jack Wertheimer, a historical sociologist at the Jewish Theological Seminary in New York was called *A Divided People* and the title is apt. A recent sociological study on American Jews by Seymour Lipset anticipate disaffiliation with Jewish religion and historical culture of millions of American Jews in coming decades. If you spoke with the younger, college-age Israelis as far back as the late 1980s, you would discover that the majority there also had lost their taste for collective energy, communal efforts, war, and the whole romantic side of Zionism. They want good education, good professional jobs, consumer goods, and quiet private and family lives. They are almost as distant from Ben-Gurion as they are from the Bal Shem Tov.

All social issues are ultimately cultural, are related to attitudes, perceptions, artistic forms, and intellectual pursuits and lifestyles grounded in sets of theoretical principles. All politics, all power systems, all social ideologies are grounded in cultural discourse and intellectual systems. The destiny of the Jews, absent a Hitler or Stalin, and assuming some kind of accommodation with the Arabs, depends on the capacity to break out of the existing narrow mainstream cultural circle to new vistas and radical horizons.

With the most widely read official organs of Jewish opinions in the English language, *Commentary* magazine, and the international edition of *The Jerusalem Post*, in the hands of militant intellectual and political conservatives who would like to narrow the present circle of Jewish thought, let alone expand it; with the Judaic Studies professors assuming partisan positions, and taking the conventional byways through the Jewish past, resisting any reconsideration of received standards and criteria; the prospect of Jewish collective survival, the forestalling of a loss of identity by half of the Jews in the world within three decades through movements of cultural revolution and intellectual renaissance is a bleak one.

But there always within Jewish culture, always in the writings of Jews who are important thinkers, always in the behavior of fringe groups or extraordinary characters, intimations of alternative values and signals of roads not yet taken that may lead to a higher or at least more widely scanning high ground.

This concluding part of *The Jewish Experience* is devoted to these alternative intimations in Jewish thought and behavior, departing from the mainstream, just as the previous chapter highlighted those legitimated by the mainstream and the power elite (even if one or other icon was not really quite as conformist as a filtered image now exhibits).

The Jews I describe, speak of, and let speak here, are an extremely diverse sort—more easily positioned along a very long, narrow spectrum than in an integrated circle. But their perspectives, their visions, their passions, deserve to be contemplated. From this congeries of viewpoints may come one or more important avenues of changes and novel forms of discourse.

Contemporary Jewish intellectual life, that is the life of the mind pursued by people called Jews, is not stagnant, redundant, or circumscribed. It often appears as such because the empowered legitimating forces of Jewish life in the U.S.A. and Israel have drawn a narrow circle around Jewish intellectuality, artful expression and progressive learning and declared that only within this

The continuity of faith: Jewish catacombs in Rome, second to third century A.D.

constricting circle of sameness and derivations is activity acceptable, kosher. But this is the mode of conservatives at all times and places.

Jewish intellectual life—as existentially defined by what people called Jews do and say—presently remains vibrant and creative in a variety of inconsistent and perhaps incompatible directions. But on its own frontiers, the culture's originality and aggressive discovery is evident. It remains to specify these alternative intimations of Jewishness, to relate them one to another, as well as to the authorized and legitimate mainstream, and build in new towers of intellect, attendant art and behavior in Jewish life.

So it has been before in Jewish history; so it is now. Will new ideas and vanguard initiatives drown in a sea of conformity and authorized expression, or will there by a breakout to new ideas and original forms of action?

Demonology

S. Ansky's *The Dybbuk*, written in 1920, became an immediate success when it was produced in Moscow two years later and it has been offered many times since in a variety of languages. In the 1930s a quite good (although over-long) film of *The Dybbuk* was made in Poland, in Yiddish, and is still available.

Ansky was a photographer and an ethnographer who was interested in the culture and society of the then-disappearing shtetl and particularly in the demonological and mystical culture arising from the Hasidic tradition.

The story in *The Dybbuk* is based on a favorite motif is Hasidic folklore—a bride just before her wedding is possessed by the demonic spirit of a dead student who feels a grudge against her family, and the rabbi undertakes an exorcism. The same motif was used by the veteran of the Jewish Art Theater on the Lower East Side of New York, Jacob Ben-Ami, in the 1940s in his *God, Man, and Devil*.

Ansky's attitude toward Hasidic demonology is ambivalent. The play seems to condemn this culture as medieval and superstitious but underneath there is nostalgia for the old way of life. This is the concluding, climatic part of the play.

LEAH (DYBBUK [*SCREAMS*])

Rebbe of Miropolye, I know how strong and mighty you are. I know that you can order angels and seraphim to do your will. But you cannot impose your will on me. I have no place to go. All roads are closed to me and all paths are blocked; evil spirits lie in wait everywhere, ready to consume me. (*in a trembling voice*) There is a heaven and there is an earth and there are worlds upon worlds in the universe, but nowhere is there a place for me. And now that my anguished and harried soul has found a haven, you want to drive me away. Have pity on me, don't hound me, don't chase me out.

REB AZRIEL

Wandering soul! I cannot help but feel deep pity for you and will do everything in my power to release you from the angels of destruction. But you must leave the body of this maiden.

LEAH (DYBBUK [*DECISIVELY*])

I will not leave.

REB AZRIEL

Mikhoel, summon ten men from the synagogue. (*Mikhoel goes out and returns quickly with ten men; they stand at the side*) Gentlemen, do you give me permission in your name and with your authority to exorcise an evil spirit who is unwilling to leave the body of a Jewish maiden?

ALL TEN MEN

Rebbe, we give you permission in our name and with our authority to exorcise an evil spirit who is unwilling to leave the body of a Jewish maiden.

REB AZRIEL

(*Rises*) Dybbuk, soul of one who has departed from our world! In the name and with the authority of this holy congregation of Jews, I, Azriel son of Hadas, command you to leave the body of the maiden Leah, the daughter of Hannah, without harming her or any other living creature. If you do not obey my command I will cover you with curses and maledictions, with conjurations and oaths, with all the power of my outstretched arm. But if you obey my command I will use all my power to reclaim your soul and drive away the spirits of evil and destruction that surround you.

LEAH (DYBBUK [*SCREAMS*])

I am not afraid of your curses and threats, and I don't believe in your assurances. No power in the world can help me! There is no more exalted realm than my present haven, and there is no deeper abyss than the one that awaits me. I will not leave!

REB AZRIEL

In the name of the Almighty God I make my final petition and command you to leave the maiden's body! If you do not leave, you will be excommunicated and given over to the angels of destruction. (*A fearful pause*)

LEAH (DYBBUK)

In the name of the Almighty God I am joined to my intended forever and will never leave her.

REB AZRIEL

Mikhoel, order white robes to be brought in for everyone. Bring seven rams' horns and seven black candles. After that, take seven Torah scrolls out of the Holy Ark. (*Fearful pause while Mikhoel is out; he returns with rams' horns and black candles; the Messenger follows with white robes*)

THE MESSENGER

(*Counts the robes*) There is one robe too many. (*Looks around*) Is someone missing in the room?

REB AZRIEL

(*Agitated, as if remembering something*) To excommunicate a Jewish soul one must first obtain the permission of the chief rabbi. Mikhoel, put away the rams' horns, the candles and the robes for the time being. Take my staff and go to Reb Shimshon; tell him in my name that he must come here immediately. (*Mikhoel gathers up the rams' horns and candles and goes out together with the Messenger, who is carrying the robes; Reb Azriel to the ten men*) You may leave for now. (*They leave; pause; Reb Azriel raises his head*) Sender, where are the groom and his parents?

SENDER

They remained in my house in Brinitz for the Sabbath.

REB AZRIEL

Send a rider to tell them in my name that they must remain there to await my orders.

SENDER

I will send a rider immediately.

REB AZRIEL

In the meanwhile you may leave; take the maiden into the other room.

LEAH

(*Wakes up; in a trembling voice*) Grandma, I

am afraid. What will they do to him? What will they do to me?

FRADE

Don't be afraid, my child. The rebbe knows what he's doing. He won't harm you; he would never hurt anyone. (*She and Sender go out with Leah*)

REB AZRIEL

(*Sits deep in thought; as if waking*) Even if it has been otherwise decreed in the higher spheres, I will reverse the decree. (*Reb Shimshon enters*)

REB SHIMSHON

May you have a good week, Rebbe.

REB AZRIEL

(*Rises to meet him*) A good week, and a good year, Rabbi. Be seated. (*Reb Shimshon sits down*) I have put you to this trouble because of a very important matter. A Dybbuk has possessed a Jewish maiden, Heaven preserve us, and he refuses to leave her body. Only one thing remains to be done and that is to drive him out through banishment and ostracism. I therefore ask your consent for this, and you will have earned the merit of saving a soul.

REB SHIMSHON

(*Sighs*) To pronounce a ban upon the living is difficult enough; how much more so on the dead. But because nothing else is left to be done, and because so godly a man as you finds this remedy necessary, I give my consent. But first, Rebbe, I must reveal a secret to you that has some bearing on this matter.

REB AZRIEL

Please do.

REB SHIMSHON

Rebbe, do you remember a young Hasid by the name of Nissen ben Rivke, a student of Kabbalah, who used to come from Brinitz to visit you regularly about twenty years ago?

REB AZRIEL

Yes, he left for distant parts and died there.

REB SHIMSHON

Well, the same Nissen ben Rivke appeared three times in my dreams last night and demanded that I summon Sender of Brinitz to a rabbinical court in his name.

REB AZRIEL

What is his claim against Sender?

REB SHIMSHON

He didn't tell me. He only said that Sender caused him the most grievous harm.

REB AZRIEL

You know that when a Jew has a claim against someone and demands a trial, the rabbi may not refuse. This is even more true in the case of a dead person who can petition the heavenly tribunal itself. But what has that to do with the Dybbuk?

REB SHIMSHON

It has a very real connection. I have heard that the young man who died and entered the body of Sender's daughter was Nissen's son. They speak of a certain promise which Sender made to Nissen and never fulfilled.

REB AZRIEL

(*Thinks a while*) In that case I will postpone the exorcism of the Dybbuk until tomorrow noon. Tomorrow right after the morning prayers, God willing, you will summon the deceased and we will cast your dream in a proper light. After that, with your permission, I will drive out the Dybbuk by excommunicating him.

REB SHIMSHON

Inasmuch as a trial between a living person and one who is deceased is very unusual and difficult I hope that you, Rebbe, will agree to be the presiding judge and conduct the trial.

REB AZRIEL

I agree. Mikhoel! (*Mikhoel enters*) Ask them to bring in the maiden. (*Sender and Frade bring in Leah, who sits down, her eyes shut*) Dybbuk! I am giving you exactly one day; if by tomorrow noon you haven't left of your own free will, I will, with the permission of the rabbi of this town, banish you by force through the agonizing means of the *herem. (Pause)* Now you can take the maiden out. *(Sender and Frade are about to take Leah out)* Sender, you remain here. *(Frade accompanies Leah out)* Sender, do you remember your old friend Nissen ben Rivke?

SENDER

(Frightened) Nissen, son of Rivke? But he died. . . .

REB AZRIEL

Do you know that last night he appeared three times in the chief rabbi's dreams? *(Points to Reb Shimshon)* He demanded that you be summoned to a trial to answer his charges against you.

SENDER

(Trembling) Me, summoned to a trial? Oh my God. What can he want from me? What shall I do, Rebbe?

REB AZRIEL

I don't know what the charge is, but you must accept the summons.

SENDER

I will do as you say.

REB AZRIEL

(In a different tone) Send the swiftest horse and rider to inform the bridegroom and his parents to be here by noon tomorrow. Let the wedding ceremony take place immediately after the Dybbuk has been exorcised.

SENDER

Rebbe, what if they have had second thoughts about the marriage and refuse to come? *(The Messenger appears at the door)*

REB AZRIEL

(With authority) Tell them that the orders are from me. And make sure that the groom is here on time.

THE MESSENGER

The groom will be here on time. *(The clock strikes twelve)*
(Curtain)

The Satmar Rebbe

The Satmarer are a Hasidic group living in Brooklyn and Rockland County, New York, and intensely bonded to their rebbe. Here is a sympathetic 1972 portrait of the Satmar rebbe and his role in the lives of his followers by a social scientist, Israel Rubin.

Reb Yoel Teitelbaum is a truly remarkable individual, even when stripped of the halo with which his followers endow him. He is, first, a most intelligent man with almost boundless mental energy. As a young man he used to sit and study Torah some sixteen hours each day, according to some informants. It is said that in his younger years he rarely went to bed during weekdays. Instead he acquired the habit, which he still has, of taking catnaps in his chair when overcome by fatigue. When I last saw him (before his stroke) he was in his late seventies and still put in a long and enormously active day, studying morning hours, praying around midday, and spending the afternoon and evening in an unbelievable multitude of activities. Reception of callers of all varieties—Hasidim seeking personal audiences, community leaders requesting decisions, outside visitors of all kinds—is a daily phenomenon which can in itself absorb all available time. On top of this, he presides over congregational executive meetings, attends official affairs, officiates at weddings, examines students at the school, and manages to save time for afternoon and evening prayer and for writing. In all, his schedule calls for a continuous active period of some ten hours, interrupted only by an occasional catnap, this in addition to several hours of study in the morning—a truly remarkable day for a man close to eighty.

His apparently high native intelligence, combined with his almost legendary diligence, enabled Reb Yoel to reach a high level of scholarship quite early in life. Already in his twenties he began to be known as a scholar, and his reputation grew with time. By the time he established his postwar position in the United States, he was respected among the great Torah scholars the world over. The fact that recognition in this respect came even from those who disagreed with his religious philosophy is important, as we shall see later.

Although scholarship is very important, in itself it is hardly sufficient for the exercise of the role occupied by Rabbi Teitelbaum. Unquestionable piety of the Orthodox Jewish variety, piety that includes both strict adherence to the written religious law and reaching beyond it when necessary, is absolutely vital. Again, it appears beyond doubt that the Rov meets this requirement. Not even his fiercest critics—and they are numerous—have ever accused him of violating any religious laws, of using his position for purposes of personal enrichment, or of hedonistic indulgence. His austere, disciplined life is an open book, available to all who wish to inspect it. His followers have done so to their satisfaction.

Persistency is another obvious trait in the Rov's character, one that his followers admire. Satmarer are quick to point out that not only is the Rov a saint and scholar now, but that he has been "saintly from the womb" and scholarly since his childhood. They emphasize the same with regard to his philosophy, especially his anti-Zionism. One informant commented: "After the war [World War II], we were temporarily back in Satmar and the Rov was in Jerusalem, with no communications at all. The general atmosphere in town was, as a consequence of the holocaust, highly pro-Zionist, since people were disgusted with the Gentiles. Once a messenger came from the Holy Land and told us that the Rov was reconsidering his anti-Zionist stand. We refused to believe. We had

absolute confidence in the Rov's steadfastness, for he never gives in to popular vogues. When communications were reestablished, we were awfully glad to hear that we were justified in our belief."

Finally, such mundane qualities as common sense, a sense of humor, a pleasant voice, a strikingly handsome and imposing countenance, and oratorical skill enable Reb Yoel to discharge his multiple duties not only authoritatively and forcefully but with a high measure of sensitivity and a distinctly pleasant manner.

Does the Rov have no weaknesses? It would be senseless to suggest such a proposition. What seems a strong point from a follower's perspective is a weakness when seen with critical eyes. Persistence turns into obstinacy, piety becomes fanaticism, and even the Rov's scholarship may be considered narrow rather than intense. Further, his "personal" response, so valued by his followers, is seen by many as interfering with objective judgment. For example, during one of my visits, the Rov once declined an invitation to an affair on the ground that one of his long-time opponents was expected to be present. The host felt hurt and saw it as part of the Rov's weakness to keep long-term personal accounts; but followers judged it a desirable trait not to seek proximity to a critic, who, they felt, was almost an enemy. From our perspective these considerations are beside the point. We are not sitting in judgment over the individual; we are merely trying to understand the basis for the tremendous sway he has over his followers. And to this end, what is important is the way he is perceived by the members of the community, rather than the way he might score on some objective value scale. Reb Yoel's subjective image is extremely positive and, further, he has evident strengths to reinforce this image and prevent it from fading over time.

As we have mentioned, originally the two leadership roles were distinct, even in those cases where one individual simultaneously occupied both posts. But in the case of the American phase of Rabbi Teitelbaum's leadership, the two components have largely merged. Here he is no town rabbi, and the congregation he heads consists of his own Hasidim, exclusively. Consequently, all facets of his leadership are affected by the charisma that separates him from his followers.

Satmarer are, as a rule, loathe to make decisions. This is so even in personal matters. On the community level, decision-making via participatory democracy is completely alien to Satmar. Consequently, the burden of deciding vital matters falls entirely upon the leader's shoulders. Not only has the Rov shaped the overall goal orientation of his community (this was virtually unavoidable in view of the fact that he created rather than inherited his following), but through all the years he has rendered strategic and tactical decisions on new problems that resulted from changing circumstances.

After World War II, the Rov made the momentous decision to establish his headquarters in the United States rather than remaining in the Holy Land, and to continue the fight against Zionism on a larger scale than ever before. Once in the United States he decided to build his own school system and, furthermore, to include in that system a girls' school, despite the lack of precedence for such a school in the community. This was part of the larger decision to try to preserve in full Satmar culture on American soil, disregarding the experience of earlier immigrants. The Rov was convinced that those immigrants had surrendered to American culture out of sheer lack of will; that they would have survived culturally had they been willing to invest the necessary effort and finances. He was determined not to let Satmarer repeat the error.

Once the necessary structures were established, the burden of deciding a myriad of tactical matters in the new environment lay squarely on Rabbi Teitelbaum's shoulders. A school in the United States must have a secular division—where does one recruit staff? What should be the curriculum for the religious division of the girls' school? What policy should be adopted with regard to the public library that has on its shelves literature considered undesirable in Satmar? Should Satmarer take advantage of the free political climate in the United States to organize demonstrations against Israel and Zionists? If so, how far should such tactics be carried? Such questions are decided almost daily by the only man in the Satmar community who is both institutionally invested with the necessary power to make a decision and personally equipped to assume the responsibility for whatever consequences it may bring.

Among the many decision-making areas, the one involving application of religious law is especially noteworthy. True, authority in this sphere is vested in all individuals who have been properly ordained, so that small daily problems (e.g., whether a given product is kosher) are handled by ordained clergy. But when larger questions with community-wide implications arise, the Rov is called upon to render a verdict. No lesser figure will take it upon himself to decide, for example, whether or not it is in accordance with Torah law for Satmarer Hasidim who live in Israel to participate in elections, or whether or not to practice birth control. The effectiveness of the Rov in this area can only be appreciated when we consider that his Torah scholarship is beyond question. In addition, the Hadisim have the absolute trust that, as a saintly individual, their master has divine assistance which prevents him from erring in any matters, let alone those involving what they see as his main mission in life, namely, to lead his flock on the only right path as prescribed by the Torah.

Finally, the providing of comfort and security to members of Satmar through a variety of public and private activities—the Hasidic rebbe element—is probably the most important component of Rabbi Teitelbaum's social rule. Publicly he discharges this part of his role at synagogue services, at the Hasidic "tables," and at occasions such as banquets or weddings to which he is invited to officiate.

At the synagogue the Rov's presence is in itself a noteworthy event. He assumes leadership in the services quite often on Sabbaths and virtually always on major holidays. He also delivers lengthy sermons several times a year, especially during the Days of Awe, when the talks reach a high emotional pitch as he calls on the congregants to repent and resolve to improve their behavior.

On the Sabbath and on major holidays the Rov conducts tables, i.e., he eats his meals publicly several hours after his followers' mealtime, so anyone has the opportunity to attend. At these semiformal occasions, which often last for hours, he recites sanctification prayers, hands out food, wishes "*lehayim!*" (to life!) to anyone who approaches him with the same wish, delivers Torah talks, and occasionally participates in comminity dancing—all highly welcomed and eagerly sought by the Hasidim, who not only visit the tables frequently but often bring their wives and children along so that they too may experience the subtle joy of these occasions.

The desirability of having the Rov officiate at one's wedding is so great that in the 1960s, as the post-World-War-II children grew up and began marrying at the rate of several a day, a canopy was set up in front of the Rov's house. Each couple came to be married by the Rov and then returned to the catering hall for the reception. No banquet in Satmar or in satellite communities is quite complete without the Satmarer Rov's presence and his few words of Torah-exposition and encouragement.

Perhaps most important and certainly most time-consuming in matters of comfort and security are the private visits of Hasidim who come with their personal problems and requests to the only individual they trust and adore. Not being used to making important decisions, Satmarer will come for consultation on just about any matter of importance.

By all objective measures, the Satmarer Rov appears to be a giant of a man, performing a huge role in the social fabric of the Satmar commuity.

Black Hats on the West Bank

There is a large colony of Haredim, ultra-Orthodox, "black hats" in East Jerusalem, in some cases going back to the nineteenth century or earlier. In the late-1970s and 1980s, the Haredim moved in substantial numbers to settle on the West Bank, only a few miles from Jerusalem but deep in entrenched Arab territory. They were encouraged to do so by the rightist Likud government of Menachem Begin and Itzhak Shamir and were offered favorable real estate deals for doing so, to such an extent that thousands of Israelis became West Bank "Settlers" for strictly economic reasons. It is the Haredim, however, who are ideologically committed to West Bank settlement as fulfilling the dictation of the covenant, to being a holy people.

These two disciples of Vladimir Jabotinsky, Begin and Shamir, were far from being Orthodox Jews themselves but they saw the Haredi "settlers" as a means of creating new political facts, very hard to undo, by establishing their colonies on the West Bank. Begin and Shamir, with just a trace of cynicism, took to calling the West Bank "Judea and Samaria" and endorsing the Haredi Biblical claims to the land.

Perhaps a third of the Haredim are from English-speaking countries, mostly New York City. Here is a view of West Bank black hats by Robert I. Friedman, a writer for the left-wing New York *Village Voice*, which is strongly pro-Palestinian. Try as Friedman does to communicate contempt for the Haredi settlers, a little bit of grudging admiration creeps through. The majority of secular Israeli, even some mainstream Orthodox, are afraid of the Haredim, not without cause.

"We are getting a raw deal," yelled Rabbi Mordechai Goldstein as he squeezed the trigger of a portable fire extinguisher, taking aim at a brush-fire that was swiftly spreading toward a large green tank that supplied heating oil to Metzad, a down-at-the-heels religious settlement built in 1984 on a remote plateau in the Judean wilderness. The fire extinguisher was defective; it wheezed and fizzed, and nothing came out. "Look at the junk the government gave us," Goldstein moaned, his white shirt untucked and darkly stained, his half-looped tie flapping, his gray beard and glasses glinting in the sun.

Swarms of small, untidy children, with filthy white shirts and dark pants, their side curls twirling in the wind, fought the fire with brooms and handfuls of dirt. "Rabbi, Rabbi, it's going to the tank," they cried out in Hebrew and English.

A lanky teenager turned on a garden hose, but not enough water dribbled out to fill a drinking glass; there was no water pressure.

"Rabbi, Rabbi, we are going to be incinerated!"

Then the wind changed, and the fire shifted toward a steep ridge and burned itself out. Good fortune had saved Metzad. But Goldstein was still angry. The rabbi complained loudly that from its inception Metzad had been orphaned by the Likud. "We came here when the Likud was trying to push in a *yishuv*" (settlement) on the eve of the 1984 national elections, he said. "They had nobody else so they took us. It's not that we don't love Israel. The RaMBaM says go together into the mountains or desert of Judea and make your own community. We followed the RaMBaM's advice—we made a community. Now we expect the government to help.

"But because we are mostly Americans here and don't know how to communicate with Israelis, we are easy to push around. Any time we asked for our rights, the government said, 'What are you complaining about?' We had a camp here one summer with one hundred and forty children. The government promised us ten thousand dollars for mattresses, then the ten thousand dollars became eight thousand dollars, and that was a lot, but we still don't have it. We can't get our feet off the ground!"

More forlorn than many Israeli slums I had visited, Metzad is a testament to the fact that not all settlements are created equal. As we shall see, Metzad has suffered because of Goldstein's unconventional religious views and lack of political savvy. The thirty families who have settled in Metzad are *horzim baale teshuvah,* so-called "repentant" Jews who have renounced their secular lives and have embraced the rigors of ultra-Orthodox Judaism. Because the men study in a Jerusalem yeshiva, their families subsist largely on small government stipends that are doled out to all full-time yeshiva students. Eking out a meager existence, Metzad's settlers live in rusted govern-ment-surplus trailers, most not larger than seven hundred square feet—though many of the families have ten or more children. Unlike nearby Efrat, a non-Gush Emunim settlement of predominantly modern Orthodox Jews from North America that boasts tennis courts, and a soon-to-be-constructed recreation center that will house an indoor basketball court, and a lavishly equipped gymnasium that would be the pride of any American high school, Metzad has little more in the way of amenities than a tiny hut that has been painted with flowers and converted into a nursery school. "We'd like maybe a prefabricated shed so our kids could have a place out of the wind and the rain," said Shabtai Herman, a South African *baale teshuvah* who gave up a promising career as an economist to study Torah and practice herbal medicine. "In winter it can be sheer hell because the winds blow with such velocity that a child cannot go outside and play. When our kids come home from school, very often they have to go around to the back of the house and climb through the windows because our houses face the wind, and you can't open the door."

There is no commerce or agriculture in this dust-blown corner of Judea. Even grapes from the local vineyards are sour. But if poverty pervades Metzad, so does the fear of Arabs. Once, two goats owned by the settlement were found beheaded. Tracks were discovered leading back to Sair, a neighboring Arab village whose land was expropriated by the government to build Metzad. Another time, a truck delivering a refrigerator was ambushed by rifle fire. During the Gulf War, Metzad's settlers worried that their homes would be overrun by marauding Arabs. "The Israeli Army said, 'Don't worry, we'll come for you with tanks,'" said a settler. "But what if those tanks were stuck on the front lines? How were we supposed to hold back thousands of Arabs with twenty-five men? Our rabbi says the Arabs could squash us like a pimple."

Everyone in Metzad seems to have a story about being stoned by Arabs during the forty-five-minute drive to Jerusalem. Gershon, a pudgy, bearded part-time art dealer originally from Canada, told me about the time he was ambushed while driving a carload of children from Metzad to Jerusalem. He had stopped his white Peugeot along the side of the road near Bethlehem so one of the boys could go to the bathroom. Suddenly,

Arabs rose from the hills with a war cry and pelted the car with grapefruit sized stones. Gershon said he deliberately aimed his Uzi low, spraying bullets several yards in front of the attackers. But the barrage of stones continued. "I trained my gun on the ringleader," Gershon recalled. "I was about to blow his head off when we caught each other's eye. He sensed his time was up, and with a whoop the Arabs withdrew."

"I'm a religious Jew, a God-fearing settler," Gershon continued. "I came to live in a Torah community. But you have to protect yourself from the Arabs. Our army uses tear gas, rubber bullets, plastic bullets—okay, sometimes they demolish a house. But the army is pretty gentle. They hope to wear the Arabs down. It's not the way to handle it. The Arabs don't fear us. The analogy is an easy teacher and one who uses a stick. Who will the kids take advantage of? You need a stick to control the Arabs. They have to live in fear. Gush Emunim wants to be able to go into an Arab village and level it if there is trouble. They understand the Arabs' mentality. If you don't use force, they don't respect you."

The use of physical force is not part of Rabbi Goldstein's repertoire. *Kvetching*, yes. Hysteria, by all means. But he is also a warm, open, caring, charismatic leader, who has formed around him a community that has endured difficult circumstances during difficult times. Rabbi Goldstein is a pioneer, not only in the political sense for having established a settlement, but also in the religious sense for having created the *baale teshuvah* movement—a revolutionary event in modern Jewish life that has had a profound effect on Israel and the Diaspora Jewish community.

The sixty-five-year-old rabbi grew up in an upper-middle-class home in the Bronx. His father was the head of the Food and Drug Administration for the state of New York; his mother was one of the first women to practice law at the turn of the century. His modern Orthodox parents were strongly committed to the Zionist experiment in Palestine. "We always dreamed about and loved Israel," Goldstein remembered. That devotion was channeled into political activism on behalf of right-wing Jewish causes. As a teenager, Goldstein joined Betar, whose American director was then Moshe Arens. When war broke out between the Arabs and the newly created Jewish state in 1948, many of

Goldstein's friends in Betar went to Israel to fight. Goldstein stayed in New York and joined the Stern Gang, becoming part of a ring that smuggled weapons to the terrorist group in Palestine.

Goldstein became an Orthodox rabbi, and in 1964 traveled to Israel with members of his New York yeshiva for advanced studies in *Halacha* and business law. He decided to remain in Israel and found a job teaching at the Hebron Yeshiva, a Haredi, or ultra-Orthodox, religious school that had moved to Jerusalem in 1936 after vicious pogroms drove the Jews out of Hebron.

It was at the Hebron Yeshiva that Goldstein met Eliezer Sachs, a young American college graduate from Rochester, New York, who had come to Israel to study Torah. Sachs had been raised in a Conservative home and had no formal Torah training. The Hebron Yeshiva wasn't set up to teach beginners, and so its chief rabbi proposed that Sachs hire Goldstein to tutor him. "I said wonderful," Rabbi Goldstein recalled. "I charged fifteen dollars an hour in those days. I had a lot of children to feed." An adept student, Sachs learned the *Gemara* in three months. More importantly, as far as Goldstein was concerned, Sachs renounced his secular life, donned the black hat and black coat of the Haredi ultra-Orthodox, and declared his desire to devote the rest of his life to Torah study.

Goldstein searched for an ultra-Orthodox yeshiva where Sachs could enroll. But the ultra-Orthodox community is intensely xenophobic and obsessed with matters of morality and purity. Little girls are taught from an early age that they are dangerous sexual objects, and Haredi women shave their heads and wear sacklike dresses that cover them from head to toe so that they can't lead men into temptation. Sachs may have opened his heart to *Hashem,* and may have been willing to follow the strict religious laws governing what is allowed and what is forbidden, but he had come from a spiritually unclean world that the Haredi believed could infect their entire community.

"He's a wealthy boy, you can charge him a large tuition, he's handsome, smart," Goldstein told the principal of a well-known Haredi yeshiva.

"Listen," said the principal, "we can't accept him. He's a *baale teshuvah*. What will be if he tells the boys in the school about girls?"

"He gave it all up," Goldstein replied. "He's not interested in girls."

In spite of Goldstein's best efforts, not a single ultra-Orthodox yeshiva in Israel would accept Sachs. "The religious schools in those days didn't open their doors for boys who didn't have a pedigree," Goldstein said. "They did not encourage people to come into their circles."

After the bout of rejections, "the boy almost collapsed," Goldstein said.

"This is Judaism?" Sachs asked Goldstein.

"So all night long I didn't sleep," Goldstein recalled. "I had taught him that the Torah was true and the best of all worlds." Then the rabbi had a revolutionary idea. In response to the discrimination Sachs had encountered, Goldstein decided to create a yeshiva entirely for *baale teshuvah*. There was nothing quite like it in Israel or the Diaspora. "That's how I started the *baale teshuvah* movement," Goldstein said. "We formed a tax-deductible organization, and the boy's father gave us some money."

On a deeper level, Goldstein believed that the time was ripe for a religious renewal within Judaism—and that the movement of Jews away from Judaism that had been going on since the Enlightenment could be reversed. At the same time, he detected a new willingness to explore Judaism, especially among the young, long-haired American Jewish back-packers who came to Israel in great numbers after the Six-Day War, turning the country into a major outpost of the burgeoning counterculture. Whether they had come to live under clouds of hashish smoke in the hippie shantytowns then rising on the outskirts of the Red Sea port of Elat, or to search for their Jewish roots while picking oranges on a socialist kibbutz, they could be the raw material of a Jewish revival, Goldstein concluded.

Goldstein had observed that in many ways, these refugees from the American suburbs were similar to the idealistic youth from Russia and Poland who settled in Palestine in the early-twentieth century and built the modern institutions of the Jewish state. The youth of the second and third *aliyah* had come with a deep faith that salvation was possible only in Palestine, that "in Palestine, under socialism, the future would take care of itself and resolve all of Jewry's social and national problems," Amos Elon wrote.

Many American Jews who journeyed to Israel in the late-60s were also in search of salvation. But they were not interested in the great Zionist socialist revolutionaries like Syrkin or Borochov (if they had heard of them at all). Israel, after all, was a *fait accompli*. And with the task completed, Labor Zionism seemed sterile and heavy with bureaucracy. These soft suburban youth were on an inner quest—for truth, clarity of purpose, utopia. Many had experimented with Eastern religions, LSD, transcendental sex. Goldstein told them that they did not have to go to an Indian ashram to find themselves—that truth was in their own backyard. He offered the Torah—a straightforward path without confusion or self-doubt, where one could find community and God.

Goldstein began to teach a small group of American *baale teshuvah* in a room on the top floor of the Hebron Yeshiva. When the number of pupils grew too large for the room, he moved to the Diskin Orphanage, a spacious building in West Jerusalem that also housed a yeshiva run by Rav Shach, a leader of a major wing of the ultra-Orthodox movement in Israel. "God gave me the gift of pedagogical methods," Goldstein said. "Some of the boys started coming from Shach's place to my place." Soon Goldstein had sixty pupils and needed a building big enough to accommodate his growing student body.

In search of additional funding, Goldstein approached Shaul Eisenberg, the richest man in Israel. Born in Galacia, Poland, Eisenberg had escaped from Nazi Europe and spent the war years in Japan, where he reportedly made a fortune, though much mystery surrounds how he was able to do that. After the Six-Day War, Eisenberg moved to Israel, where he became the nation's largest arms merchant. Because most of Eisenberg's family was lost in the Holocaust, he had a genuine sympathy for Goldstein and his mission of Jewish renewal. He made a substantial donation. But more important, he put in a good word for Goldstein with Dr. Kalman Kahane, Israel's deputy minister of education and culture, whose father had been chief rabbi of Warsaw before the Second World War.

Dr. Kahane gave Goldstein a long-term lease on a derelict medieval castle on Mount Zion, overlooking Jerusalem's Old Walled City. Although Mount Zion was within the boundaries of pre-1967 Israel, it was considered a dangerous location prior to the Six-Day War, because it was in easy range of Jordanian sniper fire. Aside from a run-down tourist shop on the mount, there was a *nahal* (paramilitary) post, several churches, and a dilapidated building allegedly holding King David's tomb, as well as the room where the Last Supper supposedly took place.

Goldstein opened the Diaspora Yeshiva in late 1967. "What good is religion if you can't open your doors and help people out?" Goldstein told me. In defiance of Jewish tradition, Goldstein actively evangelized, approaching potential recruits at Jerusalem's Central Bus Station, at the Western Wall, and on the campus of the Hebrew University, where he hung signs in the student center that asked, "How can you understand the Jewish state until you have understood Judaism?" As word spread, the Diaspora Yeshiva became a way station for scores of American Jewish hippies who were searching for God—or for free room and board. They brought with them their guitars, backpacks, and drugs, especially hashish, which was readily available in Israel. "I knew nothing about drugs then," Goldstein said. "I never had heard of hash. I was so naive."

Before long, the Diaspora Yeshiva looked as if it had been invaded by Ken Kesey and the Merry Pranksters, except that the tripsters resembled long-bearded, floppy-hatted Hasids who seemed to be fried on acid. The frenetic tones of the Jefferson Airplane and the Doors echoed from the castle, attracting curious Israelis, who were greeted with shouts of "Come and join us." Goldstein said he started a religious rock band that cut eight albums for CBS records. He also invited assorted Eastern gurus and mystics to live on the mount, confident that Judaism would win out.

There were several suicides on Mount Zion during those first few years. "There were people who died on drugs in my arms," Goldstein told me. "One boy had gotten involved with drugs in America, and his parents didn't know what to do with him, so they shipped him off to Israel. We bar mitzvahed the boy. We tried with all our heart to help him. Then he died on drugs. We can't succeed with everybody." Nevertheless, Goldstein's reputation for working with mixed-up youth grew, and soon more and more well-to-do American Jews were parking their sons with the rabbi, who often took the place of counselor and psychiatrist.

It was Goldstein's belief that these young Americans needed a kind of therapy; that they had to be cured of the ills born of the Diaspora. For all of Goldstein's seeming tolerance of the lifestyles of the counterculture, he believed the only way his students could mend was if they rejected virtually everything to do with modern life, and lived according to *Halacha*, a comprehensive code of behavior that has hardly changed since the Middle Ages. His students were required to dress in the black hats and caftans of the ultra-Orthodox; their old identities were slowly stripped away, and they were pressured to conform to the rabbi's desires. Drugs were gradually eliminated, and the yeshiva became more like traditional ultra-Orthodox schools of higher learning. "My approach was, if drugs give you a high, Torah gives you a bigger high," Goldstein said.

What remained unique about the Diaspora Yeshiva was that Goldstein mixed together practices of the two major fractions of the Haredi community—Lithuanian and Hasidic. Hasidism began in the eighteenth century as a reaction to the dry, legalistic practice of Judaism that was controlled by a small elite caste of rabbis. Hasidism stressed fervent devotion and intense prayer. The Lithuanians, so named because Lithuania was the center of opposition to Hasidism, emphasized the study of Torah and Talmud. While the Diaspora Yeshiva is Lithuanian, Goldstein adopted many of the devotional dances, prayers, and songs that are typical of Hasidism in order to appeal to students who needed an emotional experience to bind them to Orthodoxy.

Not long after the Diaspora Yeshiva opened, several Israelis asked Goldstein to establish a separate *baale teshuvah* program for native-born Israelis. Goldstein did not have the resources. So he referred them to Rabbi Avraham Ravitz, a Knesset member from the ultra-Orthodox Degel Hatorah party, who, in turn, brought them to Rav Kook, who organized two intensely nationalistic *baale teshuvah* yeshivas. By the early 1970s, a number of *baale teshuvah* yeshivas embracing both the biblical fundamentalism of Gush Emunim and the insular, pre-Enlightenment religious values of the Haredim were established and training thousands of previously secular Israelis.

Goldstein started a women's division in 1971 after Eliezer Sachs, his first student, had difficulty finding a wife. "Rabbi Goldstein realized he was running into a lot of the problems that any innovator or entrepreneur is going to have," said Shabtai

Herman. "He had made these men into *baale teshuvah,* but there was nobody for them to marry because the regular Orthodox community looked askance in those days at *baale teshuvah,* and, of course, the boys couldn't return to regular secular life to find wives." So Goldstein designed a program to train women who were Jewish but unfamiliar with Orthodoxy how best to serve their future Torah-scholar husbands and keep a proper Jewish home.

As the Diaspora Yeshiva grew into a full-fledged community with married couples and children, Goldstein decided it was time to build a settlement. "I wanted to build a place behind Hadassah Hospital [in West Jerusalem]," Goldstein told me one day in his cavernous office on Mount Zion. "I talked to city officials. Everybody agreed. I shook their hands. Then I went to America for three months to raise money. When I returned, they said, 'Listen, Rabbi, sorry, the city decided to take over the property and to build who knows what.' Then I tried to make a settlement near Carmel up north near Safed. My son said, 'I'll help you, Dad.' He went to a government minister, a woman. He gave her a box of chocolates. She was nice-looking. He said, 'Put our name down. We have the people who want to make a *yishuv.*' She took his name and told him to move to the next line. He moved from office to office. He talked nicely. He filled out the forms."

For eight years, Goldstein and his son visited government ministries, dispensing chocolates and filling out forms. Finally, on the eve of the 1984 national elections, when the Likud was desperate to create more "facts on the ground," Goldstein was offered a plot of land on a bleak desert plateau where King David is said to have hidden from Saul. "The government pushed us in," Goldstein said. "Nobody else would take it. Nobody else would take it because it's right near [the Palestinian village of] Sair. They are the worst Arabs, the toughest Arabs. Even the Arabs of Hebron are afraid of them."

Initially, Metzad's most pressing problem wasn't Arabs; it was inadequate government funding. Four families quickly left because of the financial strain. "People are only human," Shabtai Herman said. "Some people just couldn't keep it together. It was sad. These were people we loved very much."

It was not as though the Haredi community lacked the political clout to obtain government money. There are several Haredi settlements in the occupied territories, and most enjoy relatively good standards of living. Kiryat Safer has received major donations from the Reichmann family. And Betar, whose land was confiscated from the nearby Arab village of Najilin, has opulent Tudor-style homes and a world-class community center.

Metzad has remained an orphan, in part, because *baale teshuvah* are still discriminated against by mainstream ultra-Orthodox society. But Metzad has also suffered because Goldstein has only nominally aligned himself with one of the four Haredi political parties, which together had thirteen seats in the one-hundred-twenty-seat Knesset prior to the 1992 elections. Because Goldstein is not part of a larger political network, he cannot easily obtain patronage. As a consequence, Metzad is being financially strangled. "My party is the Po'alei Agudat Yisrael—the Workers of Auguda," Goldstein explained. "They don't help us with a thing. I haven't spoken to the office in six years. They gave us a *Sefer Torah,* and that's about all."

In practice, the ultra-Orthodox parties wield enormous power in Israel, which they have used cynically to extort huge sums of money from Labor and Likud in return for their political backing—essentially determining who forms the government. In 1978, as the price for their political support, the leaders of the ultra-Orthodox parties extracted from Menachem Begin wholesale military exemptions for their students. In early 1990, after the national-unity government was toppled by a vote of no confidence, Shamir and Peres vied for Haredi support with promises of huge cash gifts and even more influence over Israeli public life. Their Rabbinate already controls civil laws governing such things as marriage and divorce and has closed down public transportation and business on the Sabbath; the Haredim would also like to ban all forms of weekend entertainment, including radio and television broadcasts.

In the Haredi view, Zionism is a heresy (the true Jewish state will be created only when the Messiah has arrived), the modern world is evil, and the Jewish people have been on a destructive, downward spiral since the Enlightenment. Rav Shach infuriated secular Israelis when he declared that the Holocaust was God's punishment for sins such as violating the Sabbath and eating pork.

"The Almighty keeps a balance sheet of the world, and when the sins become too many, he brings destruction," the ninety-three-year-old Shach said. Following the collapse of the national-unity government in 1990, Rav Shach denounced Labor as the "party of pig and rabbit eaters" in a speech that was carried live over Israeli television. The two ultra-Orthodox parties under Shach's sway lined up behind Shamir, allowing him to form the most extreme right-wing government in Israel's history—a union of Likud, the Haredi parties, and three small ultranationalist lists. The Haredim were handsomely rewarded. Government funds allocated to their educational institutions skyrocketed more than two thousand percent, from less than $7 million in 1988, to more than $150 million in 1990, according to *Tikkun*. A Haredi rabbi was appointed to head the Ministry of Interior, and the Haredi parties gained control of the Knesset's powerful Finance Committee.

Rabbi Moshe Ze'ev Feldman, the black-robed head of the Finance Committee, left many of his countrymen fuming when he said during an interview on Israeli television in December 1991 that if it were up to him, women would not be allowed to vote. It was not the first time the rabbi's unenlightened views had caused an uproar. When Feldman took over the Finance Committee, he acknowledged that his only economic training was "learning from my mother that two and two equals four."

It's not surprising then that many secular Israelis fear that the Haredim will sweep Zionism away like a roiling black tide and replace it with an austere Torah society. As far as they are concerned, the so-called demographic threat is posed not by the Palestinians but by the Haredim, whose birthrate is five times higher than that of secular Israelis. Resentment of the Haredim, who are so intrusive in public life yet manage to legally dodge military service, exploded during the Gulf War, when large numbers of them fled Israel in fear. "In the past days thousands of Haredi yeshiva *buchers* have left the country," the popular columnist Nachum Barnea wrote in *Yediot*

Achronot on the day the war began. "Without shame they stormed airline ticket-sellers, wads of cash in their hands, asking to leave the country at any price."

On the other hand, during the Israeli general elections in 1988, thousands of Lubavitcher Hasidim from Europe and America who held Israeli passports had come to the country to vote for the ultra-Orthodox Agudat Yisrael party in accordance with the instructions of ninety-year-old Rabbi Menachem Schneerson of Crown Heights, Brooklyn. Agudat Yisrael, which won five seats, backed Likud after it allegedly received huge bribes. "Midnight calls were made; millions of dollars changed hands," observed an Israeli politician.

In the end, Schneerson pledged to back Shamir if he accepted the rebbe's view on The Law of Return—that only those who convert to Judaism under traditional Orthodoxy can count themselves as authentic Jews. When Shamir acceded, Agudat Yisrael and another religious party sided with Likud, tipping the electoral balance in its favor. While the Knesset subsequently refused to redraft the Law of Return according to Schneerson's wishes, the resulting debate split the Jewish world in two.

Schneerson is a bellicose advocate of "Greater Israel." Other Haredi leaders are more ambivalent about the occupied territories. Rav Shach has stated that he would support territorial compromise if it meant saving Jewish lives. But many of the poor Sephardic Jews who are Shach's disciples support the hard-line views of Kach and Likud—especially those of Sharon. On the question of Greater Israel, Goldstein stands somewhere between the two poles represented by Schneerson and Shach. While Goldstein believes in the totality of the land of Israel, creating a Torah community is his primary goal. "We came here [to the West Bank] without any political aspirations in terms of a bigger picture—advancing the politics of the land of Israel," Shabtai Herman said. "It was simply that beggars can't be choosers."

Monastic Zionism

Yeshayahu Leibowitz made his living in the 1960s and 1970s teaching science at the university in Jerusalem. But his real vocation was reconsidering Zionism and the State of Israel in light of Biblical and Talmudic theology. His criticism, especially of Ben-Gurion, in the following statement of his position comes through more clearly than his positive doctrine. Yet it seems that what Leibowitz is arguing for is a Jewish state literally committed to fulfilling the covenant, to being a holy people. The thousands of Israelis who throng the Mediterranean beaches on Yom Kippur, let alone the mainstream politicians and professors, were obviously not in agreement. The surprising thing is the patience with which Israelis heard out sermons like this one. They did not dismiss Leibowitz as a crank; on the contrary he was awarded Israel's highest prize for cultural achievement.

A careful reading of the following selection reminds one of the late medieval friars and monks, particularly the Spiritual Franciscans, the radical wing of the Franciscan Order and a bane to the papacy. Leibowitz is advocating a kind of monastic Zionism in which the people of Israel became holy in everything and transform themselves into a community committed to purity—when the Messiah comes, as they say. Yet Leibowitz makes you stop and think about what the purpose of Zionism and Israel is supposed to be as the whole coastline from Tel Aviv to Haifa gets covered by condos.

King David and Haman son of Hammedatha emphasized the "uniqueness" of the Jewish people, and their words found their way into the daily prayer of supplication, the Tahnun, and into the Sabbath Minhah (afternoon prayer). The expressions "one nation" and "one people," implying uniqueness, have become catch-words of traditional religious parlance. In literary sources of Jewish thought and in various pronouncements of Jewish thinkers to this day, these expressions have come to represent basic tenets of faith. "Uniqueness" is interwoven with other concepts such as "election," "being cherished," and even with "holiness" in usages made obscure by the ambiguity of these expressions. Adherence to this idea of uniqueness may lead to great religious exaltation. But its indefiniteness invites perversion, distortion, and eventual corruption. Today, this is an imminent danger. We must therefore examine carefully the meaning of the entire edifice of spiritual and emotional associations that has arisen around this vague idea.

The very formula "the uniqueness of the people of Israel" requires elucidation. Is the people of Israel mentioned here an ideal concept, or are we concerned with the *phenomenal* Jewish people? Are we dealing with the people of Israel as an *a priori idea*, or with the Jewish people as a historical *entity*? Is the people of Israel a nation whose uniqueness is a goal to be achieved, or an entity whose uniqueness is an empirical datum? If the subject is the historical people of Israel, are we concerned with the continuum of its history, or with the present generation, whose problems do not necessarily coincide with those of preceding ones? In other words, is the "uniqueness of the people of Israel" conceived as initially determined or as a contingent factuality? Is it an entelechy predetermining Israel's vocation or a product of its history? What came first, the uniqueness that

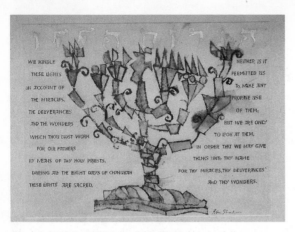

WE KINDLE
THESE LIGHTS
ON ACCOUNT OF
THE MIRACLES,
THE DELIVERANCES
AND THE WONDERS
WHICH THOU DIDST WORK
FOR OUR FATHERS
BY MEANS OF THY HOLY PRIESTS.
DURING ALL THE EIGHT DAYS OF CHANUKAH
THESE LIGHTS ARE SACRED.

NEITHER IS IT
PERMITTED US
TO MAKE ANY
PROFANE USE
OF THEM,
BUT WE ARE ONLY
TO LOOK AT THEM,
IN ORDER THAT WE MAY GIVE
THANKS UNTO THY NAME
FOR THY MIRACLES, THY DELIVERANCES
AND THY WONDERS.

Art and faith: *Menorah*, by Ben Shahn.

produced a people or a people that shaped its own uniqueness?

The term "uniqueness" itself is most perplexing. Only one uniqueness is absolute, and it is mentioned in the first verse of Shema. Within human reality there is no absolute uniqueness. Jews are human beings like all the rest, and they cannot be peculiar by nature, since by nature we are all—Jews as well as Gentiles—children of Noah. Jews could not possibly possess aptitudes that are not inherent in man *qua* man. The notion that Jewish man is endowed with characteristics that non-Jews lack (the prophetic faculty described by Judah Halevi, the "soul of the nation" proposed by Rabbi Kook, and the like) derogates the significance of Judaism. If by nature there is something special about a Jew that distinguishes him from the non-Jew, then Judaism is not a *task and a vocation* but a *factual datum*. Given facts, as such, are devoid of value; they are axiologically neutral. Values are not rooted in reality; they are objects of aspiration beyond reality toward which one must strive from within reality. It follows that to claim inherent uniqueness for the people of Israel is to deprive this uniqueness of all significance.

Some people argue that the Jewish people is empirically unique, since the Jewish fate is singular and has no counterpart among the other nations. In other words, the uniqueness of the people of Israel does not consist in a Jewish essence, but rather in the history of the Jewish people, which is an oddity in the context of general human history. If so, one should explore the sources of this uniqueness

and not evade the empirical inquiry by invoking a special calling and arguing circularly that the Jewish people was destined for a special fate, therefore its fate is peculiar.

The belief that the history of the Jewish people differs from that of all other people hinges on the use of the term "people." The existence of different people is a fact we take for granted without giving it much thought. Only rarely does it occur to us to ask ourselves what indeed is "a people." Why does a conglomeration of human beings, each of whom differs from the others, constitute a particular nation, while others, who do not differ from these individuals more than they differ from one another, do not belong to this people? A "people" is not a *natural* entity. It is a *being of the mind*. A nation exists insofar as there is a consciousness of its existence—the awareness of particular human beings that their communal existence has a framework which is "the nation," *their* nation. It is characteristic of such a framework that it does not exist *ad hoc*, for a limited period and a specific purpose. It rather persists and endures continuously over generations, throughout changes in conditions and circumstances.

The consciousness of national life is related to history. But what is the source of this shared self-consciousness? Why do the numbers of a particular human group consider themselves (and are usually considered by others) a "nation?" It seems to me that no objective answer to this question applies validly to all human groups that consider themselves "peoples" (and are so regarded by others). It also seems to me that no historian or sociologist has succeeded in proposing a criterion that would determine whether a certain human group was or was not a nation. Several defining characteristics have, indeed, been listed: racial origin, language, territory, state, and so forth. But many and diverse groups are considered "nations" and, although they lack one or even several of these characteristics, no one doubts their status as "nations." It is instructive to compare the Swedish people and the German people (the Austrians? the Swiss?), the Indian people (who lack a "national language"), the Arab people, the Palestinian people, and so on. Can an objective account be given of the peoplehood of all of these national groups?

Where does the Jewish people stand in view of these considerations? Its existence has been an empirical fact for the last three thousand years. Despite variations, changes, and structural metamorphoses, it has preserved its self-identity and continuity for approximately a hundred generations. It retained them not only in the self-consciousness of the Jews but also in the consciousness of non-Jews. Up to the end of the eighteenth century it occurred to no one to raise the question whether a Jewish nationality existed. The fact of its existence was taken for granted. What were the defining characteristics of the historical Jewish people during these hundred generations?

The biological criterion does not apply. The Jewish people is a multiracial melange. Today we can clearly discern typical facial features of all races among people who are Jews in every sense of the word "Jew." Even from the standpoint of the traditional perception, the sons of Abraham, Isaac, and Jacob have no racial or even familial peculiarity which would distinguish them from the Ishmaelites, the Edomites, the Arameans, and the Moabites. As for language, the significance of Hebrew for the Jewish people is unlike the significance of the national tongue for other peoples. During most of their history the Jews did not speak Hebrew. Even their monumental collective national literary composition, the talmudic literature, is written mostly in Aramaic. In the contemporary world, the greater part of the thirteen to fourteen million people who are considered Jews, both by themselves and by others, do not know or speak Hebrew. Yet Hebrew undoubtedly was, and is even today, the national language of the entire Jewish people, because every Jew knows that the Torah was given in Hebrew, even if he reads it in translation, and that the Shema and the daily prayer are in Hebrew.

The historic Jewish nation is not defined by territory either. Most of its history is not specifically related to the land of Israel, and today, too, most Jews have no actual tie to the land of Israel. Moreover, the heroic period of the Jewish people is precisely the period of exile. Needless to say, the historical Jewish people is not definable in terms of statehood. During the greater part of its history it had no state of its own. Even today only a minority of Jews are citizens of the Jewish state.

The Jewish people, as it existed in history, is definable only by reference to its Judaism—a Judaism that was not a mere idea in the mind but the realization of a program of living set forth in the Torah and delineated by its Mitzvoth. This way of life constituted the specific national content of Jewishness or, in other words, the *uniqueness* of the Jewish people. The Jew practiced a way of living that was exclusively his. His style of eating was not that of the Gentile—the Jewish kitchen differed from that of all other people. The sexual practices of Jews were peculiar to them since they were governed by the laws and rituals pertaining to the menstrual cycle and the "purity of the family." In the practical domain of work and industry, the observance of the Sabbath set them apart. Unlike the identities of the peoples that are characterized by race, language, territory, or state, the national identity of the historic Jewish people is *Judaism*, the actuality of which is life according to the Torah. It is not surprising that a people distinguished by a criterion absent from the defining characteristics of all other peoples should also have a history which was different from that of other nations.

The distinctiveness of the Jewish people as a historic national entity began to be blurred some two hundred years ago. Until then a Jew who cast off the yoke of Torah and Mitzvoth usually recognized that he thereby loosened his ties with the Jewish people. The innovation of recent generations is the phenomenon of Jews—a great number of them, and today the vast majority of those considered Jews—who have abandoned the Jewish way of life without severing themselves from their people. There is no authentic "Jewish" content to their lives that might distinguish them from that of Gentiles. Nevertheless, they continue to regard themselves as Jews, to present themselves as Jews and to be regarded as such by the others. Consequently a question that was hitherto meaningless arises: Who is a Jew? Who and what is the "Jewish people" with which they are affiliated? Not only is there today no Jewish national identity that actually distinguishes a Jew from a Gentile, but even among those held to be Jews, the common constitutive element that would render them *one* people is lacking. Jews who abide by Torah and Mitzvoth and Jews who have cast off their yoke cannot dine at the same table, have difficulty working together (Sabbath), and even marriage between them is problematic when both parties do not agree to observance of the laws relating to "purity of the family." Thus the appeal to national solidarity of all Jews is nowadays merely verbal and declaratory. It reflects no living reality. Even the legal Halakhic criterion for inclusion in the Jewish people is inadequate at present, since only a minority among those who consider themselves Jews regard the Halakhah as binding.

In our times we lack an objective criterion, independent of the subjective beliefs, views, and opinions of those who apply it, to determine whether someone is a Jew. In other words, we have no mark by which to define Jewish identity today. Consequently even the continued existence of the historical Jewish people is not guaranteed. The problem of the uniqueness of this people vanishes. There is a strong tendency in the religious camp to ignore this harsh reality by hiding it behind a screen of national-religious and pseudo-mystical ideology expressed in misleading phraseology. This ideology does not address itself to the real Jewish people but to a semimythological entity, "the nation," whose eternity is guaranteed in abstraction from the persons composing it. The perverse use of traditional terminology in these circles reaches its peak in application of the phrase "the eternity of Israel" to the alleged perpetual existence of Israel. When the prophet Samuel used this phrase (1 Sam. 15:29), he was not referring to an attribute of Israel, but to the God of Israel who transcends all categories of human existence.

The doctrine of Rabbi Kook identifying "the soul of the nation" with *Knesseth Israel* (the community of Israel), which in Kabbalistic context is the Shekhinah (the divine presence), or *Malkhuth* (kingdom), the tenth *Sefirah* (emanation) has been a calamitous stumbling block. In Rabbi Kook's Kabbalistic conception, the Jewish People is no longer an empirical-historical datum. From a factual reality it has been converted into a symbol of a completely different order of reality. The (intended or inadvertent) confusion of mystical and real categories is the great flaw in Rabbi Kook's doctrine that misled his disciples and continues to mislead theirs. It is imperative that we overcome this tendency to shroud reality with high-flown phraseology. There is no "soul of the nation." There are Jews who are living human beings. And the great crisis of the nation, "The hurt of my people" (Jer. 8:21), is that today we cannot tell *what* it is that makes them Jews.

The uniqueness of the empirical people of Israel is that their laws (the laws of the "King of kings of kings") are different from all peoples, whose laws are "the king's laws" (Esther 3:8). The problematic connection between the uniqueness of the actual life led by the people, and the uniqueness which the people is *intended* to achieve, can be highlighted by contrasting two adjacent verses:

You have avouched the Lord this day to be your God and to walk in His ways and to keep His statutes and His commandments and His laws and to hearken unto His voice.

And God has avouched you this day to be His peculiar people as He has promised you, and that you should keep all His commandments.

(Deut. 26:17–18).

Is there an implied cause and effect relation between these two verses? Which would be the cause and which the effect? I have no communication with what occurs behind the curtain which conceals the divine intentions, and have no opinion on the precise meaning of "God has avouched you." I am familiar, however, with the fact that "You have avouched the Lord" was the commitment of many Jewish generations. In the opinion of the greatest man of faith after the patriarchs and the prophets, these two verses should not be regarded as two distinct propositions but rather as two formulations of one proposition. In his doctrine of providence, Maimonides conceives of God's providential relation to man as identical with the state of man when he is aware of God. It is *identical* with it and not just a consequence. Similarly, one might say that the election of the people of Israel ("And God has avouched you") is identical with the assumption of the yoke of the Kingdom of Heaven by the people of Israel ("You have avouched").

Accordingly, the uniqueness of the Jewish people–also called the "holiness" of Israel–is not something that was given to the people as an abiding and an enduring possession, but is rather a demand, an assignment and a task with which they are charged–a goal toward which they are to strive eternally, without any guarantee of ever attaining it. The question is not "Did God bestow holiness upon the Jewish people"? but rather, "Is the Jewish people striving toward holiness by assuming the yoke of Torah and Mitzvoth?"

This view has been strongly opposed by many who were incapable of such lofty faith. The first to object to it was Qorah, who declared that "All the congregation are holy" (Num. 16:3), implying that the uniqueness of the people of Israel is a given fact: Israel is essentially a holy nation. The holiness of the Jewish People is not, however, a reality, but rather an end or goal which transcends reality. In reality itself there is only eternal striving towards this goal. Holiness is dependent on the doing of "all my commandments"—a condition that clashes with human nature. The author of the *Shulhan Arukh* advisedly opens his work with the words: "Let one gird up strength to rise in the morning to the service of his Creator." One cannot say simply, "man should rise in the morning to the service of his Creator," for it may well be that man is incapable of attaining the goal of serving God, but man can be charged with the trying and the effort to achieve it.

The Judaism of Moses is arduous. It means knowing that we are *not* a holy people. The Judaism of Qorah is very comforting. It allows every Jew to be proud and boast that he is a member of the holy people, which is holy by its very nature. This obligates him to nothing. There is no greater opposition than that between the conception of *Am Segulah* (a chosen people) as implying subjection to an obligation and Am Segulah as purely a privilege. He who empties the concept of the Jewish people of its religious content (like David Ben-Gurion) and still describes it as Am Segulah turns this concept into an expression of racist chauvinism.

As thus understood, the concept of the uniqueness of the Jewish people requires us to choose between two traditions of interpretation. One is represented by Judah Halevi (as the author of the *Kuzari,* not as the divine poet of the *Selihoth* and the *Yotzeroth*), some centuries later by Maharal, and, in our times, by Rabbi Kook and Ben-Gurion. The other tradition has descended from Moses, via Maimonides, to the *Shulhan Arukh*.

The uniqueness of the Jewish people is not a *fact*; it is an endeavor. The holiness of Israel is not a reality but a task. "Holy" is an attribute that applies exclusively to God. It is therefore inapplicable to anything in the natural or historical domain. He who does so apply it is guilty of idolatry. He exalts something natural or human to the level of the divine.

The uniqueness of the Jewish people is a direction and a target. Were it a reality, it would have no value. The people of Israel were not the chosen people but were *commanded* to be the chosen people. In what does its being chosen consist? This is made perfectly clear in the wording of the benediction "who has chosen us from among all peoples and has given us His Torah." The Jewish people has no intrinsic uniqueness. Its uniqueness rather consists in the demand laid on it. The people may or may not heed this demand. Therefore its fate is not guaranteed.

What has been said about the holiness of the people is also valid with regard to the holiness of the land. Exalting the land itself to the rank of holiness is idolatry *par excellence*. For a full understanding of the meaning of "holiness of the land," "the holiness of Jerusalem," and so on, one must refer to the Mishnah: "There are ten degrees of sanctity: The Land of Israel is more sanctified than all other Lands." We are not told that the land is holy but that it is sanctified. The crucial point is what its holiness consists of: From it are brought the *Omer* and the first fruits and the two loaves of bread. These things are brought from the land of Israel not because it is a holy land. The land is sanctified by the act of fulfilling the commandment to bring the offering of the Omer and the first fruits and the two loaves of bread. Similarly, the Mishnah tells us that "the area within the walls (of Jerusalem) is more sanctified than the rest of the country, since minor sacrifices and the second tithe are eaten there," and so on. The holiness of Jerusalem thus consists, among other and similar things, in the commandment enjoining the pilgrimage to Jerusalem. The Mishnah proceeds through ten stages up to the Holy of Holies, whose holiness lies in the prohibition of anyone's entering it except the High Priest on the Day of Atonement. It is only in this sense that we find holiness in the world (in nature, in sites, buildings, objects, and persons). By contrast with the intrinsic Holiness of God, there is no holiness in the world except sanctification through Mitzvoth ("who has sanctified us with his commandments"). "The Torah and faith are the very principles of the Jewish nation, and all the sanctities—the Land of Israel, Jerusalem etc.— derived from the Torah, and are sanctified by the holiness of the *Torah*. Therefore, there is no distinction of time and place relevant to any matter of *Torah*. Thus it is the same in the Land of Israel and abroad . . . *Ultimately: nothing is holy in the world* . . . only the name of God is holy . . . and every sanctity stems from a commandment of the Creator."

This is what distinguishes pagan religiosity from true religiosity. For pagan religiosity the land itself may be holy. I am aware that this paganism is spreading like wildfire today, affecting even many who, subjectively, are believing Jews. But a genuine religiosity recognizes that, in regard to the land, we are bound by certain obligations. Only the One is holy who is thrice declared holy in the Qedushah [a prayer centering on Isaiah 6:3]. Nothing other than He is holy, neither in history, nature, or man, though by virtue of their role in the service of God they may be sanctified.

New Age Judaism

One of the main trends in American Jewish religion has been an effort to develop a New Age variety of Judaism, incorporating soft-core Kabbalism (especially as told by Gershom Scholem), science fiction, and California-style transactional psychology (which in turn owes much to Martin Buber). Small Jewish publishing houses, such as Jewish Lights in Woodstock, Vermont, have turned out many thousands of these New Age books; presumably there is an active market. This selection from Lawrence Kushner's *Honey from the Rock* is typical of this genre.

There is a contemporary legend that was first told by Arthur Clarke and visualized by Stanley Kubrick in "2001" which also tries to unite the beginning and the end. Once, so the tale goes, our planet was visited by some supremely intelligent, beneficent, and curious alien. This visitor noticed that one ape seemed to be fascinated by the moon. All the others were too busy staying alive to have time for such wonderment. The visitor decided to show the moon-watcher how to extend his hand by using a simple tool. And in so doing initiated what has come to be known as human history and, incidentally, the visitor's own claim to deity. But since this visiting creator had other galaxies to explore, he devised a clever scheme whereby he might learn if his experiment would succeed. He planted some kind of cosmic alarm clock on the moon that was set to go off the moment his protégé, the moon-watching man-ape should discover it. For surely if he could rise above his fellow animals enough to reach the moon, then it would be worth the creator's time to return for a reunion.

For all these aeons of humanity, the tale suggests, we have been watched. Our progress and ascent has been hoped for. Somewhere at the furthest reaches of the cosmos there waits someone for some ape-man-child-astronaut-explorer for what will be surely the greatest reunion of them all. Standing there in space the first visitor-creator will welcome the last man-explorer. He will say something like, "So we meet again. I was not sure there for a long time whether you would ever make it. But you have and my experiment has been a success."

Now this tale also, despite its substitution for the ancient Holy One whom religious people call God with some space man (and its obeisance to technology) is also about creation and redemption. Our existence is an experiment.

Our redemption the result of some accomplishment. The end and the beginning are joined by some common purpose. And here too, one and the same life-force awareness unites all human history. Of course here the unity resides in the life of the first visitor-creator/the last visited-redeemer.

Or does it? What if there is as much unity in the countless generations separating the first man-ape and the last man-child-astronaut-explorer as there is in the single seemingly infinite life span of the cosmic visitor? What if all life is really the same life? What if what we call the end of our individual lives is only an illusion? Suppose we, each of us, are as much a part of those who precede and follow us as our childhood is of our old age? And that like some life disconnected and interrupted by flashes of amnesia, which is, nevertheless the same life, so too with the generations of human history. I cannot remember personally being freed from Egypt but nevertheless I myself was freed from Egypt.

There is another Kabbalistic legend that tells of all humankind descending from another Adam. *Adam Kadmon*, the primordial archetypic man, which the Kabbala is careful to distinguish from *Adam HaRishon*, the first mythic man of the garden, lest the distinction between man and God be confused. But by allowing them both to share the name "Adam" the blasphemous-holy confusion is nevertheless intimated. This primordial Adam was some kind of giant who contained within him the souls of us all. After the Fall they were scattered about the universe like sparks. They are never extinguished. There are only so many of them. They are each an eternal life force that gives life to one creature after another in one generation after another. And each of them began in the same *Adam Kadmon*, the same archetypic man, the same primordial giant. And at the end, they will return once again to their same ancient unity.

Perhaps in some other galaxy it is the way of life to continue from childhood to adolescence to maturity to old age without interruption or forgetting. Life awareness and continuity might span what we see as generations. But for us of this world, the continuity of lifetimes seem irreparably severed by death and inexplicably initiated by birth. Those life-sustaining sparks scattered from *Adam Kadmon* do not seem to be linked from one generation to the next. Somehow our consciousness of our journey is stricken with amnesia.

"Everybody carries the secret trace of the transmigrations of his soul in the lineaments of his forehead and his hands, and in the aura which radiates from his body." (Gershom Scholem, *Major Trends in Jewish Mysticism*, Schocken, 1941, p. 283.)

The Fascist Turn

There was a comity of interest between Haredim, the ultra-Orthodox, and the Likud party of Menschem Begin and Itzhak Shamir that formed the Israeli government and provided the Prime Minister incumbency for all but two years between 1977 and 1990 and again in 1996.

Begin and Shamir were secularist far-right nationalists, extremely hostile to the Palestinians and the other Arabs, and enamored of strong military postures. They were personal disciples of Vladimir Jabotinsky (who died prematurely in 1940), the founder of the Revisionists, the predecessor of Likud, and an admirer of the Nietzchean strong men who graced 1930s Fascism. Both the Haredim and the Likud had a penchant for authoritarian leadership, the Black Hats of rebbes, the Likud of military officers and militant politicians. The narrow band of votes that the Haredim provided in Israel's complex multiparty system (no Israeli party since Independence has actually had a majority—all governments have been ones of coalition) was important in keeping the Likud in power. In return, the Likud kept the ultra-Orthodox young men out of military service and provided lavish public aid for the Haredi yeshivas.

There was certainly a rightist trend in Israeli politics in the late 1970s and 1980s, but this fell short of Jabotinsky's legacy of Jewish Fascism. That was provided by an Israeli-born tank general Ariel (Arik) Sharon. He had performed well in the Six Day War in 1967. In 1973, after initial Israeli defeat and pullbacks on the Egyptian front, Sharon led a tank battalion in a risky but brilliant attack across the Sinai Canal, surrounded most of the Egyptian army 25 miles from Cairo, and forced the U.N. to intervene to save the Egyptians' skin by bringing the war to an end.

Sharon's thrust across the Sinai Canal, rolling up the Egyptian tank battalions, was the one of the two most brilliant actions of an armored commander in the twentieth century, standing alongside German General Hans Guderian's dash through the Ardennes Forest in May of 1940, forcing the collapse of the French army.

But Sharon was not satisfied to retire to his sheep farm and bask in his glory. He entered into a long political career, highlighted by the Israeli invasion of Lebanon and push to Beirut in 1982, for which he was principally responsible, and a dubious record, certainly marked by incompetence, perhaps by corruption, as a cabinet minister. It is in the nature of Fascism that military glory is marred by administrative failure and by corruption. So it always has been with fascist leaders; so it was with Sharon. This 1992 critique is by the Canadian-born Israeli journalist Barry Chamish.

Sharon will be remembered as the boldest and perhaps best general in Israeli military history. He salvaged a victory from the debacle of the Yom Kippur War by personally leading his troops across the Suez Canal, thereby accommodating the encirclement of two Egyptian armies. In 1977 Sharon ran under his own party, called "Shlomtzion." After the election he joined the Likud. Sharon exemplifies the impossibility of displacing a highly placed Israeli politician no matter how great a scandal. In 1982 Sharon was Defense Minister at the time of the infamous Sabra and Shatilla massacres. The Kahan Commission, which officially investigated the massacre, found Sharon guilty of gross negligence and recommended his removal from the cabinet. But the rest of the cabinet, led by Shamir, were most reluctant to let Sharon go since with him would go the votes of his followers and a good number of seats from the Likud. So expediency ruled the day and he was fired from his position as Defense Minister but allowed to stay in the cabinet, eventually as

Minister of Industry, where he caused more damage to the Israeli economy than he managed to do to Lebanon's.

Menachem Begin was once asked why he didn't appoint Sharon Defense Minister and in a now famed retort he replied that he'd be frightened to see tanks surrounding the Knesset. But even Begin, a man of great principles, was bulldozed into accepting Sharon as Defense Minister after a barrage of PLO artillery and rocket attacks against northern Israel led to a public demand for a more aggressive response.

Sharon gave most of the public what it wanted after the British Ambassador was shot and the Israeli Defense Forces (IDF) attacked Lebanon *en masse*. While giving the military their orders, Sharon was informing the cabinet of entirely different commands. At the outset of the war he told them that the goal was to secure a line forty kilometres north of the border, the range of a Katyusha rocket.

Begin, not knowing that Israeli troops were

already one hundred kilometres inside Lebanon, announced the war aim of forty kilometres. Reporters seized on what appeared to be a blatant lie by Israel but in fact, it was only Sharon who fomented the falsehood. Day after day he lied to the cabinet about the war aim and strategy. As one cabinet minister noted, the only way to get the truth out of Sharon today is to read tomorrow's papers.

The Lebanon War was a public relations disaster for Israel but up until Sabra and Shatilla, it was a beneficial war for the country. With a relatively mild Israeli loss of two hundred war dead, the PLO were forced to evacuate to lands far from easy reach of Israel's borders.

If at that point Sharon had declared victory, Israeli troops could have returned home with everlasting honour. However, Sharon's plans were more grandiose than simple military triumph. He was going to leave Israel the legacy of a friendly neighbour to the north. And he probably would have managed this to a certain extent, had his ally of sorts, President Bashir Gemayal, not been blown up by the Syrians.

Using the pretext of restoring order after the assassination, Sharon ordered his troops into Moslem West Beirut and they ended up positioned outside the Sabra and Shatilla refugee camps, which are better described as villages. Within these villages were a number of armed PLO fighters in contravention of the expulsion agreement arranged by Philip Habib and the Lebanese government. Israel wanted these men out but was wary of being responsible for any more casualties. With this in mind, Sharon, a mere two days after the assassination of President Gemayal, asked Lebanese Maronite troops to enter the camps. They did so with relish, murdering some eight hundred people over a weekend. Sharon was forced to resign as a result of sanctioning the whole debacle. He was not the only one to be rebuked by the Kahan Commission, however. When leaked news of the massacre reached Ze'ev Schiff, a journalist with *Ha'aretz,* he immediately tried to contact members of the cabinet to find out what action would be taken against the murderers. The first man he spoke to was the then Foreign Minister, Yitzhak Shamir, whose reaction was to reprimand Schiff for interrupting his holiday meal. (The massacre took place on *Rosh Hashanah,* the Jewish New Year.) Shamir's

apparent decision that his dinner was of more importance than mass murder may well have prolonged the bloodshed by a day and cost hundreds of lives. In any normal democracy, that would have been the end of his career—as it was, he escaped unscathed and went on to become Prime minister.

Sharon was now merely the Minister of Industry, a result, no doubt, of the expertise in commercial technology he had amassed as a soldier and rancher: He owns the largest sheep ranch in the country. For an Industry Minister, he took a decidedly monopolistic step. He raised tariffs on imported sheep, thus saving the nation from Scottish lamb. He then set about making local goods unprofitable by initiating a Free Trade Agreement (FTA) with the United States which is supposed to reduce and finally eliminate all tariffs and duties on trade between the two countries. Upon first glance, the idea seems advantageous to Israel which is a small market that has privileged access to the biggest market in the world. Up until the FTA, Israeli products survived in the home market as a result of high duty on foreign goods which more than doubled their prices. Once the agreement took effect, the whole plan backfired. Israel's consumer goods are shoddy compared to America's and the few manufacturers of quality items didn't have the budget to crack the highly competitive American market; nor did they possess sufficient selling skills as a result of living in a protected market for so long.

Once the prices on Marlboros dropped, the Israeli cigarette monopoly, Dubek, started going broke. Crest toothpaste cut deeply into the sales of the Israeli products, which are often akin to chalk immersed in sheep dip. Kellogg's Corn Flakes seem to out-taste Israel's Telma product and so on down the line of consumer purchases.

Sharon's foray into world trade caused other reverberations back in the Knesset. The government earns more from import duty charges than from income tax. Every time someone in Israel buys even the cheapest, smallest and flimsiest car, the government adds another $7,000 to its coffers. If American cars could come in without duty then the government would lose more revenue than it could recoup by taxing outgoing Israeli products like chocolate-covered orange peels and appliance adaptors. Sharon's plan was robbing the government of its vein of gold and there seemed no simple way of producing equal quantities of unearned cash from the weary populace. All in all, Sharon had to get Israel out of this signed, witnessed and most legal agreement between the two countries.

Sharon took an all too typically Israeli tack. He sought instances of arguable American abuses of the treaty and claimed America was taking advantage of Israel. He made such a public issue out of the minor discrepancies that the Americans set up a special commission to oversee the administration of the agreement. After a delegation of Israelis flew to Washington to air their complaints, the Americans came to the correct conclusion that the Israelis were taking great efforts to renege on the whole thing. The treaty is still on the books but the Fords and Buicks without duty are nowhere to be found in a land of Fiats and Metros.

Having shattered the treaty he fathered, Sharon decided to take a break from industrial matters for four months. He had sued *Time* magazine for libel as a result of their claim that he planned the Sabra and Shatilla massacre with Phalangist leaders. If *Time* was right, Sharon would not have been merely negligent but an accessory to mass murder. But *Time* was horribly wrong and Sharon's name was cleared.

But he spent four months in America, the first two fund-raising for his trial, the next two staying at a very expensive suite at the Plaza Hotel. Choosing not to take a temporary leave of absence, he left no one in charge of the Ministry's affairs for a third of a year. And for that time no one was in charge of creating industrial jobs, new technology or useful products. And since some eight hundred of Israel's thirteen hundred significant factories are owned directly or indirectly by the government, the period when Sharon was away from the office was one of slowdown to outright stagnation.

On the other hand, while he was away, there was a marked reduction in bare-faced patronage. To assure permanent hegemony, *Ha'aretz*, the respected newspaper, reported on 19 September 1985 that, "of the twenty-seven new directors appointed by Ariel Sharon during his tenure of Minister of Industry and Trade, twenty-three are active Likud members." Being a director means a large salary and perks. Most of these juicy and unprofitable jobs went to his own followers, not of course, to experts on trade and industry.

Miriam Ben-Porat, the respected and totally honest State Comptroller, noted in her 1990 report that "Haphazard methods, poor planning and flagrant violations of the law characterise the workings of the Ministry of Industry and Trade."

She found a number of fine examples of his work ethic, a typical instance of which was hiring one of his supporters to be his advisor on agricultural affairs. Unfortunately, no such position in the ministry existed or was approved by the Civil Service Authority—a "technicality" Sharon circumvented by hiring the man as "an outside contractor." No one knew what this man was contracted to do, though he was apparently so proficient at whatever it was he was doing that Sharon gave him yet another position, "Advisor to the Minister on Development Areas." This post never existed before but must have involved simple tasks since the new advisor was not asked to give up his outside contractor job. In short, the fortunate follower drew two salaries for doing nothing. As Ben-Porat notes: "It is clear that he was and continues to be employed in violation of the law. In the opinion of the state comptroller, the behaviour by the ministry . . . should be viewed in a grave manner."

He abused his power in other ways too, in one instance awarding substantial research and development grants to projects already completed, and in another case (after his request for their transfer had been turned down by the Civil Service Authority), luring two women from other ministries to work for him by offering them greatly enhanced salaries paid for out of public funds.

It appears that Sharon ran a crooked Industry Ministry but after the formation of the new government in May 1990, he was given an even more important task to mishandle: creating new accommodation as Minister of Housing. The timing of this appointment, the most ideological position in the cabinet short of prime minister, was important. By May 1988, perestroika and glasnost had engendered the emigration of Soviet Jews, resulting in a tidal wave of new Israelis. Israel's population might be increased by twenty-five percent as a result of the human flood.

Israel has been waiting a long time for an increase in its Jewish population to offset the frightening birthrate of the Arabs within its borders. Jewish emigration was still a ticklish question in the Kremlin with all its vital ties to the

Arab world and nothing was allowed to upset the testy feelings of the Soviet leadership.

But the cabinet decided to put massive emigration at risk for the sake of ideology. Sharon had many times publicly given his vision of several million Jews settling in the Jordan Valley (better known as the West Bank). The Soviets implicitly stated that populating the West Bank with their Jews would endanger the whole enterprise. What better man to placate their fears than Sharon at Housing?

And he didn't let anyone down. Sharon owns a thousand-acre ranch but still felt a little constricted, understandable in his case, so he bought a home in the Moslem Quarter of the Old City of Jerusalem. There is an unwritten law dividing the Old City and keeping its residents in separate quarters. Sharon's home was a deliberate provocation and a message that a Jew could live anywhere he chose in his own land—perhaps a noble sentiment, but costly to Israelis who don't share it. Besides the cost of the house, an eight-man guard is stationed permanently outside it, their salaries paid by an already beleaguered and overtaxed public.

The Easter before there had been another surprise, this time for residents of the Christan Quarter of the walled city. A hundred and fifty Jews moved into a building in their quarter. The churchmen protested and the world watched Israel suffer another blow to its image as black-garbed priests carrying large crosses clashed with soldiers in Easter processions. This was not a constituency Israel could afford to alienate. Religious Christians, especially in America, are amongst Israel's most devoted supporters, largely because they see the Jewish state as prophetic and presaging the Second Coming.

The purchase of the building was legal. The owner received $4.6 million for the property, far above its actual value and he set up shop well away from Israel with the money. The land was not holy, in fact it was quite run down, and in any other city, the transaction would have been ethi-

cal. But in Jerusalem it was viewed as an intrusion guaranteed to spark violence. Still, it was a private transaction, wasn't it?

No, it wasn't. The Housing Ministry, at the time run by David Levy, had contributed significant funds towards the purchase of the property. Public money had once again been used to stir up trouble in the promotion of Likudan ideology. The Americans were so incensed by the revelation that the government had had a part in the purchase of the building that they subtracted the government's contribution from their next economic aid package.

And the provocations continued. Shamir announced that with the big new population coming from Russia, a big new Israel would be required. The Arab states are terrified by the Soviet emigration and used this statement as proof that the government was using Soviet Jews to fill the disputed territories. They succeeded in forcing Gorbachev to threaten to stop the emigration if Shamir was stating policy. In fact, he may have been, but less than 1% of Soviet Jews have chosen to live in the territories and James Baker took great offense at the Soviet leader's threat to emigration and forced him to back down. Soviet Jews continued to flock to Israel despite Sharon's mismanagement of the housing operation.

Sharon continued to be deliberate in his timing. When James Baker visited Israel after the Gulf War to push his new "window of opportunity" peace initiative, Sharon authorised the dedication of two new settlements. As a result, when Sharon arrived in Washington a month later, Baker called him an obstacle to peace and refused him the right to attend a White House meeting with American Housing Secretary, Jack Kemp.

Sharon's tenure at Housing [was] a disaster not only for young couples who have been priced out of the housing market by government policies, but especially for new immigrants who were initially being housed either in army camps or three families to an apartment in civilian areas.

Sociology

Three-quarters of what professors and students do in sociology departments today are lines of thought and research that were developed by the first professor of sociology at the University of Paris, Emile Durkheim, who died in 1917. He was the son of a French rabbinical family. Here are his key statements on the sociology of religion: First, that religion is functionally related to other social actions; and second, that religious belief is in inevitable decline in modern, secularizing society.

It has often been said that religion was, at each moment of history, the totality of beliefs and sentiments of all sorts relative to the relations of man with a being or beings whose nature he regarded as superior to his own. But such a definition is manifestly inadequate. In point of fact, there is a vast number of rules, either of conduct or of thought, which are certainly religious, but which apply to relations of an entirely different sort. Religion forbids the Jews to eat certain meats and orders them to dress in a certain fixed way. It imposes such and such an option concerning the nature of man and things, or concerning the origin of the world. It often governs even juridical, moral, and economic relations. Its sphere of action extends, then, beyond the interaction of man with the divine. We know for certain, moreover, that a religion without a god exists (Buddhism). This alone should be sufficient to show that we should not continue to define religion in terms of the idea of god. Finally, if the extraordinary authority that the believer attributes to the divinity can account for the particular prestige of everything religious, it remains to be explained how men have been led to give such authority to a being who, so everyone avers, is in many cases, if not always, a product of the imagination. Nothing comes from nothing; this force must come to the individual from somewhere, and consequently, this formula does not get to the heart of the matter.

But this element aside, the only characteristic that all religious ideas and sentiments share equally seems to be that they are common to a certain number of people living together, and that they are also normally very intense. It is, indeed, a universal fact that, when a conviction of any strength is held by the same community of men, it inevitably takes on a religious character. It inspires in men's minds the same reverential respect as beliefs which are properly religious. It is, thus, very probable—this brief exposition, of course, is not rigorous proof—that religion corresponds to an equally very central area of the *conscience collective*.

Truly religious beliefs are always common to a specific group which professes to adhere to them and to practise the rites connected with them. They are not merely received individually by . . . There is something eternal in religion which is destined to survive all the particular symbols in which religious thought has successively enveloped itself. There can be no society which does not feel the need of upholding and reaffirming, at regular intervals, the collective sentiments and ideas which give it its unity and individuality. Now this moral reconstruction cannot be achieved except by means of reunions, assemblies and congregations, in which individuals, being brought together, reaffirm in common their common sentiments. From this source arise ceremonies which do not differ from properly religious ceremonies, either in their object, the results which they produce, or the processes employed to attain these results. What essential difference is there between an assembly of Christians celebrating the principal dates of the life of Christ, or Jews remembering the exodus from Egypt or the proclamation of the decalogue, and a gathering of citizens commemorating the institution of a new moral or legal system or some great event in national life?

. . . If there is one truth that history teaches us beyond doubt, it is that religion tends to embrace a smaller and smaller sector of social life. Originally, it pervades everything; everything social is religious. The two words are synonymous. Then political, economic, scientific functions gradually free themselves from religious control, establish themselves separately and take on a more and more openly temporal character. God, if one may express the matter this way, was at first present in all human relations, but progressively withdraws from them;

he abandons the world to men and their disputes. At least, if he continues to dominate it, it is from on high and at a distance, and the power which he exercises, becoming more general and abstract, leaves more place to the free play of human forces. The individual really feels himself less *acted upon*; he becomes more a source of spontaneous activity. In short, not only does the domain of religion not grow at the same time and in the same measure as temporal life, but it contracts more and more. This regression did not begin at some certain moment of history; we can follow its development from the early phases of social evolution. It is thus linked to the fundamental conditions of the development of societies, and this shows that there is a decreasing number of collective beliefs and sentiments which are both collective and strong enough to assume a religious character.

Social Anthropology

If Durkheim, the founder of sociology as an academic discipline was from a French rabbinical family, the greatest social anthropologist of this century (who is still at work), Claude Lévi-Strauss, also a Parisian academic, was from a Belgian rabbinical family. He studied in Paris in the 1930s with Durkheim's heir and nephew, Michel Mauss, and started field work in the Amazon while teaching at the University of San Paolo. During World War II he taught in New York City, where he called himself Mr. Strauss so students would stop asking him if he was related to the family that made blue jeans.

Lévi-Strauss' memoir and intellectual testament, *Tristes Tropiques*, published in 1956, is one of the three most important books of the twentieth century. The others are *The Interpretation of Dreams*, by Sigmund Freud, a Jew, published in 1900; and *Ulysses* by the modernist James Joyce, published in the early 1920s and at least ostensibly about a day in the life of a Dublin Jew in the year 1904.

Tristes Tropiques developed the radical program of the later twentieth century—that of the structural polarity between the destructive, technical West and the pristine, environmentally friendly Other of non-Western societies. This concept proved more troublesome for the Israelis to contend with than the whole tradition of Christianity and Islam.

Here, in the splendid Weightman translation, Lévi-Strauss describes how he became an anthropologist and how his view of the world began to take shape.

Lévi-Strauss ignores his rabbinical background in this memoir. But the theory he developed was directly opposed to the rabbinical idea of the Chosen People. Instead Lévi-Strauss structuralism posited the universality of a common code—based on the binary principle—running through all mind and society. The mind of the physicist and the savage mind have the same structure which is also found in kinship, diet, etc. And it is the Other, the nonindustrial, nontechnological world that is closest to the underlying universal structure. In the West, the universal structure has been overlaid with the corrupting effects of environmentally ravaging technology, money, and power. It is the Other, the colonial world, that is in tune with the universal code of the universe.

Since the mid-1960s, Lévi-Strauss' structuralism has dominated social anthropology. Ideologically it is the diametrical opposite of the traditional Jewish view of the special nature of the Jewish people. Lévi-Strauss' doctrine has proven very useful to anti-Jewish Arab writers like Edward Said. Israel with its importation of Western imperialist ways into the Orient and its denigration of the Arab peoples as backward, is in conflict with the authenticity of the structural Other, it is alleged.

I was studying philosophy with a view to sitting the *agrégation* competitive examination, but this was the result less of a genuine vocation than of a dislike for the other subjects I had sampled up till then. When I reached the top or "philosophy" class in the lycée, I was vaguely in favour of a kind of rationalistic monism, which I was prepared to justify and support; I therefore made great efforts to get into the section taught by Gustave Rodrigues, who had the reputation of being "advanced." He was, it is true, a militant member of the SFIO, but on the philosophical level all he had to offer was a mixture of Bergsonism and Neokantism which I found extremely disappointing. He expounded his dry dogmatic views with great fervour and gesticulated passionately throughout his lessons. I have never known so much naïve conviction allied to greater intellectual poverty. He committed suicide in 1940 when the Germans entered Paris.

It was in that class that I first began to learn that every problem, whether serious or trifling, may be solved by the application of an always identical method, which consists in contrasting two traditional views of the question; the first is introduced by means of a justification on common-sense grounds, then the justification is destroyed with the help of the second view;

finally, both are dismissed as being equally inadequate, thanks to a third view which reveals the incomplete character of the first two; these are now reduced by verbal artifice to complementary aspects of one and the same reality: form and subject-matter, container and content, being and appearance, continuity and discontinuity, essence and existence, etc. Such an exercise soon becomes purely verbal, depending, as it does, on a certain skill in punning, which replaces thought: Assonance, similarity in sound and ambiguity gradually come to form the basis of those brilliantly ingenious intellectual shifts which are thought to be the sign of sound philosophizing.

Five years of study at the Sorbonne boiled down to acquiring skill in this form of mental gymnastics, the dangers of which are nevertheless obvious. In the first place, the technique by which intellectual balance is maintained is so simple that it can be applied in the case of any problem. To prepare ourselves for the examination and for the supreme ordeal of the *leçon d'agrégation* (the oral part, which consists in dealing with a question drawn from a hat, after a few hours' preparation), my fellow-students and I set ourselves wildly unlikely subjects. I was confident that, at ten minutes' notice, I could knock together an hour's lecture with a sound dialectical framework, on the respective superiority of buses and trams. Not only does this method provide a key to open any lock; it also leads one to suppose that the rich possibilities of thought can be reduced to a single, always identical pattern, at the cost of a few rudimentary adjustments. It is rather as if music could be reduced to a single melody, once the musician has realized that this melody can be read either in the treble or the bass clef. In this sense, our philosophical training exercised the intelligence but had a desiccating effect on the mind.

I can see an even graver danger in confusing the advancement of knowledge with the growing complexity of intellectual structures. We were asked to produce a dynamic synthesis, by starting from the least adequate theories and progressing towards the most subtle; but at the same time (since all our teachers were obsessed with the historical approach), we had to explain how the latter had gradually emerged from the former. Basically, it was not so much a system of discovering what was true and what was false as of understanding how mankind had gradually overcome certain contradictions. Philosophy was not *ancilla scientiarum*, the servant and auxiliary of scientific exploration, but a kind of aesthetic contemplation of consciousness by itself. It was seen as having evolved, in the course of the centuries, ever higher and bolder structures, as having solved problems of balance or support and as having invented logical refinements, and the result was held to be valid, in proportion to its technical perfection or internal coherence. The teaching of philosophy might be compared to instruction in a form of art history which proclaimed that Gothic was necessarily superior to Romanesque, and, within the Gothic, the flamboyant style more perfect than the primitive, but which did not raise any questions about what was beautiful and what was not. The signifier did not relate to any signified; there was no referent. Expertise replaced the truth. After years of this training, I now find myself intimately convinced of a few unsophisticated beliefs, not very different from those I held at the age of fifteen. Perhaps I see more clearly the inadequacy of these intellectual tools; at least they have an instrumental value which makes them suitable for the service I require of them. I am in no danger of being deceived by their internal complexity, nor of losing sight of their practical purpose

through becoming absorbed in the contemplation of their wonderful elaborateness.

However, I suspect that there were more personal causes for the disgust which quickly made me abandon philosophy and turn to anthropology, since it offered a way of escape. After spending a happy year at the Mont de Marsan lycée, teaching and preparing my course of lessons as I went along, I was dismayed to discover at the beginning of the next school year, after being transferred to Laon, that I would have to repeat the same course for the rest of my life. A peculiar feature—no doubt a weakness—of my mental make-up is that I find it difficult to concentrate twice on the same subject. Normally the *agrégation* is held to be an inhuman ordeal, at the end of which, one is entitled, if one so wishes, to be left in peace for ever. In my case, it was just the opposite. I passed the *agrégation* at the first attempt and as the youngest candidate in my year, and I had been in no way exhausted by my foray through doctrines, theories and hypotheses. My torment was to begin later: I realized that I would be physically incapable of delivering my lessons, unless I evolved a new course every year. This handicap proved to be still more embarrassing when I found myself having to act as an oral examiner: As the questions cropped up at random, according to the accidents of the draw, I was no longer sure what answers the candidates were supposed to give. The dimmest of them seemed to say all there was to be said. It was as if the subjects were melting away before my eyes, through the mere fact that I had once applied my mind to them.

Today I sometimes wonder if anthropology did not attract me, without my realizing this, because of a structural affinity between the civilizations it studies and my particular way of thinking. I have no aptitude for prudently cultivating a given field and gathering in the harvest year after year: I have a neolithic kind of intelligence. Like native bush fires, it sometimes sets unexplored areas alight; it may fertilize them and snatch a few crops from them, and then it moves on, leaving scorched earth in its wake. At the time, however, I was incapable of achieving any awareness of this deeper motivation. I knew nothing about anthropology, I had never attended any course and when Sir James Frazer paid his last visit to the Sorbonne to give a memorable lecture—in 1928, I think—it never occurred to me to attend, although I knew about it.

It is true that, from my earliest childhood, it had been my hobby to collect exotic curios. But it was an antiquarian interest, the direction of which was governed by the cost of things I could afford. As an adolescent, I was still so uncertain about what I wanted to do that the first person to give an opinion, André Cresson, one of my early philosophy teachers, suggested that law studies would be most suited to my temperament; I remember him with gratitude because of the half-truth concealed in his mistake.

So I gave up the idea of competing for the Ecole Normale Supérieure and enrolled as a law student, while at the same time studying for the *licence* in philosophy; I adopted this solution because it was so easy. A strange fatality hangs over the teaching of law. It is caught between theology, which at that time it resembled in spirit, and journalism, towards which it was beginning to swing as a result of the recent reforms, and so it seems unable to find any basis for itself that is at once solid and objective; it loses one of these virtues in trying to gain or retain the other. The jurist, who is himself an object of study for the social scientist, always makes one think of an animal trying to show the magic lantern to the zoologist. Fortunately, in those days, it was possible to get through examinations after only a couple of weeks' work, thanks to manuals which had to be learned by heart. But I was put off by the people studying law even more than by the barrenness of the subject. I doubt whether the distinction is still valid, but around 1928 the various first-year students could be divided into two distinct species, one might almost say two distinct races: law and medicine on the one hand, the arts and the sciences on the other.

However unattractive the terms extrovert and introvert may be, they are no doubt the most appropriate ones for the expression of the contrast. On the one hand there was "youth" (in the sense in which traditional folklore uses this term to signify a certain age group), noisy, aggressive, anxious to assert itself even at the cost of the worst kind of vulgarity, and politically to the extreme Right (of the period); on the other, prematurely aged adolescents, discreet, withdrawn, usually Left-wing, and whose aim was to be admitted to the ranks of the adults they themselves were busily trying to become.

There is a quite simple explanation for the difference. The extroverts, who are studying to enter the professions, behave as they do to celebrate their release from school and the fact that they already accept a definite place in the system of social functions. Finding themselves in an intermediary state between the undifferentiated role of the schoolboy and the specialized activity for which they are intended, they feel themselves to be in a marginal situation and claim contradictory privileges appropriate to both positions.

In the case of arts and science students, the usual openings—teaching, research and various miscellaneous careers—are quite different in kind. The student choosing them does not bid farewell to the world of childhood: On the contrary he is trying rather to remain with it. The teaching profession, after all, offers adults their only possibility of remaining at school. The arts or science student is characterized by an attitude of refusal towards the demands of the group. An almost monk-like tendency inspires him to withdraw either temporarily or more permanently into study and to devote himself to the preservation and transmission of a heritage independent of the passing moment. As for the future scholar or researcher, his aim is commensurable only with the time-span of the universe. Nothing could be more mistaken, then, than to lead them to believe that their choice is a form of commitment; even when they think it is, the commitment does not consist in their accepting a particular datum and identifying themselves with one or other of its functions and in accepting the personal opportunities and risks it involves, but in judging it from the outside, as if they themselves were not part of it; their commitment is just their own special way of remaining uncommitted. In this respect, teaching and research are not to be confused with training for a profession. Their greatness and their misfortune is that they are a refuge or a mission.

In this opposition between, on the one hand, the professions, and, on the other, ambiguous activities which can be classed either as a mission or a refuge, partake of both, but are always rather more definitely one than the other, anthropology certainly occupies an exceptional position. It is the most extreme form of the second term of the contrast. While remaining human himself, the anthropologist tries to study and judge mankind from a point of view sufficiently lofty and remote to allow him to disregard the particular circumstances of a given society or civilization. The conditions in which he lives and works cut him off physically from his group for long periods; through being exposed to such complete and sudden changes of environment, he acquires a kind of chronic rootlessness; eventually, he comes to feel at home nowhere, and he remains psychologically maimed. Like mathematics or music, anthropology is one of the few genuine vocations. One can discover it in oneself, even though one may have been taught nothing about it.

To these individual peculiarities and social attitudes must be added other promptings of an essentially intellectual nature. It was during the decade from 1920 to 1930 that psychoanalytical theories became known in France. They taught me that the static oppositions around which we were advised to construct our philosophical essays and later our teaching—the rational and the irrational, the intellectual and the emotional, the logical and the prelogical—amounted to no more than a gratuitous intellectual game. In the first place, beyond the rational there exists a more important and valid category—that of the meaningful, which is the highest mode of being of the rational, but which our teachers never so much as mentioned, no doubt because they were more intent on Bergson's *Essai sur les données immédiates de la conscience* than on F. de Saussure's *Cours de linguistique générale*. Next, Freud's work showed me that the oppositions did not really exist in this form, since it is precisely the most apparently emotional behaviour, the least rational procedures and so-called prelogical manifestations which are at the same time the most meaningful. Rejecting the Bergsonian acts of faith and circular arguments which reduced beings and things to a state of mush the better to bring out their ineffability, I came to the conclusion that beings and things could retain their separate values without losing the clarity of outline which defines them in relationship to each other and gives an intelligible structure to each. Knowledge is based neither on renunciation nor on barter; it consists rather in selecting *true* aspects, that is, those coinciding with the properties of my thought. Not, as the Neokantians claimed, because my thought exercises an inevitable influence over things, but because it is itself an object. Being "of this world," it partakes of the same nature as the world.

However, this intellectual development, which I underwent along with other members of my generation, was given a particular colouring in my case by the intense interest geology had inspired in me ever since childhood. I count among my most precious memories not so much some expedition into an unknown region of central Brazil as a hike along the flank of a limestone plateau in Languedoc to determine the line of contact between two geological strata. It was something quite different from a walk or a simple exploration of space. It was a quest, which would have seemed incoherent to some uninitiated observer, but which I look upon as the very image of knowledge, with the difficulties it involves and the delights it affords.

Every landscape appears first of all as a vast chaos, which leaves one free to choose the meaning one wants to give it. But, over and above agricultural considerations, geographical irregularities and the various accidents of history and prehistory, the most majestic meaning of all is surely that which precedes, commands and, to a large extent, explains the others. A pale blurred line, or an often almost imperceptible difference in the shape and consistency of rock fragments, are evidence of the fact that two oceans once succeeded each other where, today, I can see nothing but barren soil. As I follow the traces of their age-old stagnation despite all obstacles—sheer cliff faces, landslides, scrub or cultivated land—and disregarding paths and fences, I seem to be proceeding in meaningless fashion. But the sole aim of this contrariness is to recapture the master-meaning, which may be obscure but of which each of the others is a partial or distorted transposition.

When the miracle occurs, as it sometimes does; when, on one side and the other of the hidden crack, there are suddenly to be found cheek-by-jowl two green plants of different species, each of which has chosen the most favourable soil; and when at the same time, two ammonites with unevenly intricate involutions can be glimpsed in the rock, thus testifying in their own way to a gap of several tens of thousands of years suddenly space and time become one: The living diversity of the moment juxtaposes and perpetuates the ages. Thought and emotion move into a new dimension where every drop of sweat, every muscular movement, every gasp of breath becomes symbolic of a past history, the development of which is reproduced in my body, at the same time as my thought embraces its significance. I feel myself to be steeped in a more dense intelligibility, within which centuries and distances answer each other and speak at last with one and the same voice.

When I became acquainted with Freud's theories, I quite naturally looked upon them as the application, to the individual human being, of a method the basic pattern of which is represented by geology. In both cases, the researcher, to begin with, finds himself faced with seemingly impenetrable phenomena; in both cases, in order to take stock of, and gauge, the elements of a complex situation, he must display subtle qualities, such as sensitivity, intuition and taste. And yet, the order which is thus introduced into a seemingly incoherent mass is neither contingent nor arbitrary. Unlike the history of the historians, that of the geologist is similar to the history of the psychoanalyst in that it tries to project in time—rather in the manner of a *tableau vivant*—certain basic characteristics of the physical or mental universe. I can take the simile of the *tableau vivant* further: The game called "charades" provides a simple illustration of a procedure which consists in interpreting each action as the unfolding in time of certain eternal truths, the concrete aspect of which the charades are meant to recreate on the moral level, but which in other fields are referred to specifically as laws. In all these instances, the arousing of aesthetic curiosity leads directly to an acquisition of knowledge.

When I was about sixteen, I was introduced to Marxism by a young Belgian socialist, whom I had got to know on holiday, and who is now one of his country's ambassadors abroad. I was all the more delighted by Marx in that the reading of the works of the great thinker brought me into contact for the first time with the line of philosophical development running from Kant to Hegel; a whole new world was opened up to me. Since then, my admiration for Marx has remained constant, and I rarely broach a new sociological problem without first stimulating my thought by rereading a few pages of *The 18th Brumaire of Louis Bonaparte* or the *Critique of Political Economy*. Incidentally, Marx's quality has nothing to do with whether or not he accurately foresaw certain historical developments. Following Rousseau, and in what I consider to be a definitive manner, Marx established

that social science is no more founded on the basis of events than physics is founded on sense data: The object is to construct a model and to study its property and its different reactions in laboratory conditions in order later to apply the observations to the interpretation of empirical happenings, which may be far removed from what had been forecast.

At a different level of reality, Marxism seemed to me to proceed in the same manner as geology and psychoanalysis (taking the latter in the sense given it by its founder). All three demonstrate that understanding consists in reducing one type of reality to another; that the true reality is never the most obvious; and that the nature of truth is already indicated by the care it takes to remain elusive. For all cases, the same problem arises, the problem of the relationship between feeling and reason, and the aim is the same: to achieve a kind of *superrationalism*, which will integrate the first with the second, without sacrificing any of its properties.

I was therefore opposed to the new metaphysical tendencies which were then emerging. Phenomenology I found objectionable in that it postulated a kind of continuity between experience and reality. I agreed that the latter encompasses and explains the former, but I had learned from my three sources of inspiration that the transition between one order and the other is discontinuous; that to reach reality one has first to reject experience, and then subsequently to reintegrate it into an objective synthesis devoid of any sentimentality. As for the intellectual movement which was to reach its peak in existentialism, it seemed to me to be anything but a legitimate form of reflection, because of its overindulgent attitude towards the illusions of subjectivity. The raising of personal preoccupations to the dignity of philosophical problems is far too likely to lead to a sort of shop-girl metaphysics, which may be pardonable as a didactic method but is extremely dangerous if it allows people to play fast-and-loose with the mission incumbent on philosophy until science becomes strong enough to replace it: That is, to understand being in relationship to itself and not in relationship to myself. Instead of doing away with metaphysics, phenomenology and existentialism introduced two methods of providing it with alibis.

Between Marxism and psychoanalysis, which are social sciences—one orientated towards society, the other towards the individual—and geology, which is a physical science—but which has also fostered and nurtured history both by its method and its aim—anthropology spontaneously establishes its domain: for mankind, which anthropology looks upon as having no limits other than those of space, gives a new meaning to the transformations of the terrestrial globe, as defined by geological history: This meaning is the product of the uninterrupted labour which goes on all through the ages in the activities of societies as anonymous as telluric forces, and in the minds of individuals whom the psychologist sees as particular case histories. Anthropology affords me intellectual satisfaction: as a form of history, linking up at opposite ends with world history and my own history, it thus reveals the rationale common to both. In proposing the study of mankind, anthropology frees me from doubt, since it examines those differences and changes in mankind which have a meaning for all men, and excludes those peculiar to a single civilization, which dissolve into nothingness under the gaze of the outside observer. Lastly, it appeases that restless and destructive appetite I have already referred to, by ensuring me a virtually inexhaustible supply of material, thanks to the diversity of manners, customs and institutions. It allows me to reconcile my character with my life.

This being so, it may seem strange that for so long I should have remained deaf to the message which, even during my lost years at school, was being transmitted to me through the works of the leading French sociologists. As it happened, the revelation did not occur until 1933–34, when by chance I came across Robert H. Lowie's *Primitive Society*, which was by no means a recent work. The point was that instead of presenting me with ideas taken from books and immediately changed into philosophical concepts, it described the writer's actual experience of native societies, and presented the significance of that experience through his involvement. My mind was able to escape from the claustrophobic, Turkish-bath atmosphere in which it was being imprisoned by the practice of philosophical reflection. Once it had got out into the open air, it felt refreshed and renewed. Like a city-dweller transported to the mountains, I became drunk with space, while my dazzled eyes measured the wealth and variety of the objects surrounding me.

So started that long and intimate acquaintance with Anglo-American anthropology—carried on first, at a distance, through the medium of books, and later maintained by personal contact—which was to give rise to serious misunderstandings. In Brazil, to begin with, where the university professors expected me to join in teaching the kind of Durkheimian sociology towards which they themselves inclined, both because of the positivist tradition which is still very much alive in South America, and because of their desire to provide a philosophical basis for that moderate liberalism, which is the usual ideological weapon used by oligarchies to combat personal power. I arrived in a state of open revolt against Durkheim and against any attempt to use sociology for metaphysical purposes. At a time when I was doing my best to widen my horizons, I was hardly in a mood to rebuild the prison walls. Since then I have often been criticized for showing too slavish an obedience to Anglo-American thought. This is absolute nonsense. Apart from the fact that, at this moment, I am probably more faithful than anyone else to the Durkheimian tradition—and abroad everybody is aware of this—the authors to whom I willingly proclaim my debt, Lowie, Kroeber and Boas, seem to me to be as far removed as possible from the James or Dewey kind of American philosophy which has been out of date for so long, or from what is now called logical positivism. Since they were Europeans by birth and had been trained in Europe or by European professors, they represent something quite different: a synthesis reflecting, on the level of knowledge, that other synthesis which Columbus had made objectively possible four centuries earlier: The synthesis of a strong scientific method with the unique experimental field offered by the New World at a time when American anthropologists not only had the best available libraries, but could leave their universities and visit native communities as easily as we could go to the Basque country or the Riviera. What I am praising is not an intellectual tradition but an historical situation. It must have been an extraordinary advantage to have access to communities which had never yet been the object of serious investigation and which were still quite well preserved, since their destruction had only just begun. Let me quote an anecdote to illustrate what I mean. An Indian, through some miracle, was the sole survivor after the massacre of certain savage Californian tribes. For years he lived unnoticed in the vicinity of large towns, still chipping stones for the arrow-heads with which he did his hunting. Gradually, however, all the animals disappeared. One day the Indian was found naked and dying of hunger on the outskirts of a suburb. He ended his days peacefully as a porter at the University of California.

Psychoanalytic Theory

Sigmund Freud, who died in 1939 in London after leaving his beloved Vienna two years earlier when the Nazis took over, shares with Albert Einstein the status of being the most influential Jewish thinker of the twentieth century. Certainly he is the most controversial. He came from a family of comfortable middle-class Jews who migrated like many others from the hinterlands of the Austro-Hungarian Empire to Vienna. It was Freud's early wish to become an academic research neurologist, but given the anti-Semitic quotas at the University of Vienna at the time, he knew this would be impossible, so in order to support himself and his fiancee, he gravitated to medicine.

A year's postdoctoral work in Paris brought Freud into the field of psychiatry and he established an office for this kind of practice on the ground floor of his house in an unfashionable section of Vienna. It is still there, preserved as a museum. It must be stressed that Freud was throughout his career a practicing therapist and he gained the data upon which he developed his theories almost entirely from psychoanalysis of the patients from his early years, mostly affluent Jewish women. Even after, by the 1920s, he had become world famous, Freud had no more than an adjunct status on the faculty of the Vienna medical school.

Freud discovered early on that neuroses—psychological dysfunction—were the consequences of sexual repression, which upon returning caused the neuroses (he never dealt with psychotic patients). Furthermore he concluded that sexual drive exists as early as the age of two. He noticed that many of his patients reported childhood sexual abuse, but concluded that this was usually repressive fantasy—a conclusion in his work that has become immensely controversial in recent years. Through transference between analyst and patient in psychoanalysis, incidents of sexual repression will be restored to consciousness, and this release will revoke the neurotic consequences. Oedipal feelings—the attachment of the child to the parent of the opposite sex—are critical to an individual's sexual history. The root of many neuroses lies in unresolved Oedipal feelings.

These views were not all singular or original with Freud, but most of it was innovative, and taken together they comprised a whole theory of personality shaped by sexuality. In Catholic Vienna this won Freud many enemies, including most of the psychiatric faculty at the University. Yet Freud, a completely autonomous person of great courage (like Einstein) persisted and he rapidly gathered around himself from Vienna and from elsewhere in the German-speaking world, a whole generation of innovative psychoanalysts, most of them Jewish. By the 1920s he had gained many adherents throughout the Western world. It was a wealthy and well-connected Parisian female psychiatrist who in 1938 saved Freud and his family from the Nazis.

There are two ways that a particularly Jewish quality can be seen in Freud's thought. First, he drew a line in human behavior and consciousness between the restrained, civilized qualities that were visible, that were above the line; and the biologically driven primordial impulses that lie below the visible surface. Civilization requires an enlightened, liberated interaction between what is above and below the line, helped by psychoanalysis. This sharpness of division of above and below is characteristic of Jewish life and indeed in central to the Talmudic rabbis' view of sexuality—anything goes as long as it is within marriage and confined to the bedroom.

Second, the Kabbalists had seen in the sexual act the symbol of the union of the Shekinah, Divine Presence, with mankind. Human history is an act of copulation. Freud well believed in the same thing and he tried again and again in his books to expand his psychoanalytic doctrine from the individual and personal to the collective and group level. He never really succeeded in making psychoanalysis a social theory, nor has anyone else. His Swiss German Protestant disciple, Carl Jung, with whom he had a great falling out, only achieved a theory of the collective unconscious by desexualizing it, infuriating Freud.

One of Freud's famous efforts at a social version of psychoanalysis was his explanation of the origins of Judaism, *Moses and Monotheism*. The book has never ceased to be condemned by rabbis, but a close reading offers insightful and provocative ideas. Freud was not an observant Jew, but the book is written by a lover of the Jews. Here is a selection from key parts of the book; the translation is by Katherine Jones.

Freud had an anthropological vision, to which he reverted again and again and is most fully developed in *Totem and Taboo*. It is grounded in his Oedipal doctrine. A primordial horde, a family of brothers slew their father. After a period of latency, or repression of this event, guilt drives the group towards reorganizing themselves according to ethical principles. First violence, then repression, then civilization. This is the pattern of all society.

Freud held that Moses was an Egyptian. He was a disciple of Ikhnaton, the Egyptian Pharaoh who tried to get his people to subscribe to the worship of the monotheistic sun-god Aton; he failed. Moses, assuming the role of liberator of the enslaved Jews, tried to get them to accept the monotheistic Jahve. The Jews killed Moses. After the latency period of psychological repression, the wandering in the desert, the Jews entered Canaan and the monotheistic religion of Moses was eventually reconstructed into the highly ethical prophetic form. As empirical history, this is doubtful, but Freud was not writing history: He was propounding psychoanalytic anthropological theory. Behind puritanical control lies primordial violence. Ritual and ethics are the consequence of the return of the repressed. Freud's theory is worth thinking about.

Among all the events of Jewish prehistory that poets, priests, and historians of a later age undertook to portray, there was an outstanding one the suppression of which was called for by the most obvious and best of human motives. It was the murder of the great leader and liberator Moses. Moses, trained in Ikhnaton's school, employed the same methods as the king; he gave commands and forced his religion on the people. Perhaps Moses' doctrine was still more uncompromising than that of his master; he had no need to retain any connection with the religion of the sun-god since the school of On would have no importance for his alien people. Moses met with the same fate as Ikhnaton, the fate that awaits all enlightened despots. The Jewish people of Moses were quite as unable to bear such a highly spiritualized religion, to find in what it offered satisfaction for their needs, as were the Egyptians of the Eighteenth Dynasty. In both cases the same thing happened: Those who felt themselves kept in tutelage, or who felt dispossessed, revolted and threw off the burden of a religion that had been forced on them. But while the tame Egyptians waited until fate had removed the sacred person of their Pharaoh, the savage Semites took their destiny into their own hands and did away with their tyrant.

Nor can we maintain that the Biblical text preserved to us does not prepare us for such an end to Moses. The account of the "wandering in the wilderness"—which might stand for the time of Moses' rule—describes a series of grave revolts against his authority which, by Jahve's command, were suppressed with savage chastisement. It is easy to imagine that one of those revolts came to another end than the text admits. The people's falling away from the new religion is also mentioned in the text, though as a mere episode. It is the story of the golden calf, where by an adroit turn the breaking of the tables of the law—which has to be understood symbolically (= "he has broken the law")—is ascribed to Moses himself and imputed to his angry indignation.

There came a time when the people regretted the murder of Moses and tried to forget it. . . .

Whenever it was that the different tribes were united into a nation by accepting the same religion, it might very well have been an occurrence of no great importance for the history of the world. The new religion might have been swept away by the stream of events, Jahve would then have taken his place in the procession of erstwhile gods which Flaubert visualized, and of his people all the twelve tribes would have been "lost," not only the ten for whom the Anglo-Saxons have so long been searching. The god Jahve, to whom the Midianite Moses led a new people, was probably in no way a remarkable being. A rude, narrow-minded local god, violent and blood-thirsty, he had promised his adherents to give them "a land flowing with milk and honey" and he encouraged them to rid the country of its present inhabitants "with the edge of the sword." It is truly astonishing that in spite of all the revisions in the Biblical text so much was allowed to stand whereby we may recognize his original nature. It is not even sure that his religion was a true monotheism, that it denied the character of God to other divinities. It probably sufficed that one's own god was more powerful than all strange gods. When the sequence of events took quite another course than such beginnings would lead us to expect, there can be only one reason for it. To one part of the people the Egyptian Moses had given another and more spiritual conception of God, a single God who embraces the whole world, one as all-loving as he was all-powerful, who, averse to all ceremonial and magic, set humanity as its highest aim a life of truth and justice. For, incomplete as our information about the ethical side of the Aton religion may be, it is surely significant that Ikhnaton regularly described himself in his inscriptions as "living in Maat" (truth, justice). In the long run it did not matter that the people, probably after a very short time, renounced the teaching of Moses and removed the man himself. The tradition itself remained and its influence reached—though only slowly, in the course of centuries—the aim that was denied to Moses himself. The god Jahve attained undeserved honour when, from Qadeš onward, Moses' deed of liberation was put down to his account; but he had to pay dear for this usurpation. The shadow of the god whose place he had taken became stronger than himself; at the end of the historical development there arose beyond his being that of the forgotten Mosaic god. None can doubt that it was only the idea of this other god that enabled the people of Israel to surmount all their hardships and to survive until our time.

It is no longer possible to determine the part the Levites played in the final victory of the Mosaic god over Jahve. When the compromise at Qadeš was effected they had raised their voice for Moses, their memory being still green of the master whose followers and countrymen they were. During the centuries since then the Levites had become one with the people or with the priesthood and it had become the main task of the priests to develop and supervise the ritual, besides caring for the holy texts and revising them in accordance with their purposes. But was not all this sacrifice and ceremonial at bottom only magic and black art, such as the old doctrine of Moses had unconditionally condemned? There arose from the midst of the people an unending succession of men, not necessarily descended from Moses' people, but seized by the great and powerful tradition which had gradually grown in darkness, and it was these men, the Prophets, who sedulously preached the old Mosaic doctrine: The Deity spurns sacrifice and ceremonial; he demands only belief and a life of truth and justice (Maat). The efforts of the Prophets met with enduring success; the doctrines with which they reestablished the old belief became the permanent content of the Jewish religion. It is honour enough for the Jewish people that it has kept alive such a tradition and produced men who lent it their voice, even if the stimulus had first come from outside, from a great stranger. . . .

I thus believe that the idea of an *only* God, as well as the emphasis laid on ethical demands in the name of that God and the rejection of all magic ceremonial, was indeed Mosaic doctrine, which at first found no hearing but came into its own after a long space of time and finally prevailed. How is such a delayed effect to be explained and where do we meet with similar phenomena?

Our next reflection tells us that they are often met with in very different spheres and that they probably come about in various ways which are more or less easy to understand. Let us take for an example the fate of any new scientific theory, for instance the Darwinian doctrine of evolution. At first it meets with hostile rejection and is violently debated for decades; it takes only one generation, however, before it is recognized as a great step towards truth. Darwin himself was accorded the honour of burial in Westminster Abbey. Such a

The liberator: *Freud*, by Ben Shahn.

case provides no enigma. The new truth had awakened affective resistances. These could be sustained by arguments that opposed the evidence in support of the unpleasant doctrine. The contest of opinions lasted a certain time. From the very beginning there were both adherents and opponents, but the number as well as the importance of the former steadily increased until at last they gained the upper hand. During the whole time of the conflict no one forgot what was the matter at issue. We are hardly surprised to find that the whole process took a considerable time; probably we do not adequately appreciate the fact that we have here to do with a manifestation of mass psychology. There is no difficulty in finding a full analogy to it in the mental life of an individual. In such a case a person would hear of something new which, on the ground of certain evidence, he is asked to accept as true; yet it contradicts many of his wishes and offends some of his highly treasured convictions. He will then hesitate, look for arguments to cast doubt on the new material, and so struggle for a while until at last he admits it himself: "This is true after all, although I find it hard to accept and it is painful to have to believe in it." All we learn from this process is that it needs time for the intellectual work of the Ego to overcome objections that are invested by strong feelings. This case, however, is not very similar to the one we are trying to elucidate.

The next example we turn to seems to have still less in common with our problem. It may happen that someone gets away, apparently unharmed, from the spot where he has suffered a shocking accident, for instance a train collision. In the course of the following weeks, however, he develops a series of grave psychical and motor symptoms, which can be ascribed only to his shock or whatever else happened at the time of the accident. He has developed a "traumatic neurosis." This appears quite incomprehensible and is therefore a novel fact. The time that elapsed between the accident and the first appearance of the symptoms is called the "incubation period," a transparent allusion to the pathology of infectious disease. As an afterthought we observe that—in spite of the fundamental difference in the two cases, the problem of the traumatic neurosis and that of Jewish monotheism—there is a correspondence in one point. It is the feature which one might term *latency*. There are the best grounds for thinking that in the history of the Jewish religion there is a long period, after the breaking away from the Moses religion, during which no trace is to be found of the monotheistic idea, the condemnation of ceremonial, and the emphasis on the ethical side. Thus we are prepared for the possibility that the solution of our problem is to be sought in a special psychological situation. diction of the written history. It was less subject to

distorting influences—perhaps in part entirely free from them—and therefore might be more truthful than the account set down in writing. Its trustworthiness, however, was impaired by being vaguer and more fluid than the written text, being exposed to many changes and distortions as it was passed on from one generation to the next by word of mouth. Such a tradition may have different outcomes. The most likely event would be for it to be vanquished by the written version, ousted by it, until it grows more and more shadowy and at last is forgotten. Another fate might be that the tradition itself ends by becoming a written version. There are other possibilities which will be mentioned later.

The phenomenon of the latency period in the history of the Jewish religion may find its explanation in this: The facts which the so-called official written history purposely tried to suppress were in reality never lost. The knowledge of them survived in traditions which were kept alive among the people. According to Ernst Sellin, there even existed a tradition concerning the end of Moses which contradicted outright the official account and came far nearer the truth. The same thing, we may suppose, happened with other beliefs that had apparently found an end at the same time as Moses, doctrines of the Mosaic religion that had been unacceptable to the majority of Moses' contemporaries.

Here we meet with a remarkable fact. It is that these traditions, instead of growing weaker as time went on, grew more and more powerful in the course.

Spinoza's Rationalism

In addition to the bold new frontiers of Jewish thought presented in art history, cultural studies, sociology, anthropology, and psychoanalysis, there are important alternative intimations, outside of the mainstream, from the Jewish past. It is worth reconsidering them as possible suggestions for new or enriched avenues of thinking for the present and future.

The first of these past roads not taken, but maybe now ready to be followed is the rationalism of Baruch (Benedict) Spinoza who was excommunicated by the Jewish community of Amsterdam in the mid-seventeenth century *for his strictly rationalist ethics and historical approach to the Bible. Here is an original and long-range assessment of Spinoza, "the Marrano of Reason," made in 1989 by the Israeli scholar Yirmiyahu Yovel.*

Spinoza's image of Judaism is anchored in a thesis which proved useful to later Jewish reformers and anti-Semites alike. For Spinoza, Judaism is fundamentally a political religion that was designed specifically for the ancient Hebrews as the basis for a theological regime. When the temple was destroyed and the Jews were deprived of their political existence, their religion also lost its meaning, and Judaism became historically obsolete and self-contradictory.

This view would appear to smack of Christian logic. After all, the Christians were the first to claim that since Jesus had redeemed the world, Judaism had been superseded: God's "chosen people" were now those who adhered to the Christian church. But this is mere rhetoric. Spinoza does not consider Judaism anachronistic because God's elect are now the Christians: Spinoza rejects the very notion of election. What makes Judaism obsolete is not a theological argument but a purely profane analysis, which treats history as a natural causal system, uninformed by divine providence.

Judaism lost its historical rationale, according to Spinoza, because the political nature of the Jewish religion no longer corresponded to the nonpolitical existence of the Jews in the Diaspora. In the absence of a Jewish body politic, Jewish religion is superfluous. To sustain this view Spinoza must turn to a sociohistorical analysis, showing that the essence of the ancient Jewish religion was theocratic, that is, a political regime where the laws of God are also the supreme civil authority. Crucial sections of chapters 3 and 17 of the *Theologico-Political Treatise* are given over to this analysis, which is Spinoza's alternative to traditional theological interpretations of Judaism.

While his methodological principle is sound, Spinoza's detailed explanation is imprecise. As we know, the ancient Jewish state was racked throughout its existence by a relentless struggle to convert it into a theocracy. That struggle, however, was never quite resolved. Even if, as Spinoza

contends, the Jewish religion projected the ideal of a theocratic state, it was never strong enough to impose it on concrete reality. Prior to the destruction of the second temple, the influence of the Pharisees (which came closest to the theocratic model) considerably increased, but its great achievement came, paradoxically, after the destruction of the second temple. Then Rabban Yochanan Ben-Zakkai requested and received from the Roman emperor authority over "Yavnch and its provinces," in order to establish there a center of Jewish culture and law. Rabban Yochanan, with whom Spinoza is quite familiar, is thus considered to have laid the cornerstone for autonomous Jewish life in the Diaspora as well. Such autonomy is based on the sanction of the Gentile government and the voluntary develop-

"The Marrano of Reason": Baruch Spinoza, mid–seventeenth century.

ment of a system of rabbinical commandments as a substitute for the Jewish body politic. This development is also seen, to a certain extent, as a triumph of the Pharisaic approach.

From Spinoza's point of view, it is an absurd and incongruous state of affairs when the laws of a religion, whose entire purpose is the political constitution of some concrete and actual theocratic state, succeed in gaining ascendancy over reality only *after* the state itself is annihilated. Henceforth, the Pharisees are able to dictate the shape of future Jewish history. Yet, under these circumstances, the theocratic laws have taken over in a distorted and absurd manner. In the absence of a concrete state, a phantom substitute has been created by the imagination, nourished by piety and a hatred of other nations, and this phantom "homeland" is carried by the Jews everywhere in their exile. The Jews continue to regard themselves not only as a separate nation but even a separate polity, however bizarre and incongruous in reality.

Of course, Spinoza's main interest is in the present—with his analysis of Jewish existence in the exile, from which he also projects back into the Jewish past. The Jews in Palestine never lived under an absolute theocracy. The almost full coalescence of law and religion emerges only in the phantom state Spinoza criticizes—and with which, we may add, he had an existential clash. Only in the exile is it possible to say as Spinoza says in painful reproach that "everyone who fell away from religion ceased to be a citizen, and was, on that ground alone, accounted an enemy" (*Theologico-Political Treatise,* chapter 17, pp. 219–20). In this type of reality, a critic of religion like Spinoza was forced to relinquish his membership in the Jewish community. In the ancient Jewish states, however, both in the first and the second temple periods, there were many Jews who disavowed religious authority or transgressed against its laws without being considered enemies; or who took issue (like the Sadducees) with the Oral Law and with the very principle of theocracy, and yet were legitimate, even influential, citizens of the polity. . . .

Even if Judaism has lost its raison d'être with the destruction of the temple, the Jewish people continue to survive. For centuries they zealously preserve their phantom "homeland," rooted, as it is, in religious superstition. Moreover, like Spinoza's own parents and fellow Marranos, they prevail even in the face of forced conversion and cruel persecution, returning openly to Judaism after generations of secret practice. From a logical point of view, there is something incomprehensible in all this, a kind of theoretical scandal; and empirically, at least prima facie, this poses a riddle.

Thus Spinoza, in his own way, faces the same problem that has perplexed Jews and Christians alike: the amazing survival of the Jewish people. The Jews maintain that they are God's chosen people who, even though sinners, yearn for redemption. Christians, on the other hand, maintain that the Jews *were* God's chosen people who, because they rejected Jesus as the Messiah, are themselves rejected by God.

Spinoza of course, must dismiss both explanations as transcendent. What is demanded is a purely natural explanation, based upon social and psychological causes. Significantly, the twofold explanation Spinoza offers is drawn in part from his Marrano background. What preserved the Jews, he says, was Gentile hatred of the Jews from without and the power of their religious faith ("superstition") from within.

Gentile hatred of the Jews, in Spinoza's view, enhanced their survival. So intensely do the Jews differentiate themselves from other peoples, that they cannot help but arouse animosity and revulsion. As a result, even if many individuals are ostracized and lost to their people, the external pressure reinforces the Jews' survival as a group. This is a modern, essentially secular, explanation which has by now become banal (the last important writer to use it was Sartre). Spinoza, however, was among the first, if not actually the first, to express it so succinctly. Spinoza's outlook derives from the accumulated experience of the Jewish people in general, and from his own Marrano forefathers in particular.

The Rise and Fall of Yiddish

Centering in Odessa and New York in the early decades of the twentieth century was a thriving international Yiddish literary culture that has been not only dissolved but largely excised from collective Jewish memory. The following assessment of the rise and fall of the great Yiddish culture by the Israeli scholar Benjamin Harshav not only stimulates advocacy of resurrecting familiarity with the Yiddish world but also raises the issue of creating a new international Jewish culture, this time perhaps in impregnable English.

Yiddish had a considerable body of folklore and a large written literature which flourished in the sixteenth century and again between 1862 and the present. Its international recognition culminated in the awarding of the Nobel Prize for literature to Isaac Bashevis Singer in 1978, and the Israel Prize to A. Sutskever, poet and editor of the prestigious literary quarterly *Di Goldene Keyt,* in 1984. In the last third of the nineteenth century, three "classical" writers of Yiddish literature, Mendele Moykher Sforim, Sholem Aleichem, and I. L. Peretz, lent prestige to a rapidly expanding literary institution. In a short period, dozens of important writers created a literature with European standards, moving swiftly from rationalist Enlightenment through carnivalesque parody to Realism, Naturalism, and psychological Impressionism, and then breaking out of these conventional European modes into the general literary trends of Expressionism and Modernism.

This became possible because of the secularization of the Jewish masses and the trend to join the general world of modern culture and politics in the language they knew. The growing political parties, especially the Diaspora-oriented Folkists and Socialists, but many Zionists as well, supported Yiddish culture and education, seeing it at first as a tool for propaganda and as a way to break out of the traditional religious framework and, later, as a goal in itself. The Orthodox Agudah ("Agudas Isroel") responded by developing their own Yiddish school system for girls. Hundreds of periodicals and newspapers appeared in Yiddish (the earliest was the newspaper *Kurantn* published in Amsterdam in 1686). Libraries sprang up in hundreds of towns. A modern secular school system developed all over Eastern Europe and was echoed in part in both Americas. Massive translation efforts brought to Yiddish readers the works of Tolstoy, Kropotkin, Ibsen, Zola, Jules Verne, Rabindranat Tagore, Lion Feuchtwanger, Shakespeare, Sergey Yesenin, Ezra Pound, and many others.

It was, however, a tragic destiny. As Leo Wiener put it in 1899, "there is probably no other language . . . on which so much opprobrium has been heaped." Traditionally, Yiddish was considered the "servant maid" to the "Lady" Hebrew. With the onset of the Enlightenment among German Jews, Yiddish became the ugly symbol of everything that kept the Jews from entering civilized western society. Indeed, when viewed from the point of view of a "pure" normative literary German language based in the northern city of Berlin, Yiddish—based on oral, medieval, southern German dialects and thoroughly "melted"—did look like a contortion, a corrupted medley with no grammar or aesthetic values. Moses Mendelssohn wrote: "This jargon contributed no little to the immorality of the common Jews" and he demanded "pure German or pure Hebrew, but no hodgepodge." (Hebrew was also "purified": the synthetic language into which it had developed in the Rabbinical tradition, employing components from various layers of its history of more than three thousand years, was despised and abandoned by the "Haskalah" writers for the limited but "classical" and "pure" language of the Bible.)

It was not merely a matter of language: Yiddish became the externalized object of Jewish self-hatred. Pressured by a Gentile society, Jews internalized many anti-Semitic stereotypes, blaming "Jewish" character traits, mentality, and behavior for their lot among Christian nations. Moving out of the Jewish towns in areas of minority nationalities and into the centers of the state languages like Warsaw, Vienna, Berlin, Moscow, London, Paris, Tel Aviv, or New York, masses of Jews eagerly embraced the new dominant language and culture. In centralized modern societies, speaking Yiddish would have isolated and stigmatized them. Furthermore, the language seemed to symbolize the devious, irrational ways of "Jewish" behavior, the ugly, unaesthetic image of the caricature Jew, and the backward, lower-class existence of most of its Eastern European speakers. The movement of many young, bright, and successful Jews away from Yiddish again left the language mostly with lower-class readers of limited culture and thus strengthened the vicious circle. In Israel, too, there was an extreme emotional hatred of Yiddish—the "potato tongue" of the poor, embodying all the weak traits of the subservient and parasitic "Diaspora mentality"—reinforced by the guilty feelings of a society created by young people who had abandoned their parents and the world of their parents in Eastern Europe to rebuild their own lives, the image of the Jews, and human society itself.

As Joshua Fishman summarized it: "Just as those Jews themselves stand accused in the eyes of many outsiders of simultaneous but opposite derelictions (capitalism *and* communism, clannishness *and* assimilation, materialism *and* vapid intellectualism) so Yiddish stands accused—within the Jewish fold itself—of being a tool of the irreligious *and* of the ultra-Orthodox, of fostering ghettoization *and* rootless cosmopolitanism, of reflecting quintessential and inescapable Jewishness *and* of representing little more than a hedonistic differentiation from the ways of the Gentiles, of being dead or dying, *and* of being a ubiquitous threat to higher values."

A grotesque, not to say tragic, footnote to the self-effacement of Yiddish speakers vis-à-vis. German was written in the Holocaust. Forced to speak the language of the Master Race when com-municating with Germans, Yiddish speakers "germanized," that is, they selected what they thought to be German words in Yiddish and adapted them to a "German" pronunciation; they were thus reduced to speaking a minimal language divested of the expressive vigor of Yiddish, the stylistic effects and subtleties of meaning of its Hebrew and Slavic elements and subtexts, and its idioms and proverbs which depend on those layers. Germanizing Yiddish in ghettos and death camps was a linguistic dehumanization of people reduced to baby-talk or to a grammatical subhuman stammer vis-à-vis the Master Race, whose orders they subconsciously accepted. One is flabbergasted to see how West German courts in recent trials of Nazi criminals (like the Maidanek trials) again reduced the Jewish witnesses to this minimal, mock-language; the witnesses themselves, when faced with their former tormentors, instinctively succumbed to the "higher" language of the "Masters." Even in Claude Lanzmann's carefully documented film, *Shoah*, based on witness accounts, his witnesses automatically accept German as the "culture language" and some of them are reduced to speaking a minimal vocabulary rather than speaking a full-blown Yiddish (which would then be translated, as was Hebrew). When toward the end of the film, a woman sings a Yiddish song from the camps, she rhymes TRERN–WERDEN, Germanizing the Yiddish VERN, which was obviously the original rhyme for TRERN. All this after the Holocaust!

To be sure, there was a vigorous Yiddishist movement counteracting both assimilation and self-abasement. It was celebrated in the famous "Czernowitz Conference" of Yiddish writers and activists in 1908 which freed Yiddish from the derogatory label "jargon," and pronounced it "a Jewish national language." For the first time in its long history, Yiddish literature was seen not as a handmaiden to Hebrew but as an equal, even a preferred cultural force; indeed, as the very justification for having a separate, autonomous culture. Yiddishism, too, was part of the trend that was profoundly critical of the old ways of Jewish Diaspora existence (for which it usually blamed religion and "backwardness" rather than language). A network of schools, libraries, clubs, publishing houses, a Writers Union, and scientific academies were established, especially in post-World-War-I Poland and the Soviet Union. Its culmination was the foundation of a Yiddish Scientific Institute, YIVO, in Vilna, in 1925, a combination of a research center and cultural policy institute. Textbooks were written, terminologies developed, and elitist theatre and poetry cherished.

In the long-range perspective of Jewish history, however, it is clear that Yiddish culture served as a bridge between the traditional religious Jewish society and assimilation into western languages. Indeed, Yiddish literature as an institution existed for seven centuries. But for each individual writer, it was a matter of one (in rare cases, two) generations. Most Yiddish writers still grew up with some Hebrew education in a religious environment and their children were already steeped in the culture of another language.

It is true that Hitler and Stalin destroyed Yiddish culture in its European stronghold. The Jewish people lost a third of their numbers but nonetheless survived; the destruction of Yiddish, however, was total: Stalin killed the Yiddish writers, Hitler killed the writers and their readers alike. The Yiddish-speaking masses are no more.

But it is also true that the trend of assimilation was overpowering everywhere, even before the Holocaust. In 1897, 97.96 percent of all Jews inhabiting the Russian Empire claimed Yiddish as their mother tongue. But this percentage has rapidly diminished everywhere: in Russia and Poland, in France, Canada and Argentina, as well as in Israel and the United States.

The lot of Yiddish was never easy. For example, the fight for Yiddish in the public schools failed in New York (compare the attitude toward Spanish in a later generation). Still, in the 1920s, it was impossible to predict that, in the competition between the two languages, Hebrew, with its base in a tiny community in Palestine, would survive and become a full-fledged state language while Yiddish, a "World Language," with its mass newspapers and millions of readers, would disappear. For those who wanted to preserve a Jewish culture in a secular world, this was the choice.

There was, however, no free play of cultural choices but brutal historical facts. The attempt to create a modern, cosmopolitan culture in a separate Jewish language, culturally autonomous and steeped in historical values and associations, was doomed to failure. For the writers sensing the loss of their readership, this was an indescribable tragedy.

Reconstructionism

Highly visible and promising in the 1940s and 1950s was the Reconstructionist movement led by Mordechai Kaplan, who taught at the Jewish Theological Seminary. He would have had a greater impact if he had accepted one of two invitations he received in his career to teach at the Reform Hebrew Union College in New York, which was much more hospitable to his ideas that his dour conservative colleagues on Morningside Heights.

Heavily influenced by John Dewey's pragmatism, Kaplan saw Reconstructionism as a method rather than a sectarian program. The method aimed to incorporate any and all facets of the higher cultural and artistic life into synagogue service and activity to achieve unity and integration among Jewish denominations. Kaplan did move conservative and reform synagogues towards greater involvement as community and educational centers, although they remain the most underutilized upscale buildings in the country. Otherwise, Kaplan failed. Reconstructionism today is simply a weak fourth synagogue denomination. Little or nothing has been done to integrate the

synagogue into vanguard American culture. While Catholic and Protestant churches use rock music in their services, conservative and reform synagogues are stuck in the musical and dramatic world of the 1940s, and the orthodox keep thinking up new ways to create divisiveness in American Jewish life.

Kaplan's vision of Reconstructionism, once so widely applauded, merits rereading—if only the man could write.

The Reconstructionist movement is a method rather than a program. As a method, its validity should not be tested by its organizational success. Its function is not to form an additional sect or denomination. What will prove whether Reconstructionism is valid is the extent to which it will succeed in preventing the existing sects or denominations from doing the harm they do at present to Jewish life, and in eliciting and reinforcing the good they are capable of doing. Each trend in Jewish life must learn to recognize its limitations and to eliminate from its philosophy and program whatever smacks of curtainship that shuts off communication with the rest of Jewry. At present that exclusivist spirit is virtually the dominant evil of every trend in Jewish life. To overcome it, the contemporary trends have to find in the survival and enhancement of the Jewish people the highest common denominator, of which each trend is merely the numerator.

For Reconstructionism to achieve that goal, it must state in no uncertain terms wherein each of the existing trends in Judaism is unable to make of the Jewish tradition and the Jewish way of life an asset rather than a burden. Let us pass the trends briefly in review:

Orthodoxy is definitely committed to supernaturalism and to a literalist acceptance of the miraculous events and the self-revelations of God as recorded in the Bible. Its conception of world history is Israel-centered. That the world was created for the sake of Israel is no mere figure of speech, but has to be believed in as fact. This and nothing less is the significance of the divine chosenness of the Jewish People. What all this calls for in the way of life to be lived by the Jew is summed up in the legal code known as *Shulhan Arukh*. For those to whom human life must speak in accents of certainty and absolutism, if it is to have any

meaning at all, and for those who can will to believe whatever contributes to certainty and absolutism, Orthodoxy is an ideal solution. But their name is by no means legion.

Reform advocates a libertarian attitude toward the Jewish tradition. It grants the freedom to select from that tradition whatever is compatible with our sense of reality and reinforces our highest idealism. Were that combined with a realistic desire to maintain the continuity of the Jewish People, and a tireless striving to save it from disruption and absorption by the rest of the world, there would have been no need for the Reconstructionist movement. But, unfortunately, the only evidence that the Reform movement has given of such striving has been "a way of talking" instead of a way of living and creating. Instead of creating Jewish environment and producing Jewish culture, both ethical and esthetic, for that environment, Reform is content with harping upon the idea of the Jews as a Chosen People on Sabbaths and Festivals, and doing nothing about it during the rest of the week.

Conservatism is conspicuously of a divided mind, so that it is not even loath to make a virtue of inconsistency. It shies away from consistency as the questionable virtue of small minds. It makes a point of being true to historical fact, even when such fact hurts one's *amour propre*. Indeed, more than any other Jewish movement, Conservatism, both in the Old and in the New World, has made a vast contribution to the knowledge of the Jewish—not the Biblical—past. Yet it has never attempted to draw the logical consequences for Jewish life today from what it has learned about the past. It is half-hearted in its belief in the divine or supernatural authorship of the Pentateuchal Torah, and yet it insists upon treating the ancient *Halakha* as inherently infallible and unalterable, *as though* it were of supernatural origin and not a fallible product of the human will. It combats democratic legislation in any area of Jewish life where *Halakha* has had its say. It subjects even ritual practice, like the observance of the Sabbath and *kashruth*, to the same legalistic status as civil and marriage law. . . .

As a method of converting Jewish life from a liability into an asset, Reconstructionism spells clarity of vision and strength of will. The vision we Jews need most desperately is that which would enable us to confront reality without shrinking, from its most terrifying aspects, and at the same time penetrate sufficiently beneath the surface of reality to behold the possibilities not only of recovery but of health and growth. Coupled with such vision must be the power and the drive of will, both as a prerequisite and as a follow-up. A prerequisite to clarity of vision is the will to live a Jewish life and the determination to transmit the Jewish heritage. That heritage is the accumulated moral and spiritual energy of a hundred generations. In a world that abounds in the uranium that can be used to blow the world into smithereens, mankind can ill afford to waste the uranium of the spirit latent in the Jewish heritage. Once having beheld the vision of the greater Judaism of the future, we need the power of will that spells patience, wisdom and energy to translate it into living reality. . . .

The one unmistakable purpose which our past can yield is that of recovering our sense of collective responsibility. That purpose can unite us amid all our intellectual and cultural divergencies, and enable us to contribute our share toward the metamorphosis of mankind. It would mean reactivating the sense of moral responsibility which was an outstanding Jewish trait and extending the scope of that responsibility so that it embrace the whole of mankind.

Epilogue: The Coming of the Messiah

This appropriate epilogue to *The Jewish Experience* is from "The Coming of the Messiah" by Franz Kafka.

The Messiah will come as soon as the most unbridled individualism of faith becomes possible—when there is no one to destroy this possibility and no one to suffer its destruction; hence the graves will open themselves. . . .

The Messiah will come only when he is no longer necessary; he will come only on the day after his arrival; he will come, not on the last day, but on the very last.

Author Index

COPYRIGHT ACKNOWLEDGMENTS

Acknowledgment is made of copyright permissions to reprint selections from the following books.

Jason Aronson Inc.
From *Great Yiddish Writers of the Twentieth Century*, translated by Joseph Leftwich. Reprinted by permission of the publisher, Jason Aronson Inc., Northvale, N.J. Copyright ©1987.

Chaim Bermant
From *The Walled Garden*, by Chaim Bermant. Reprinted by permission of author.

Georges Borchardt, Inc.
From *Tristes Tropiques*, by Claude Lévi-Strauss. Reprinted by permission of Georges Borchardt, Inc. for the author.

Georges Borchardt, Inc.
From *Merchant Princes* by Leon Harris. Copyright ©1979 by Leon Harris. Reprinted by permission of Georges Borchardt, Inc. for the author.

B'Nai B'Rith
From *Flavius Josephus: Selections From His Works*, by Abraham Wasserstein. Reprinted by permission of B'Nai B'Rith.

Brandt & Brandt Literary Agents, Inc.
From *I Can Get It For You Wholesale*, by Jerome Weidman. Copyright ©1983 by Jerome Weidman. Reprinted by permission of Brandt & Brandt Literary Agents, Inc.

Breslov Research Institute
From *Rabbi Nachman's Wisdom* by Rabbi Nathan Of Nemirov, translated by Rabbi Arych. Reprinted by permission of Breslov Research Institute.

Canongate Publishers
From *The Fall of Israel*, by Barry Chamish. Reprinted by permission of Barry Chamish and Canongate Publishers.

IMG Literary
From *Genesis 1948, The First Arab-Israeli War*, by Dan Kurzman. Copyright © 1992, by Dan Kurzman, published by Da Capo Press. Reprinted by permission of the author.

Doubleday Books
From *Anne Frank: The Diary of a Young Girl*, by Anne Frank. "Excerpts", from *Anne Frank: The Diary of a Young Girl*, by Anne Frank. Copyright ©1952 by Otto H. Frank. Used by permission of Doubleday, a division of Bantam Doubleday Dell Publishing Group, Inc.

Doubleday Books
From *Anne Frank's Tales from the Annex* by Anne Frank. Copyright ©1949, 1960 by Otto Frank. Copyright ©1982 by Anne Frank-Funds, Basel. English translation copyright ©1983 by Doubleday. Used by permission of Doubleday, a division of Bantam Doubleday Dell Publishing Group, Inc.

DVIR Publishing House
From *Stories of the Sages*, by Chaim Pearl, from Sefer Ha-Aggadah by H.N. Bialik and Y.H. Rawnitzky. Copyright © DVIR Publishing House.

Farrar, Straus & Giroux, Inc.
From *Call It Sleep*, by Henry Roth. Reprinted by permission of Farrar, Strauss & Giroux, Inc.

Farrar, Straus & Giroux, Inc.
From *Enemies, A Love Story*, by Issac Bashevis Singer. Reprinted by permission of Farrar, Strauss & Giroux. Inc.

From *Jews of Arab Lands* by Norman Stillman. Reprinted by permission of the Jewish Publication Society, copyright © 1979.

The Jewish Theological Seminary of America

From *The Users of Tradition,* by Jack Wertheimer. Reprinted with permission of The Jewish Theological Seminary of America.

KTAV Publishing House, Inc.

From *The Shetel Book,* by Diane K. Roskies and David G. Roskies. Reprinted by permission of KTAV Publishing House, Inc.

Lilith Publications

Excerpts from the Ester Singer Kreitman short story. This article was originally published in *Lilith,* the independent Jewish women's quarterly: subscriptions are $18.00 per year, from Lilith, 250 West 57th Street, New York, N.Y. 10107. It is being reprinted here by permission.

Macmillian Publishers

From *I and Thou,* by Martin Buber. Reprinted by permission of Macmillian Publishers.

Macmillan Publishers

From *The First Israelis,* by Tom Segev. Reprinted with permission of the Free Press, an imprint of Simon & Schuster. Copyright ©1986 by the Free Press.

William Morrow & Co., Inc.

From *I Never Played The Game,* by Howard Cosell with Robert Bonventre. Copyright ©1985 by Howard Cosell. Reprinted by permission of William Morrow and Company. Inc.

Mosaic Press

From *Burnt Pearls,* translated by Seymour Mayne. Burnt Pearls, from Ghetto Poems, by Abraham Sutzkver, translated by Seymour Mayne, published by Mosaic Press, 1252 Speers Rd., Unit a & 2, Oakville, ON L6L 5N9, Canada, copyright ©1981, published with permission of the publisher.

Oxford University Press

From *The Holocaust: The Fate of European Jewry, 1932-1945,* by Leni Yahil. Copyright ©1990. Reprinted by permission of Oxford University Press, Inc.

Oxford University Press

From *Lewis Namier: A Biography,* by Julia Namier. Copyright © Lady Namier, 1971. Reprinted by permission of Oxford University Press, London.

Oxford University Press

From *Modern British Jewry,* by Geoffrey Alderman. Copyright © Geoffrey Alderman 1992. Reprinted from Modern British Jewery by Geoffrey Alderman (1992) by permission of Oxford University Press.

Penguin Books USA, Inc.

From *A Book of Miracles by Ben Hecht.* Copyright ©1939 by Ben Hecht; Renewed copyright ©1967 by Rose Hecht. Used by permission of Viking Penguin, a division of Penguin Books USA, Inc.

Penguin Books, USA

From *Eichmann In Jerusalem* by Hannah Arendt. Copyright ©1963, 1964 by Hannah Arendt. Used by permission of Penguin Books, USA, Inc.

Penguin Books USA

From *Everyman's Talmud* by Abraham Cohen. "Angelology" from Everyman's Talmud by Abraham Cohen. Copyright ©1949 by E.P. Dutton, Inc., renewed ©1977 by Rev. Dr. Boaz Cohen. Used by permission of Dutton Signer, a division of Penguin Books, USA. Inc.

Penguin Books, USA

From *Henrietta Szold: Life and Letters,* by Marvin Lowenthal. Copyright ©1942 The Viking Press, renewed ©1970 by Harold C Emer and Harry L. Shapiro, Executors of the Estate. Used by permission of Viking Penguin, a division of Penguin Books Usa, Inc.

Penguin Books, USA

From *Personal Impressions,* by Isiah Berlin. Copyright 1949, 1951, 1955, © 1958, 1964, 1965, 1966, 1971, 1972, 1973, 1975, 1976, 1980 by Isaiah Berlin. Used by permission of Viking Penguin, a division of Penguin Books USA Inc.

Penguin Books, USA

From *The Penguin Book of Modern Yiddish Verse* by Irving Howe, Ruth R. Wisse and Khone Shmeruk. "The Mound" by Perets Markish, from the Penguin Book of Modern Yiddish Verse by Irving Howe, Ruth R. Wisse and Khone Shmeruk. Copyright ©1987 by Irving Howe, Ruth Wisse, and Khone Shmeruk. Introduction and Notes copyright ©1987 by Irving Howe. Used by permission of Viking Press, a division of Penguin Books USA, Inc.

Penguin Books, USA

From *The Spanish Inquisition,* by Henry Kamen. Copyright ©1965 by Henry Kamen. Used by permission of Dutton Signet, a division of Penguin Books, USA Inc.

Penguin Books, USA

From *Survival in Auschwitz,* by Primo Levi. *If This Is A Man (Survival in Auschwitz)* by Primo Levi, translated by Stuart Woolfe. Translated copyright ©1959 by Orion Pres, Inc., ©1958 by Giulio Einaudi Editore S.P.A. Used by permission of Viking Penguin, a division of Penguin Books USA Inc.

Penguin Books USA

From *A Treasury of Yiddish Stories* by Irving Howe and Eliezer Greenberg. "Bontsha the Silent" by I.L. Peretz and Hilde Abel, translator, from A Treasury of Yiddish Stories by Irving Howe and Eliezer Greenberg. Copyright ©1953, 1954, 1989 by Viking Press, renewed ©1982 by Irving Howe and Eva Greenberg. Used by permission of Viking Penguin, a division of Penguin Books, USA Inc.

Penguin Books

ILLUSTRATION CREDITS

Page ii: Jewish Museum/Art Resource, NY. Page xxiv: Foto Marburg/Art Resource, NY. 15, 30: Giraudon/Art Resource, NY. 43, 58: Jewish Museum/Art Resource, NY. 68: Photo Marburg/Art Resource, NY. 72: Jewish Theological Seminary, NY. 86: Giraudon/Art Resource, NY. 90, 108: Jewish Musem/Art Resource, NY. 111: Giraudon/Art Resource, NY. 115: Snark/Art Resource, NY. 118, 123, 126, 132: Jewish Theological Seminary, NY. 137, 140: Jewish Museum, NY. 153: Giraudon/Art Resource, NY. 183: Prado Museum, Madrid. 190: Foto Marburg/Art Resource, NY. 197, 215: Jewish Museum/Art Resource, NY. 218: Library of Congress. 222: Jewish Theological Seminary, NY. 230: Alinari/Art Resource, NY. 246: Snark/Art Resource, NY. 254, 256, 260, 264, 286: Jewish Museum/Art Resource, NY. 310: Snark/Art Resource, NY. 317: Jewish Theological Seminary, NY. 314: Jewish Museum/Art Resource, NY. 347: Foto Marburg/Art Resource, NY. 355: Giraudon/Art Resource, NY. 376: Foto Marburg/Art Resource, NY. 357: Jewish Theological Seminary, NY. 393: Jewish Museum/Art Resource, NY. 397: Scala/Art Resource, NY. 405: National Portrait Gallery, Smithsonian Institution/Art Resource, NY. 417, 424: Jewish Theological Seminary, NY. 429: Snark/Art Resource, NY. 435: Alinari/Art Resource, NY. 450: Art Resource, NY. 471: Snark/Art Resource, NY. 473: Giraudon/Art Resource, NY.

NORMAN F. CANTOR is professor of history, sociology and comparative literature at New York University. He is the author of numerous books, including *The Sacred Chain, The Civilization of the Middle Ages, Medieval Lives* and *Inventing the Middle Ages*, which was nominated for a National Book Critics Circle Award.